"A compelling and comprehensive single volume on one of the most controversial conflicts of the modern age. Wawro is at the top of his game in this stunning book, full of wisdom and insight and convincingly arguing this was both a highly political and unnecessary war. Superb."

—James Holland, author of *Normandy '44*

"In *The Vietnam War*, master historian Wawro wades into the historical world of the Vietnam War, where nearly everything is an argument. Wawro brings fresh eyes and a new perspective to the struggle for the history of America's lost war. The result is a readable, entertaining, and indispensable account of this most controversial of conflicts."

—Andrew Wiest, author of *Vietnam's Forgotten Army*

"Fifty years after it came to an end, the Vietnam War still casts a shadow over American life. Wawro has written a brilliant, gripping account of that conflict and its effects, rigorous in military and political detail but never lacking in empathy when considering the human cost. A definitive account."

—Rana Mitter, author of *Forgotten Ally*

"Wawro has written an excellent history of the Vietnam War that includes important lessons learned from that war. These are valuable insights that our political and military leaders would be wise to consider before committing our forces in future conflicts."

—General Anthony Zinni, USMC (ret.)

"Wawro's *The Vietnam War* pits one of the sharpest historians of his generation against the most controversial war in US history. Sparks fly throughout, as Wawro zeroes in relentlessly on the mistakes, misjudgments, and the hubris that led to American defeat in Vietnam. It is not a pretty picture: Politicians and generals floundering in a sea of tables, charts, and graphs, young men in the field fighting and dying as they try to learn the art of jungle warfare on the fly. Featuring deep research, unsparing analysis, and Wawro's always brilliant writing, *The Vietnam War* delivers across the board."

—Robert M. Citino, senior historian, National World War II Museum

THE
VIETNAM
WAR

Also by Geoffrey Wawro

Sons of Freedom: The Forgotten American Soldiers
Who Defeated Germany in World War I

A Mad Catastrophe: The Outbreak of World War I
and the Collapse of the Habsburg Empire

Quicksand: America's Pursuit of Power in the Middle East

The Franco-Prussian War: The German Conquest
of France in 1870–1871

Warfare and Society in Europe, 1792–1914

The Austro-Prussian War: Austria's War
with Prussia and Italy in 1866

THE

VIETNAM

WAR

A MILITARY HISTORY

GEOFFREY WAWRO

BASIC BOOKS
New York

Basic Books
Hachette Book Group
1290 Avenue of the Americas, New York, NY 10104
www.basicbooks.com

Printed in Canada

First Edition: October 2024

Published by Basic Books, an imprint of Hachette Book Group, Inc. The Basic Books name and logo is a registered trademark of the Hachette Book Group.

Print book interior design by Bart Dawson.

Maps copyright © 2024 by Patti Isaacs

Library of Congress Cataloging-in-Publication Data
Names: Wawro, Geoffrey, author.
Title: The Vietnam War : a military history / Geoffrey Wawro.
Description: First edition. | New York : Basic Books, 2024. |
    Includes bibliographical references and index.
Identifiers: LCCN 2024000142 | ISBN 9781541606081 (hardcover) |
    ISBN 9781541606098 (ebook)
Subjects: LCSH: Vietnam War, 1961–1975—United States. |
    United States—History, Military—20th century.
Classification: LCC DS558 .W397 2024 | DDC 959.704/3373—dc23/eng/20240325
LC record available at https://lccn.loc.gov/2024000142

ISBNs: 9781541606081 (hardcover), 9781541606098 (ebook)

MRQ

Printing 1, 2024

For Sherry Zhang

CONTENTS

List of Maps   ix
List of Abbreviations   xi

Introduction   1

1. Parody of High Strategy   11
2. No-Win War   31
3. Eve of Destruction   51
4. Strength Only for Defeat   73
5. Ia Drang   91
6. "Nail the Coonskins to the Wall"   109
7. "The Country Is Behind You—50 Percent"   129
8. Jive at Five   145
9. "We'll Just Go On Bleeding Them"   169
10. "Victory Is Around the Corner"   193
11. Zenith of Fatuity   221
12. Year of the Monkey   247
13. Tet   261
14. "We Can Keep On Winning the War Forever"   281

CONTENTS

15. Khe Sanh   301

16. Mini-Tet   317

17. A Better War?   331

18. Hamburger Hill   349

19. Search and Avoid   365

20. "I Will Not Be the First President to Lose a War"   377

21. "Cambodia Is a Man's Job"   401

22. Quiet Mutiny   423

23. "The Heaviest Defeat Ever for Nixon & Company"   445

24. "We've Made the War Too Much of a Good Thing"   467

25. "Defeat Is Not an Option"   479

26. The Fall   503

Conclusion   531

Acknowledgments   *541*
Select Bibliography   *543*
Notes   *553*
Index   *625*

LIST OF MAPS

Indochina After 1954	14
The Four Corps Areas of South Vietnam	36
The Central Highlands Region	93
Spreading VC Control in South Vietnam	110
Operations Cedar Falls and Junction City	159
The Mekong Delta	176
Northern "Eye Corps," aka "Marineland"	210
The Tet Offensive	262
The Cambodian Incursion	414
Lam Son 719	456
The Easter Offensive	484
Hanoi's Final Offensives	516

LIST OF ABBREVIATIONS

AO	area of operations
AOR	area of responsibility
APC	armored personnel carrier
ARVN	Army of the Republic of Vietnam (South Vietnamese army)
AWOL	absent without leave
CAP	combined action platoon
CIA	Central Intelligence Agency
CIDG	civilian irregular defense group
CINCPAC	Commander in Chief, Pacific Fleet
CORDS	Civil Operations and Revolutionary Development Support
COSVN	Central Office for South Vietnam (Viet Cong political and military HQ)
DEROS	date eligible for return from overseas
DIA	Defense Intelligence Agency
DIOCC	District Intelligence and Operation Coordinating Center
DMZ	demilitarized zone
DRV	Democratic Republic of Vietnam (North Vietnam)
FAC	forward air controller
FANK	National Khmer Armed Forces (American-backed)
FO	forward observer
FSB	fire support base, aka "firebase"
GDP	Gross Domestic Product

LIST OF ABBREVIATIONS

G.O.P.	Grand Old Party (Republican Party)
GRUNK	Royal Government of the National Union of Kampuchea (Chinese-backed)
GVN	Government of Vietnam (South Vietnamese government)
H&I	harassment and interdiction fire
ID	infantry division
I&M	improvement and modernization
JCS	Joint Chiefs of Staff
JUSPAO	Joint United States Public Affairs Office
KIA/BNR	killed in action, body not recovered
LAW	light antitank weapon
LCU	landing craft utility
LP	listening post
LZ	landing zone
MACV	Military Assistance Command Vietnam
MIA	missing in action
MONEVAL	monthly evaluation
MR	Military Region
MSS	Military Security Service (ARVN intelligence agency)
NATO	North Atlantic Treaty Organization
NCO	noncommissioned officer
NLF	National Liberation Front (communist front organization for the unification of Vietnam)
NSC	National Security Council
NVA	North Vietnamese Army
NVN	North Vietnam
PIOCC	Provincial Intelligence and Operation Coordinating Center
POL	petroleum, oils, and lubricants
POW	prisoner of war
PROVN	Program for Pacification and Development of Vietnam (study)
PRP	People's Revolutionary Party (Viet Cong political party)
PRU	Provincial Reconnaissance Unit (Phoenix Program death squads)

LIST OF ABBREVIATIONS

PSDF	Popular Self-Defense Force (South Vietnamese militia)
PT	patrol torpedo boat
PX	post exchange
R&D	research and development
R&R	rest and recreation
RD	revolutionary development (fortified hamlet in South Vietnam)
RF/PF	Regional Forces/Popular Forces, aka "ruff-puffs" (South Vietnamese militia)
ROK	Republic of Korea (South Korean forces in Vietnam)
RPG	rocket-propelled grenade
RTO	radio telephone operator
ruff-puff	South Vietnamese militia forces
SAM	surface-to-air missile
SDS	Students for a Democratic Society
SEATO	Southeast Asian Treaty Organization
SecDef	secretary of defense
SVN	South Vietnam
TOC	Tactical Operations Center
USAID	United States Agency for International Development
USIA	United States Information Agency
USIS	United States Information Service
VC	Viet Cong (South Vietnamese communists)
VCI	Viet Cong infrastructure
VNAF	Vietnamese Air Force (South Vietnamese air force)
WP	white phosphorous

INTRODUCTION

Vietnam was a war of choice. Understanding it requires a reckoning with this stubborn fact. The United States was not provoked into war, and none of the Cold War justifications of containment or the "domino theory" required the US military to intervene. If South Vietnam fell to a communist insurgency, the Chinese or the North Vietnamese were not going to "land on the beaches of Waikiki"—as Vice President Lyndon Johnson rather daringly warned in 1961. It was not a war fought in self-defense or for democratic ideals. What motivated the United States to go to war and stay there was a fear of appearing weak.

John F. Kennedy was the first president to fully appreciate the danger Vietnam posed, not to the United States but to himself. Just as Eisenhower had feared Senator Joe McCarthy's Red-baiters, Kennedy and Johnson feared being tarred as liberal doves by conservatives. Johnson scaled up the war effort out of the same fear, while Nixon dreaded becoming "the first president to lose a war."

It was a peculiar war from the start, inseparable from the government debates and political calculations that launched it. Kennedy set the tone when he tiptoed in, hoping to "hold the line" until he was safely reelected for a second term in 1964, at which point he planned to "explore all options," including getting out. His likely opponents in 1964 ridiculed his caution in the matter of Vietnam. After Kennedy's assassination in 1963, they were even harder on his successor, Lyndon Baines Johnson.[1]

Johnson took no comfort from the entirely American irony that he routed Barry Goldwater in the 1964 elections chiefly because the public feared that Goldwater would drag the country into the Vietnam War. And yet the moment LBJ was inaugurated, the braying for an escalation of the war resumed from the right. Ronald Reagan demanded "full mobilization" and a blockade of Haiphong harbor: "I don't see how a nation our size, engaged with a nation that size, can talk about a ten- or twenty-year war. We ought to go in and get it over with." Richard Nixon warned that Vietnam would be *the* issue in 1968 if Johnson didn't "win the war, and end it." LBJ's waking nightmare for the rest of his presidency was that he'd be running for reelection against one of these hawks "with Ho Chi Minh running through the streets of Saigon."[2]

In the world of the 1960s, America was incomparably rich, commanding 40 percent of global GDP, compared with about 15 percent today. American wealth added to American confidence made *anything* seem possible. President Kennedy, after all, had pledged in 1962 to put a man on the moon before the end of the decade, and it was done—American astronauts walked on the moon in 1969. Militarily, the United States had fueled and equipped the Allies in World War II and put 16 million troops into Europe and Asia to defeat the Germans and Japanese. No one expected North Vietnam, which armed the twenty-year insurgency in South Vietnam, to pose much of a problem. It was, President Johnson snorted, "a raggedy-ass little fourth-rate country."[3]

And yet the United States had to fight North Vietnam cautiously. Politicians of both parties talked tough when it came to communism, but the Korean War, waged from 1950 to 1953, made presidents exceedingly cautious. In Korea, American-led forces had effectively won the war by October 1950, at which point Mao Zedong unexpectedly launched 300,000 Chinese troops into Korea and turned a short war into a long one that exasperated Americans, drove President Harry Truman from office, and was terminated with no formal peace treaty and a permanent garrison of American troops on the 38th parallel.

When President Johnson weighed sending American troops, aircraft, and ships to Vietnam in 1965, Korea was foremost in his mind. The Korean War had sunk the Truman presidency, and President Eisenhower had ended that war only by threatening to use nuclear weapons. With big, costly plans for his Great Society and War on Poverty, Johnson wanted to keep the conflict in Vietnam short and cheap. Above all, he wanted to forestall a Chinese intervention that would lengthen the war and suck funds from his cherished domestic programs. Like Eisenhower and Kennedy before him, he yearned to wash his hands of the war. But he didn't dare.

The consequences would have been severe. Senator Joe McCarthy's Red Scare had only flickered out in 1954, and Washington in the 1960s was still in the grip of a "China Lobby" inflamed by Mao Zedong's victory over Chiang Kai-shek in 1949. Henry Luce's popular *Time* and *Life* magazines, which gave busy Americans their worldview, purveyed the opinions of the China Lobby, chief among them the need to prevent any more defeats in Asia to communism. American voters wanted their politicians tough too. They didn't want Goldwater, but they didn't want to lose either. Getting out of Vietnam never would have been easy.

And so LBJ launched America's Vietnam War under the most bizarre circumstances. To fight the war on a low-cost basis without giving China any excuse to intervene, he opted for "graduated pressure" in North Vietnam. Instead of overwhelming the North with military power, LBJ would increase air strikes and ground troops *gradually*, each added increment theoretically demonstrating to the North Vietnamese the futility of resistance to the richest power in the world, which, the enemy would have to assume, was only getting started. Johnson didn't come up with this strategy on his own. It was fashioned for him by the presidential advisers he had inherited from Kennedy, chiefly Secretary of Defense Robert McNamara, Secretary of State Dean Rusk, and National Security Adviser McGeorge Bundy.

LBJ hoped that graduated pressure would also reassure the Chinese and Soviets that he was not aiming at the total destruction of North Vietnam. He hoped that his decision not to attack the neutral sanctuaries of Laos and Cambodia, where North Vietnamese troops and supplies moved on their way into South Vietnam, would serve as proof that Washington sought nothing more than a "free and independent South Vietnam." Naturally, this graduated pressure strategy succeeded only in persuading Hanoi, Beijing, and Moscow that Washington was not serious. A superpower that shrank from invading or even heavily bombing North Vietnam and that feared the odium of invading the "neutral" sanctuaries of Laos and Cambodia to close the Ho Chi Minh Trail was clearly a superpower fighting with one arm tied behind its back.

Graduated pressure, unfortunately, was never applied in South Vietnam. America's ally in the war was exposed to the full fury of the American arsenal: B-52s, batteries of field artillery, helicopter gunships, airmobile assaults, and "herbicide operations" with Agent Orange that stripped and poisoned much of the lush green country. Whatever affection the South Vietnamese people had for Americans withered away on a battlefield that spanned the entire country and led to the death of half a million civilians, mainly from American firepower.

The contrast between the deference and delicacy afforded North Vietnam and the ultraviolence unleashed in South Vietnam highlighted one of the war's great sins—its lack of strategy. Kennedy saw it not as a war but as a problem to be managed. Johnson saw it as a war that had to be artfully contained. "I am going to control from Washington," he said in 1965, a position from which he never deviated.

Neither JFK nor LBJ came up with a winning strategy, some way to fit military operations to political outcomes. The presidents talked about fighting to create a free South Vietnam, but they knew—and, one or two years into the war, most Americans knew—that the South Vietnamese nation was hopelessly corrupt and divided. As a result, there was no viable strategy, no way to segue from war to peace in an environment where the Viet Cong communists were always more feared and respected than the government in Saigon.

Starting in 1965, General William "Westy" Westmoreland filled the strategic void with his concept of "search and destroy." Westmoreland reasoned that if he would not be given the forces and authority to defeat North Vietnam and invade the neutral sanctuaries, he would defeat the enemy by killing so many of them that Hanoi would reach a "crossover point," where American-inflicted casualties would outnumber Viet Cong recruiting and North Vietnamese infiltration.

Search and destroy was what the American military did in Vietnam from 1965 to 1969. In view of its colossal ineffectiveness—only about 10 percent of search and destroy operations actually found the enemy—the body count it did inflict on the communists was a grim tribute to the efficacy of American firepower. An estimated 1 million enemy troops were chewed up by American ground and air attacks during the war.

And yet search and destroy failed because North Vietnam had 2.4 million young men of military age with 120,000 more reaching military age every year, and because corrupt, dysfunctional South Vietnam produced a steady stream of young recruits for the Viet Cong. Search and destroy failed because the Johnson administration and its generals did not appreciate just how different North Vietnam and the United States were. The United States was an affluent Western democracy that would tire of Vietnam as soon as it became a painful burden. North Vietnam was an authoritarian state fighting to unify and revolutionize Vietnam. Its aims and energy, buttressed by the resources of Moscow and Beijing, were unlimited.

And search and destroy failed because instead of securing South Vietnam, it destroyed it—literally. The United States defoliated one-seventh of South Vietnam's territory, obliterated countless villages, and created 5 million internal refugees in the course of the war. Through it all, Westmoreland was unmoved, obtusely assuring a journalist in 1967 that this self-inflicted devastation served a purpose: "It does deprive the enemy of the population, doesn't it?"

Westmoreland's robotic approach to the war explained why President Kennedy had been so wary of letting the US military into Vietnam. "Watch the generals," JFK remarked, "and avoid the feeling that just because they are military men their opinion on military matters is worth a damn." Once the US military got into any contingency, JFK complained, the demands of the generals—for money, personnel, and facilities—always soared. True to form, Westmoreland paved South Vietnam, built container ports and air bases, and positioned field artillery everywhere in the country, but never even sniffed victory. He made the war about operational art, not strategy. He focused entirely on planning, launching, and sustaining his costly and inefficient operations without ever fitting them to an achievable endgame and an enduring peace.[4]

Critics argued then, and still do, that had Johnson only permitted Westmoreland to do *more*—to attack Laos and Cambodia, to invade and pulverize North Vietnam—then the war could have been won. Beguiling as such arguments are, they are founded on nonsense. In fact, the Johnson administration looked at all of these possibilities and rejected them all not because of Johnson's caution but because none of them were *feasible*.

Vietnam became such a big war so quickly that there was never any slack in the system that would permit new commitments in Cambodia, Laos, or North Vietnam. There were many reasons for this. All are explored in this book. Casual observers regard 1969's peak American strength of 543,000 troops in Vietnam as a lot of manpower. It wasn't. Half a million American troops never yielded more than 80,000 combat troops, so great were the demands of logistics, maintenance, and other support functions. There was a moment in 1968 when Secretary of Defense Robert McNamara, crushed by the war and its demands, calculated the total number of American personnel on the ground, in the sky, and on the seas around Vietnam and responded this way to a request from Westmoreland for more troops: "You have 1.2 million forces in Southeast Asia, and yet you've only got 50,000 or 60,000 in combat." In view of the military's high tail-to-tip ratio, there were never enough troops even to fight effectively in South Vietnam, let alone Laos, Cambodia, and North Vietnam.[5]

Ninety percent of American operations in South Vietnam never even located an enemy who would have been far more elusive in the vast forested spaces of Laos and Cambodia. Airpower availed far less than anticipated. Laos, site of the Ho Chi Minh Trail, was the most heavily bombed country in the history of the world during the Vietnam War, and yet all of that bombing never prevented the North Vietnamese from moving troops and supplies into South Vietnam. Only ground troops could, but there were never enough of them. There were over 1 million South Vietnamese troops paid for by American taxpayers. Pushed into Laos in 1971 to close the Ho Chi Minh Trail and demonstrate the success of "military Vietnamization," they met with a fate that revealed the true nature of the South Vietnamese military and its appalling leadership.

There was also the financial pinch. The war in Vietnam could not be broadened because there was no money for it. America was rich, but not so rich that it could afford both the new federal programs of LBJ's Great Society—an initiative even bigger than FDR's New Deal—and a costly foreign war. But even if LBJ and his Republican successor had chosen guns over butter, the price of Vietnam, even on LBJ's reduced-cost basis, was already backbreaking: half a million troops, 12,000 helicopters, 2,000 jets, and all of the ships, sailors, and aircraft of the Seventh Fleet. And this just scratched the surface. The daily consumption of fuel, parts, ammunition, and medical care was immense, and training and equipping 3.5 million South Vietnamese regulars and militiamen cost billions more.

Vietnam spending triggered inflation, which doubled in the United States between 1965 and 1967, and doubled again by 1970. The war created huge budget deficits, a run on America's gold reserves, and a hollowing out of America's defense preparedness, as every other account at the Pentagon (NATO, Korea, ICBMs, R&D) had to be plundered to pay for the insatiable costs of Vietnam. Quite simply, the war could not be expanded without even greater harm to the American economy and national security. Critics who wanted to expand and intensify the war never bothered explaining where they would have found the money and the troops to do so. Such is politics and, latterly, "revisionist history."

This book briefly summarizes the prehistory of LBJ's decision to commit ground troops to the war in Vietnam and looks closely at the years of American combat. It focuses as much on Nixon's war as on LBJ's, for the two were equally bloody and significant. Nixon ran in 1968 against LBJ's vice president, Hubert Humphrey, who took up the cudgels after Johnson, ruined by the war, declined to run for a second term. Nixon linked Humphrey to LBJ's "gradualism" and "camouflaged surrender" and vowed to do better. "Never has so much military, economic, and diplomatic power been used so ineffectively as in Vietnam," one of Nixon's campaign spots intoned.

But Nixon's presidency began with an act of subterfuge as disgraceful as any in "Tricky Dick's" shady political history. Nixon deliberately wrecked a peace deal that LBJ was close to sealing in October 1968 by opening a back channel to the South Vietnamese president, Nguyen Van Thieu, and urging him *not* to make peace. Thieu was assured through cutouts that Nixon would get him a better deal than Johnson or Humphrey could.

This naked act of ambition, consecrated on a second, entirely avoidable mountain of American dead and wounded, got Nixon elected in a close race by denying Humphrey an "October surprise." But Nixon now had to end the war himself and reveal his "secret plan."

The secret plan, such as it was, held that Nixon would repeal all of LBJ's self-denying ordinances—no bombing in North Vietnam, no invasions of Laos or Cambodia—and mend relations with Moscow and Beijing in order to detach them from Hanoi. In a war in which far too much was spent on the relatively minor issue of Southeast Asia, Nixon and Kissinger gave away the store to Mao Zedong, who had ruthlessly overseen the deaths of 45 to 80 million of his own people in purges and famines. In the hope that Mao would rein in Chinese support for Hanoi, Nixon offered Mao the prospect of diplomatic normalization and a "One-China" policy from which Kissinger meekly removed every mention of America's military alliance with Taiwan. Nixon's attempt to expand the war into the neutral sanctuaries broke against the hard limits of the war. Congress refused to fund ground operations in Laos and Cambodia, and American citizens protested in unprecedented numbers when Nixon invaded Cambodia in 1970. The fury of those protests was in no way diminished by Nixon's timid rules of engagement, which were nearly as restrictive as Johnson's.

Another unhelpful facet of Nixon's "secret plan" was de-Americanization of the war, which his secretary of defense named "Vietnamization." It was supposed to proceed in careful, measured steps, but when Americans read about the Battle of Hamburger Hill in 1969 and others like it, they were so appalled by the brutish tactics and casualties in an obviously lost cause that Nixon felt compelled to pull American forces out precipitously, effectively wrecking Vietnamization and abandoning South Vietnam to certain defeat.

The military that Nixon led in Vietnam was demoralized by all of this self-serving chicanery. Johnson's "no-win war" had been bad enough, but the grunts were even more demoralized by Nixon's official change of the war aim—from battlefield victory to "peace with honor" and "buying time for South Vietnam."

To speak of any great military possibilities in the Nixon years is pure fantasy. The "Vietnam-only Army" inherited by Nixon was a curious phenomenon. Neither Johnson nor Nixon dared call up America's 1 million trained reserves, so the military in Vietnam relied entirely on draftees and "volunteers," young men who volunteered for noncombat jobs in order to avoid being drafted into combat units, where 88 percent of the grunts were draftees. This force began to fall apart in 1969, when the war was acknowledged by all to be futile. Drug use surged, race relations worsened, and the combat units began to practice "search and avoid" rather than search and destroy. Officers and noncommissioned officers (NCOs) who tried to coerce their soldiers into combat were ignored or murdered (fragged). Nixon's attempt to reform the broken system in 1970 with a draft lottery only made things worse, as we shall see.

The dirty secret of Nixon's Vietnamization plan was that it was more about removing America's demoralized armed forces from Vietnam before they disintegrated, or before they suffered a series of catastrophic defeats in the field or even inside their bases. Force security and vigilance had become so slack by 1970 that commanders and politicians feared massacres of American draftees at communist hands.

The war, when viewed across all of its phases, tells us a great deal about the arrogance and limits of power. Compared to World War II or even Korea, Vietnam was fought with a derisory share of American GDP—only 3 percent in 1967. This led decision-makers to believe that they could eat their cake and have it too. They couldn't. The costs of the war kept rising, and funds could be found only by raising taxes and cannibalizing the defense budget. Media and popular opinion turned against the war and made it even harder to escalate.

For the historian, the most striking feature of the war was the cavalier way in which it was managed from beginning to end. Kennedy kicked the can down the road and was spared dealing with Vietnam in a more agonizing way only by his assassination in 1963. Johnson talked tough—"Nail the coonskins to the wall!"—but waged a war hemmed in by punctilious rules of engagement, economic limits, and a failure to decide what the war was really about or what the strategy was. Nixon promised to make "big plays" in Southeast Asia to break the deadlock, but the new president bumped up against the same political and financial limits that had constrained LBJ. Nixon ended up settling for the same peace deal that LBJ had negotiated four years earlier, a scandalous return on investment for all of the dead, wounded, and billions of dollars expended on Nixon's watch.

The Vietnam War is an unsettling, illuminating story of American power at its zenith. In the world wars of the early twentieth century, the United States had intervened with extreme reluctance. The nation had viewed wars as catastrophic in every way. After 1945, the United States was more willing to go to war. This was partly hubris and partly because national security was politically weaponized during the Cold War. Politicians had to project toughness or risk ridicule and defeat. Wealth, power, and anti-communism inclined ordinary Americans toward intervention abroad in the early 1960s. Vietnam would reveal the weakness of Congress, the power of the presidency, the complicity of the general public, the might of the bureaucracy and armed services, and the ease with which these power centers can make and prolong even the most ill-considered wars, with ruinous consequences.

Chapter 1

PARODY OF
HIGH STRATEGY

America's commitment to South Vietnam began under the most unpromising circumstances. China had fallen to Mao Zedong's communists in 1949. North Korea had nearly overrun South Korea in 1950, and then France, whose ten-year war to retain "French Indochina" had been funded by the United States, abruptly abandoned Southeast Asia in 1954. In Vietnam, France left behind two states: a communist North Vietnam with its capital at Hanoi, and a noncommunist South Vietnam governed from Saigon. North Vietnam held all the cards: a legendary leader, an industrial base, an army hardened by war, an inspiring message, and a land border with China. South Vietnam had little besides liabilities: an unpopular leadership, an agricultural economy, vulnerable land borders, an uninspiring message, and an army recruited from the old French colonial force. South Vietnam's long borders with Laos and Cambodia, great wilderness areas of old French Indochina, were simply too big to defend. Following the French retreat, they were left to their weak monarchies and to Chinese-supplied communist "forest armies" that were already jostling for power—the Khmer Rouge in Cambodia and the Pathet Lao in Laos.

Sixty-three-year-old Dwight Eisenhower was president when France abandoned Indochina. Some of his military advisers had pressed him to

11

intervene at Dien Bien Phu, France's final defeat in 1954. The US Navy and Air Force had wanted to bomb the Vietnamese troops besieging the French, but the Army, led by General Matthew Ridgway, had reminded Ike of the American precept since Korea that there must be "no land wars in Asia." The continent had a history of luring armies to their death in its undeveloped spaces. Were ground troops needed in Indochina, Eisenhower was told, there would never be enough of them to pluck victory from such a vast theater of revolutionary war.[1]

Eisenhower stood down, but, fearful of the Red-baiting anticommunists gathered around Senator Joe McCarthy of Wisconsin, he poured military and economic aid into South Vietnam to prove that he took the communist threat seriously. Eisenhower wanted to do just enough for South Vietnam to keep Joe McCarthy off his back, but not too much. South Vietnam had so many liabilities that Ike did not want to be yoked to the place if it fell, which was always a strong possibility.

North Vietnam had a history. It was located in Tonkin, the most populous and developed part of Indochina. Its capital, Hanoi, was the finest colonial city in Asia. And its leader was sixty-four-year-old Ho Chi Minh—modest, affable, self-effacing, and admired by the Vietnamese people for having founded the Viet Minh national independence movement and driven out the French.

South Vietnam had no history. It was located on the southern tip of the Indochinese peninsula, named Cochin China by French imperialists deliberately in order to deny the existence of a Vietnamese nationality. Its capital was Saigon, an entirely new city built on a finger of delta land washed by the South China Sea. Cochin China's antipode was Annam, the northern half of South Vietnam, where the proud inhabitants of older cities such as Hue and Da Nang looked down their noses at the nouveau-riche hustlers of Saigon. South Vietnam's leader was an inherited French puppet emperor, Bao Dai, who gave way after just a year to his conniving prime minister, Ngo Dinh Diem, who kicked the emperor out of the country in 1955 and converted the monarchy to a republic, with himself as president. The fifty-four-year-old Diem was an austere Roman Catholic zealot in a lively nation in which Catholics, who were widely regarded as French collaborators, never amounted to more than 20 percent of the population.

Eisenhower and Secretary of State John Foster Dulles greet South Vietnamese president Ngo Dinh Diem on his state visit to the United States, May 1957. Eisenhower took the measure of Diem and was unimpressed, but still gave South Vietnam $1 billion in aid to appease American anticommunists. (National Archives)

Eisenhower took the measure of Diem and was not impressed, but he still funneled over a billion dollars of aid into South Vietnam before he left office. The two Vietnams were supposed to submit to elections for a unified country in 1956, but, knowing that the revered "Uncle Ho" would win those elections easily, Eisenhower instructed Diem to cancel the elections and declare the independence of South Vietnam instead. Eisenhower did this on the assumption that the more populous communist North Vietnam would simply absorb the less populous South Vietnam by fair means or foul. Still, it was not a good origin story for a new nation committed to "democracy" under "free-world" tutelage.

When Diem canceled the elections, the 10,000 Viet Minh "stay-behind" guerrillas, who had gone quiet for two years awaiting the nationwide ballot,

CHINA

NORTH VIETNAM

Lao Cai

Red River

Phuc Yen

Dien Bien Phu

Hanoi ★

Haiphong

LAOS

Thanh Hoa

Gulf of Tonkin

Hainan

Mekong River

Vientiane ★

Vinh Vien

Dong Hoi

Demilitarized Zone

Partition Line, July 1954

THAILAND

Hue

Da Nang

Chu Lai

Quang Ngai

Ho Chi Minh Trail

Kontum

Pleiku

Bangkok ★

CAMBODIA

Binh Dinh

Qui Nhon

SOUTH VIETNAM

Tonle Sap

Mekong River

Nha Trang

Cam Ranh Bay

Phan Rang

Phnom Penh ★

Gulf of Thailand

Bien Hoa

Gia Dinh

Saigon ★

Long Xuyen

Mekong Delta

SOUTH CHINA SEA

0   150 mi

0   150 km

Indochina After 1954

resumed their struggle in South Vietnam to unify the country under the rule of Hanoi.

President John F. Kennedy took office in 1961 and was horrified by the situation he inherited from Eisenhower. Diem, who had lived in exile at the Maryknoll Seminary in Lakewood, New Jersey, in the 1950s and sold himself to politicians and journalists as a promising man of action, was not working out. Initially lauded by JFK as a "miracle man," a "third-force" statesman untarnished by association with the French or communists, Diem was none of those things. He was an unpopular, celibate, straitlaced loner who surrounded himself with family members and cronies, most of whom descended into corruption and tyranny.[2]

Eisenhower's billion had paid for a massive expansion of the Army of the Republic of Vietnam (ARVN, always pronounced "arvin"). Kennedy continued the funding and inserted thousands of American military advisers to assist. Eisenhower had sent 700 advisers; Kennedy sent 15,000. All of this should have been sufficient to defeat the Viet Minh stay-behind guerrillas. To puncture their aura of saintliness, Diem renamed the Viet Minh "Viet Cong," which was a pejorative meaning "Vietnamese commie." He then reduced their numbers by 80 percent, to an estimated 2,000, through a vicious multiyear "Denunciation of Communists Campaign." That American-advised program of mass incarceration, torture, and massacre, which played out during Eisenhower's second term, had the unwanted effect of *increasing* the appeal of the Viet Cong. Diem jailed 20,000, killed thousands more, and ultimately generated more Viet Cong than he destroyed.[3]

Diem ordered whole villages believed to be in thrall to the Viet Cong to be annihilated in the late 1950s—places like Huong Dien, where ninety-two people were killed, two-thirds of them women and children. Diem authorized province chiefs to execute detainees on suspicion alone; there was no need for a trial. He ordered "mopping-up operations" in critical areas around Saigon like Bien Hoa, gouging out eyes, cutting off tongues, burning hands and feet, and displaying decapitated victims. The luckiest suspects were spared but forced to recant in ceremonies in which they would be ordered to spit on, trample, and burn portraits of Ho Chi Minh and the Viet Minh flag—still proud symbols of nationalist resistance to the French in every part of Vietnam—and to kneel and beg a merciful Diem for clemency.

Diem ordered the desecration of Viet Minh war memorials and graves, further alienating the Vietnamese.

It was a five-year-long flurry of unfocused violence and score settling all over the country as local officials took the "anti-treason laws" at the heart of the campaign as a convenient pretext to eliminate or dispossess their enemies, creditors, or rivals. Most of the victims had little or no connection to the communists, many of whom remained concealed in the villages and the government. The arbitrariness of it all merely deepened the sense of insecurity in South Vietnam and the impression of weakness around Diem. British novelist Graham Greene called Diem "the patriot ruined by the West."[4]

The US advisers sent to train the ARVN reported that it would not fight. The ARVN generals were as afraid of the Viet Cong as they had been of the Viet Minh, for they were the same dogged enemy. The generals were also afraid of reporting casualties to Diem, for he viewed fighting generals as a threat to his rule and demoted them or shunted them into powerless administrative jobs. The corps and division commands were given to loyal, passive Catholics. Initiative, valor, and aptitude were discouraged. The generals were expected to limit casualties, keep Diem in power, share their plunder, and take a cut of American aid dollars, 75 percent of which went to the ARVN.

With so much moral hazard on display, President Kennedy lost his early enthusiasm for Diem. But JFK didn't dare pull the plug. Like Eisenhower, he had to *appear* tough. Having begun his presidency with the Bay of Pigs fiasco, Kennedy needed a win somewhere to beat back Republican criticism that he was too callow to lead the global fight against communism.[5]

Kennedy's administration was full of hawks, chief among them Robert McNamara, the secretary of defense; Dean Rusk, the secretary of state; McGeorge Bundy, the national security adviser; CIA director John McCone; and White House military adviser Maxwell Taylor. These men prodded Kennedy deeper into Vietnam. Forty-five-year-old Bob McNamara, who had come to the administration from the Ford Motor Company, bubbled with optimism. America was so rich and powerful that it would prevail where the French hadn't.

Fifty-two-year-old Dean Rusk was a fervent anticommunist who saw the hands of Nikita Khrushchev and Mao Zedong behind every national liberation movement. Forty-one-year-old McGeorge "Mac" Bundy, the youngest dean in Harvard history, was the professor, who silkily explained that war could be waged in thin slices: pressure could be first "signaled" and then artfully increased to nudge an enemy as small and insignificant as North Vietnam toward surrender. Max Taylor was a retired general with a glittering resumé and the author of *The Uncertain Trumpet*, a book published in 1960 that called massive nuclear retaliation a strategic "dead end" and argued instead for "flexible response"—the ability to muster varying levels of force or capability to cope with the "entire spectrum of possible challenges," from insurgencies such as the one in Vietnam to nuclear war between the superpowers. Kennedy endorsed the book's arguments and brought Taylor onto his White House staff.[6]

These hawks in the Kennedy cabinet were reinforced by the Military Assistance Command Vietnam (MACV). This was the headquarters first established by Truman and Eisenhower to coordinate deliveries of military assistance to the ARVN. The American generals sent to Vietnam in the 1950s and early 1960s to run the advisory group had one thing in common: none of them ever submitted a candid report on the situation in South Vietnam. The nature of peacetime military organizations is to check boxes, fulfill requirements, and generate positive performance reviews. All of this could be achieved in South Vietnam in spite of the glaring defects of the operations there. ARVN units could be equipped, trained, and deployed. Their regular reverses in the field could be converted into victories on paper. The timidity of the well-armed South Vietnamese units and their failure to defeat the communists in battle could not be acknowledged without threat to the four-star MACV commander's career.

This scam became particularly notorious under the MACV commander selected by Kennedy. Fifty-seven-year-old General Paul "Ramrod" Harkins was sent out to Saigon in 1962 on the recommendation of Maxwell Taylor. Taylor's fingerprints would be all over the American intervention in Vietnam. He picked top commanders for it, and he pushed Kennedy in deeper.[7]

During Harkins' three-year tenure in Saigon, there was growing friction between his staff and the advisers attached to South Vietnamese units in the field. The most notorious example of this was Harkins' feud with Lieutenant Colonel John Paul Vann, described in detail in Neil Sheehan's Pulitzer Prize–winning *A Bright Shining Lie: John Paul Vann and America in Vietnam* (1988). Vann advised the ARVN 7th Division in the Mekong

Delta for two years. He reported in granular detail the failings of the ARVN, but also their total lack of interest in improvement. Other advisers besides Vann noted the incipient demoralization of a force in which urban French-speaking Catholic officers treated their rural Buddhist troops "like dirt." One adviser wondered if the United States was not unwittingly playing the role of "the British Redcoats during the American Revolution" by backing the ARVN. Harkins angrily suppressed such reports and sent Lieutenant Colonel Vann home to a desk job in the Pentagon, where General Max Taylor, whom Kennedy had reactivated in 1962 and made chairman of the Joint Chiefs of Staff, took pains to ensure that Vann was given no opportunity to brief the lessons he'd learned in Vietnam to an influential audience.[8]

Everyone knew what Harkins was up to. The general routinely manipulated statistics and charts to show progress, and converted questions from the White House or the Pentagon about progress into templates for entirely fictional "headway reports" that would please the faraway civilians. "We are winning, this we know / General Harkins tells us so," jaded American advisers sang to the tune of "Twinkle, Twinkle, Little Star." President Kennedy tolerated this "lying machine" because it served his own political need to show progress in Vietnam and to keep the commitment small and cheap. Were Harkins to reveal the true state of the ARVN and the extent of his own incompetence, Kennedy would come under immediate pressure from hawks to commit more money, airpower, and personnel to Vietnam. It was easier, Kennedy reasoned, to pretend that all was well. In this way, reporter and historian David Halberstam observed, "the lie became truth" with JFK's connivance.[9]

Secretary of Defense McNamara also connived at war, from a strange mixture of fear and hope. The "SecDef," as he was known, feared the Joint Chiefs, who had no executive authority but nevertheless packed a heavy punch. They could whisper dissent to Congress or the press and trigger backlash against the administration. McNamara—increasingly the engine of the war, so much so that Vietnam was at this early stage referred to as "McNamara's war"—was himself a prisoner of that military bureaucracy.[10]

On the SecDef's regular trips to Vietnam in the early 1960s, he inevitably encountered dissidents—reporters, Army advisers, diplomats, aid workers, CIA agents—who told him that MACV's frothy progress reports were

An American infantry adviser wading through a rice paddy with an ARVN machine gun crew in August 1964. US advisers reported in granular detail the failings of the ARVN, but also their total lack of interest in improvement. (National Archives)

fabricated, what one reporter called "a parody of high strategy." But, like the president he served, McNamara didn't dare contemplate the alternative—a *real* strategy—for the simple reason that such a step would embolden the generals to ask for *more* force and resources in Vietnam. This they would assuredly do, either to reinforce the war in Vietnam or merely to get additional resources for Europe, Korea, and other theaters under the cloak of needs for Vietnam. This, in turn, would force McNamara to request more defense dollars from the president, which had to be avoided if McNamara was to remain a privileged insider at a time when Kennedy was trying to pass billions of dollars in tax cuts to energize the economy. McNamara became a vehicle for slow and steady escalation by claiming that things were going well enough for the war to continue.[11]

The one precaution Bob McNamara did take was to bring in the "whiz kids," bright young civilians from think tanks and universities, to check Harkins' work. They discovered the same trickery reported by Vann and tolerated by Kennedy. Alain Enthoven, a thirty-one-year-old whiz kid from the RAND Corporation who ran McNamara's computerized Systems Analysis Office, discovered that the ARVN was faking operations to justify its existence. But none of this dulled McNamara's appetite for war in Vietnam. Like most of his peers in the can-do "GI Generation," the SecDef brimmed with confidence. Kennedy's conventional and nuclear force buildups and America's unrivaled economic might had redrawn the "map of power," McNamara declared in a speech. Even if the United States waged a carefully limited war in Vietnam to forestall Chinese intervention, McNamara thought it inconceivable that little North Vietnam could withstand even small increments of American power. "We have a $50-billion-dollar budget and this is our only war," McNamara chuckled to a general in 1961. "Don't worry about money."[12]

There were a few Cassandras in the Kennedy administration who warned against this overconfidence. Fifty-one-year-old George Ball, undersecretary of state, was one of them, cautioning Kennedy in November 1961 that "within five years we'll have 300,000 men in the paddies and jungles and we'll never find them again." But Kennedy shooed away these voices of reason. To secure reelection in 1964, he felt compelled to posture in Vietnam. His likely opponent, Senator Barry Goldwater of Arizona, was already accusing Kennedy of "losing Indochina." Polls in 1963 showed Kennedy trailing Goldwater by 20 points in all eleven states of the old Confederacy and losing ground in the suburbs as well. Kennedy feared electoral defeat and another "Joe McCarthy scare" if South Vietnam fell to the Viet Cong insurgency.[13]

By the fall of 1963, the 25,000 Viet Cong (VC) guerrillas in South Vietnam controlled 80 percent of the country's 12,000 rural hamlets. Organized on Maoist lines, the VC waged revolutionary warfare. They went into rural areas that were corruptly administered by Diem and introduced clean administration. They insisted on the rights of the Vietnamese nation against foreign-controlled "puppets" such as Diem. They played Robin Hood, breaking up landed estates and distributing small plots to the villagers. Where incentives and propaganda failed, they inserted *dich van*, "moral intervention cadres." These were communist assassins, who killed thousands of hamlet chiefs, youth leaders, paramedics, teachers, police, and their families—making clear who was *really* in charge. Everywhere the

VC took control, they redirected taxes from the government to themselves. Their numbers kept growing through the 1960s.[14]

Diem by 1963 was under attack by his own people. Buddhist monks, sick of the corruption, tyranny, and casualties of the war with the Viet Cong, launched a campaign of conscience against Diem. This "Struggle Movement" attracted thousands of ordinary people to its ranks—students, mothers, schoolchildren, and even government workers. The demonstrators made the connection between Diem and his American enabler. The cry went up: "The United States must either make Diem reform or get rid of him." Two years earlier, Attorney General Robert F. Kennedy had waved away a question about Diem, saying, "We've got twenty Vietnams a day to handle." Now the one and only Vietnam came into focus.[15]

Diem, assisted by his brother Nhu, who ran South Vietnam's secret police and intelligence services, cracked down on the Struggle Movement, raiding and trashing the Buddhist pagodas of Saigon, Hue, and the other major towns of South Vietnam. Monks in their saffron robes were shot and beaten, others jailed. Students, thought to be a nexus between the Buddhists and the Viet Cong, were pulled from their university classrooms and tortured. Kennedy's vast increase in military aid and personnel in South Vietnam had resulted in a great increase in the press corps there too, from just two full-time American reporters at the start of his administration to a dozen in 1963, some of them with television cameras, which they now turned on the scenes of violence. Bill Bundy, one of Kennedy's whiz kids in the State Department, observed that in the summer of 1963 the president became "more preoccupied with Vietnam than at any previous time."[16]

Worse was still to come. On June 11, 1963, a seventy-three-year-old monk named Thich Quang Duc took the anti-Diem protest to a shocking new level. He sat in the middle of Saigon's busiest intersection, crossed his legs in the lotus position, drenched himself with gasoline, and set himself on fire. While the press shot photos and video and a horrified crowd gathered, the monk burned for ten minutes, sitting upright, his hands folded in his lap.

Images of the burning monk flashed around the globe. Six more monks and nuns burned themselves in the following weeks, inspiring massive demonstrations against the regime. What had been a South Vietnamese

Kennedy's administration divided over the issue of support for Saigon. Here a worried JFK discusses Vietnam with Secretary of Defense Robert McNamara and Chairman of the Joint Chiefs of Staff General Maxwell Taylor in October 1963. (JFK Library)

crisis—downplayed by the US embassy and MACV—suddenly became a political crisis for the White House that implicated Camelot in Diem's human rights abuses. Kennedy, one reporter observed, gave every appearance of subsidizing "a religious war against the country's Buddhists."[17]

Kennedy's administration now divided over the issue of a coup in Saigon. McNamara, Rusk, Mac Bundy, McCone, Taylor, and Harkins argued that the war was going as well as could be expected under Diem and that it would be unwise to rock the boat. The State Department split, Rusk supporting Diem but two of his powerful deputies—Averell Harriman and Roger Hilsman—urging JFK to begin laying the groundwork for a "clean coup," in which the ARVN generals would seize power, unite the country, and fight the VC more effectively.

Kennedy's counterinsurgency adviser, Colonel Edward Lansdale, warned against a coup, characterizing the ARVN generals as "highly selfish and mediocre people squabbling among themselves for power while the Communists take over." The prime loyalty of each of South Vietnam's forty-eight generals was to his mentor, himself, and his hangers-on—certainly not to his country. Forty-eight generals, one contemporary wisecracked, provided forty-eight reasons for changing the status quo. Diem, at least, had the solid support of South Vietnam's Catholics. That was more grassroots support than any one general had. Taking it all in, the newly arrived American ambassador, sixty-one-year-old Henry Cabot Lodge Jr., counseled caution. With the ARVN generals so clearly lacking unity and courage, a coup now would be "a shot in the dark."[18]

A coup began to materialize—more from chance than from cold calculation. Playing a deadly game of musical chairs, the generals, many of whom were under surveillance by Diem and Nhu, finally rushed to end the game on their terms before Diem could end it on his. They were prodded along by Hanoi's most notorious double agent, ARVN colonel Pham Ngoc Thao, who used his crucial role as a regime security chief, trusted by Nhu, to push along the coup, which he correctly predicted would further destabilize South Vietnam. An already narrow political base would be made even narrower, "setting," as journalist Marguerite Higgins observed from Saigon, "the Vietnamese army at the throat of the Diem regime in the middle of a war."[19]

Colonel Thao, whose brother was Hanoi's ambassador to East Germany, assembled a force of 3,000 coup troops on his own initiative, but then yielded control to the two heavyweights: forty-seven-year-old General Duong Van Minh, known as "Big Minh" because he was six feet tall and 200 pounds, and the forty-six-year-old chairman of the Joint General Staff, General Tran Van Don. Decisive force was lent by thirty-eight-year-old General Ton That Dinh, who commanded Saigon and the thousands of troops of the III Corps region surrounding it. One of Dinh's more ambitious subordinates, General Nguyen Van Thieu, was the commander of the ARVN 5th Division at nearby Bien Hoa. Thieu had recently converted to Catholicism to ingratiate himself with Diem. He now hastened to join the plotters, securing his own brilliant future.[20]

The coup happened in the middle of the afternoon on November 1, 1963. With pro-coup forces surrounding the presidential palace, which was the old French Government House, Diem and Nhu fled to the fortified basement, where a $200,000 bomb shelter, radio transmitter, and command center with phones and maps had just been installed. They frantically called Ambassador Lodge, who had received a cable from Mac Bundy the previous day instructing him to let a coup under "responsible leadership succeed." Lodge told Diem that the United States government had no position on the unfolding coup. The frightened brothers then ran down a secret tunnel with nothing but a briefcase stuffed with dollars, emerged outside the palace, and found their way to St. Francis Xavier Church in Cholon—Saigon's Chinatown.[21]

Half of South Vietnam's army remained loyal to Diem, but that half was in the provinces and could not make its way to Saigon over blocked roads and bridges. Early the next morning, with coup forces searching the city for Diem and Nhu, Diem phoned General Dinh at the Joint General Staff and asked for safe conduct to the airport so that he and Nhu could go into exile. Diem had assumed Dinh would launch a countercoup, but Dinh did nothing of the sort. He first berated Diem and his brother—"Dinh saved you mother fuckers many times, but not now, you bastards. You shits are finished. It's all over"—and then he sent three armored cars to collect the Ngo brothers and drive them to the airport.[22]

Until the last, Diem and Nhu believed that the coup was a fake one to flush out plotters and that loyalists like Dinh would rally back to the regime at the critical moment. During the drive, the two leaders began to grasp that the coup was real. None of the highest-ranking generals came to escort them, and the general who did had been demoted by the Ngos and hated them. He placed them in an armored car with a major and Big Minh's forty-three-year-old bodyguard, Captain Nguyen Van Nhung. Nhung was Big Minh's aide-de-camp and in-house assassin. He had killed his forty-eighth victim for Big Minh the night before the coup, when he shot the commander of the ARVN Special Forces in the head for refusing to join the revolt. He was about to kill two more. Witnesses observed Big Minh make a pistol of his fingers and wave them at Nhung as he departed—a signal to kill the brothers and remove them as threats to the coup regime.

Back at Joint General Staff headquarters, most of the coup plotters still assumed that Diem was headed to the airport and into exile. But inside their armored car, Diem and Nhu, their hands tied behind their backs, began to quarrel with Captain Nhung, who then stabbed Nhu twenty times with a bayonet before shooting him and Diem in the head. When the armored cars arrived at the Joint General Staff headquarters, the waiting generals feigned anguish. None of the plotters wanted Diem and Nhu to escape abroad to found a competing government in exile, but they had promised the brothers safe conduct and an "honorable surrender." In the space of an hour, they had given their word and broken it.[23]

President Kennedy, apprised of the news in the White House, left the room "somber and shaken," as one witness recalled. Arthur Schlesinger Jr., then a special assistant in the White House, found JFK more depressed than at any other time since the Bay of Pigs. The president had been trying to extricate the United States from Vietnam, yet this coup, which the world would assume he had facilitated, pulled him in deeper and tied him to whatever regime followed. "*Our* soldiers," adviser John Kenneth Galbraith had warned Kennedy on the eve of the coup, "cannot deal with *the* vital weakness": Saigon's inability under *any* regime to defend and legitimize its government. Galbraith pleaded with JFK to stop listening to the hawks, or "we shall replace the French as the colonial force in the area and bleed as the French did."[24]

Three weeks later, Kennedy himself lay bleeding in Dallas. Hours after that, his fifty-five-year-old vice president, Lyndon Baines Johnson, unexpectedly ascended to the Oval Office. As vice president, LBJ had been a minor player on Vietnam. Never privy to Kennedy's inner doubts about the war—only aware of the president's public statements of support—Johnson felt that by taking a hard-line position on Vietnam he was continuing Kennedy's policy, an illusion encouraged by Kennedy's hawkish advisers, all of whom Johnson retained. Just days after Kennedy's murder, LBJ baldly stated his position on the war to Ambassador Lodge, who had flown to Washington to meet with the thirty-fifth president but instead met with the thirty-sixth. "I am not going to lose Vietnam," Johnson vowed. "I am not going to be the president who saw Southeast Asia go the way China went."[25]

The junta that Kennedy had tepidly encouraged proved even worse than Diem. It was unconnected to the masses, and arguably more French than Vietnamese: General Tran Van Don had been born in the Gironde and educated in France. Big Minh had attended the top French colonial high school in Saigon before going abroad to study at the École Militaire in Paris. He was almost theatrically lazy, skipping meetings to tend his orchids, feed his exotic birds, or play tennis. General Le Van Kim, Don's brother-in-law and co-conspirator, had attended film school in Paris. Nguyen Ngoc Tho, the civilian premier, was the Catholic son of a rich southern landowner and Diem's former vice president. Having no idea what to do, the generals had kept him on in the hope that he would, despite the fact that he had blood on his hands from the Buddhist crisis.

These compromised men were nothing like the hard-core, admired nationalists of Hanoi and the VC. They were soft and doubting, and surprised to find themselves in charge. They would draft land and tax reforms to ease the burdens of the South Vietnamese peasants and to appease Washington, and then internally sabotage those same reforms because they and their political allies owned the lands and benefited from tax loopholes that they had no intention of closing.[26]

It was exactly the opposite of the successful system implanted by Ho Chi Minh, where VC fighters penetrated villages or refugee camps and established shadow governments that addressed the needs of the poor, rooted out corruption, and exposed the precariousness of government control. As a senior VC official put it, "We never propagandized communism; instead, we say: the peasants are the main force of the revolution." They pitched it as a battle between rich and poor, town and country, corrupt and incorruptible. Neil Sheehan, who covered Vietnam for the Associated Press and the *New York Times* in the 1960s, noted that the communists were the only truly national organization spanning North and South Vietnam and, Sheehan noted, "the only party representing revolution and social change, for better or worse according to a man's politics." Most South Vietnamese were poor, and their politics increasingly aligned with the Viet Cong and their promise of security, rice, land, and dignity.[27]

A second coup followed three months after the first. This one, headed by thirty-six-year-old General Nguyen Khanh, was propelled by younger officers who felt snubbed by the first junta, among them the two generals who would overshadow South Vietnamese politics for the remainder of the war: thirty-three-year-old Nguyen Cao Ky and forty-year-old Nguyen Van Thieu. Khanh's coup was nearly bloodless. The only casualty was the officer who had assassinated Diem and Nhu, Nguyen Van Nhung, now a major. Big Minh's bodyguard was hustled into the garden of a Saigon villa by one of Khanh's officers and shot in the back of the head as he knelt over his own grave. It was the same method Nhung had used to execute the commander of ARVN Special Forces three months earlier. No one was ever charged with the murder of Major Nhung, a detail that perfectly illustrated the murky, incestuous politics of South Vietnam.[28]

The military impact of both coups was disastrous. After the second coup, President Johnson sent McNamara to tour the country with General Khanh at his side—to make clear that Khanh was "America's man"—and to gather information on what Dean Rusk was calling "the dirty, untidy, disagreeable war." Big Minh had been deposed for taking seriously a proposal by French president Charles de Gaulle that South Vietnam proclaim itself a neutral state as a possible means of ending its civil war. Khanh had been thrust forward by his colleagues and the US embassy team because he made all the right noises about fighting to the bitter end, growling that he would be equally hard on communists and "the traitors who advocate neutralism."[29]

McNamara came back from his muddy-boots tour discouraged, reporting in March 1964 that, in their zeal to remove their rivals, the two juntas had effectively destroyed the rural administration of South Vietnam *again*. Thirty-five of forty-one province chiefs had been replaced. Ten provinces had run through three or four different chiefs in three months. "Almost all of the major military commands had changed hands twice"—once after the Diem coup, and then again after Khanh's January coup. No one was taking charge of the situation, and the Viet Cong were advancing. The Vietnamese air force, always on "coup alert," was not interdicting the enemy or supporting the ARVN. Panicked US advisers raised the alarm. More villages were falling under communist control. The VC seemed unstoppable.[30]

LBJ agonized over the optics of this emerging fiasco and sought for ways to cram Vietnam back into the shadows. A bellicose Joint Chiefs faction led by General Wallace Greene of the Marines and General Curtis LeMay of the Air Force were pestering him to "either get in or get out." Johnson convened the Joint Chiefs on March 4 and described his "hold-until-November" strategy: "I've got to win the election...and *then* you can make a decision."[31]

LBJ feared the service chiefs as much as Kennedy had—they could leak and make him "look like an ass," as he put it—and the president kept Maxwell Taylor on as chairman to keep them in line, which Taylor did, for now, assuring the chiefs that LBJ was going to use Vietnam as "a laboratory, not only for this war, but for any insurgency." Johnson expressed growing doubts about Vietnam to McNamara. There couldn't be anything "as bad as losing," LBJ told the SecDef, but the president couldn't see "any way of winning."[32]

Strategy for the unfolding war would have to fit the requirements of Johnson's 1964 reelection campaign. McGeorge Bundy's military aide said the obvious—that Vietnam was being treated as "a political football," so that LBJ could pose on the eve of the election as the candidate of peace and stability against Goldwater, who was notorious for his casual advocacy of war. LBJ despised the cigar-chomping, warmongering LeMay, but he renewed the general's term as Air Force chief of staff in January 1964 so that LeMay would not retire and go public with his opposition to the "hold-until-November" strategy.[33]

LBJ's frivolity in the matter of war contrasted with Hanoi's severity. By now, fifty-six-year-old Le Duan had moved from the southern insurgency back to Hanoi, where he had been named first secretary of North Vietnam's communist Workers' Party. Le Duan saw a closing window of opportunity—the Americans still not fully committed and the South Vietnamese floundering from one junta to the next. He wanted to deploy every available resource to the war effort immediately. But first Le Duan had to override the caution of Ho Chi Minh in the politburo. He did this with remarkable audacity, inventing a "theory of two mistakes." Le Duan accused Ho Chi Minh of failing to prevent the French return to Indochina in 1945 (the first mistake) and then accepting the two-state solution for Vietnam at Geneva in 1954 (the second mistake). Le Duan then impeached his other rivals for power with this theory and purged them as "revisionists," "humanists," and "rightists." Le Duan retained seventy-three-year-old Ho Chi Minh as a beloved but increasingly powerless figurehead while acquiring dictatorial powers for himself.[34]

McNamara, Mac Bundy, and the Joint Chiefs hoped that US bombing would turn the tide against this energized communist regime. If the South Vietnamese generals could not keep their country on the warpath, maybe American bombing would. The Joint Chiefs of Staff recommended that LBJ "put aside his self-imposed restrictions" and "take bolder action." The chiefs wanted a devastating air campaign to hit every node of power in North Vietnam. Johnson, fearful of Chinese intervention and the probability of heavy civilian casualties, didn't dare authorize *that*. And so McNamara selected "graduated pressure" instead of the "hard knock" pushed by the chiefs. The SecDef falsely assured the president that the generals considered graduated pressure "acceptable."[35]

In this way, McNamara, Mac Bundy, and Max Taylor got their way with minimal opposition. Air strikes could be increased to punish Hanoi and reduced if Hanoi slackened its support for the Viet Cong. The rationale for Operation Rolling Thunder—the forty-four-month air campaign against North Vietnam that would begin in 1965—was being worked out. The Joint Chiefs (privately) judged it "well below the minimum activity that the situation demands." Like everything else in the war, it was notable for its conceptual muddle and divorce from Vietnamese realities.

Flexible response, Kennedy's overhaul of Eisenhower's massive nuclear retaliation strategy, permitted a leader to work up the ladder to whatever level of force was needed to defeat an enemy. But LBJ's "graduated pressure" concept blocked the upper rungs—major ground war, nuclear war—and sought to deter an enemy merely by "signaling" that more damage *might* follow if the enemy did not negotiate. "The history of warfare contained no precedent for such a policy," General William Westmoreland, who would soon replace Harkins, later observed. The only rationale for graduated pressure, in Westmoreland's view, was if means were accumulating slowly, as in the world wars or Korea. If you already had the means—and the mighty United States certainly did—the only rational course was to use them at once to win. McNamara was not so sure. Why pursue "victory," the SecDef deftly countered, if the United States could achieve its political goals simply by threatening more air strikes?[36]

The theory, with its emphasis on winning without fighting, might have been cribbed from the pages of Sun Tzu's *Art of War*. But how well could it work in this scenario? Hanoi under Le Duan was determined to win at any cost, and air raids in the North would not make the ARVN fight harder, or create peace and stability in the South, which seemed to be imploding, not improving. Bob McNamara held a pivotal position in all of this. Johnson was in awe of him, called him the "smartest man" he had ever met, and liked to say that when McNamara was in the room "you could almost hear the computers clicking."[37]

But McNamara's brilliance was also his Achilles heel. He did not factor in the fog and friction of war. The SecDef believed, as he put it, that America's "vast power" could be carved into slices—this much for Europe, this much for the Middle East, this much for East Asia—and then "unleashed to the precise degree required by whatever threat we face." To control that "vast power" and mollify LBJ, McNamara had to control the generals as well, which was becoming more difficult. The Joint Chiefs read MACV accounts of the worsening military situation in Vietnam and wanted big hunks of power, not thin slices. The Air Force and the Navy wanted to bomb targets in North Vietnam, and the Army wanted to attack the VC in South Vietnam, Cambodia, and Laos.[38]

The Joint Chiefs ran a war game in April 1964 called Sigma I, which tested the "graduated pressure" idea conceived by Mac Bundy and McNamara and concluded that it would fail. The guerrilla war in South Vietnam would intensify if the United States shifted resources to a bombing campaign in the North. "Graduated pressure" would merely lengthen the war without winning it—stiffening Hanoi's resolve and weakening America's. McNamara so feared upsetting Johnson that he did not even mention Sigma I and its conclusions to the president.

By 1964, the SecDef hardly even bothered consulting with the Joint Chiefs. Their meetings were increasingly content-free, likened by one participant to "a mating dance of turkeys" that "solved no problems." This was because McNamara was turning the brewing war in Vietnam over to his whiz kids, treating their quantitative analysis—body count, kill ratio, weapons captured, air sorties—as more predictive of how the war might go than the extrapolation of a war game, where players did what their gut, analysts, and history told them that hostile and friendly forces would do under different levels of stress.[39]

The State Department's Policy Planning Council did its own forecast of an American bombing campaign and came to the same conclusion as Sigma I: that it would fail and that it would drag the United States deeper into an unwinnable war. Bombing would fail because the North Vietnamese were not fighting a limited war and would not flinch at bluffs and physical destruction. It would fail because damage to North Vietnam's industrial plant and infrastructure would merely cause the Soviets and Chinese to pour in more aid, or even intervene militarily. It would fail because the United States and its free-world allies would appear to be killing innocent civilians from the air. It would fail because instead of deterring Hanoi it would provoke Hanoi to escalate the war, sending more infiltrators, weapons, and supplies into South Vietnam to punish the American pressure. Bombing would do little to stiffen South Vietnamese resolve or morale. If bombing failed—which it almost certainly would—American troops would have to be sent to stabilize the Saigon government. With American troops on the ground, pressure would build for LBJ to take over *every* aspect of the war. "Once on the tiger's back," George Ball warned, "we cannot be sure of picking the place to dismount."[40]

Chapter 2

NO-WIN WAR

The State Department report of February 1964 spelled out the reality that would dog the war effort in Vietnam: it was unwinnable under all conceivable scenarios. An embarrassment to the administration, the report was closely held and hastily revised. In April 1964, Johnson ordered a National Intelligence Estimate on the same question, and this one—orchestrated by the CIA and shaped by military assertions of the efficacy of bombing—came back positive. Bombing *would* work. This suited LBJ better. He wanted to force a consensus and get everyone on board early. He confined discussion of the growing Vietnam problem to Tuesday lunches, where the three heavyweights, McNamara, Bundy, and Rusk, would "coordinate" their counsel before going into the lunchroom—to placate Johnson with what Rusk called "common conclusions." In LBJ's administration, Mac Bundy observed, "anything less than 100 percent support was rank desertion." Doubters were taken as signs of weakness—and silenced or sidelined.[1]

Irving Janis, a research psychologist at Yale University, studied the inner workings of the Kennedy and Johnson administrations and coined a new concept: "groupthink." In essence, it was what was happening now—presidential advisers were valuing membership in the in-group higher than any other consideration. They "overcommitted to past decisions and ignored challenging intelligence reports" to keep in step with the boss and each other, and to avoid relegation to the powerless out-group—

the humiliating fate of doubters such as Bill Trueheart (recalled from the Saigon embassy for finding fault with the South Vietnamese government), Roger Hilsman (replaced in the State Department by Mac Bundy's brother Bill), and Averell Harriman (exiled to African relief operations). Even George Ball, who remained with the in-group, did so only because, as a colleague put it, he let himself be "cuckolded" by the president: heard but ignored. All of this was a welcome development for administration hawks, the "mindguards" of the in-group, who were now spared the ironic asides and second-guessing of Jack Kennedy's skeptics.[2]

One of those skeptics, Mike Forrestal, who would himself be banished to the out-group in July 1964, was startled to receive clandestine visits in the White House from Bob McNamara's hawkish deputy John McNaughton in the spring of 1964. McNaughton, who did not dare host Forrestal at the Pentagon because the White House aide was regarded as a dove on Vietnam, would slip into the White House after hours to share his doubts about the war with Forrestal. Bombing, McNaughton feared, was nothing more than a "gimmick" in the absence of strong and popular government in Saigon. The war could be won only by an effective South Vietnamese regime, precisely what was lacking and what would probably never emerge. In one of their chats, Forrestal assured McNaughton that if everything failed, the United States would cut its losses and get out. No, McNaughton replied: "The trouble with you, Forrestal, is that you always think we can turn this thing off, and that we can get off of it whenever we want. But I wonder. I think if it was easy to get off of it, we would already have gotten off."

Working killer hours at the Pentagon as McNamara's deputy, McNaughton knew just how overpowering the US military's commitment to any major operation like Vietnam was. "I think it gets harder every day," he told Forrestal. "Each day we lose a little control, each decision we make wrong, or don't make at all, makes the next decision a little harder because if we haven't stopped it today, then the reasons for not stopping it will still exist tomorrow, and we'll be in even deeper."[3]

In May 1964, the *Wall Street Journal* characterized American policy in Vietnam as "error upon error." There was no apparent plan, the paper wrote: "It is almost impossible to figure out what is U.S. strategy." To quiet criticism like that and keep the generals onside, Mac Bundy's National Security Council (NSC) worked on a plan to "hurt" but not "destroy" North

Vietnamese capabilities in the hope that Hanoi would see the trend lines and withdraw its support for the VC. This blossomed into an NSC "Projected Course of Action on Southeast Asia" on May 25 that called for "military action with more deterrent than destructive impact." Pressure, in other words, would be applied gently—to avoid goading the enemy into overrunning South Vietnam.

LBJ's war planning resembled a political science seminar. There was no military involvement, no major targets, no clear objectives, just a lot of words. McNamara boasted of his newfound ability to "fight a limited war without the necessity of arousing the public ire." The Joint Chiefs tried to break into this closed civilian circle, insisting in a memo on May 30, 1964, that the objective must be to "accomplish the destruction of North Vietnamese will and capabilities, to compel them to cease providing support to the insurgencies in South Vietnam and Laos," but Max Taylor, in his last act as chairman of the Joint Chiefs before departing to replace Lodge as ambassador in Saigon, suppressed the memo and threw in with the political scientists, recommending on June 5 nothing more than "demonstrative strikes against limited military targets to show U.S. readiness and intent."[4]

Taylor made a virtue of this deceit, which he defined as seeing the problem "through the eyes of the president," being "more than a military man," and "attenuating the differences between the civilian and military authorities within the Department of Defense." In a word: groupthink. With Taylor shutting off military advice and straining to remain relevant and powerful in a new administration, the president's approach to the conflict appeared flabbier and more purposeless than ever.[5]

To give it some muscle and purpose, LBJ accepted the resignation of Ambassador Henry Cabot Lodge Jr., and in July 1964 named Max Taylor to be the new ambassador to South Vietnam, with broad powers and instructions to right the ship in Saigon. Johnson had kept Lodge on to give Vietnam policy a bipartisan flavor, but he now saw opportunity in letting Lodge go home to battle Goldwater for the Republican nomination. Taylor, a now twice-retired general with a heroic military record, offered bipartisan cover without Lodge's cantankerousness.[6]

Taylor, a virtuoso of the org chart, secured from LBJ total control of "the whole military effort in South Vietnam," including the appointment of one of his most loyal protégés, fifty-year-old General William "Westy"

Westmoreland, first as Harkins' deputy, and then to replace Harkins as MACV commander that summer. Max Taylor was now, as the deputy director of the CIA put it, "the coach, the quarterback, and the captain of the team" in Vietnam.[7]

But the coach's glittering career was starting to dim. Averell Harriman, one of JFK's favorite contrarians, had tartly taken the measure of Taylor: "He is a very handsome man, and an impressive one, and he is always wrong." But Johnson, like the Kennedys, was still in awe of Max Taylor and hoped that the smooth-talking general might succeed in forging consensus between all of the groups warring over Vietnam policy—the Army, the CIA, the State Department, and the Joint Chiefs of Staff. With the election drawing near, LBJ also saw Taylor as insurance against Republicans who might call the president "soft" on communism and too enamored of nation-building. "Win the war," Johnson told Taylor, and stop fussing with "social concerns" in Saigon.[8]

Harkins had departed Saigon in June 1964, leaving the four-star MACV command to General Westmoreland. Westy was a prodigy—the scion of a South Carolina military family that had served in the Revolutionary War. First in his class at West Point, Westy had fought in the North African and Italian campaigns in World War II, where he met and impressed Max Taylor. After the war, Westy commanded the 101st Airborne Division, served as superintendent of the US Military Academy, and was a young three-star general in 1963 when he attracted the attention of Kennedy and McNamara, who viewed Westmoreland as the energetic type who would clean up the mess left by Harkins and carry the ball to victory in Vietnam.

"Accentuate the positive," "Bring best thought to bear," and "Avoid frustration and stagnation" were Westmoreland tag lines that endeared him to McNamara. On his way to Vietnam, Westmoreland stopped at West Point to lecture the gathered cadets on leadership and remind them that "knowledge is not the chief aim of man—action is." The mark of a true leader, Westmoreland declared, is the "positive approach." A general who had served under Westy in the past foresaw disaster ahead: "He is spit and polish, two up and one back. This is a counterinsurgency war, and he would have no idea how to deal with it."[9]

Arriving in Vietnam, Ambassador Max Taylor was shocked to discover that the war was being lost far more rapidly than he had imagined from his perch in Washington. There were more VC than he had believed, and more VC activity. To tame and harness the southern guerrillas, Le Duan had reinforced the Viet Cong with teams of northern infiltrators, and taken control of the Central Office for South Vietnam (COSVN), which was the VC's political and military headquarters. COSVN cemented northern control of the southern insurgency and brooked no opposition.

The most tangible result of this power struggle was the expansion of well-equipped, well-trained Viet Cong main-force units. These were VC battalions organized as regular troops, entirely interchangeable with North Vietnamese Army (NVA) battalions if for no other reason than that most of their replacements during the long war of attrition would be NVA recruits and officers. Le Duan and COSVN would use VC main forces—trained, directed, and manned by NVA personnel—as the surest way to bring South Vietnam's Viet Cong under North Vietnamese control.[10]

In 1964, Le Duan sent General Nguyen Chi Thanh, who had monitored ideological purity in the NVA, to run COSVN and centralize all Viet Cong resources. This he did, improving VC regiments and deploying the first VC divisions as main-force "fists" capable of shattering larger ARVN units in conventional battles. By the time Max Taylor arrived in Saigon, the reorganized VC had taken more than half of South Vietnam's territory and population under its control. This explained Taylor's shock. Using his broad new powers, Taylor instructed Westmoreland to skirt Pacific command in Honolulu, known as CINCPAC, as well as the Joint Chiefs, the usual channels for force requests, and go straight to the White House with a call for 4,200 additional US military advisers that was immediately (and secretly) granted, raising the number of US troops in Vietnam to 22,200. From Washington, Rusk cautioned Taylor not to "confirm total numbers" and to "refuse to describe future plans." LBJ needed to hide the war from the public until after the November 1964 election.[11]

Phony optimism, rebranded as the "positive approach," would characterize Westmoreland's headquarters no less than Harkins'. Westmoreland and his deputy, General Dick Stillwell, became instant virtuosos at the game. One of Westy's "headway reports" from the summer of 1964 showed how it was done. The report, which covered South Vietnam's four corps areas from north to south, was supposed to summarize American adviser reports for decision-makers in Washington. Unfortunately, the adviser reports were

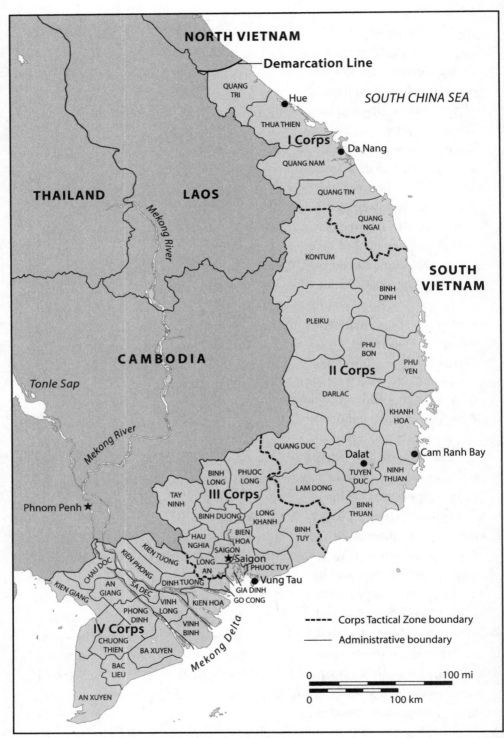

The Four Corps Areas of South Vietnam

universally negative. In I Corps, always pronounced "Eye Corps," the northern region abutting the demilitarized zone (DMZ) separating North and South Vietnam, US advisers described a crisis atmosphere. South Vietnamese militia forces summoned to "hold" ground "cleared" by the ARVN were all but useless. Hue and Da Nang were deeply divided between political factions. Key province chiefs were under investigation for corruption. In the II Corps region, where the Central Highlands and the mountain passes of the Ho Chi Minh Trail descended to South Vietnam's coastal plain, there was open conflict between the South Vietnamese government and the ethnic minorities who lived in the mountains. Only 25 percent of military recruits conscripted in this region actually heeded the draft call, and most of that small number vanished before they could be inducted.

In III Corps, the densely populated region around Saigon, the ARVN was resorting to defoliation missions to beat the VC, spraying their hideouts from the air, but not daring to meet them in battle. Whenever they drove out to find the VC, their convoys were blown up by mines and ambushes, and their helicopters shot down by .50-caliber machine guns seized from careless ARVN units. Civic action cadres—the young South Vietnamese social workers who were supposed to live in the rural hamlets, organize basic services, and propagandize against the VC—refused to spend the night in *any* of the hamlets of III Corps. They knew that they would be murdered or abducted if they did.

In IV Corps, the Mekong Delta, VC kidnapping was up 300 percent month over month, and acts of sabotage were up 25 percent. American advisers measured a 94 percent increase in VC activity that was met with a 10 percent *decrease* in ARVN contacts with the VC. ARVN divisions hardly maneuvered. They lived in army camps alongside their dependents, who feared VC reprisals if they remained in their villages. This need to defend parents, wives, and children against communist attacks meant that the ARVN rarely strayed from its base camps, and never for long periods of time. When Westy had arrived in Vietnam in January 1964 he was startled to discover this fact as well as another: that "the South Vietnamese simply called off the war—or ignored it—on weekends and holidays and took long siestas at lunch time." Nothing had changed in the meantime.[12]

Everywhere, US advisers described South Vietnamese counterinsurgency measures as "nullified" or "paralyzed" by apathy, fear, and corruption.

The colonels and generals responsible for the defense of South Vietnam's cities and provinces spent most of their time selling government jobs and draft exemptions or embezzling funds and materials. They routinely used their troops and vehicles to smuggle drugs and other contraband, or sell American-supplied fuel and other commodities to the Viet Cong.

American advisers warned that control of the country was fast slipping away—if not already gone—and yet here is how Generals Westmoreland and Stillwell summarized for the White House the dismal reports that they received from all four corps areas in 1964: "In general, though deficiencies and problem areas still exist, optimism among U.S. advisory elements continues to grow. A sense of purpose and direction is beginning to materialize." Overall, the MACV commander lied, "the month [of June] has had the effect of crystalizing thinking into a firm philosophy of winning the war on all fronts." Of September 1964, for which the adviser reports were even more dire, Westmoreland assured the president that, "overall, morale and combat effectiveness is satisfactory." Westy, no less than Harkins, was willing to traffic in fibs if they served his purpose of expanding the war and validating his command.[13]

Groupthink like this, however, could get President Johnson only so far. It ensured the loyalty of his handpicked inner circle, but not of Democratic liberals carping about the waste and hypocrisy of the war. Nor did it appease Goldwater Republicans and anticommunist Democrats, who complained about the meagerness of American support for South Vietnam, or the uniformed military, whose loyalty to Johnson was contingent on getting what they wanted from him. Leaks were already becoming a problem. Senator Goldwater, groping for a foothold in his run against the incumbent president, accused Johnson of having "weakened the bonds of confidence between civilian leaders and the nation's top military professionals" and having "bypassed seasoned military judgment in vital national security issues." It wasn't hard to figure out where those slurs were coming from.[14]

President Johnson suffered a series of setbacks in 1964 that made him look weak on national security. In February, VC guerrillas attacked the US advisory compound in Kontum City in the Central Highlands, and then bombed a theater in Saigon—killing three Americans and wounding fifty. In April, the VC overran Kien Long, a district capital in the Mekong Delta, killing 300 ARVN troops. In May, two VC commandos attached explosives to the hull of an American ship docked in Saigon harbor and sank it, killing five American sailors. On the Fourth of July, the VC seized the US Special Forces camp at Nam Dong, killing two more Americans, as well as fifty South Vietnamese. In Washington, Republicans railed that LBJ was preparing for "retreat or defeat." In Saigon, General Khanh challenged Johnson to do more: "The United States must take a firm course, so that North Vietnam knows it is not a paper tiger."[15]

A majority of American voters as yet ascribed little importance to foreign policy questions—least of all Vietnam—but Johnson wanted to forestall *any* election-eve embarrassments. He increased aid and shipments of matériel, and in June 1964 he began angling for a congressional resolution of support for his Vietnam policy—a resolution that would force politicians of both parties to support him on patriotic grounds, persuade the military brass that he would stand and fight, frighten Hanoi and Beijing, and release him from his political restraints on Vietnam. But for that he needed an *incident*, something that would galvanize the American public and turn them herd-like against North Vietnam.[16]

The incident arrived in the first days of August 1964. It sprang from another facet of Johnson's "hold-until-November" strategy—covert operations. With Khanh's junta pressing for more muscular American assistance, which LBJ did not dare offer before the elections, McNamara had been busy cooking up various "black ops" against North Vietnam to keep Khanh quiet and test the SecDef's graduated pressure theory. South Vietnamese saboteurs and spies were parachuted across the 17th parallel with little success, often because the paratroopers, knowing they were on suicide missions, reported for duty drunk so that they could not be flown into action. More promising, from McNamara's perspective, were covert raids on North Vietnamese targets by high-speed South Vietnamese patrol boats guided by US Navy destroyer patrols in the Gulf of Tonkin. These raids, launched from Da Nang, drew more North Vietnamese motor gunboats into the area to resist the incursions. By shelling communist radar stations along the littoral, McNamara hoped to "send the message" that at sea no less than in the air the United States could tighten its grip at any time. "Leave your neighbors alone," Rusk challenged Hanoi. "If you don't, we will have to get busy."[17]

On August 2, 1964, two American destroyers—the *Maddox* and the *Turner Joy*—had a run-in with three fast North Vietnamese patrol torpedo (PT) boats. With no international agreement on territorial waters until 1982, US destroyers had been routinely pushing to within four or five miles of the North Vietnamese coast since 1962 on "watchdog patrols" to study coastal defenses and locate Soviet radars and antiaircraft missiles in the Tonkin Gulf. This time, three North Vietnamese PT boats, reacting to the presence of the American warships near the mouth of the Red River Delta, motored out on August 2, fired torpedoes, missed, and were set upon and destroyed by F-8 Crusaders launched from the USS *Ticonderoga*. The two destroyers returned on August 3 to "show the flag," and that night they fought a confused action in a rainstorm against a phantom enemy.

No one aboard or in the air actually detected any North Vietnamese boats on August 3 or 4. The skipper of the *Maddox*, Captain John Herrick, later allowed that his crew had made no visual sightings of enemy vessels. Commander James Stockdale, who flew from the *Ticonderoga* to counter this second communist "attack," also saw no targets on the sea beneath him. Sonar operators on the American ships reported what they thought *might* be approaching torpedoes, but there were no impacts.[18]

LBJ knew that his administration had provoked the attacks with its own covert operations against North Vietnamese radar sites. Those attacks, code-named OPLAN 34-A and delivered by South Vietnamese PT boats, had been kept secret from Congress and the American people for three years. The president also knew that the communist naval attacks alleged on August 4 may not even have happened. Neither of the American warships had seen an enemy boat, or even a wake. Sonar operators could mistake any noise for a torpedo contact. "For all I know, our Navy was shooting at whales out there," Johnson laughed. But it was no laughing matter for the congressional leaders he summoned to the White House at 6:15 p.m. on August 4. LBJ, who had already given the order for carrier air strikes on several North Vietnamese targets, informed the lawmakers that North Vietnamese attacks had been confirmed, even as his Pentagon was confessing (internally) that it had no "positive evidence."[19]

Just before midnight, Johnson went on television from the Oval Office and informed the American people that he had ordered strikes against North Vietnam for its "open aggression on the high seas against the United

States of America." For Johnson, this phony "Tonkin Gulf incident" offered political cover at a pivotal moment. He had just passed the bruising Civil Rights Bill of 1964, which overrode Jim Crow laws in the South but had to survive a furious sixty-day filibuster by Republicans and southern Democrats. With the November elections approaching and liberal voices criticizing LBJ's commitment to South Vietnam as too generous and conservative voices decrying it as insufficient, the Tonkin Gulf dustup, if deftly converted into a congressional resolution, would allow LBJ to do four things: wrap himself in the flag, neutralize Vietnam as a political issue, hide the scars of civil rights, and bind both parties to a "wartime president."[20]

Lyndon Johnson, whose political deftness was legendary, got what he wanted out of the Tonkin Gulf incident. The president had maneuvered his protégé, Arkansas senator J. William Fulbright, into the chair of the Senate Foreign Relations Committee in 1959 when Johnson had been Senate majority leader. LBJ now called in the debt, pressuring Fulbright, who opposed the escalating war in Vietnam (and had filibustered against civil rights), into cramming discussion of the Tonkin Gulf Resolution into just nine hours of committee work and floor debate, totally dominated by the deceitful testimony of McNamara and Rusk.

Opponents of the resolution had wanted real hearings, to call military and civilian critics of the war, and to limit or defeat the resolution. Bill Fulbright, answering to Johnson, had refused, citing the "emergency" situation in Vietnam. The real reason was that Johnson did not want to be confronted with "disagreeable questions," such as: Was this a blank check? What amounts of force were being authorized? Why was such a resolution needed at that moment, or ever? With the floor to themselves, McNamara and Rusk cloaked themselves in secrecy, assuring the senators that they knew things that they could not divulge in an unclassified setting, that the North Vietnamese had ambushed the American ships, and that there had been no American provocation. President Johnson accused Hanoi of "shooting at our ships over 40 miles from their shores." This was the beginning of the "credibility gap," which would bring down the Johnson presidency. The president, McNamara, and Rusk were not telling the truth.[21]

In fact, the *Maddox* and the *Turner Joy* had been part of a McNamara-devised covert operation to goad the enemy into switching on their radars so that they could be targeted, and to protect South Vietnamese PT boats, which were attacking North Vietnamese naval bases under a secret program managed by the CIA. The North Vietnamese had actually been defending themselves, not launching unprovoked attacks. Johnson, McNamara, and Rusk told Congress none of this. McNamara lied to Congress, assuring both houses that there had been no American involvement in the raids on North Vietnam. General Earle "Bus" Wheeler, who had replaced Max Taylor as chairman of the Joint Chiefs, did not contradict the lies. Bus Wheeler was a new kind of general, one who had been groomed as an organization man by McNamara. He was a uniformed bureaucrat who would do what he was told. And Wheeler's connivance was ultimately unnecessary. With Fulbright himself managing the floor debate and cutting off inconvenient questions, the joint resolution passed 88–2 in the Senate and 416–0 in the House on August 7, 1964.[22]

Johnson successfully cast the incident as an attack on American honor and his response as "limited and fitting." Determined to reassure voters that he was not a war hawk like Goldwater, LBJ weirdly pledged that "my firmness will always be measured." The two senators who voted against even measured firmness, Wayne Morse of Oregon and Ernest Gruening of Alaska, had nearly been joined by several others, including Republican Jacob Javits and Democrat George McGovern, who feared that the resolution would be used by the White House to usurp the Senate's war powers.

Johnson, through Fulbright, assured wavering senators that he too had no appetite for a "land war in Asia," and that the resolution was intended merely to speed the delivery of urgent air or naval attacks "to deter the Chinese Communists and North Vietnamese from spreading the war." To doves, Johnson stressed his "peace motive and readiness to negotiate." When the votes were tallied, Morse called the Senate's acquiescence "a historic mistake." The resolution gave the president broad war powers. "Like grandma's nightshirt," LBJ joked, "it covered everything."[23]

But how exactly could Johnson *use* that new power? In his campaign against Goldwater, who had been nominated at the Republican convention in July, Johnson was promising that he would "not send American boys nine or ten thousand miles away to do what Asian boys ought to be doing for themselves." LBJ was running as a peace candidate against a Republican nominee promising finally to win the "no-win war" prolonged by Kennedy and Johnson. That left air strikes—war with as few *American* deaths as possible—as the only feasible option.

LBJ insisted that the strikes be sharply limited to avoid the kind of images that would blemish a Johnson candidacy: blasted schools or markets, dead civilians, broken dikes, flooded villages, or, if the bombing crept too far north, Chinese intervention. Ambassador Taylor wanted aggressive reprisals to reassure Saigon that the United States would not "flinch from direct confrontation with the North Vietnamese." The Joint Chiefs wanted a "heavy effort" to establish what they called an "outer parameter" of violence that America was willing to inflict. Specifically, they wanted to bomb Hanoi and the port of Haiphong, but Johnson did not dare go that far. "We are not going to take it lying down," he told a Republican senator, "but we are not going to destroy their cities."[24]

A new war game at the Pentagon was organized in September 1964 to test the effectiveness of limited bombing in shoring up South Vietnam and deterring North Vietnam. The game would test Mac Bundy's thesis that air strikes could be meted out in a calibrated way to hurt the North Vietnamese just enough to "reduce or eliminate their support for the insurgency." Inevitably, the Air Force again sent their "heavy effort" man: "Old Iron Ass" himself—Curtis LeMay, chief of the Air Force staff. Kennedy had famously wrestled with "Bombs Away LeMay" during the Cuban missile crisis, when the four-star general had wanted to bomb and invade Cuba, even at the risk of nuclear war. LeMay, who months earlier had been satirized in Stanley Kubrick's film *Doctor Strangelove*, joined Bill Bundy and John McNaughton on the Blue (US) Team in the war game, and squared off against a Red (Hanoi) Team led by Army chief of staff Bus Wheeler.[25]

The game, code-named Sigma II, was played over ten days in mid-September 1964 and ended badly for the United States. Bombing the infiltration routes from North to South Vietnam had scant effect because the infiltrators traveled light, with little or no logistics tail to betray their movement. Bombing North Vietnamese military installations had little impact because they could be moved and camouflaged. If the United States mined or blockaded the port of Haiphong, the North Vietnamese would "punish" the escalation by sending additional infiltrators into South Vietnam. With an army of 250,000 men constantly replenished by more than

2 million draft-age males and presumably backstopped in an emergency by the hordes of China, the North Vietnamese could reinforce the VC by sending as many battalions south as the Ho Chi Minh Trail infiltration routes could handle.[26]

If the United States bombed North Vietnamese airfields, the Red Team moved women and children onto their remaining airstrips and announced to the world that they were there—daring the Americans to slaughter them under the glare of television cameras. Inside South Vietnam, the VC, directed by General Wheeler's Red Team, shifted their attacks to places known to contain American advisers and support troops. To prevent those Americans from being killed or captured—politically disastrous for LBJ— LeMay's Blue Team felt compelled to send in US Marines for force protection. The Red Team responded to *that* escalation by sending yet more infiltrators down the Ho Chi Minh Trail. Washington could not credibly accuse the North Vietnamese of aggression or interference in the affairs of South Vietnam when the United States was itself bombing the North and sending ground troops into the South, radically upsetting the military balance on Hanoi's southern border.

When LeMay's US Marines arrived in-country, Wheeler's VC set to work mining and ambushing all of the roads and railways used by the logistics-heavy Americans, forcing them to supply themselves by air, and then shooting down the resupply aircraft with their heavy machine guns. That would not be a good look for Johnson either, in any year, let alone an election year. The Viet Cong themselves, Ambassador Taylor would shortly report from Saigon, had invincible morale and "the recuperative powers of the phoenix." They fought to the last man and had no difficulty replacing their casualties with eager new recruits. "Fresh recruits believed entirely what they were told," a VC defector reported in 1964. "That's why most of the Front's real achievements are made by the young."[27]

With LeMay's Americans stalemated, a second game was played, this one loosening the rules of engagement. LeMay shifted the aerial bombing farther north, cutting the rail links between North Vietnam and China. China reacted by sending 50,000 troops into North Vietnam to take over essential labor and defense tasks and free up still more North Vietnamese troops for infiltration to the South. The air campaign having failed to "coerce" North Vietnam out of the war, the US Blue Team began introducing American ground troops in an expanding torrent. By game's end, the United States had *ten* 15,000-man US infantry divisions in South Vietnam, but they still failed to win, or even turn the tide.

Sigma II predicted the losing or deadlocked course of the war to come. The communist Red Team played with the assumption that the American public's support for the war would wane the moment they grasped that it was protracted and costly. The game mocked the academic conceits behind graduated pressure: that the "U.S. would not buckle," that "the U.S. could meet *any* level of escalation that the enemy might mount." In fact, the rural, agricultural economies of North and South Vietnam made it hard to escalate decisively, as did the unknown positions of Beijing and Moscow. Yet none of the major players were prepared to accept the inevitability of failure. George Ball thought that priority should be given to publicizing "rules of engagement which would appear 'fierce'"—a perfect encapsulation of the mincing LBJ approach.[28]

LeMay reacted bitterly to the Blue Team's inability to inflict real damage on Hanoi. Between games, the Air Force general complained to Mac Bundy about the strict rules of engagement and insisted that more targets be made available—levees, cities, ports, factories, oil depots—even at the risk of heavy civilian casualties, exactly what Johnson needed to avoid if he was going to keep Congress, the press, overseas allies, and the American people on board. We're swatting at flies, LeMay grumbled, when really we should be going after the manure piles—the sources of North Vietnamese power. This was the occasion for LeMay's most famous line: "We should bomb them into the Stone Age." Noting the paucity of major industrial targets and infrastructure, Mac Bundy suavely replied: "Maybe they're already there."

LeMay had argued for hitting ninety-four targets in North Vietnam after the Tonkin Gulf incident. LBJ had consented to a small number of them, leaving the big "manure piles" untouched. But even when they hit all ninety-four targets during Sigma II—the "hard knock" desired by LeMay—it did nothing to deter the North Vietnamese, weaken their support for the southern insurgency, or get peace talks started. These findings implied a long, grinding, indecisive war, which the American people would reject. The games, held to fine-tune an American bombing campaign intended to scare the North Vietnamese to the peace table without alarming the American public with evidence of a real war, returned a dismal verdict. American ground troops *would* be needed to backstop Saigon. Mac Bundy urged the president to consider a "grim alternative"—two brigades of US Marines as "good medicine everywhere." He warned LBJ that if the president was the "first to quit in Saigon," he'd lose at least as much domestic political support as Truman had lost after Mao's victory in China.[29]

And yet America could not "tear it all down" from the skies, as LeMay advised, for all of the usual reasons plus another: Soviet premier Nikita Khrushchev had explicitly warned LBJ that to do so would risk nuclear war between the superpowers. Even if LBJ had been willing to risk that—he wasn't—the political fallout at home and abroad would have been too toxic. How could the mighty leader of the free world inflict a humanitarian catastrophe on little North Vietnam and emerge with its benevolent image intact? The bombing would *have* to be limited, yet the American generals could point to no scenario in which Hanoi's will to continue the war to victory was broken by limited bombing—what Bob McNamara and Mac Bundy called "slowly walking up the ladder."[30]

The generals themselves were deeply divided, making it easier for McNamara to ignore the results of Sigma II and continue with graduated pressure. Fifty-two-year-old General Harold "H.K." Johnson, a survivor of the Bataan Death March, replaced Wheeler as chief of staff of the Army when Wheeler became chairman of the Joint Chiefs. In internal debates, H.K. rejected LeMay's view that heavy bombing could be decisive. He also spurned General Wallace Greene's view that US Marine "enclaves" sprinkled around South Vietnam could turn the tide. The war, General Johnson said, was an indigenous insurgency and had to be fought at its roots with larger troop numbers than the Marines could ever provide—in South Vietnam, but also in Laos and Cambodia, where the communists sheltered on neutral territory and moved their infiltrators and supplies.

But the Army chief of staff had no appetite for such a war. He told LeMay and Greene, thirsting for that "hard knock" against North Vietnam, that they were being "illogical." Modest American pressure was already backfiring, spurring more, not less, communist activity. "More severe pressure," H.K. predicted, will only "increase and intensify the insurgency in the South." When the chiefs finally agreed on a joint memorandum outlining a Vietnam strategy in October 1964, it read just like McNamara's: use air strikes to "demonstrate resolve, increase pressure," and force Hanoi to "cease support of the insurgency" by hitting targets "in ascending order of severity." This was hope, not strategy.[31]

From Saigon, Ambassador Taylor warned McNamara that war games weren't enough. South Vietnam was failing, and the United States would have to take over the war against the VC. Previously, Taylor had opposed an American air campaign on the grounds that it would relieve pressure on Saigon to fix its internal problems and fight and win the war. Now he wanted not only American planes and pilots but as many as 100,000 ground troops as a "last resort." To critics such as George Ball, who argued that South Vietnam was too fragile to justify the commitment, Taylor argued that it was precisely because of that fragility that troops and aircraft had to be put in: "Failure in Southeast Asia would destroy and severely damage our standing elsewhere in the world." Vietnam, Taylor argued, was an "experiment" in thwarting communist insurgencies, and the experiment *had* to succeed.[32]

President Johnson remained torn, even after his landslide victory over Goldwater on November 3, 1964, when he won 61 percent of the popular vote and 90 percent of the Electoral College, gained 37 seats in the House, and achieved control of the Senate with more than a two-thirds majority. Johnson was keenly aware that his landslide was *not* a mandate for military escalation—quite the contrary. Fearing Goldwater's pugnacity, Americans had elected Johnson to keep the peace and launch his Great Society. There was scant media or political pressure for escalation in Vietnam in 1964. Only about 25 percent of Americans supported military action in Vietnam at the time. Seventy-five percent supported negotiations with Hanoi. Eighty percent opposed the introduction of US ground troops. LBJ had considerable freedom of action to wind down the war, if only he could hit upon a face-saving formula.[33]

With a massive legislative agenda teed up to crown and surpass FDR's New Deal, LBJ understood that a big war in Southeast Asia might unravel everything. The president had declined to react two days before the election when the Viet Cong had mortared the air base at Bien Hoa, killing five Americans, wounding seventy-six, and torching a half dozen aircraft sent to Vietnam after the Tonkin Gulf incident to "signal" American resolve. Taylor and LeMay had called for immediate reprisals, but Johnson had paused to consult the pollster Lou Harris. Harris warned the president that reprisals were just "the sort of thing people would expect from Barry Goldwater and probably the main reason they are voting for *you*." LBJ stood down, privately assuring the Joint Chiefs and Taylor that *after* the election he'd take the gloves off and hit hard.

The VC exploded a bomb in Saigon's Brink Hotel on Christmas Eve, killing two more Americans and wounding fifty-eight, narrowly missing the delayed arrival of entertainer Bob Hope and his troupe—there for the first of nine annual Vietnam Christmas tours. The president hesitated again. The most obvious complication was the certainty that if America sent its own forces into South Vietnam, North Vietnam, which already interpreted the Tonkin Gulf Resolution as a declaration of war, would reinforce the Viet Cong with more infiltrators as well as regular army units—trained, camouflaged, motivated, well-armed divisions of the North Vietnamese Army. In November 1964, the first NVA units began marching down the Ho Chi Minh Trail to infiltrate South Vietnam. If Washington dropped its advisory charade, Hanoi would drop its VC charade and accelerate this takeover of the war in the South.[34]

Like Kennedy, Johnson squirmed in frustration. There was no "cause" in Saigon, just a quarreling junta of generals described by Ambassador Taylor as "lethargic, irresponsible, discouraged, and divided." The Air Force chief of staff, General Curtis LeMay, wanted to skirt the political problem with a massive knockout blow: hit every target in the North, pierce the dike, levee, and dam system that protected the low-lying Red River Delta from catastrophic flooding, and do it all at once. If you weren't allowed to hit it, you shouldn't be allowed to go to war, LeMay reasoned.[35]

Johnson worried that bombing and drowning civilians would be a public relations catastrophe, and that targeting harbors, factories, and military bases would almost certainly kill Chinese and Soviet advisers, possibly bringing those powers into the war as active combatants. Khrushchev, who had ceded the Vietnam issue to Mao's China, had been forced into retirement in October 1964 and replaced by the more aggressive leadership of Leonid Brezhnev, who regretted Khrushchev's failure to react forcefully to the Tonkin Gulf Resolution, and offered Hanoi a military alliance and the promise of advanced weaponry such as surface-to-air missiles (SAMs). Mao, now in direct competition with Moscow for the leadership of world communism, could do no less.[36]

George Kennan had predicted that the two great communist powers would fall out, weakening international communism, and they had. But for North Vietnam, their split in the early 1960s was a blessing. It meant that Ho Chi Minh and Le Duan would have two great powers behind them, both anxious to outbid the other in their support. Looking at the situation, Army chief of staff Harold Johnson shared LBJ's doubts. A war in Vietnam, he said, would be a lot like Korea, with the United States forced to fight another interminable "accordion war," launching attacks, pulling them back, and ceding initiative and sanctuaries to the enemy to limit escalation.

President Johnson, who had been offered nothing but light, medium, or heavy bombing as options by his advisers in November 1964 after the Bien Hoa attack, recoiled in doubt and disgust. "This bombing bullshit," he snarled, would not be enough. Yet what *might* be enough was not politically feasible. He raged at the CIA's inability to tell him what was going on in Hanoi—*who* were the key players, *what* were they thinking, *how* would they respond to American bombs? "I thought you guys had people everywhere, that you knew everything, and now you don't even know anything about a raggedy-ass little fourth-rate country," he growled to CIA director John McCone. The president burned with frustration. He had trounced Goldwater and secured Congress' assent to an escalation of the war effort, yet no one could tell him how to win, or even how to get the North Vietnamese into peace talks. Incredibly, the nature and eventual outcome of the Vietnam War were acknowledged before Johnson even began his massive escalation of the conflict.[37]

Chapter 3

EVE OF DESTRUCTION

L BJ had seemed poised to escalate the war the minute victory over Gold-water was in the bag. He had promised General Earle Wheeler that he was "going to do something" after the election, but he now drew back from the brink—again. In late November 1964, the president reviewed plans for action against North Vietnam and chose the one least likely to inflame Hanoi and its superpower allies: "present policies plus additional forceful measures, followed by negotiations." Johnson clearly wanted to rid himself of the war as quickly as possible, a fact not lost on Hanoi. Two months of administration war planning in November and December 1964 by an interdepartmental group and the Joint Chiefs yielded more political science—a plan dubbed "progressive squeeze and talk."

As LBJ prepared for his new term with commanding majorities in the House and Senate, he totted up the projected cost of his Great Society programs and discovered that there was no room in the budget for a war in Vietnam. A short list of Great Society "asks" included tax cuts, medical care for seniors and the poor, college tuition grants, farm subsidies, infrastructure, welfare, low-income housing, clean air and water, and urban renewal. With the peacetime military already eating up half of the federal budget and 10 percent of GDP, where would LBJ find the money for such an ambitious domestic agenda? Even if the war in Vietnam went well, rising defense expenditures would hand Republicans and southern Democrats a club to kill the Great Society. Many of them had opposed Kennedy's tax cuts on the grounds that they were fiscally irresponsible. They would leap at the chance to kill the Great Society.[1]

President Johnson would have dimly recalled that every communist removed from the battlefield in the Greek Civil War, waged with American aid from 1946 to 1949, had cost the CIA about $50,000. Numbers like that made Johnson flinch. At conservative estimates, there were already at least $15 *billion* worth of communists needing to be removed from the battlefield in South Vietnam, a fact confirmed by the president's economic advisers, who pressed him to seek a $10 billion pay-for-the-war tax increase. Johnson was horrified. The Republicans, he burst out, would "take the war as their weapon; they'll be against my programs because of the war; they'll say we're not against the poor, but we have this job to do, beating the Communists."[2]

Senate majority leader Mike Mansfield implored the president to pull back and not go "further out on the sagging limb" of Vietnam. But just after the inauguration in January 1965, Mac Bundy and Bob McNamara pushed the president further out on the limb. They warned LBJ that he faced a "disastrous defeat" if he did not move beyond "the middle course" he had been on since Kennedy's assassination. "Harder choices" had to be made.[3]

It was no longer enough to "prop up the authorities in South Vietnam," McNamara argued. The only sure way to contain China was "with a determined display of military power." Dean Rusk concurred. Losing South Vietnam, he said, would mean losing Southeast Asia: "Country after country would give way and look toward Communist China as the rising power of the area." Bill Bundy recommended sending US ground forces and increasing air attacks to "signal" Hanoi and "stiffen" Saigon. Mac Bundy, Bill's younger brother, sniffed that Americans would just have to "pull up their socks" and go to war if the South Vietnamese wouldn't do it themselves. He urged the president "to *use* our military power in the Far East to force a change of Communist policy."[4]

Johnson's vice president, fifty-three-year-old Hubert Humphrey, warned Johnson *not* to escalate. "American wars," Humphrey wrote the president in February 1965, "have to be politically understandable by the American public." This one was not—and, in view of the chaos and drift in Saigon, never would be. American citizens "looked in vain for a cogent, convincing case." They were "worried and confused." They could not be made to understand "why we would run grave risks to support a country which is totally unable to put its own house in order." Humphrey warned LBJ that escalating the war would fracture the Democratic Party and make the president the "prisoner of events" in Vietnam.

President Johnson angrily put Humphrey "in limbo" after this exchange, excluding the vice president from NSC meetings on the war and shifting him from the in-group to the out-group. Outwardly bluff—laughing that "Humphrey is all heart and no balls"—the president inwardly shared the vice president's doubts. LBJ felt trapped and miserable. There seemed to be no path to peace other than surrender. Calls for a cease-fire in South Vietnam were simply ignored by the VC and Hanoi, who knew that Johnson had no appetite for war.[5]

On the eve of the 1964 election, candidate Johnson had told a rally in New Hampshire that, if elected, he would "get [the South Vietnamese] to save their own freedom with their own men." The *New York Times* was already breathing down his neck, asserting on November 25 that "if an Asian war is to be converted into an American war, the country has a right to be told what has changed so profoundly in the past two months to justify it." There were now 23,300 American military personnel in South Vietnam, and 168 of them had been killed or captured in the course of 1964. More would surely follow those men to the grave. The First Lady recalled that Johnson had trouble sleeping at night. "I can't get out," he told her, and "I can't finish it with what I've got, and I don't know what the hell to do."[6]

While LBJ tossed and turned, the VC intensified their attacks in South Vietnam. Having struck Bien Hoa air base in November 1964 and Saigon at Christmas, the VC struck again in February 1965, this time mortaring Camp Holloway, the sprawling American base at Pleiku in the Central Highlands, where many of the North Vietnamese forces descending the Ho Chi Minh Trail turned into South Vietnam. Eight more Americans were killed, 126 were wounded, and twenty-five aircraft went up in flames as VC mortars raked the airfield and VC guerrillas breached the perimeter and sprayed the compound with fire. The attack coincided with Mac Bundy's visit to Saigon and also with a visit to Hanoi by Soviet premier Alexei Kosygin with an entourage of Soviet generals to fine-tune military assistance programs for the NVA and VC.[7]

Mac Bundy flew immediately to Pleiku with Generals Khanh and Westmoreland. They surveyed the damage and recommended the heavier air strikes that LBJ had been resisting: Operation Flaming Dart I. These would be the first strikes on North Vietnam since the raids following the Tonkin Gulf incident six months earlier. Three American carriers were on station in the South China Sea ready to bomb North Vietnam. In Washington, President Johnson convened an NSC meeting to consider options, and all present, including George Ball, recommended retaliation, as did the Joint Chiefs. "All the services were anxious to get a foot in the door," an Army general on the Joint Staff recalled. Mac Bundy sent LBJ a memo warning that if he did not strike now defeat was "inevitable, within the next year or so." American "prestige," Bundy wrote, was "directly at risk."[8]

Until now, Mac Bundy had shrugged off American casualties in Vietnam as no more numerous or problematic than the number of traffic fatalities in the streets of Washington, DC. But after Pleiku, the national security adviser threw caution to the wind and persuaded Johnson that launching a serious "policy of graduated and continuing reprisal" was the best course. Even if we suffer heavy casualties and lose, Bundy assured the president, we will strengthen American "credibility" by fighting. "Pleikus are like streetcars," Bundy joked; when one comes along, you have to be ready to hop on. Support for escalation in the White House was owed again to groupthink—Humphrey's exclusion from the inner circle a warning to all—as well as Ambassador Taylor's panicky calls from Saigon for action. The CIA station had counseled against bombing, predicting that any benefit would be outweighed by massive North Vietnamese escalation of the war on the ground. Taylor forwarded the CIA analysis to the White House only after removing all references to Hanoi's likely escalation.[9]

Johnson, oblivious to Taylor's subterfuge, then called in Senate majority leader Mike Mansfield and sought his opinion. Until now, the United States had tried to keep on the fringes of the war, with 23,000 military personnel in an "advise and support" capacity in South Vietnam. Direct American military action would raise the stakes and potential for escalation enormously. "I would negotiate; I would not hit back; I would get into negotiations," Mansfield advised. Intervention, Mansfield continued, would not only ensnare the US military in an open-ended conflict, it might lead to war with China, and might even repair the Sino-Soviet split.

It would not do, Mansfield cautioned, to *help* the two great communist powers mend fences through American overreach. Bill Bundy, who was there, felt the tension in the room, respect for Mansfield colliding with a determination to do *something* and to appease Republican hawks such as House minority leader Gerald Ford, who was also at the meeting—pressing for more and heavier air strikes.[10]

"I just don't think you can stand still and take this kind of thing," President Johnson cut in. "You just can't do it." Doing nothing would be "another Munich," a reference to the Western democracies' notorious appeasement of Hitler on the eve of World War II. Voters would not respect him if he let the VC "kill American boys in their tents." Johnson surveyed the room and added: "I've kept my shotgun over the mantel and the bullets in the basement for a long time now." It was time to take the shotgun down and bring the bullets upstairs. The president then went on television to address the American people—"We shall pay any price to make certain that freedom shall not perish from this earth"—and gave the order to launch Operation Flaming Dart I: strikes by forty-nine attack aircraft from two carriers in the Gulf of Tonkin.[11]

The jets stormed aloft and hit NVA barracks and radio shacks just north of the 17th parallel. The South's Vietnamese Air Force (VNAF) chipped in a wave of its own strike fighters, one of them flown by junta member Air Marshal Nguyen Cao Ky. When the first American jets attacked Dong Hoi, General Khanh, who called the VC "the arms of the enemy monster [whose] head is in Hanoi," popped the cork on a bottle of champagne to celebrate America's active involvement. Congress signaled its willingness to "pay any price," promptly voting $2.4 billion for combat operations in Vietnam.[12]

Undeterred, the VC attacked a hotel housing Americans in Qui Nhon the following day. They killed the ARVN guards at the front door, placed a massive charge under a central staircase that supported the hotel, and blew it. Four stories flopped to the ground, crushing twenty-three more American soldiers to death. Johnson now authorized Flaming Dart II—ninety-nine American attack aircraft from three Navy carriers, and about thirty US Air Force F-100 Super Sabres flying from bases in Thailand to hit targets north of the line drawn for Flaming Dart I.

The raid was designed by the Joint Chiefs to hit seven targets but was restricted by Johnson to two, neither of which was destroyed. Johnson and McNamara were this time spared LeMay's fulminations because the Air Force chief of staff had just retired and been replaced by a "McNamara man," sixty-three-year-old General John P. McConnell, who, in auditions for the position with Lyndon Johnson, had assured the president that, unlike LeMay, he would go along to get along. His job, he told LBJ, would be to give the president "suitable alternatives." Johnson would "choose the one which best solves the problem *as you see it*." That said, McConnell began pressing inside the Pentagon for a massive air campaign against North Vietnam (with over 1,000 aircraft) that might as well have been designed by LeMay.[13]

Khanh's champagne had barely lost its fizz before he was removed by a coup in late February 1965—this latest one led by Air Marshal Ky and General Nguyen Van Thieu. It hadn't taken long for the once plucky Khanh to grasp the futility of the war. His efforts to expand conscription and military activity to defeat the Viet Cong had been shouted down in the streets by student- and Buddhist-led protests. The Buddhists and their many supporters had become stridently anti-American, attacking the United States Information Service (USIS) centers in Hue and Saigon, shouting "Taylor go home!," and deriding the Khanh junta as "American lackeys." The CIA warned that "social and political revolution" was under way. The whole scene, George Ball observed, had "the smell of death" about it.[14]

Khanh had briefly reinvented himself as "the Sihanouk of Vietnam," a nod to the neighboring leader of Cambodia, who was attempting to walk a neutral line between communists and anticommunists. That was enough to provoke the junta, now known as the Armed Forces Council, to move with Ambassador Taylor's encouragement against Khanh, who earlier had moved on the exact same pretext against Big Minh. By this point the VC controlled most of South Vietnam's territory and were hacking away at the government-controlled areas with near impunity. The South Vietnamese regional commanders were devoting their time to politics, not war, and it showed. ARVN casualties rose steeply, to 1,500 a week, and 350 ARVN soldiers were deserting the colors every day, putting the American advisers in their midst at greater risk. In a single week in mid-February, 36 Americans were killed, 196 wounded, and another dragged into the jungle never to be seen again.[15]

President Johnson, who had been led to believe by Mac Bundy that he could switch the war on and off and "shape" communist behavior with "graduated pressure," began finally to grasp that such an approach was a fallacy. General Westmoreland remarked on the "folly of running the minute details of a war by a committee of presidential advisers thousands of miles away" and now called for US forces "in division strength" to protect US personnel and facilities. Former president Eisenhower came to the White House for a three-hour meeting with Johnson on February 17, 1965. The thirty-fourth president had clearly shaken off his old misgivings about the mischief of the "military-industrial complex" and now breathed fire. The thirty-sixth president, Ike insisted, must prepare six to eight infantry divisions for immediate intervention in the war. "We cannot let the Indochinese peninsula go," the old general exhorted. That same day, LBJ's UN ambassador, Adlai Stevenson, argued against the "harder military line" sought by Westmoreland and Eisenhower, but confessed that he saw no viable path to peace. Beijing and Moscow would veto in the Security Council any American effort to stop infiltration or impose a cease-fire, and Hanoi was not negotiating.

Throughout his meeting with Eisenhower, Johnson displayed remarkable servility—more evidence of his lack of confidence on military matters. On February 20, the Joint Chiefs put meat on the bones of Ike's advice: they recommended sending 65,000 American troops and a half-dozen Air Force squadrons for counterinsurgency combat operations. There was no point in negotiating, the generals contended, because South Vietnam's position was too weak to extract *any* concessions from Hanoi.[16]

On February 25, General Khanh was bundled onto a Pan Am flight to Paris. Ambassador Taylor called for a "Victory Government" of new South Vietnamese personalities who would "set their sights on victory and vigorously pursue it." The CIA mocked Taylor's cheerleading, observing that Khanh's flight into exile with no clear successor "merely opens up new opportunities for numerous aspirants to the role of military strongman." General Nguyen Van Thieu, competing for that role with Air Marshal Nguyen Cao Ky, was described in a CIA report as the perfect cat's-paw: "intelligent, highly ambitious," and entirely focused on "personal advancement."[17]

MACV noted that the rise of Thieu and Ky changed nothing: the "consummate interest in politics" that had gained them the junta leadership had entailed a neglect of the war effort and led to more monthly declines in ARVN operations and effectiveness. And none of the American air raids intended to stand in for the floundering ARVN did much damage. Their greatest impact was on the Soviets' attitude. Senator Fulbright warned the president that escalation in Vietnam would "intensify the Cold War" and cause "a revival of jingoism," and it did. Kosygin was in Hanoi during Flaming Dart I and II, and he would return to Moscow determined to avenge the slight to Soviet pride and equip Hanoi with the latest air defenses.[18]

On March 2, 1965, Johnson ordered the start of Operation Rolling Thunder, an open-ended air campaign conceived by Johnson's inner circle as a "slow squeeze," what Mac Bundy called "a policy of *sustained reprisal* against North Vietnam." Instead of knocking the North Vietnamese out with massive air raids that might trigger Soviet and Chinese intervention or inflict a humanitarian disaster and harden North Vietnamese resolve, the United States would increase pressure on Hanoi delicately, adding or subtracting targets—barracks, depots, bridges—to "shape" North Vietnamese actions and opinion.

The aims of the air campaign were deliberately "soft": assist South Vietnam, avoid Soviet or Chinese intervention, and "allay" American domestic concerns about the bombing of North Vietnam. American pilots, LBJ boasted, "can't hit an outhouse without my permission." Any target that might cause Soviet or Chinese intervention or, as Mac Bundy put it, "make it hard for Hanoi to shift its ground" was scratched from the list, all but ensuring that the bombing would be ineffective.

Seventy percent of North Vietnam's imports arrived at Haiphong harbor and the other 30 percent came by rail over the Chinese border, but both areas were left unscathed, as Johnson and his advisers were fearful of what they called the "flash point"—the one provocation that might bring the Chinese into the war or make it impossible for Hanoi to negotiate without losing face. Bob McNamara made a virtue of this delicacy: "We are trying to induce them to get out of the war without having their country destroyed and to realize if they do not get out, their country will be destroyed."[19]

Rolling Thunder was hugely controversial—Johnson's caution about getting into another Korea weighed against military complaints (most cut off by McNamara or Wheeler before they reached his ears) that the air campaign was inadequate. But Johnson forbade a real strategic air offensive of the sort LeMay had pushed during the September 1964 Sigma II war game. He and McNamara agreed that airpower would be used to defeat the "insurrection" in the South as well as North Vietnamese attempts to feed that insurrection with infiltrators and supplies, but it would not be used "to overthrow the Communist government of North Vietnam" or destroy its capacity to wage war. To critics of this micromanagement, Johnson replied: "As long as I am Commander in Chief, I am going to control from Washington."[20]

Civilian hawks like McNamara, Bundy, and Rusk envisioned a measured air campaign as a cattle prod, to "touch up" North Vietnam and persuade them to cut ties with the VC and recognize South Vietnam. There would be no loss of face in failure, Mac Bundy assured the president on February 7, because people all over the world would see that "we did all that we could." He then told LBJ that he put the odds of South Vietnam surviving the war as an independent nation at about 25 percent. But bomb anyway, he advised, for "even if it fails, the value of the effort seems to exceed its cost." The war had not even begun in earnest, and it was already draped with an air of futility and defeatism.[21]

Instead of thousand-bomber raids over Hanoi, Westy sourly commented in his memoirs, we got "two to four raids a week by a few dozen planes at a time." Taking it all in, *New York Times* columnist Russell Baker observed on March 2, the day Rolling Thunder began: "It is almost impossible to find out what United States policy is in Vietnam, unless you are the kind of person who can get an all-night bull session with Dean Rusk or McGeorge Bundy." And even if you were such a person, he continued, "this is the most dangerous possible moment to be caught with an opinion about the policy." Most Americans, Baker concluded, "felt that while there probably was a United States policy on Vietnam, it would be hopeless for them to try to understand it in the limited lifetime available to them." He titled the column "Befuddled in Asia."[22]

MACV's monthly evaluations, known as MONEVALs, described a war in South Vietnam that was now hanging by the slender thread of US airpower. "USAF F-100s and B-57s doing all the work" was a well-worn phrase. After the coup of February 1965, operations by the ARVN's 300,000 troops all but stopped because of "the diversion of commanders' interest by political intrigues in Saigon," which, in turn, led to more "administrative confusion" all across the country as provincial budgets were frozen by the frequent changes of regime. Militia forces—the 300,000 villagers the Americans were arming to provide rural security in South Vietnam—were surrendering in droves and handing their weapons to the VC, in some cases handing over their American advisers as well. The latest junta, McNamara warned, was already "on the brink of total collapse."[23]

Reading MONEVALs like these, which every month got worse, not better, Westmoreland concluded that the war would have to be Americanized. He knew that Hanoi would respond to a bigger American effort by infiltrating NVA divisions into South Vietnam and increasing aid to the VC, but he seems to have viewed this more as an opportunity than as a risk. He would destroy the VC's state sponsor in battle with the method enshrined in the Army's 1962 *Field Service Regulations*: use "United States military forces to terminate the conflict rapidly and decisively."[24]

Westy was itching for war, for the big promotion from adviser to field commander. He was so eager that when his military intelligence shop predicted in the spring of 1965 that American escalation would provoke the North Vietnamese to march tens of thousands of troops into South Vietnam to reinforce the Viet Cong, Westy "revised the number downward" before transmitting it to the White House. "Jesus," one of Westmoreland's aides said to another after reading the truthful estimate, "if we tell this to the people in Washington we'll be out of the war tomorrow." Harkins had prevaricated to keep the advisory mission going. Westmoreland was prevaricating to get combat operations going.[25]

Rolling Thunder required more jets and air bases, none of which—after the bloody attacks at Bien Hoa, Saigon, Pleiku, and Qui Nhon—could be safely entrusted to the ARVN. Westmoreland requested a 6,000-man Marine expeditionary brigade to defend the American facilities, which the president whittled down to 3,500 Marines, who were sent to guard the airfield at Da Nang on March 8, 1965. "I'm scared to death of putting ground forces in," LBJ told McNamara, "but I'm more frightened about losing a bunch of planes from lack of security." These 3,500 Marines—half had been circling in ships off the shore of Vietnam for more than a month, the other half flew in from Okinawa—were the first pebbles in a coming avalanche of American manpower.[26]

If LBJ had supposed that the Marines—a combined-arms force with their own tanks, artillery, and aircraft—would suffice to turn the tide in combat or even as a bargaining chip, he was quickly brought to his senses. Even a bare-bones program limited to guarding American bases would require troop numbers far in excess of what the Marines could provide. The

Army reckoned that 15,000 troops would be needed to provide security for Pleiku, and a similar number for each of the sprawling American bases at Da Nang, Qui Nhon, Bien Hoa, Saigon, and Cam Ranh Bay. In all, Westy said, he'd need at least 75,000 troops just to safeguard US personnel and bases.[27]

LBJ pressed ahead, despite the total absence of strategy or even a reliable strategic partner. He never paused to consider the key flaw in his strategy. "Escalation dominance" was America's decisive advantage—its ability to raise the level of pain in North Vietnam to unbearable levels. But LBJ could not invade or devastate North Vietnam without risking war with China or the Soviet Union. The limited war he *could* wage against Hanoi would never push it to the brink. He flailed angrily, hoping to land a lucky punch. "You get things bubbling, General," he barked at the Army chief of staff in a White House elevator. But the president didn't specify what he meant. Johnson was feeling pressured to display a little more "go-north attitude," as he put it. He worried that Republicans would view him as a patsy, and he needed them to side with him, not with the southern Democrats, who were trying to kill the Great Society programs as zealously as they had tried to kill civil rights. "If I don't go in now," LBJ snapped, "and they show later I should have gone, then, they'll be all over me in Congress. They won't be talking about my civil rights bill, or education, or beautification. No sir, they'll push Vietnam up my ass every time. Vietnam. Vietnam. Vietnam. Right up my ass."[28]

Meeting with the Joint Chiefs in April 1965, LBJ sowed the seeds of what would shortly become the "search and destroy" strategy. He rejected Marine General Wally Greene's plea for an intensification of the war against North Vietnam, but he placed no limits on the war in South Vietnam: "We are limited to what we can do in North Vietnam, but we have almost free rein in South Vietnam, and I want to kill more Viet Cong." He officially authorized a change in posture from static defense to "counterinsurgency combat operations." In short, the US military was commanded to fight the war against North Vietnam in South Vietnam, where there would be few restrictions on the use of American force.[29]

Ordered by President Johnson to come up with answers and solutions—"win the game in South Vietnam" and "start killing more Viet Cong"—the Army got to work. Their 1963 field manual on "counter-guerrilla operations" called for restless "combat patrolling," "continuous pressure," and "aggressive action" to destroy the insurgents. In March 1965, Westmoreland submitted his "Commander's Estimate of the Situation," which adverted the desirability of crossing into Laos to cut the Ho Chi Minh Trail but settled for high-intensity operations inside South Vietnam, which he called "free maneuver of American and Allied units throughout South Vietnam."[30]

It was a critical moment, spanning the spring and summer of 1965. Some in the administration wanted no more than seventeen battalions sent to Vietnam to secure the air bases critical to Rolling Thunder, with combat left to the South Vietnamese. If the South Vietnamese collapsed, the Americans could depart with a minimum of fuss.[31]

But Westmoreland and the chiefs thought that such a strategy was too passive, reactive, and indecisive. They wanted forty-four battalions, with at least twenty-four more in the pipeline, to take the fight to the communists and, as Westy put it, "stomp them to death." Westy shrewdly cloaked the request in the "signaling" language of the Johnson White House: forty-four maneuver battalions, he alleged, would "give us a substantial and hard-hitting capability on the ground *to convince the VC that they cannot win.*"[32]

Johnson edged closer to war on the ground. He authorized McNamara to begin using American ground troops to exert graduated pressure in the same way as air strikes—to "signal" stiffening American resolve. Air raids, LBJ told reporters in April, were "carefully limited," aimed at "concrete and steel, and not human life." He assured the American people in a speech that he knew of no "far-reaching strategy that is being suggested or promulgated for Vietnam," as if that were a *good* thing. Noting that the University of Michigan had just held the first "teach-in" of the war, a twelve-hour event in four auditoriums and six classrooms that drew 3,000 students wearing "Stop the War in Vietnam" buttons and vowing to organize marches and legislative action against the war, the president grumbled that Americans should show more respect for "our soldiers who are dying in Vietnam."[33]

LBJ unveiled plans to lavish foreign aid on South *and* North Vietnam if only Hanoi would agree to an "honorable peace." He would fund a Mekong River development program "on a scale to dwarf our [Tennessee Valley Authority]," and finance education and healthcare in both Vietnams as well. There was a pleading tone to it all, Johnson in speeches saying things like "I'll never be second" in the search for peace, and "I'll go anywhere at any time and meet with anyone" for peace in Vietnam. Le Duan and Ho Chi Minh, recognizing the president's desperation, rebuffed the offer immediately. Peace, the politburo announced, would come only after the United States stopped the bombing, withdrew from South Vietnam, and permitted a coalition government in Saigon that would finish the task of national unification. So long as the Americans and their "puppets" remained, the Viet Cong would serve as the legitimate representative of the South Vietnamese people.[34]

McNamara, meanwhile, flew to Hawaii to meet with Westmoreland and Taylor. In Honolulu on April 20, 1965, the die was cast. Bombing was not working, Westmoreland argued; the North had endured 2,800 sorties over ten weeks of bombing and would continue to endure whatever bombing the United States unleashed because Hanoi knew that it was close to winning the war in the South. Westmoreland outlined what he called his "victory strategy." He should be given more troops, Westmoreland said, to beat the NVA and the VC on the ground in the South, and prove to the communist leadership that they couldn't win. Only then, he argued, would Hanoi yield, or negotiate.

With McNamara, the Joint Chiefs, and the president leaning toward a major ground commitment, Westmoreland secured 30,000 more troops at the Honolulu meeting, raising the total number of US forces ticketed for South Vietnam to 82,500—a 150 percent increase. He wanted at least three divisions to defend the coastal plain against the VC and begin offensive operations in the Central Highlands against NVA infiltrators. Westy changed the American aim from merely signaling the futility of continued war—by bombing the North and installing US troops in a few invincible southern "enclaves"—to seeking and destroying the communist forces in the South with American maneuver battalions. The CIA director observed (again) that such a strategy would produce "no definite result" for the simple reason that North Vietnam could easily match and exceed every American surge with troops of its own.[35]

The stickiness of the liability created by Westmoreland's "victory strategy" was almost immediately felt. There were 50,000 US troops in South Vietnam on June 1, 1965, with 30,000 more on the way. Westy now requested 72,000 more, for a total of 152,000. The new CIA director, Admiral William

Raborn, proved no more supportive than McCone had been. Every month the ARVN was losing 10,000 troops to desertion, not combat. What was the point of reinforcing such an army with American boys? asked Raborn. He cautioned LBJ against the surge: "We will find ourselves pinned down," unable to get out, forced to "broaden the conflict in quantum jumps." The war, Raborn said, was more political than military and needed to be won "at the hamlet level" by the South Vietnamese. White House counsel Clark Clifford warned that the surge would lead LBJ into "a quagmire," an "open-end commitment without a realistic hope of ultimate victory." Clifford advised taking a settlement instead; "It won't be what we want, but we can learn to live with it."[36]

LBJ temporized, whittling Westy's latest request for 72,000 troops down to 18,000—"to hold the situation." The president would immediately send the nine battalions (16,000 troops) of the airmobile 1st Cavalry Division, better known as the "Cav." The president told Wheeler that he wanted "maximum protection at the least cost." The situation appeared hopeless: the North Vietnamese and VC "think they are winning," LBJ said, "and we think they are too." The war continued without any real strategic direction—its only apparent aim to burnish Johnson's national security credentials and postpone defeat by inserting American forces.[37]

Westy's request for forty-four battalions coincided with more coup attempts in Saigon, as the junta members, goaded by the VC double agent Colonel Pham Ngoc Thao, marched in and out of Saigon with loyal troops until the Americans and the junta agreed in June to formally anoint Air Marshal Nguyen Cao Ky prime minister and General Nguyen Van Thieu president. Ky was, among other things, a drug trafficker who used his command of the South Vietnamese air force to smuggle Laotian opium into Saigon on military flights. Ky told a British interviewer in 1965 that he had "only one hero: Hitler." The Johnson administration scrambled to deny the remark and accuse the interviewer of fabricating it, at which point Ky reaffirmed it. Hitler was indeed his man.[38]

Thieu too was a polarizing figure, an ambitious officer who had converted in his thirties from Buddhism to Catholicism to improve his career prospects. The first act of the two leaders was to decree a "no-breathing week," during which newspapers were shut down and civil liberties suspended. Predictably, the "no-breathing week" would extend into years as the most effective way to silence rising demands for reform. The more Washington asserted the need to support South Vietnamese democracy, the less their South Vietnamese protégés worked at it. The Thieu-Ky rivalry would shortly begin to gnaw at South Vietnam like a cancer, for these two men, who would become avatars for Saigon politics until the downfall of the regime ten years later, commanded rival factions that spread their corrosive influence into every corner of the South Vietnamese government and military.

The thirty-five-year-old Ky was a flamboyant hustler who dressed like his idea of an air ace, with purple scarf, flight suit, and Ray-Bans. To complete the look, he divorced his wife to marry a beautiful Air Vietnam flight attendant who often appeared in public at his side in matching flight suit, scarf, and sunglasses. General Khanh had fueled Ky's rise from obscurity, using Ky's control of the air force around Saigon to secure his own coup and fend off rivals. The forty-two-year-old Thieu, commander of the ARVN 5th Division, had been sidelined by Khanh, a snub that proved helpful after Khanh's ouster in 1965, when Thieu was made chairman of the new junta's National Leadership Council.

The competition of these two strivers for control of South Vietnam distracted from real nation-building. To secure their own positions, they pursued a spoils system for the next ten years, Ky trying to place his men in every powerful ministry, and Thieu doing the same. Every South Vietnamese military headquarters, police unit, and civilian ministry was gradually divided into opposing camps, one for Thieu, the other for Ky. The two leaders discovered that American-ordered "anti-corruption campaigns" could be helpful, not to cleanse South Vietnam of corruption but to purge each other's supporters. "Americans are big boys," Ky laughed. "You can talk them into almost anything. All you have to do is sit with them for half an hour over a bottle of whiskey and be a nice guy."[39]

None of these machinations could be concealed indefinitely from the American press and public. An antiwar mood was slowly spreading. Barry McGuire's "Eve of Destruction" surged to number one on the charts with its haunting lyrics: "The eastern world it is explodin' / Violence flarin', bullets loadin'." Twenty thousand demonstrators—reminded by McGuire's hit that they were "old enough to kill, but not for votin'"—gathered around the White House on April 17, 1965, demanding that "the U.S. get out of

Vietnam." Johnson zigged and zagged, proffering some (barely) positive war aims in early 1965—none of them compelling or concrete. Now he spoke wanly of redeeming a "national pledge," taking "the path of peaceful settlement," creating "confidence in the value of an American commitment," and dulling "the appetite of aggression."[40]

These were insipid aims for a president who had spent five years around this emerging war. Privately, Johnson beseeched his inner circle in June to tell him what the war was *really* about: "Who sees our purpose and means of achieving it out there?" he asked. "Will it be so costly? How do we expect to win?" In this meeting—with Mac Bundy, Rusk, McNamara, Ball, and McNaughton—Johnson fretted that he might lose reelection in 1968 to an Eisenhower-like candidate, who would make the whole election about terminating the no-win war. Ike had chased off Truman and beaten Adlai Stevenson this way in 1952, LBJ reminded the group. "How do you expect to wind things up? You'll get, 'I go to Korea,'" a reference to Eisenhower's pledge during the Korean War that, if elected, he would "go to Korea" and end the frustrating conflict.[41]

Reelection obsessed LBJ. He couldn't be on the ballot in 1968, the president exclaimed at another meeting, with "Ho Chi Minh running through the streets of Saigon." Republican Richard Nixon was already warning that Vietnam would be *the* major issue in the 1968 elections if Johnson failed "to win the war, and end it." Another likely challenger, Ronald Reagan, was calling for "full mobilization" and a blockade of Haiphong harbor, saying, "I don't see how a nation our size, engaged with a nation that size, can talk about a ten- or twenty-year war. We ought to go in and get it over with."[42]

In a meeting at Camp David on July 25, 1965, to brainstorm *how* to "get it over with," General Earle Wheeler proposed sending 750,000 US troops to defeat the VC insurgency once and for all. Johnson interrupted to say that such numbers would *never* be sent to Vietnam. Clark Clifford, who could see that Johnson was not facing facts, interrupted: "But even if it *is* the figure, and it *works*, my question is, what *then*?" Would the United States be free to depart, leaving South Vietnam to enjoy its freedom and independence? No, Wheeler replied. The United States would have to leave a large force in South Vietnam for twenty or thirty years to keep the peace.

There was something unhinged about the process: a president trying to wage a war by stealth and muddying every important detail, from the cost to the scope and length of the commitment; generals not insisting on clarity; and all of the in-group power players endorsing the travesty because they believed that, despite the flaws in planning and messaging, the war would be short and easy once the VC and NVA found themselves at the sharp end of American mobility and firepower. The fifty-eight-year-old Clifford looked around the room—at the generals, the cabinet officers, and the White House aides—and declared: "I see catastrophe ahead for my country."[43]

Three days later, LBJ finally handed Westmoreland a blank check—in a press conference: "Additional forces will be needed later, and they will be sent as requested," the president told reporters and the MACV commander. This was all the more astonishing because Johnson's rationale for the war, relayed at the same press conference, remained soggy: "We are there because for all our shortcomings, for all our failings as a nation and a people, we remain fixed on the pursuit of freedom as a deep and moral obligation that will not let us go." The president's expressed aims were even soggier, all about what Washington did *not* want: "We do not want an expanding struggle...but we will not surrender or retreat." "We will not abandon the men that are there." But what was the war *for*? Clearly there was little to recommend this war, but Johnson did not dare pull out.[44]

Mac Bundy had been transformed by his trip to Pleiku in February 1965 when he had seen American dead and wounded for the first time. LBJ was alarmed by the transformation, for Bundy had previously occupied a more thoughtful space between the doves and hawks: "Well, they made a believer out of you, didn't they," Johnson greeted Bundy on his return to Washington. Always cool and calculating, Bundy came back hot and emotional. The spilled American blood had to be avenged. The troops had to be protected. McGeorge Bundy at war, Johnson laughed to a friend, reminded him of the pious preacher's son who went to a whorehouse. When asked how he liked it, the boy said: "It's really good, I don't know what it is, but I like it, it's really good."[45]

The report Mac Bundy delivered to the president after his Vietnam trip was hugely influential. Without US action, the national security adviser warned, South Vietnam would collapse. Negotiated withdrawal was "surrender on the installment plan." The "international prestige and influence of the U.S.," Bundy said, were "directly at risk in Vietnam." And yet in the same report Bundy confessed that the Viet Cong had "astonishing" perseverance and frightening ubiquity: "They can appear anywhere—and almost at any time." Against such a foe, there was no "shortcut to success."[46]

Bundy was aware of the mounting VC terror in South Vietnam: 400 government officials beheaded, disemboweled, or otherwise killed in 1965 alone, hundreds of South Vietnamese people murdered in VC mine and grenade attacks on buses, restaurants, airports, and stadiums, and VC raiders torturing villagers to extract information and obedience. The American people would have to prepare for a long struggle against such a ruthless enemy. Bundy's ultimate recommendation, in short, was fatuous on its face: limited boots on the ground and a lightweight air and naval reprisal policy. The United States would deploy intermittent bombing to avenge the murder of a hamlet chief or a terrorist bomb in a restaurant against the concerted decades-long struggle of Vietnamese revolutionaries.[47]

When McNamara presented Johnson with the "maximum-force options" pushed by the Joint Chiefs—70 maneuver battalions, 235,000 reserves, and more air wings—the SecDef had to admit that even if such colossal forces won on the battlefield, suffering a projected 500 killed-in-action every month and twice as many wounded, they would *solve* nothing. "It would merely drive the VC back into the trees and back to their 1960–64 pattern—a pattern against which U.S. troops and aircraft would be of limited value. Even in success," McNamara concluded, "it is not clear how we will be able to disengage our forces from Vietnam."[48]

Johnson opted to keep this emerging disaster as secret, cheap, and low-key as possible. The chiefs wanted $12.7 billion for the new deployments, 27 additional maneuver battalions and a call-up of 235,000 reserve troops. Johnson replied with a no—not a penny more than the $1 billion already budgeted. And no reserves. LBJ had been vice president when JFK called up 150,000 reservists during the Berlin crisis of 1961, an event most notable for its political toxicity.[49]

They had to lower "the political noise level of escalation," Johnson told his advisers. Raising taxes, asking for a $12 billion war supplemental, declaring a "national emergency," and calling up 235,000 reserves to fill out the forces bound for Vietnam would be the opposite of low-key. It would disturb every community in America and would give congressional conservatives a pretext to choose guns over the butter of the president's Great

Society programs, which he hoped to see passed into law by January 1966. After *that*, he assured the chiefs, moving the goalposts yet again, he would get them more money for the war. As Johnson later put it to Doris Kearns Goodwin: "If I left the woman I really loved—the Great Society—in order to get involved with that bitch of a war on the other side of the world, then I would lose *everything* at home."[50]

The result? Strategic chaos, or, as Mac Bundy put it, "a premium put on imprecision." The war would be fought, General Harold Johnson said, with "peacetime practices." The quality of the Army would "erode" without proper funding and reserve capabilities, he warned. The reserves were key. The United States had 1 million trained reserve troops in 1965. They were kept on the payroll for a reason: to bridge the gap between peacetime active-duty forces and the expanded manpower demands of a war such as this. By not calling up the reserves, LBJ commenced the degradation of the armed forces. Without enough trained troops, the services would have to deplete America's strategic reserve—the uncommitted active-duty forces in the United States—and then rely entirely on draftees and troops plucked from other overseas commands, where they were needed at least as much as in Vietnam.

But these concerns were bulldozed by LBJ's determination to keep the war cheap and hidden. In an NSC meeting on July 27, 1965, where the decision was taken to expand the war without properly budgeting or even declaring it, Johnson explained his casuistry: "I don't want to be overly dramatic and cause tensions. I think we can get our people to support us without having to be too provocative and warlike." The next day he announced to the American public that the US troop level in Vietnam would be raised from 75,000 to 125,000 "almost immediately," and then to 200,000, but that this provision of thirty-four more maneuver battalions plus 35,000 combat support troops and essential air squadrons would be accomplished by doubling monthly draft calls, from 17,000 to 35,000. The reserves would not be called up.[51]

LBJ's "credibility gap" was widening. The president was determined to cloud the war in mystery, so that its true cost in blood and dollars would not reveal itself. The more specific he was about ends and means, the easier it would be for Congress or the media to price the unfolding war. He had recently assured the public that the war would cost no more than $2 billion

LBJ and Clark Clifford listen to Henry Cabot Lodge Jr. during the pivotal July 27, 1965, National Security Council meeting. There the decision was taken to expand the war without declaring or even budgeting it. (LBJ Library)

a year, but legislators on Capitol Hill, after pricing the commitments made to Westmoreland and the Joint Chiefs, put the real cost at closer to five times that—$10 billion a year, a sum that was certain to increase. But how could the United States finance new programs such as Medicare and Medicaid in addition to a hot war in Southeast Asia without also raising taxes to pay for it all and stifle the inevitable inflation?

It couldn't. US inflation would double in the next two years, and then double again by 1970. The federal deficit would balloon to $10 billion by 1967, $27 billion by 1968. But Johnson didn't dare raise taxes to deal with the inflation and deficits. If he did, he complained, the powerful Democratic chairman of the House Ways and Means Committee would cut him off: "Old Wilbur Mills will thank me kindly and send me back my Great Society, and then he'll tell me that they'll be glad to spend whatever we need for the war."[52]

McNamara in 1965 solved this particular problem by hiding the true cost of the war. The total cost, from beginning to end, he assured Congress, would not exceed $10 billion, a trifling share of GDP. It was a fantasy number, plucked from the air and based on the assumption that the war and all spending associated with it would conveniently terminate on June 30, 1967, the end of a fiscal year. Privately, McNamara knew that the cost would be far higher, at least $21 billion, and probably much more than that. Horace Busby, a White House aide who sat in on many of these discussions, scribbled an urgent warning to LBJ in July 1965: "What we are considering is not whether we continue a war—but whether we start (or have started) a *new* war. The 1954–64 premises, principles, and pretexts no longer apply. This is no longer South Vietnam's war. We are no longer advisers. The stakes are no longer South Vietnam's. The war is *ours*. We are participants. The stakes are ours—and the West's."[53]

Chapter 4

STRENGTH ONLY
FOR DEFEAT

On July 28, 1965, having wrestled his advisers into agreement on the troop surge for Vietnam, Johnson began revealing the true scope of the war to the American people. Some of his aides had wanted the president to deliver a major speech to the nation, announcing the expanded American commitment in Vietnam. Daniel Ellsberg, the analyst who would later leak the Pentagon Papers, actually drafted such a speech for LBJ. It challenged Americans to rise to the occasion and battle international communism "till hell freezes over."[1]

Johnson froze in horror. That was asking far too much of a nation that had just reelected him to keep the peace and was already on the hook for the Great Society. Instead, LBJ declared the Vietnam War quietly, at a press conference. "Why must young Americans, born into a land exultant with hope and with golden promise, toil and suffer and sometimes die in such a remote and distant place?" he asked. "We did not choose to be the guardians at the gate," he answered, "but there is no one else." America *must* fight "against the grasping ambition of Asian communism." The president would send 125,000 troops immediately and double the monthly draft call, to 35,000—not to win, but to coax Hanoi into negotiations. "We are going to continue to persist, if persist we must, until death and desolation have led to the same conference table where others could now join us at a much smaller cost."[2]

Later, Johnson cleaned it up. No mother wanted her son to die for *negotiations*, and for a rich superpower with 200 million citizens to fight a poor third-world country of 20 million for the prize of a "conference table" sounded pathetic. Privately Johnson told worried congressional leaders that the aim really *was* negotiations—that he could get Hanoi to quit in six months' time—but publicly he spoke of victory, as did the Joint Chiefs. McGeorge Bundy summarized LBJ's perplexity: "He had decided to do whatever he had to do, but he had not decided how much he had to do."[3]

In the Pentagon, where McNamara had struggled to assemble the manpower for the more limited mission—to force Hanoi to the conference table—there was a clear realization that Johnson's call for victory had landed the US military in what McNamara aide John McNaughton called "the dilemma." America, McNaughton wrote McNamara in mid-January 1966, could force Hanoi to negotiate only if it deployed the force necessary for victory. Yet North Vietnam was a young developing country with a galloping birth rate, and 120,000 North Vietnamese males reached draft age every year. Additionally, there were more than a million North Vietnamese men of military age not yet serving in the NVA. That number could be more than doubled by making more North Vietnamese age cohorts draft eligible. Hanoi had only to send a fraction of all these young people south to counter every American troop surge and replace casualties.[4]

This was McNaughton's "dilemma" in a nutshell: "the force necessary for victory" in South Vietnam was going to keep rising—to unthinkable heights. With large numbers of NVA reinforcing the VC in the South, Westmoreland and the chiefs, who had seemed content with 400,000 American troops, now estimated that 750,000 American troops would be needed for victory. But that was two-thirds of the entire active-duty strength of the US Army and Marine Corps. President Johnson would never authorize that many troops for a limited war in a faraway country, McNaughton noted, yet smaller troop numbers wouldn't get the job done, and would be interpreted by the enemy as an admission of weakness, emboldening Hanoi to prolong the war and wait America out. "If we go for compromise," McNaughton warned, "we have the strength only for defeat."[5]

To assemble more than "the strength for defeat," President Johnson sought help from America's allies, but he found few that were willing. The NATO countries met his requests for "more flags" in the coalition with a deafening silence. McGeorge Bundy and McNamara went so far as to offer the British $1 billion in aid if they would agree to send a brigade to Vietnam. Harold Wilson refused the offer, put off by the explanation that LBJ "wanted a few British soldiers to die in Vietnam alongside Americans" to give the appearance of a coalition. Only regional allies Australia and South Korea sent troops, the Australians averaging about 6,000 men in-country in any given year, the South Koreans 47,000. It wasn't much. Johnson would have to find most of his "free-world forces" in the United States.[6]

But the drafted "Vietnam-only Army"—shorn of its trained reserves—would be a two-edged sword. Taking young men was easier than pulling older men out of their civilian jobs, but it would become politically explosive as the war lengthened and the small draft calls of the late fifties and early sixties abruptly soared. Already in August 1965, Johnson was forced to extend the draft law to previously exempted married men to fill up the first deployments to Vietnam. Big draft calls would also pose political and morale problems because of the way they placed the burden of the war on a relatively small and disadvantaged cohort.

The Vietnam draft, based on the Selective Service Act of 1948, was anything but fair. Young men's draft status was decided by local draft boards, which were largely white—entirely white in many southern states—and tended to "defer" or exempt white middle-class youth, drafting working-class and minority men instead. African Americans, just 11 percent of the US population during the war, would furnish 16 percent of draftees and 23 percent of combat troops.[7]

Overall, of the 27.5 million American males eligible for the draft during the war, only 1.7 million would be drafted and sent to Vietnam. The rest either would not be called at all or would find sanctuary in illness (real or feigned), family hardship, the clergy, missionary work, college, graduate school, or other pursuits deemed exemptible. That this tendency to shift the burden of combat down the social scale was a deliberate piece of Cold War policy—to conserve America's intellectual capital in the event of war—did not lessen its perceived unfairness.[8]

While LBJ began deploying ground troops to Vietnam, the jungle paths through Laos and Cambodia to South Vietnam—collectively named the Ho Chi Minh Trail—hummed with activity. Regiments of 2,000 newly trained North Vietnamese conscripts were moving quietly down the forested tracks in groups of 200. They would change their unit numbers—critical for estimates of enemy strength and intentions—to confuse American and South Vietnamese intelligence. So, for example, as McNaughton did his thought exercise on what force level it would take to get North Vietnam to negotiate, Hanoi's NVA 33rd Regiment reported for training at the headquarters of the NVA 325B Division, renamed itself the NVA 101st Regiment, and took the cover name Song Lam (Blue River) for its march south to Cambodia in July and its infiltration into South Vietnam through the cut of the Ia Drang Valley. This meant that even before the 2,000-man unit infiltrated, it had begun to sow doubt in the minds of American and South Vietnamese military intelligence. Were they one regiment or three? If one, where were the other two? Such vagueness, compounded by the rare North Vietnamese deserter or prisoner, who might give one of three different unit designations, would make an attrition strategy hard to calibrate. If you never knew the enemy strength, you could never know what percentage of them you were killing.[9]

The man in charge of defending South Vietnam against these southbound NVA regiments was fifty-two-year-old General William Westmoreland, the straitlaced organization man chosen by Max Taylor to energize MACV. The shift from advising to fighting was converting Westy into a public figure. He would be named *Time* magazine's "Man of the Year" in January 1966—"a jut-jawed, flat-bellied six-footer, the sinewy personification of the American fighting man." Having already secured President Johnson's assent to give him 200,000 troops in 1965, 300,000 by 1966, and a blank check for the future, Westmoreland considered that he finally had the means to push the NVA and Viet Cong over what his operations chief called their "threshold of pain." Kill and maim enough of the enemy, General Bill DePuy asserted, and they would give up.[10]

"Stay loose," Westy jauntily wrote all of his Vietnam-bound division commanders. Major combat operations were imminent. French operations against the Viet Minh had been feeble by comparison. Westmoreland would dip into America's towering cash pile to fight the kind of war that no other power in the 1960s could even contemplate. With the United States generating 40 percent of world GDP in 1965, there seemed no limit to what America could do—in Vietnam or anywhere else.

South Vietnam was immediately transformed by an American construction boom. The French had made do with just six air bases in Vietnam. America added forty-three new ones, including Bien Hoa, which during the Vietnam War became the busiest airport in the world. American construction companies built eleven new ports and naval bases, and hundreds of miles of road to connect South Vietnam's coastal cities with over a hundred new "agricultural settlements," which were really Special Forces camps sited on the high plateaus overlooking South Vietnam's long borders with Laos and Cambodia.

When the first Marines splashed ashore at Da Nang in 1965, there was no logistical system to support them. Everything had to come "over the beach." Two years later, there would be enough ports, airfields, and storage facilities to handle more than a million tons of supplies every month—enough to sustain a million troops in the field.[11]

When they found the elusive enemy, the Americans planned to destroy him with superior tactics and technology, which they gave a name: airmobile operations. For the first time in the history of warfare, a large field army would rely on a fleet of thousands of helicopters as its primary method of tactical movement. America's decision to fight in Vietnam coincided with the introduction into combat of the icon of the war: Bell's UH-1 Iroquois "utility helicopter," better known as the "Huey." The UH-1s began rolling off production lines in 1963. They could be configured as an air ambulance (known as a "medevac") with nine litters, as a gunship ("guns") with pilot-fired machine guns, rockets, and grenade launchers, or as a troop carrier ("slick") with space for a dozen soldiers and crew.

This streamlined, powerful marvel replaced the gawky Korea-era helicopters, whose 5,000-pound, thirteen-cylinder radial engines had eaten up most of the cargo space. When troops were crowded into what little space remained, those early helicopters couldn't even hover. They were too heavy. That's why they had four wheels—they had to make running takeoffs.

With its 500-pound gas-turbine engine and forty-eight-foot main rotors, the Huey changed the game. Even with two pilots, a crew chief, a door gunner, and six soldiers with full gear aboard, the Huey could hover

A battalion of Airborne troops setting down in II Corps. For the first time in the history of warfare, a large field army would rely on a fleet of thousands of helicopters as its primary method of tactical movement. (National Archives)

up to an altitude of 10,000 feet, fly 315 miles out and back, slip in and out of crude landing zones (LZs) on their skids, and whiz through the air at 125 mph, significantly faster than the 80 or 90 mph managed by its predecessor. And that was just version 1.0: the UH-1A and UH-1B models in use when the first American ground troops went to Vietnam in 1965. Version 2.0 was the UH-1H model, introduced in 1967–1968. The "Hotel" added 500 horsepower to the engine and stretched the fuselage to create 12 percent more space for men and supplies.

The Pentagon, the Joint Chiefs, and Westy all imagined that "search and destroy" operations with the Huey would be the decisive advantage in the war. The road-bound French had been continually ambushed, evaded, or wrong-footed. The airmobile Americans would be able to rush fresh troops to even the remotest battlefields. The helicopters, or "birds," erased the problems of time and space.[12]

The US Army had tested this "vertical envelopment" concept at Fort Benning, Georgia, in the early 1960s and then created the 1st Cavalry

Division (Airmobile) in 1965. The Cav would be by far the best-equipped outfit in Vietnam, and the idealized model for everything that followed. Their single "air-assault division" of 16,000 men in three brigades had 434 helicopters of its own to move assault troops in and out of LZs and resupply them during battle.

Four hundred and thirty-four helicopters were a lot: four or five times as many birds as were attached to a normal Army division in Vietnam. The helicopters were grouped in battalions, each usually consisting of three companies of troop ships ("slicks") and one company of gunships. The companies, in turn, were further subdivided into lift and gun platoons. For probes and reconnaissance missions, there were squadrons of air cavalry troops, which were equivalent in number to battalions and companies, respectively. These air cavalry squadrons contained fewer slicks, more guns, and eight or nine light observation helicopters (known as "loaches"), which darted above the jungle canopy searching for the enemy.

Each of the Cav's nine infantry battalions would have sixty-four helicopters dedicated to it alone during combat operations. The complexity and cost of moving, supplying, reinforcing, and coordinating operations with different types of helicopters—assault, assault support, and rocket-firing gunships—was so immense that British defense analysts judged the looming campaign in Vietnam "uniquely American." There would be seventy 30-ship assault helicopter companies and twenty 27-ship air cavalry squadrons operating at any given time in South Vietnam. And that sum did not include the many Hueys assigned to medevac detachments or command functions. Nor did it take account of companies of CH-47 Chinooks and CH-54 Skycranes for medium and heavy lift. No other great power could even envision spending like this on a limited war in a peripheral theater.[13]

Airmobile warfare was also uniquely American in its total emphasis on battle, with little strategic regard for the day after. Westmoreland always twinned his battle plans with calls for pacification—"an imaginative and aggressive civic-action program"—but securing the South Vietnamese population against VC penetration was never his priority, as we will see. It was a half-hearted sop to critics of search and destroy, and little more than that.

Westy's troops would be rapidly inserted and just as rapidly withdrawn. In theory, they would hopscotch between battles, gradually defeating the enemy, who would be mauled by "vertical envelopments" wherever he appeared. In reality, the enemy would quickly grasp the strengths and weaknesses of this light-footed approach and learn to either avoid the Americans or wait them out. "Search and destroy" did not translate into "clear and hold." Noisy tactical victories here and there never produced "pacification"—the lasting defeat of insurgents and the restoration of government control. This would be the whole frustrating story of the war.[14]

Initially, however, such doubts did not cloud the high hopes of McNamara and Westmoreland. Flying in helicopters, US troops would, as their commanders put it, "move aggressively to contact with the enemy." They would use their mobility to trap and destroy North Vietnamese infiltrators and Viet Cong units, along with their essential caches of arms and food.[15]

Artillery would be the queen of this battlefield because it could be physically located just about anywhere and instantly activated in all weather, including monsoon rains, which drenched South Vietnam's regions at different times of the year, pouring down on Saigon and the Delta from April to September, soaking the central region from September to December, and washing across the northern provinces between October and April.

In a feat of engineering (and expenditure), the US Army and Marines began in 1965 to pre-position batteries of medium field artillery around South Vietnam in networked "fire support bases," which were simply called "firebases" or FSBs. These triangular or star-shaped artillery positions—whose outlines and asphalt helipads survive to this day on hilltops all over southern Vietnam—contained four- and six-gun batteries of 155 mm and 105 mm artillery.

These howitzers could be slung into even the most remote and trackless regions by twin-engine heavy-lift helicopters and would fire in support of any ground operation within their fifteen-mile effective range or against enemy attempts to overrun neighboring firebases. When infantry contact with the enemy was reported from the ground or the air, the gun crews in the firebase took those coordinates, determined range, angle, and fuse settings for their howitzers, and then opened fire. The infantry in the field were just bait, a "tethered goat" to lure communist troops into battle. The real killing would be done by the gunners in the firebases. "Theirs was an odd war," a visitor remarked. "A hundred shirtless men worked, sweating, in practiced synchronization in the hot, stagnant air....

Howitzers could be slung into even the most remote regions by heavy-lift helicopters to fire in support of any ground operation within their fifteen-mile effective range. Here a Chinook lowers a 105 mm howitzer into a 1st Infantry Division firebase in July 1966. (National Archives)

Working feverishly in tree-walled clearings dotted here and there, away from everyone else, their enemy remained unseen, and the measure of their success or failure was a radio call from an aerial observer counting bodies."[16]

The firebases, which could double as headquarters and helipads for units in the field, were, in turn, supplied by a web of American-built ammunition supply points. The supply system of "ammo humpers" around Saigon for the III and IV Corps areas became the model for all others. A 120,000-ton ammunition supply depot was built at Long Binh Post—a US Army base so large that it had its own city bus service, garbage collection, golf course, and water treatment plant. Twelve hundred trucks connected Long Binh's ammo dump to six regional ammunition supply points and three gunship rearming points. The overall concept was summed up by the commander of the US 4th Infantry Division: "If we are going to beat the enemy in the jungle we must take full advantage of our supporting firepower and avoid man-to-man engagements with small arms. This requires artillery in massive volumes."[17]

An American platoon or squad leader, surprised by an enemy ambush, had only to glance at his 1:25,000 map—gridded in squares, streams picked out in blue, hamlets in red, connected by white roads flanked with buff-colored huts beside green paddy fields. Assuming that he knew where he was—not always a safe assumption with inexperienced leaders in rugged wilderness—he would radio the enemy's grid coordinates to a forward air controller (FAC) or, if the monsoon was raging and ceilings were low, to the nearest firebase, which usually had a helpful sign like this one over its main gate: "You Yell + We Shell—Like Hell. Open 24 Hours Daily."[18]

American infantry in Vietnam also enjoyed the protection of *flying* artillery, first the Huey gunship model, known as the "Firebird," and then, from 1967, Bell Helicopter's Cobra gunships. The "Snakes," as the Cobras were known, were killing machines. Whereas the Huey gunships were armed versions of the slick, the Cobra would be the first helicopter designed as a "rotorcraft gunship." It had tandem seating like a strike fighter, with the gunner and pilot seated one behind the other, both with clear views of the airspace and battlefield. Whereas Huey Firebirds looked like the ad hoc contraptions they were, mini guns and rockets bolted to the airframe and skids, the Cobras mounted missiles and rocket pods on four hard points on its stub wings and carried a six-barrel mini gun in its nose that spat 100 rounds per *second*.

Each of the Cobra's 2.75-inch rockets had the destructive impact of a 105 mm shell. The Snake was a marvel, arriving on station in half the time of a Huey gunship, with twice the ammo and three times the loiter time. The gunships always escorted the "slicks" or troop carriers into a landing zone. They could "prep" the LZ with machine gun, cannon, and rocket fire to suppress any defenses, or circle around to block the retreat of enemy forces, buying time for ground troops to catch up and surround them.

The gunship cannons could fire four hundred 40 mm rounds a minute. The machine guns, known as flex or mini guns, were six-barreled electrically operated Gatling guns that spewed 6,000 rounds a minute, enough fire to plow up a football field from end zone to end zone in three seconds. If troops on the ground were attacked, they would "pop smoke" to mark their position. The gunships, organized in twelve-ship companies with roguish names like "Stacked Deck," "Smiling Tigers," or "Wolf Pack," would immediately "go hot"—running in to strafe the ground around the embattled troops. "Death is our Business and Business is Good" was the motto of a typical gunship company.[19]

Casualties, bound to be a sensitive issue in the United States, stood a better chance of survival in this war than in any previous war, thanks to the use of helicopters as ambulances. These ships, reconfigured with space for stretchers, were called "medevacs" or "dust-offs." They allowed for the fast pickup of casualties in the field and their delivery to a forward clearing station or, in severe cases, to one of the 8,000 hospital beds located around South Vietnam by American taxpayers. Casualty evacuation in Vietnam averaged fifteen minutes—"stand by for three U.S. litters, multiple frags," a pilot would radio—less time than it would take to summon an ambulance at home in the United States. Fast dust-offs meant that only 1.5 percent of American wounded were dying in Vietnam in 1966, compared with 2.5 percent in Korea and 4.5 percent in World War II.[20]

Tactical air support—called "tac air" in the field—was another vital component of airmobile operations. It gave infantry commanders access to "on-call" fighter bombers such as the F-100 Super Sabre or the F-4C Phantom, as well as fixed-wing gunships, which were C-47 and C-130 transport aircraft fitted with three mini guns firing 14,000 rounds of .30-caliber rifle ammo a minute. Like the Cobras, they could rake a football field from end to end with a three-second burst. Nicknamed "Spooky" or "Puff the Magic Dragon," the fixed-wing gunships were never more than thirty minutes away in Vietnam. They could fly in at 2,500 feet strewing flares to turn night into day and machine-gunning any enemy caught in the open. They flew higher during daylight missions, but they were no less lethal when equipped with the "Hand of God"—the Gatling-style Vulcan rotary cannon that fired 6,000 rounds of 20 mm ammunition a minute. The Spookies could fire uninterrupted for an hour or more, pummeling the ground below them until nothing was left standing or alive.

To position tac air where it was most needed, the US government built fifty more airfields around South Vietnam in the 1960s, for a total of one hundred. Twenty of them could be used for jet aircraft. The rest could land cargo planes such as the C-130 Hercules, which became a mainstay of the war effort, moving reinforcements, supplies, ammo, and casualties. By 1966, every tactically important area in South Vietnam was within twenty miles of an airfield. During infantry operations, the strike fighters orbited the combat zone around the clock and could be directed against enemy attacks or withdrawals at supersonic speed.

A jet crew, streaking along at 500 miles per hour, made no decisions about targets. How could they? They were moving so fast that they never saw what they were bombing. In this pre-GPS, pre-smart-bomb era, they relied on FACs, who circled the battlespace in little Cessna prop planes—called "bird dogs"—and spoke by radio with the troops on the ground. There were 700 FACs operating out of seventy forward locations in South Vietnam by 1968. Either they would tell the aircrew what to bomb and provide the map coordinates, or the FAC would see and mark the enemy himself with a smoke rocket. It was a dangerous job in such a slow, unarmored plane. One of every twenty FACs was killed in action during the war.[21]

If even more firepower was needed, the Air Force repurposed its B-52 Stratofortress strategic bombers to drop conventional bombs on targets in South Vietnam. This was Operation Arc Light, which spanned the entire war. These strikes, by the big swept-wing bombers designed to deliver thermonuclear bombs against the Soviet Union, were especially devastating because they plastered a small area with concentrated fire. Really concentrated: with more than a hundred 500- and 750-pound bombs loaded in its belly and wings, each B-52 carried the bomb payload of four B-29 Superfortresses. In the first Arc Light strike flown in Vietnam, in June 1965, 30 B-52s dropped 558 tons of bombs onto a jungle area near Saigon that was just one mile long and two miles wide. Flying from Guam or Thailand, B-52s could literally vaporize any enemy unit unfortunate enough to be caught aboveground when the "Buffs" flew silently overhead at an altitude of 30,000 feet.[22]

Already in 1965, American aircraft were dropping more bombs on North and South Vietnam every *day* than the French had dropped during the entire fifty-six-day Battle of Dien Bien Phu in 1954. The American love affair with airpower was on. It allowed statesmen and citizens to wage war without guilt. From a safe distance, John Saar wrote in *Life*, "our air power seemed as innocuous and reliable as home electricity."[23]

A massive fuel network like the ammunition network was built from scratch to keep all of these aircraft in action. In III and IV Corps, the Army's Support Command built a vast petroleum, oils, and lubricants

(POL) terminal at Long Binh Post. With pipelines, boats, barges, trains, and a fleet of 5,000-gallon tanker trucks, it fed the big air bases such as Tan Son Nhut and Bien Hoa as well as myriad smaller airfields and helipads. To keep the fuel flowing, US construction firms built seven deep-draft ports, storage for 3 billion barrels of oil, 600 miles of roads, and five miles of bridges. Until the summer of 1965, Long Binh had been a jungle of rainforest and rubber trees. The Americans then cleared 19,000 acres and constructed the biggest military base in Southeast Asia, with twenty-eight miles of perimeter, thousands of buildings, and 10 million square feet of barracks, warehouses, and maintenance shops.

Long Binh alone delivered 45 million gallons of fuel every month to its air bases and units in the field. Da Nang's POL terminal delivered similar quantities across I and II Corps. Augmented by this apparently limitless airpower, search and destroy was considered invincible. It would, one American officer insisted, "convince the enemy that he cannot hide, cannot hold the initiative, and cannot win."[24]

Westmoreland would have more of everything, and his forces would use the weapons in concert, as was intended, rather than singly, as the ARVN usually did, halting the infantry and air columns whenever the artillery started up. Every American operation would be finessed behind the scenes by liaison officers from the artillery and air squadrons, who—in theory—would always clear targets on the ground for fire that would be safe for all but the enemy. Westy crunched the numbers and concluded that if he could kill 8,000 communists every month, he would annihilate the VC and overwhelm North Vietnam's ability to reinforce the insurgency.[25]

In Washington, Bill Bundy in the State Department was already cautioning Westmoreland *not* to fight this enormously complex high-tech war independently with his US combat divisions. It would remove all incentives for the less well-equipped and less well-trained ARVN to fight or even improve, and "turn the conflict into a white man's war with the U.S. in the shoes of the French." If the ARVN was squeezed out in this way, Bill Bundy warned, the United States would be left holding the bag. Already the smart set in Saigon were using the phrase "*xai tien nhieu my*"—"to spend like Americans"—to describe not only the lifestyle of Americans in South Vietnam but also their extravagant use of artillery and airpower to secure even minor objectives.[26]

Until 1965, American diplomats and military advisers had struggled to put together anticommunist operations with balky South Vietnamese governments and troop commanders. As more and more Americans entered the country, entire operations could be planned and launched without the participation of a single Vietnamese. General Ed Lansdale, who had been pushed into retirement in 1963 for opposing just this sort of high-intensity war, considered Westy's airmobile divisions and all of their firepower a perversion of sound counterinsurgency doctrine that did *nothing* to secure "hearts and minds." Bernard Fall, the French historian and war correspondent who had written some of the best books on France's war in Indochina before turning to cover America's, was even more critical: "If tomorrow morning Mickey Mouse became prime minister of South Vietnam," Fall observed, "it would have precious little influence on the men of the U.S. Army...or on the fighting ability of the 3rd U.S. Marine Division." They would continue to pursue their strategy of "success through firepower," terrifying the people they were supposed to protect, widening the gap between themselves and the ARVN, and creating a crisis of confidence in Saigon.[27]

In the short run, Fall surmised, this American war was "militarily unlosable" because of the influx of US combat divisions and firepower, but in the long run? Casting his eyes back to the French experience, Fall felt certain that Hanoi would simply revert to guerrilla warfare and dodge Westmoreland's heaviest punches. In the meantime, all that could be predicted with any certainty was that a "prostrate South Vietnam, still in the hands of a politically irrelevant regime, would be plowed under by bombers and artillery." This was not a recipe for American success.[28]

Bernard Fall plunged deeper into this problem of American spending and overkill. He published a piece in the *New Republic* in October 1965 titled "Vietnam Blitz: A Report on the Impersonal War." Successful counterinsurgencies, Fall argued, had above all to be "personal"—they had to connect vulnerable civilians with their government and armed forces. When powerful allies like the United States were involved, they too had to get personal with the threatened populace, earning their loyalty and trust.

It was less about money and munitions and more about security and good governance. This failure to connect had doomed the French, and was now dooming the Americans. Technology and systems developed to protect

American troops would cost them the support of the Vietnamese people, who would be regular victims of "collateral damage" from bombs, shells, and napalm.

Touring South Vietnam in 1965, Fall was struck by the degree to which America's "Blitz" into Vietnam had already shouldered the Vietnamese out of the war, and not just the South Vietnamese allies but the North Vietnamese and the VC too. "There are no 'Wanted' posters in Vietnam offering rewards for the capture of a Communist leader," Fall marveled. The Americans showed no serious interest in the guerrilla war. They planned to destroy the enemy with big-unit operations. "For all one cares," Fall quipped, "the chairman of the [Viet Cong] could work as a cleanup boy in a U.S. mess hall in Bien Hoa, and nobody would recognize him."

Fall spoke to one American officer who told him that in the province he operated in, the Americans typically fired half a million dollars' worth of howitzer ammunition per month at unobserved targets while spending only $300 on information and intelligence gathering. Fall warned that this "progressive irrelevance of the human aspects of the Vietnam war," this "crass and constant" willingness to bombard civilian areas in the hope of hitting the shadowy VC, would undermine the war effort and demoralize the US forces.[29]

For now, Westmoreland treated cavils like these as the maundering of liberal critics. He confidently placed search and destroy at the core of a three-phase approach that he called a strategy. In Phase I, from mid-1965 to mid-1966, he would build US strength up to 400,000 troops and 500 aircraft, construct a vast logistical base, expand and "revitalize" the ARVN, and hold the line against the encroaching NVA and VC. In Phase II, from mid-1966 until late 1967, Westy would launch search and destroy operations in the border areas to defeat the infiltrating NVA main-force units. In the populated interior of South Vietnam, ARVN and US forces would launch "clearing" operations to kill or capture Viet Cong and secure the countryside. The goal was to "attrite VC and North Vietnamese forces at a rate higher than their capability to put men in the field," effectively knocking them out of the war. And yet the longer Westy delayed in the vital job of "pacification," weeding out the local insurgents and their communist commissars, the harder it would be to reach Phase III, when the war would be handed over to a more experienced and confident ARVN.[30]

The Viet Cong had agents everywhere, from peasants in hamlets to senior officials in Saigon. Here a US Marine takes VC suspects to a collection point in October 1965. (National Archives)

The VC were already embedded in most of the country, with functioning chapters of the People's Revolutionary Party (PRP) in every province. Most villages were controlled by thirty-five-man platoons of local guerrillas, who managed the flow of intelligence, manpower, transport, ammo, and food to main-force units, and resorted to harassment, sabotage, and assassination to remove government officials and enact their own tax gathering and propaganda.

It was the local guerrillas who provided the VC and NVA main-force units with their astonishing mobility. Guided everywhere they went by locals, the main-force battalions could move twenty-five miles in five hours, attacking a government post at night and vanishing without a trace before daylight. "The ARVN has more troops and better equipment than the VC," a senior communist defector told his captors. "But ARVN intelligence is very poor. The ARVN would be more effective if it had intelligence like the VC's. The Viet Cong have agents everywhere, from peasants in hamlets to high-ranking army officers in Saigon. I've never seen evidence that the ARVN has infiltrated the VC."[31]

For now, Westmoreland avoided that granular work in the hamlets, designating battles against large communist main forces as "the gold standard." He assumed that American tactics, speed, and technology would inflict catastrophic losses on the communist battalions in Phase II, severing them from their critical tunnel complexes and base areas inside South Vietnam near the population centers. Local guerrillas could then be picked off at will by more "clearing" operations, better police work, and the insufficiently exploited incentives of Chieu Hoi (Open Arms), an amnesty program that paid VC guerrillas to come in from the cold. As local security improved, free elections would be held and a civilian government seated in Saigon and the provinces by the end of 1967.

In Phase III of Westmoreland's "strategy," beginning in 1968, the American military would push the enemy regular forces out of South Vietnam, uproot the local VC and their infrastructure, accelerate the expansion and modernization of the ARVN and its territorial forces, and begin the "Vietnamization" of the war by handing over responsibility to Saigon and starting the drawdown of US forces.[32]

It was a lot to manage, and from the standpoint of Phase I, Phase III must have seemed a long way off, but Westmoreland embraced the war eagerly. It fit with what he knew from his education and career—offensive operations with overwhelming force to defeat the enemy—and also promised a tide of appropriations, battle, promotions, glory, and victory. But only if Westmoreland's assumptions were met: that the enemy would not react effectively to the American moves, and that the continuing failure of rural pacification by the ARVN would not sink Westmoreland's big-unit war on the periphery. What was the point of fighting the NVA in their remote sanctuaries if the populated and most vital parts of South Vietnam were steadily falling under VC control? Why erect a "shield" of American combat power for a nation-building effort that was rotting from within? Why send American troops to defend the South Vietnamese when, if properly motivated, they could defend themselves?

Westmoreland did ponder these questions. The war, he later said, seemed to have been fashioned by Lewis Carroll's Red Queen: "It took all the running you could do just to stay in the same place." Troops sent in major operations to destroy enemy main-force units exposed villages and militias that had been protected by those same troops in pacification roles. Troops scattered in pacification roles—a squad here, a platoon there—could be destroyed or merely evaded by enemy main-force units. Because the enemy did not have to occupy a village to control it—nocturnal visits, terror, threats, and indoctrination did the trick—their forces could be spread far more thinly than the ARVN. They could do more with less. The only way to break out of this stagnation was to motivate the South Vietnamese to fight in the field and defend the villages. Search and destroy by Americans could never be more than a partial solution, and one sure to fail if the South Vietnamese did not themselves rise to the occasion. For a moment in 1965, Westmoreland had the opportunity to do what MacArthur had done in Korea: pull the ARVN under his own unified command and *make* them fight under American direction. But Westy was no MacArthur. Diffident, punctilious, and bureaucratic, Westmoreland looked at the ARVN and its quarreling personalities and recoiled in fright. They were too much to handle. And so Westy did what he did best: he emitted high-sounding explanations about "respecting" South Vietnamese pride and sovereignty, and then, like Sisyphus, he began pushing his boulder up one side of the hill, while the South Vietnamese began pushing theirs up the other.[33]

Chapter 5

IA DRANG

President Johnson's Rolling Thunder air campaign and ground buildup achieved exactly what the Pentagon war-gamers had predicted: it increased the flow of North Vietnamese regulars into South Vietnam, effectively raising the "threshold of pain" and matching Westmoreland's troop increases. If the US military was coming to save the ARVN, the NVA would fight to save the VC and cement Hanoi's influence in the contested South. The air strikes that Johnson had assumed would deter Hanoi and increase his leverage had instead enraged the communist leadership and made them more determined than before to conquer South Vietnam.[1]

Between July and November 1965, the number of North Vietnamese soldiers in South Vietnam quadrupled as Hanoi brought South Vietnam's Central Highlands and the adjacent strips of Laos and Cambodia under the control of the NVA high command. Seven new NVA regiments hiked into South Vietnam, raising communist strength in South Vietnam to an estimated 200,000 trained main-force troops.[2]

Even as Westmoreland moved to implement search and destroy in 1965, the MACV commander complained that whatever advantage he had enjoyed in June, when Johnson had authorized a surge in forces to 200,000 men, was fast withering away. His combat units were swallowed up by a vast wilderness, described this way by a newly arrived Marine: "triple-canopied jungle, mountains unfolding into higher mountains, ravines and gorges and fast-moving rivers and waterfalls and steep cliffs and smoky little hamlets and great valleys of bamboo and elephant grass." Worse, the VC/NVA buildup rate was double that of US forces. Every ninety days the enemy would add fifteen maneuver battalions, the United States just seven.[3]

Westmoreland looked for a place on the map where he could physically block NVA infiltration and impose a teachable moment on the communist enemy, who would be hit with the concentrated fury of American mobility and firepower. He found that place in the Ia Drang Valley in South Vietnam's Central Highlands in November 1965. NVA units moved up the valley and into South Vietnam in regular echelons. Westy planned to find them and hit them hard to accent MACV's shift from defensive enclaves to offensive search and destroy.

The tactic had been tried out against concentrations of Viet Cong in August and September with good results. Accustomed to the casual tempo of the ARVN, the VC had been surprised by the vigor of the Americans. They had been raked by air strikes and artillery, set upon by American rapid-reaction forces, and then hit with B-52s, which could be dispatched on "quick runs" from Guam to crush even the sturdiest bunker and tunnel complexes. A kill ratio that had hovered around 2:1 for the ARVN soared to 6:1 under the more effective Americans. Hopes for the operation in the Ia Drang Valley were so high that it became the centerpiece of a battle that Westmoreland grandly named "the Pleiku Campaign."[4]

Ia Drang lay at the heart of the Central Highlands region, which Hanoi was using as a route to infiltrate troops and supplies into South Vietnam from the Ho Chi Minh Trail's Cambodian outlets. For Westmoreland, this Pleiku Campaign was a key to the war. If he could defeat the North Vietnamese in the field and then turn the Central Highlands over to Saigon for territorial defense and development, he would have sealed the leaky Cambodian border and would be able to turn to other problems, like the equally leaky Laotian border, the DMZ, and the Mekong Delta, gradually reducing or eliminating the problems until Hanoi saw the writing on the wall and quit.[5]

This theory of victory was as improbable as had been the French theory at Dien Bien Phu, which had sought to "seal" North Vietnam's border with Laos. The Pleiku Campaign originated in the same delusions that had beset the French. There would be no "sealing" the Cambodian border, by

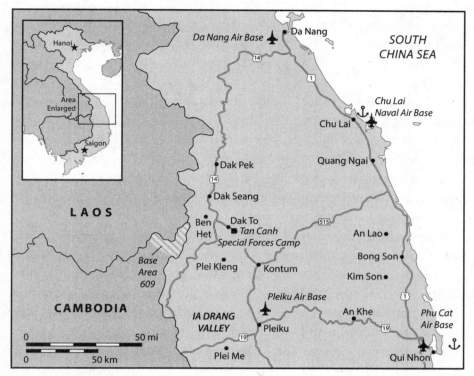

The Central Highlands Region

Westmoreland or anyone else. The French had lost control of Cambodia in the 1950s when anti-French guerrillas had taken over the colony's eastern provinces and moved into alliance with the Viet Minh. The Cambodian people, bludgeoned then by French reprisals, were in no mood to engage in this latest round of fighting. Even if the Cambodian sanctuary problem could be solved, Westmoreland in South Vietnam would struggle just to *find* the enemy infiltrators or supplies, and would have to go searching for them.

If he found them, after days or weeks of "saturation patrolling," the NVA would either fight if the odds were in their favor or melt away to fight another day if the odds were against them, as the VC units pulverized in August and September had done. Even if they fought and were chewed up by US firepower, the NVA infiltrators could retreat into Cambodia or Laos, technically neutral nations where American troops would not pursue. There they would replace their casualties with new recruits coming down the trails from North Vietnam, and lie low until the Americans tired of looking for them and flew away to other areas. Then they would reemerge in South Vietnam to take back all of the ground they had briefly lost.[6]

This inevitable denouement could be prevented only by a strong, respected, and determined Saigon government, willing to push into the secured area, rebuild or improve it, and then defend it against future incursions with troops and police. And yet this is precisely what the American–South Vietnamese war effort lacked from beginning to end—respected government troops and administrators who would doggedly "hold" districts that had been "cleared" of Viet Cong.

Doubts also arose as to the value of the terrain that Westmoreland was contesting. Ia Drang lay in II Corps, a vast but unpopulated area of operations (AO). It contained half of South Vietnam's territory but less than a fifth of its population. Winning there would do nothing to check the rise of the VC insurgency in South Vietnam's populated areas. In short, the Pleiku Campaign, even if successful, would fail because it would not deter VC activity elsewhere and would leave no formidable stay-behind force to close the door to the *next* North Vietnamese infiltration. As an American platoon leader in the Central Highlands put it: "We would fight and bleed to take ground that the [NVA] would pull away from after they had exacted their toll. We always left afterward so they could always come back if they liked that particular place."[7]

But Westmoreland had a conventional mind that preferred to isolate the military elements of the equation and pursue them alone. If the "op" succeeded but the AO later fell back under communist control, well, that could not be blamed on Westy, who would have already declared victory and moved on to other areas of operation—citing a high kill ratio and tons of enemy supplies destroyed as proof of his prowess.

He would blame subsequent defeats in the briefly conquered AO on the South Vietnamese government, or on US civilians charged with advising provincial reconstruction and defense. In the worst case, where shaming the ARVN or US civilians was not sufficient, Westy promised a "clean-up phase" after the major battles were fought, where all communist remnants would be located and destroyed by American troops fresh from battle.

How they would be "located," let alone "destroyed," was never explained. Thus, even at the outset, the American war effort was fatally flawed, self-deluding, and without an effective strategy. The Army, in effect, was waging a war it could not win, but pushed ahead to uphold its own service interests, placate the president, and send political messages about American "toughness."[8]

In October 1965, Westmoreland received intelligence that three NVA regiments had concentrated in Pleiku province around the Ia Drang Valley, with plans to clean out the American-run Special Forces camps in the region and then drive eastward to the coast, splitting South Vietnam in two. This would be the heaviest blow of what appeared to be a looming NVA general offensive. Hanoi's strategy, as understood by MACV, was to recruit more "organic" VC units in the heavily populated coastal plains of South Vietnam and reinforce them with infiltrating NVA units to rip away South Vietnam's northern provinces and convert Saigon into a beleaguered rump state. Having just taken delivery of the three brigades of the US 1st Cavalry Division (Airmobile), Westmoreland planned to use the Cav's power and mobility to nip the threat in the bud.[9]

There would be nothing subtle about it. The Cav built its base camp at An Khe, halfway between Qui Nhon and Pleiku. It sat in a valley among the Central Highlands along two important arteries—Route 19 and the Song Ba River. An Khe was broad and flat enough to accommodate 20,000 troops and a 300-acre heliport dubbed "the Golf Course." "The Cav," an officer boasted, "will be the first unit to locate right in the middle of VC-land and the idea is to be right there in the middle of 'em, to clean 'em out of here, pronto." Westy's persistent fear was that the NVA would hew to the old Vietnamese proverb "He who controls the Central Highlands controls South Vietnam" and strike from the hills along Route 19 to the coast, scissoring the country in two. This came to be called Westy's "scissors theory."[10]

Westmoreland ordered up two operations to find and destroy the NVA infiltrators and their local VC infrastructure in October 1965. In Operation Happy Valley, two brigades would fly into the Vinh Thanh Valley near Pleiku to "search and clear," a search and destroy variant applied in populated areas to destroy or remove the VC and "restore government control." In Operation Silver Bayonet, the third Cav brigade would fly into the largely uninhabited Ia Drang Valley, find those elusive NVA battalions, and bring them to battle, where they could be hemmed in by the airmobile American infantry and killed by artillery and air strikes. Both air assault operations would be textbook examples of search and destroy. Westmoreland believed that they would demonstrate how to shatter Hanoi's insurgency and general offensive. A Cav helicopter pilot flying into An Khe for the first time was not so sure: "Vietnam looked very big and very green, it looked like the perfect place to have a guerrilla war, if you were going to be the guerrilla."[11]

Operation Happy Valley took aim at a river valley used by the NVA to infiltrate South Vietnam. It was in the middle of nowhere on the western edge of the least populated region of South Vietnam. Steep foothills wreathed in clouds rose from high wooded ridges. Amid the chaos of Diem's downfall, its village and hamlet leadership had been chased away by the Viet Cong, who now ran the valley as a VC territory. All of that brutally changed when two brigades of the Cav arrived at the populated southern end of the valley on October 13 for seven days of what the division called "domination." The week of "domination" would be followed by a week of "resettlement and construction" and crowned by a week of "consolidation." In other words, the Cav assumed that in just three weeks they would not only defeat the enemy but permanently remove him.

The Army's own reporting on Happy Valley signaled a determination to ignore facts. The VC had taken over the valley and burned every public building to illustrate the destruction of government authority and slow any attempt by the ARVN to retake the area. They had begun planting and harvesting food for communist units. The American attack, preceded by air strikes and artillery "prep fires," certainly stunned the enemy, but by no means drove them out or restored government authority. In fact, reading the Cav and MACV reports on the operation, it appeared that the Army was not so much fighting to win as to create the *appearance* of winning.

MACV flourished Operation Happy Valley as an example of how to do search and clear right. The enemy was surprised by the artillery fire and air strikes, and then set upon by company-sized air assaults that were not particularly well coordinated because there was no friendly intelligence issuing from the VC-held valley. The Cav carved the valley into thousand-acre "boxes" and cleared each one as they moved south to north. They lifted troops onto the high ground overlooking the valley and swept downward to a blocking force on the valley floor. The "grunts," so named for the grunt they emitted when heaving their backpacks over their shoulders in tropical heat, spent a week advancing two miles a day up the valley.

They discovered caches of rice but few VC, most of whom withdrew or hid in tunnels. The enemy, a Cav pilot observed, were not losing at all. They "controlled the situation" and were "bending with the force to learn more about how the Cav operated." They knew every LZ in every thousand-acre box and attacked them with .50-caliber machine guns during every insertion and extraction. To at least one pilot those .50-caliber rounds, an inch long and a half inch wide, moving at 3,000 feet per second, looked "big as baseballs."

That was enough punishment for MACV. At this point, Westy's staff concluded that "a peaceful and stable environment" had been created. They were clearly just checking every box except the most important one: effectiveness. "With all our mobility, the VC still called the shots," a veteran of the operation confided. "We fought on *their* terms." No matter: MACV now spent a week checking the next box: "resettlement and reconstruction." Army helicopters circled the heights with loudspeakers urging the peasants, who had taken to the hills to escape the fighting, to return to their hamlets on the valley floor. Few did. Some descended in the mornings to poke through the abandoned huts and take whatever belongings and food they could find, but then returned to the hills in the afternoon.[12]

National Police were bused in to take over security of the still empty valley, and construction of a CIDG (civilian irregular defense group) camp was begun. None of this was reassuring. The police did not linger long, and the civilian irregulars were local Jarai tribesmen, an ethnic minority most famous for their ritual drunkenness. Whenever the Army loudspeakers started up, the VC, hidden on the ridges, banged pots and pans loudly to drown out the broadcasts. They also fired on the helicopters, forcing them to higher altitudes where the loudspeakers warbled inaudibly. Army engineers appeared to smooth and repair the valley road that had been cratered by the VC, and this, MACV disingenuously declared, made clear to the locals "that a permanent, stabilizing force would remain in the valley and that security would not vanish as soon as the American troops left and the VC returned."[13]

The "resettlement and construction" of the still deserted valley was judged complete after a week, when a Cav battalion lingered long enough to check the third box: "consolidation." A burnt school and church were repaired, vaccinations were administered to those who came down from the hills, and pro-government leaflets were handed out—all of the loud-speakers having failed or proven useless. The leaflets would fail too, for, as a counterinsurgency adviser scoffed, "peasants don't follow leaflets; they follow people," just exactly what was missing here where there were no government officials to protect and organize the frightened country folk. At night, batteries of the US 77th Artillery raked the surrounding hills with 105 mm "harassment and interdiction fire" (H&I) to discourage "curfew violators," which was what the VC were called after the "domination" phase had worked its magic.

After a few days of this, the Cav threw a party—Operation Friendship—in which the district and hamlet chiefs, shamed into returning to their dangerous valley by the exploits of the Cav, joined with the American battalion commander to make speeches and hear a concert by the Cav band. The Cav then departed, after distributing 550 pounds of used clothing as well as pallets of milk, orange juice, and C-rations. It was, MACV declared, a great victory that "showed the essential elements of a successful pacification program." As naive as that sounded, the underlying analysis was even more guileless. Happy Valley had succeeded because ground was taken and held, and because the operation had persisted "for sufficient duration to insure lasting effect." Even the military authors could not have believed what they were writing. When the last Cav slick departed the valley, the hamlet chiefs ran for their lives and the Viet Cong moved back in. Ops like this, the Cav's counterinsurgency expert scoffed, were "gimmicks—a bunch of activity reports but no real results."[14]

In Operation Silver Bayonet, which would flare into the Battle of Ia Drang, the Americans searched for two weeks, taking light fire from the occasional sniper, and pausing in every highland village to offer vaccinations and medical care and distribute food aid, which the troops called "civic action." The Cav used Caribou two-engine aircraft, each able to carry thirty-two troops and take off and land on dirt runways, to move quickly into areas thought to contain enemy troops. From there, the men fanned out in "saturation patrols" to locate the enemy. If they found him, firebases would grab the coordinates, strike fighters would load the correct ordnance, and helicopters would rush reinforcements to the scene.

After searching for two weeks, the Cav finally bumped into some NVA stragglers, and Lieutenant Colonel Hal Moore's battalion of the division's

3rd Brigade was dispatched in Hueys to the Ia Drang Valley to engage the main enemy force, whose exact size remained unknown. Moore's grunts, men of Colonel George Armstrong Custer's old unit, the 1st Battalion of the 7th Cavalry Regiment, were ordered to pin down the NVA infiltrators long enough for them to be destroyed by Cav reinforcements, two batteries of 105 mm howitzers, and air strikes.

Moore touched down in the midst of three NVA battalions and triggered a three-day battle in which two entire NVA regiments attempted to surround and destroy a single American battalion, an operation that must have reminded Moore and his staff of the US 7th Cavalry's most notorious action—the Battle of Little Bighorn.

The Battle of Ia Drang showcased the technologies that Westmoreland counted on to bring victory. Every search and destroy operation in South Vietnam would follow the pattern of Ia Drang. Military intelligence would piece together information on enemy routes, hideouts, and strength, and then the operation would be drawn up. The infantry would never be alone. B-52s would bomb suspected enemy base camps and tunnel complexes. Ground operations would be conducted under the long shadow of tactical air support and artillery firebases. The helicopter-rich Cav even had an airborne artillery battalion—a dedicated force of three firing batteries that could be lifted in quickly by Chinooks to support the infantry operations.

As Moore's battalion flew from Plei Mei into the Ia Drang Valley on November 14, 1965, to commence its search and destroy operation, it felt the protective embrace of two batteries of 105 mm artillery. The guns, thudding away from a nearby firebase—LZ Falcon—plowed up the ground around Moore's landing zone, blowing away trees, high grass, and anything else that might conceal enemy infantry. As the first assault company prepared to descend to LZ X-Ray, the howitzers ceased fire, so as not to hit the helicopters in the air or on the ground. The battalion's escorting gunships swarmed over the LZ firing rockets and machine guns to hit anything the artillery might have missed, and then ascended to orbit the landing zones with "on-call fire." With door gunners in the slicks blazing away at the trees and the high grass, Moore's command group and half of his Bravo Company then descended in steep turns to the ground in sixteen Hueys.

Moore's infantry slid off the birds and ran toward the surrounding trees, firing their M-16 rifles. The job of the first lift was always the same—secure a perimeter and hold it until the combat assault was complete. While squads of one platoon staked out a perimeter around LZ X-Ray, Moore was joined by his command group and a Montagnard translator, who spoke English, Vietnamese, and Hmong—the last the language of the mountain people in this wedge of the Central Highlands.

Moore's command and control helicopter orbited overhead. In it was Moore's operations chief and a trio of liaison officers—one to communicate with the supporting artillery, another to arrange efficient lifts of helicopter transport to and from the LZ, and the third (the FAC) to de-conflict all of the flights and artillery and summon fixed-wing air strikes as needed.

With Moore's sixteen Hueys returning to Plei Mei to pick up the rest of Company B and the vanguard of Company A, Moore massed the few men he had in the center of LZ X-Ray as an "offensive striking force." While he worked, one of his squads on the perimeter brought in a prisoner. He

The job of the first lift was always the same—secure a perimeter and hold it until the combat assault was complete. (National Archives)

was NVA, and he gave every evidence of the misery that North Vietnamese infiltrators suffered on their long march from North to South Vietnam. He was unarmed, and dressed in a ragged khaki shirt and pants. His canteen was empty, and he said that he had eaten nothing but green bananas for five days. He had a shocking bit of intelligence. There were three NVA battalions on the mountain above them, he said, adding, "We want to kill Americans, but have been unable to find any."

They had found them now. Two hours after landing in the LZ, with Bravo Company on the ground and lead elements of Alpha and Charlie Companies flying in, the NVA began to strike at the root of the operation. They began to hit LZ X-Ray with 60 mm and 81 mm mortar fire. Moore finished the lift with difficulty and reported that he was already caught in a blistering firefight, one of his Bravo Company platoons on the right flank nearly cut off and surrounded. Moore deployed his three companies in a rough circle, to support each other and prevent the loss of the LZ. He radioed his command helicopter and directed the liaison officers aboard to place heavy fire by air strikes, gunships, and artillery on the mountain slopes around the LZ and every approach to it.

The difficulty of search and destroy, even when the enemy was found, immediately emerged. With the troops battling under trees, scrub, and clouds of dust and smoke, Moore's FAC and his artillery liaison officer—searching in vain for well-defined terrain features in a uniform and featureless landscape—could not tell where the forward elements of their own infantry were. The bushes and the trees all looked alike from the air and the ground, and the isolated Bravo Company platoon on the right flank could not be rescued with air strikes or artillery because it could not say with any certainty exactly where it was. The problem became insuperable when 100 enemy troops crabbed forward to the edge of the lost platoon's position, making "close fire support" too risky to be attempted.

Moore then tried to bring in his D Company, but as its lead units landed they were mangled by well-aimed enemy fire—the commander's radio operator killed the instant he stepped off the bird, both his door gunner and pilot wounded. Moore, who estimated that he was fighting at least 500 enemy troops, with more on the way, now requested another rifle company, and was told that B Company, 2nd Battalion, 7th Cavalry, was assembling at its pickup zones.

Between 3 and 5 p.m. Moore made two attempts to reach the isolated platoon of his own Bravo Company. Each time he failed to break through to them, noting the skill of the North Vietnamese infantry and the priority they assigned to killing American officers, NCOs, and radio operators. "These enemy were aggressive," he reported. "They came off the mountain in large groups, well camouflaged, they used cover and concealment, they were good shots, armed with automatic weapons and potato-masher grenades." Moore was struck by the toughness and bravery of the North Vietnamese: "Even after being hit several times in the chest, many continued firing and moving several steps before dropping dead."

To slip inside the protective envelope of American firepower, the enemy had wriggled right up to the beleaguered platoon's perimeter. Some of the NVA were in trees; others had dug spider holes or burrowed into the walls of anthills. "Grazing fire" from their well-placed machine guns had already killed or wounded twenty of the platoon's twenty-seven men. The platoon leader, the platoon sergeant, and the weapons squad leader were all reported killed in action (KIA).

Unable to dislodge the surrounding troops, Moore fell back to the increasingly hot LZ for the night. Each American struck down trying to rescue the lost platoon was one less American to defend LZ X-Ray, which had become Moore's only line of retreat or reinforcement.

He called for white phosphorous (WP) around the LZ to burn, create smoke, blind the NVA mortars, and permit the evacuation of his growing number of casualties by helicopter. The most he could do for the surrounded platoon was ring it with nonstop artillery fire to make it harder for the NVA to overrun it.

The isolated platoon of Moore's Bravo Company—now the focus of the battle—spent the night inside a ring of 105 mm artillery fired from LZ Falcon. The NVA launched three 50-man attacks during the night, with the men they had pushed inside the ring of fire, and each attack was driven off. The grunts used their light antitank weapons (LAWs), 66 mm rocket launchers, to blow away the anthills sheltering the enemy, and fired their M-79 grenade launchers into the tall grass and trees to flush out the enemy, whose prowess in camouflage was already acknowledged. "Without his own overhead fire support," Moore noted, "he relies on camouflage, mass attacks, infiltrators, and stay-behind killer parties." To stymie mass attacks and infiltration, tactical air swooped in to drop fragmentation and cluster bombs around the ring, and helicopter gunships fired salvos of rockets. As night fell, flare ships circled overhead scattering parachute flares to prevent the enemy from advancing under cover of darkness.

The troopers of the Cav recalled hearing the enemy all around them. "Their shouts and screams told of good results" by the howitzers and air strikes. The North Vietnamese feared napalm and white phosphorous the most. Napalm is jellied gasoline that burns hot and sucks the oxygen from the air, suffocating anyone not burned alive. White phosphorous—better known as "Willy Pete"—was even more terrifying. If any of its burning fragments brushed you, they would burn until deprived of all oxygen, causing untreatable, agonizing wounds. Communist troops would "hit the dirt" under high explosive shelling but get up and flee in panic when firebombed. The helicopter gunships had a shock effect whenever they appeared, because their desolating fire was instant; it did not have to be adjusted by observers or "walked" onto the target gradually.

The battle culminated the next morning, November 15, when the NVA attacked Moore's LZ from three directions, with three fresh 100-man companies. Without radios, the NVA coordinated their charges with shouts and bugles. They pushed right up to the foxholes on the perimeter, and two hours of savage fighting ensued. The enemy used the same tactics they had used to such good effect against the French. They would surprise the Americans with heavy fire, inflict casualties, force the Americans to stop firing to aid their wounded, and then press in closer, gradually eroding the combat effectiveness of the American unit. This explained the American emphasis ever since on always firing—"to forestall the enemy firing first."

The enemy, Moore observed, "was a deadly shot," hitting many of the American casualties in the head and chest. The NVA infantry were trained to aim at leaders, which, in a chaotic battle, were invariably the men shouting, pointing, and talking on radios. They were also trained to kill the men carrying radios on their back and to shoot at all men wearing rank insignia—especially NCOs with stripes on their arms.

With his battalion withering away under this patient, accurate enemy fire, Moore, having received Bravo Company in the night, urgently requested another company of the 7th Cavalry but was told that no troops could land because the LZ was being scorched by enemy mortar and machine gun fire.

Hueys were unarmored and could set down only in secure LZs. Moore's surrounded, shrinking force threw colored smoke grenades out to the perimeter, to mark the tightening noose of enemy troops so that they could be pushed back by tac air, gunships, and the howitzers at LZ Falcon. One of the Americans took stock of the men around him. They were scratched, cut, and smeared with blood; their clothes were torn; and "they all had that look of shock. They said little, just looked around with darting, nervous eyes."

By now, Moore's force had been whittled down to such small numbers that enemy attacks on all faces of the perimeter nearly broke through. Private Jack Smith watched it happen close to his sector: "There weren't enough GIs there and they couldn't shoot them down fast enough." They were saved by an American Douglas A-1E Skyraider, a big twin-engine plane that could carry massive amounts of ordnance and loiter for long periods over the battlefield. This one dropped napalm just in front of Smith's ragged line. "I couldn't see the gooks, but I could hear them scream as they burned. A hundred men dead, just like that."[15]

Unable to take the LZ and repulsed by gales of American fire, the NVA broke off the attack at around ten o'clock that morning. The 105 mm howitzers at LZ Falcon, five miles east of X-Ray, had fired 33,108 shells into the encroaching NVA troops in the course of the forty-eight-hour battle. Moore's weary troops on the perimeter cautiously searched the blasted trees and shrubs around them and discovered that the enemy, so close to victory, had pulled back. The NVA reformed that night and launched several 100- and 200-man attacks. These too were lit by the flare ships and driven off.

By now, Moore had been backstopped by four batteries of field artillery and reinforced with a third infantry company. Together, these forces drove the NVA off after two days and nights of combat. By turning night into day, the Cav appeared to have "won" the battle, but in a fluid war of infiltration and attrition, "winning" ground like this was meaningless. The enemy would resume using it the moment the Americans departed. Moore ordered his men to "police the battlefield" and produce evidence of victory that could be relayed to MACV and the Pentagon. They were told to collect all abandoned weapons, count enemy corpses and body parts, and follow blood trails into the woods to capture or kill any enemy who had dragged himself away.[16]

"There must have been about 1,000 rotting bodies out there, starting about 20 feet from us and surrounding the giant circle of foxholes," one grunt recalled. Moore reported a kill ratio of 8:1. He had suffered 79 dead and 121 wounded or missing. The enemy had lost 634 confirmed dead, 6 prisoners, and an estimated 1,215 wounded.[17]

The troopers of the Cav scrutinized their dead adversaries. They had well-maintained automatic weapons with plenty of ammunition, and each of them had been issued three to five Chinese-made hand grenades. They were self-contained fighting machines, each man feeding himself from a softball-sized wad of cooked rice and sleeping under a sheet of waterproof plastic. Some of them had wallets or dog tags taken from American KIAs in their pockets.

Moore's troops captured 150 enemy weapons, which they piled in a shell crater and burned. The troops of the Cav noted what Moore called the "fanatical efforts" made by the North Vietnamese to remove their dead. They found many of the KIAs far from the scene of their demise, ropes tied around their ankles. They had been dragged away for burial, and abandoned only when the American pursuit got too close. The wounded, Moore noted, were no less fanatical—they shot any Americans who approached them. All of this would make an accurate "body count" difficult to compute.

Moore's after-action report expressed deep concern at the various ways in which the North Vietnamese enemy, in one of his first major clashes with the US Army, was *already* learning how to fight and beat the Americans by blunting their technological edge. The NVA soldiers were adept at shooting down helicopters and shutting down landing zones. They recognized the problem of American firepower and were solving it. They knew they had to close fast with the Americans, Moore wrote—"get very close, 25 meters or less, even intermingled"—so that the Americans could not safely call in artillery or air strikes.

Once inside that envelope, Moore wrote, the North Vietnamese could force the Americans to "fight on their terms," as US close fire support and tac air would have to be shut down and the grunts would have to fight with their rifles, grenades, and squad machine guns. The enemy persisted with these "hugging tactics" even when the Americans retreated, so that supporting weapons could never be used. "We must make imaginative and constant use of our tremendous fire support to kill the enemy *before* he gets close enough to fight on his terms."[18]

American firepower, in other words, was not going to solve all problems. Even in a battle as small as this one, major difficulties had emerged. "Friendly fire" was already emerging as a problem on the ground with the NVA emphasis on in-close fighting. Since World War II, the United States military had leaned on firepower as a casualty-reducing panacea. But it worked only when the enemy could be held at arm's length. Once he closed in, as the NVA had done to the French and were now doing to the Americans, the panacea became a two-edged sword, as dangerous to friendlies as to the enemy. Internally, MACV rued the "major losses" of Westmoreland's Pleiku Campaign and fretted about the "deterioration of our foxhole strength."[19]

It was easy to see why. The "victory" of Ia Drang on November 16 was followed by a crushing defeat the following day, two miles east of the battlefield. Marching overland from Moore's position to nearby LZ Albany, the 500 troopers of the 7th Cavalry's 2nd Battalion were ambushed by a hidden NVA battalion and savaged: 155 grunts were killed and 124 wounded in the sixteen-hour battle. This amounted to over 50 percent casualties. This drove US casualties in Operation Silver Bayonet to nearly 300 dead and hundreds of wounded.

The ambush was so well prepared and the Cav troopers so unsuspecting that there was no margin for the safe use of tac air and artillery. Nor could the troops apply the basic ambush survival technique of sprinting into the enemy's midst to check his otherwise uninterrupted fire. The whole battalion was trapped in a narrow, wooded sack near the LZ and mowed down by NVA machine gunners and snipers roped into the upper branches of trees and companies of infantry concealed in tall grass.

For the NVA, with a clear view of the "beaten zone," it was like shooting fish in a barrel. Private Jack Smith, who survived the massacre, noted that they might as well have doubled the number of American KIAs because "almost all of the wounded were crippled for life." He recalled the horror around him as he crawled, badly wounded himself, from one group of terrified grunts to another: Cav troopers with their heads or arms or legs ripped off. Dozens of the men had belly wounds and they never stopped screaming. "They kept on until they were hoarse, then they would bleed through their mouths and pass out; they would wake up and start screaming again. Then they would die."

Of the 500 grunts who set off for LZ Albany, only 84 would return to the unit. The rest were either buried or invalided home. Smith recalled that everyone still alive or conscious when the battle ended was weeping with pain, fear, and grief. They had seen their buddies killed or mutilated and, in the darkness, listened helplessly as the enemy prowled around killing the wounded. ("Every few minutes I heard some guy start screaming, 'No, no, no, please,' and then a burst of bullets.")

Many of the wounded Americans shot themselves before they could be captured. When the 7th Cav's 2nd Battalion returned to base, Jack Smith discovered that all of his friends in the unit had been killed. In Pleiku, where the dust-offs flew with the dead and wounded, "a small crowd of living stood watching a growing pile of dead." Corpses were stacked in one pile, severed body parts in another. Mortally wounded men were injected with morphine and left to die outside the operating tent. "Compared to Happy Valley," a Cav officer observed, "this was action, but living through a year of it seemed unlikely." The NVA colonel who commanded the action later explained how he had neutralized American firepower: "I gave my orders to the battalion: 'Move inside their column, grab them by the belt, and avoid casualties from their artillery and air.'" The lessons learned from the Americans at Ia Drang, a captured enemy document proclaimed, "were worth the cost of 100,000 men."[20]

Chapter 6

"NAIL THE COONSKINS
TO THE WALL"

Back home in the United States, the media focused more on the Cav's victory at Ia Drang than on their defeat at LZ Albany. Ia Drang was "just the beginning" of a massive, winning offensive, an American general exulted in *Life* magazine: "We cut the enemy's throat." Army chief of staff Harold Johnson concurred, sighing gratefully, "The worst is behind us." SecDef McNamara flew all the way to An Khe to congratulate the Cav. *Time* magazine named Westmoreland its "Man of the Year" for his "victories" in the Central Highlands. Ia Drang, Westy beamed, "demonstrated beyond any possible doubt the validity of the Army's airmobile concept."[1]

And yet for all of the bravado, Westmoreland's Pleiku Campaign was a bust. It did nothing to slow NVA infiltration. It merely distracted from a worsening situation everywhere else in South Vietnam that McNamara privately likened to a sticky "bowl of jelly" that would engulf hundreds of thousands of American troops, with no promise of success.[2]

Had you placed a map of South Vietnam in 1961 beside a map of the country in 1965, the areas shaded to signify VC control had expanded drastically. In 1961, the VC had controlled small sanctuaries on the Cambodian and Laotian borders, and pockets of territory around the

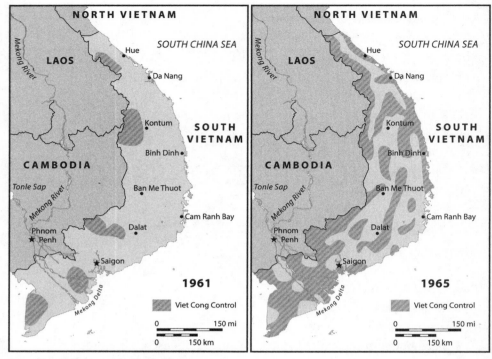

Spreading VC Control in South Vietnam

DMZ and the Mekong Delta. Four years later, they were everywhere—in the cities, on the coastal plain, in the Central Highlands, in the Saigon region, and all through the Mekong Delta. The Americans were killing more enemy than the ARVN was, but it was like a game of whack-a-mole. The enemy would break up, withdraw, and then reemerge when the American helicopters were moving elsewhere and the coast was clear. Tactical victories here and there got the United States no closer to winning the war or getting Hanoi to negotiate. "Nothing happening to the Vietnamese Communists is bad enough to make them stop fighting," a 250-page CIA study concluded.[3]

The US Marines, always stretched thin, had only three or four battalions available for operations along the DMZ, a buffer zone separating North and South Vietnam that was fifty miles long and six miles deep. The Marines could push more force in at any time to check NVA infiltration, but that meant relaxing pressure on the VC units in the coastal plain. Every deployment on the DMZ pulled the Marines out of clear and hold operations in the populated areas of I Corps and into the high country around the Khe Sanh plateau, where they found themselves strung out in a string of fortified outposts just four miles from the Laotian border and fourteen miles south of the DMZ.[4]

At Khe Sanh, the Marines were shelled and mortared regularly by the NVA in what appeared to be an exercise in futility. Nothing decisive could ever be achieved because the NVA units had only to retreat back across the 17th parallel to find sanctuary. "Our patrols kept going out to fight in the same places they had fought the week before and the week before that," Marine Lieutenant Philip Caputo wrote of this period. "The situation remained the same.... We fought no great battles. There was no massive hemorrhaging, just a slow, steady trickle of blood drawn in a series of ambushes and fire-fights."[5]

This was the plan of the fifty-four-year-old NVA commander and defense minister General Vo Nguyen Giap, who had masterminded the victory over the French. In 1965–1966, the Marines in I Corps, the most hazardous piece of Vietnam because of its proximity to the North Vietnamese border, had launched thousands of squad- and platoon-sized actions to push the VC out of populated areas. In just twelve months the Marines had brought 1,600 square miles and 500,000 people under government protection, and increasingly dared the North Vietnamese to come out and fight on the open terrain of I Corps' coastal plain, where NVA supply lines would be overstretched and the Marines' supporting arms could be concentrated. To avoid this fate, Giap worked to thwart the successful Marine counterinsurgency by pushing more units into the border area, stringing the Marines out along the whole length of the DMZ in defensive operations.[6]

Giap's aim, a senior communist official explained, was to "lure the Americans closer to the North Vietnamese border and bleed them there without mercy." In 1966, the Americans took the bait. General Lewis Walt moved the 3rd Marine Division headquarters from Da Nang to Phu Bai in Quang Tri province. The division's forward command post went all the way to Dong Ha, which became the "brain and nervous system" of a network of artillery bases along the DMZ. The largest base, eight miles southwest of Dong Ha, was Camp Carroll. Its abandoned battery positions can still be glimpsed today between rows of rubber trees. The Rockpile, a jagged peak ten miles west of Camp Carroll, was another artillery base, this one with

175 mm guns that could fire twenty-five miles—all the way west to the Marine combat base at Khe Sanh near the Laotian border. More Marine battalions were placed in other strongpoints along the DMZ such as Gio Linh and Con Thien.[7]

It was a momentous shift in emphasis. The Marines were best at "small wars," fighting and winning among the people, as they had done in their first year in-country. The eleven battalions of the 3rd Marine Division were now being placed along the northern border in defensive positions, "taking the D out of DMZ," they muttered. Their big sweeps through the wilderness of I Corps made little contact. "Mostly," a journalist wrote, "it was an invasion of a thousand operation-miles of high summer dry season stroke weather, six-canteen patrols that came back either contactless or chewed over by ambushes and quick, deft mortar-rocket attacks, some from other Marine outfits."[8]

Lew Walt chafed at this vulnerability, recognizing that McNamara's concept of an "anti-infiltration barrier" along the DMZ—defended by Marines—was just more of the ineffective political science that had pushed American troops into the war. But Westmoreland kept ordering the Marines to cling to that 300-square-mile border strip they named "Leatherneck Square." Westy and the Joint Chiefs hoped eventually to strike into Laos and cut the Ho Chi Minh Trail. Khe Sanh overlooked the north–south routes into the Laotian panhandle and blocked enemy movement through Quang Tri province to the coast. It was the logical place to launch a cross-border operation—if such an operation were ever approved by a president who shrank from adding yet another front to the war in Vietnam.[9]

In Washington, Bob McNamara could already see that Westmoreland's search and destroy concept was faltering. So could LBJ. Belatedly, the president demanded a *strategy*. "Bob," he told McNamara in a cabinet meeting in January 1966, "you need to get from Westmoreland his plan for using our resources and what *results*—what happens by July, and next January? What's his estimate of NVN [North Vietnamese] response? In other words," Johnson continued, "I want the coach to give me the season's schedule—what the other teams will do—and what we'll do."

Having flogged the war into life, McNamara suddenly lost heart. He began to express the defeatism that would characterize his last years in office. With the NVA and VC deploying sixteen new battalions every *month*, the United States and its allies would never be able to keep pace. "In 1967," McNamara answered Johnson, "we will be faced with a military standoff at a much higher level, with pacification still stalled, and with any prospect of military success marred by the chances of an active Chinese intervention." Just to secure this military "no-decision," McNamara warned, "U.S. killed-in-action can be expected to reach 1,000 a month."[10]

It was already clear that technology was not going to be the silver bullet that would snatch victory from this expanding morass. Westy characterized his own operations as a partial fix at best, and one not calculated to please LBJ: "Patrolling relentlessly, we prevented the North Vietnamese from massing for major attacks." True, but a war of "relentless patrolling" might go on forever. Invading the enemy sanctuaries in Laos and Cambodia was not a realistic option. It would lumber the already overstretched American and ARVN combat units with more areas of operation, and might hasten Chinese intervention.

LBJ would have liked to co-opt the regime of Prince Norodom Sihanouk, who had run Cambodia since 1941 and taken on a right-wing prime minister, General Lon Nol, in 1966. But facts had to be faced. Even Lon Nol saw no way to oppose the massive Chinese-backed NVA and VC forces in Cambodia's eastern provinces, or their use of Cambodia's port of Sihanoukville. Those Vietnamese units were bigger and better equipped than Cambodia's little army, and they had agreed to give Sihanouk a 10 percent cut of their supply deliveries from China. They also agreed not to support Pol Pot's Khmer Rouge communist guerrillas if the prince would let Hanoi's forces rest and resupply in sanctuaries along the South Vietnamese border. It was the best deal the Cambodians were going to get. To stay in power and keep the Khmer Rouge at bay, Sihanouk and Lon Nol recognized Communist China, fended off an anticommunist coup attempt, and adopted a policy of "live and let live" with NVA and VC forces on Cambodian soil. They called this "extreme neutrality."[11]

The Cambodians really had no choice. Even MACV admitted in 1966 that "Cambodia has no ability to restrict VC use of its territory." Trying to *force* Sihanouk to do so, the Americans concluded, would merely "push Sihanouk closer to the Chinese and to more active support of the VC and the NVA." Laos, with its vast hinterland and tiny population, was also in the grip of its great neighbors, China and North Vietnam, and would remain so absent a massive invasion and occupation, for which there was neither appetite, funds, nor manpower in Saigon and Washington. Westmoreland would complain in his memoir that LBJ's refusal to let him invade Cambodia and Laos to fight the NVA was tantamount to FDR forbidding Eisenhower to cross "France to get at Germany." The complaint was ludicrous on its face.[12]

Westy was already rooting around for excuses because his theory of victory, that fast-moving American infantry in helicopters would pounce on unsuspecting enemy units and destroy them, was not working as advertised. In the months leading up to the Battle of Ia Drang, US battalion days of operation had risen 44 percent, armed helicopter sorties had more than doubled, and tac air strikes had increased to 132 a day in October and 446 a day in November. And yet none of this hugely expensive military activity was proving decisive, or even effective. "The game in the jungle," the commander of the US 1st Infantry Division observed, "is to send in a small force as bait, let the enemy attack, and be able to react with a large force in reserve nearby. But if the enemy doesn't want to fight, then the jungle just goes off in 360 directions."

Over 90 percent of American and ARVN-initiated operations were making no contact with the enemy in *any* of these 360 directions. The communists usually avoided American and ARVN patrols and engaged on their own terms when *they* wanted. US bombers and strike fighters were flying four times as many sorties over South Vietnam as over North Vietnam, also with no decisive effect. On a visit to Vietnam in 1966, Henry Kissinger observed that it had been eighteen months since the first Marines had landed in Da Nang, yet "it is still impossible to go four kilometers outside the city without running a real risk of being shot." Nothing, Kissinger concluded, had changed since the American intervention.[13]

During the Sigma II war games at the Pentagon in 1964, players had noted that while Vietnam looked small on the map, it became enormous when decisions had to be made about where to put troops and bombs. The United States was already overextended. Johnson tried everything to get Hanoi to negotiate—a thirty-seven-day "bombing pause" in early 1966, appeals to Moscow and neutral intermediaries—but nothing worked. "We can't get anyone to the table," Johnson told congressional leaders in January 1966. "If you produce them, we'll meet them."[14]

Westmoreland tried to suppress or ignore the failures. He wanted to move to Phase II of his strategy in 1966, which called for the invasion and destruction of enemy sanctuaries and base camps. The Army staff in Washington, headed by General Harold Johnson, recognized the ineffectiveness of what Westy was doing. MACV was wasting lives and dollars searching for a phantom enemy on South Vietnam's periphery, while the VC took more and more of South Vietnam's inhabitants under its control.

At the same time, Westmoreland's restless operations were driving up the costs of the war in alarming ways. By the middle of 1966, the Americans were losing 200 to 300 KIAs every month, 1,000 to 2,000 wounded, and fifty to seventy-five aircraft, shot from the sky in growing numbers by improving communist air defenses. Yet nothing lasting was being accomplished. "Technology, airmobility," they were just "stunts," reporter Michael Herr observed. "Mobility was just mobility, it saved lives or took them all the time," but "you weren't *going* anywhere" so long as the enemy refused to yield control of the people.[15]

A Cav pilot recalled returning over and over to fields of supposedly decisive battle: "We had to go back out to patch up a few holes in the victory. Somebody forgot to tell Charlie he lost, so he was still out there shooting down helicopters, the dumb fuck." Operation Silver Bayonet in the Ia Drang Valley, Hal Moore's relatively small and fruitless operation against a tiny fraction of the enemy army, had nevertheless consumed 25 percent of America's Southeast Asian airlift capacity for two entire weeks. It had opened gaps in the war's ravenous supply chain that would have to be filled with more defense dollars and manpower. The number of American personnel would have to increase, along with their creature comforts. The cost of this buildup, even for a short war, would be mind-boggling—far in excess of anything imagined by LBJ when he had casually thrown down the gauntlet after the Tonkin Gulf incident.[16]

Westy continued to flail at an invisible enemy. He sought desperately for targets. The more troops he put in—twelve new maneuver battalions arrived in early 1966—the less the VC and NVA fought. Ops increased, sorties increased, and yet the number of enemy KIAs fell 30 percent. It was easy to see why. The war had just begun and already the Americans were predictable. A brigade or division would be given an AO to clean out. In those boonies, they would construct battalion bases. Each rifle company would then fan out from the battalion base to establish its own company base. Platoon and squad patrols would search for several days from these company bases—the proverbial "walk in the sun"—scouring a 140-square-mile area, always under the protective umbrella of their tac air and firebases.[17]

To achieve surprise, helicopter assaults could be added to the menu, but even at this early stage of the war they were no longer surprising to the enemy. To limit American and ARVN casualties, every LZ had to be prepped with air strikes and artillery fire. General Glenn Walker, the operations chief of the US 25th Infantry Division, observed in August 1966 that the enemy knew exactly what prep fires portended: "The enemy usually leaves the area, hides, or moves into prepared or advantageous positions to fight on his own terms."

Communist troops rarely even waited for the American battalion to arrive. Once they noticed that a new AO was being created with company firebases and a maneuver battalion at its center, they fled, returning only when the op was over and the battalion removed. "The enemy has observed our tactics and techniques," Walker concluded. "After one has observed artillery preps and air strikes and large numbers of helicopters moving into an area, it is not difficult to determine what is taking place. Therefore, the enemy is becoming more difficult to find."[18]

Operation Rolling Thunder, the air campaign that President Johnson had launched in March 1965 to raise the cost of the war for Hanoi, was instead reminding Americans of the rising cost of the war *they* confronted. By inching into the conflict with "graduated pressure" instead of the "hard knock" pushed by the Joint Chiefs, LBJ had failed to exploit Hanoi's period of maximum vulnerability in 1965, when North Vietnamese air defenses had been almost nonexistent: two dozen radar sets and 700 flak guns for the entire country. Now the North Vietnamese were much better defended, with early-warning and fire-control radars, more antiaircraft guns, SAMs, and MiG fighters.

The total number of Rolling Thunder sorties against North Vietnam rose from 55,000 flights in 1965 to 148,000 in 1966, and total bomb tonnage rose from 33,000 to 128,000, but the number of American aircraft lost surged from 171 to 318, and direct operational costs of the air campaign rose from $460 million to $1.2 billion. And yet, Pentagon analysts grimly concluded, the increased bombing and aircraft losses "accomplished little more than in 1965."[19]

President Johnson continued to hold the bombers on a short leash, spooked by fears of Chinese intervention as well as *New York Times* editor Harrison Salisbury's visit to Hanoi in 1966, when Salisbury had detailed widespread bomb damage and reported that "the principal sufferers are the people," giving the lie to Johnson's claim that the air campaign was interdiction-only, surgical, and even humane. Rolling Thunder, a Pentagon spokesman allowed, was ripening into yet another "credibility disaster" for an administration that was still holding on to public and congressional support, but for how long?[20]

Everywhere LBJ turned seemed to be a dead end. Bob McNamara, once so eager, now balked at everything. "The military-action approach" wasn't working, said the SecDef, and wouldn't work. Words like "victory and win," McNamara scoffed, were distracting "color words." The best that could be hoped for was a "favorable settlement," but the North Vietnamese made clear that they wouldn't come to the table unless LBJ agreed to accept their "four points," which they published in April 1966: the United States must stop bombing, must annul any alliance it had with Saigon, must withdraw all forces, and must permit the unification of Vietnam by Hanoi and the Viet Cong. To accept those points would be to accept defeat.[21]

LBJ was terrified by the growth and cost of the war, and by Hanoi's indifference to his "peace offensive"—that monthlong Christmas 1965 bombing halt as well as White House appeals to the pope and ninety governments around the world to join in America's "search for peace." At the start of 1965 there had been 23,000 American troops in Vietnam. At the end of the year there were over 181,000. Over 1,600 had been killed in action. The war had become so expensive that LBJ had to request a $13 billion supplemental from Congress in January 1966 to cover the cost overrun of the previous year.[22]

In his January 1966 State of the Union address, LBJ confirmed that the war might go on endlessly: "The days may become months and the months may become years, but we will stay as long as aggression commands us to battle." In an interview after the address, he let slip that he had no control over events, and no plan to win or exit the war. "Who knows how long, how much?" the president blurted out. He paused, and added: "The important thing is are we right or wrong? I believe we are right." The strategy, in other words, was unchanged: violence mixed with pieties, with no end in sight.[23]

Learning that an estimated two NVA regiments had reinforced a VC regiment on the coastal plain east of Pleiku and taken an entire province and its 800,000 inhabitants under communist control, Westmoreland launched Operation Masher in January 1966 with his 1st Cavalry Division, aided by the ARVN 22nd Division and South Korea's Capital Division. Masher, which aimed to destroy VC bases near the heavily used Route 1, lasted into March. The American units fired 132,000 rounds of artillery, which worked out to 1,000 shells for every estimated enemy fatality. Masher was so destructive that President Johnson demanded that MACV rename the op White Wing after only a week so that the South Vietnamese would not get the wrong idea about their American saviors.[24]

Masher/White Wing was about as good as it got for Westy, which was to say not good at all. The "body count" he published was fishy. He claimed to have destroyed most of two enemy regiments—killing 1,742, capturing 430, and detaining 2,000 VC suspects—but at the end of the operation he could only produce 365 captured weapons, leading many, including Senator Fulbright, who was televising hearings on the war in early 1966, to infer that hundreds of civilians had been slaughtered by Operation White Wing's air strikes and artillery. "If he's dead and Vietnamese, he's VC" was standard Army guidance in this period.[25]

Westmoreland's boasts about a rising kill ratio in Vietnam (4:1 in mid-1966) seemed more dubious than ever. Operation White Wing, designed to uproot the VC and NVA on the coastal plain below Da Nang, had instead created 125,000 refugees and killed more than 10,000 South Vietnamese civilians. Washington and Saigon insisted that they were fighting the good fight against a communist regime that murdered its adversaries, but even liberal estimates of communist assassinations in the decade since the French withdrawal rarely exceeded 20,000. Careless American fire could assassinate that many villagers in a few weeks. A Special Forces lieutenant scolded Westmoreland for his overreliance on air strikes and artillery: "These wide-screen raids the Cav and other units are doing are wrecking everything these people have. Sure, they beat the NVA units and the VC, but they're ignoring the stomping they're doing to the people we're trying to help."[26]

Senator Bill Fulbright's Senate Foreign Relations Committee estimated that the US Army and its free-world allies had killed six civilians for every dead communist combatant in the course of Operation White Wing. That estimate was almost certainly correct. Later it was revealed that the South Koreans, deployed here to secure the coastal highway as well as the route running west from the coast to Cambodia, had massacred more than 1,000 civilians of all ages during White Wing and listed them as "enemy KIA." One American commander compared this sort of combat in populated areas to an orchestra—sometimes emphasizing the drums, other times trumpets, bassoons, or flutes alone. "The Koreans," he commented, "play one instrument—the bass drum." When deductions of civilian casualties were made from Westy's body count, the general's results were paltry: several hundred enemy casualties measured against 1,300 dead and wounded Americans.[27]

Vice President Hubert Humphrey, ostracized by LBJ since February 1965 for having urged the president to terminate the war, was sent to South Vietnam nearly a year to the day after his disgrace to redeem himself. Humphrey, eager to be readmitted to the White House in-group, this time spoke his lines perfectly. Antiwar liberals were horrified. They recalled a Humphrey who had declared a year earlier that the United States had no business in "that faraway conflict, where no lasting solution can be imposed by a foreign army." The vice president now flip-flopped, describing the war as not only justified but winnable, and part of a worldwide mission to spread peace and prosperity. In Saigon, he toured a suspiciously clean and comfortable "relocation center" with Air Marshal Ky and was photographed laughing with healthy, well-attired refugee children.[28]

Humphrey met with Ambassador Lodge and General Westmoreland and inhaled their hawkish optimism. On his return to Washington, a startled *Newsweek* judged the vice president "the scrappiest warrior in the White House phalanx." Once a dove, Humphrey had become a hawk. This eagerness to please by the erstwhile "gabby extremist of the Left" was a perhaps inevitable reaction to the abuse Johnson had heaped on him in 1965: excluding him from important meetings, editing his speeches, cutting his office staff, and boorishly refusing him access to perks like the presidential yacht and Air Force Two. "Hubert," Johnson once grunted, needs "to kiss my ass in Macy's window at high noon and tell me it smells like roses." Mission accomplished.

Here was another example of the lifelong "Humphrey duality," which was a polite phrase for hypocrisy. The vice president now made outlandish statements that would doom him when he ran for the Democratic nomination and presidency in 1968. The war, Humphrey declared in 1966, was a "matter of survival," his turn to embrace it a "matter of conscience," for "Vietnam today is as close to the U.S. as London was in 1940," and the communists, if not checked in Southeast Asia, would be coming next for "Honolulu and San Francisco."[29]

Although the Senate crushed an attempt to repeal the Tonkin Gulf Resolution in March 1966 by a vote of 92–5, that lopsided win concealed mounting frustration with the war among American elites. Fulbright's nationally televised hearings included testimony from Cold Warrior George Kennan, who marveled at LBJ's massive diversion of scarce resources to Vietnam, which Kennan defined as "*not* a region of major military, industrial importance, where *no* decisive developments of the world situation will be determined," where there were *no* "dangers great enough to justify our military intervention." Sent by the White House to defend the war, Max Taylor flopped. The United States was not trying to "defeat" North Vietnam, he assured senators, but was just trying to make them "mend their ways." America's objective, he unhelpfully added, was "an Appomattox or something of that sort."[30]

This floundering triggered a panicky response from the president. LBJ convened an emergency three-day summit in Honolulu in early February 1966 with the leaders of South Vietnam to give the appearance of a united front. The summit revealed again the lack of strategy and, worse, Johnson's continuing attempt to hide that fact behind what columnist Walter Lippmann called "the vaguest, most ambiguous generalities about aggression and freedom."[31]

The Honolulu summit was convened on a day's notice, and used by Johnson to woo liberals by committing Thieu and Ky to "build true democracy" in South Vietnam and to keep hawks on board by promising "to nail the coonskins to the wall"—more military action to reach Westmoreland's "crossover point."

Thieu and Ky read from the White House script, pledging to "build a better life for their people." Westmoreland steeled Americans for "many campaigns and many operations" to "ferret out" the enemy. Back in Washington, containment theorist George Kennan continued his testimony, unimpressed by LBJ's antics in Honolulu. Kennan judged the unfolding American war in Vietnam "unsound" in every way. In the first place, Kennan wanted to know *why* America was taking up the cudgels for the Saigon regime. LBJ's hastily arranged Declaration of Honolulu essentially "invented an obligation" that did not exist in any formal alliance. This faux obligation, Kennan continued, risked war on the most unfavorable terms with China and burdened America with the thankless task of nation-building in South Vietnam. "Determining *their* political realities," Kennan snapped, is "not *our* business."[32]

Westmoreland described the president at Honolulu as "intense, perturbed, and uncertain how to proceed...torn by the magnitude of [Vietnam]." An increasingly nervous LBJ pressed McNamara and Westmoreland to tell him how long the war would last, but they couldn't.

The answer, McNamara hazarded in March 1966, "could not be framed in years or months" because everything there depended not on what the United States did but on what Hanoi did. "We win if North Vietnam leaves South Vietnam alone" was the SecDef's unhelpful conclusion. America would have to keep "stepping up" its force levels in Vietnam until the NVA and VC stopped stepping up theirs. Westmoreland explained that the length of the war could not even be guessed at because there were still "too many imponderables." This would become a pattern, with Johnson yearning for an "end date" as if the war could be magically terminated.[33]

To give the president some solace, McNamara and Rusk now handed Westmoreland a list of goals for 1966: MACV must increase the South Vietnamese population in secure areas by 10 percent, open 20 percent more roads and railroads, and destroy 30 percent more communist base areas. If MACV could do that, they said, all might be well. They were handing Westmoreland the very weapon with which he would destroy his own reputation—the weapon of official fibs and legerdemain. As long as he plotted his numbers on an ascending curve, he could claim that he was winning.[34]

The cost of meeting the new goals pushed the price of the war higher. For fiscal 1966, McNamara had projected that the war would cost $2 billion. It ended up costing four times that sum. For fiscal 1967, he projected costs of $11 billion, which would balloon to $21 billion. Johnson stubbornly refused to acknowledge the fiscal danger posed by the expanding war. In his 1966 State of the Union address, he claimed that America could eat its cake and have it too. He would not "wring sacrifices from the hopes of the unfortunate here in the land of plenty." No, Johnson insisted, "I believe that we can continue the Great Society while fighting the war in Vietnam."[35]

Butter, the president promised, would be spread as lavishly as guns. For 1966, LBJ planned to create two new federal departments, expand the Department of Health, Education, and Welfare, rebuild America's cities, develop Appalachia, modernize hospitals, build schools, enact clean air and water plans, fund city parks and highways, eradicate smallpox all over the world, and on and on. He submitted 113 bills in all to the Eighty-Ninth Congress in 1966 to, as one of his aides put it, "get his Great Society while he fought the war." Taking it all in, Senator Fulbright condemned this "arrogance of power": the Johnson administration's failure to grasp "what exactly is within the realm of its power and what is beyond it."[36]

To prosecute the war in Vietnam more effectively, Johnson had put three trusted generals in key positions: Harold Johnson as Army chief of staff, Creighton Abrams as Army vice chief, and Westmoreland as MACV commander. Now the triumvirate began to divide as Generals Johnson and Abrams, pressed by the president, began to ask awkward questions about Westy's conduct of the war. The most important question was voiced by a Pentagon insider: "The indices for measuring progress," he confessed, "measure nothing." Body count and kill ratio as metrics of victory in a war with a resolute enemy were like a man "taking his own temperature and using that to diagnose the existence of plague."[37]

Army chief of staff Harold Johnson ordered a review of Westmoreland's performance in March 1966 that came to be known as the "PROVN study"—shorthand for "Program for the Pacification and Long-Term Development of Vietnam." Vice Chief of Staff Abrams, who had graduated from West Point in 1936 in Westmoreland's class, led the study and concluded that Westy was artificially separating high-intensity operations and pacification and not "understanding the nature of the conflict."

The South Vietnamese people, Abrams argued, were the true "strategic determinant," and indeed the war's whole raison d'être. The people were the "object" for which everyone was fighting, and their future was the aim that lay "beyond the war." And nothing that Westmoreland was doing was winning their loyalty or securing their future. Despite all of the flailing, slaughter, and boasts of a 4:1 kill ratio in South Vietnam, enemy force totals in Saigon kept rising, not falling as projected. The "crossover point" Westmoreland had vowed to reach by year-end 1966 seemed as distant and illusory as ever.[38]

There were big battles whenever the enemy stood and fought—usually on terms the communists judged favorable—but the standard operation in this period was neatly summarized by journalist Michael Herr: "Patrols went out, patrols collided, companies splintered the action and spread it across the hills in a sequence of small, isolated firefights that afterward were described as strategy." Ambush is the basic tactical technique in both guerrilla and counterguerilla warfare, and there were ambush positions everywhere in Vietnam—cliffs, streams, embankments, narrow trails, paddies, and roads with canals on either side. In places like these, Herr observed, battles didn't so much end as vanish, as swiftly as they had arisen. After drawing in whole American brigades, "the North Vietnamese collected up their gear and most of their dead and 'disappeared' during the night, leaving a few bodies behind for our troops to kick and count."[39]

And yet American casualties kept ticking up—from mortar rounds, grenades, bullets, mines, booby traps, punji stakes, helicopter and plane crashes, accidents, burns, malaria, diarrhea, pneumonia, hepatitis, dengue, typhus, venereal disease, and fevers of unknown origin. Only 15 percent of American hospital admissions in Vietnam in 1966 were caused by enemy action. Army chief of staff Harold Johnson went to South Vietnam to see things for himself while Abrams put finishing touches to the PROVN study. Johnson met with a group of colonels to get their impressions. One told him that he had implored Westy "to end the big-unit war," to no avail. "We're just not going to win it doing *this*," the colonel told Johnson.[40]

The PROVN study deplored the waste and pointlessness of Westy's big-unit war, which harmed South Vietnamese villagers far more than the elusive enemy. VC propaganda in the villages was accenting US and ARVN violence, destruction, plunder, and rape. Population security and loyalty had to be the focus, PROVN argued: not only protecting the population from the VC but protecting them from careless American and ARVN fire and other abuse as well. "All other military aspects of the war," the study concluded, "are secondary." South Vietnam's villages were "the true point of decision in Vietnam." Abrams, who would succeed Westmoreland as field commander in 1968, began to sketch the concept of "one war"—integrating big-unit operations and pacification, so that each would serve the other.[41]

The Marine Corps was making the same arguments, and had been since 1965. General Victor "Brute" Krulak, who commanded Marine forces in the Pacific theater, warned McNamara that by devastating uninhabited areas in the usually fruitless search for enemy forces, Westmoreland was claiming "victories in the search and destroy operations that were not relevant to the total outcome of the war." Not only were they not relevant, they were not even victories. General Lew Walt, the Marine commander in Vietnam, added that the Army was repeating the error of the French: conflating control with security. Calling a village "government-controlled" did not make it secure when the VC stole in every night to recruit and punish. "Control over the people," Walt pointed out, "must be *absolute* to be effective."[42]

To make their control absolute, the Marines experimented successfully with combined action platoons (CAPs). Squads of Marines would move into a village to live, eat, sleep, and fight with the local militia. The CAPs, usually fifteen Marines plus thirty-five village militia members, were a great success—one of the few good-news stories of the war. Knowing that the Marines were with them, the militiamen stood their ground and fought, and the VC and NVA avoided CAP villages. Marines in CAPs inflicted casualties on the enemy out of all proportion to their numbers. Marines in CAPs were only 1.5 percent of total American strength in Vietnam, yet they accounted for 8 percent of total enemy killed and wounded.[43]

But despite the Marine arguments, their prodigious body count, and the Army chief's bureaucratic turn to new methods in the war, bad facts on the ground were hardly disturbed by MACV's still minuscule commitment to pacification and to clear and hold operations. Westmoreland rejected the PROVN study and the Marine CAPs. As Westy's intelligence chief put it, "He could not embrace the study's concept without admitting that he and his strategy were wrong." And with Westmoreland's units still out in the uninhabited border regions, civic action and police forces could not deploy where most needed because they could not be secured against VC attacks.[44]

Even the cities weren't secure. The Buddhist protests, briefly quieted by Diem's fall, roared back with a vengeance in 1966. This time they were focused in the north, where I Corps commander and junta member General Nguyen Chanh Thi allowed demonstrations against the Thieu-Ky regime to rage unchecked in Da Nang and Hue. General Thi enjoyed total control of the five provinces of I Corps and its two ARVN divisions and made no secret of his desire to supplant Thieu and Ky in Saigon.[45]

Air Marshal Ky relieved Thi of his corps command and his seat in the military government and eagerly sent reinforcements into I Corps, not to fight the enemy but to fight ARVN troops loyal to General Thi and the Buddhist Struggle Movement, which called for the ouster of the junta, removal of US forces, a new democratic *civilian* government, and immediate negotiations with Hanoi and the VC to end the war and unify Vietnam. The Buddhists believed, not without reason, that they had supplied most of the effort to remove Diem three years earlier and had been rewarded with a Saigon junta in which they had no part or representation.[46]

The civil war in Hue and Da Nang served as yet another humiliation for President Johnson. "An American public sending its sons to die in Vietnam saw these events as distressing," Westy explained in his wooden way. The president's approval rating fell to 46 percent. The percentage of Americans who believed it was a mistake to send troops to Vietnam jumped 11 points.

One of LBJ's advisers, on a summer vacation in Rhode Island, noted that most of the people he met were wealthy Republicans, and even they had no idea what America was doing in Vietnam: "I heard the old refrain about the president 'not explaining why we are there' a dozen times." The civil war in I Corps—so intense that the White House considered using it as a pretext to abandon Vietnam altogether—increased the confusion. It was as clear an indictment as there could be of LBJ's inability to conjure real leadership and nation-building in Saigon, or to forge a coherent strategy.[47]

The Buddhist Struggle Movement said a great deal about the state of play in 1966. The Saigon government remained weak, a ten-man military directorate, with Thieu as head of state and Ky as prime minister, and each of the four corps areas controlled by a warlord general such as Thi in Hue. Until now, Saigon had acquiesced to the power of the warlords, asking only that they serve loyally and share with Saigon whatever they gleaned in corruption. But Ky, emboldened by LBJ's embrace in Honolulu, now set out to tame the regional barons and put his own creatures in their place. The Americans, who viewed the Buddhists as pawns of the communists, were happy to assist. They did not fully appreciate that the real issue—apart from Thi's sprawling empire and ambitions, which were no different from Ky's—was that growing numbers of South Vietnamese in Hue and elsewhere simply wanted peace under *any* flag.[48]

South Vietnam's Buddhists wanted to negotiate with the VC and settle the war with an all-party coalition government. Ky, who would have been driven from power by such a result, persuaded Johnson to back him, not the Buddhists, and so another opportunity to end the war faded, the Americans deciding that having a reliable client for the prosecution of the war—even a war going badly—was better than cultivating a new client who might bring an end to the war by ushering in the communists. Assistant Secretary of State Bill Bundy recalled a feeling of abashment and disgust in Washington. "Ky's winning team," Bundy wrote, "seemed to all of us the bottom of the barrel, absolutely the bottom of the barrel."[49]

While American forces fought the VC and NVA in 1966, the ARVN waged a civil war against itself for three months, during which twenty-five Americans were killed defending Da Nang airfield against General Thi's ARVN troops. Another 228 Americans died fighting the communists elsewhere in I Corps to keep them from exploiting the infighting in Hue and Da Nang. By July, Ambassador Lodge, who had returned to Saigon in 1965 after Max Taylor's move to the White House, was crediting Ky with "a solid political victory," although it was anything but that.[50]

Anger seethed below the surface. The South Vietnamese officers in I Corps trained in "political warfare," a US program begun twelve months earlier to infuse the ARVN with patriotism, had sided with the Struggle Movement forces against their own government. So too had the senior leadership of the militia forces and 500 of their troops. Several professors at the University of Hue had left their posts to join the Viet Cong. Desertion surged on the back of the unrest, and dozens of recently secured hamlets had to be downgraded to insecure, the VC having reinfiltrated them amid the chaos of the Struggle Movement.[51]

Even Saigon was not safe. Six VC main-force battalions were operating at any given time within ten miles of the capital, and three VC special action units were nested inside the city. Ky's political settlement, devised to buy off rivals and please the Americans, merely saddled an already inefficient Saigon government with more inefficiency. To remain premier, Ky agreed to boost the pay of all government and military employees, convert the ten-man junta into a twenty-man National Leadership Council, and establish a People's and Armed Forces Congress to "oversee" government affairs. As head of state, Thieu decreed that there would be elections in "three to five months" for a constituent assembly that would write yet another constitution—South Vietnam's third in a decade—and begin the transition to democratic rule by civilians.[52]

None of this supported the war effort. With the South Vietnamese leaders consumed by their turf wars, the Americans would have to do more. Westmoreland responded in August 1966 with a new "Concept of Military Operations in South Vietnam" that, for the first time, stressed the need to give "maximum practical support to area and population security." In theory, this made perfect sense. Westmoreland had told the president that he would destroy the VC and NVA with intensifying American firepower in 1966–1967 and then "clean up" their shattered remnants in 1968. Any remnants would hide among the people, making population security no less important than the heavy fighting in the hills and jungles. The president was so impressed by the plan—briefed to him by Westy at LBJ's ranch in Texas—that he boasted to the television cameras of certain victory: "A Communist military takeover in South Vietnam is no longer just improbable, it is *impossible*."[53]

To move the plan along, Westmoreland brushed off the PROVN study and aggressively committed 95 percent of his maneuver battalions to search and destroy operations. Worried that the success of the Marine CAPs at population security would cost him manpower, Westy declared war on the Marines as well. To this point, the Marines had garrisoned only eighty villages with CAPs, all of them in I Corps. CAP advocates wanted a nationwide effort—2,500 CAPs or more, using Marines *and* Army troops. They countered Army critics, who argued that the CAPs were too vulnerable, with the observation that only one of eighty CAPs had been wiped out, and that one had been successfully reestablished within twenty-four hours. And whereas the Army routinely destroyed villages, the Marines were defending them—a crucial distinction.[54]

Westmoreland sent his operations chief, General Bill DePuy, to visit and evaluate the CAPs. DePuy returned the desired verdict. The "spreading ink-blot process" of the CAPs, he said, was too slow. The Marines did a good job of defending villages, but at the cost of leaving "all but a tiny part of I Corps under the control of the VC, who have freedom of movement outside of the Marine enclaves." The ARVN and militia did not "fill in behind the Marines," leaving most of South Vietnam's territory to the enemy, who could, as Westy summarized, "come and go as he pleased."

Lew Walt, who commanded the Marine divisions in Vietnam until May 1967, reminded Westmoreland of the obvious. The enemy did not need to "come and go." Their allies *lived* around American bases and could host VC soldiers and mortar units anytime they wanted. "One hundred and thirty thousand Vietnamese live within mortar range of the Da Nang airfield," Walt liked to say. The Americans needed to worry more about winning *them* over than chasing the Viet Cong.

To weaken what he regarded as this pernicious Marine influence, Westmoreland stepped up his attacks on the Marines in 1966, one analyst noting that "this argument between the U.S. Army and the U.S. Marine Corps seems at times more intense than the war between either of them and the VC." Westy told the Marines that despite their success here and there, they were on their own. Any Marines they wanted to put into the CAP program would have to be subtracted from Marine units already in the field. William Corson, the Marine colonel who directed the CAPs, was bluntly told to go away: "If you want to play around with such foolishness, you'll have to eat the personnel spaces out of your own hide. No additional Marines will be made available to support combined action. We'll starve you out." In this way, the promising CAPs became a minor footnote to the war, permitting Westmoreland to focus everything on search and destroy.[55]

Chapter 7

"THE COUNTRY IS
BEHIND YOU—
50 PERCENT"

In August 1966, even Senator John Stennis of Mississippi, the hawk-ish Democratic chairman of the Armed Services Committee, began to grasp the folly of Vietnam. Stennis cautioned the White House that even current expenditures in South Vietnam were excessive. Hanoi was tying down "a substantial amount of U.S. manpower and matériel" and burning through the $20 billion annual war cost in addition to other non-Vietnam Pentagon accounts that underpinned the war in South-east Asia. Strategy for the war was still nonexistent, Stennis complained, replaced with "hastily prepared statements, information and estimates presented to us by the Executive Department in time of emergency or semi-emergency."

The Johnson administration, Stennis admonished, "had to face up realistically to the situation and make a hardheaded and realistic assess-ment of the problems with which we would be confronted if two, three, or more of such contingencies should occur simultaneously." Other allies in other theaters might need American assistance. Everything must not be poured blindly into military operations in South Vietnam.[1]

Westmoreland was not listening. From June to November 1966, he was busy launching five major ops in the Central Highlands that were given the names Hawthorne and Paul Revere I, II, III, and IV. Ward Just, a thirty-year-old reporter covering the war for the *Washington Post*, tagged along on Operation Hawthorne in June 1966. Hawthorne, which MACV advertised as "the campaign for control of the Central Highlands," sent General Willard Pearson's 1st Brigade of the 101st Airborne Division and a Cav battalion into the jungles west of Pleiku to find and destroy an NVA regiment that had nearly overrun an American firebase north of Dak To, another of the many Special Forces camps erected along South Vietnam's western border to monitor communist infiltration routes.[2]

Pearson was the author of a new approach to the war, which he worked out with one of his battalion commanders, thirty-five-year-old Major David "Hack" Hackworth. If the key problem in Vietnam was finding the enemy, who had learned to sidestep American and ARVN sweeps, Pearson and Hackworth resolved to fight them the way they fought the Americans, which was quietly and stealthily—to, as Hackworth put it, "outguerrilla the guerrilla."

Hack and Pearson created a forty-two-man "recondo" platoon—short for reconnaissance/commando—whose job was to slip unnoticed into the mountains and snake deep inside enemy-controlled territory, seizing enemy stragglers and searching for base camps with large numbers of enemy troops and weapons. If camps were found, the recondo platoon, called Tiger Force in the 101st Airborne, would radio the coordinates and summon the artillery, air strikes, and maneuver units needed to wipe out the enemy.[3]

Ward Just had flown to Pleiku and then on to Dak To to cover Operation Hawthorne. In Dak To, Just had hitched a ride on a helicopter to the American firebase that had been nearly overrun the night before by an NVA battalion. It was in a place called Toumorong, ten miles northeast of Dak To. Alighting there, Just noted that there were still body parts scattered about and long smears of blood from the perimeter into the bush where the enemy had dragged away his casualties.

Just watched Hackworth assemble Tiger Force. They were all paratroopers, all volunteers, and half of them were Black. "Goddamnit," Hack called to the men as they assembled their gear, "I want forty hard-charging fuckin' dicks. And if anybody ain't a hard-charging fuckin' dick I want him out."

Recondo platoon and squad leaders searching for their elusive enemy in March 1967. They tried to "outguerrilla the guerrilla." (National Archives)

Like players breaking a huddle, the paratroopers called out "Fuckin'," Hackworth answered "Right," and they were off, Ward Just in their midst. As they climbed into their helicopters, Hackworth, who would remain behind in headquarters, shouted encouragement: "My God, we chased them for five days over every flipping hill in Vietnam. Five days! And they hit us back here. They kept one hill ahead of us. Well, now they've had it." The grunts flew north over the rugged, hilly ground and then set down in a clearing. The slicks departed and Tiger Force threaded into the jungle to begin the hunt. The trees had two or three levels of canopy, blotting out the sun. It was like "moving inside a great green-glass bottle."[4]

Setting off on a well-used path toward the Laotian border, the recondo platoon found abandoned positions and camps. As the daylight faded, they bumped into an NVA straggler and exchanged fire, killing the straggler and one of their own. The American KIA was Pfc. Richard Garcia, shot in the chest. Captain Lew Higinbotham, who commanded Tiger Force, told

Just that Garcia had probably been killed by friendly fire: "Most likely he was killed from our own lines. It's a matter of fire discipline. There's never enough of it, and too many people are killed needlessly."

They spent the night in a star-shaped defensive formation, each point of the star a group of three men, one of them awake at all times, with the command group in the center. They were always within range of the 1st Brigade's artillery, but fire support would not save them if they were hit and overrun quickly. In the morning, they were awakened by another burst of fire. Three NVA stragglers, taking the Americans for an NVA unit, had walked into their midst and then run away, pursued by gunshots.

Battalion headquarters had already warned Higinbotham that he was effectively surrounded by the NVA 226th Regiment, which was known to be hidden in these hills. So long as Tiger Force proceeded quietly and unnoticed, they could do their job and find the enemy companies and battalions that could then be targeted by higher headquarters. But by now they had fired twice, betraying their presence. And this time three North Vietnamese had escaped with knowledge of their strength and location.

The corpse of Private Garcia added to their difficulties. They would either have to drag him on the mission on a stretcher (too cumbersome) or have him extracted by a helicopter (too noisy). Higinbotham pressed on, moving up a two-foot-wide jungle trail, everyone on edge. They blundered into a company-sized position, exchanged fire with an outpost, took another casualty, and then took stock.

Their mission was blown, and they were exceedingly vulnerable. The company they had flushed from cover now returned to attack them from three sides. It was hard to know the enemy strength or location, for the communist infantry were moving and firing, working in close, very deliberately making it hard for Higinbotham to call in artillery and tac air. When he did, a ring of shell bursts blowing up the jungle around Tiger Force, the enemy fire hardly slackened. Many of the North Vietnamese had already pushed *inside* the ring.

And Tiger Force's fight for survival was just one of several happening that day as other paratrooper companies fanned out north and west of Dak To, searching for the enemy. Captain Bill Carpenter, Army football's famous "Lonesome End," was fighting a similar battle several miles to the south against an NVA battalion, which gripped Carpenter's paratroop company so tightly that he had to napalm his own position. "They are overrunning us," Carpenter radioed. "Lay it right on top of our position. We might as well take some of them too." These were the "hugging tactics" the communists had perfected in the months since Ia Drang, getting so close to the embattled American infantry that the grunts couldn't call in air or artillery support without risk to themselves.

Ward Just, lying at the center of Higinbotham's disintegrating position—"a tiny area about the size of a basketball court"—was struck by the captain's cool under fire. Six of his men were already dead and many more wounded, but the commander spoke quietly and calmly into the field radio, pulling the American artillery fire closer and closer to his own men as the NVA crept nearer, trying to get near enough to lob grenades into the American position.

By late afternoon, when the platoon had been under fire for over three hours and its wounded were crying out for help—"You got to get me out of here!"—Major Hackworth came on the radio and ordered Higinbotham to hold out a little longer. The major had sent another company to reinforce. It was on foot, a mile away. "If you don't get here soon, we're all gonna die," Higinbotham snapped. They nearly did, a last attack stopped just yards from their position, but the reinforcing company arrived and Tiger Force, reduced by twelve dead and nineteen wounded, would live to fight another day.

MACV called Operation Hawthorne in its entirety a victory, flourishing the body count as evidence—1,200 enemy dead and only 250 friendly KIA (270 if you counted the 20 missing in action [MIA] and never recovered in that dark jungle). But Ward Just, who had trembled through that hellish day, clutching a borrowed .45 pistol, knew that any victory here was illusory: "There was no real epilogue to the reconnaissance patrol of Tiger Force." The 101st Airborne Division was just reprising what the Cav had done before and what others would do after, described this way by a participant: "When the net was closed, no fish were found. The dumb little barbarian had got away, showing not the least respect for superior technology."[5]

Two helicopter pilots involved in the op argued over its significance. "If they're gone and we killed 2,000 of them, we won," said one. "What did we win?" asked the other. "We don't have any more real estate, no new villages are under American control, and it took everything we had to stop them."

NVA infiltration would resume afterward and, eleven months to the day after Just's recondo patrol had barely survived that desperate fight, another US platoon would be ambushed in the same place and wiped out. Coincidentally, Lew Higinbotham would be operations officer that day. He remembered his last call with the platoon, which was retracing Higinbotham's old route north of Dak To. "How is it?" Higinbotham radioed at 10 a.m. "Good clean fun," the lieutenant on the ground cheerily replied. Twenty minutes later the platoon leader's radio went dead, and every man in the platoon was killed, wounded, or captured. If this was victory, what did defeat look like?[6]

All four Paul Revere operations mingled the same tragedy and futility as Hawthorne. The futility should have been expected. The Cav's Pleiku Campaign in 1965 had fought over the same ground, and yet here the enemy was again—just a few months later and in even greater strength, with even bolder aims. While the Americans searched for the six regiments of the NVA 1st and 10th Divisions in a 500-square-mile wilderness, the NVA, hidden by dense jungle, crabbed forward into South Vietnam and constructed new base areas and bunker complexes. Whenever they met American resistance, they looked for opportunities to isolate and ambush American units, who came in and out of the area for periods ranging in length from two weeks to two months in the four operations.

This became the standard enemy game plan: move boldly ahead until countered by the Americans, and then revert to a tactical defensive until the Americans finished their operation and went elsewhere. For the Americans, ops in the Central Highlands posed unprecedented challenges. There were hardly any roads in the rugged mountain region. That's why market towns like Pleiku and Kontum City were so important. They were the crossroads and airfields where what little infrastructure there was converged.

And yet the roads that went in and out of these hubs were mined every night by the VC. Convoys were always at risk, and so everything urgent and vital had to move by air—men, artillery, ammo, and supplies. But there were few natural clearings for LZs or firebases, just a seamless wall of teak and mahogany, the trunks of these great trees six or seven feet in diameter and impervious to the light-duty chainsaws issued to infantry units.

This meant that a ponderous development phase, closely observed by the enemy, had to precede every operation. Air strikes were called to thin the wooded mountain slopes. Engineers slung bulldozers in under Chinooks and then went to work with two-man chainsaws and C-4 explosive to clear landing zones and firebases. Then more heavy-lift helicopters lowered 105 mm howitzers into battery positions, which were entrenched, wired, and sandbagged, as they were everywhere else in Vietnam.

A single firebase would require sixty or more sorties by Chinooks and Hueys to deliver the howitzers, ammo, fuel, supplies, and personnel. Each time the firebase moved, the process was repeated, thirty or forty Chinooks lifting the guns and ammo out of one clearing and moving them to another. The grunts in the jungle had to be commanded and fed, so more helicopters flew in and out to create forward battalion command posts and resupply points, where pallets of ammo, C-rations, and drinking water would be stored and flown out every day to sustain the companies in the field. For the enemy, it was a simple matter of connecting these dots to descry the course and direction of the pending operation.[7]

Once a protective web of firebases, forward supply areas, and LZs was in place, the American infantry went to work as best they could. Four of the nine rifle companies in any three-battalion brigade were never available for combat assault missions because they were tied down defending the brigade forward base and the battalion firebases. The five that *were* available went in search of the elusive NVA through forests so dense and dark that even in daylight you couldn't see more than fifteen yards in any direction.

Having already identified the key support points of the American operation, the NVA had little trouble finding the stealthier American infantry because they usually arrived on helicopters and could be attacked in their LZs or on the few paths leading away from the LZs; in the unlikely event that VC "trail watchers" lost sight of them, they could be tracked by the support helicopters sent to feed and hydrate the American troops, dropping three-gallon collapsible water containers through the jungle canopy and landing wherever possible to deliver hot meals.[8]

Like Operation Hawthorne, the Paul Revere operations became a series of sharp, disconnected clashes—NVA battalions hitting American companies, NVA companies hitting American platoons, and then running away from the retaliatory fire when it arrived. Tons of shells and bombs fell into the narrow space between the Se San River and the Cambodian border, a major communist infiltration route fitted with base camps, overnight rest areas, bunkers, and a web of "high-speed trails," which were six times wider than a normal one-foot-wide jungle trail and could handle the fast movement of NVA troops and supplies.

But even the high-speed trails, hidden beneath the jungle canopy, were hard to locate. The base areas and rest camps were even more difficult to spot, never on a trail, always fifty yards or more away from it, and well camouflaged with trees and brush and defended by machine gunners in spider holes and bunkers. While the grunts combed through this wilderness looking for the enemy, enemy patrols were always following and reporting the American location, strength, and direction of movement back to higher headquarters with their own radios and landlines.

The Americans were usually stunned by the sudden appearance of battalion-sized enemy units around them. The enemy patrols followed until the Americans stood down for the night and then positioned their infantry and mortars for a devastating attack, usually just after dusk. The communists marked their own lines of attack and retreat with gray telephone wire, and wriggled forward on their bellies to pinpoint the American night position. They quietly snipped the wires to any trip flares and claymores the Americans had placed around their perimeter.[9]

Battles in the field by these small units were confined but ferocious, typified by the attack on two rifle platoons of the US 4th Infantry Division at 6:45 p.m. on October 28 by two NVA companies about forty-five miles west of Pleiku. The fifty Americans were searching for NVA units believed to be massing for an assault on the Special Forces camp at Plei Djereng, and had just halted for the night when 180 North Vietnamese troops, who had been stalking them through the jungle, attacked. Most of the Americans were eating a dinner of C-rations. The daylight security outposts were filing back to the safety of the circular positions chosen by the platoon leaders.

The men assigned to the night listening posts (LPs)—one of the most frightening jobs in Vietnam—were leaving the platoon positions for a sleepless night in a hole beyond the perimeter. Their job was to lie silently in the bamboo thickets on the jungle floor, listening for the preparatory noises of an enemy attack. If the men in an LP heard the enemy approaching, they threw grenades toward the sound, alerting the grunts in the perimeter that an attack was imminent. It was certain death if the LPs revealed their position, so they rarely fired their rifles.[10]

Grunts in the field hastily stringing concertina wire to strengthen their perimeter before nightfall. (National Archives)

The two NVA companies crept unseen to within thirty yards of the perimeter and then fired into the American positions with everything they had—rifles, grenades, and machine guns. In the American night positions, no one panicked. American platoons were far better armed than the enemy. The grunt's basic load was around 400 rounds of M-16 ammo. The three-man M-60 machine gun team humped 1,200 rounds between them. The M-79 grenadiers carried around twenty-four rounds. The M-79 "thumper" fired a 40 mm projectile out to 200 yards, producing a fragmentation pattern 30 feet wide. It could make all the difference in stopping an enemy assault. Man for man, an American unit in Vietnam had at least six times more firepower than enemy units, which had to lug their smaller quantities of ammunition over the paths from Cambodia and Laos, and could not be resupplied by helicopter like the Americans and their free-world allies.

Within five seconds of the initial enemy fusillade, the grunts' outgoing fire was three times heavier than the incoming fire, the infantry buying time while the platoon leaders called for close-in artillery support. Those radio calls were less reliable in terrain like this than on the coastal plains. With forward units separated from brigade headquarters by thirty miles of tall jungle and high hill masses, a lot could go wrong. In the terrifying interval, while the radios crackled quietly, the M-79 grenadiers pumped out high-explosive and shot rounds, and for twenty minutes the two platoons fought for their lives, some of the NVA infantry getting within five yards of the two circular positions.

It was for fights like these that American platoons carried shotguns. No less effective were the young draftees who now made up most of the rifle strength in every platoon. They were intelligent, motivated, resourceful, and in good physical shape. They held the perimeter for twenty minutes, until the first rounds of assault artillery began to impact among the enemy troops closing from the south and east and the attack weakened. The communists pulled back and the Americans counted their casualties—two KIAs and eleven wounded.[11]

At 10 p.m., a medevac chopper thudded overhead to extract the most seriously wounded men. There was no LZ in such a remote place, so the chopper hovered overhead, floodlights on, and lowered a winch through the tree canopy to pull the casualties out. When the last casualty was loaded, an NVA soldier, taking advantage of the deafening noise and the blinding floodlights, fired a rocket-propelled grenade (RPG) into the medevac, which caught fire and fell into the middle of the American position.

While the ship burned, the men on the ground cut the injured pilot and co-pilot out just before the fuel ignited. The wounded were killed in the crash, along with a crew member. All night long the enemy threatened, and was kept back only by continuous fire from the perimeter and by the faraway artillery. In the morning, the two platoons went out to count the enemy dead and found seven corpses and eleven weapons, which was taken to signify a body count of nineteen. With five Americans killed and eight wounded, the kill ratio was not good, and all too typical of the largely forgotten actions like these that were happening all over South Vietnam in 1966.

Operation Paul Revere IV continued in this vein for another two months. For revisionist historians and strategists, who would later argue that the United States should have invaded Cambodia to wipe out the sanctuaries there, it prefigured the extreme difficulty of such a course. American troops, stretched thin in South Vietnam, would have been stretched even thinner if extended into Cambodia. In 1966, Westmoreland admitted as much, officially restricting operations close to the Cambodian border "to retain adequate maneuver and reinforcement flexibility." The Army lacked the resources to carry the war into Cambodia. It was too far from American sources of power and too close to Hanoi's.[12]

The Paul Revere operations were later characterized as "spoiling attacks" and a "reconnaissance in strength," aimed at destroying bunker complexes and trapping and killing as many NVA troops east of the Cambodian border as possible, but the futility was as obvious in this AO as in the others. The enemy avoided American operations, except when vulnerable targets presented themselves, and then reemerged in strength as soon as the Americans left. As one American platoon leader put it: "To win a battle, we had to kill them. For them to win, all they had to do was survive."[13]

At this point, Secretary of Defense McNamara, who had done so much to start the war and only recently had begun to look at it more critically, seemed to give up on it entirely. Returning from a trip to Vietnam in October 1966, he described to the president the failure of Westy's "victory strategy." The communists, the SecDef explained, were thwarting it by dodging the heaviest blows, replacing casualties with infiltration and recruitment, and driving up the mammoth cost of the war for Americans by prolonging it with "a strategy of attriting our *national will*." Westmoreland's claims of progress were mirages: "We control little, if any, more of the population." The number of Viet Cong in South Vietnam had doubled in 1966. Westmoreland's body count totals were massively inflated. McNamara put the rate of inflation at 30 percent. Another study put Westy's rate of inflation at 100 percent. Operation Rolling Thunder, intended to eviscerate North Vietnam's war effort, was a bust. Aid flowing in from Russia and China was "about five times the total damage caused by Rolling Thunder air attacks." Overall, McNamara inclined increasingly to the arguments of his deputy John McNaughton: that the United States had no vital interest at stake, could not dominate Vietnam "at the subnuclear level," and had embarked on "an enormous miscalculation."[14]

Knowing that McNamara was turning against the war and pressing Johnson to place a hard ceiling over rising troop levels in Vietnam, Westmoreland stepped on the gas. In September 1966, Westy had twenty-three operations going, with names like Attleboro, Prairie, Golden Fleece, Hastings, Irving, and Dragon Eye. US aircraft pummeled the South Vietnamese countryside, dropping 175 to 200 tons of bombs every day on friend and foe, for many of the operations were launched in populated areas east of the Central Highlands. This led to a sharp rise in "collateral damage," when hamlets were destroyed, crops burned, and peasants killed in the clumsy effort by the Americans and the ARVN to separate the VC from the villagers.[15]

The VC and NVA often fortified contested hamlets with trenches, bunkers, and tunnels, leaving the Americans and ARVN the choice of assaulting them on the ground or shelling and bombing them. They generally chose the latter, to reduce their own casualties. The VC policed every battlefield after dark and killed any wounded they found, which had a way of discouraging ARVN aggressiveness. The Americans and ARVN preferred to spray any areas suspected of harboring the VC with chemical defoliants, destroying tens of thousands of acres of rice land.[16]

"Only You Can Prevent Forests" was the motto of the "Ranch Hand" pilots—the most shot-at people in the war. Starting in 1965, these American pilots flew the lumbering twin-engine C-123 Providers that cruised at a slow, nearly stalling speed of 130 knots just 150 feet off the ground to spray chemicals onto fields and treetops. A 1,000-gallon load cost $5,000, took four minutes to spray, and killed everything green in a 300-acre area. The Ranch Hands sprayed the perimeters of American airfields and other bases, to create a deeper field of fire, and also sprayed along the edges of roads, railways, and riverbanks, to make it harder for the VC to move and place mines and ambushes. They sprayed all along the DMZ and any jungle trails and truck routes used by North Vietnamese infiltrators. They called what they were doing "removing tropical jungle from the Republic of Vietnam," as if it were crabgrass. They sprayed crops that might feed the VC or NVA—enraging friendly, neutral, and hostile peasants alike. "We are the most hated outfit in Vietnam," a Ranch Hand pilot remarked in July 1966. "Nobody likes to see the trees and crops killed. But we're in a war." Their drinking songs showed as little remorse as that pilot: "See them line up in the market / Waiting for their pound of rice / Hungry, skinny, starving people / Isn't killing harvests nice?"[17]

Each MACV monthly report would puzzlingly present the structures destroyed and the acres poisoned in South Vietnam as indicators of *progress*, as if the people turned out of those blasted deserts would not hate the free-world forces for ruining them. Of the metrics that mattered most—enemy troop totals in South Vietnam, hamlets secured, levels of violence—all of them were running *against* the free-world coalition.

The NVA now had six full divisions operating in South Vietnam with the ability to "launch offensives at any time." In Hanoi, this year of escalating American offensives had featured a fierce debate on strategy between the rival generals of Ho Chi Minh and Le Duan. Ho's general, Vo Nguyen Giap, had deplored the NVA's heavy casualties and pressed for a more cautious, dispersed approach to American firepower. Le Duan's general, COSVN commander Nguyen Chi Thanh, derided "armchair generals" in Hanoi—a not so subtle jab at Giap—and argued that the shortest route to victory was to kill Americans and challenge their "endurance" by waging a "bigger war." There were already 385,000 American troops in Vietnam. The North Vietnamese should make them put in *more*, Thanh insisted. Backed by Le Duan, Thanh's aggressive approach won out. The stars of Ho Chi Minh and Giap, the heroes of the war against the French, continued to wane.[18]

President Johnson nervously authorized yet more troops, but now he placed a ceiling over forces for Vietnam: 470,000 US troops, plus 68,000 coalition forces from South Korea, Australia, New Zealand, the Philippines, and Thailand. An army this size would give Westmoreland thirty-one maneuver battalions for combat in 1967—enough, he hoped, to win before the crisis of pacification collapsed South Vietnam from within.

Westmoreland planned to use his augmented American manpower immediately, battling south to north in the largely dry season that would extend from November 1966 until May 1967, when the monsoons would return, slowing operations and pacification. He'd find and destroy the enemy in the Mekong Delta, III Corps, and the Central Highlands, and then take on the three or four enemy divisions in I Corps—the northern tip of South Vietnam. He'd destroy the enemy with linked offensives, knocking their best sword from their hand.

Westy was somehow encouraged by Operation Attleboro, the two-month struggle around the Michelin Plantation in III Corps, which had ended in November. There the VC 9th Division had stood and fought for a mile-long jungle base camp, taking over a thousand casualties, but killing and wounding 650 Americans. US forces were winning, Westmoreland insisted. The war would be over by the summer of 1967. He sat down for an interview with *Life* magazine in November 1966 and boasted: "We're going to out-guerrilla the guerrilla and out-ambush the ambush...because we're smarter...and we've got more guts."[19]

Westmoreland was clearly in over his head. He could not win the war, or even make progress, so he took refuge in the only thing he knew—combat operations and the data points they generated. But none of it was working. Through the fall and winter of 1966, the American commander kept citing "favorable trends" in battalion days-in-action, kill ratio, force ratio, weapons loss ratio, and body count. And yet Westmoreland had always to admit at the end of his reports that in spite of the favorable trends the number of secured hamlets in every province was still declining, not rising, and that—in what would become a well-worn phrase—"there is no evidence of the collapse of the enemy forces or a cessation of his efforts to dominate the country despite continuous pursuit and losses of men, food, and war materials."[20]

As 1966 ended, the Americans in Vietnam found themselves in a trap. Westy's theory of victory had been to annihilate the VC and NVA with American firepower in 1966–1967 and then "mop up" the shell-shocked remnants in 1968. But the ease with which the Viet Cong penetrated the villages of South Vietnam—controlling and fortifying them in the absence of determined South Vietnamese local defense—meant that American firepower could not be used to maximum effect. "Strategic hamlets" were supposed to have solved the problem, concentrating the rural population in a handful of protected areas, leaving the rest of the country as "strike zones" or "free-fire zones." But these were not without their own problems. "Moving everybody out and then sweeping the place as if it were the Fort Benning battery range," a visitor to Vietnam observed, served only to infuriate the peasants and scourge the landscape.

An American officer who patrolled through a free-fire zone in this period could not believe his eyes: "The earth was churned up by artillery and pocked with huge, water-filled craters from B-52 strikes. Pieces of shrapnel, iridescent with heat scars, glittered underfoot. The dikes had been breached. The paddies were full of brackish water covered by green, undulant slime." And yet there were still *people* living there, he marveled. The villas and hooches were deserted, "but we kept coming across their garbage and cooking fires. Cooking fires—just like a Western." These terrified, hunted people

Singer, actress, and sex symbol Ann-Margret entertaining the troops during Bob Hope's 1966 Christmas Show in Da Nang. (National Archives)

would probably never rally to the Saigon government, for American firepower had confirmed to them all of the propaganda of the VC.[21]

Comedian Bob Hope flew to Saigon for his third Vietnam Christmas Tour in 1966. "What I've seen of the war has turned me into a hawk," he assured the American servicemen lucky enough to catch his show. Seventy-seven-year-old Cardinal Francis Spellman took a turn onstage to remind the troops that they were the "soldiers of Christ." The war, the cardinal said, "is being fought to preserve civilization. Any solution to the war except victory would be inconceivable." But Bob Hope's Christmas show did signal awareness of soft support in America: "If you don't get better ratings," Hope waggishly admonished 20,000 troops gathered at Da Nang, "this whole war may be canceled." But don't worry, he added, "the country is behind you—50 percent."[22]

Chapter 8

JIVE AT FIVE

B ob Hope wasn't wrong. Solid support for the war in Vietnam was beginning to slip as 1966 ended and 1967 began. American draft calls soared, from 231,000 in 1965 to 382,000 in 1966. In 1967, another 300,000 young Americans would open the letter that began: "Greetings: You are hereby ordered for induction in the armed forces of the United States." This was unfamiliar territory for Americans. When JFK had won the White House in 1960, annual draft calls had totaled 86,000. They had quadrupled on Johnson's watch. McNamara had boasted in 1966 that "never before in history has the United States been in better economic position to fulfill its commitments abroad." But limits were emerging.

The escalating war was distracting from all of LBJ's domestic priorities, yet the president's January 1967 State of the Union message offered no relief. LBJ warned America to expect "more cost, more loss, and more agony" in the *years* ahead. "For the end is not yet. I cannot promise that it will come this year—or come next year." The president pleaded for "patience—and I mean a great deal of patience." He confided his strategy, which, to listeners, sounded like the absence of strategy. It was "the strategy of accumulating slowly but inexorably every kind of material resource, and teaching troops the elements of their trade."[1]

The costs were agonizing. Nearly 50,000 Americans had already been killed or wounded in the war. In 1965, President Johnson had spent $103 million on the war. That number had leaped to $6 billion in 1966. The administration had budgeted $10.5 billion for the war in 1967, and now discovered that it would really cost at least $22 billion. Johnson requested a $12.3 billion supplemental for 1967—on top of the $10.5 billion already budgeted—and then asked for another $21.9 billion for 1968. The 1967 federal budget deficit, which Johnson had projected at $1.8 billion, soared to $9 billion thanks to Vietnam.[2]

LBJ dispatched Bob McNamara to Capitol Hill to assure the Senate Armed Services Committee that there would be no more $12 billion surprises. Everything would be more scrupulously budgeted. And yet the aim of all this spending remained abstract. The president still seemed to be "inventing" reasons for America to be in Vietnam. It was hard to discern the vital interest. "We are acting to meet the common danger of aggression," Johnson said. (UN stuff.) "We have chosen to fight a limited war in Vietnam to prevent a larger war" against an emboldened China. (Cold War stuff.) To these intangible objectives, he added another—"an honorable peace."

On January 2, 1967, General Westmoreland sent the Joint Chiefs a memorandum that could only be characterized as despairing. The enemy, Westy wrote, was able to move and shelter with impunity in the DMZ, Laos, and Cambodia. He was able to recruit or infiltrate 12,000 new fighters every *month* in South Vietnam—none of whom could be located. Despite heavy attrition and high kill ratios, there were 42,000 more communist troops in South Vietnam on New Year's Day 1967 than there had been 365 days earlier. Enemy attacks on US forces had more than doubled in the same period.

"Hanoi's counter-buildup," Westy continued, had thwarted his search and destroy strategy by negating the effects of attrition. You could never grind all of the meat in a pile if someone kept adding to the pile. The White House's attempt to stop Hanoi from adding to the pile by bombing more targets in North Vietnam availed nothing. Ho Chi Minh, coached by Le Duan, rejected a personal appeal from President Johnson for "direct talks" to end the war in February 1967. The communist counterbuildup, which could be indefinitely sustained by the youthful Vietnamese population, portended a war that might go on forever. Westmoreland called for a new strategy, one based not on attrition but on decisive maneuver *beyond* the borders of South Vietnam.[3]

Westmoreland was returning to the strategy he had mentioned in his "Commander's Estimate" of 1965. He now sought 206,000 additional troops so that he could mass at least three US divisions around Khe Sanh and move them twenty-seven miles west into Laos on Route 9 to seize and hold Xepon, a key crossroads of the Ho Chi Minh Trail.

Westy expressed frustration with the reactive and political way in which the war was being managed in Washington. In a memo he prepared on February 3, 1967, he criticized the "amazing lack of initiative in planning for the future in higher echelons of government" and a no less "amazing lack of boldness in our approach to the future." He complained that in his conversations with the president and the SecDef, the two civilians dwelled on the length and cost of the war but shrank from giving him additional means to win it, insisting that he make do with a maximum of 470,000 troops.[4]

Westmoreland felt betrayed by these cautious civilians. The way to beat Hanoi and the insurgency, he now argued, was to seize their Laotian and Cambodian trails and sanctuaries. This would restrict the flow of NVA infiltrators and supplies and isolate the VC inside South Vietnam. For such an operation, which Westmoreland planned to augment with an amphibious hook around the DMZ to pin Hanoi's reserves inside North Vietnam, he would need to lift the troop ceiling from 470,000 to nearly 700,000.

The earliest Westy could have launched such an operation—if a troop surge had been approved—would have been late 1968. But even if Johnson had wanted to implement Westy's new plan, he would have struggled to do so. Without activating the reserves, it was impossible to surge forces quickly in Vietnam. There was always a yearlong lag as new forces were budgeted, and then drafted, trained, and eventually deployed. LBJ and McNamara tried to make a virtue of this sluggishness, describing it as yet another facet of "graduated response," but it made American military execution in Vietnam balky and slow. In the "stay loose" days of 1965, Westmoreland had promised to win the war by 1967. Exposed to reality in the months since, he now pledged to win it by 1972—at the earliest.[5]

General George C. Marshall had famously said after World War II that "a democracy cannot fight a Seven Years' War." Westy was embarked on just that sort of conflict, but he saw no other way than to keep going and *intensifying* the war. Combat would continue to sputter and would become "unreasonably protracted," he warned, unless President Johnson took the gloves off and went all in. Westy wanted those 206,000 additional troops and authorization to strike into Laos, Cambodia, and North Vietnam in order to increase pressure on Hanoi, cut the supply routes south, and attack the communist sanctuaries in a war-terminating "exploitation phase." The communists would be starved of resources, run to ground, and destroyed. Westy called this a "two-fisted strategy." Punch North Vietnam with one fist, flattening every important target in Hanoi–Haiphong and launching an amphibious attack north of the DMZ. Invade and destroy Hanoi's Cambodian and Laotian sanctuaries with the other fist.[6]

General Earle Wheeler, after a visit to Saigon in February 1967, heard Westy's plan and returned to Washington brimming with optimism. "The adverse military tide has been reversed," he assured LBJ. "The enemy can no longer hope to win the war. General Westmoreland now has the initiative," Wheeler declared. "We can *win* the war if we apply pressure upon the enemy relentlessly in North and South."[7]

As always with Westmoreland and Wheeler, there was an air of fantasy, wishful thinking, and mendacity about their plan. Westy kept insisting that the ARVN was getting better under his watch. But if that were so, why did he need 206,000 more American troops? "Every time Westy makes a speech about how good the South Vietnam army is," one American general grumbled to a reporter, "I want to ask him why he keeps calling for more *Americans*. His need for reinforcements is a measure of our failure with the Vietnamese."[8]

Westy had not dented the NVA's resolve in South Vietnam, had made no progress in pacification, and could not even eliminate communist sanctuaries inside South Vietnam, such as the ungoverned A Shau Valley in I Corps, which ran along the Laotian border, harbored roads and supply dumps of the Ho Chi Minh Trail, and had been under North Vietnamese control for *years* while the Marines chased breathlessly around the rest of I Corps on indecisive search and destroy operations. And yet here Westy was, two years in, arguing—with a straight face—that by adding just 206,000 troops he could finally "go for broke" and win in South Vietnam, Laos, and Cambodia, and even throw in an "Inchon-like" amphibious attack around the DMZ and into North Vietnam "once I Corps was cleaned up." Even a hawk like Walt Rostow, who had replaced McGeorge Bundy as national security adviser, was unimpressed. Westy's plan, Rostow said, was like "ladling some water out of the bath tub while the tap is still turned on."[9]

In Saigon too, leading minds were turning against search and destroy. Ambassador Lodge had so soured on the countrywide scourge of attrition strategy that he contemplated resigning and publicly protesting Westy's conduct of the war in early 1967. General Fred Weyand, who commanded II Field Force, the US corps around Saigon, also dissented from search and destroy, arguing that "the key to the war was in providing security to the villages and towns of Vietnam." To muffle these dissident voices, Westy relied increasingly on an in-country PR machine known as JUSPAO—the Joint United States Public Affairs Office—to sell his high-intensity big-unit war.

JUSPAO was run by Barry "Zorro" Zorthian, a colonel in the Marine Corps Reserve, who had his own office building on Avenue Le Loi, where, in the second-floor auditorium, the Saigon press pool was invited to daily briefings so content-free that they were known as the "Jive at Five" or the "Five o'Clock Follies."

Ward Just called the five o'clock briefing "an articulate framework for the half-coherent mumblings of officials and their dramatists." The dramatists were colonels, a ground briefer and an air briefer, who would pass out three handouts—one from each service—and then stand behind a lectern on a well-lit stage and describe "the last 24 hours of free-world military activity." The colonels were understood by all present to be, as one of their own put it, "leading graduates of the Pentagon school of escape and evasion." Nothing significant or controversial was divulged or explained. Ops were just "continuing." Body count was recited, along with sorties flown and artillery missions fired. Some battles went entirely unreported.[10]

The press found it hard to come up with anything to write about. Every op seemed the same: grunts sweeping an area and making contact, or not. This gave rise among the reporters to a yearning for any kind of "first," "most," or "least"—something fresh to put in a headline. They called it the "left-handed battalion commander syndrome," as in "for the first time, a left-handed battalion commander led the outfit into battle." Most of the reporters understood that they were being gamed—forced, as Ward Just put it, to count "angels dancing on the heads of pins."[11]

Real information on the war was hard to come by. MACV's press center was, as one reporter put it, "nothing but a huge fact-suppression machine." The journalists were made to debate abstract trivia—the accuracy of body and weapons counts, or the precise location of search and destroy missions.

MACV briefings, one reporter wrote, provided "an articulate framework for the half-coherent mumblings of officials and their dramatists." Nothing significant or controversial was divulged or explained. (National Archives)

There were all sorts of taboos. MACV briefers were forbidden to use the word "napalm." They referred instead to "soft ordnance."

These insipid briefings were what gave Americans at home, reading the paper or watching the news, their narrow and sanitized view of the war. At least one reporter found it curious that American media took MACV's briefings and communiqués seriously while dismissing each of Hanoi's radio broadcasts and press releases as useless propaganda. Were they that different? The more enterprising American reporters left Saigon and went into the field to discover the truth. Vietnam was the last war in American history where journalists could go wherever they could find a truck or heli-copter willing to take them.[12]

Stripped of spin, the counterarguments to Westmoreland's "two-fisted strategy" wrote themselves. How would the general cope with all of the new territorial responsibilities and casualties, plus the international odium of invading technically neutral countries and bombing the densely populated

Hanoi-Haiphong area? Laos had been neutralized by agreement of the major powers in July 1962, but the North Vietnamese had ignored the requirement to withdraw their forces from Laos. They had seized additional territory in the intervening years, all the way down to the vital crossroads of Xepon, which extended the Ho Chi Minh Trail's reach into South Vietnam.

The four Laotian factions that had made peace in July 1962 had gone back to war with each other ninety days later, with the Hanoi-backed communist Pathet Lao gaining the upper hand. President Kennedy had authorized a CIA-run "secret war" to battle the Pathet Lao and NVA supply routes in 1962. The secret war had continued under LBJ, arming one of Laos' ethnic minorities, the Hmong, and setting them against the communists in tandem with undisclosed American bombing. One-fourth of the Hmong population would die in this so-called secret war—most of the 15,000-man army and a large part of the 300,000 or so Hmong refugees who were brutally driven from their villages by the inevitable communist reprisals.

The irony, an American journalist among the Hmong observed, was that the power that Washington gave the Hmong and other mountain tribes in weapons and aid was their downfall: "It made them a force the North Vietnamese *had* to crush" to maintain their sanctuaries and trails in Laos. And after the defeat of the Hmong army, Washington had shot its bolt. With the cost of the war in Vietnam already wildly out of control, nothing bigger than this failed and tragic proxy war in Laos could be contemplated.[13]

Westmoreland, egged on by the Joint Chiefs, nevertheless contemplated something much grander for Laos. Yet each of Westy's proposed operations into Laos to hit Hanoi's sanctuaries and supply routes looked hopeless on its face. There was another seventy miles of Laotian territory west of Xepon—the road hub that the NVA had seized in 1962. Why wouldn't the NVA simply detour around American troops inserted into Xepon? If they did, how many more American or ARVN divisions would be required to pursue them deeper into Laos and its proliferating "liberated zones," which was what Hanoi called its trails and sanctuaries in Laos?

And who was going to *pay* for all of those new US troops in Vietnam and Laos? McNamara put the two-year cost of even a modest troop surge at $15 billion, in a war that was already costing $20 to $25 billion a year.[14]

In all, Westy was requesting four new infantry divisions and thirteen new tactical fighter squadrons for a new "optimal force ceiling" of 670,000 troops. Always a pleaser, he included a "minimal force" option of two additional divisions with smaller Air Force and Navy elements—100,000 additional troops—but noted that those troops would be sufficient only to defend areas already cleared of communist troops, not to execute the "decisive" cross-border maneuvers.

Both requests were massive asks of a beleaguered and war-weary president who was struggling to find ways to pay for the troops he already had in Vietnam, let alone 206,000 new ones. In his January 1967 State of the Union address, Johnson asked Congress to pass an immediate 6 percent surtax on personal and corporate incomes to pay for the war, but Congress, where forty-seven House seats and three Senate seats had flipped Republican in the 1966 midterms, balked. Wilbur Mills, the Democratic chair of the House Ways and Means Committee, refused even to consider new taxes for the war until Johnson scaled back the Great Society.[15]

With Westmoreland beginning to assail the administration's lack of boldness, LBJ flew out to Guam to meet the general for a day of meetings on the war in the last week of March 1967. Crammed into the Guam officers' club, rain drumming on the roof, speakers paused each time a B-52 noisily took off for Vietnam or roared in for a landing. Westy warned that though progress was being made, the war would probably go on "indefinitely" unless the VC fell apart or Hanoi withdrew its backing, both unlikely scenarios. He was fighting "bullies" and "termites" at the same time. "It will take time and patience" to beat them both. With Gallup polls registering a steady decline in his approval rating, LBJ pleaded with Westy for signs of progress. Are we winning? the president implored. "Yes sir," we are, Westy assured him.[16]

Westmoreland, impatient with the apathy of the ARVN as well as LBJ's limits on the war, could only hope that the casualties he was inflicting on the communists with search and destroy would cause them to give up. American intelligence on North Vietnam and its capabilities was patchy at best, but what MACV and the CIA did know in early 1967 was that the American war effort was worrying leaders in Hanoi, as well as the commander of the communist forces in the South, General Nguyen Chi Thanh. Thanh had earlier challenged Defense Minister Giap and pressed for a "bigger war" in the South. But the casualties inflicted by American firepower had become so horrific that the two generals mended fences and agreed that something new had to be attempted to lengthen the war and stanch the bloodletting.[17]

Ho Chi Minh's communist Workers' Party Central Committee met for several days in late January 1967 and concluded that the military outlook was grim. The party needed a quick and decisive victory to return the country to peace and prosperity, but the Americans weren't cooperating. The seemingly limitless power of the United States worried the communist leadership. American bombers were hitting North Vietnam with 1,000 tons of high explosive every day, blowing away bridges, cratering roads, and incinerating fuel and supply depots. American ground troops in South Vietnam, who had launched over a dozen major search and destroy operations in 1966 and had many more scheduled for 1967, made it impossible to win on the ground. They were killing more communist troops every year than the United States had lost in the entire three-year Korean War, and even the best NVA units could not maintain a battalion in the field for more than twenty-four hours once it had been located and targeted by American air strikes and artillery.

This is why Bernard Fall had judged Westmoreland's war "unlosable"— not because Westmoreland was a brilliant commander, but because, as Fall put it, "there is *so much* of everything available in Vietnam that almost any kind of military error, no matter how stupid, can be retrieved on the rebound."[18]

The Rolling Thunder air attacks—in the DMZ, eastern Laos, and the Hanoi-Haiphong region—were further eroding the communist war effort, and could be intensified and expanded on a presidential whim. The only leverage Hanoi had was the fact that the grisly war was never popular in the United States and among America's allies. By 1967, there were regular antiwar rallies in Lafayette Park, across from the White House, where protesters would gather to chant "Hey, hey, LBJ, how many babies did you kill today?" It had been a year since the president's confidant Jack Valenti had warned LBJ that the war was raising "walls of hate" inside America, and the walls were rising higher every year.

Hanoi's communist Central Committee resolved to keep doing what it had been doing for years—fighting on "three fronts," military, political, and diplomatic. Wins in the military and political realm inside South Vietnam would provide leverage in diplomacy. One insight the North Vietnamese had was to use diplomacy—the quest for peace—in an "innovative" way. They would launch a global information campaign to blacken the reputation of the United States and vaunt their own virtues—a rugged little postcolonial nation fighting for survival against a violent neocolonial superpower. They dared not mention their own tyrannical methods, nor did they have good answers to American airpower, and so they grimly settled on the line that there would be no negotiations with the Americans until President Johnson ordered a halt to all bombing north of the 17th parallel.[19]

For now, at least, that wasn't happening. Johnson had conceded a thirty-seven-day bombing halt in late December 1965 and received nothing in return. He was not about to offer another pause now that Westmoreland and the Joint Chiefs smelled blood. "The primary role of U.S. forces in 1967," Westmoreland declared, "will continue to be the destruction of enemy main-force units." To those who had expected a turn away from search and destroy toward pacification, Westmoreland temporized: "Accenting search and destroy missions simultaneously provides the conditions that would be conducive to pacification," he assured Washington. Large concentrations of US forces near priority areas for pacification would miraculously "enhance security," where actual South Vietnamese troops *in* those areas had not. By this stage of the war, few were fooled by such transubstantiation. It was the usual MACV legerdemain. High-intensity operations and pacification were two different animals, requiring entirely different structures and methods.[20]

Belatedly it dawned on the White House that whatever was happening in Westmoreland's big-unit war, good or ill, the United States was definitely losing the "other war"—the struggle for the security, hearts, and minds of the South Vietnamese people. Saigon controlled about 60 percent of the South Vietnamese people for no other reason than that they lived in the big cities, provincial capitals, and refugee centers, and were easier to police and defend. The remaining 40 percent of the country's population was contested—22 percent under outright VC control, and 18 percent in areas that were up for grabs.[21]

The Saigon government in 1967 controlled only 1,944 of the nation's 12,537 rural hamlets—fewer than one in six. Little effort was made to tackle the other five-sixths. Instead, MACV and Saigon set their sights on another one-sixth, about 1,100 hamlets in forty-four provinces, and named them "national priority areas." Even this modest ambition proved too much. In late 1967, pacification ran behind schedule in twenty-six of the forty-four provinces, and pacification workers and cadres proved as hard to keep in the ranks as the ARVN. They were being killed by the VC at the rate of fifteen a week and complained that the fifty-three ARVN battalions deployed to protect them did not protect them at all.

Often the Viet Cong spared the pacification official but murdered or mutilated his wife, children, and parents to underscore the point that resistance was futile and costly. Corpses of the official or his family members would be found with torturing wounds—bullets through the palms and soles of the feet, breasts hacked off, and a note like this one stabbed into the body: "Tuan Cao Ky has been found guilty by the People's Court of aiding the American imperialists in their suppression of the Vietnamese people. This is the justice that will be brought to all who consort with Americans." Under pressure like this, pacification cadres, recruited and trained at great cost, were deserting at higher rates than the armed forces, with thirteen of every hundred workers walking off the job in 1967.[22]

One American official estimated that, given the brutality, tenacity, and mobility of the communists, it would take 8 *million* allied troops to clear and hold all of South Vietnam, a country the size of Montana. That was why pacification was so important. It was the only way to win without that 8-million-man army—by turning local security over to the locals and making *them* defeat the communists. But to make the locals defend themselves, you had to kindle a spirit of resistance. That had to come from within. It clearly wasn't. So, like everything else, President Johnson decided to impose it from without. He would remove pacification from South Vietnamese hands and Americanize it too.[23]

In early 1967, LBJ appointed White House special assistant Robert Komer to be Westy's deputy for pacification in MACV. "Blowtorch Bob" Komer, a graduate of Harvard Business School, created an entirely new bureaucracy, which was called Civil Operations and Revolutionary Development Support, or CORDS for short. The idea behind CORDS was that it would take the pacification support mission, which previously had been handled by the ARVN, the US embassy, and various civilian agencies, and place it under "single-manager" MACV control.[24]

The forty-five-year-old Komer would receive ambassadorial rank—equivalent to four stars—and a rung on the MACV ladder just below

Westmoreland and right beside Westy's military deputy, General Creighton Abrams. This militarized CORDS would bring together 6,500 personnel from the armed services plus the State Department, CIA, USAID, USIA, and White House, and put them to work training South Vietnam's militia forces and pacification workers and devising better ways to evaluate and secure hamlets that lived in the shadow of the VC.[25]

Komer created a computerized Hamlet Evaluation System, which would rate every hamlet and village in South Vietnam not under VC control on eighteen criteria. Each of the senior US military advisers in the four South Vietnamese corps areas would get a new civilian CORDS deputy to energize and drive pacification. And yet the most common complaint—that ARVN and militia forces were not providing real security—was not addressed. Westmoreland promised no more than 15,000 US troops for pacification, not enough to make a dent in the problem.[26]

CORDS became as unwieldy and disappointing as the joint US-ARVN military effort. It brought an alphabet soup of agency programs under Bob Komer's management: Revolutionary Development, refugee management, the Chieu Hoi program, USAID's New Life Development, the CIA's Census Grievance program, Montagnard recruitment, MACV's Civic Action and Civil Affairs programs, JUSPAO's Field Psychological Operations or "psyops," and the militia forces, which were officially renamed Regional Forces/Popular Forces (RF/PF) and nicknamed "ruff-puffs" by their advisers. The 6,500 American CORDS personnel managed by Bob Komer were expected to drive pacification and establish a school for the South Vietnamese pacification workers, who were given the name "Revolutionary Development cadres."

The cadres, young people taken from the same draft pool used by the ARVN, the ruff-puffs, and the National Police were generally mediocre, for manpower priority was always given to the armed forces. Cadres would train for ninety days at a central Revolutionary Development (RD) school, and then be placed in a fifty-nine-man team and sent to work for six months in one of two situations, either a hamlet under "construction" or a hamlet undergoing "consolidation." Construction meant bringing a hamlet under government control. Consolidation meant taking a hamlet that had slipped from government control back to secured status.

The fifty-nine-man teams were expected to secure only two hamlets a year—"by far the most realistic target ever set in Vietnam," a British observer drily noted. They had groups for militia, reconstruction, and development. The first group trained the ruff-puffs, the second group documented and administered the local population, weeding out the VC and talking up the achievements of the Saigon government, and the third group undertook land reform, medical care, farming assistance, and public works.

Like Westmoreland's big-unit operations, Komer's CORDS quickly became a sink of computerized nonsense and obfuscation. Blowtorch Bob's obsession with appearances and good numbers undercut progress toward real achievements. In 1967, 60 percent of Westy's operations were search and destroy. The other 40 percent were pacification and local security operations to aid CORDS. But the latter two operations ended up looking like the first, for the simple reason that commanders emphasized "security"—of their own troops and base camps—and launched spoiling attacks to achieve it, further alienating locals, who could not see how search and destroy differed from pacification. Once ushered into the field, CORDS teams avoided the hamlets under VC control and never stayed more than six months in the "contested" ones, which was not enough time to make a difference against a patient adversary like the Viet Cong.[27]

Yet US advisers in the program had no trouble manipulating numbers that were difficult to verify and usually meaningless. The measure of success for "secured hamlets" was a census of all inhabitants, destruction of VC infrastructure, creation of an intelligence net to give early warning of a VC return, ruff-puffs recruited and trained, hamlet chiefs selected, peasant grievances heard, village elections held, and economic and social development projects initiated. All of these "achievements" could be "scored" on a computer punch card, which they inevitably were. Emphasis could easily be placed on form over function. A pacified Potemkin village could hide VC cadres on its outskirts waiting to move back in at night or at the end of six months.[28]

With both pacification and search and destroy failing, Westmoreland sought desperately for what he called an "Achilles heel" in the enemy effort. In 1967, he thought he had found it: the enemy's supply system. Without pre-positioned food, ammo, and medicine, the enemy could not operate in

South Vietnam. So Westy made plans to attack the VC supply lines in 1967 and wipe out the most critical enemy base areas that fed the fighting in the four corps areas. "If we can neutralize the enemy base areas and prevent replenishment of the material captured or destroyed, we will have taken a long stride toward ultimate victory," Westy assured President Johnson and the Joint Chiefs.[29]

The most notorious enemy base area of all was the aptly named "Iron Triangle"—210 square miles of VC-controlled territory just twenty-five miles northwest of Saigon. Communist insurgents had been installed in this forested wedge of land between the Saigon and Thi Tinh Rivers since the 1940s. The Triangle was dotted here and there with monuments to French units that had been ambushed by the Viet Minh in the decade after World War II whenever they went in to clean it out. Three American divisions had been roughed up here a year earlier during Operation Attleboro.

But with the Americans able to rake the whole region with artillery and air strikes, most of the VC activity, previously run from communist camps in the rubber plantations of the Iron Triangle, had gone entirely underground in tunnel complexes such as Cu Chi, which contained barracks, headquarters, field hospitals, kitchens, and arsenals. The villages and hamlets of the Iron Triangle were entirely under VC control and well supplied from a VC base area called War Zone C, which spread from the Iron Triangle west to the Cambodian border.

To remove the threat once and for all, Westmoreland again resorted to technology. This time he wouldn't search for the enemy with small patrols; instead, he would trap and kill them like rats in a cellar. In the last weeks of 1966, MACV had put finishing touches to Westy's most ambitious operation yet. He would surround the Triangle in January 1967 with twenty-eight combat battalions and twenty-five artillery batteries—a force of 30,000 men and 140 howitzers. Then he would unleash the B-52s to pound the Triangle with bombing to collapse the tunnels, which ran twelve to twenty feet underground. When the B-52s weren't overhead, artillery barrages and tac air strikes would pummel the Iron Triangle, to prevent the VC from moving around or escaping. After a week of this, Westy would launch Operation Cedar Falls on January 8, 1967.

On the appointed day, General Fred Weyand's US 25th Infantry Division and the 196th Light Infantry Brigade held the base of the triangle,

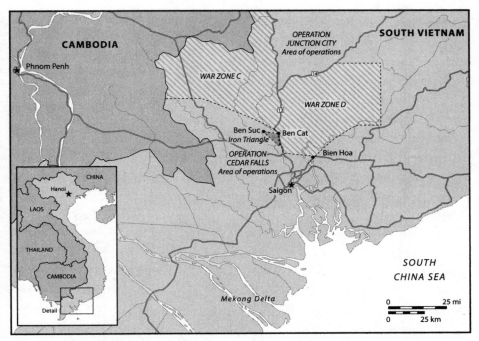

Operations Cedar Falls and Junction City

formed by the Saigon River, while General Bill DePuy's US 1st Infantry Division (nicknamed "the Big Red One") and the 173rd Airborne Brigade, reinforced by tanks of the 11th Armored Cavalry Regiment, struck the northern and eastern faces of the triangle. The 1st ID moved into Ben Suc to begin rolling up any Viet Cong who remained alive. Loudspeaker helicopters flew overhead ordering the population of 3,500 to remain in their huts: "Anyone seen running away will be considered Viet Cong."[30]

Eighty bulldozers were flown in, dangling from the bellies of Chinook and Skycrane helicopters. They set down to begin ripping out the jungle that provided cover to the enemy. They were followed by flamethrower tanks and infantry units that burned everything: huts, hamlets, and felled trees, as well as the 3,200 tons of rice found hidden in caches. The villagers were rounded up—women, children, and old men, not a young man among them—and shipped downstream to a refugee camp. Then the B-52s returned to bomb the scourged Iron Triangle again and collapse any tunnels still intact.

Twenty-three-year-old reporter Jonathan Schell, who poked through the ash and dust of Ben Suc, was struck by the madness of what his compatriots were doing: "The unmistakable fact was that the general population despised the United States and if they hadn't despised it before we arrived, they despised it after we destroyed their villages. The more we'd win on the battlefield, the more we lost the political war."[31]

Bernard Fall, who interviewed one of the American brigade commanders as he prepared to pull the infantry out, asked why the Americans weren't planning to hold the Iron Triangle after so much effort had been expended clearing it. "We just haven't got the troops to stay here, and the Arvins simply won't," the general sighed. "In other words," Fall clarified, "the VC will move right back in again?" "Sure," replied the general, "but we'll have helicopter LZs all over the place. Next time's going to be easier to get back in." This American assumption that there would be a "next time," that American troops could be ordered into the same places again and again to fight the same battles and take the same heavy casualties—400 Americans killed and wounded in this operation—clashed with American reality, where pressure was increasing on the home front to obtain results or terminate the war.[32]

Jonathan Schell's coverage of Operation Cedar Falls filled the *New Yorker*'s July 15, 1967, edition, and would shortly become a 130-page book. The last time the magazine had devoted an entire issue to a single article had been 1946, when it had published John Hersey's "Hiroshima." Schell, like Hersey, shined a light on the ethics of what the Americans were doing with their firepower advantage: "Having once decided to destroy it, we were now bent on annihilating every possible indication that the village of Ben Suc had ever existed."[33]

Bernard Fall interviewed a VC prisoner taken in the operation, who seemed unfazed by his "defeat" and hopeful for the future: "Do the Americans think they can stay with this kind of war for 30, 40 years? Because that is what it is going to take." Seven hundred and fifty enemy were killed and large caches of food, ammunition, and weapons were captured. Half a million enemy documents were seized, among them one confirming that entertainer Bob Hope had been the target of the Brink Hotel bombing two years earlier. But MACV's claim that "the Iron Triangle is no more" was plainly false. The area had been the headquarters of communist efforts against Saigon since the 1940s, and would be again. Just days after the conclusion of Cedar Falls, the Iron Triangle returned to VC control. "It was literally crawling with what appeared to be VC," an American observer noted.[34]

At home in the United States, Cedar Falls was a PR disaster, for the op had been preceded by the destruction of the villages from the air and the forced evacuation of about 6,000 inhabitants to the squalid Phu Loi refugee camp on the outskirts of Saigon. There had been scenes of bedlam inside the Triangle as the refugees struggled to avoid being sent to the camp. Like all villagers, they had buried their life savings in earthenware jars to avoid VC taxation and ARVN looting, and they now had to assume that all was lost. "Even as the last of the evicted still poked around their wood and thatched huts assembling their belongings, U.S. troops began to burn and bulldoze their villages to the ground," *Newsweek* reported. It was in this climate of misery that the Democratic chairman of the Senate Foreign Relations Committee, J. William Fulbright, published his book *The Arrogance of Power*, sharply disputing the American tendency, as the senator put it, "to equate power with virtue."[35]

Cedar Falls was followed by the biggest American offensive of the entire war: Operation Junction City, which began in February 1967, after the number of US troops in South Vietnam had reached the magic figure of 500,000, which Westmoreland reasoned was sufficient for a year of what he hoped would be annihilating offensives against the outgunned enemy. Junction City was the mother of all operations to come, for Westmoreland saw it as a model for attacks on base areas and an essential first step in a steady south-to-north reconquest of South Vietnam. Like most Vietnam operations, it was long, lasting eighty-two days. And it was big—45,000 troops, a three-division operation aimed at securing the northwestern wedge of III Corps along the Cambodian border, the same AO worked over by Operation Attleboro in 1966.[36]

With this bigger operation, Westmoreland planned to pivot on the Cambodian border, clean out VC base areas, and continue pressing north. Operation Junction City would try to locate and seize COSVN, the "VC Pentagon" that the communists called the B-2 Front headquarters. COSVN was correctly believed to be somewhere around Tay Ninh City, employing an estimated 2,000 staff to coordinate NVA and VC operations. Junction City was a classic Westmoreland search and destroy operation, and it targeted the III Corps area with troops from some of the same US 1st and 25th Infantry Division units involved in Attleboro and Cedar Falls plus the US 4th ID and several battalions of ARVN Rangers and Marines.

It was a hammer and anvil operation, with eight US battalions deploying in a horseshoe-shaped cordon on the northern edge of III Corps' War Zone C while two brigades of American infantry pushed whatever they found in the rough terrain south of the horseshoe north and into the blocking position near the Cambodian border. The two brigades worked their way toward the anvil in the last week of February and found...nothing. They reported fifty-four enemy KIA and twenty-eight friendlies, not an acceptable "kill ratio." The enemy *had* been there—the grunts found bunkers, tunnels, underground chambers, and sixteen base camps sized for regiments, battalions, and companies, but no enemy troops.

This was the pattern in the war. Tipped off before the hammer fell by American movements and VC agents in Saigon and the various ARVN headquarters, the communists had dispersed to avoid contact. In the rough, wooded country, they had found it easy to break into small parties and slip through the paradropped and heliborne American cordons. Compared to Americans, who traveled "heavy" with over 100 pounds of noisy gear—rifle, helmet, flak jacket, ammo pouches, grenades, knife, canteens, first-aid and gun-cleaning kits, sunscreen, mosquito repellent, and cans of food and

Men of the 196th Light Infantry Brigade waiting to lift into a VC-occupied area during Operation Junction City, April 1967. (National Archives)

foot powder—the NVA and VC traveled light, carrying little besides their weapon, ammo pouch, a change of clothes, a hammock, a poncho, a water bottle, and a ball of cooked rice. They could slip through cordons as quietly as ghosts.[37]

The grunts then fanned out to east and west, searching for the enemy. Sixty-nine B-52 strikes were called in to pulverize any area suspected of harboring communist troops. The strikes killed enemy troops in the open and flattened their bunkers, but many of the bombs bounced around in the jungle canopy and fell to the ground without exploding, providing the VC, who had learned to recycle "dud" artillery rounds as booby traps in their war with the French, with a new source of explosive charges for the "emplaced munitions" they rigged in the path of every American and ARVN operation.[38]

American infantry encountered these booby traps everywhere—in captured rice caches, on roads and trails, in huts, beneath enemy corpses, and in trees and bushes. If you spent enough time in the field, one would find you, as one found forty-year-old Bernard Fall, by this time a professor and acclaimed analyst of the war, during his sixth trip to Vietnam in 1967. Fall was trudging along Route 1 north of Hue with a US Marine unit when he, or the Marine beside him, stepped on a booby trap, killing them both.

Whole fields could be sown with dozens of dud artillery rounds or aerial bombs fitted with electrical detonators. A weary grunt, who might already have stepped over a tripwire fastened to a bomb and chosen not to open a gate pressed shut with a firing device, could as easily be killed by a tiny fishhook dangling from a tree branch or the narrow opening in a hedgerow. If the hook snagged his shirt, pants, or helmet cover, his next step would pull the tension wire tight and explode the charge hidden in the brush. Afterward, the man would be dead or maimed, his belongings scattered among his amputated body parts and uniform scraps. "Nothing could prepare you for the sight of the mangled bodies," a nurse recalled. Many of the victims would be triaged, labeled "expectant" (as in expected to die), medicated, washed, and left behind a screen to perish. Those who went under the knife often had wounds so big and ghastly that surgeons had no name for the operations they were performing. They called them "horridzomas" or "horriblectomies."[39]

A second monthlong phase of Operation Junction City commenced on March 18, 1967, this time with thirty battalions, and it too disappointed. The searching American brigades found the enemy only where he elected to appear, in battalion-strength assaults to cover the retreat to Cambodia of the NVA 9th Division. More evidence of the tactical cunning of the VC emerged in the fighting. They cut fire lanes in the thick jungle growth just a few inches above the ground. As the taller Americans approached, hacking with their machetes and not noticing the fire lanes at their feet, the VC would open up, hitting the Americans in the legs. When the Americans fell to the ground to save themselves, they exposed their heads and torsos to the concentrated fire of the VC automatic weapons.

The enemy booby-trapped LZs, sowing the clearings with mines, tripwires, and punji stakes. If lift commanders paused between prep fires and landing to mark an LZ with smoke, the enemy, who was always monitoring the American and ARVN radio frequencies, would race back to the LZ and fire on the grunts when they were most vulnerable: framed in the doors of the hovering slicks, trying to get off. Or the enemy would simply pop smoke where *he* was, luring the slicks into a perfect ambush. For this reason, grunts had to carry smoke grenades in four colors—red, yellow, green, and purple—so that the aircraft commanders could call the color before shooting the approach, defeating this latest enemy deception.[40]

The major fights that developed during Operation Junction City were initiated by the communists. The platoons of a US 25th ID company were guided through heavy jungle to a VC base camp by an aerial observer, who failed to spot a waiting ambush by an entire VC battalion. The American company, completely surrounded, was saved by close artillery fire and the arrival of a second American company that had to hack its way through a half mile of jungle. The only other major action was at a place called Suoi Tre on March 21, 1967, where the 272nd Regiment of the VC 9th Division, undiminished by Operation Attleboro, massed six battalions of infantry and a regiment of artillery to hit the Americans as they pushed closer to the Cambodian border sanctuaries. The battle, a rare daytime operation by the VC, targeted American troops when they were most exposed, lifting into areas that had been cleared during Operation Attleboro but were already back in enemy hands.

The first choppers that landed on March 19 in the football-field-sized clearing at Suoi Tre were met by command-detonated mines that destroyed three Hueys, damaged thirteen others, and killed or wounded forty-three Americans. Four hundred and fifty American troops arrived in the course of the day along with eighteen 105 mm howitzers. The troops spent most of that day and the next building a firebase and arranging the guns in a circle inside the perimeter.

The 2,500 men of the VC 272nd Regiment struck at 6:30 a.m. on March 21, first firing a barrage of 1,000 mortar rounds, recoilless rifle fire, and RPGs. They then attacked for four hours in groups of 200. The startled defenders of the newly constructed FSB Gold gave up the outer perimeter and retreated into a tightening circle around the emplaced guns, firing with their rifles and machine guns at the VC, who were seen climbing over the abandoned bunker line to reach them.

Eleven of the eighteen howitzers placed the day before were knocked out. Those that survived lowered their barrels to zero elevation and fired "beehive rounds"—a special shell for point-blank combat like this. Each beehive round contained 8,000 steel darts or flechettes that sprayed into the enemy in a shotgun-like burst. Many of the VC killed that day were later found with their hands and arms nailed to their faces and chests by the flechettes. American F-4 Phantom jets, scrambled from Bien Hoa air base, dropped napalm all around the shrinking perimeter. Howitzers from two neighboring firebases fired barrages that crept right into the LZ, where the VC pushed to within fifteen yards of the battalion command post.

FSB Gold was nearly wiped out. Half of the defenders were killed or wounded. A battalion of the US 25th ID sweeping the area west of the firebase to find sites for additional LZs was called back to rescue the two besieged infantry companies and their battalion of artillery. It took them three hours to hack a path through a jungle infested with snipers and ambush groups. Most of the men in that relief column, like most of the men inside FSB Gold, were draftees who had never seen battle before. One of them recalled being amazed by the sound of the fighting at Suoi Tre, even from a mile away: "I was overwhelmed by the noise emanating from the battle site. I thought to myself, 'Wow, imagine what it was like on D-Day if this battle is producing such devastating sounds.'"[41]

The tanks and armored personnel carriers (APCs) of an armored battalion south of FSB Gold lost valuable time searching for a suitable place to cross the Suoi Samat River and also arrived just in the nick of time, when the VC battalions were seen prodding their walking wounded into the front lines and mustering for a last charge at the depleted defenders with everything they had. For the enemy, it was one of the biggest single-day losses they would suffer in the entire war: 647 killed. Westmoreland called it "a great victory," but was it? Two battalions of the Big Red One had fought the same kind of seesaw battle in this area four months earlier during Operation Attleboro against two VC regiments and had defeated them, killed 399, and seized a vast enemy base camp at Ap Cha Do that extended for over a mile through the dense forests and bamboo. And yet here the enemy was again, in the same places, and even better armed than last time.

The VC dead at Suoi Tre carried brand-new RPGs, AK-47 assault rifles with folding bayonets, more ammunition than in the past, and Chinese-made radios modeled on the American PRC-25, which increased the independence and striking power of VC units that could no longer be paralyzed by breakdowns in their primitive communications networks. The VC were less inclined to throw themselves away in human-wave attacks. They attacked like Americans instead, first developing a tremendous volume of small-arms fire, and then advancing by leaps and bounds behind this covering fire. A sergeant in the Big Red One, a veteran of World War II, Korea, and now Vietnam, mocked the briefers in Saigon who denigrated the VC: "The Viet Cong is the best fighter I have ever seen anywhere. Man-for-man, he is as good—maybe better—than we are."[42]

After-action reports joined Westmoreland in proclaiming Operation Junction City a great success, but the fine print betrayed nervousness. Communist base camps were destroyed and weapons, ammo, supplies, and documents captured, but lasting security was not ensured, just more pointless combat: "Now we can focus on improving road networks and LZs in the area to enhance *future* ops." Americans, it appeared, had died here merely to "enhance" future battles in the same place. This was the Vietnam War in a nutshell. And all of this American activity concealed another problem, noted by an ARVN officer. The international press was transfixed by these big, noisy battles "with so much firepower and such large formations" that gave the "erroneous impression that the Americans were doing all the fighting for the Vietnamese. This gave the communists more propaganda ammunition for the political war: 'The Viet Cong were fighting the Americans to save Vietnam.' It was a very effective line," he drolly concluded. "It even convinced a lot of Americans."[43]

Once the enemy had slipped away, II Field Force headquarters at Long Binh proclaimed victory and largely withdrew from the area. General Jonathan Seaman yielded command to General Bruce Palmer, who left Special Forces camps in the mountains east of Tay Ninh, but little else. Elements of the 25th ID's 3rd Brigade remained for a time in the plain at the foot of those mountains "to keep tabs on the rehabilitation of the Communist forces," but, the 3rd Brigade commander admitted, it was really the VC who were keeping tabs on him from the slopes of the mountains, where they lived and moved freely. "The Communists know immediately every time one of my units moves."[44]

Overall, the Americans had suffered 282 dead and 13,500 wounded in the three phases of Operation Junction City, but had killed an estimated 2,700 enemy, wrecked 5,000 structures, and seized 850 tons of food. It was the US Army's biggest airborne operation since General Matthew Ridgway's 16,000 paratroopers had attacked the Rhine bridges in March 1945. And yet strategically the battle was another bust, certainly not the "turning point" claimed by MACV. It had failed to find COSVN, or trap and destroy the NVA 9th Division, which escaped into Cambodia. Of the estimated 600 communist installations in War Zone C, only 100 had been located and destroyed.

COSVN was no "Asian Pentagon." It was now understood to be a subsidiary of the North Vietnamese Workers' Party and high command. As North Vietnam's command post in the South, it was like everything else Hanoi sent south—a mobile complex with the ability to pack up quickly, move, and set up where needed. With the VC bugging out to avoid American pressure, the massive Junction City onslaught with thirty US battalions briefly improved security in the countryside. After the operation, II Field Force boasted that it had brought 82 percent of III Corps under government control.

But with 10,000 NVA infiltrators crossing the border into South Vietnam every *month* by this date, how real or lasting was that control? When Operation Junction City was terminated in May 1967, the VC returned, the

ARVN remained passive, and the locals naturally concluded that the government remained incapable of protecting them. Returning to Saigon from the Iron Triangle in a helicopter after a visit in April, the military intelligence chief of II Field Force looked down and remarked, "The Communists are already reoccupying it—the headquarters of VC Military Region VI is already back there." By August 1967, the VC had reconstituted their control of all fifty-three districts in III Corps, with a 10-man squad in every hamlet, a 30-man platoon in every village, an 80-man company for each district, and a 350-man company for each of III Corps' twelve provinces. It was as if Operations Cedar Falls and Junction City had never happened.[45]

Chapter 9

"WE'LL JUST GO ON BLEEDING THEM"

The mounting waste, aimlessness, and folly of the war were hard to deny. Like a plucky flyweight, Westy danced around an empty ring, throwing punches that only required an adversary to be regarded as dangerous. As it was, the opponent kept slipping through the ropes and reappearing only when an exhausted Westy was back in his corner, mopping sweat and preparing for his next foray.

Westmoreland followed Cedar Falls and Junction City with Operation Sam Houston in February 1967. Just as the two ops in III Corps had aimed to tie up loose ends left by Operation Attleboro, Sam Houston aimed to finish the job in the Central Highlands of II Corps left unfinished by the four Paul Revere operations in 1966. Unfortunately, Sam Houston failed in the same way as its predecessors. A US 4th Infantry Division brigade lifted in, set up battalion forward operating bases in the dense hardwood jungle—where the trees soared to a height of 150 feet—and began searching again for the nine elusive NVA battalions targeted by the Paul Revere operations.

As they had done the previous year, the four NVA regiments vanished into the double-canopy jungle, appearing only when they glimpsed a tactical advantage—to overrun a vulnerable LZ or ambush a small patrol.

American tactics, generally predictable, were even more so here, where the choice of LZs was limited by the dense forest.

The Americans lost 155 killed and several hundred wounded in Operation Sam Houston, to no apparent effect. Enemy body count was hard to calculate. It seemed subject to wild and whimsical swings, as in the case of two 4th ID companies that fought an NVA battalion west of the Se San River on March 22 and reported 25 American dead, 39 US wounded, and 42 enemy KIA. The commanding general, in receipt of those embarrassing numbers, hiked the enemy body count to 160 and gave a final tally for the operation of 792 enemy KIA.[1]

MACV auditors were shocked by the waste of Sam Houston and every operation like it. Two American brigades had fought for two months; 80,000 helicopter sorties had been flown, 230,000 rounds of artillery had been fired, and 2,500 air strikes had been delivered—for a small number of enemy dead and no victory on the ground. As in the Paul Revere operations, much of the Army's strength and energy had been spent during Sam Houston carving bases out of the wilderness and defending them. Three more ops would be launched in this area in 1967, with the same disappointing results—Operations Francis Marion, Greeley, and MacArthur, all culminating in the Battle of Dak To in November, which would prove bloodier but no more decisive than the preceding operations.[2]

Hoping to demoralize the NVA troops, who seemed always just out of reach, the Americans blanketed the Central Highlands with Chieu Hoi (Open Arms) leaflets to encourage communist desertions. They included provocations such as this one: "Do you constantly worry about being spied upon, even when going to the latrine?" But, as the commander of Operation Sam Houston himself allowed, most of the leaflets stuck in the trees, 150 feet above the ground. Those that drifted to the forest floor resulted in not a single surrender. Efforts to induce South Vietnamese psyops personnel to join American combat units to communicate directly with the enemy in the Vietnamese language were unavailing: "The South Vietnamese resisted attachment to rifle battalions and companies and developed a multitude of personal problems and demanded that they be returned to Pleiku to solve their difficulties, or they went AWOL [absent without leave]."[3]

This pusillanimity contrasted with the fierce dedication of the NVA political officers and combat troops. Though hungry, anemic, ill, poorly shod and equipped, and depleted by casualties, the NVA withstood every-thing that was thrown at them. Their medical care was all but nonexistent. An American study in 1969 would discover that nearly half of commu-nist forces in the field at any given time suffered from malaria or dysen-tery. Eighty-seven percent of communist troops wounded in combat died of their wounds, as the average NVA "medevac" took eight to twelve hours on a hammock or a bicycle and at the end of it there were few if any sterile instruments, antibiotics, painkillers, intravenous fluids, or blood bags.[4]

And yet the communists persevered. The keys were the endurance and the patriotism of the troops and the savvy of their political officers. The troops, an NVA defector explained, were "very young men who were flat-tered to think that they were fighting for something great, something super-human." The political officers, he continued, made "the communist army work" far more than the military commanders. They came from worker or peasant families and had to endure hardships more stoically than anyone

NVA prisoners in the POW compound at Bien Hoa. Such troops, an NVA defector explained, were "very young men who were flattered to think that they were fighting for something great, something superhuman." (National Archives)

else in their outfit. They were harsh and unyielding but fair. They explained the aims of the war to their troops—"to liberate the nation and gain human rights for themselves"—which "gave the men something to fight for more than their pay." Before battles, the political officers would challenge their battalions to outdo others in "emulation campaigns," and they briefed the men on the war crimes—real or fabricated—of the units facing them, "to make the men angry."[5]

Westmoreland proclaimed March 1967 "the most successful month of the conflict to date." He measured success in a body count somewhere between 9,000 and 15,000—"the enemy's heaviest losses of the war." But, as the fluctuating number suggested, the body count was "aggregated" by large numbers of Viet Cong "estimated" to have died of wounds. Westy also boasted of 5,125 defectors but made no mention of MACV's growing awareness that the Chieu Hoi program to incentivize enemy desertion was as rife with corruption and false reporting as body count.

With multiple operations in train, Westmoreland alleged that, for the first time since American troops arrived in-country, "total enemy losses exceeded personnel inputs." The Americans and ARVN had killed over 100,000 VC and NVA since President Johnson had put combat troops into Vietnam two years earlier. This was how you reached the "crossover point," when rising losses on a graph crossed the descending line of available replacements. Westy threw in more hopeful statistics on the ARVN and the enemy for good measure, but the report ended on the usual bleak note: "The enemy continues to fight determinedly. There is no indication that he is lessening his attempt to dominate South Vietnam."[6]

In public, Westmoreland tried not to appear bleak. On April 14, 1967, he told reporters at a press conference that "we'll just go on bleeding them until Hanoi wakes up to the fact that they have bled their country to the point of national disaster for generations. Then they will have to reassess their position." In another presser, Westy untruthfully explained that the "real objective of the war is people" and that he had already beaten the communists at that game—denying them Saigon and the densely populated Mekong Delta. Behind the scenes, Westmoreland was anything but hopeful. In March and April 1967, the recommendations he had sent to the Joint Chiefs for a wider war and 206,000 additional troops had been answered by President Johnson with a token increase of just 55,000, which was not sufficient to undertake any new initiatives.[7]

In White House meetings in March and April 1967, Walt Rostow was the first to grasp that what Westy was asking for was LBJ's commitment to a bigger, wider, faster war—an entirely new strategy. Yet no one, apart from Rostow and Westmoreland, was interested. Recent polls showed that a small majority of Americans still supported the war, Harris reporting that 55 percent of Americans supported "maintaining military pressure in Vietnam" and 67 percent supported continuing the bombing of North Vietnam. But most poll respondents distrusted Johnson, who still floundered in his efforts to articulate a plan or even a good reason for the war. "American opinion is increasingly uneasy about Vietnam because there appear to be no defined limits to the levels of force and danger that may lie ahead," a White House adviser summarized. John McNaughton was distraught: "We are carrying the thing to absurd lengths," he wrote the SecDef. "The increased polarization signals the worst split in our people in more than a century."[8]

In a March 1967 speech, the best LBJ could do was this: "We have to face the hard reality that only military power can bar aggression and can make a political solution possible." In plain English: more combat, casualties, and billions merely for the *possibility* of negotiating with Hanoi—not a good look. The president's approval rating was sinking because of the interminable war and the 6 percent price inflation it was causing. With 60 percent of Americans disapproving of him and his conduct of the war, how likely was he to ask Americans to make even greater sacrifices for Vietnam?[9]

Not likely at all. The Joint Chiefs tiptoed around these hard facts. Their interest was less in escalating the war in Vietnam than in filling all of the preparedness holes that were appearing in American forces around the world because of Vietnam. Knowing that Johnson would shy away from an aggressive, expansive new strategy, the chiefs slyly assured him that the new troops and aircraft requested by Westy were needed not to expand the war but merely to reinforce the existing war effort, to "retake the initiative."

But what they *really* wanted was to replenish the nation's training base and strategic reserve of active division forces in the continental United States, Hawaii, and Okinawa. Until 1965, America's strategic reserve had totaled nine Army and three Marine divisions. In the course of 1967, the insatiable demands of Vietnam had reduced it to just four Army divisions and a single Marine division. With most of that diminished force earmarked for NATO, that left only two divisions available for other "contingencies": the 82nd Airborne and the 2nd Marine Division.[10]

And without calling up the reserves, the generals had no "surge" capability in Vietnam or anywhere else. Slow, incremental escalation, as intakes of draftees were funded, trained, equipped, and deployed, was all that could be managed. Summoned to meetings with President Johnson at the White House in April 1967, Westy went along with the ruse propagated by the Joint Chiefs, talking up the benefits of a wider war but implying that the troops were needed above all to cope with rising infiltration and the current demands of search and destroy.

On this visit, the first time in American history that a field commander had left an active war theater while still in command to address a joint session of Congress, Westy threw himself into the political game. He told the Joint Chiefs that "we couldn't expect any new initiatives until the 1968 election was over." The willingness of the Joint Chiefs and the field commander in Vietnam to conceal their intent and tell LBJ what they thought he wanted to hear instead of offering a clear and credible plan goes some way toward exonerating the commander in chief for his half measures and blundering. These men, after all, were his professional military advisers.[11]

SecDef McNamara continued to lose faith in Westmoreland. The general had given a press conference in New York during his April 1967 visit and blamed the enemy's continuing success not on his own failed attrition strategy but on the antiwar movement in America. Pentagon computers, which had begun quantifying everything in Vietnam, now crunched the numbers on attrition and concluded that it simply didn't work. McNamara trusted data more than men, especially ambitious, ingratiating ones like Westmoreland.

The SecDef, advised by Bill Bundy and John McNaughton, now argued the exact opposite strategy of the one advocated by Westy. "Cool" the hot war down, McNamara advised the president. Use allied combat troops to contain the NVA, accelerate pacification, and negotiate. Like the Joint Chiefs, McNamara was more worried about fading American readiness around the world than the outcome in South Vietnam. So was McGeorge Bundy, LBJ's old national security adviser, who had left the administration in early 1966 but remained in regular contact with the White House. The young hawk had soured on the war in the months since and now judged search and destroy ineffective and unsustainable.[12]

For now, there was no "cooling" of the war, for the mounting doubts of the SecDef and Mac Bundy coincided with the arrival in-country of all of the American troops they had authorized—a total that now surpassed 500,000. *Something* had to be done with all of these men. In April 1967, the first US combat units splashed into the watery Mekong Delta, the IV Corps area that previously had been left to the ARVN. The region, which produced three-quarters of South Vietnam's rice crop and was home to one-third of its population, was critical to the fortunes of South Vietnam, but Westmoreland had no interest in fighting there. He didn't have enough troops to counter the threats in the other three corps areas as it was, and the swampy terrain, poor roads, and dense settlement of the Mekong Delta would hamper the application of American firepower and tactics and make "collateral damage" inevitable.

But the ARVN failure to stop the growth of the VC in IV Corps forced Westmoreland's hand. A twenty-seven-year-old VC prisoner taken in a rural district near Can Tho in March 1967 revealed just how far gone the region was. The man, a poor farmer and a father of two, loathed the war but concluded that the VC had the real support of the people because the communists gave them land and other forms of aid. The villagers fed and quartered the VC at great risk of retaliation by the Americans and the ARVN, and the man's comrades, despite the allied advantage in firepower, "did not think it possible that the Americans could win the war."[13]

To show that he *could* win the war, Westmoreland sent two brigades of the US 9th Infantry Division into the Mekong Delta to "set an example of tactical aggressiveness." The results were not what he expected. In the first place, there was literally nowhere for the big American units with their long logistical tails to go. All dry ground in the watery Delta was occupied, so farmers and villages had to be moved and dikes, roads, and crops plowed under to create new firebases, airstrips, and armed camps.

Westmoreland invested two years and $8 million in the construction of Dong Tam Base Camp, an artificial port and airfield on the Mekong created by dredging mud from the river bottom to create 640 acres of usable terrain. VC sappers sank three of the dredgers, and a fourth, in what was

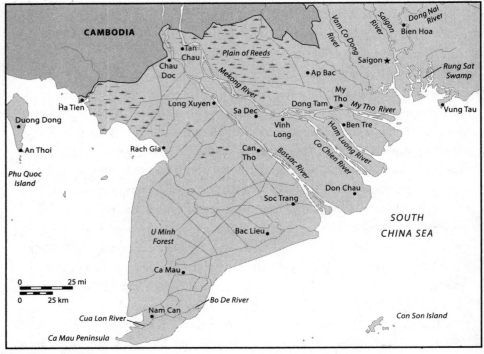

The Mekong Delta

surely a metaphor for the American war effort, sank itself when it accidentally dredged unexploded shells from the river bottom and exploded. Even before the shooting started, the locals complained bitterly about the damage, traffic, trash, inflation, forced relocations, and disrespect for graves, shrines, and the elderly. "School teachers saw a difference in their kids after the Americans came," Major General George O'Connor, the commander of the 9th ID, wrote after his tour. "Their manners worsened."[14]

When the shooting did start, American infantry began to understand why the ARVN had made no progress here. In the dry season, the fields of the Mekong Delta were bare and dusty, offering no concealment from an enemy who set ambushes in palm thickets and hedgerows, waiting till the lead squad or point element had walked right into their midst before opening fire. In the rainy season, the paddies were flooded and it was "a constant battle with water," O'Connor reported, crossing deep canals and tidal estuaries that often rose above a man's head. The grunts all developed crippling fungal lesions—"jungle rot"—from wearing wet boots day and night, and had to be removed from the field every two days just to dry their feet.

"Rules of engagement" that had been worked out over the past year else-where in South Vietnam proved hard to apply in the Delta. Every inch of high ground was thickly settled, which meant that VC lookouts were inevi-tably there, cheek by jowl with the locals. They couldn't be blasted away with artillery or air strikes—the usual practice—without the formal approval of a faraway province chief, which meant that infantry units had to enter them warily, trying to figure out who was VC in villages where every family dug bunkers for personal protection under their huts.

The VC goaded the Americans into committing atrocities by firing shots from civilian homes, or setting claymore mines in the lanes between them. When grunts were killed or wounded, the rest of the unit would burn the hamlet down, just as the VC intended. "Once started," O'Con-nor recalled, "this is difficult to stop." The Army found itself always on the back foot—paying "solace money" for damaged property or killed civilians, making condolence visits to grieving families, rebuilding homes, schools, roads, and churches, and dealing all the while with booby traps and low morale in the division. "It was mentally depressing to live in the hot, humid, muddy, and unclean environment."[15]

That environment, pierced by 2,500 miles of waterways, naturally favored the VC, who knew it; they controlled the night (and therefore the locals) and used the rivers, swamps, islands, and floating markets of the Delta to move, hide, supply themselves, and launch opportunistic attacks that bled the 9th ID, the ARVN, and the ruff-puffs slowly. The 9th ID tried to turn things around. Its 3rd Brigade launched Operation Enterprise in April 1967 in Long An province. It was like every other search and destroy operation in Vietnam—only muddier. Each of the brigade's three batteries was placed in a different district, and then the grunts swept "every foot of the area" before returning the province to ARVN control. The VC waited until the American whirlwind had passed, then reemerged to continue doing everything that they had been doing before.[16]

Unable to win the war as it actually was in the Mekong Delta, the Army tried to make it something that it wasn't. They converted the 9th Infantry Division's 2nd Brigade into a "Mobile Riverine Force" based on Navy bar-racks ships. In June 1967, the 2nd Brigade of the 9th ID launched Operation

Coronado I, which used eighty landing craft to put two infantry battalions ashore to surprise and destroy enemy troops on the Rach Nui River. The VC lured the Americans off the riverbank and into an ambush, where 50 grunts were killed, 150 more were wounded, and four helicopters were lost.

To save his command, Colonel William Fulton submitted a false casualty report, claiming that he had killed 256 VC in the debacle. Operation Coronado I became Operation Coronado II, III, IV, and so on, all the way up to Operation Coronado IX in November 1967, by which time Fulton had been promoted to general. The results of these ops were disappointing: a small (9 percent) increase in the population under government control and 1,000 VC KIAs, out of an estimated 50,000 VC in the Delta. The Coronado ops featured a high kill ratio, 15:1, but there was the usual body count inflation in every action and, more significantly, in seven months of violent combat, Westmoreland's own numbers disclosed that the Coronado ops had killed just 2 percent of the enemy forces in the Mekong Delta. "At this rate of attrition," an Army officer later joked, "Westmoreland would be able to destroy all remaining Viet Cong in the IV Corps Tactical Zone by 2016, just eleven years after his death in 2005 at the age of ninety-one."[17]

In May 1967, Bob McNamara crunched other numbers from Vietnam and was stunned to learn that the NVA and VC were *still* the ones who started the shooting in over 90 percent of company-sized firefights. Eighty percent of all combat engagements in South Vietnam began with a well-orchestrated enemy attack, not an American bolt from the blue. The inference was clear. The enemy almost always fought voluntarily and on his own terms in accordance with his "bait and lure tactics."

He bided his time and came out to fight, as MACV put it, only when he had to defend vital infrastructure or glimpsed the opportunity "to cut off or annihilate careless units." The enemy could stop the bleeding of attrition by simply not fighting—by remaining in the background and dominating the countryside through terrorism, sabotage, and indoctrination. In the big ops on the Cambodian border, the NVA had massed in battalions whenever a US unit or base had appeared vulnerable, but then dissolved into groups as small as three men to escape the American retaliation when it came.[18]

Westmoreland had pitched American mobility and firepower as game-changers. They weren't. On the contrary, Alain Enthoven, who led systems analysis for the SecDef, warned McNamara that attrition and

Westy's constant demands for reinforcements might even be favoring the enemy: "If their strategy is to wait us out, they will control their losses to a level low enough to be sustained indefinitely, but high enough to tempt us to increase our forces to the point of U.S. public rejection of the war."[19]

Westmoreland turned a deaf ear to civilian critics such as Enthoven. He had the total support of the only man who mattered—the commander in chief. By now, LBJ had successfully enlisted Westy in the president's 1968 reelection campaign. The new national security adviser, Walt Rostow, had told LBJ that the president's situation was like Abraham Lincoln's on the eve of the 1864 elections, when a promising war effort was nearly undone by George McClellan's peace candidacy. The president had to "pour it on in Vietnam so that our people can see clearly the end of the road in 1968, even if the end is not fully achieved by November."[20]

Westmoreland bought eagerly into his new role: cheerleader for the administration, the general who would produce dramatic victories like Grant in the Wilderness or Sherman at Atlanta. During the summer of 1967, he masked his earlier pessimism and cited "continuous and steady progress toward the accomplishment of our objectives in South Vietnam" through Operations Greeley, Pershing, and Francis Marion. As proof of this "steady progress," Westy submitted a high body count (12,516 enemy killed in July 1967), an average kill ratio of 5.5:1 ("the best on record"), more "ARVN-initiated" operations, and 92 percent of roads and 88 percent of waterways open to traffic in the "national priority areas," which were a small slice of the entire territory of South Vietnam. "These are measurable indicators of progress," Westmoreland pleaded. Except, of course, they were not. The infatuation with numbers, to "keep score," was increasingly seen as a joke, particularly by the grunts in the field, who were closest to the enemy and had a cleaner grasp of what they called "Vietnam realities."[21]

Operation Pershing, a yearlong operation led by the Cav in Bin Dinh province, was designed to kill two birds with one stone—destroy VC and NVA main-force units on the fertile central coastal plain and also support the CORDS pacification program. The AO's Bong Son Valley was, a Cav officer recalled, "one of the most valuable of all Vietnamese valleys because of its bountiful rice crop." It opened from the Central Highlands toward the coast at Qui Nhon. With Navy ships shelling from the sea, the

Marines landing on the coast, and the Cav air-assaulting into the heart of Bong Son, Operation Pershing generated a startling body count. Nearly 8,000 enemy were reported killed in eighteen major engagements on the populous plain, which the VC had been treating as sovereign territory for years.

But when a visitor toured the province hospital during the operation, he found all 400 beds filled with civilian, not military, casualties. The hospital director, a surgeon from New Zealand, railed against the Cav's lavish use of firepower: "The only way to stop this slaughter is to withdraw American troops."[22]

War correspondent Martha Gellhorn, who had posed as a nurse to cover the D-Day landings twenty-three years earlier, set herself the task of visiting South Vietnam's hospitals and orphanages to document the friendly-fire problem in a small, poor nation, where there was only one doctor per 120,000 inhabitants, compared with one doctor for every 685 in the United States. "The disaster now sweeping over its people is so enormous," Gellhorn wrote in 1967, "that no single person has seen it all." The French had built a free hospital for civilians in every province, but those places were entirely overwhelmed by 1967. Wounded lay two to a bed and on the floors of every ward and corridor. And these were the lucky ones, who had actually made it to a hospital. Most of the provincial hospitals were doing at least 300 major surgeries every month. "Most of the bits and pieces I take out of people," a doctor told Gellhorn, "are identified as American." An American surgeon in Da Nang expressed anguish at all of the women and children he treated. There were no young men because they had all been drafted into the ARVN or the VC. "When a village is bombed you hit women and children almost exclusively, and a few old men.... The United States is grossly careless."[23]

Securing the population against VC control proved more difficult and was accomplished only by carving the Bong Son plain into mutually supporting firebases of 105 and 155 mm howitzers and then pouring more money into the construction and defense of 157 fortified hamlets so that the plain could be treated as a "free-fire zone." Carl von Clausewitz had famously cautioned strategists never to let expenditure of effort exceed the value of a political object, and yet here many American millions were spent to declare 200,000 South Vietnamese temporarily "secure." Asked by a visitor if the people in these new fortified hamlets were truly secure, the most that the US Army adviser to the largest cluster of villages could say was this: "We'll have to wait and see."[24]

Operations Francis Marion and Greeley, two of the other "successes" flourished by Westmoreland, were just two more of the now depressingly common and fruitless three-month battles fought in the same Central Highlands AO already traversed by the Silver Bayonet, Hawthorne, Paul Revere, and Sam Houston operations. In Francis Marion, which ebbed and flowed between April and July 1967, General William Peers' US 4th Infantry Division lost 135 killed and 362 wounded in ten small, sharp battles through the zone of thick trees with high canopy, bamboo, dense undergrowth, hills, and steep ridges.

The desultory combat, when it erupted, was horrific, with American rifle companies isolated, surrounded, and forced to fight for their lives against battalion-strength or larger NVA attacks. Supporting artillery would have to fire to within fifty yards of the grunts to rescue them, causing numerous friendly-fire deaths. In these forested hills there were few LZs, just widely spaced single-ship clearings sawed with difficulty from the hardwood wilderness. The NVA lost 854 men in the operation, but they unveiled new methods to hurt the Americans. They would cut the grunts off from their supplies and medevacs, decapitate command groups with mortar fire, and organize simultaneous attacks on patrolling platoons as well as the company patrol base behind them, making it harder to rescue those outnumbered units with artillery, tac air, and reaction forces, because they would all be hit at the same time. The fighting was often so desperate that one battalion commander recalled making his men learn to fire the entire NVA arsenal—their RPGs, heavy and light machine guns, and AK-47s—because his platoons could so easily run out of ammo or jam their weapons in that rough, unforgiving terrain.

Operation Greeley followed Francis Marion and spanned the summer monsoon season (June–August 1967) in the jungles around Kontum City. Westmoreland put two American brigades—the 173rd Airborne Brigade and the 3rd Brigade of the Cav—into a task force under the command of Peers' US 4th Infantry Division, headquartered at Camp Holloway in Pleiku. Their mission was what it always was around here: "locate and destroy VC/NVA forces."

Like every other operation in the Central Highlands, Greeley was largely reactive—this one triggered by the murder near the Dak To Special Forces camp of five ARVN soldiers and their American adviser. The South Vietnamese had been executed, hands tied, gunshots to the back of the head. The Green Beret had been used for bayonet practice and left to die of his wounds. They had been scouting along the Cambodian border, where three NVA regiments were moving from their sanctuary toward Dak To and Kontum City. Guided by local VC, the NVA units were making good progress—mortaring and rocketing the Dak To and Dak Seang Special Forces camps northwest of Kontum City, and threatening the fortified hamlets that had been set down in this area as proof of the Saigon government's staying power.

The communists were also maneuvering to cut Route 14, which was the main road from Saigon through the Central Highlands. It passed through Kontum City and the CIDG camps and branched to the coast along Route 19 at Pleiku. In the monsoon season, which was settling over the Central Highlands when Operation Greeley commenced, Routes 14 and 19 would be more important than ever. Men, ammo, medevacs, and urgent fire support that would normally move by air in a crisis would be grounded by the weather and forced to crawl along those muddy roads. Holding the roads and keeping them open was critical—to defeat the enemy, hold II Corps, and deny Hanoi a "liberated zone" inside South Vietnam.

The 4th Battalion of the 173rd Airborne Brigade's 503rd Airborne Infantry Regiment, searching an area eight miles from the Cambodian border near Dak To, collided on July 10, 1967, with what they took to be a company of NVA on Hill 830, a 2,700-foot height overlooking a known path into South Vietnam from the Ho Chi Minh Trail. The battle that developed was another perfect illustration of communist tactics. The US battalion, climbing in a long column up the face of Hill 830, was pinned down by machine gun fire from low earthen bunkers blocking the only track up the hill. Alpha Company, on point, hit the dirt, returned fire, and sent two platoons crawling through the brush to the right to outflank the bunkers. But they couldn't. There were more bunkered machine guns and trenches extending that flank.

Delta Company, arriving behind Alpha Company, was immediately hit with heavy mortar rounds, which whistled in from the other flank. The battalion commander ordered Delta Company to move left to outflank those 82 mm mortars. As they struggled to cut a path to the left, the grunts received heavy fire from there but also from the unsubdued and still invisible positions in front and to the right. Every grunt on the hill was pinned down—by mortars, RPGs, machine guns, and rifle fire. A position estimated to hold a single enemy rifle company was now spitting the fire of at least two companies plus attached artillery—the NVA revealing their strength gradually, luring as many American infantry as they could into their killing field before showing their hand.

The American battalion commander, completely pinned down, called for artillery fire on the enemy positions, and sent his Bravo Company, the last in line, on a move right to outflank the enemy position that was flanking his pinned Alpha and Delta Companies. As Bravo tried to wriggle beyond the trapped platoons of Alpha Company, they stumbled into more machine gun and mortar positions, which mowed down the battalion operations officer, the artillery forward observer team, and the commander of Bravo Company. All of this happened in just thirty-five minutes. The battalion commander, who had only a single platoon of Bravo Company in reserve, ordered Alpha Company to fall back on that platoon, while Delta Company crossed through enemy fire to unite with the rest of Bravo Company just as darkness descended, two hours after the battle had exploded at 3:45 in the afternoon.

It was critical that the companies "harbor" for the night together—to make it harder for the NVA to overrun them in the darkness, and to make it easier for dust-offs to come in to get the casualties, which numbered twenty-six American dead and sixty-two wounded. The grunts spent a wretched night under a pelting rain that prevented air strikes and the evacuation of casualties. They manned their perimeters through the night, knowing by now that they faced at least a battalion in the trenches around them.[25]

The rain finally let up at 7 a.m. on July 11, and medevacs, escorted by gunships, began carrying away the dead and wounded. The sodden grunts moved uphill again, this time against no resistance. The enemy had chewed their pound of flesh and withdrawn to fight another day, knowing that clear weather would be used to direct accurate air strikes and artillery fire on their positions. Delta Company, searching the ridgeline, discovered two abandoned fighting positions—one with eighty bunkers, the other with thirty, with a complex of command bunkers behind them. Everything was well built, interlocked, and camouflaged, with two feet of dirt packed atop the bunker positions to absorb the impact of bombs and shells.

Enemy casualties seemed negligible—the battalion reported a body count of only nine. There *had* to be more. American artillery had pounded the height and the most likely withdrawal routes all through the night to stop the enemy from hitting and running. It was, as Michael Herr, *Esquire* magazine's correspondent in Vietnam, put it, "spooky. Everything up there was spooky.... The towns had names that laid a quick, chilly touch on your bones," and every time Herr imagined his own death it was up in the Central Highlands. The sheer remoteness, he concluded, "was enough to make an American commander sink to his knees and plead 'O God! Just *once*, let it be our way. We have the strength, give us the terms!'"[26]

That was the whole story of the American war in Vietnam—trying and failing, over and over, to fight with American strength on American terms. The communists, who had defeated every French tactical innovation and technology upgrade, were doing the same to the Americans. "American patrols," one officer wrote, "hacked through the brush only to become hopelessly lost." Platoon leaders reported men missing who were only ten feet away, swallowed up by jungle that the NVA, forced to live here, had made his "home field." A pilot flying slicks for the 101st Airborne Division recalled embarrassing confusion: "The 101st had lost units looking for lost units looking for lost units." In the Central Highlands, the communists could reinforce and retreat rapidly. Like an agile boxer, they shuffled forward, jabbed hard, slipped punches, and then darted out of reach. The American casualties they inflicted were a cancer gnawing at LBJ's war effort.[27]

Tactical "victories" never lasted. They staved off enemy attacks, but only for the moment. The enemy would pull back, resupply, and resume his march into South Vietnam as soon as the Americans or ARVN departed, which they always did. More interventions would be required to blunt enemy infiltration—a never-ending cycle. And the cost of each intervention was not nearly so trivial as the bloody but inconsequential engagement on Hill 830.

While that American Airborne battalion had fought for its life, an ARVN battalion had fought the same kind of battle nearby on Hill 1258. For the obscure fight on Hill 1258 involving a few hundred ARVN troops, American taxpayers had funded 150 air strikes, 200 helicopter sorties, 10,000 rounds of artillery, 81 tons of aerial bombs, 33 tons of napalm, 12,000 cluster bomblets, 3,000 2.75-inch rockets, and too many 20 mm cannon rounds to count. In a single month in Vietnam in 1967, American aircraft were dropping 77,000 tons of bombs, which was equal to the monthly tonnage Allied bombers had dropped across the entire European theater in the peak bombing years of World War II.

Every *day* in Vietnam, American aircraft and vehicles were burning 45 million gallons of fuel. By 1967, two-thirds of American aircraft losses in Vietnam were helicopters shot down by ground fire in operations like this one. The early promise of the Huey had dimmed. Against enemy countermeasures, the helicopters could be safely deployed only if a whole list of restrictive conditions were met: clear weather, smoke screens, preplanned artillery barrages around the objective, and, if troops were being brought in, the ability to choose between multiple LZs to wrong-foot the enemy. There also had to be enough slicks available to land the entire assault force in one go, not multiple lifts. The last two conditions could never be met in forested mountains like these, hence the extreme isolation and vulnerability of American and ARVN troops operating in the Central Highlands.[28]

No wonder McNamara's Pentagon had erred by 100 percent in their estimate of the war's cost for fiscal 1967. They had estimated $10 billion, and the war had ended up costing the United States over $20 billion that year. Britain's defense attaché in Saigon could not comprehend or even express the extravagance: "Where does one begin to work out the cost effectiveness of such weaponry? Tons of bombs per VC killed? Number of bunker complexes or trenches destroyed? A comparison of friendly forces to enemy forces killed? Or an amalgam of the whole issue? Clearly a meaningful study of the cost effectiveness of the mighty weaponry in use in Vietnam today is beyond the ken of the writer. No doubt many brilliant minds in the RAND Corp. and kindred organizations are hard at work endeavoring to make sense of the various assessments—politics aside."[29]

After Operation Francis Marion, which flared through the mountains of II Corps for most of 1967, General William Peers had a revealing and rare exchange with one of his 4th ID battalion commanders on the nature and futility of what the Army was doing in the Central Highlands. The battalion commander, Lieutenant Colonel Corey Wright, had just supervised a disastrous defeat on the northern edge of the Ia Drang Valley, a place that kept killing Americans despite so many "victories" there. Wright challenged the Army assumption that search and destroy handed the initiative to US forces. No, Wright insisted, the *enemy* was acting with initiative, tracking the noisy Americans through the jungle, pinpointing their location and posture, and then closing in for the kill whenever rain, fog, and low ceilings combined with the craggy terrain to make fire support and reinforcement difficult.

Even in clear weather, the American weapons were blunted in this mountainous, jungle-cloaked wilderness, where accurate map reading was difficult even from the air, and units on the ground struggled just to find their own location on a map. In this operation, like the ones before and after it, American units could hardly move. They followed jungle trails where they existed, but the need to place security elements on the flanks, where they had to hack their way through virgin forest and bamboo with machetes, meant that the rate of movement in these rainswept woods was less than 300 yards an hour.

With no LZs available—they were too hard to cut from the hardwood forest—and a required "reinforcing time" of sixty minutes or less to save ambushed units from certain death, the American and ARVN maneuvers were easy for an enemy to predict. Friendly companies could not be spread wide to sweep up and envelop any enemy in their path. If they were, they would need many hours, not sixty minutes or less, to come to each other's aid. As a result, the three companies of an American battalion would advance side by side, no more than 500 yards apart, a grimy phalanx reeking of menthol, crud, and sweat that the enemy would simply let pass, attacking only when one of the American platoons or companies veered far enough away from the others to become vulnerable.[30]

General Peers reacted blimpishly, writing a memo back to Wright that blamed the problems observed by Wright—and so many other troop commanders in Vietnam—on the battalion commander himself. Wright's battalion, Peers scolded, was apprehensive and not prepared for combat. If it had been, Peers continued, Wright wouldn't have been surprised by the enemy. "There were intel indications at the division, brigade, and battalion level to deduce the NVA intentions." Wright's forces should have been positioned to accept combat and reinforce.

Wright pointed out the fantasy of such a view in the US Army of 1967. Lyndon Johnson's "Vietnam-only Army" was already full of holes. Sergeants, who usually required several years to attain the rank, were being produced by the thousands in a twenty-four-week course at Fort Benning, Georgia, because NCOs were being killed and wounded in such large numbers in Vietnam. DEROS, an acronym for "date eligible for return from overseas," was the Pentagon policy that promised grunts in Vietnam that their tour would last 365 days and not an hour more. This is why so many helmets and flak jackets had days, weeks, and months crossed off—troops literally counting the days to their DEROS. But it meant that units were in constant upheaval, losing combat veterans every day and waiting for their inexperienced replacements—the "newbies" or "FNGs," short for "fucking new guys."[31]

DEROS was a public relations policy, meant to reassure parents, spouses, and the troops themselves, but it had dire military consequences. Twice as many grunts were killed in the first half of their tours as in the second half, which revealed the high price of inexperience. Those who survived were constantly and randomly leaving. Wright's line companies had just been reduced from 130 to 90 men by "DEROS departures." Unit cohesion eroded as the shrinking number of battle-hardened grunts had to be spread evenly across the platoons and squads. The officers and NCOs had also turned over, causing, as the colonel put it, "a drastic reduction in the tactical experience of companies and platoons." Many of the leaders were as green as the led. The young draftees, nineteen- and twenty-year-olds, most of them with just a month or two in-country, had fought tenaciously against overwhelming odds, but what more could be expected of them? The NVA wrapped overwhelming force around the company and read it like a well-thumbed book. When the Americans popped smoke to mark their ground location for the FACs, who flew overhead whenever the clouds broke to direct air strikes, the NVA poured mortar and rocket fire onto the smoke grenades, knowing that there would be grunts crouched around them for safety.[32]

DEROS was the Pentagon policy that promised soldiers in Vietnam that their tour would last 365 days and not a day more. Here a Cav grunt keeps track of time left in-country on his helmet cover. (National Archives)

There was another problem, Wright added. Using FACs to guide fire onto the enemy was good in theory, but on the day of his disastrous patrol the FAC who was actually in the cockpit was new and became confused trying to coordinate air and artillery strikes, and he repeatedly "checked fire" so that the attacking aircraft would not be hit by incoming artillery, leaving Bravo Company defenseless for long, terrifying intervals, even when the weather cleared. Peers allowed that DEROS and inexperience caused "turbulence and reduced combat capability" but insisted that Wright should have anticipated all of this and deployed accordingly and made his own arrangements for rapid reinforcement. This was the definition of "punching down."[33]

Wright continued punching up. He asserted that it was suicidal to maneuver against *this* enemy. To Peers, this was another shocking case of heresy. Maneuver to contact with the enemy was a Westmoreland mantra, drummed into every combat unit. Wright poured cold water on the by now trite concept: "Junior leaders must be made fully aware that to attempt to maneuver against NVA forces often leads to disastrous results." The enemy knew the area and were in prepared ambush positions designed to kill the Americans in a cross fire. In the operation under discussion, one of Bravo Company's platoons had tried to maneuver against those enemy positions, lost its command group, and then lost contact with the rest of the company. The artillery and air strikes needed to save the other platoons of the company, huddled in an all-around defensive position, could not be called in without risk to the lost platoon. The casualties piled up. In that desolate place, many of them would never be recovered and would join the lengthening list of MIAs, their names engraved on "POW/MIA bracelets" worn by Americans at home.

Most of the lost men from Wright's 1st Battalion of the 12th Infantry were later listed as "ground casualties, small-arms fire," but several of them were taken alive and carried back to die of their wounds or hunger in the NVA's Cambodian sanctuary, where American prisoners of war (POWs) were locked in bamboo cages, their feet in stocks, iron collars around their necks. Men who tried to escape would be buried in the ground up to their throats. The forward artillery observer, a twenty-five-year-old reserve lieutenant whose tour would have been up in ten days and who was about to return for his junior year at Brigham Young University, was killed after his company commander was cut down by the enclosing battalion of North Vietnamese infantry.

The survivors of the company, none of whom had been in Vietnam more than a few months, must have felt sheer terror when they saw their last radio destroyed in the mortar blast that killed the headquarters platoon, and waited, totally cut off from the world, for the reinforcements that belatedly arrived overland to push the NVA back. Here again, Peers talked past Wright, arguing for the war he wanted to fight rather than the war as it was: "You must maneuver with company and platoon sized units, find the enemy's weak spots, and be aggressive and in sufficient strength to do the job."[34]

While Peers quarreled with Wright, Le Duan sent delegations to Moscow and Beijing to secure greater quantities of aid for the struggle against the United States. By 1967, when Moscow was celebrating the fiftieth anniversary of the Russian Revolution, the Sino-Soviet rift that had begun to open a decade earlier was complete. Now Mao Zedong cast China as the true and uncorrupted leader of the world communist revolution and mocked the pragmatic Soviet Union, which had embarked on a policy of peaceful coexistence with the West. Mao, in the midst of his own bloody and internecine Cultural Revolution, damned the "revisionist traitors" of Moscow and demanded an ideological and material intensification of the war in Vietnam to drive the Americans out and place the whole country under totalitarian rule. But it was the Soviets who had the best weapons and provided the most aid—at least three times more than the Chinese—and *they* wanted a quick, negotiated end to a war that was becoming a costly distraction for Moscow; they saw it as a chip that Russian negotiators might trade with the Americans in other areas.[35]

The North Vietnamese politburo maneuvered deftly between the two communist giants, neither of which was willing to cede control of the war to the other. Hanoi pursued the Chinese line of a war to the finish, which Mao called "the strategy of annihilation," but appeased the Soviets by suggesting that they could pull it off without bankrupting Moscow. They would use politics and war—more converts in the South, more victories on the battlefield, and more "information war" against the United States and its anxious allies—to pressure the Americans to deescalate, halt the bombing of North Vietnam, and withdraw.[36]

Observers on the ground in North Vietnam reported scattered devastation but a willingness to go on. Two-thirds of Hanoi's population had been evacuated and the city's broad boulevards and French villas were now semi-deserted, but the capital remained clean and well-kept. Knowing their punctilious adversary, the NVA packed the city center with trucks, fuel, ammunition, antiaircraft guns, and SAM carriers, on the assumption that LBJ would not risk an international outcry by bombing the populated heart of Asia's finest colonial city. When air raids did occur, factory and office workers would file into bomb shelters, and pedestrians and cyclists would drop into foxholes rammed into every sidewalk with concrete cylinders. Brian Stewart, Britain's consul general in Hanoi, summarized the mood in the North Vietnamese capital: "Effectively supported by the whole Soviet bloc and China, hopeful of a weakening of U.S. resolve and inured to struggle over more than a generation, they are prepared to fight until their adversaries become tired of war."[37]

Air strikes on the Ho Chi Minh Trail also disappointed, for the NVA and VC required a fraction of the logistics required by the Americans, just fifteen to twenty tons of supplies a day, and they could move this quantity and more along the trail despite heavy bombing. President Johnson had assumed that Rolling Thunder attacks would force the North Vietnamese to the peace table. Instead, Le Duan feigned indifference to the blackouts, shortages, and bomb damage, and continued to insist that there would be no talks until the bombing stopped. LBJ's theory of victory, that communist morale and combat power would be crushed by bombs and airmobile operations, now resonated like a bad joke. A major reboot was needed.[38]

Chapter 10

"VICTORY IS AROUND
THE CORNER"

Westmoreland had until now been an island of gung-ho denial, but in the summer of 1967 the general belatedly understood that search and destroy was not working. High American kill ratios were not bringing victory, the conditions for a lasting peace, or even negotiations. The war was stalemated, a situation that favored the communists. Intuiting his own demise if he didn't turn things around, Westmoreland began to push for a more dynamic strategy that might rescue his failing command and compel Hanoi to end the war. He wanted to thrust across South Vietnam's borders to attack the communist sanctuaries in Cambodia and Laos, and invade North Vietnam as well.

Westy began to build up bases like Dak To, opposite the Laotian panhandle, and he and Ambassador Ellsworth Bunker, who had replaced Henry Cabot Lodge Jr. in April, pressured Thieu and the ARVN Joint General Staff to increase the size of the South Vietnamese armed forces. How could Westmoreland persuade LBJ to raise American force ceilings in Vietnam and authorize a bigger war if the South Vietnamese were still refusing to draft eighteen- and nineteen-year-olds?

Westmoreland and Bunker prodded the ARVN commanders to plan a bold operation into Laos to cut the Ho Chi Minh Trail. Westy floated again the idea of a massive US troop surge. To break the stalemate, he argued, it would be necessary to stop "swatting flies" inside South Vietnam and instead strike into Cambodia, Laos, and even North Vietnam to hit the sources of communist power and prevent the NVA from continuously reinforcing their position in South Vietnam.[1]

Westmoreland's theory of victory had been to use American mobility and firepower to annihilate the NVA and VC main-force units in a "strategy of attrition." The theory and the strategy were all too obviously failing. Infiltration was rising, not falling. The NVA was pushing an average of 8,500 troops into South Vietnam every month in 1967, an average that would rise sharply late in the year and more than double in 1968—to 20,350 troops every month. The strategy of attrition foundered as the enemy replaced every one of his casualties, added new units, and pushed deeper into South Vietnam.[2]

When Westmoreland tried to interest President Johnson and Secretary of Defense McNamara in an expansive new strategy to stop the infiltration by invading North Vietnam, Laos, and Cambodia, the general was rebuffed. Bob McNamara looked at Westy's request for an additional 206,000 troops and a force ceiling of 670,000 and recoiled in disgust. There were already 1.3 million Americans in uniform in Southeast Asia, he scolded Westy, yet on any given day only 50,000 or 60,000 of them were in a ground combat role in South Vietnam. The SecDef assumed that more troops would just be frittered away in the same fashion, staffing the post exchanges (PXs), mailrooms, depots, maintenance shops, supply ships, air bases, and warehouses of the military's fathomless rear echelons. He had Alain Enthoven and the whiz kids calculate how many communists 206,000 additional US troops would kill every week under various scenarios, and the answers fell in the range between 139 and 431. Even assuming the high number, McNamara noticed, they would not have killed all of the enemy by 1977—ten years off. In the course of their analysis, the whiz kids discovered that Westy had been lying a few months earlier when he had boasted of reaching the mythic "crossover point." That too lay far in the future.[3]

President Johnson, gearing up to run for reelection in 1968, was unwilling to go before the American people, who had been assured that they were winning the war, and tell them that in fact they had lost 20,000 dead for a stalemate, and that they were expected to provide yet more draftees, money, lives, and time for a total reset of US strategy, which would entail bomb-ing Hanoi-Haiphong, hitting the railways south from China, and invading North Vietnam, Laos, and Cambodia to close the communist supply and infiltration routes. Clark Clifford, the influential LBJ adviser and consum-mate Washington insider, tried to see things Westy's way: "We can't get the war over as long as the faucets are on," Clifford reminded the president. But if Johnson massively escalated the war to close the faucets, he might not secure the Democratic nomination. Even if he got the nod, he'd probably lose the election.[4]

Richard Nixon, the president's likely Republican opponent, was already hammering Johnson for wasting American strength in "gradual escalation" instead of "massive pressure" all at once. LBJ rejected massive pressure for another reason besides cost and optics—his fear, encouraged by Rusk, that further escalation might prompt a Soviet move against Berlin or a Chinese move against South Korea. Polling during the "long, hot summer of 1967," when race riots exploded in Detroit, Newark, and dozens of other American cities, showed that voters linked the riots to the war—that funds needed to revitalize cities and schools were instead being spent on a foreign war of choice, a point made by Martin Luther King Jr. in August: "We are losing the war against poverty here at home precisely because of the energies, the resources, the money, and all of the other things that we are putting in that tragic, unjust, evil, brutal, senseless war in Vietnam."[5]

What LBJ needed to do as the 1968 presidential campaign season kicked off was persuade the American people that Westmoreland *was* winning. "Don't let communications people in New York set the tone of the debate," Mac Bundy admonished from his new job at the Ford Foundation. "Empha-size the 'light at the end of the tunnel,'" Bundy counseled the president, "not battles, deaths, and dangers." Westmoreland must be encouraged to speak the phrase that would shortly become notorious: "Victory is around the corner." This Mac Bundy recommendation, eagerly conveyed to Westy by the president, confronted the MACV commander with a moral quandary: Should he go along with LBJ and his political gambit, or should he stake his career on the change in strategy he considered necessary?[6]

He went along. Westmoreland flew to Washington in July 1967 and gave an upbeat news conference. "The statement that we are in a stalemate is complete fiction," the field commander scoffed. "During the past year, tremendous progress has been made." The NVA had lost so many troops in 1967 that they could no longer put enough forces across the DMZ to reinforce VC units that were being run down by US, ARVN, Korean, and Australian forces. "Every indicator belies stalemate or loss of initiative."

Westy had been pushed into partisan politics, persuaded that no new strategy or force could be announced and that he'd have to put a brave face on what he had. None of the smart people around LBJ really thought America could win. They had stopped referring to the MACV commander in meetings as "Westy," such was their newfound contempt for him. Most of them agreed that Westmoreland had lost the war and needed to be fired. That's why LBJ had sent Army vice chief of staff Creighton Abrams out to Saigon in May 1967. He would be Westy's replacement.[7]

But LBJ, as always in the war, temporized, and took the counsel of his fears. How could he fire Westmoreland on the eve of elections? It would only confirm what his critics said, that he and his general were inept. No, he would keep Westy on, promote the prospect of victory until the election, and then, safely seated in office, be free to fire Westmoreland and wind the war down or announce some "peace with honor."[8]

Of course, the essential precursor for any "peace with honor" needed to be a robust South Vietnamese government, just exactly what Saigon, well into its fourth year of military rule, was not. Johnson had always assumed that military rule would work more effectively than civilian government, but could any regime be less effective than the infighting Thieu-Ky junta? To give South Vietnam a democratic veneer, elections were ordered for September 1967. The early front-runners, unfortunately, were Thieu and Ky, both of whom announced their intention to run for president. The new constitution, drafted in six months by a national assembly elected in September 1966, created an American-style republic with an elected bicameral legislature and a strong president who would wield the powers of head of state and head of government.

Fifty-one-year-old General Duong Van Minh—the key player in the Diem coup—announced from his Bangkok exile that he would return and run. Air Marshal Ky began a barnstorming campaign that pulled each of the many levers he controlled in the South Vietnamese military and bureaucracy. He used military aircraft to fly his voters to rallies. He moved likely Thieu voters into VC-controlled areas to stop them from voting. He paid bribes for votes that rivaled even Thieu's payoffs. Thieu, who had none of Big Minh's bonhomie or Ky's seedy charisma, sensed defeat and threatened the Americans that he'd sponsor yet another coup if Ky won.

Prime Minister Ky solved the Big Minh problem by forbidding the general's return from exile. Bunker and Westmoreland then urged the South Vietnamese generals to reconcile Thieu and Ky, which, after a grueling conclave, they finally did—by forcing an enraged Ky to accept a junior role as vice president on a Thieu-led ticket.

Problem solved in Saigon, but it was yet another disaster and embarrassment for Washington. For the October 1967 presidential election that was supposed to "civilianize" the South Vietnamese government, the junta had chosen a ticket that paired two generals and disqualified all but the most lackluster civilian candidates. To dispel any illusions in the White House as to what they were dealing with in Saigon, Bob Komer characterized Thieu and Ky as "smart crooks, rather than dumb honest men."[9]

Meanwhile, in Hanoi the North Vietnamese communists were not relenting. But they were worried and far from unified. From the British embassy in Hanoi, John Colvin shined a light into the fissures within the six-man North Vietnamese politburo, which gave insight into the regime's strengths and vulnerabilities in 1967. Ho Chi Minh was the aging figurehead of the political bureau, summoned now and then "to sign agreed papers." Defense Minister Giap's star shined brightest when he delivered victories in the field and dimmed whenever the news was bad. Prime Minister Pham Van Dong, Ho's most trusted adviser, was overshadowed by Le Duan, the party's first secretary. Le Duc Tho, Le Duan's closest ally, controlled every appointment in the communist bureaucracy and made sure to push Le Duan's people to the top. Rivals were purged or demoted. The "brothers Le," as they were known, were deeply committed to what Hanoi called "the Southern War," but not on the extended timeline pushed by China. Le Duan wanted to take delivery of advanced Soviet weapons and launch heavy combined-arms offensives against the South Vietnamese cities—ending the war and its misery quickly by smashing the ARVN in battle and pushing the Americans to their breaking point.[10]

In the spring of 1967, Hanoi reviewed the military situation in the South and heard from General Nguyen Chi Thanh, who commanded COSVN, which coordinated NVA and VC strategy. By June, the NVA general staff was forced to the conclusion that something urgent had to be done. Viewed from Hanoi, where people were living a dark, hungry, and miserable life, the wealth and power of the United States seemed so immense that it was easy to infer that America's protection of South Vietnam might go on forever. For the Americans, relatively small increments of power could be dished out to sustain the Saigon regime and brutalize the North. As bleak as things may have looked in Washington, they looked far bleaker in Hanoi.[11]

At a politburo meeting chaired by Ho Chi Minh in July 1967, the ailing leader heard just how bleak. The North Vietnamese, who had been poised to win the war in 1965 before the introduction of American troops, now seemed blocked everywhere they turned. The NVA had planned to propel the VC to victory in South Vietnam but were instead spending most of their strength merely operating the Ho Chi Minh Trail through Laos and Cambodia—finding ingenious ways to move those fifteen to twenty tons a day of essential supplies from North Vietnam to the battlefields in the South.

And every crumb of food sent south was one less crumb that could be eaten by hungry northerners. Taking stock of the misery in Hanoi, a British diplomat wrote: "For the first time I am beginning to believe that this extraordinary people must have a physical limit." Rolling Thunder air attacks had crippled essential infrastructure, making it hard to move food and other critical items around the country. North Vietnamese children wandered around with swollen bellies, prominent ribs, worms, and scabies. Even the best food, reserved for soldiers and factory workers, was barely fit to eat, "containing items that are visually repellent." Famished people, drained of energy, shuffled slowly around the city.[12]

A politically threatening stalemate had emerged. To break it, Le Duan supported General Thanh's proposal for a massive uprising and offensive in early 1968 to win the war. He was opposed by Ho's chief military adviser and defense minister, General Vo Nguyen Giap, who worried that American firepower would not only thwart the offensive but *destroy* it with backbreaking casualties.[13]

Giap argued that it would be more sensible to continue with a low-intensity guerrilla war until the Americans could be nudged off the field by their own casualties and lack of progress plus a widening wave of domestic and international opposition. Operations like Junction City showed Giap just how dangerous and costly it was to seek battle with the better-armed and more mobile Americans. To limit casualties, the VC had already been forced in early 1967 to curtail battalion-strength assaults and operate instead in companies and platoons. Battalions were just too big a target for American artillery and airpower. What, Giap inquired, had changed, to make his colleagues hopeful that a sudden general offensive by large units might succeed?[14]

But Giap's colleagues, led by the "brothers Le," worried about their casualties, their lack of progress, and the unpredictable support arising from the Sino-Soviet split. How long would the North Vietnamese people and the regime's communist allies back a government that could fight endlessly but never *win*? China talked tough but was economically weak and mired in its Cultural Revolution. The Soviets were preoccupied with a massive defeat in the Middle East, where Israel had just routed Moscow's Arab clients in the Six-Day War, all of whom would have to be rearmed. Who could say how long Moscow would support Hanoi's long-game strategy? Giap's cautious approach lost out, and the politburo resolved in a series of meetings that a mortal blow had to be struck in 1968—to demoralize and evict the Americans, and permit North Vietnam to deal with South Vietnam one-on-one.[15]

Le Duan crowned his success in the politburo by rudely demoting Giap. Le Duan feared the fifty-six-year-old Giap for good reason. The general was younger and more charismatic, and he came attired with military glory, Ho Chi Minh's trust, and devout backing from the Russians, who suspected Le Duan of being too close to Beijing. The party secretary now moved ruthlessly against the great hero, for Giap was too cautious, too famous, a rival for power, and capable of a coup. In July 1967, Le Duan put General Van Tien Dung in charge of planning the 1968 Tet Offensive and arrested several of Giap's most loyal staff officers, charging them with "anti-Party agitation." This was a not-so-veiled warning to Giap himself.[16]

Le Duan's rise was complete. Ho Chi Minh, undercut by the first secretary's grip on the party's security apparatus, would leave Hanoi in September for medical treatment in Beijing. General Giap would continue as defense minister and assist in planning the Tet Offensive, but he would never recover his early power and influence. The general would depart Hanoi in October 1967 in what could only have been a prudent act of self-exile. Giap made a tour of Eastern European capitals and then settled in Budapest. The defense minister would be gone for eight months, missing the entire Tet Offensive.[17]

While Hanoi began to plan that massive offensive, Westmoreland puzzled over what *his* proper strategy should be. Increasingly, he was just launching search and destroy operations in the hope that they would generate impressive body counts and through attrition reduce the enemy to untenable levels. His plan to expand the war—which offered little hope of victory but plenty of controversy—was predictably dead on arrival in the White House. So search and destroy muddled on. But the NVA was destroying Westmoreland even as he attempted to destroy it. The North Vietnamese had figured out his methods and were beating him at his own game.

The communists lacked aircraft and firebases, but they had better intelligence and motivation. The high quality of VC recruits, including large numbers of English-speakers, meant that their signals platoons could eavesdrop on US forward air controllers and infantry radio nets and warn of impending attacks. They also gained access to American and ARVN codes from agents in the South Vietnamese military and were able to lay ambushes in the path of South Vietnamese and American operations.

A Soviet trawler on station off Guam gave early warning of every B-52 strike launched from the island. Communist units in contact with allied forces would be warned to disperse before the "Buffs" arrived overhead, five hours later, after their 2,500-mile flight. Meanwhile, US units had begun to sag under their own losses, some inflicted by the enemy, others by DEROS, which whisked troops home on their 365th day in-country whether their replacement had arrived or not. Usually he hadn't. Battalions could lose 60 percent of their strength in a single day. Experienced officers were already becoming scarce. Troops too: in the 1st Infantry Division, some platoons were down to eleven men instead of the normal thirty or forty.[18]

With most of South Vietnam contested or under VC control, there were never enough American troops. Airmobile operations looked good in theory, but in practice they created as many problems as they solved. They allowed the rapid movement of forces over great distances, but every increase in the number of airmobile troops required increases in support personnel for staffs, bases, airlift, air traffic control, repair, refueling, resupply, food service, and medical care. Half a million American troops would not be enough when deductions were made for "combat support" and "combat service support." Each of the four corps areas had massive support command facilities and truck fleets that skimmed off 85 to 90 percent of US manpower, leaving just 10 to 15 percent of the over 500,000 US troops in South Vietnam available for combat.[19]

This paltry number of men with their "ass in the grass"—80,000 or fewer at any given time—was immediately swallowed up by the vastness of South Vietnam and the deadly game of hide-and-seek played by the VC and NVA. The enemy would either ambush isolated American combat troops or attack the combat support units as they worked to sustain the grunts in the field. The daily mortar and rocket attacks launched by the VC on American and ARVN bases all around Vietnam were more than a nuisance. They contributed to a crippling supply chain problem. The mortar attacks, always launched and broken off in under five minutes, the "scramble time" for nearby aircraft, would aim to crater the airstrip and ignite the bladders of fuel and crates of ammunition held at every firebase and headquarters.[20]

The small number of grunts with their "ass in the grass" was immediately swallowed up by the vastness of South Vietnam and the deadly game of hide-and-seek played by the VC and NVA. (National Archives)

Each successful attack would crimp the already tenuous supply chain. Maneuver operations, helicopter combat assaults, and casualty evacuations would have to be halted or decreased while 150 or more trucks were sent along dangerous roads, sown with mines and ambushes, to replace the lost "stockage." Sorties of C-130s and helicopters would have to be sent with the most urgent requirements, exacerbating the already difficult problem of "air traffic density" and "blade time." Manpower and equipment would have to be shifted from military to logistical uses. Officers would have to cannibalize units for vehicles, find troops to clear and police the roads, remove wrecks, fight fires, and dispose of all of the damaged ordnance in the roads and bases.[21]

The war had become ravenous. President Johnson had put in 160,000 additional troops in 1965, 210,000 more in 1966, and another 96,000 thus far in 1967, raising the total force to 500,000. Of this number, nearly 16,000 had been killed and nearly 100,000 had been wounded since he took office, yet he seemed no closer to victory, or even a face-saving "peace with honor." LBJ was desperate to get out. He wanted to trade the Rolling Thunder air campaign over North Vietnam for something concrete, like a cutoff of Hanoi's aid to the VC, or Hanoi's agreement to a cease-fire. He proffered such a deal in September 1967 in a speech in San Antonio, Texas, where LBJ offered to stop the bombing of North Vietnam if Hanoi would "promptly" sit down for "productive discussions" to end the war.

Johnson also used the San Antonio speech to move away from his ineffective arguments for the war to more concrete ones. But they still seemed soggy and conjectural. The president suggested that if America did not fight in Vietnam, an Asian communist bloc, strengthened by the conquest of Southeast Asia, *might* in due course control two-thirds of the world's people and *possibly* threaten America with a much larger, *possibly* nuclear war: "One could hope that this would not be so, but... I am not prepared to risk the security—indeed, the survival—of this American Nation on mere hope and wishful thinking."

Smarter analysts would have noted that the real threat was not some "third world war" arising from the "loss of Vietnam" but rather the stress of Vietnam on America's deterrence and defense posture. Keeping the combat and supporting units up to strength at a time when America faced serious challenges in every corner of the world was becoming impossible.

The problem of "personnel fill," replacing casualties and departures in Vietnam, pitted every US regional command against MACV. Rampant and unauthorized "reprogramming" in the Defense Department, shifting funds to Southeast Asia from other accounts, was hollowing out the military. Pentagon R&D and procurement budgets were being slashed to the bone to pay for Vietnam. In the course of 1967, the number of fixed-wing aircraft lost to hostile action and accidents in Vietnam reached 1,709, with the number of downed helicopters standing at 1,081. That $12 billion Vietnam supplemental Johnson had asked Congress for in January had included $4 billion for replacement aircraft alone, the Senate Armed Services Committee deploring "the alarming decrease in our tactical assault and airlift capabilities" due to the soaring losses in Vietnam.

Sensing Johnson's weakness and America's strategic overstretch, Hanoi rejected LBJ's "San Antonio Formula," scoffing that Washington was asking Hanoi to deescalate without first deescalating its own effort—and a glance at the alarming budget numbers suggested this was true.[22]

Faced with this communist intransigence, it increasingly looked as if LBJ was going to have to concede a bombing halt without getting *anything* in return, because America simply could not afford the accelerating losses of pilots and aircraft. Hanoi's own assessment of the war in late 1967 was summarized by the Defense Intelligence Agency in this way: "In general, the communist view of the war is basically that half a million U.S. troops have been fighting in South Vietnam for more than a year, and yet they have been forced onto the defensive."

Hanoi estimated that the NVA and VC, despite chronic shortages of ammo, food, medicine, and transport, had survived all of the major sweep operations launched by the Americans in 1967 and inflicted punishing casualties on at least twenty US battalions, ratcheting up pressure on Johnson, who would have to run for reelection in 1968 against a backdrop of death, debt, and defeat.

Johnson's frustration mounted. By the summer of 1967, there were an estimated 300,000 communist troops in South Vietnam—about 60,000 NVA and 240,000 VC. To defeat them, Johnson had sent 500,000 American troops and paid for a million-man ARVN, and yet he was still on the back foot—"winning" indecisive battles here and there but never approaching victory or even a semblance of leverage. "We might ask ourselves," an expert on the war challenged the Senate in August 1967, "why the Vietnamese we support are less effective fighters than the Vietnamese Hanoi supports?"[23]

Internally, MACV knew the answer to that question. Selected for their political and family connections, no South Vietnamese general officer was rated "fully competent" in any aspect of warfare. With over half of the ARVN generals and 70 percent of the field-grade officers drawn from the old French-officered colonial army, they were inevitably regarded by their own troops as tools of a foreign power, earlier the French, today the Americans. The ARVN captains and lieutenants who led the infantry companies and platoons were, by law, drawn exclusively from the 15 percent of the population who had completed twelve years of school and a rigorous exit exam. There were so few of these men—not least because most of them fled abroad or used their connections to get safe rear-echelon jobs—that the ARVN was reduced to plucking 3,000 teachers and professors from their classrooms and forcing them to lead infantry units that were in no way encouraged or reassured by their embittered, frightened new officers. This contrasted with the NVA, where officer candidates were required to spend five years in the enlisted ranks before they could even be considered for a commission.[24]

Kept in the dark by MACV about the ARVN's worst characteristics, LBJ struggled to understand the situation. If putting in eight times as many American troops as North Vietnam fielded and funding an ARVN that was four times larger than the VC were not sufficient, what on earth would be? It was "as if the entire United States and its military were being defeated by the Sioux nation," Ambassador John Kenneth Galbraith snorted during a visit to Washington.[25]

And despite American largesse, there was no end to the requirements in Vietnam at a time when US forces in other theaters were stretched dangerously thin. A gap had already opened in American factories between production and attrition, and the costs for this limited war of choice were becoming prohibitive. Over 800 American soldiers were dying every month in Vietnam. Replacing a single Air Force B-52 Stratofortress cost $16 million ($128 million today), with an F-100 Super Sabre costing $700,000 ($5.6 million today), and every Huey that went down cost $250,000 ($2 million).[26]

Compared to World War II or Korea, which had sucked up 48 percent and 12 percent of American GDP, respectively, the war in Vietnam, costing 3 percent of GDP in mid-1967, was still relatively cheap, but it was sparking inflation, widening the budget deficit, and cutting into LBJ's domestic programs. In August 1967, Johnson, who had spent the year wrangling with House Ways and Means Committee chairman Wilbur Mills over the president's proposed 6 percent surtax on personal and corporate incomes to fund the war, now unveiled a new proposal, a 10 percent surtax. He wrapped himself in the flag to overcome Mills' obstruction: "The inconveniences this demand imposes are small when measured against the contribution of a Marine on patrol in a sweltering jungle, or an airman flying through perilous skies, or a soldier 10,000 miles from home, waiting to join his outfit on the line."

Congressman Mills, however, had his revenge, forcing Johnson to accept a 10 percent cut to his discretionary spending in exchange for the surtax, which would take effect in 1968. Forced to trade butter for guns, the American people, who now discovered a new line on their tax returns *after* "tax due"—this one called "special surcharge liability"—recoiled. "The president's tax proposal made a lot of new doves," Dean Rusk groaned to his staff. For the first time, a plurality of Americans—46 percent—judged the Vietnam War a "mistake."[27]

Now Congress and the White House had to assess other costs of the war as well. Financially, America's gold reserves were plummeting as foreign governments, spooked by the wartime inflation in the United States, converted their dollars and Treasury bonds to American gold. This threatened a run on the dollar and undermined America's role as the financial mainstay of the free world.

Militarily, the deficits were just as worrisome. Planes urgently requested by the government of Laos to defend their territory against incursions such as Hanoi's border-busting Ho Chi Minh Trail could not be supplied so long as Rolling Thunder and its loss rates continued. Helicopters sought by the three Australian battalions fighting in Vietnam could not be spared. In Europe, weapons required by America's NATO allies could not be supplied. The explanation was always the same: "due to priority requirements for Southeast Asia." This was happening at a time when Britain, a key European ally, was devaluing the pound and cutting its defense budget by $416 million and the other NATO allies were also cutting their defense outlays in the face of the economic slowdown that had set in after the boom years of the early 1960s.

Helicopters, C-130s, strike fighters, tracked and wheeled vehicles, artillery, and munitions were now being taken from the European theater and sent to South Vietnam, creating a readiness crisis in NATO. In Asia, the situation was even worse. Around Taiwan, the military balance had shifted sharply in favor of Communist China. In South Korea, the 50,000 US troops had not even been issued M-16 rifles; the weapons were that scarce. The South Korean army was, by the Pentagon's own admission, "abysmally equipped" and not ready to handle North Korea's 430,000 troops if they invaded again. Daily North Korean provocations—assassination attempts, incursions, harassment—were tolerated for lack of retaliatory means. The *Pueblo* incident of 1968 would encapsulate the failings. The North Koreans would seize an American spy ship, the USS *Pueblo*, in international waters and hold and abuse the eighty-three-man crew for eleven months with no reprisal from President Johnson, who had no force to spare for yet another conflict. Vietnam had hollowed out the American military, sucking up all of its "residual force capability." Something would have to give, and soon.[28]

In the field in Vietnam, the steady attrition of American power in pursuit of insignificant objectives continued apace. Main-force VC and NVA looked for opportunities to ambush overzealous American units still committed to search and destroy and destroy *them*. This is what happened to the US 1st Infantry Division after Junction City. In mid-June 1967, Westmoreland sent the Big Red One on a two-week mission called Operation Billings to flush out and destroy elements of two NVA divisions known to be operating in III Corps and denying Route 13 and other critical roads to the US military.

Apprised of the 1st ID's approach, NVA general and COSVN commander Nguyen Chi Thanh laid a trap for them. The commander of Operation Billings, General John Hay, had ordered his 1st ID to find those two NVA divisions operating in III Corps and bring them to battle. Hay's method was the usual. The American commander planned to leapfrog into a position that he assumed the enemy needed, and then absorb their attacks long enough for urgently summoned artillery, air strikes, and maneuver units to envelop and destroy the overeager enemy.

Instead of taking the bait, Thanh ignored the dangled air assault and withdrew deeper into the wilderness of III Corps. He then lured a battalion of Hay's 3rd Brigade to a remote LZ, where he hit it with two NVA battalions, killing 57 Americans and wounding 196. Thereafter, Hay groped in the dark for those two elusive NVA divisions. Wherever he pushed his troops, they were wasted by booby traps, snipers, mortars, and ambushes, driving up the casualties. The only time he met the enemy in force was whenever Thanh massed briefly against an isolated American unit, such as the battalion of the Big Red One savaged in its LZ. The operation petered out in heavy monsoon rains. No major gains or accomplishments were recorded.

A few months later, Hay would take another stab at it, launching Operation Shenandoah II. He used the same method as before, pushing his mobile units into spaces used by the enemy to provoke contact. These "tethered goat" operations were getting more and more dangerous as the enemy now understood exactly how to kill the goat before its heavily armed shepherds could intervene to save it with artillery and tac air.

Recognizing that American troops constantly swept their areas of operation for signs of the hidden enemy, the VC and NVA units in those AOs began to fight back with "countersweep" operations of their own. They studied and observed every American and ARVN action to determine the patterns and tactics of the free-world forces. Knowing which trails the allied forces would patrol, they prepared countersweep ambushes along those trails, with snipers, machine gun nests, and booby traps. A common ruse was to place VC stragglers in the path of an approaching platoon. The Americans or ARVN would run after the VC and into a prepared ambush—a track crisscrossed by mortars and machine guns, or a bunker complex hidden by woods or cliffs.

The first shots in such an ambush were typically taken by communist snipers, who aimed first at the radio telephone operators (RTOs), easily spotted with their backpack radios and ten-foot whip antennas. A platoon leader might run through six or more RTOs in a single year. The snipers would then train their rifles on the platoon leaders, who would be right beside the RTOs, and any grunt carrying "the pig," the M-60 machine gun, which would provide most of the unit's fire. The RTO and the platoon leader were the crucial link to fire support and medevacs. They were picked off because they were the ones keeping track of terrain features, pace count, map coordinates, and azimuth, and able to call in accurate supporting fires quickly. When RTOs went down, the enemy kept firing at them, so no one else could reach the lifesaving tactical radio alive. It all happened with

The first shots in every ambush were aimed at the radio telephone operator and the platoon leader. The RTO and the platoon leader were the crucial link to fire support and medevacs because they were the ones keeping track of terrain features, pace count, map coordinates, and azimuth. (National Archives)

scathing abruptness, which explained the commonly cited adage that the life expectancy of an RTO in an ambush was five seconds, that of a lieutenant just sixteen seconds. If machine gunners survived the first ten seconds, they'd usually be dead within five minutes. "War is hell," the grunts joked, "but contact is a mother fucker."[29]

On October 17, during Operation Shenandoah II, at a place called Ong Thanh, the NVA sprang a trap like this and killed fifty-eight men of Lieutenant Colonel Terry D. Allen's battalion of the 28th Infantry Regiment. Seventy-five more were wounded. Allen, whose father had commanded the Big Red One in World War II, was among the dead. He had walked into a skillfully prepared ambush and paid the price.

The Americans had entered the war confident that helicopters, firebases, and fast-moving tac air would give them the ability to surprise and annihilate the enemy everywhere. Instead, the Americans had become predictable.

By now, the enemy could estimate accurately how much time they had to operate before the American artillery could respond to radioed fire requests and before attack aircraft arrived over the battlefield. They would fire with everything they had—AK-47s, RPGs, machine guns, mortars, and recoilless rifles—and then scatter. As General Hay put it, defeats like Allen's were due to "the overuse of proven tactics on the ground," the very thing that made communist countersweep tactics so effective.[30]

Bad as the situation was in III Corps, it was worse in I Corps, where 65 to 70 percent of American KIAs were generated every year. Eye Corps bordered the DMZ and the first exits from the Ho Chi Minh Trail, which meant that it was the fastest point of infiltration for NVA troops and matériel. Under unceasing attack between the mountains and the sea by three NVA divisions and thousands of VC, the two Marine divisions and the Marine air wing in I Corps would lose 14,500 killed and 88,000 wounded in the war. New lieutenants arriving to lead rifle platoons knew that their odds of being killed or wounded in Vietnam were greater than 50 percent. Few Marines would pass unscathed through a full thirteen-month tour in Quang Nam or Quang Tri, the most bitterly contested provinces.[31]

The US Marines were mainly volunteers—only 10 percent of Marines in Vietnam were draftees—and they would earn fifty-seven Medals of Honor for valor. With a total worldwide strength of 190,000 Marines in 1965, there were never enough of them to defend the space of I Corps. Westmoreland now agreed to reinforce Lew Walt's III Marine Amphibious Force, the 70,000 Marines in I Corps, with three Army brigades plucked from less violent parts of Vietnam and given the name Task Force Oregon. Eye Corps, also known as "Marineland," would henceforth be a joint Marine-Army undertaking, so severe were the threats and casualties there.[32]

In the spring of 1967, Task Force Oregon, commanded by Westmoreland's chief of staff, General Bill Rosson, relieved Walt's 1st Marine Division at Chu Lai on the South China Sea coast. Just two years earlier the coastal plain around Chu Lai had been so quiet that Marine General Victor "Brute" Krulak had chosen it as the perfect place to establish the Marine Corps' second major airfield in I Corps, to supplement the crowded runways and helipad at Da Nang. The place, fifty-six miles south of Da Nang, sprawling along a sandy beach, wasn't even marked on maps. Krulak wittily named it for himself: Chu Lai, which was "Krulak" in Mandarin.[33]

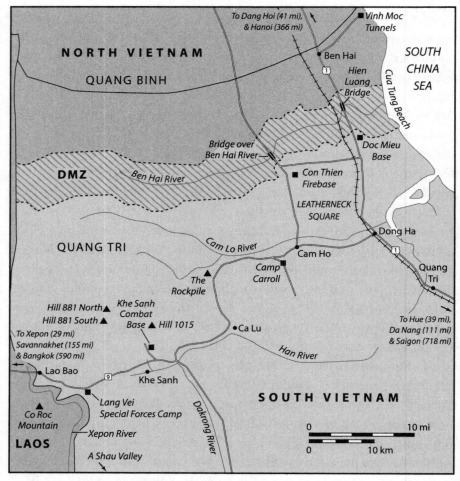

Northern "Eye Corps," aka "Marineland"

Chu Lai was no longer quiet. With the Army's arrival in 1967, it became home base and headquarters for an entire US infantry division, who called it variously "Chucky Lucky," "Chicken Little," or "Wonderful Downtown Chu Lai by the Sea." Four types of enemy forces had pushed into its area of responsibility (AOR), which was a 2,000-square-mile corridor encompassing the three southern provinces of I Corps: Quang Nam, Quang Tin, and Quang Ngai, a flat scrubby plain from the sea to the Central Highlands, with a population of 1.2 million people, largely fishermen, rice farmers, and artisans.

Ho Chi Minh had been born here. American analysts called it "a private little world" where "ideologies like democracy and communism are meaningless abstractions." By 1967, dozens, sometimes hundreds, of Americans were being killed every month in this backwater. "Lay chilly, man!" the Marines joked. "There are lots of ways to die in Quang Nam." Westmoreland's "strategy of the periphery"—his plan to find and destroy the NVA infiltrators on the empty frontiers before they descended to the populated coastal plain—was founded in part on the MACV commander's insistence that the cancer eating Chu Lai and its environs must not be allowed to spread to the rest of South Vietnam.[34]

Trying to defend the region around Chu Lai had become next to impossible due to infiltration. NVA and main-force VC had moved into the AO in regimental strength. Unable to supply themselves in battle thanks to restless American artillery and airpower, they had hidden caches of arms, food, and ammunition around the three provinces for use in their countersweep ambushes. The ARVN and Americans spent much of their time sweeping the area to find these caches in an attempt to disarm the enemy. Each time they did, they usually encountered an ambush, or a string of booby traps fashioned from the 27,000 tons of dud ordnance that the Americans were strewing across South Vietnam every year. With the allies focused on the NVA and main-force VC, a third type of enemy troops—the local forces—kept the ruff-puffs and Revolutionary Development cadres busy, raiding their hamlets and outposts, ambushing their patrols, and then melting into the villages or the countryside whenever ARVN or American reaction forces showed up.[35]

The local VC moved in squad- or platoon-sized "cells" and would force their way into a village for food, for medical care, or simply to hide from American or ARVN troops. The villages rarely resisted because of the ubiquity of a fourth type of enemy combatant, by far the most numerous: the so-called irregulars. The irregulars were the backbone of the communist organization in South Vietnam. Organized at the hamlet, village, and district levels, they carried out the daily low-level missions that eroded all semblance of government control: terrorism, sabotage, reconnaissance, espionage, tax collection, and propagandization of the population. They assisted the main-force units in transport, intelligence, and combat, snuck men and women into American bases to spy on their operations, and were trained in the conversion of dud ordnance into booby traps.[36]

Under constant attack by these four tentacles of the Viet Cong, the Chu Lai region had become one of the most dangerous places in South Vietnam, so thoroughly penetrated by the enemy that most of it had been declared a free-fire zone, where US troops were ordered to shoot "at everything not American, ROK [South Korean], or ARVN."

While the US 1st Marine Division moved north to Da Nang, Task Force Oregon swept the region around Chu Lai, Quang Tin, and Quang Ngai, with the by now usual result. These were areas that were never pacified in the entire course of the war. They earned nicknames like "Dodge City," "Happy Valley," and the "Gaza Strip." The grunts patrolled into partially deserted hamlets, through streams and hedgerows, and in dense woods. Rice paddies and loose sand alternated with pineapple forests, palms, banana trees, and "wait-a-minute vines"—vines so sticky that when you walked into one it took a minute to peel it off you.[37]

The whole area was riddled with mines and booby traps, which killed and maimed Americans at a steady, demoralizing pace. Most feared was the "Bouncing Betty," a mine that when trod on would "bounce" out of the ground and explode at waist height, cutting men in half, sawing off their legs and groins, and amputating their arms at the elbow. Some platoons would lose half or more of their strength in a fortnight from booby traps alone. New slang was coined on those bloody trails: "He really stepped on it," or "Get it all in one bag." For the grunts, the war appeared more absurd than ever, trudging back and forth over ground sown with mines in the vain hope that a single VC might emerge on a deserted village lane or poke his head out of a tunnel.[38]

Westmoreland woodenly reminded Rosson to keep on keeping on. He was to measure success, Westy commanded, by the three established metrics: body count, kill ratio, and weapons captured. Westmoreland was, as reporter Michael Herr noted after a dud of an interview with the general, strikingly literal: "I came away feeling as though I'd just had a conversation with a man who touches a chair and says 'This is a chair,' points to a desk and says, 'This is a desk.'" Now General Obvious continued to bet all on body count and kill ratio, even as their falsity and irrelevance were acknowledged in the field and everywhere else.

In the Chu Lai operation, body counts were about three times higher than weapons captured, suggesting that the KIAs were as likely to be civilians or ARVN draft dodgers as VC. The fact that captured weapons came largely from main-force caches discovered after the fighting, not from fallen troops, raised more doubts about the accuracy of Westmoreland's reporting and his claimed 10:1 kill ratio in the operation. *Esquire* reporter Michael Herr met a Special Forces captain in this period who told him: "I went out and killed one VC and liberated a prisoner. The next day the major called me in and told me I'd killed 14 VC and liberated six prisoners."[39]

Westmoreland seemed hell-bent on making things worse, not better. Task Force Oregon destroyed 70 percent of the villages in its AO, sending their inhabitants away as refugees. The war, Michael Herr observed, had "passed into the hands of the firepower freaks out to eat the country whole, and with no fine touches either."[40]

Blundering blindly, finding no enemy in three "base areas" that were supposed to be crammed with troops, General Salve Matheson, commanding the 1st Brigade of the 101st Airborne Division, decided to yank out the remaining population and shower the area with bombs, shells, and herbicides. The herbicide of choice—Agent Orange, named for the orange stripe on the barrels in which it was stored—could not have been better designed to terrify and alienate the rural population. It contained two chemical weedkillers mixed with diesel, kerosene, and dioxin, the last of these "the most toxic molecule synthesized by man." It burned away Vietnamese crops and shade trees, and soaked the ground with the dioxin that would eventually kill or deform Vietnam's children. It was splashed across 500,000 acres of South Vietnamese farmland to deny crops and cover to the VC.

Village security would have been a far more effectual way to secure the loyalty of the South Vietnamese peasants, but that was something the Americans and ARVN could never manage—the "government of the night" always impressing the peasants more than the government of the day. None of this seems to have troubled Westy or Matheson. If they couldn't locate the enemy in the hills overlooking the coastal plain, they'd turn the lush coastal plain into a desert, denying it to the enemy.[41]

Westmoreland kept creating new problems like this, one after another. Just as his search and destroy missions alienated the peasantry with their careless fire, the herbicide missions alienated them with their careless crop destruction. Matheson added 7,000 more refugees to the 12,000 already squatting in filthy camps around Duc Pho.

Saigon's population increased by one-third in the course of 1967, from 2 million to 3 million, most of the new arrivals refugees fleeing West-moreland's search and destroy operations to live in filth and poverty. South Vietnam's other cities grew as fast, squalid slums and shantytowns filled with uprooted peasants sprawling through their outskirts and populating their city centers with beggars and bar girls. VC propaganda kept a tally of villages destroyed, people moved, children conscripted, and food, livestock, fields, and forests destroyed. There was no need to workshop the message: "Americans kill many people and we want revenge!"[42]

By July 1967, fifty-three-year-old General Thanh, who commanded communist forces in the South, had made his roundabout way to Hanoi—via Cambodia and China—and presented what came to be known as the "COSVN proposal," which was ultimately the blueprint for the Tet Offensive of 1968. Thanh argued, and Le Duan's politburo agreed, that a quick victory was needed, but that the only feasible way to get one was to strike in such a stunning and brutal way that the South Vietnamese regime would fall and the Americans would give up. Thanh recommended that the NVA continue to lure the American and ARVN divisions into peripheral areas such as the Central Highlands, the Cambodian border, and the DMZ, while the massed Viet Cong launched a military takeover of South Vietnam's major cities and provincial capitals. Those critical towns—there were 105 of them—would presumably be thinly defended because the allied regular troops would be out in the border areas battling the infiltrating NVA. Thanh reasoned that such an onslaught—sudden, unexpected, and overwhelming in areas presumed secure—would collapse the Saigon regime and chase the Americans out of Vietnam.[43]

As plans went, it was a moonshot, reflecting the growing nervousness of the North Vietnamese leadership in the face of American power. Hanoi received a billion dollars of aid from the Soviets and the Chinese in 1967, a sum that was dwarfed by the $20 billion or more poured into South Vietnam by the Americans every year. In spite of their success tormenting American grunts, the North Vietnamese politburo were by no means certain that they could defeat the most powerful country in the world. Hanoi could keep prolonging the war, but how long could they keep their people's nose to the grindstone, especially if the Americans inserted yet more troops and hardware and intensified the bombing of North Vietnam?

Resistance to Le Duan's bloodthirsty methods in North Vietnam was growing. Political and military officials were whispering about the need for negotiations. Le Duan was compelled to launch more purges in 1967–1968, suspending "party democracy," cutting off politburo debate on the war, and arresting hundreds of communist officials and NVA officers for the crime of "sowing dissension within the party and undermining the unity of the army."[44]

Thanh himself was killed after making his case to the politburo. The Americans later credited his demise to a B-52 strike on his COSVN head-quarters that required his hasty evacuation to Hanoi. But it appears more likely that he died from a heart attack brought on by the bottles of 40-proof rice wine that he and his comrades drank in Hanoi to toast the decision to press ahead with the Tet Offensive.

Some suspected that Thanh may have been poisoned by Giap, his chief rival, or even Le Duan, who now hastened to replace Thanh with fifty-five-year-old Pham Hung, a Le Duan loyalist, who would oversee General Hoang Van Thai, sent south at the same time to coordinate the VC uprising from the COSVN headquarters. Thai began implementing orders to draw the American and ARVN forces away from the populated areas and into the remote ones, where they would be helpless to intervene effectively against the coming VC onslaught in the cities and towns of South Vietnam.

In the last months of 1967, the NVA launched a series of offensives against remote areas that seemed to have little strategic value—Khe Sanh, near the Laotian border; Con Thien, along the DMZ; Loc Ninh, on the Cambodian border; and Dak To, in the Central Highlands. Westmoreland, as was his habit, took this as proof of nothing more than infiltration, and hastened to counter it with big troop deployments. Others were puzzled by the enemy's choice of objectives.[45]

Normally, the NVA skirted bastions like these to infiltrate the South. Around Khe Sanh, NVA infiltrators had always given the Marine combat base a wide berth, marching into South Vietnam on what the Americans called the "Santa Fe Trail," an infiltration route along the Laotian border, just beyond the maximum range of American artillery. Now they were probing the combat base itself, sniping its outposts, cutting its defensive wire, and moving two entire NVA divisions—25,000 men, 50 percent of their strength in I Corps—into positions to attack it. Why?[46]

Westmoreland interpreted all of this activity as justifying his controversial "strategy of the periphery"—to meet the enemy on the frontier and defeat him there. He continued to believe that he was exercising initiative in the war, when in fact he was dancing like a puppet on Hanoi's string. Battles like these were part of Hanoi's plan to draw the Americans and their ARVN ally into the remote badlands, where few South Vietnamese lived, and expose the populous cities and coastal plain to the Tet Offensive of 1968. It was a crude strategy that hinged on Westmoreland's eagerness to take the bait and move his maneuver battalions from populated areas to unpopulated ones.

As usual, Westy did not disappoint. President Johnson looked at a place like Khe Sanh and warned that it might be just another "damn Dinbinfoo," meaning a marginal place that the Americans would be tricked into defending at a high cost. Westmoreland looked at the same place and pictured it as "a Dien Bien Phu in reverse," meaning that he would accept the gift of the North Vietnamese massing forces there and then slaughter them with air strikes and artillery. The beleaguered Americans in these places would be left as the "tethered goat," certainly yet another cause of the cynicism that was taking hold on the home front and now in the ranks too. "Eat the apple, fuck the Corps," Marines had begun to scrawl on their helmets and flak jackets.[47]

In April 1967, Westmoreland had ordered the Marines to take and hold three hills north of the Khe Sanh combat base, which they had done, after suffering 160 dead and 746 wounded in murderous struggles for the summits. Fifty percent of the Marines sent into action in these "hill fights" were killed or wounded, but they secured the high ground overlooking Khe Sanh, which Westmoreland considered essential—to protect the base and to fire across the border into Laos and the DMZ. For the rest of the year, Westy ordered the Marines to launch a sequence of operations around Khe Sanh: Crockett, Ardmore, and then Scotland, all aimed at scouring the wooded mountains around the combat base with two battalions to find and destroy all communist units there.

The fighting was intermittent and the kill ratios—about 4:1—not particularly favorable. Antagonism between the Army and Marines sharpened. From the Marine perspective, there were two hubs of combat in I Corps:

the DMZ and the densely populated coastal plain between Da Nang and Chu Lai, which had become an operating area of the NVA 2nd Division. The Marines continued to insist that their relatively small numbers would be far better employed at pacification in that critical populated area of South Vietnam.[48]

Westmoreland wasn't listening. In July 1967, Westy took one of the two Marine battalions at Khe Sanh and sent it east, where the NVA was attacking America's northernmost bastion in South Vietnam, the 525-foot height of Con Thien, which overlooked the DMZ and anchored what some called "the McNamara Line." The McNamara Line, officially the Strong Point Obstacle System, was designed to narrow the options available to NVA units trying to infiltrate across the DMZ. Its sensors and barriers would channel the enemy into certain areas, such as the ground below Con Thien, where they could be detected and shelled.[49]

Con Thien, with its bunkers, batteries, and bulldozed red-dirt airstrip, absorbed heavy bombardments every day. The Marine epigram "Shut up and die like a man" was nowhere more apt than here. On September 25, 1967, alone, 1,200 mortar and artillery shells struck the base, drawing in more Marines to replace casualties. "Don't worry baby, God'll think of something," a Black Marine at Con Thien was overheard muttering to no one in particular during one such barrage.[50]

American commanders had to weigh the benefits of Con Thien against its chief liabilities—that it squatted within range of 130 North Vietnamese howitzers dug in just beyond the DMZ, and that it was hard to supply over a single road that was mined and ambushed by the enemy every day. Surely the McNamara Line and the DMZ could be no less effectively monitored from a more secure base farther from the NVA artillery, such as the staging area of Dong Ha, ten miles to the south. But that's not how Westy thought or behaved. Westmoreland fought back, regarding Con Thien as another "Dien Bien Phu in reverse," where he could call in air strikes, artillery, and naval bombardments on the lonely hilltop just fourteen miles from the sea.[51]

The battle for Con Thien turned into a monthslong stalemate, both sides oddly believing that they were winning. The Marines and their air and naval support killed an estimated 7,500 North Vietnamese, but the Marines would lose over 1,000 dead and 9,000 wounded, and the stories about Con

Thien reported in the press were hard on morale and public opinion. Take the tragedy of two companies of the 1st Battalion of the 9th Marine Regiment, which descended from Con Thien for a routine sweep of the two-mile gap between the base and the DMZ only to be ambushed by an NVA force that had evaded the sensors of the McNamara Line and the eyes of Marine pilots overhead.

Eighty-six Marines were killed, and 176 wounded; only 27 returned unscathed. The Marines would later judge it "the worst single disaster to befall a Marine Corps rifle company during the Vietnam War." The corpses roasted in the sun for two days before they could be recovered—this time by two entire battalions of Marines, who were shocked by the sight and stench. A news crew shot the scene for television—it was never aired—but reports of what had happened leaked out. The dead Marines had been mutilated. One had had his genitals cut off and sewn to his face. A picture of the grunt's girlfriend had been stabbed into his chest. In the first nine months of 1967, the 3rd Marine Division lost 10,000 killed and wounded along the DMZ at places like Con Thien, to no appreciable effect. No ground changed hands, and enemy infiltration continued unchecked.[52]

Westmoreland's alternately leaden and light-footed operations contained a fatal flaw. He vacillated between reinforcing peripheral strongpoints and sweeping the countryside with search and destroy missions. Neither approach promised or even approached victory for the simple reason that there were not enough friendly troops. Westy saturated areas briefly with sweeps and heavy fire and then left, permitting the NVA and VC to reoccupy temporarily abandoned camps and push deeper into the South Vietnamese countryside, this time with greater popular support after the population had been scorched by American fire and defoliants or forced into refugee camps.

In the "robbing Peter to pay Paul" way that was the nature of American deployments in Vietnam, Westmoreland now desperately "realigned" his troop strength, reactivating a forgotten World War II unit—the 23rd "Americal" Infantry Division, so named because twenty-five years earlier it had been pulled together from three US Army regiments rushed out to the South Pacific island of New Caledonia after Pearl Harbor to defend it against Japanese invasion. This "American, New Caledonian Division"—"Americal" for short—had been the only American division in history to be formed of troops already overseas.

It now repeated the feat, reactivated in Chu Lai in September 1967 with three brigades and a cavalry squadron plucked from II and III Corps. Those three brigades, organized as Task Force Oregon, had just torn through South Vietnam's three northern provinces, uprooting over 20 percent of the population and laying waste to the countryside. Jonathan Schell, who embedded himself in five of the task force's operations, wrote another scathing piece for the *New Yorker* that summed up Westmoreland's approach: "We are destroying, seemingly by inadvertence, the very country we are supposedly protecting."[53]

The Americal Division was ordered to reinforce the overstretched 1st Marine Division and pacify the space between Da Nang and Chu Lai once and for all. When the officers of the Americal were later asked by MACV, "What makes duty at this base different from others?" they responded: "Searching for Charlie." It seemed harder in this fiercely hostile AO than anywhere else. The winning of hearts and minds was never prioritized. "Civic action," MACV's blanket term for CORDS activities such as farm aid or vaccination programs, was assumed at best to be a future benefit. "Americal clears and secures so this can happen" was all that the division's commander, forty-eight-year-old General Samuel Koster, had to say on the matter. Koster's three Americal brigades made plans to subdivide into battalions and sweep the AO constantly with helicopter assaults designed to "destroy the enemy before he can fade into the jungles."[54]

As in other combat units, the Americal's immersion in battle yielded a distinctive slang. Putting your M-16 on full automatic was "rock & roll." The M-60 machine gun was "the pig," the M-79 grenade launcher the "chunker" or "thumper." Hand grenades were "frags." Contact was "quakin' and shakin'." The grunts called their division patch—a blue shield emblazoned with the Southern Cross—"the Blue Cross Hospitalization Group."

When the troops weren't on an op, their firebases—one per battalion, three to five per brigade—would spit H&I onto every important terrain feature in the area. Visiting one of these firebases, Michael Herr fell in with a gunner, who assured him "that their record was the worst in the whole Corps, probably the whole country, they'd harassed and interdicted a lot of sleeping civilians and Korean Marines, even a couple of Americal patrols, but hardly any Viet Cong."[55]

Nevertheless, Koster clung to the plan to keep the enemy moving, taking casualties, and running out of supplies and recruits. It worked for a time, but the grittiness of the area and the growing hatred of the locals led the Americal Division in six months' time to a place called My Lai, where their plans would spectacularly unravel, along with the American war effort.[56]

In some corner of his brain, Westmoreland must have seen it all coming. On a flight during that summer of 1967, the general found himself seated next to journalist Neil Sheehan. Sheehan asked about the agony of the Vietnamese people and its impact on the war. "Aren't you bothered by all of the civilians killed by shelling and bombing?" Sheehan asked the general. "Yes," Westmoreland replied, casually adding: "But it does deprive the enemy of the population, doesn't it?" Westy, in other words, knew exactly what he was doing but felt certain that amid the slaughter and destruction, he was drying up the sea in which the VC swam and reaching the "crossover point"—the point at which he would be killing more enemy troops than the communist recruiters could replace. Westmoreland could only hope that one final push might break Hanoi's will to go on before his own casualties and dearth of results broke LBJ's confidence in him. But the general was running out of time.[57]

Chapter 11

ZENITH OF FATUITY

Khe Sanh and Con Thien were just two American backwaters attacked by Hanoi in late 1967 to lure the Americans away from the population centers. In the 31,000 rugged, empty square miles of II Corps, there was another: Dak To, a lonely Special Forces compound in the Central Highlands.

Westmoreland fixated on four regiments of the NVA 1st Division, which were believed to be moving through the mountains and gathering for an overwhelming attack on Dak To. With Giap departing for his "self-exile" in Budapest, General Van Tien Dung was resuming the attacks that had triggered the Hawthorne, Paul Revere, Sam Houston, Francis Marion, and Greeley operations of 1966–1967. In those earlier battles, the NVA had waged small "bait and lure" operations, to draw free-world forces into the jungle-clad mountains and kill them in their small patrol units. Westmoreland had taken the bait each time, intoning his obtuse mantra: "If we avoided battle, we would never succeed." It had become an article of faith for Westy that you *had* to fight in the Central Highlands and along the entire length of the DMZ to prevent "the enemy pushing his base areas closer to the centers of population."[1]

With Vice President Hubert Humphrey arriving in Saigon to attend President Thieu's inauguration at the end of October 1967, Le Duan and his entourage now played for bigger stakes. LBJ and Humphrey were

Protesters march on the Pentagon in October 1967 during the first great national demonstration against the Vietnam War. (LBJ Library)

looking increasingly vulnerable at home. More than half of Americans polled in 1967 declared that the draft was "unfair." Muhammad Ali had refused induction in April—"I ain't got no quarrel with those Viet Cong"— and had been barred from boxing and convicted of draft evasion in June. The first mass protest against the war occurred in October 1967, on the eve of Dak To, when 100,000 people gathered at the Lincoln Memorial and a third of them marched on to the Pentagon, where 682 were arrested.[2]

Campus protest had become a feature of the Vietnam War because of the dramatic way American society had changed over the past decade. The population had grown 7 percent but college enrollment had surged 102 percent, not least because college and grad students were exempt from military service until 1967, when the Johnson administration began dismantling the automatic student deferment. This naturally stimulated campus resistance to the war.[3]

With the baby boom and the affluent society intersecting, college campuses were radicalized by the 300,000 draft calls in 1967. For the first time, college students would have to submit to a standardized "college qualification test" and score in the highest percentiles to avoid the draft and continue in college. Grad students would lose their deferments after a single year of study. By 1967, most students considered the war a gross misuse of American power. "They can't understand why we are using our air power against a primitive people that has no air power," George Ball explained to the president.[4]

Dak To, established to monitor the infiltration routes through the 6,000-foot peaks that ran along the Laotian and Cambodian borders, unexpectedly became one of the biggest battles of the war. Westmoreland was in Washington briefing President Johnson on what the general was grandly calling his "Year of Progress" when the threat to Dak To emerged.

American signals intelligence detected the installation of new NVA forward command posts and their direct radio communication with Hanoi—always a tip-off of impending offensives. The five regiments of the NVA 1st Division appeared to be devising a three-pronged attack on Dak To.

General Creighton Abrams, who had left Washington in May to take up his new role as Westmoreland's deputy, found himself acting commander during Westy's political trip to Washington. Abrams rushed the US 4th Infantry Division and 173rd Airborne Brigade into action. Twelve thousand trucks were put on the road from the American bases at Kontum City and Pleiku to supply Dak To with a mountain of ammunition, fuel, and food. Thwarted by Abrams' rapid reinforcement of Dak To, the NVA changed their plan. Instead of overrunning Dak To, they took up defensive positions in the hills south and southwest of it, trained their mortars and rockets on the Dak To combat base and airstrip, and dared the Americans to climb into those mountains to root them out.[5]

The carnage inside Dak To mounted as the NVA artillery pounded the base, hitting C-130s on the ground and blowing up tons of ammunition and fuel. With the stealthy NVA infantry and artillery springing ambushes on American patrols and dug in on the peaks around Dak To, Abrams ordered them driven out in a big op he named MacArthur. The conditions for Operation MacArthur around Dak To were appalling—"the endless rain seemed to beat against the place, driving it, and everyone in it, deeper into the depressing goo," Private John Ketwig wrote. Ketwig described the mood inside Dak To during the long battle: "Thousands of guys like myself, torn away from home and family, crouched in the mud, wishing they weren't here." They'd have ample opportunity to complain and make those complaints heard, for Dak To drew a crowd of network TV crews and reporters, including emerging stars such as Peter Arnett, Edwin White, Dana Stone, and Hugh Greenway.[6]

In the hills overlooking Dak To, the NVA took full advantage of the favorable terrain: caves, cliffs, dense jungle, triple-canopy vegetation, streams and rivers, foot trails, and only one hard-surface road to serve the American guns. A battalion of the US 4th ID took Hill 1338, south of Dak To, while two ARVN battalions cleared Hill 1416, northeast of the place. With American strength surging in the area and the arrival of the B-52s, which pounded the enemy-held peaks, the North Vietnamese began a retreat to their sanctuaries in Laos and Cambodia. They clung to key heights on the way back, most notoriously Hill 875, southwest of Dak To.[7]

The fighting there, in the week before Thanksgiving, was vicious. "As far as brutal fighting goes," General William Peers told journalists, "I would say that this is the worst that we've had." Two battalions of the NVA 174th Regiment were in camouflaged, bunkered positions, their faces blackened, their weapons wrapped in burlap. Early on November 19, three companies of the 173rd Airborne Brigade, about 330 men, climbed the north slope of Hill 875, intending to push the enemy out of their positions and off the hill. "The Herd," as the 173rd were known, had suffered 79 killed and 287 wounded just reaching the mount against NVA rearguards. They now met even fiercer resistance. Companies C and D of the 2nd Battalion of the 503rd Regiment went first, followed by Company A, which waited in reserve and busied itself hacking an LZ out of the jungle.[8]

The assault formation, "two up and one back," the reverse wedge formation preferred by American commanders for fifty years, immediately broke down in the rough, wooded terrain. The paratroopers, struggling to stay on line, were continually surrounded and mortared by aggressive, stealthy enemy infantry, who sheared off squads, platoons, and command groups, then slid a force in between the two forward companies and the reserve company behind to prevent them from combining. "Jesus, they were all over the place," one of the grunts recalled. "The noncoms kept shouting 'get up the hill, get up the goddamn hill,' but we couldn't; we were surrounded, and we were firing in all directions."[9]

Alpha Company ended up having to "escape forward" to join Charlie and Delta Companies on the slope, its envelopment narrowly averted by the heroics of Pfc. Carlos Lozada, a twenty-year-old Puerto Rican, who walked backward up the hill firing his M-60 machine gun long enough for the company to slip out of the trap, a feat for which Lozada received an NVA bullet in the head and a posthumous Medal of Honor. Helicopters sent to resupply the American troops with pallets of ammo, food, and water were driven off by enemy ground fire. Six slicks went down in flames. NVA infantry, hidden in tunnels, camouflaged in trees, and firing from invisible, defiladed positions, yelled *"Chieu hoi!"*—"Open arms!"—to mock the Americans, who crouched in frightened, disoriented groups on the hillside.

An air strike sent to relieve the battered 2nd Battalion as night fell on November 19 went terribly wrong and pointed to the growing difficulty of bombing safely in Vietnam, where the bombs were still "dumb" and unguided and the opposing forces were so close together that the danger of a "short round"—ordnance falling on friendly forces instead of the enemy—had become a fact of life. "Air Force bombs are very, very accurate," grunts joked. "They hit the ground."

In this particular case, Lieutenant Colonel Richard Taber, a Marine pilot who had flown ninety hours in combat, was directed by his FAC, an Air Force captain orbiting the battlefield in a Cessna, to drop his bombs

"Air Force bombs are very, very accurate," grunts joked. "They hit the ground." Friendly fire deaths were a constant menace. Here an F-100 drops its bombs into jungle canopy. (National Archives)

on a napalm fire that Air Force jets had just ignited along the enemy trench lines. Taber, swooping in at 500 miles per hour, released his two Snake Eye Mark 81 bombs. They landed 220 yards short. The bombs, each filled with 100 pounds of TNT and aluminum powder, the latter added to increase the heat and blast of the bomb, tumbled onto the very spot where the command group and first aid station for two of the American companies trapped on the hillside were sheltered. One of Taber's bombs failed to explode; the other glanced off a tree and burst on top of the Americans.[10]

The Mark 81 bomb, the lightest bomb in the Air Force arsenal and heavily used in Vietnam to mitigate the chances of "fratricide," tore through the grunts on the ground. One company commander was killed, the other severely wounded. Forty-one others were killed, and forty-four were wounded by the blast. An Air Force pilot passing over the scene immediately detected the error: "Oops," he blurted into his microphone, "we just got friendlies."[11]

At the point of impact, Specialist Jon Wambi Cook, who had been shielded by a tree trunk, heard moaning and crying, crawled to the edge of the smoking crater, and peered inside. The carnage was dimly lit by flares drifting over the battlefield. "All you saw was parts and pieces." Cook recognized the face of a friend. "Hey," the face called, "can you come and get me?" Cook squinted into the darkness: "I could see that he'd been cut off below the thighs; there was nothing there."[12]

With the 2nd Battalion of the 503rd Infantry Regiment pinned down on the north slope of Hill 875 and kept alive only by a steady application of artillery and air strikes, the three companies of the regiment's 4th Battalion flew into a firebase north of the hill on November 20 and then moved overland in diamond formations—one platoon in the lead, one on each of the flanks, and one in the rear—to rescue the 2nd Battalion, which had crammed inside a narrow perimeter, barely 100 yards wide and 100 yards deep. The besieged battalion was under constant fire, was running out of everything, and could not even evacuate its wounded because LZs could not be cut and medevacs could not approach through intense enemy antiaircraft fire, much of it from captured American M-60 machine guns.

The communists were so close to the perimeter that the Americans inside could hear the almost instantaneous cough and impact of the enemy mortars—five-round volleys either focused on targets or walked through the position in a searching pattern that, given the crowding, always hit something.

Casualties piled up in the packed square. Direct hits on holes crowded with grunts would kill or wound half a dozen men at a time. The three companies of the 4th Battalion marched all day through scrub and thick bamboo on November 20 to reach the 2nd Battalion. They passed through several abandoned NVA base camps, and knew they were close when they arrived at a 2nd Battalion observation post, occupied by a single paratrooper, lying dead on his side in a pile of empty shell casings, still clutching his jammed machine gun. After that, they passed so many dead paratroopers of the 2nd Battalion that one grunt asked aloud if there could be any friendlies left alive. Sweeping into the perimeter, they found the survivors of the 2nd Battalion spent, many of them with tears in their eyes.

All night long the enemy artillery raked the reinforced perimeter. Reporter Peter Arnett, who was there, noted that "the living and the dead had the same gray pallor on Hill 875." The casualties mounted: "Men joking with you and offering cigarettes writhed on the ground wounded and pleading for water minutes later." Instead of withdrawing, the Americans resumed the attack on November 21.

One thousand helicopters arrived overhead to drop in LAWs (the latest version of the bazooka), flamethrowers, mortars, and ammo. The paratroopers of the 4th Battalion were given hasty instruction in the use of flamethrowers and LAWs. They then formed up to watch five air strikes on the hill above them—ten F-100s and a pair of F-4C Phantoms shuttling in to drop 15 tons of high explosive and 7.5 tons of napalm on the summit of Hill 875. The enemy bunkers and tunnels withstood it all. They would shiver, quake, burn, and then resume firing. "We've tried 750 pounders, napalm and everything else, but air can't do it," a despairing platoon leader said to Peter Arnett. "It's going to take manpower to get those positions."[13]

The sky soldiers attacked at three in the afternoon, moving out of the shell-gouged perimeter and into the tangle of blown-down trees around it. The air strikes seemed to have accomplished nothing. The fire from above was as intense as ever. The paratroopers lost another 19 killed and 108 wounded trying to move up the hill.

The grunts looked anxiously for targets for their LAWs and flamethrowers and found none. The NVA on the slopes were hidden in bunkers that were almost flush to the ground, and they were firing from six-inch slits covered with leaves and branches. While the M-60 machine gunners stood erect to spray the trees around them in a desperate bid to suppress the snipers nested there, thirty-four-year-old Master Sergeant William Cates hustled forward with satchel charges to fling at the bunkers. He was hit by a mortar round, which disintegrated him, his satchel charges, and the men around him.

The 4th Battalion's Bravo Company suffered devastating casualties—all of its platoons mauled. The survivors retreated 100 yards, some muttering an altered "Battle Hymn of the Republic": "Gory Gory What a Hell-of-a-Way to Die." They sat down to allow the Air Force and the artillery to resume pounding the hill. All day and night on November 22 the medium and heavy artillery fired at maximum rates, and air strikes came in every fifteen to thirty minutes.[14]

The next morning, Thanksgiving Day, the 4th Battalion attacked again up the north slope, this time with help from two companies of the 1st Battalion of the 12th Regiment, which advanced up the south slope—a tactical precaution that Peers should have taken days earlier. They were preceded by another storm of American artillery—10,000 rounds—and a final massive air strike: four tons of high explosive and three tons of napalm in forty-five minutes. Then the two battalions attacked, crying "Airborne!" and "Geronimo!" as they neared the bald, burned, cratered summit.

This time the Americans took the hill in just twenty-five minutes. The enemy had left. Some of the paratroopers wept with relief and pride as they examined the captured fortifications: a trench system deep enough for the NVA infantry to walk upright, six feet of overhead cover to protect against shrapnel and high explosive, and caves dug into the back of the trenches so that dead or wounded men could be shoved out of the way. The grunts ate C-ration turkey loaf until helicopters arrived with a hot Thanksgiving meal, which they devoured sitting in the dust atop Hill 875. "It was the best meal I ever ate," one of the paratroopers recalled.[15]

MACV hastened to pronounce Dak To a victory. "It's the beginning of a great defeat for the enemy," Westmoreland told the *New York Times*. "We smashed Giap's attack," Westy's military intelligence chief added. That Westy's intelligence shop didn't know that Giap was 5,000 miles away in exile in Hungary was disturbing. Still more disturbing was the tactical result.

Nearly 2,000 Americans were "smashed" in the battle—376 killed and 1,441 wounded. The 4th ID's medical company discovered that it had used more units of blood in those five days on Hill 875 than the hard-fighting division had consumed in the previous eleven months: 300 pounds of blood, and for what? A place that the North Vietnamese had abandoned the instant it lost its tactical advantage. The enemy suffered an estimated 1,000 killed on the hill, mostly to artillery and air strikes, but the battle rendered three 4th ID battalions and the entire 173rd Airborne Brigade "combat ineffective," while MACV sought desperately for fillers.[16]

The American rifle companies had lost an astonishing 51 percent of their strength in the monthlong battle. The heavy American casualties and the successful escape of the NVA 1st Division from an area "secured" by no fewer than seventy-eight American, ARVN, and South Korean maneuver battalions belied again Westmoreland's theory of victory: that the communist forces could be surprised, flushed from cover, "fixed" in place by infantry, and annihilated with firepower.[17]

It was the Americans who were continually surprised—by the enemy resistance and tactics. The four-day struggle for Hill 875 saw the heaviest use of tac air and artillery yet unleashed in the war: 152,000 rounds of artillery and 2,096 sorties of tac air dropping 3,400 tons of ordnance on a small target. Nine hundred tons of food, fuel, and ammo had been flown and driven into Dak To every day to supply the onslaught, and yet, as always in Vietnam, the "great victory" changed nothing on the ground.

By late 1967, Hanoi was infiltrating 14,000 NVA replacements into South Vietnam and recruiting 7,000 new VC every *month*. It was hard to bleed out an enemy whose army was growing, not shrinking, and showing no willingness to compromise or retreat. General Giap later observed of this moment in the war that Westmoreland "could have put in 300,000 more men, even 400,000, but it would have made no difference." The theater was too big, the terrain too difficult, the resistance too stout, and the ARVN too cautious. Nevertheless, General Peers wrote his after-action report in the "we are winning" political tones preferred in Washington and Saigon. He proclaimed Dak To "the turning point of the war in the Central Highlands."[18]

The officers of the 173rd Airborne Brigade knew better. Their analysis took account of facts on the ground: "The enemy continues to choose the time and the place in which decisive engagements are fought. He fights only where the tactical situation, terrain, battlefield preparation, and the relative strength of the opposing forces favor enemy action—only then does he initiate significant contacts." The lack of any meaningful success at Dak To confirmed the observation of another senior officer: "Trying to win the war tactically was like swimming up Niagara Falls with an anvil around your neck."[19]

By now, it must have been clear to Westmoreland and Abrams that US casualties, even if smaller than the enemy's, were a strategic factor that had to be accepted with extraordinary caution given the small number of American combat troops, the fading of morale inside the Army and Marine Corps, and the rise in opposition to the war in the United States. In the last three months of 1967, 200 Americans died every *week* in Vietnam. Michael Herr, who wrote one of the most powerful books about Vietnam as well as narration and screenplays for *Apocalypse Now* and *Full Metal Jacket*, got his first taste of the war at Dak To. He arrived during the struggle for Hill 875, in which those two battalions of the 173rd Airborne Brigade lost 400 killed or wounded in the battle for a cold, foggy, rain-lashed mount whose only value was the presence on its summit of a fleeting number of enemy troops.[20]

Herr watched a Chinook full of paratroopers returning from the hill set down on the landing strip of Dak To, where a welcoming party of Red Cross "donut dollies" had been assembled to cheer the troops up with coffee and donuts. The dollies were one-year volunteers who would try to distract shocked and frightened grunts with games or banter. "Where you from, soldier?" "Hi soldier, what's your name?" the girls called. "And the men from the 173rd just kept walking without answering, staring straight ahead, their eyes rimmed with red from fatigue, their faces pinched and aged with what had happened during the night." Only one of the men paused to answer the shouted queries; he said something in a girl's ear and she began to cry. "The rest just walked past the girls and the large olive-drab coffee urns. They had no idea where they were."[21]

What exactly was Westmoreland "containing" with these bloody operations that were killing and wounding far more Americans than expected? In the course of 1967, the big battles such as Dak To, Cedar Falls, Attleboro, and Junction City hiked the monthly average of 477 American KIAs, which had seemed high in 1966, to a far more alarming 816 American KIAs. US casualties in Vietnam had more than doubled in 1967—from 44,382 killed and wounded on New Year's Day of that year to over 100,000 killed and wounded on New Year's Eve twelve months later. Eight hundred and fifty US aircraft had been shot down in a single year. "Victory is not close at hand. It may be beyond reach," the *New York Times* ventured. The war had been entirely "Americanized"—troop strength surging in two years from 50,000 to 500,000—and yet nothing decisive had been accomplished. Westy spoke of "tremendous progress," but his subordinates in the field didn't. "American officers talk somberly about fighting here for *decades*," one journalist reported from Saigon. "Stalemate," a dirty word in Washington, was on everyone's lips in Vietnam.[22]

In October 1967, *Life* magazine, an early and influential cheerleader for the war, ran up the white flag, declaring that the Vietnam War was no longer "worth winning," no longer "imperative," and no longer worth "asking young Americans to die for."

Congress, which could have cut funding for the war, remained on the sidelines, the senators and representatives finding it politically expedient to "support the troops" with funding rather than risk their "national security" credentials by advocating the withdrawal craved by the vast majority of troops. Attempts to repeal the Tonkin Gulf Resolution or forbid the deployment of draftees to Vietnam in 1966 had received just six and two votes, respectively, Senate majority leader Mike Mansfield, an early critic of the war, explaining his pusillanimity this way: "We are in too deep now."[23]

In November 1967, Bill Fulbright's Senate Foreign Relations Committee took another stab at curtailing the president's war powers, his rule by "executive supremacy," but the resolution went nowhere. LBJ's lawyers argued that "declarations of war are out of date" and that the president needed instant power to react to crises with "an immediate riposte." Congress weakly agreed, despite the fact that the Vietnam "riposte" had been going on long enough to call it a war. Congress would not seek to impose a single limit on the war until 1969, when it would *try* (and fail) to forbid the president sending US troops into Laos or Cambodia.[24]

His flank secured by a compliant Congress, Westmoreland turned his fire on another threat: the media. He deplored the influence of Western journalists on public opinion, calling them cat's-paws of Hanoi and purveyors of fake news, and instructed MACV's public affairs office, JUSPAO, to put the rising American casualties in a positive light. They were trifling beside the enemy's heavier losses, Westy explained.[25]

At Dak To, a battle initiated by the NVA in November 1967 to draw the Americans into the jungled mountains of the tri-border area and away from the populated cities and lowlands, Westmoreland assured Americans that the US losses of 1,800 killed or wounded paled beside total enemy losses of 4,000 or more. Yet when the 173rd Airborne Brigade took Hill 875 at the climax of the battle, they found only forty-four corpses, not the hundreds that might have been expected, and Westy was later discovered to have personally intervened to inflate body count. A US company commander had suffered seventy-nine KIAs and twenty-three wounded to kill small numbers of NVA; Westmoreland had increased the captain's body count to 475. "Too late, it's already gone out," Westy snapped when challenged about the lie.[26]

In November 1967, the NVA launched another border battle. Like Dak To, it was intended to pull American, ARVN, and Korean forces away from the populated cities and coastal plain and into the mountain wilderness—the essential prelude to the Tet Offensive, planned for January 1968. Four NVA regiments, about 25,000 men heavily supported by artillery and antiaircraft guns, began to close around the Marines' Khe Sanh combat base, which sat close to the Laotian border and the Ho Chi Minh Trail on the western edge of I Corps and the DMZ. This border battle seized President Johnson's attention more than the others. The president took the unusual step of demanding a letter from the Joint Chiefs "guaranteeing" that Khe Sanh would not fall if the Marines remained dug in there. "Sign it in blood," the president grunted. The NVA command planned not only to humiliate the Americans at Khe Sanh, seizing the combat base and its battalion of Marines, but also to tear a hole in their border defenses through which NVA divisions could funnel south to reinforce the Tet Offensive.[27]

For anyone viewing this dismal picture, optimism was hard to summon, but Westmoreland summoned it anyway, with the mendacious alacrity that characterized his tenure in Vietnam. He wanted more and more troops—a "minimum force" of 550,000, or an "optimal force" of 672,000—and he insisted that his "Year of Progress" was going well, despite all evidence to the contrary.

"During 1967," Westy wrote, "the enemy lost control of large sectors of the population." The VC were having morale and recruiting problems and had been forced to disperse to avoid American attacks. The US military, Westmoreland alleged, had truly reached the "crossover point," where free-world forces were killing more men in South Vietnam than Hanoi could infiltrate to replace them. Body count in 1967 exceeded infiltration by 31,000. He boasted of "tremendous progress." Attrition was working.[28]

Unfortunately, MACV's own figures belied the rosy nonsense purveyed by Westmoreland in his effort to wring more troops from President Johnson. By year-end 1967, there were 500,000 US troops and 750,000 ARVN and allied troops in South Vietnam against 300,000 VC and NVA troops, yet efforts to destroy the VC were failing, and efforts to interdict the continuing flow of manpower from North Vietnam were also failing. NVA forces in South Vietnam increased from 58,600 in December 1966 to 80,000 in December 1967. An estimated 36,300 infiltrators had entered South Vietnam in 1965, 92,287 in 1966, and 101,263 in 1967. This had prompted the construction of the McNamara Line, as well as the bloody struggle for border posts such as Dak To and Khe Sanh.[29]

Westmoreland hoped eventually to stanch this flow of northern infiltrators and matériel by invading Laos to deny its trails and "sanctuaries" to Hanoi, but that was a pipe dream under any circumstances prevailing in 1967. There were fourteen NVA battalions in Laos, 100,000 Pathet Lao communist guerrillas, and thousands of Chinese troops posing as "volunteers." Looking at this communist horde, CINCPAC made clear to MACV that it could not spare even a squadron of aircraft to expand the war into Laos, where the roads of the Ho Chi Minh Trail continued to multiply.

Farther south on the Ho Chi Minh Trail, Cambodia remained a weak, divided country, where officers of the Royal General Staff were actively selling arms and rice to the VC camps inside their own border. Cambodia's government—still led by forty-five-year-old Prince Norodom Sihanouk—was in constant conflict with Saigon over offshore drilling rights, free navigation on the Mekong, the exact location of the border between the two nations, and the status of several disputed islands that had not been settled when the French scuttled from Indochina in 1954.

Even the election in 1966 of a conservative, anticommunist Cambodian government had done nothing to change the policy of "extreme neutrality" in eastern Cambodia, which amounted to Sihanouk authorizing Hanoi to use Cambodia as a sanctuary in exchange for not destabilizing the Sihanouk regime with support for Pol Pot's Khmer Rouge "forest army."[30]

With obstacles like these—to say nothing of the poor roads and forbidding terrain—CINCPAC warned Westmoreland not even to contemplate operations against the cross-border sanctuaries. With everything committed to South Vietnam, neither troops nor aircraft could be spared for what would have to be massive and sustained operations in Cambodia and Laos, with little chance of success.[31]

Critics who argued that the war could have been won if only the will had been summoned to "take" those communist sanctuaries always neglected to explain how they could have been "taken" and held without troops and aircraft and against the forces of nature, weather, time, domestic opinion, enemy action, and hostile populations and governments. Even as Westmoreland assured the press, the president, and the Congress that he was defeating the enemy, he actually knew the opposite to be true. Laos and Cambodia had become communist highways and sanctuaries, beyond the reach of American capabilities, and MACV's own numbers showed an increase, not a decrease, in enemy strength across South Vietnam, giving the lie to Westmoreland's assertion that the goal of breaking the enemy through attrition "had in good measure been achieved."[32]

What was certifiably being achieved was the breaking of the South Vietnamese people. Their presidential election in September 1967 was a sham, with the all-military Thieu-Ky ticket winning only 34 percent of the vote despite their best efforts at vote rigging. When the National Assembly's committee on elections voted to invalidate the election due to the small plurality and "widespread cheating," Vice President-Elect Ky's National Police commander slouched above them in the gallery, swigging beer and loudly spinning the chamber of his snub-nose .38 Smith & Wesson. The committee's recommendation was rejected, and Thieu and Ky moved into the brand-new, 100-room, 65,000-square-foot presidential palace that had been commissioned by Diem in 1962, entrusted to architect Ngo Viet Thu, and was finally complete.[33]

The elections had been intended to showcase the vibrancy of South Vietnamese democracy, refute the arguments of the Viet Cong, and elect a national figure capable of challenging the aura of Ho Chi Minh. The elections instead exhibited the calcification of Saigon "democracy" in the authoritarian hands of the military. The also-rans in the race were "peace" candidates, leading to credible speculation that they had been defeated more by vote rigging than by the popular will. LBJ rushed to congratulate President Thieu. He called the election "a milestone on the path to a free, secure, and peaceful Vietnam."

Thieu's election, after every serious opponent was banned in advance, "legitimized," the *New York Times* observed, "an unchanged central government, continuation of heavy-handed police tactics, the same generally corrupt officials in the provinces, the same dispirited army, and more war." Painful as this prospect was to Americans, the newspaper concluded, "it is far worse for the South Vietnamese." Of Vice President Ky, a young ARVN officer said this: "No South Vietnamese really looks up to or respects Ky. He could never be our national hero—too young, too flashy, too American, too much the playboy, too much the pilot."[34]

While Thieu and Ky moved into the luxurious palace, a breezy and elegant homage to Edward Durrell Stone's New Formalism, with teak floors, fountains, chandeliers, and reception rooms finished in gold and lacquer, the number of impoverished refugees in South Vietnam had doubled *again*, as crop destruction, defoliation, compulsory relocations, combat operations, B-52 strikes, and round-the-clock H&I barrages by American and ARVN artillery made much of South Vietnam uninhabitable for all but the Viet Cong. On a tour of South Vietnam in 1967, Army chief of staff Harold Johnson was startled to discover that only 10 percent of Army artillery fires and 4 percent of air strikes were actually observed. Nine in ten bombs and shells were dropped blindly into areas that *might* contain VC. This obliterated villages, woods, and farmland. Rice production cratered, as 625,000 acres of farmland were abandoned when their owners were drafted into the army or put out of business by shelling, bombs, and defoliants.[35]

American officials in Saigon continued to pretend that what they were doing was beneficial. They cited Mao Zedong: "We can catch the fish only by drying up the water." In October 1967, Maxwell Taylor published a piece in the *New York Times Magazine* under the title "The Cause in Vietnam Is Being Won." The former chairman of the Joint Chiefs and ambassador to South Vietnam sounded more quixotic than ever, arguing, with a straight face, that herding one-quarter of South Vietnam's 17 million people into refugee camps was a good thing, for "they are withdrawn from among the human assets so necessary to support the guerrilla movement."[36]

People closer to the action than Max Taylor noted the flaw in his argument. In Quang Ngai province, where the Americans and ARVN had deliberately razed 70 percent of the villages and pushed their inhabitants into refugee camps, an American colonel involved in the exodus reported that apathy and defeatism were the predictable result. "Look, the V.C. get their people to support them. They *organize* the people. Those people are *alive*; they are highly *motivated*. But the people who are supposed to be on our side are just *blobs*. The refugees sit around all day doing *nothing*, and *we are doing nothing about it*."[37]

LBJ's patience with this floundering was wearing thin. Saigon had become the biggest American embassy in the world, with 800 people.

Razing South Vietnamese villages and pushing rural people into refugee camps backfired. Defeatism and apathy were the predictable result. Here dispossessed peasants in Quang Ngai province await processing. (National Archives)

MACV's headquarters staff alone now numbered 3,300 officers and men—so many that Westmoreland spent $25 million building "Pentagon East," a new headquarters complex at Tan Son Nhut Airport that featured the largest air-conditioning plant in Asia, four acres of parking lots, and a fifty-page staff directory. And yet what was there to show for it all? Just more smoke and mirrors.[38]

Settled facts were the first casualty of America's war in Vietnam. "It was no trick to find facts to back up the preconceptions," Ward Just wrote from Saigon in 1967. "Facts were everywhere, and with suitable discrimination could be used to support almost *any* argument." Westmoreland, like Harkins before him, found it expedient to argue that the war was going well. He now went to work tailoring the latest depressing facts to support the argument. He knew that the VC and NVA troop numbers were growing, so he manufactured a decline in their numbers by simply subtracting 56,000 VC who had previously been counted in the enemy order of battle. They had political jobs in the hamlets under VC control, he reasoned, as if they would not take up arms the minute their enterprise was threatened. This phony revision of the numbers undergirded Westmoreland's claim that 1967 had been a great success and that "the picture gives rise to optimism for increased success in 1968."[39]

Westmoreland could fake the numbers all he wanted, but rising US casualties and the continuing inertia of the ARVN posed political problems at home, where voters were asking why American boys were being forced to do the fighting for the boys of South Vietnam. "Maybe the people of Nam are worth saving," a platoon leader in the 4th ID wrote in December 1967, "but their army isn't worth shit." Jonathan Schell overheard some American pilots singing during Operation Benton in August 1967: "Throw candy to the ARVN / Gather them all around / Take your twenty mike-mike / And mow the bastards down." *Time*, *Newsweek*, and *U.S. News & World Report* all published withering exposés of the ARVN in 1967. The *Newsweek* piece—"Their Lions, Our Rabbits"—was a brutal takedown of the South Vietnamese military, referencing cowardice, desertion, and an inability even to pacify hamlets. American advisers in Vietnam competed among themselves for the distinction of serving with "the absolute worst South Vietnamese division." Johnson was ready to spend just about any sum to make the ARVN better but, to his dismay, Saigon did not want to be made better, particularly when General Thieu, elected president with only a third of the popular vote in September 1967, got a taste of what "getting better" would involve.[40]

South Vietnamese men were needed, above all, to fill ranks depleted by the ARVN's habit of desertion and draft dodging, and to reconquer all of the areas controlled by the VC. And so MACV proposed to fund a million-man ARVN equipped with M-16 rifles, M-60 machine guns, LAWs, helicopters, M-41 tanks, 105 mm howitzers, and the latest PRC-25 radio sets.

Funding all of that equipment on the back of the American taxpayer turned out to be the easy part. The hard part remained getting a million South Vietnamese into uniform. To get that many, a draft of all eighteen-to-thirty-three-year-olds was required, as well as "specialists" and "experts" as old as forty-five. And to keep a million South Vietnamese under arms, the term of service had to be made open-ended—"for the duration of the war." Eighteen-year-olds drafted in 1968, in other words, would be forced to serve until their thirty-fourth birthday if peace, death, or dismemberment did not intervene. Thieu hesitated even to *propose* conscription on this scale. It would provoke draft riots against the government, and it would never pass the parliament.[41]

With the South Vietnamese shrinking from the fight, Westmoreland ordered an "image-building campaign to publicize the ARVN and off-set the common belief that the South Vietnamese won't fight." Westy's PR flack, Colonel Barry Zorthian, called the program "Creating More ARVN Heroes." Westmoreland's lack of seriousness was plain. Washington had pressed him twice in 1967 to create a Korean War–style unified command that would have given him control over the ARVN. Both times Westy refused, breezily explaining that his personal relationships with top ARVN generals ensured unity of effort. In fact, Westmoreland did not dare tackle the problem. He was so frightened by what he might find if he popped the hood on the ARVN Joint General Staff and combat divisions that he came to rely on Zorthian's fluff instead. Fluff, however, would not put rifles on shoulders, boots on the ground, and troops in combat. President-Elect Thieu, who had not even been inaugurated yet, agreed under American pressure to slip an expansive new conscription law into force as an unchallengeable "emergency decree" *before* South Vietnam's new constitution took effect on October 31, 1967.[42]

If Thieu waited for his own inauguration and for the new constitution to take hold, this new "national mobilization" law would have to be debated and approved by the two houses of the National Assembly. Both houses were hotly opposed to the law, knowing that their voters opposed it. Thieu's decree beat them to the punch, but the president-elect was stung by the backlash when he announced the ARVN expansion just five days before his inauguration.[43]

Thieu knew that he had no choice but to mobilize more citizens. The Johnson administration was wavering, apparently willing to negotiate with the Viet Cong to end America's involvement. Thieu had to demonstrate that the South Vietnamese were willing and able to fight on. MACV's analysis of the ARVN in 1967 revealed it to be only 44 percent as effective as US forces—the measure of success being the number of communist troops killed per 1,000 free-world troops engaged in offensive operations. Even more troubling was MACV data showing American combat deaths continuing to exceed ARVN combat deaths in the last half of 1967, putting more pressure on President Johnson to deescalate the war.[44]

American pilots killed or captured during Rolling Thunder raids added still more pressure. The Russians had given the North Vietnamese radar-guided SAMs to counter the Rolling Thunder attacks. Climbing at Mach 3—three times faster than the US jets they were pursuing—the missiles could be evaded only by diving for the ground, a maneuver that dropped pilots out of the path of the SAM but into seamless barrages of 37 mm, 57 mm, and 85 mm antiaircraft guns, whose sights computed altitude, range, and lead instantly. More and more American aircrews were being killed or captured by the enemy.

The facile "signaling" and "graduated pressure" breezily pushed by McGeorge Bundy and McNamara in 1965 were not facile anymore. American air sorties were increasingly flown not to hit important targets but just to take out SAM sites and antiaircraft guns, which blocked the Navy's approach from carriers in the Tonkin Gulf as well as the Air Force's approach along "Thud Ridge"—a line of peaks guiding American jets toward Hanoi and Haiphong from air bases in Thailand. American pilots reported that the enemy's high-low air defense system was so dense that "it was like trying to fly through a rainstorm without hitting a drop." By 1967, North Vietnam was firing 25,000 tons of antiaircraft ammunition every month, hitting American aircraft at every altitude between 1,500 and 45,000 feet.

LBJ's fastidious rules of engagement remained in force, abbreviated by one pilot this way: "You had to see the target to attack it. You had to see an impact if possible. You had to!" The Americans flew two-seater aircraft, the joke went, so that one pilot could fly while the other read him the rules of engagement. The count of Americans shot from the sky and held as POWs in brutal conditions in North Vietnamese prisons continued to tick upward. One of the latest additions was Lieutenant Commander John McCain III, the son of the Navy admiral poised to take command of all US forces in the Pacific. John McCain was shot down over Hanoi in October 1967.

The war seemed unresolvable. Just packing up and quitting might be the only way to end it. Michael Herr turned on Armed Forces Radio in Saigon in the first week of December 1967 and heard this bulletin: "The Pentagon announced today that, compared to Korea, the Vietnam War will be an economy war, provided that it does not exceed the Korean War in length, which means it will have to end sometime in 1968."[45]

Musings such as this one seized Saigon's attention. To preclude an American deal with the Viet Cong, the new South Vietnamese Senate ratified Thieu's mobilization law on December 8, 1967, but took care to box the Americans in by simultaneously declaring the VC National Liberation Front an "enemy of the nation" and an "instrument of aggression of North Vietnam." Any American deals with the VC, the South Vietnamese Senate avowed, "would infringe the right of self-determination of the Vietnamese people." This official stance would make it harder for Johnson or any other president to negotiate an end to the war.[46]

Saigon's new mobilization law expanded the draft from men in their twenties to men between the ages of eighteen and thirty-eight. In theory, it would nearly double the size of the armed forces—from 600,000 to 1.1 million. But it was already being riddled with loopholes for the well-connected, who were allowed to remain in school or university, or even civilian jobs, where they could be "mobilized in place" in "posts of national interest" while peasant sons served in the field.[47]

In the eyes of the South Vietnamese government, LBJ's fervor for war-terminating negotiations was at least as threatening as his push for national mobilization. Thieu, Ky, and the ARVN generals knew that negotiations with the VC could not be undertaken because a coalition government of all parties would have had no place for politicians and generals like them, who were stained by corruption and too close to the Americans. Like Diem before them, the South Vietnamese leaders now began to lean on South Vietnam's Catholics as a bulwark against American retreat, creating a lobbying group in 1967 called the Greater Unity Force to attack "defeatist tendencies in the United States," lead "Anti-False Peace" demonstrations, and insist on a continuation of the war until communism was defeated.[48]

"Peace"—that condition sought most avidly by the Vietnamese people—had paradoxically become a "dirty word" in Saigon government circles, a British diplomat observed. He watched the Saigon police race to tear down a banner with the anodyne message "In 1967, the military forces and the people of Vietnam along with the allied forces will succeed in their quest for peace." To Thieu and Ky, "peace" was American code for regime-ending negotiations with the VC. They banned all references to it in the press and public demonstrations. In meetings with Thieu, LBJ pressed him to compromise with the VC to split them from Hanoi. Thieu refused even to consider the idea. Senator Fulbright, who was urging LBJ to negotiate directly with the VC, was savaged by the Saigon press, most spitefully by the papers controlled by Thieu and Ky. Bill Fulbright, they wrote, was a "dotard," a "colonialist par excellence," a "dictator," a "dirty imperialist."[49]

LBJ was horrified by the spectacle, and groped again for a way out of this poorly managed war. The exit, however, remained blocked by the same irreducible facts. Johnson believed that Operation Rolling Thunder—his ability to drop 1,000 tons of bombs a day on North Vietnam—was his hole card. He would concede a "bombing halt" only in return for Hanoi's agreement to stop infiltrating troops into South Vietnam. Hanoi refused even to consider such "reciprocity."

Le Duan believed that Ho Chi Minh's greatest error, and the reason for the national hero's eclipse now, had been Ho's willingness to negotiate from a position of weakness in 1945 and 1954. That had led to the division of Vietnam and the introduction of first French and then American forces. The lesson for Le Duan was simple: negotiate only when you have the enemy beaten, on the ropes, and willing, even eager, to accept *your* maximum aims.

But Hanoi's war aims still clashed irreconcilably with America's. Hanoi insisted that the Geneva Treaty of 1954 be respected. The Americans would have to stop bombing North Vietnam, withdraw all of their troops from South Vietnam, and then permit the nationwide elections that were supposed to have been held eleven years earlier. Washington's war aim was for a Korean-style solution—partition of Vietnam into two countries at the 17th parallel. A compromise between the two positions would necessarily involve the Americans agreeing to nationwide elections and a role for the Viet Cong in South Vietnamese elections and politics.[50]

Johnson was powerless to make Hanoi negotiate, and he knew it. "You can't tell American voters one day that the United States plans to get out of Vietnam, and then on the next day tell Ho Chi Minh that we'll stick it out for 20 years," the CIA's special assistant for Vietnamese affairs reminded the president. "Why would anyone in North Vietnam *believe* it?" Le Duan certainly didn't. He knew that Johnson was flagging. The last thing the North Vietnamese leader would do now was concede anything that might alleviate LBJ's predicament and permit the president to keep forces in South Vietnam. The Americans, Le Duan believed, needed to be driven out, to be confronted with unending loss and futility.[51]

In December 1967, Secretary of Defense McNamara made clear that Westmoreland's leash had run out of slack. If there couldn't be peace, then there must be less war. Max Taylor offered the president four alternatives, pullout, pullback, all-out, and stick-it-out, but insisted that the first three, a year before the 1968 elections, would disappoint American voters by reinforcing the impression of "self-stagnation" in "a hopeless struggle." It would be more expedient to advertise something that at least *sounded* dynamic.

President Johnson agreed and now committed to what he called "the gospel of pacification." The Pentagon's "five urgent requirements" for 1968 were formulated to shift the focus from search and destroy to pacification, with the aim of getting the United States out of South Vietnam by fixing the roads and waterways, building jails, increasing the number of advisers for pacification and intelligence exploitation, expanding the ARVN and ruff-puffs, and adding more Revolutionary Development cadre teams through the CORDS program.[52]

In Washington, National Security Adviser Walt Rostow, still keen as ever on the war, pressured the CIA's Office of Current Intelligence to portray pacification as a great success story. Rostow was told that such a portrayal would be at odds with the facts. The fifty-one-year-old national security adviser, derided by Senator Fulbright as "LBJ's Rasputin," kept up the pressure, warning the CIA's George Allen that there would be consequences if he did not truckle. "I am amazed at your unwillingness to support your president in his time of need," Rostow threatened. Allen caved and provided data that statistically showed improvement, but he added a cover letter that described the continuing failure of the program. Rostow detached the cover letter, threw it in the trash, and handed Allen's data to the president. "At last," Rostow sighed, "an objective appraisal from CIA."[53]

The CIA also disputed MACV's numbers on enemy strength. Westmoreland, now in full political campaign mode on behalf of the president, was trying so hard to show progress in Vietnam that he simply refused to count all of the VC operating there. When CBS News later reported how much he had prevaricated, airing a special titled *The Uncounted Enemy: A Vietnam Deception*, Westmoreland would seek $120 million in damages from the network for its "defamatory falsehoods," a rather wild act of chutzpah by the then seventy-year-old retired general. The case collapsed before it could be heard before a jury, Westy settling without a penny of damages to avoid the likelihood that he—having indeed lied in 1967—might have to pay CBS' legal fees in 1985.[54]

In 1967, the fifty-three-year-old Westy was still large, in charge, and accustomed to obedience. He insisted that only "hard figures" of VC forces would be used. There would be no more extrapolation from captured documents and prisoner interrogations. The only VC that MACV would count would be those physically identified in the field by the combat commands.

By the end of 1967, the gulf between the CIA and MACV numbers had widened dangerously, the CIA reporting that there were 600,000 VC in South Vietnam—a full 300,000 more than MACV was reporting. The CIA was counting not only armed combatants but also all of the irregular forces the VC used for information, food, shelter, labor, recruiting, and logistics. Sam Adams, a CIA analyst in Saigon, revealed that an Army officer in MACV told him off the record that MACV's military intelligence personnel had been ordered to keep the VC total under 300,000 for political reasons. Wheeler ordered Westy to reject the CIA numbers: "If these numbers reach the public domain," the chairman of the Joint Chiefs wrote, "they'll literally blow the lid off Washington."[55]

Military intelligence, Michael Herr observed, had by 1967 become little more than a "jargon stream," a "carnival bear, broken and dumb, an Intelligence beast, our own." Nothing it told you got you any closer to winning the war. The CIA director, Richard Helms, was pressured to agree to the deflated MACV figures, and he went along, rejecting the "exaggerated military strength" estimates of his own agency with "arguments so complex," Sam Adams recalled, "that I became confused." The argument was more than academic. Westmoreland was about to be hit in the places he considered most secure by the full force of the Viet Cong.[56]

In a weird, split-screen moment, Westmoreland was back in Washington taking a kind of victory lap while the politburo in Hanoi authorized the Tet Offensive. Westy had been quietly trying to persuade the president to escalate the war and adopt a more offensive strategy. Now, with US elections a year away, he reverted to the blarney that was his trademark. He appeared before House and Senate committees and sat down for television interviews. At the National Press Club on November 21, 1967, Westy presented his "Progress Report on the War in Vietnam." The enemy, he declared, was nearly beaten, "unable to mount a major offensive" of any kind. He hadn't won "a major battle" in over a year, was "losing control of the scattered population under his influence," and, Westy improbably added, had been "dealt a mortal blow by the installation of a freely-elected representative government."[57]

Westmoreland recited LBJ's talking points for the 1968 presidential race: "Whereas in 1965 the enemy was winning, today he is certainly losing." Victory, Westy continued, "begins to come into view." He mooted a "withdrawal strategy" in which the successful war could soon be "phased down" and turned over to the South Vietnamese. On the last day of 1967, Westy assured the White House that the number of VC and NVA troops in South Vietnam had fallen to just 115,000 under MACV's punishing attacks—hardly enough to survive a 1968 campaign against 1.2 million allied forces.

This was the context for Westy's notorious statement during a meeting with LBJ that there was "light at the end of the tunnel." It was a time, Tom Buckley of the *New York Times* recalled, "when American optimism about the course of the war was reaching a zenith of fatuity." But only on the surface. The generals knew that their strategic objective, defined in 1965 as "seeking an independent non-Communist South Vietnam," had to be sharply curtailed to something more along the lines of "buy time for Saigon to grow in capacity and popular support so that it can survive on its own." Pullback, in short. But such a plan would inspire no one. With elections around the corner, it was better to feign victory.[58]

In December, LBJ awarded Westmoreland a new oak leaf cluster. "All the challenges have been met," the president grinned. Inwardly, he seethed. "I am like the steering wheel of a car without any control," Johnson fretted. Westy's barnstorming had pushed the president's approval rating back up, from 39 to 50 percent, but not for long. The war just rolled on—with no end in sight.

Westmoreland, who had suppressed his desire for a troop increase and a wider war throughout 1967, felt increasingly confident that he had played the game right. Bob McNamara, wrung out by six years of twelve-hour days, discredited, and on the verge of a nervous breakdown, had announced his resignation in November. President Johnson, who felt personally betrayed by resignations, would keep the exhausted McNamara in harness until February 1968. In his valedictory memos to LBJ, the SecDef pronounced the war unwinnable: increasing US forces from 465,000 to 525,000, he warned the president in November, "will not produce any significant change," just more encounters, and more casualties, followed by requests for yet more ground forces.[59]

But McNamara would soon be replaced at the Pentagon by a hawk: sixty-one-year-old Clark Clifford. Clifford had assailed Bob McNamara's pessimism in November and argued for an intensification of the war: "The war is a success, so we should go right on doing what we're going to do." Clifford was known as Johnson's "war minister." If LBJ won reelection, Clifford would continue as secretary of defense. If Nixon won, the new president would almost certainly put in someone even more hawkish than Clark Clifford. Either way, Westy would probably get the troops he needed to move into the NVA's Cambodian and Laotian sanctuaries, cut the Ho Chi Minh Trail, and win the war.[60]

Chapter 12

YEAR OF THE MONKEY

In November 1967, the communist leadership in Hanoi officially adopted Le Duan's "Strategy of the General Offensive and General Uprising," which had been worked out over the previous several months. It would proceed in three phases; the first, still under way, was the fighting along the borders of South Vietnam to lure allied troops away from the population centers and into wilderness areas like Dak To and Khe Sanh.[1]

The second phase, now imminent, was a general offensive to collapse the South Vietnamese government and military. One hundred and twenty thousand NVA and VC main-force troops in South Vietnam would be reinforced by 200,000 NVA infantry now moving south on the Ho Chi Minh Trail with 80,000 tons of supplies. On the appointed day, they would break from cover and wrest away South Vietnam's towns and cities in a stunning coup de main.

Le Duan expected the communists to seize power in every corner of South Vietnam and hand it to "revolutionary administrations" and "national peace-force alliances," which would be Hanoi's fig leaves for annexation. That would be the signal for phase three, a "general uprising" against all remnants of the Saigon regime by the entire war-weary South Vietnamese people.[2]

For Hanoi, it was a major shift from the doctrine of protracted guerrilla war to a conventional attack on US and ARVN forces that might inflict devastating casualties and open the door to a total destruction of

Saigon's rural pacification program and a VC uprising in the cities. It aimed to capitalize on Westmoreland's failure to achieve anything decisive in 1967.

Le Duan, who by now had shouldered Ho Chi Minh out of the picture, judged that LBJ had escalated in 1967 as far as the American people were willing to go. The war had entered a "strategic stalemate." The time, Le Duan declared on January 18, 1968, was ripe for "thundering blows" to "change the face of the war," "shake the aggressive will" of the Americans, and force them to "change strategy and de-escalate the war."

The communists would not have to defeat every American formation— how could they? American forces, which Westmoreland had conveniently scattered in the border regions, would be fixed in place with diversionary attacks or bypassed, permitting stealthy VC and NVA units to strike what Le Duan called "the major center" of South Vietnam: the towns and cities. "In the innermost areas," an NVA planning document elaborated, "there are nothing but puppet and police authorities. The U.S. forces are outermost."[3]

Le Duan hoped that the general offensive during the Tet holiday in February 1968 would sweep all before it. In the event that it didn't, the NVA planned a second general offensive in May and a third in August. The Tet Offensive would overwhelm South Vietnam with a countrywide assault on military bases, government offices, and every major city, town, and village. The May offensive, if needed, would focus the attack on the South Vietnamese military headquarters in Saigon. If the August offensive was needed, it would hit the "Saigon Circle"—the area north and west of the capital containing the big American military bases at Long Binh and Bien Hoa.[4]

Defense Minister Giap later described Hanoi's approach in this way: "We were not strong enough to drive out a half-million American troops, but that wasn't our aim." The aim, he said, was "to break the will of the American government to continue the war" with a great *psychological* blow. Of Westmoreland's belief in troop numbers and technology, Giap scoffed: "If we had focused on the balance of forces, we would have been defeated in two hours." The Americans, Giap said, had to be persuaded that the North Vietnamese would go on until victory, that there would be no easy exit: "another twenty years, even a hundred years, as long as it took to win, regardless of cost." He called this war *à la manière vietnamienne*—"war Vietnamese style," in a land that had struggled against foreign invaders for 4,000 years. The enemy would be pinned in a quagmire and exhausted.[5]

The communists relied on a combination of deceit, surprise, and faith in the inefficiency of the allied armies. The VC had been offering Tet cease-fires since the arrival of American troops in 1965. They were intended to drive a wedge between the Americans and the South Vietnamese—as VC leaders put it, "to discriminate between the invading American soldiers and the puppet Vietnamese soldiers, to protect the people and stir up patriotism among the Vietnamese soldiers during the sacred holiday."

Tet cease-fires were always the occasion for VC-organized demonstrations before the offices of province and district chiefs and in the big cities. Crowds would appear waving signs—"Down with artillery fire and air strikes on villages, down with the military draft." Demonstrators would demand poor relief, slum clearance, the release of political prisoners, and a Tet bonus for workers, all calculated to incite criticism of the South Vietnamese government.

If the Americans attacked during the holiday, it would further harm their image and raise the prestige of the communists. The VC themselves always abused the cease-fire. The communists had what American officials called "a contemptuous attitude toward truce arrangements," viewing them as just another way to take advantage of a gullible enemy. A VC cadre killed south of Da Nang on the eve of the 1966 cease-fire carried an order that read: "We've requested a ceasefire during Tet, and during the ceasefire we will attack the enemy."[6]

Though Hanoi had planned to launch the offensive in March 1968, they moved it up to coincide with that year's Tet cease-fire, which conveniently had been extended from twenty-four to thirty-six hours at Pope Paul VI's request. Tet Nguyen Dan—the lunar new year—fell each year in late January or early February and marked the start of spring in Vietnam. It was celebrated with a week of vacation to greet the new year and the new animal spirit brought by the twelve-year Chinese calendar cycle.[7]

The spring festival was a time of merriment and family reunion. For the Vietnamese, it was like a combination of every Western holiday rolled into one—their only real holiday of the year. The departing animal spirit (1967's goat) would be sent off with a midnight meal and gifts to ensure that he gave a good account of the family's activities during the expiring lunar year to the Jade Emperor. The incoming spirit of 1968 (the monkey) would be honored in the same way.[8]

For 1968, the Tet cease-fire was scheduled to go into effect at 6 p.m. on January 29. At that time, half of the ARVN, many of the ruff-puffs, and most of the National Police would already have taken leave for Tet, and the various bases and garrisons around the country would be held by skeleton forces, or Americans alone.[9]

This was just the break that Hanoi needed to make a success of the general offensive. Hanoi's respect for American combat troops did not extend to the ARVN: "If attacked fiercely," an NVA directive alleged, "they will disintegrate; their morale is poor; they fear our regular units; their paper strength is large but their combat strength is low." Organized in the image of the US Army, the ARVN was a pale imitation: "They are diversified among branches that become confused in combat."[10]

Assessing the political scene in Washington, Hanoi calculated that it would be enough to savage the ARVN in combat, wound the Americans, overrun the government-held villages, provoke uprisings in the towns and cities, and demonstrate conclusively that Saigon could not protect its own people or even itself against the communists. If these things happened, the North Vietnamese politburo reasoned, "the military, political, and psychological conditions would be conducive to opening negotiations for the withdrawal of U.S. forces." The Americans would leave because there would be nothing to defend—an already weak cause would be rendered hopeless.[11]

For the NVA military planners, the ultimate success of the Tet Offensive hinged on two things: the communist ability to defeat the allied forces in battle, and the reluctance of LBJ to widen the war. In January 1968, the Americans had ninety-six infantry and sixty-four artillery battalions in Vietnam. Those 150,000 combat troops, reinforced by 23,000 South Koreans and 4,000 Australians, were barely enough to hold the line in South Vietnam. If LBJ responded to the aggression of Tet by putting in *more* troops and bombers, crossing the DMZ, and invading North Vietnam, the whole offensive plan of Generals Giap and Van Tien Dung would backfire, and COSVN's general uprising, organized by Pham Hung and General Hoang Van Thai, would be crushed.[12]

But the probability of a US invasion of North Vietnam had to be reckoned as quite low. LBJ feared Chinese or Soviet intervention if he invaded, and the president knew that the limited war in Vietnam had been expanded to its political limits. There were already half a million US military personnel in Vietnam, plus 5,900 aircraft. America's commitments in more vital theaters continued to be starved of resources to maintain these high levels of manpower and equipment. Invading North Vietnam risked not only a wider war but also the further hollowing out of America's armed forces and finances, as well as a surge of antiwar protest. The American dilemma of Vietnam, seen from Hanoi, was that there was not enough force to win, and yet the force could not feasibly be expanded due to American frustration with the war and other commitments in Europe, Korea, the Middle East, and elsewhere.

To test LBJ's resolve, further thin the number of American troops near the cities, and open another path into South Vietnam, General Dung preceded the Tet Offensive with a major assault on the Marine combat base at Khe Sanh on January 21, 1968. Khe Sanh had been quiet since the "hill fights" of the previous year. These days it was entrusted to a single battalion of the US 26th Marine Regiment. A crushing NVA barrage now hit it—from long-range, heavy-caliber guns in Laos as well as from 82 mm mortars and 122 mm rockets positioned in the hills around Khe Sanh, some on the lower slopes of heights controlled by the Marines.

Inside the combat base, American helicopters were destroyed, trucks and tents blown away, the mess hall flattened, and the base's fuel storage and ammo dump set on fire. Eleven thousand rounds of ammo cooked off over the next forty-eight hours, pelting the Marines with their own ordnance as well as clouds of tear gas. The cannonade, backed by an estimated 20,000 troops of the NVA 320th and 325C Divisions, was intended to draw Westmoreland's attention back to the periphery, to pull American troops away from the populated areas that were about to be hit by the Tet Offensive, but also to feel out LBJ. Would the president punish the attack by invading North Vietnam, or would he remain on the defensive, leaving the initiative to the enemy?[13]

Westmoreland conferred with General Robert Cushman, who had replaced Lew Walt in command of III Marine Amphibious Force. They decided to hold and reinforce Khe Sanh with four additional battalions. Westy believed that the North Vietnamese were bluffing, that here and elsewhere they were "conducting a short-term surge effort...to improve their chances of gaining their ends through political means, perhaps through negotiations." To deny them *any* wins, Westmoreland declared that the alternately dusty and rain-lashed Khe Sanh plateau would become "the Western Anchor of our defense."[14]

With NVA infiltration accelerating, Westmoreland's priority remained what he called "border-sealing." American maneuver battalions would be pushed out to the borders to block infiltration and stop the steady creep of NVA sanctuaries in Laos and Cambodia into South Vietnam. Westmoreland was playing into Hanoi's hands, putting his best units out on what MACV termed the "extreme border" and leaving the interior of South Vietnam, where 82 percent of the population lived, thinly guarded.[15]

With Khe Sanh garrisoned by Marines, Cushman went along with Westy's rationale that the combat post needed to be held not only for military reasons—to slow enemy infiltration of men and supplies—but for political reasons as well. It was important to avoid "taking a step backward" at a time when Americans were being told that victory was "coming into view." But the counterarguments were at least as compelling. With two NVA divisions threatening Khe Sanh and two more in the vicinity, a single Marine regiment there would be exceedingly vulnerable. The Marines lacked the helicopters and troops to launch the airmobile assaults that could relieve pressure on the garrison. Far from an "anchor," Khe Sanh was a place that could easily be skirted, as it had been for years.[16]

The NVA would use their superior numbers to cut Route 9, forcing the Americans to fly everything into Khe Sanh, and yet if the combat base, built for a battalion, was reinforced to a strength of five battalions, as Westy planned, its daily supply needs would balloon from 50 tons to 185 tons. Somehow all of this would have to be flown in despite enemy artillery fire and regular "below minimum" visibility. In the White House, Max Taylor, who these days was running LBJ's war room, argued against remaining at Khe Sanh. "Withdraw," he advised the president. "Whatever the past value of the position, it is a positive liability now." But Westmoreland forged ahead, grumbling about all of the "one-upmanship" by "armchair strategists" in Washington. To some, Westy seemed undone by the challenges, one of his colonels remarking that "everybody here is wandering around without any clear-cut direction or management."[17]

Khe Sanh would provide a focus of sorts. Westmoreland viewed the combat base as the logical place to launch offensive operations into Laos if

LBJ or his successor ever endorsed the general's proposal to widen the war and attack the Ho Chi Minh Trail. Like Westy's "scissors theory," which held that his major operations on the periphery in 1967 were intended to stop the North Vietnamese from cutting South Vietnam in half—never a real possibility until the Americans left Vietnam—Westy now vaunted the importance of Khe Sanh, reinforcing it in the hope that he could fight a major battle there and notch another "victory."[18]

Unable to maneuver there, Westmoreland would, as he put it, "box in the slippery NVA and VC." If the enemy is "willing to stand and fight, it's a good idea to oblige him," Westy said in his peppy way. He correctly estimated that at least two of the four NVA divisions known to be in I Corps were now at Khe Sanh. Westy asserted that 5,000 Marines and 1,000 ARVN Rangers at Khe Sanh, crammed hurriedly into a base built for 1,000, would be able to "fix the enemy in position around the base while the Allied air and artillery battered him into senselessness," keeping those enemy divisions far from the "vital internal organs of South Vietnam."[19]

As the reference to "the vital internal organs of South Vietnam" attested, Westmoreland's rationale for Khe Sanh was assembled later, with the benefit of hindsight, when he knew about Tet and could claim that he was pinning down units at Khe Sanh that would otherwise be overrunning the cities and towns of South Vietnam. But, in truth, the operation never made much sense and was a poor use of the Marines sent there. General Lowell English, deputy commander of the 3rd Marine Division, thought that the defense made no sense at all. Marines at Khe Sanh did little to stop infiltration. The enemy could just continue to bypass it. "When you're at Khe Sanh," General English groused, "you're not really anywhere. You could lose it and you really haven't lost a damn thing."[20]

But Westmoreland was fixated on body count, in the hope that he could lure elusive communist troops onto the plateau at Khe Sanh and kill them. That was the real reason for Khe Sanh—that, and his determination not to suffer anything resembling a Dien Bien Phu. President Johnson had installed a sand-table model of the Marine combat base in the White House Situation Room, such was his own obsession with the place, which LBJ inevitably compared to the Alamo. Khe Sanh, Westy agreed, was "not just another battle." It was a *symbol* of American determination to hold the line in Vietnam. He gave Operation Scotland, the Marine mission at Khe Sanh, priority over every other operation in South Vietnam, and he layered Operation Niagara over it.

Niagara, as the name suggested, would be a torrent of airpower: close air support, radar-controlled bombing, and B-52 Arc Light strikes. The scale of Niagara was stunning. From January to April 1968, when the siege of Khe Sanh would be lifted, American jets would fly more sorties over the combat base every day than they flew over the rest of I Corps, which was the most violent theater of the war. In that same period, Air Force B-52s would fly 85 percent more sorties and drop 82 percent more bombs around the flyspeck of Khe Sanh every day than they dropped on all of South Vietnam and the DMZ. The Marine outpost became, as one visitor put it, the "passion, the false love object in the heart of the Command." In the absence of a real strategy, it focused allied efforts. But then, a few days later, the focus abruptly shifted.[21]

Legend has it that the Tet Offensive came as a surprise. It did not. The portents and much hard evidence of its imminence were everywhere. It was Westmoreland, determined to get on with fighting the war on the frontiers, who ignored or downplayed them. He continued to quarrel with the CIA about the true number of enemy combatants and support troops inside South Vietnam. By late 1967 he claimed that he had ground the communist main forces down to 115,000, whereas the CIA put the number (conservatively) at 225,000, noting that enemy recruitment was increasing, not declining, and that communist units were taking a more "offensive posture" in every corps area.[22]

None of this would come as a great surprise to Westmoreland. His own field units were reporting signs of an impending and massive attack, and his corps commanders questioned his complacency in the face of the gathering storm. Two new NVA divisions had been infiltrated south of the DMZ. Captured documents instructed VC local and main-force units all over South Vietnam to "prepare the battlefield" for attacks by moving caches of food, weapons, and ammo closer to the cities and towns. In I Corps, the Americal Division captured prisoners and documents in December 1967 that stated plainly that all of the main towns were going to be hit "in early '68," and that Route 1 would be cut and Chu Lai airfield attacked to prevent American and ARVN counterattacks. Other reports spoke of a "pressurized VC conscription drive" of all men between sixteen and thirty-five years of age to "meet the *imminent* requirements of the battlefield." ARVN agents reported that all village communist party chapters were being staffed with female cadres to free the males for combat.[23]

The enemy plan was to attack towns and installations in the I and II Corps areas on January 29, 1968, and then, before daylight on January 31, with most of the South Vietnamese military on leave, to launch the nation-wide Tet Offensive on the first night of the Vietnamese lunar new year.

Thirty-nine of forty-four provincial capitals would be hit, plus seventy-one district towns and the autonomous cities of Saigon and Da Nang. All would be attacked suddenly with mortars, rockets, and ground assaults. The goal was to wipe out centers of political authority and essential military infrastructure: base camps, airfields, and logistics hubs. Tactically, the enemy intended to confuse the Americans, send them rushing off to defend the remote places hit on January 29, and pin the rest down in defensive positions in the populated areas.

Hanoi and COSVN also planned to destroy the pacification program and take over all of the rural areas that had been clawed back under government protection by the CORDS program. Strategically, the communists sought to provoke a general uprising and topple the Thieu-Ky regime, opening the door to a coalition government controlled by the communists.[24]

General Fred Weyand, who commanded II Field Force, the Army corps command that guarded III Corps and Saigon, opposed Westy's plan for 1968 to concentrate on the frontiers and "seal the border." Weyand had fifty-three battalions in III Corps, and Westy wanted thirty-nine of them committed to operations in the jungles, hills, and swamps along the Cambodian border, more than 100 miles from Saigon, to which it would be exceedingly difficult to return them in an emergency.

Weyand gaped at Westmoreland's detachments to the frontiers: Westy sent the 1st Brigade of the US 101st Airborne Division plus two ARVN battalions on Operation San Angelo, which was to locate and destroy any NVA units trying to infiltrate over the Cambodian border during the Tet truce. Westy also sent two brigades of the 25th ID out to the wilderness around Tay Ninh, sixty miles west of Saigon, to resume the clearing operations that had ended inconclusively with Operation Junction City in 1967. He then sent four battalions of the 101st Airborne Division up to I Corps, where, as always, threats were multiplying along the DMZ. "If we do not violently contest every attempt to get NVA units into South Vietnam," Westmoreland wrote the Joint Chiefs, "we permit him to expand his system of bases in-country, levy taxes on the people, get their rice, and prove to the people that the NVA is very much alive in South Vietnam."[25]

These detachments to the border areas left just fourteen American and ARVN battalions in the zone around Saigon, Long Binh, and Bien Hoa, where South Vietnam's key political and military assets were located and where 80 percent of the population lived. This was the "Saigon Circle," the critical zone surrounding the capital, which included Weyand's headquarters and supplies at Long Binh Post. It was also the seat of the vast American air base at Bien Hoa, which, with 857,000 landings and takeoffs a year, was the busiest airport in the world. At the center of the circle were MACV headquarters, the South Vietnamese Joint General Staff, and the Saigon airfield at Tan Son Nhut.

The border, Weyand argued, was not the main threat. Troops operating there would be useless if the enemy struck at Saigon. They would be too far and too scattered to get back by helicopter. They would have to return on fixed-wing aircraft, slowly, and into air bases like Bien Hoa and Tan Son Nhut that might already have fallen into enemy hands.[26]

Weyand's intelligence on the eve of Tet showed five NVA regiments moving toward Saigon and the VC 5th Division approaching Bien Hoa. NVA "fillers" were replacing casualties in the VC units, and they were all equipped with AK-47s, RPGs, and heavier weapons like the 120 mm mortar and 122 mm rocket. Something really big was happening, for the major battles signaled by all of the inflowing intelligence violated the enemy's inveterate caution: the VC habit of moving stealthily and undertaking attacks only when favorable strength ratios were guaranteed.

Still, it was hard to get the complete picture—the communists gave plans of attack only to select leaders. The troops received their movement orders at the last minute. Faced with this uncertainty, Weyand persuaded Westmoreland to dial back the border operations, leaving twenty-two battalions in those peripheral areas and locating twenty-seven battalions, twice as many as Westy had planned, in the Saigon Circle, all within assault helicopter range of the vital points.[27]

It would prove to be a lifesaving decision. The same radio chatter and headquarters spread that had alerted the Americans to the impending attack on Dak To now indicated that the communists were massing for an attack on the major towns and cities of South Vietnam, including Saigon. In early January 1968, Weyand showed Westmoreland a map that sketched the movement of three NVA divisions and three main-force VC regiments toward Saigon. "I can see these guys moving inward," Weyand said. "They're not staying in their base areas." He pointed on the map to the Cambodian border and added: "*We're* going to be up here in the base areas and *they're* going to be down here somewhere." His hand traveled to the Saigon area. "I don't know what they've got in mind, but there's an attack coming."[28]

There was indeed. The NVA plan for III Corps was to hold the Americans on the periphery with the NVA 7th and 9th Divisions, which would pin down as many battalions as they could before infiltrating and blocking the roads most critical for reinforcement of threatened areas. The VC 5th Division would attack the Bien Hoa complex, the hub of American airpower in Vietnam. Eleven more VC battalions would attack Saigon. In all, COSVN committed thirty-five of fifty-four available VC main-force and local battalions to the initial assault.

The VC who infiltrated into the heart of Saigon *before* the fighting began did it easily, for they were just 4,000 guerrillas coming into a city of 3 million in the midst of a noisy, busy holiday period. Many of them infiltrated in 100-man companies, walking right past Saigon's police and military checkpoints. Many came in disguised as small ARVN units. With so many ARVN troops passing in and out of the city to take leave for Tet, no one noticed. Others arrived in civilian clothing, riding buses and taxis, the latter driven by sympathetic Saigon cab drivers. Still more simply walked across the paddies and swamps that bordered the city, or alighted from barges and sampans that were constantly plying the city's waterfront and canals. They recognized each other by using secret signals—sleeves rolled up or down, a white band on the left arm, or an incomplete uniform. They armed themselves at cache sites inside Saigon that had been filled with weapons over the previous sixty days, and then swapped their white armbands for red ones when they went into action.[29]

The VC had studied traffic patterns and security routines and smuggled weapons into the city on food, rubber, and lumber trucks or under heaps of clothing in the three-wheeled carts of market vendors. Communist secrecy was maintained by a general ignorance of the plan among the attackers.

They were told the bare minimum—where to assemble once inside Saigon's city limits—but not told how long to fight or where to retreat if necessary. This must have alarmed the more prudent among the VC, for they were lightly armed for such a big mission: an assault rifle, 450 rounds of ammo, and just one grenade per man, with each squad issued a light machine gun and one RPG as well.[30]

In I Corps, the other main objective of the Tet Offensive, the NVA planned to strike decisively at Hue with three infantry regiments, three sapper battalions, and an artillery battalion. In contrast with Saigon and III and IV Corps, where the fighting was led by the VC, two-thirds of the communist troops deployed in I and II Corps were NVA.

Hue, Vietnam's imperial capital in the nineteenth century, was the NVA's prime target. With its walled forbidden city and royal tombs along the Perfume River, the communists called it "the nest of feudalist mandarins and monarchs, the brain of the reactionary spirit." Hue and Saigon had competing elites and networks and competing visions of the future. The communists knew this, and they also knew about the festering Buddhist Struggle Movement as well as the political rivalry between the Thieu-Ky government and the ARVN garrison in Hue that had exploded into civil war in 1966. They planned to exploit every one of these fissures to seize and hold a major city in South Vietnam for the first time.[31]

The communists looked at the allied forces around Hue—the US 3rd Marine Division and the 1st ARVN Division, plus ten companies of Regional Force militia and fifty platoons of Popular Forces—and concluded that they were not enough. Between them, they mustered only about 7,000 troops "able to fight well"; the rest would surrender or run away.

More critically, the NVA learned that "the inner perimeter"—Hue and the populated coastal strip—was "nearly unprotected." Westy had taken the bait and gone hunting at Khe Sanh, Dak To, and elsewhere on the wild frontier. Frustrated by his inability to fight the enemy in populated areas without massive collateral damage to civilians, he leaped at the opportunity to meet them in the unpopulated areas, where he could use his firepower without restraint. He believed that he had inflicted so many casualties on the communists in 1967 that they lacked the strength to fight simultaneously on the border and in the interior.[32]

The NVA plan took full advantage of Westmoreland's yearning for decisive operations on the frontier. Hanoi would use VC and NVA units in I Corps "to attack the unguarded inner area" and then move outward, rolling up the more than 100 strong points the ARVN had established as an outer defense system. For the rest, Hanoi estimated that it had 400,000 VC sympathizers in I Corps who would rise up to defeat the ruff-puff units while the main-force battalions were attacking the harder targets. "The people *must* stand up because our armed forces alone will fail to win."[33]

Chapter 13

TET

The first attacks of the Tet Offensive were delivered in faraway II Corps on January 29. Thirty-five hundred communists attacked the towns of Kontum province, while 4,600 hit Pleiku and its surrounding camps and towns. The allied defenses there shook under the blow, for they had been drained of troops after the long, bloody fight for Dak To, when Westy had proclaimed "victory" and pronounced II Corps ready for broader pacification by CORDS.[1]

In Pleiku, Private John Ketwig awoke from a deep sleep in his compound at the foot of Artillery Hill. Most firefights in Vietnam were over quickly, enemy mortar or rocket units firing a salvo and scuttling away before they could be targeted by a firebase or a gunship, but this one was different. It went on for hours—waves of rockets, mortar rounds, small-arms fire, and then return fire from the American batteries on Artillery Hill. The enemy fire struck everywhere: Pleiku City, Artillery Hill, Camp Holloway, and the US 4th ID headquarters on Titty Hill.[2]

Kontum City was saved by the rapid reaction of its American garrison. The helicopter gunships were on "strip alert" and the perimeter bunkers were fully manned. When the communists attacked, it was their turn to be surprised, as the gunships roared aloft instantly and engaged targets at will, catching hundreds of NVA attackers on the open ground between the jungle and the perimeter defenses.

261

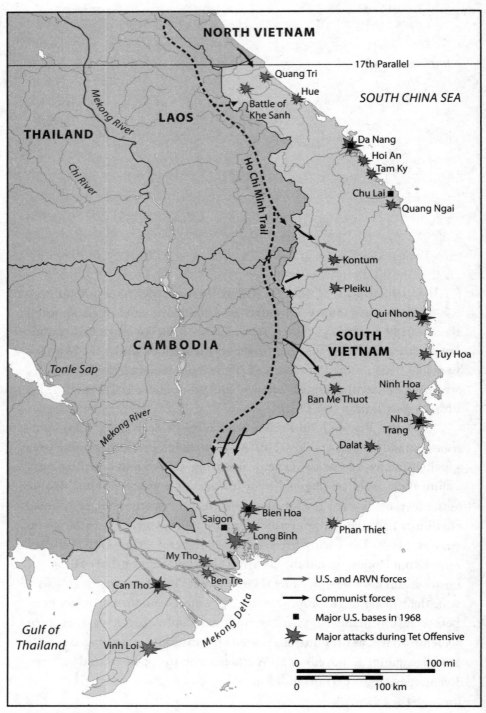

NORTH VIETNAM

17th Parallel

Quang Tri

Hue

SOUTH CHINA SEA

Battle of
Khe Sanh

LAOS

THAILAND

Mekong River

Chi River

Da Nang

Hoi An

Tam Ky

Chu Lai

Quang Ngai

Kontum

Pleiku

Qui Nhon

SOUTH
VIETNAM

Tuy Hoa

CAMBODIA

Ninh Hoa

Tonle Sap

Ban Me Thuot

Nha
Trang

Mekong River

Dalat

Bien Hoa

Saigon

Long Binh

Phan Thiet

My Tho

Ben Tre

Can Tho

Mekong Delta

*Gulf of
Thailand*

Vinh Loi

U.S. and ARVN forces

Communist forces

■ Major U.S. bases in 1968

Major attacks during Tet Offensive

0   100 mi

0   100 km

The Tet Offensive

Fast American reaction repulsed all of the opening attacks in II Corps—at Ban Me Thuot, Kontum City, Pleiku, Darlac, Qui Nhon, and Nha Trang—with devastating losses for the enemy. The Americans and ARVN lost 427 dead and 1,524 wounded, but the enemy lost twelve times as many: 5,405 killed and 704 captured, although, as always, that 12:1 kill ratio was almost certainly inflated by the inclusion of civilians on a battlefield where 16,000 homes were flattened by allied artillery and air strikes. In Ban Me Thuot, a lovely town of 65,000 in the Central Highlands, journalist Don Oberdorfer described "a horror of blood, bullets, death, and destruction."[3]

The first shots in I Corps were aimed at Da Nang's sprawling air base on January 29. The communists hit it with forty rocket and mortar rounds, killing and wounding seven, crippling thirteen strike fighters, burning three hangars, and setting a bomb dump on fire.

The following night, the general offensive struck every major town in I Corps, including Hue and Da Nang. Initially, the Americans recorded "GVN [Government of Vietnam] and ARVN paralysis brought on by the shock of the attack and the impression of VC strength." ARVN soldiers of all ranks were alleging a vast conspiracy and refusing to fight. American troops, they said, were deliberately letting the communist attacks roll inward to put pressure on President Thieu to negotiate with Hanoi and the VC to end the war.[4]

In IV Corps, the VC attacked thirteen of the sixteen province and district capitals in the Mekong Delta. They cratered, blocked, or dropped every essential road, waterway, and bridge. The thirty-nine battalions of ARVN infantry that garrisoned the Delta had been reduced to such a weak strength by Tet leaves that the US 9th Infantry Division and American combat support units had to weigh in everywhere. They would have had to weigh in anyway, for the few ARVN who remained in IV Corps proved reluctant to venture out of their bases to confront the unfolding hell of Tet. Five years earlier a plucky American adviser in the Mekong Delta named John Paul Vann had risked his career to detail all of the failings of the ARVN that MACV had tried so sedulously to conceal. Lieutenant Colonel Vann had been forced into retirement for his candor, but clearly none of the problems he had explored in his reports had been solved. "The ARVN remain in static defensive positions," a US adviser complained as the communists rampaged through the Delta. "They do not pursue the VC forces."[5]

The ARVN IV Corps commander, General Nguyen Van Manh, did not ride to the sound of the guns. Instead, he took refuge in his residence in Can Tho, behind a barbed wire fence and heavily manned bunker positions. Taking no chances, he ordered his two Ranger battalions not to fight the VC but to secure his headquarters and house and the streets around them. For two entire weeks, all ARVN ground movement in the Mekong Delta stopped. Revolutionary Development hamlets that had been listed by Bob Komer as "secure" were abandoned to the communists.

The ARVN units assigned to defend those CORDS pacification projects were pulled back to the provincial capitals, along with the RD teams. The ruff-puffs who remained took one look at the encroaching VC and abandoned their outposts with little resistance. The civilian population of the Delta, terrified by the VC attacks, fled the major towns, clogging the already cratered roads with throngs of refugees. The ARVN had made no arrangements for such a crisis. There was no checkpoint or control system, which meant that the enemy could hide among the refugees, gathering intelligence, traveling in their midst, and blocking the movement of reaction forces. The National Police stuck to the cities, not daring to venture onto the roads outside. General Manh's dereliction of duty in IV Corps was so extreme, even by ARVN standards, that MACV forced his removal. Despite commanding three South Vietnamese divisions, five Ranger battalions, and several Marine battalions, General Manh had left the Mekong Delta to its fate. In Saigon, a complicit Thieu awaited the disgraced corps commander and immediately promoted him to the post of inspector general of the army.[6]

MACV had earlier delegated all supply support in IV Corps to the ARVN, as a first step toward handing the entire war over to them. The experiment failed under the stress of Tet, and the Americans had to hurry back in. A US adviser in the Delta remarked that "the chaos here anticipates exactly what will happen during 'Vietnamization.'"[7]

Despite ample warning of Tet, the ARVN and ruff-puffs had been caught unprepared. Though they had canceled cease-fire leaves in I Corps on January 29 and leaves everywhere else on the thirtieth, those measures initially had no effect, for the ARVN had no way to contact troops who had already left for home.

Even President Thieu had ignored urgent appeals from Westmoreland to remain at his post in Saigon and departed for his wife's home at My Tho in the Mekong Delta. ARVN combat battalions everywhere remained at 50 percent of their duty strength throughout the Tet Offensive. In the Delta, none of them had bothered to stockpile ammo or even top up their fuel tanks, which meant that some units couldn't fight at all and others had to ration their fire and movement. They couldn't be resupplied by road or river. The roads were blocked and the canals were under constant attack by the VC. The South Vietnamese forces could hardly even communicate. The VC had cut every one of their phone lines.[8]

Seventy-two ARVN and ruff-puff firebases and garrisons in the Delta were cut off for over fourteen days and had to be resupplied by MACV's already overused air assets, chiefly the 164th Aviation Group, which had been established at Can Tho to backstop the ARVN just two weeks earlier.

Medical care in the Delta also fell to the Americans, most of the Saigon government's medical personnel having run away when the communists attacked, and stayed away. An American captain attached to IV Corps headquarters in Can Tho marveled at the exertions of the American pilots: "The ARVN survived only because of these emergency deliveries." US pilots delivered everything—aviation and motor gas, diesel, lubricants, ammo, rations, and water. They also flew in thousands of ARVN troops who had been stranded on leave, moved maneuver units from place to place, and handled the evacuation of ARVN casualties, which was particularly urgent because the ARVN had not pre-stocked blood or oxygen, and the VNAF helicopters in the Delta refused to fly because of their "restrictive regulations," which were always risk-averse and never more so than during a holiday or a battle.[9]

The commander of II Field Force Vietnam, General Fred Weyand, had felt the storm brewing and, three weeks earlier, had received Westmoreland's permission to move most of his corps back to the Saigon Circle. With twenty-seven US maneuver battalions and six ARVN divisions, Weyand had the combat power to take on the thirty-five VC battalions that launched the Tet assault in III Corps. He was immediately put to the test.[10]

Late on January 30, an armed VC caught at a checkpoint in Saigon divulged that he was on his way to attack Tan Son Nhut Airport. The Capital Military District went on full alert at 10 p.m., warning troops in the city to stop every ARVN vehicle and search it for impostors. At 2:45 a.m. on January 31, a nineteen-man VC sapper platoon blasted a hole in the wall of the US embassy and crawled inside. They knew exactly where they were going, for two of their number were VC employed by the US State Department inside the embassy. Two MPs guarding the embassy grounds fired on the VC sappers as they wriggled through the hole in the wall, killing the two team leaders, but both MPs were shot in the back by the two VC already inside the compound, men who had quietly worked as embassy drivers before the offensive.[11]

There was only a small group of Marines and MPs defending the embassy when the VC sappers broke in, but they reacted smartly, sealing the embassy building, alerting the rest of the Marine contingent to return to the embassy from their barracks five blocks away, and picking off the VC in the compound one by one.

The VC sappers had forty pounds of C-4 with them—more than enough explosive to blast their way into the chancery building, where a half dozen embassy employees huddled fearfully. But their leaders had been shot and killed coming through the wall. The surviving sappers had been told that they would be reinforced by VC infantry and that crowds of pro-VC, anti-war students would join them on the embassy grounds. None of that support materialized. Instead, the embassy defenders began to strike back. Five Americans were killed in the shoot-out, but their hard-pressed fellows pinned the confused attackers in the embassy gardens long enough for additional MPs and Marines to arrive, as well as a platoon of 101st Airborne troops, who landed on the embassy roof to secure the chancery and grounds. By 9 a.m., Westmoreland and Bunker declared the embassy secure. All nineteen VC were dead, and only one of the American reaction forces was wounded.[12]

But tremendous damage had been done at home in the United States. On the networks, the evening news at 6:30 p.m. on January 30 carried the first reports of the assault in Saigon, where it was 5:30 a.m. the next day. News that the Viet Cong had penetrated the US embassy was reported to a disbelieving public. America had been fighting on the ground since 1965, had over 500,000 troops in-country, had suffered over 20,000 killed, and Westmoreland had just pronounced victory imminent. And yet here were the VC, inside the South Vietnamese capital, inside the walls of the US embassy, and fighting toward Thieu's presidential palace.

On Capitol Hill, even sympathetic senators deplored LBJ's failure to preempt the offensive, and his underestimation of the VC. "You have been saying the situation with the Viet Cong was one of diminishing morale," Senator Robert Byrd confronted the president. "What has happened?"[13]

In Saigon, the invaders made early gains against a defenseless capital. The eleven VC battalions that had infiltrated Saigon before the offensive assembled at their regrouping points and began attacking their objectives—police posts, headquarters, radio transmitters, and government buildings. Skirmishes flared across the city as the VC battalions, fighting in company, platoon, or squad strength, tried to capture key objectives.

ARVN units in Saigon were posted in camp areas on the outskirts and were not supposed to operate in the city's crowded precincts. Saigon's defense was entrusted to the commander of the National Police, General Nguyen Ngoc Loan, a Ky crony and an Air Force officer. Loan, who had taken the precaution of defending his own headquarters with a battalion of South Vietnamese Marines, was fortunate that he had, for without them he probably would have been swept up and killed.

In theory, 3,000 National Police were supposed to garrison the capital. There were 200 of them in each of Saigon's nine precincts and 1,000 more at the National Police headquarters. But with most of the police at home with their families, only a third of Saigon's National Police were on duty—fewer than 1,000 for the entire city. For emergencies such as this one, Loan also had three 400-man paramilitary Police Field Force battalions based in Saigon. But these units, well armed and trained, were also gutted by Tet leaves, some of the 400-man battalions having fewer than thirty men on duty when the communists struck. The older cops, who had joined during the French administration, generally skulked out of harm's way. The younger ones did most of the fighting, but not well. They had to be yanked off the line and provided with thirty minutes of "improvised refresher training" in the middle of the battle to familiarize themselves with weapons and tactics.

General Loan, who had built this 100,000-man police empire, had done it in the usual Saigon way—piling up budgets, perks, and influence, with no regard for performance. The cops lacked cars and radios, and their "reserves" turned out to be clerical workers, most of whom were on leave or had fled. Loan ordered all officers up to the age of thirty-five to combat duty on February 7. Two days later, he ordered all men up to age forty-five to join the fighting, with no noticeable effect. The cops who turned up were exhausted and hungry. Unlike the army, they were not given rations. With the markets closed and combat raging, Saigon's policemen were observed knocking on doors to beg for food and water.[14]

General Loan committed one of the only acts of police daring in the first days, shooting a handcuffed VC prisoner in the head in front of NBC's television cameras, an exploit that stunned American viewers, who had supposed that the Saigon regime was more lawful than the communists.

Loan's televised execution of a prisoner may have been, as *New York Times* reporter Tom Buckley put it, "the turning point—the moment when the American public turned against the war." Eddie Adams' photo of the murder, showing the agonized face of the VC captive at the instant when Loan pulled the trigger, found its way onto the cover of the next *Newsweek*, and leered accusingly from America's newsstands, coffee tables, and waiting rooms.[15]

In Saigon, VC attacks on the presidential palace, broadcast facilities, and the Joint General Staff headquarters were all repulsed. The lightly armed Viet Cong struggled to make a dent in weak defenses that, thanks to American mobility, were swiftly reinforced. VC documents captured in the battle revealed deep frustration with the communist failure to stop American air and overland reinforcement of the capital, as well as the absence of spontaneous popular support from the inhabitants of Saigon. "VC/NVA elements failed to motivate the local populace," one report read. It concluded that the early gains could not be consolidated "because there were not enough replacements from locals" to replace VC casualties in the offensive.[16]

The communist attacks spanned the entire Saigon Circle: Saigon, Tan Son Nhut Airport, Bien Hoa Airbase, and Long Binh Post, which was the headquarters of II Field Force and the seat of the Army's 1st Aviation Brigade. Long Binh was the prize. Everything was there: signals, engineers, two evacuation hospitals, the biggest supply dump in the country, and over 40 percent of American helicopters in Vietnam. In Saigon, where there were no US combat troops besides the Marines guarding the US embassy, three VC local-force battalions breached the wire at Tan Son Nhut, the headquarters of the VNAF and the US 7th Air Force, and nearly seized the two

10,000-foot concrete runways as well as Westmoreland's headquarters in the neighboring MACV compound.

Westmoreland was stunned by the speed with which the recently opened "Pentagon East" was encircled and attacked. He and his staff descended to the command bunker for a last stand, pausing only to transfer Westy's authority to US Army headquarters in Long Binh, in case MACV was overrun. The enemy was held just short of its objectives by US Air Force reaction forces and two ARVN companies and then, after three hours of combat, was defeated by a squadron of the US 4th Cavalry Regiment, which rolled in at 6 a.m. from its camp northwest of Saigon to hit the VC in the rear with tanks.[17]

VC mortars cratered the runway at Bien Hoa at 2:48 a.m. on January 31, preventing any jets from taking off. The VC 274th and 275th Regiments then stormed the air base, getting into the bunker line and nearly breaking through the perimeter. The air base was saved by the arrival at 9 a.m. of a battalion of the 101st Airborne Division and a troop of armored cavalry from the 9th ID, but also by the heroics of its Army gunships, which, as everywhere, were on "strip alert" and got aloft in thirty seconds or less.

Sixty-eight gunships, grouped in "light fire teams," were all the air cover available in the Saigon Circle until about 1 p.m., when the first fighter jet was able to take off from the hastily repaired runway at Bien Hoa. The gunships swarmed over Saigon, Bien Hoa, and Long Binh, attacking enemy mortar and rocket sites, following the river lines and destroying 520 sampans used to ferry enemy troops and ammo, and then mowing down nearly 2,000 men of the two VC regiments. In 18,000 sorties, the restless gunships fired over 100,000 rocket and artillery rounds and 6.4 million rounds of machine gun ammo. The VC attackers, who had closed so eagerly on the Bien Hoa–Long Binh complex, were torn to shreds.[18]

The communist plan had been for local forces to infiltrate the cities and to be quickly reinforced by inflowing waves of main-force units, who would exploit the prevailing chaos to move into the cities. In Saigon, the plan was foiled by the fast reaction of the US 101st Airborne Division, which clung to the Bien Hoa–Long Binh complex, and by the US 1st Infantry Division, which repulsed a VC attack on their base camp and then made heavy contact with the VC 273rd Regiment at Phu Cuong City, the provincial capital, which lay just east of them.

Phu Cuong was the sort of critical junction the communists needed to take and hold in order to reinforce the combat in Saigon. A river and three highways converged there, but the Americans caught the VC on the move and killed nearly 400 of them. The fighting was confused, the initial VC boldness replaced by caution as the Americans scrambled "lightships" with searchlights to illuminate the VC companies and then target them with air strikes and artillery.

The VC, stunned by the speed of the American reaction, backed into the surrounding hamlets to shelter among the inhabitants and buy time while the Big Red One sought "political and provincial clearance" to fire into the village of An My, on the northwestern edge of Phu Loi Base Camp. The clearance was given, and the Americans obliterated the village and its hamlets under 5,000 rounds of field artillery and air strikes with cluster bomblets and 500-pound bombs. Picking through the wreckage on February 1, the grunts of the 1st ID would find another 197 corpses of the VC 273rd Regiment.[19]

Brutal counterattacks like these stopped the VC main-force units short of Saigon, depriving the infiltrators in the capital of crucial reinforcements. The US 25th Infantry Division did the same to the VC 271st and 272nd Regiments, halting their drive on the capital. The tanks and APCs of the US 4th Cavalry Regiment that saved Tan Son Nhut Airport at 6 a.m. on February 1 traveled on Route 1, which the VC were supposed to have cut, and across bridges that the VC were supposed to have dropped. VC troops missed their assignments there, and also on Route 13, where another American armored battalion at Loc Ninh was able to race right past a VC division on the outskirts of Saigon to relieve the ARVN III Corps headquarters. "The communists were snared by their own strategy," Weyand's ops chief observed. "They needed local forces to cut the key roads and bridges, but they sent those local forces into the urban fighting and left non-local NVA and other units who didn't know the area to cut the roads."[20]

Because of these prompt and effective American counterattacks, the VC and NVA units in the Saigon Circle could not reinforce the sputtering attacks inside the capital. On the contrary, they were themselves destroyed. Scheduled to enter Saigon in the days after February 2, they instead found themselves trapped between their base areas and Saigon—easy meat for American airpower and artillery. "They took a terrific pasting," General

Weyand's headquarters reported. In the first week of February, Weyand estimated that his troops killed and captured 8,500 communists in the Saigon Circle. The victory hadn't been cheap—1,000 allied forces died in the same period—but it was lopsided.[21]

By midnight on January 31, Weyand had brought more maneuver battalions into Saigon than the communists had managed to infiltrate. The VC who *had* infiltrated could now be contained, run to ground, and killed. Most of the VC prisoners captured in Saigon came from central Vietnam. This fact suggested that the VC had far fewer Saigon adherents than they claimed, and was another explanation for the poor performance of the VC in the capital. They did not know the city and became utterly lost when separated from their guides. Even the guides got lost, failing in many cases to find street addresses where weapons and ammo were cached.[22]

All of Le Duan's optimistic assumptions about the Tet Offensive proved false. All of Defense Minister Giap's caution, which had led to his exile, proved warranted. The ARVN and ruff-puffs did *not* crumble under the onslaught of 84,000 communist troops, and the Americans did *not* retreat. With many of its battalions down to just 200 men because of Tet leaves, the ARVN stumbled early but then pulled itself together. Still, Weyand found his South Vietnamese ally far from effective. They didn't collapse tactically, but they did allow themselves to be pushed out of many areas, at which point they displayed the "perennial ARVN problem of counter-attacking," which was to say, *not* counterattacking, until the Americans showed up.[23]

The longest battle of the Tet Offensive flared through Hue in I Corps, where the fighting dragged on for three weeks. Hue exerted a special fascination for the North Vietnamese. Sited far to the north on Route 1, it sat halfway between the 16th and 17th parallels and was vulnerable to a communist land grab because of its nearness to the DMZ. It also had special significance to the South Vietnamese. It was a cradle of their country, its imperial palace the ancient seat of the Vietnamese emperors. The Viet Minh had tried to destroy the palace in 1945 "to sever Vietnam from its past," but the French had renovated and expanded it to give their puppet emperor a more imposing court and to accent traditional values of family loyalty and ancestor worship that the Viet Minh had tried to eradicate.

The three-week battle for Hue proved a couple of things. First, like the fighting around Saigon, it proved the truth of Bernard Fall's observation that for the United States the war was, "in the short run, militarily 'unlosable'" owing to "the immense influx of American manpower and firepower." By no means had the now deceased Frenchman believed that it was winnable, just that it was "unlosable," in the sense that neither the NVA nor the VC had answers for American maneuverability, command of the air, and firepower. The communists lacked even a basic capability to sustain large-scale attacks. The US 1st Infantry Division made the same point after chewing up two VC main-force regiments that had attacked their base camp and attempted to drive on Saigon: "The enemy's problem is how to carry out his intentions based on *capability*." This gulf in capabilities between American and communist forces was too wide to bridge.[24]

The bitter combat in Hue also proved that the war, pitched by Westmoreland as nearing its end, was far from over. The tenacity of the communist fighters in Hue foreshadowed a conflict that would go on and on, beyond the "short run" favored by Americans, into a "long run" that, for the Americans, *would* be militarily losable. The White House struggled to understand how the situation could have flipped so quickly. "I have a question," Secretary of State Dean Rusk asked the Joint Chiefs at a meeting in the Cabinet Room during the battle. "In the past, we have said the problem really was finding the enemy. Now the enemy has come to us. I am sure many will ask why aren't we doing better now that we know where they are."[25]

For a man who had been congratulating himself on preventing the communist "scissors" from slicing across the country to the seacoast and its important cities of Hue and Da Nang, Westmoreland failed in Hue, as elsewhere, to prevent 6,000 NVA regulars from filtering through I Corps, infiltrating the city, and launching a reign of terror there. Don Oberdorfer, a Korean War vet who reported from Hue for the *Washington Post*, put this failure down to the usual mix of sloth and aloofness that characterized American and South Vietnamese cooperation.

Hue's police chief, a former sportscaster who sipped Johnnie Walker Black Label throughout the workday, did not send whatever intelligence he gleaned to the city's ARVN 1st Division, nor did the small CIA office in Hue communicate with the US military advisory team there. Radio intercepts of the NVA advance on Hue picked up by the US field station at Phu Bai, just eight miles south of Hue, were sent not to the city's defenders but to Da Nang for "analysis," where they languished.[26]

At 2:00 a.m. on January 31, three battalions of the NVA 6th Regiment and several VC units crossed the Perfume River in two places, attacked the Imperial Citadel at Hue, penetrated the forbidden city (that "nest of mandarins and monarchs"), and raised the yellow-starred flag of the Viet Cong over the Citadel. In the New City on the southern bank of the Perfume River, where most of Hue's 140,000 people lived, the NVA 4th Regiment assembled after picking its way through the rural districts around the city. They struck toward the MACV compound.

Long off-limits to US combat forces for political reasons, Hue nearly fell to this communist swipe. But a single company of General Ngo Quang Truong's ARVN 1st Division held fast in the division headquarters in the northeast corner of the Citadel. The general was reinforced that evening by his 3rd Regiment and three ARVN Airborne battalions. South of the city, small parties of Americans fought to slow the communist infiltration of South Vietnam's third-largest city, secure the MACV compound, and clear the south bank of the river.

After the initial onslaught, the communists held most of Hue except for tiny enclaves—the ARVN 1st Division headquarters inside the Citadel, the MACV headquarters in the New City on the south bank, and, most critically, the "LCU ramp." The ramp was Hue's south-bank river port, the place where troops, supplies, and ammo were shipped by sea from Da Nang and then up the Perfume River to Hue in LCUs (landing craft utility). Purely by chance, a platoon of four tanks and two self-propelled guns destined for Quang Tri City had just landed at the port when the attack began, providing the allied reaction forces with critical armored support.[27]

The battle would play out in three distinct areas: the Citadel, the New City, and the country surrounding Hue, an area of low hills, old imperial tombs, scrubby brush, and rice paddies. The NVA would have to hold this ground if they wanted to remain in Hue. Removing them from it was a key to saving the city. The Marines would focus on defending their own main supply route, which was the LCU ramp as well as Route 1, which ran right past the front gate of the beleaguered MACV compound. The ARVN 1st Division successfully retook the Citadel's airfield on February 1, allowing them to fly in reinforcements.

More ARVN reinforcements arrived by road that same day. Two ARVN Airborne battalions and a troop of twelve APCs shot their way into the

Citadel on February 1, losing 130 killed and wounded, many of them in four APCs that were pierced by NVA antitank guns. On February 2, the US 1st Cavalry Division began sending companies of its 3rd Brigade to take up positions north and west of Hue to prevent the communists from reinforcing the two NVA regiments, the sapper and rocket battalions, and the six local-force companies known to be inside the city.[28]

Hue's Citadel sprawled along the north bank of the Perfume River and enclosed a square mile of palace buildings erected over the years by the Vietnamese emperors. This was the old or forbidden city of Hue, shielded from the eyes of commoners by two stone walls, three feet thick and fifteen feet high, and a moat, fed by the river, that surrounded most of the Citadel. Between the outer and inner walls of the Citadel was a town of narrow lanes, heavy stone houses and buildings, high walls, and hedgerows. The residents of Hue had fortified their homes, with bunkers beneath them, broken glass cemented on the tops of the walls, and barbed wire laced through the hedges to deter assailants. Every home inside the old city was a defensive position. In southern Hue, the New City, the streets were wider and the houses easier to breach. Here there would be more room to maneuver.[29]

To take back the vital space around Hue and strangle the communists inside, the 3rd Brigade of the Cav and a battalion of the 101st Airborne Division air-assaulted into positions north and west of Hue on February 2 to attack the three additional NVA regiments and the 3,000 local forces who were holding a corridor into Hue and supporting the two NVA regiments already inside the city.

NVA battalions were trying to hold a ring around the city and move reinforcements into it by creeping unseen down the canals that surrounded the Citadel. In this they were aided by heavy rains and fog, which made American artillery, air strikes, and the 8-inch guns of Navy cruisers in the Gulf of Tonkin harder to target. The Citadel's western wall was the vital link. Everything the communists consumed—troops, ammo, medicine, and rations—flowed through it. US forces, checked by foul weather, low ceilings, and visibility of 500 feet or less, fought to close that route. For ten miserable days, four American battalions pressed down from the northwest toward that wall, the NVA defending their key supply lines—Route 554 and the Perfume River itself—with mortars, machine guns, RPGs, and 122 mm rockets.[30]

MACV documents spoke of "the weather greatly limiting supporting fires," but those fires were still prodigious: 7,700 rounds of 8-inch shell, 53,000 rounds of 105 mm artillery, and 200 tons of aerial bombs and napalm. By February 22, the Cav and Airborne had closed to within a mile of the wall. Two days later, they reached the wall itself. Sixty-eight Americans had been killed and 453 wounded in the effort to cut this main supply line and chew up the battalions defending it. In the course of their advance, they counted 400 enemy dead in collapsed bunkers and trenches. The NVA units, MACV noted, were secure only "when they walked through jungles, and avoided the population." That advantage disappeared everywhere they deployed in Tet, especially in Hue. "As soon as he moved, we did also," MACV observed.[31]

Undeterred by the ARVN, which lacked heavy direct-fire weapons to blast the communists out of their hardened positions, the two NVA regiments inside Hue embarked on a bloody purge of what the VC called "the enemy's restrictive administrative machinery." The political cadres embedded in the combat units had lists and photos of South Vietnamese citizens to be "eliminated" and were given more names by some of the students, teachers, and Buddhist monks who welcomed the invaders. To make the purge more palatable, the communists stood up a "Coalition Front for Peace." This was the usual communist front organization that was entirely supine: two Viet Cong, a Buddhist monk, a professor, and sixty-year-old Mrs. Luan Chi.[32]

The purges were carried out inside Hue but also in its outer districts, the "kill lists" vetted by NVA and VC officers. In just two of the outer districts, the communists killed over 2,000 "puppet authorities," who were legislators, policemen, army officers on leave, hamlet and village chiefs, civil servants, clergy, professionals, or just merchants or landowners indicted as "tyrants, reactionaries, and spies." The corpses of two Benedictine priests from France were found, one bound hand and foot and buried alive, the other shot in the back of the head.

The NVA, guided by their "coalition front" in Hue and by snitches in the occupied outlying districts, killed about 6,000 South Vietnamese citizens. The victims of the communist purge were later discovered in mass graves on both banks of the Perfume River. Many had been shot; others had been clubbed to death or buried alive. During and after the atrocity, the communists were unrepentant: "The entire control machinery of the feudalists and bourgeois was centered in Hue," they alleged. The proletariat had risen up to kill its masters, they lied. "Hatred and vengeance prevailed everywhere, in the hearts of children and old people alike."³³

For the first several days, Hue's defenders were handcuffed by rules of engagement that banned "supporting fires" in a city that was notorious for its culture of political resistance to Saigon. "The invaders," a witness reported, "were all over the area, walking back and forth through the streets with leafy camouflage hanging from their shoulder packs, carrying mortar tubes and projectiles, machine guns, and other weapons." They seemed untroubled by thoughts of a counterattack. The restrictions were finally removed on February 3, when two US Marine battalions, which had been rushed up from Phu Bai as a reaction force on January 31, began fighting house-to-house to take back the New City.³⁴

Michael Herr, who was there for *Esquire*, recalled the drive into Hue from Phu Bai in an eight-truck convoy, refugees lining the sides of the road: "All the grunts were whistling, and no two were whistling the same tune; it sounded like a locker room before a game that nobody wanted to play." The fighting in the New City sloshed back and forth, Marine battalions measuring their AOs not in square miles but in city blocks. They learned urban warfare quickly, avoiding the streets and closing on the enemy by blasting through the walls of houses until they arrived inside the enemy strongpoints. They took and held the Hue University campus. Based there, they undertook six major assaults on enemy troops in the Treasury and Post Office buildings. Half of the New City was reduced to rubble.³⁵

The US determination to recover Hue reflected high-level meetings in Washington, where administration officials worried that the NVA needed only *one* major city. If they held Hue, they could call it the "first liberated zone" and the "true capital" of South Vietnam. It would become a magnet for antiwar South Vietnamese "coalitionists." Clark Clifford urged Johnson to drop bombs into the "restricted areas" around Hanoi and the Chinese border to make clear that the United States would not be pushed around in this way. Hanoi was not taking up the president's peace feelers, Clifford argued, so Johnson should hit them *harder*. But Johnson squirmed away from the decision. Too many planes and pilots would be lost to the North

Vietnamese air defenses, LBJ countered. "Bob McNamara says the loss is not worth the gain."

General Earle "Bus" Wheeler, the chairman of the Joint Chiefs, urged the president to "stop applying rigid restrictions to ourselves" and to counterpunch brutally before it was too late. On February 8, Wheeler wrote Westmoreland: "There is a theory that overall enemy strategy is to attack and attrite the ARVN and thereby destroy them and ultimately gain acceptance by the people of a coalition government that would request the withdrawal of U.S. forces in South Vietnam." In meetings with the president, Bus Wheeler spoke not of theory but of fact. Reinforcements were urgently needed to "contain the enemy offensive" in I Corps.[36]

On February 12, the 1st Battalion of the 5th US Marine Regiment and two South Vietnamese Marine battalions relieved the ARVN Airborne troops inside the Citadel. Using the critical LCU ramp, the Marines brought in five M-48 tanks and four M-50 Ontos tank destroyers, the latter a lightly armored tracked vehicle mounting six 106 mm recoilless rifles. The two South Vietnamese Marine battalions arrived with five 105 mm howitzers,

Men of the 5th Marine Regiment during the combat in Hue City. Inside the Citadel, the Marines lost one killed or wounded for every yard gained. (National Archives)

which finally gave them the firepower to dislodge the small, scattered enemy detachments that were holding up whole companies of ARVN infantry.[37]

The fighting inside the Citadel intensified. The troops fought house-to-house, the US forces suffering one killed or wounded for every yard gained. The US Marines were held up inside the northeast wall of the Citadel, their advance checked by enemy fire from the palace grounds on their right flank, which, for "political and cultural" reasons, they were forbidden to suppress.

Here and there shivering refugees would appear from a cellar or through a gap in a wall to try to reach their abandoned homes. The Marines would shoo them away: "Di, di, *di*, you sorry-ass motherfuckers, go on, get the hell away from here!" The refugees would smile, bow or shrug, and dash up the ruined streets. Three companies of the 1st Battalion of the 5th Marines were reduced to below platoon strength. By now, Michael Herr observed, "everyone wanted to get wounded," just to get out alive. On February 16, radio intercepts revealed that the NVA officer commanding the force inside the Citadel had been killed by artillery. His deputy commander requested permission to withdraw, as the soldiers could no longer be supplied. American artillery, air, and naval fires were making all movement through the western wall impossible. His request was denied, and he was ordered to "defend in place"—to the last man.[38]

On that same day, scenting victory, Vice President Ky, Prime Minister Nguyen Van Loc, ARVN I Corps commander General Hoang Xuan Lam, and a dozen other South Vietnamese grandees flew to MACV's Forward HQ in I Corps to show themselves to a gaggle of reporters before being briefed on the recapture of the Imperial City. Westy's deputy, Creighton Abrams, was there, along with the Marine commander Robert Cushman. They briefed Ky and the others on the fighting, and spoke of the "cultural" constraints posed by an enemy fighting from pagodas, palaces, churches, schools, and hospitals. By now, 150 of the 160 historic structures inside the Hue Citadel were smoking ruins. Ky, who had declared war on Hue two years earlier when its garrison commander had challenged his rule, assured the gathered generals that they were free to raze everything that remained standing: "I will take responsibility for damage or destruction if necessary to drive the enemy from the city."[39]

On February 21, the ARVN 1st Division was finally relieved by the Cav, which broke through enemy positions on the western and northern faces of the Citadel. The communists by now had been pressed into the south-eastern corner of the Citadel. All hope of resupply and reinforcement was ended. The 1st Brigade of the 101st Airborne Division had deployed on the southern outskirts of Hue to close those routes, and the Cav had stopped all movement in and out of Hue from the north and west.

None of it had been easy. Those Army units took two-thirds as many casualties in five days as the Marines had suffered in three weeks. On February 23, a battalion of the ARVN 1st Division as well as the division's crack reaction force—known as the Black Panther or Hac Bao Company—seized the flag tower on the southern wall of the Citadel. They fired 300 rounds of 105 mm artillery into the wall to kill the defenders there before fighting their way up the steps of the flag tower, the surviving NVA retreating before them, triggering claymore mines and defending barricades to the last man.[40]

Early on February 24, ARVN troops tore down the fifty-foot-wide VC flag that had fluttered over the Citadel for more than three weeks. They raised the red-striped yellow flag of South Vietnam in its place. President Thieu, a former ARVN 1st Division commander, arrived the next day to congratulate the division's current commander, General Ngo Quang Truong, on his successful defense of the city. Mopping up communist stragglers would continue for another week, but Operation Hue City was effectively over. The battle ended on March 2, with 70 percent of the city destroyed or badly damaged. Enemy casualties were estimated at 5,000 killed and 100 captured. The ARVN and South Vietnamese Marines lost 384 killed and 1,830 wounded. The US Marines lost 142 killed and 857 wounded, the Army 74 killed and 507 wounded. Both sides were chastened by the result here and elsewhere. Le Duan's general offensive had shattered against superior allied mobility and firepower, failing to ignite a general uprising, or any uprising at all. But the American and South Vietnamese success had to be netted against the tremendous damage done to South Vietnam, high casualties, a collapse of the pacification program, and the psychological blow of the offensive to American hopes and plans.[41]

Chapter 14

"WE CAN KEEP ON WINNING THE WAR FOREVER"

The Tet Offensive ripped visible gashes all across South Vietnam. It did equal, less visible harm to the South Vietnamese government. General Le Nguyen Khang, the III Corps commander and a Ky protégé, told the CIA in February 1968 that Thieu had shown himself to be a weak and uninspiring leader, and that Ky was no better. Still, Khang added, there was no appetite for a coup among senior military officers. No one wanted responsibility for the mess in South Vietnam. The only thing all of the generals could agree on was that, like Thieu and Ky, they would never permit the VC to join a South Vietnamese coalition government. Above all, the generals were survivors, and they knew that they would not retain their posts under a power-sharing deal with the communists. France's puppet emperor Bao Dai had tried that twenty-three years earlier, and he had lasted only five months on the throne before being brushed aside by his Viet Minh coalition partners. "I have no solution to the leadership problem," Khang confided to the CIA, "and I doubt anyone else has one."[1]

With so much defeatism swirling around him, Westmoreland could see that his war in Vietnam was running out of time and gas. President Johnson froze in panic, woodenly insisting that, although critics abounded, "our military and diplomatic men in the field know more than any of our congressmen and senators back here." And yet when the military men wanted to start bombing Hanoi and Haiphong to punish Hanoi's aggression and war crimes inside South Vietnam, Johnson authorized just fourteen targets, hardly enough to sway the politburo.

On February 18, 1968, the president flew to California to appear on the flight deck of the carrier *Constellation* to address the crew before they sailed for Vietnam. LBJ dripped fear and indecision. He asked for questions, and none were asked, so he called on the gathered sailors. "If you were president," he asked one, "what would *you* do to change things?" "Hit them more," the young man replied. Johnson then launched into a tortured explanation as to why he couldn't. It was impossible, he insisted, to close all of their roads and sea lanes. And the Russians and Chinese might intervene if he did: "The whole family might jump on us."[2]

LBJ was trying to kick the war away to reduce its impact on his reelection chances. That was more difficult now than earlier, for the press corps in Saigon had nearly doubled in size during Tet. There had been 350 reporters in Saigon when the offensive began. There were now 650. With the media filled with news of Tet and its casualties, the president's approval rating sank to 32 percent.

LBJ's meetings in February and March 1968 rang with indignant denunciations of the press and Bill Fulbright's Senate Foreign Relations Committee. "People have the view that we took a great defeat," the president grumbled. "*Our* version is not being put to the American people properly." Yet MACV's lawyerly assertion that Tet had resulted in "favorable operational statistics for the quarter" charmed no one.

Clark Clifford, who was poised to replace McNamara as secretary of defense, pointed to the contradiction in the Army's position: "On the one hand the military has said we had quite a victory out there last week. On the other hand, they now say that it was such a big victory that we need 120,000 *more* men." This was a reference to Westmoreland's plea for reinforcements during the Tet Offensive.

McGeorge Bundy, once an ardent booster of the war, had fled the administration. McNamara, voice of so much rah-rah optimism, was in his last, thoroughly dispirited month on the job. President Johnson, abandoned by his most trusted hawks, was stricken with fear and doubt. The

CIA director, Dick Helms, told him that the best that could be expected from the great bloodletting of Tet was more stagnation, "neither side capable of registering decisive gains." For the moment, LBJ held the line against Westmoreland's call for more troops. There would be "no great new overall moves" in the war, the president assured a press conference. The manpower ceiling would be kept at 525,000. Up for reelection in nine months, the president dared not raise it again.[3]

But Westmoreland wanted to counterpunch. He wrote directly to LBJ on February 12. The heavy communist casualties, Westy argued, "afforded near and long-term opportunities" to pursue and destroy the wounded enemy. Until now, the United States had waged "a limited war with limited objectives, fought with limited means, programmed for the utilization of limited resources." It was time to go all in to win with "a bold offensive campaign."[4]

Westmoreland had inflicted enormous casualties on the enemy during Tet and now wanted to implement the new strategy he had floated during the summer of 1967. He told the president the bold outlines—"the enemy has changed his strategy, we must change ours"—but he kept the rather alarming details to himself and the Joint Chiefs. Westy wanted to increase troop levels and take the offensive north across the DMZ and west into the sanctuaries in Laos and Cambodia, to cut the Ho Chi Minh Trail and isolate the South Vietnamese battlefield.

Three weeks before Tet, Westmoreland had ordered his staff to work up Operation El Paso. El Paso would harden Route 9 across I Corps, through Khe Sanh, and into the Laotian road and trail junction of Xepon. With that line of supply complete and secured by US Marines, Westy planned to strike to Xepon with the Cav, the 101st Airborne Division, and the ARVN Airborne Division to seize that "critical choke point" before retiring down the Ho Chi Minh trail to Kontum City in the Central Highlands, destroying enemy troops and supply caches as he went.[5]

Westmoreland planned to pair El Paso with Operation Pacific Grove, an amphibious feint with Okinawa-based Marines toward the North Vietnamese city of Vinh. He assumed that the feint toward Vinh, 150 miles north of the DMZ, would pin down North Vietnamese reserve forces and make it safer for the Cav and Airborne to operate in Laos. For these operations, he renewed his plea for 206,000 additional troops, which would have breached the already strained ceiling of 525,000 US troops in South Vietnam that had been agreed in July 1967.

Westmoreland reckoned that he would get his wish list this time. Even if President Johnson lost the 1968 race, his successor almost certainly would want a war-winning strategy. McNamara was leaving and Clark Clifford was taking over at the Pentagon to run the war. Clifford had been hawkish on Vietnam. And, oddly, polls favored Westy at this point. True, there had been a rally of 100,000 against the war in Washington in October 1967, and antiwar demonstrations spread to a growing number of American colleges in 1967 and 1968. But 60 percent of Americans still opposed the protests.

When polled about strategy in December 1967, a plurality of Americans had called for a more *aggressive* prosecution of the war. Asked whether America should invade North Vietnam with troops, 49 percent had said yes, 29 percent had said no, and 22 percent were unsure. Forty-seven percent had approved occupying the DMZ, with only 21 percent opposed. Forty-two percent of Americans had supported mining Haiphong harbor, even at the risk of sinking Soviet ships. Only 33 percent opposed the risky measure. This was soft support for escalation, but support nonetheless.[6]

And yet Westmoreland and the chiefs, fearful of LBJ's temper and moods, once again failed to specify what they *really* wanted. The chairman of the Joint Chiefs, General Earle Wheeler, had been thoroughly cowed by the president. These days he entered the White House, a witness observed, like "a wary beagle, his soft dark eyes watchful for the origin of the next blow." What followed, in February and March 1968, was a deliberate and ultimately self-defeating program of deception by Wheeler, Westmoreland, and the Joint Chiefs.[7]

Already on February 8, four days after Westmoreland had assured Wheeler that the communists had been soundly defeated and lacked "a basic capability to sustain attacks" anywhere in South Vietnam, Wheeler instructed Westmoreland to go ahead and request reinforcements anyway because "the U.S. is not prepared to accept defeat in Vietnam." Westy read between the lines and understood what Wheeler was up to: scaring the president into sending more troops. Westmoreland obediently went along with the ruse. Right you are, he replied to Wheeler. "It's only prudent to plan for the worst contingency, in which I will need more troops."[8]

Wheeler, knowing that Westy wanted the troops to enable a new offensive strategy in Southeast Asia, did not dare say as much to the president, who wanted the war to end, not widen. Nor were Wheeler's and Westy's interests aligned. Westmoreland wanted the troops to win in Vietnam. Wheeler wanted to use the troop request to pressure the White House into finally calling up the reserves so that he could begin to fill the US military's personnel shortages all over the world.[9]

Bureaucratically, Wheeler had high hopes for 1968. McNamara, who had held the Joint Chiefs on a short leash for three years, was departing and being replaced by Clark Clifford. The chiefs assumed that Clifford would be an ally—"a tabula rasa," as one analyst put it, "on which to write their plan." He wasn't. In mid-February, as SecDef designee, Clifford made his revised position on the war crystal clear: "The idea of a U.S. military victory in Vietnam is a dangerous illusion because both the Soviets and the Chinese have the capacity to preclude it—probably by supply operations alone, but if necessary by intervening with their own forces."[10]

In 1968, Wheeler and Clifford were looking at overlapping crises everywhere: in South Vietnam, to be sure, but also a Soviet invasion of Czechoslovakia, China's successful test of a thermonuclear bomb, North Korea's seizure of the USS *Pueblo* spy ship and attack on the South Korean presidential palace, continuing conflict between American and Soviet proxies in the Middle East, and the communist Pathet Lao's rout of US-backed Royal Laotian forces, effectively handing that critical nation to the communists—the worst possible prelude to Westy's proposed incursion into Laos.[11]

Pentagon planners tasked with responding to these emergencies reported that, due to the nonstop demands of Vietnam and the dwindling strategic reserve, they had sufficient forces and funds to cope with none but the most trivial. LBJ's dogged refusal to call up even a fraction of America's 1 million reserve forces exacerbated this "manpower crisis of 1968."[12]

Asking an already spooked LBJ to double down on Vietnam, abandon the policy of gradual escalation, call up 120,000 reserves, and lift the ban on ground operations in North Vietnam, Laos, and Cambodia—which might finally trigger Soviet or Chinese intervention in the war—seemed obtuse in an atmosphere in which inflation and deficits were rising and nearly every US Army unit in the United States, Europe, and Korea was judged "not combat ready" owing to diversions of men, vehicles, and munitions to Vietnam.[13]

Clark Clifford saw nothing but disaster in a larger war because it would merely apply Westy's attrition methods to a bigger theater, creating massive additional liabilities and casualties in the process. As it was, President Johnson was close to despair. "What makes the North Vietnamese fight so well, with so much more determination than the South Vietnamese," he blurted out in a meeting of his senior advisers. The South Korean government was threatening to withdraw its 50,000 troops from South Vietnam to cope with Kim Il Sung's threats along Korea's 38th parallel, and Johnson had no troops (or willing allies) to replace them. Now here was General Westmoreland requesting more troops, "shock action," and a "more dynamic strategy" at a time when honest analysis of Tet revealed that, far from being a victory and a launchpad for more aggressive operations, Tet might have been an American *defeat*.[14]

Tactically, Tet *seemed* at first blush to have spelled disaster for the communists. But really, the communists suffered less from Tet than Westmoreland alleged. Initial MACV accounts spoke of a VC that was effectively destroyed during Tet. In January and February, MACV put communist losses at 45,000 killed and 5,800 captured. That was 20 percent of their total strength if you used MACV's pre-Tet estimate, but only 10 percent if you used CIA numbers.

CIA analysts now argued that the victory was not nearly as decisive as it appeared. They noted that 58,000 communist main and local forces had been fed into battle in the two weeks of fighting that ebbed on February 13, 1968. That was about 50 percent of their regular forces inside South Vietnam, and if you assumed, as MACV seemed to be doing, that most of the communist KIAs and prisoners during Tet were NVA and VC main-force troops, then they should have been devastated, with a casualty rate of 88 percent.[15]

But that, the CIA argued in February 1968, was nonsense. Many of the enemy casualties were not trained, seasoned regular troops. They were local-force guerrillas, peasants drafted to move VC supplies, new recruits, or civilians killed in populated areas taken under attack. The CIA concluded that the VC/NVA losses were "high, but not as serious as first believed." And the enemy, who had flooded the countryside during the offensive, was accelerating recruiting in those rural areas that had not so much been "liberated" by the enemy as abandoned by their own security forces.

After Tet, the NVA continued to infiltrate 14,000 troops every month, and the VC continued to recruit 7,000 new fighters every month. Setting infiltration and recruitment against Tet casualties, the net communist loss was probably closer to 29,000 men, which was far from backbreaking. "In sum," the CIA concluded, "communist losses were high, but not as serious as first believed."[16]

Strategically, Tet paid enormous dividends to Hanoi and the Viet Cong. Free-world forces had been attacking the communists and reporting huge body counts every year since 1965. Westmoreland had assured the American public in 1967 that the enemy was nearly broken. And yet Tet brought the heaviest fighting of the war for the Americans—a massive upsurge, not the last gasp mooted by Westy.

American casualties in 1968—17,000 killed and 87,000 wounded—increased the dismay. In 1966, only about 1.5 percent of American wounded were dying of their injuries. With the communists using more potent weapons and tactics, that ratio had climbed to 19 percent, making the number of Americans wounded as "political" as the number of KIAs.

Lulled by MACV's prediction of imminent victory, the shocking attack on South Vietnam's cities had, in the words of the US embassy, "stunned and confused" the South Vietnamese (to say nothing of the Americans watching on their televisions at home). South Vietnam's city dwellers had believed themselves safe. They had always thought of the war as a rural one. Suddenly they were confronted with urban combat, death and destruction, water and power cuts, housing and food crises, and mobs of refugees. As MACV put it: "The VC got into the towns as they said they would." And now everyone believed they could do it *again*.[17]

This psychological victory had knock-on effects. The VC, MACV warned, could continue "to force a non-committed attitude on the people, to oppose every government call for 'unity of effort' and 'national purpose.'" General Fred Weyand's staff, which monitored the intense VC activity in III Corps and Saigon, concluded that "the most clear-cut gain of the VC" from Tet was the success of this "strategic terrorism." They had made even the safest areas feel dangerous.

"Everywhere," Weyand's operations chief wrote, "there is fear of the VC now." Supporting the Saigon regime had become a life-threatening choice. The VC followed Tet with a very deliberate program of terrorism, assassinations, and kidnappings to ram home the point that neither the Americans nor the Thieu government could protect the South Vietnamese people. Every week, all over South Vietnam after Tet, an average of 85 civilians were assassinated, 160 wounded, and 250 abducted, causing the US embassy in Saigon to begin tracking yet another implacable statistic: "Weekly Terror Activity." How would the Saigon government ever get *this* scourge under control?[18]

How indeed? South Vietnam was thrown into chaos and confusion by the Tet Offensive, which destroyed towns, halted business activity, drove up prices, and generated refugees on an enormous, destabilizing scale. After the offensive, CORDS analysts discovered that Westy's ops in 1967 and the communist attacks in 1968 had created at least 1.5 million new refugees—meaning that one of every eleven South Vietnamese was now a displaced person.

The destroyed towns and villages were all the more problematic because they were largely destroyed by American and ARVN fire. "The strafing of populated areas," an ARVN officer told the CIA, "must cease. *We* are killing more innocent civilians than the VC." In I Corps, most of Hue was destroyed, 4,000 civilians were killed, and 90,000 of the region's population were made refugees. In II Corps, all of the major towns were destroyed. An American soldier who went into Pleiku after the VC withdrew wrote that "the destruction was staggering," everything burnt and pulverized, "like Berlin or London after the bombings of World War II." John Paul Vann, now a civilian CORDS adviser in II Corps, noted the irony that "the battles we win may add up to losing the war" for "the destruction exceeds our capability for recovery."[19]

In III Corps, the losses were most severe in Saigon, where 17,000 civilians were killed and wounded and 19,000 houses were destroyed, creating 206,000 new refugees. Before Tet, there had been only 14,000 refugees in IV Corps' Mekong Delta. Now there were 170,000. The Revolutionary Development and New Life pacification programs, designed to bring secure housing, healthcare, and education to rural areas, were halted and thrown backward by the Tet Offensive. Teachers and social workers were killed, kidnapped, or driven away. Youth groups and ruff-puff forces were penetrated by the VC, during and after the offensive, and could no longer be considered reliable.[20]

The scale of the Tet destruction all across South Vietnam was so great and demoralizing that President Thieu had announced Operation Recovery on February 4, before the smoke had even cleared on the battlefields and while combat was still raging in Hue and Saigon. It was a $400 million program to repair the estimated $1.4 billion of damage done by the communist attacks on the cities and towns. Even on such a reduced scale, none of it went smoothly. A US adviser was appalled by the inefficiency. "The Tet disaster," he wrote, "produced classic examples of the 'I-have-to-ask-Saigon' syndrome." There were thousands of problems to solve everywhere you looked, yet no one dared solve them. Local officials and officers had been trained that "authority comes from Saigon and so do all decisions." American advisers noted that South Vietnamese military and civilian organizations functioned neither horizontally nor even vertically: "It was difficult to determine which government official was in charge of what section, and what problems he was to solve."[21]

The buck never stopped. It just turned in demoralizing circles, a problem made worse by a prolonged breakdown in the mail and phone systems. Even teams from Saigon's Ministry of Social Welfare, dispatched to aid the refugees, refused to do anything for them without "specific and unambiguous instructions." There was no sanitation, medical care, education, recreation, or even food and water distribution in squalid camps that were increasingly run by gangs. The government assured its citizens that despite the late and stumbling start, all Operation Recovery claims would be settled by May 1968. By May, only one-third of the claims had been funded.[22]

Overall, the communist Tet Offensive and the allied reaction had killed or wounded 32,000 South Vietnamese civilians, destroyed 200,000 homes, and made 627,000 homeless. A fragile South Vietnam, its military reduced by 3,000 casualties in the fighting, had been made even more fragile, the VC occupying 205 more South Vietnamese hamlets after Tet than they had controlled before it. Saigon would have to claw those places back, fight the war, upgrade its military, and rebuild its shattered infrastructure and society—all at the same time, and at a moment when American patience with the war and its costs was near the breaking point.[23]

To the American people, who sat in judgment of this distant and futile war, the scale and fury of the fighting in every corner of Vietnam made clear that Westmoreland's boast that the corner had been turned in the war—a boast he almost certainly had not believed even as he uttered it—was yet another irresponsible lie. "We have been too often disappointed by the optimism of the American leaders, both in Vietnam and in Washington, to have any faith any longer in the silver linings they find in the darkest clouds," *CBS Evening News* anchor Walter Cronkite told his nearly 30 million viewers on February 27. Watching the broadcast in the White House, LBJ groaned: "If I've lost Cronkite, I've lost the country."[24]

He certainly had. Nineteen sixty-eight would be the crossover point in polling on Vietnam—the first year in which a majority of Americans called the war a "mistake." Three hundred and forty-six Americans had been killed and nearly 2,000 wounded repulsing the Tet attacks. Cronkite, who

CBS Evening News anchor Walter Cronkite in Hue City during the fighting there. MACV and the president, Cronkite observed, "are finding silver linings in the darkest clouds." For LBJ, this was the end: "If I've lost Cronkite," he groaned, "I've lost the country." (National Archives)

roved from Saigon to Hue, challenged the MACV line that the Americans had won the battle, observing that it was far from clear "who won and who lost in the great Tet Offensive for the cities."[25]

But even if the Americans and ARVN were credited with victory, what exactly had they won? The American people had now been at war in Vietnam for longer than they had fought in World War II, and for what seemed to all of them much smaller stakes. Cronkite expressed the rising sense of futility: "It now seems more certain than ever that the bloody experience of Vietnam is to end in stalemate." Even the conservative *Wall Street Journal* despaired: "Get ready to accept that the whole Vietnam effort may be doomed."[26]

It was against this gloomy backdrop that Westmoreland continued to nurse his fantasy that the United States was winning and that he just needed one more massive troop surge to deliver victory. Earle Wheeler, who had tried and failed to interest the president in a 500,000-man expansion of the US military to handle Vietnam and all other contingencies, flew out to Saigon on February 23 to meet with Westmoreland and coordinate their approach to the president.

Westy argued that it was essential "to give a highly-visible manifestation of the nation's resolve" that would shock Hanoi into major concessions. But Wheeler didn't dare go there, knowing that the last thing LBJ wanted on the eve of the presidential election was a "highly visible" reminder of the sacrifices demanded by the war in Vietnam. In White House meetings in the second week of February, LBJ had studied every option to increase combat power—mobilize reserves, enlarge the draft calls, lengthen the twelve-month combat tour, or send Vietnam veterans back for a second tour. He had rejected them all as political poison.[27]

In their Saigon meetings two weeks later, Wheeler and Westmoreland agreed on some fibs to tell the president to galvanize him. It was a perfect example, as one analyst put it, "of that mysterious inner odds-making process by which Southeast Asia policy decisions were reached in the Johnson Administration." The two Army generals would warn the president that 206,000 additional troops were needed—not for new offensive operations but as "emergency reinforcements" to avert collapse. "Why argue strategy *then*," Wheeler later rationalized. "Why argue *that* far down the line?" First, he argued, "get the capability." Troops, not strategy, were "the stronger talking point."[28]

Wheeler cabled the president from Saigon on February 26 and falsely asserted that Westmoreland had a "paper-thin margin" after Tet and was barely hanging on. Westy urgently needed reinforcements. LBJ's advisers met to discuss the cable the next day. President Johnson was worried: "I don't like what I'm smelling from those cables from Vietnam." He worried about an American defeat on the eve of elections. "I don't want them to ask for something," the president fretted to his advisers, "not get it, and then place all the blame on *me*." But LBJ had to fear his own defeat in the elections if he assented to Westy's request and increased US forces in Vietnam to 675,000 troops.[29]

Nearly all of his advisers agreed that a new troop surge would further Americanize a war that was already too Americanized. Undersecretary of State Nicholas Katzenbach called the proposed surge "pounding troops down the rathole." First, Katzenbach advised, it was important to ask, "What is our *purpose*? What is *achievable*?" These were the two crucial questions that Wheeler and Westy were deliberately avoiding. White House counsel Harry McPherson called the surge plan "unbelievable and futile." McNamara, now in his last week on the job, also argued against Wheeler and Westmoreland. They were asking for too much, he said. In order to deploy 206,000 additional troops to Vietnam, the SecDef explained, the Pentagon would have to increase active-duty strength by 400,000, pull troops from Europe, activate 150,000 reserves, increase draft calls, extend tours for six months, expand production of aircraft, artillery, ordnance, and vehicles, and bust through congressionally authorized "manning levels." At a minimum, McNamara estimated, such a surge would cost an additional $28 billion. The correct number of reinforcements for Vietnam, the SecDef concluded, "is zero."[30]

Wheeler flew back to Washington to brief LBJ on his meetings with Westmoreland and warned the president on February 28 that the damage of Tet had been so severe that more troops really *were* needed just to avoid setbacks. Without them, he cautioned the president, the ARVN would collapse, and allied forces would have to abandon Hue and Quang Tri City to the communists. Elsewhere, the NVA and VC would be free to undo all of the progress of the past three years. They would overrun Khe Sanh and the DMZ. They would take the Central Highlands and the Mekong Delta, and they would attack Saigon again, "and indeed anywhere where the conditions are favorable."

Westmoreland, of course, had privately assured Wheeler that defeat had already been averted and that the surge forces were needed not to hold the line but to widen the war and win. Wheeler's real interest was not Vietnam. He wanted to add US troops around the world to plus-up theater commanders and restore the nation's strategic reserve to its pre–July 1965 level. Westy tagged along obediently, displaying passive-aggressiveness even in his metaphors: "I stayed within the ballpark, but I played it right up to the fence." On one of Wheeler's letters, Westy scribbled in the margin: "Wheeler knew that I knew what was available, but Wheeler wanted a substantial reserve for worldwide use.... I wanted a 'bank' of reserves from which to draw." Westmoreland applauded Wheeler's "bureaucratic tactics" and the chairman's skill as "a soldier and a diplomat."[31]

He shouldn't have. Bus Wheeler did his job too well. He cast the war and the aftermath of Tet in such a gloomy light that LBJ—whose approval rating was sinking below 30 percent, the lowest of his presidency—turned to the incoming defense secretary, Clark Clifford, and instructed him not to fulfill the troop request but instead to undertake an across-the-board review of Vietnam strategy. Whatever Clifford decided would be law. A titan of the Democratic Party for twenty years, Clifford had organized Truman's upset victory in 1948, had overseen the Kennedy transition, and was old, wealthy, and confident enough to be immune to LBJ's groupthink.[32]

The media had all but declared war on the administration. NBC, for example, frankly admitted that its war coverage was unrelentingly negative not because America was losing but because "Tet was already established in the public's mind as a defeat," and so the network gave the viewers what they wanted. *Washington Post* satirist Art Buchwald, whose syndicated column appeared in over 500 newspapers around the country, played to this growing antiwar audience, publishing an "exclusive interview with General Custer at the Little Big Horn" in February. "We've turned the corner and can see light at the end of the tunnel," Buchwald's Custer barked. "We have the Sioux on the run."[33]

This mockery and malice gnawed at LBJ. Clark Clifford recalled that at a breakfast meeting with Bus Wheeler, "President Johnson was as worried as I have ever seen him." The president displayed far more strategic sense than the chiefs at the meeting, directing Clifford to give him recommendations by March 4 that would answer the critical questions raised by the war: What specific goals would surge forces achieve? How would the communists react to the surge? How would Congress and the American public react to further escalation?[34]

Clark Clifford's fast, caffeine-fueled review scrutinized all of America's largely wasted effort and expenditure. Clifford was advised by his two principal deputies, Paul Nitze and Paul Warnke. The sixty-one-year-old Nitze, deputy secretary of defense and the number-two man at the Pentagon, argued that the war had to be sharply curtailed and fought on a reduced-cost basis because of the "interrelationship between U.S. Vietnam strategy and global objectives." It was high time, Nitze said, to shift resources from the "bottomless pit" of Vietnam to more important missions elsewhere. As things stood, Nitze concluded, America was "paying too much for a single foreign policy objective." The war in Vietnam had pushed the American defense budget to 10 percent of GDP—an unsustainable level. To dead-enders such as Max Taylor, who wanted to add more ground troops and increase bombing after Tet, Warnke snapped: "We can't slug them any more than we have already done—and we didn't break their will before; why should we be able to break it now?"[35]

Assistant Secretary of Defense Warnke headed the Pentagon's "Little State Department"—the Office of International Security Affairs. That was John McNaughton's old post, vacated when McNamara's closest adviser had been killed along with his wife and twelve-year-old son in a Piedmont Airlines crash in July 1967. For Clifford's review, Warnke's shop evaluated Westmoreland's search and destroy operations and posited some "alternative strategies."[36]

Warnke agreed with Nitze, attacking the "misconception that Southeast Asia [is] an arena of superpower confrontation." In fact, the forty-eight-year-old Warnke said, Vietnam had only marginal importance to the Soviet Union, and its importance to the United States was no greater. As for the panacea of bombing North Vietnam, Warnke called it "irrational." Rolling Thunder air strikes, Warnke argued, "are infinitely more costly to us than to the North Vietnamese." To blunt Rolling Thunder, Hanoi had added a high-performance air force, early-warning radars, SAMs, and radar-directed antiaircraft guns. They had exacted a heavy toll, downing 950 American aircraft with more than 1,000 pilots and aircrew. The price of these trained men and aircraft plus the million tons of bombs strewn across North Vietnam far exceeded the value of North Vietnamese facilities destroyed, and this was not even accounting for the "self-defeating" damage to America's image around the world caused by North Vietnam's civilian casualties from American bombing, which averaged more than 1,000 every month.[37]

Warnke recalled that in the fall of 1967, McNamara had asked him to project where the United States would be in Vietnam in one year's time. "My general conclusion," Warnke later told an interviewer, "was that a year later we would be exactly where we were then, except that another 10,000 Americans would have been killed. I turned out to be wrong. There were another *14,000* Americans killed."

Warnke judged the American war in Vietnam "unlosable"—so long as US forces remained—but, he asked, what end was served by the sacrifice if Saigon could never stand on its own? "We can keep on winning the war forever... and it won't ever make any difference... because there is no way in which we can bring about political progress in South Vietnam." Tet, Warnke said, "exposed that what we had thought was political progress was just so thin as to be illusory."[38]

For "alternative strategies," Warnke's office urged the rapid "Vietnamization" of the war. The North Vietnamese still had plenty of manpower and will, so the war might go on forever for Americans unless they disengaged. US forces should serve as a "mobile shield" around the main population centers only until the war could be handed off to a more confident and competent ARVN. In the meantime, American forces should abandon search and destroy in the border regions, cede that empty space to the enemy, and pull back to guard the more important border—"the demographic frontier" of the big cities and the densely populated coastal plain.

On March 1, Nitze handed Clifford a detailed memo formed from frank conversations like these. It argued for a radical overhaul of LBJ's Vietnam strategy. Victory was impossible. Now was the time to seek a nonmilitary solution. Search and destroy operations should be wound down, America's profile in Vietnam lowered. More responsibility had to be given to the South Vietnamese government and armed forces, and the bombing of North Vietnam should be halted. The San Antonio Formula—a bombing halt in exchange for peace talks—should be swiftly implemented as part of a new "reduced-cost strategy." Westmoreland should be given no more than

50,000 additional troops—and those only to buy time for the "South Vietnamese to pick themselves up."[39]

Bombing, the preferred American way of war in the twentieth century, was losing support even among senators afraid of seeming soft on communism. It just didn't seem to work. Bombing the Ho Chi Minh Trail never hobbled the NVA and VC in South Vietnam because they subsisted on a mere 20 tons of supplies a day, not the 20,000 tons required each day by American forces. North Vietnamese air defenses had become almost invincible in the three years since Rolling Thunder began. A country defended by just 700 flak guns in 1965 now had 8,000 antiaircraft guns, 400 radar systems, 150 fighter aircraft, and 40 SAM sites.[40]

Nitze and Warnke had already pointed to the cost-ineffectiveness of Rolling Thunder—that the bombs, aircraft, and aircrews expended cost far more than the damage inflicted on the ground. Now Democratic senators like William Proxmire of Wisconsin and George McGovern of South Dakota pressured the White House to "stop the B-52 bombing escalation." In three and a half years of air war, Proxmire argued, the United States had dropped more bombs on Vietnam than it had dropped on all theaters in World War II. And half of those bombs had been dropped on allied South Vietnam, a percentage that would soar if Johnson halted the bombing in the North as an incentive for peace talks. "If we don't set a limit," Proxmire said, "there will be nothing left in South Vietnam." Senator McGovern added that bombing had *increased* NVA ground infiltration—from just 400 troops in South Vietnam in 1965 to 60,000 in 1968. The "colossal military mistake" of bombing had *spread* the war, not confined it, and helped make a minor problem a major one.[41]

Clifford's strategic review was assisted by another meeting of the "Wise Men"—former cabinet secretaries, ambassadors, lawyers, bankers, judges, and generals, many of whom had been pondering Vietnam for twenty years. They met in Rusk's office in the last week of March 1968—Dean Acheson, George Ball, Omar Bradley, McGeorge Bundy, Arthur Dean, Douglas Dillon, Robert Murphy, Abe Fortas, Matthew Ridgway, Cy Vance, Maxwell Taylor, and Henry Cabot Lodge, Jr. This was the same group that had expressed support for the war in November 1967, when Westmoreland had assured them that the conflict would be all but won within a year. Now they were informed, in a more realistic round of briefings organized by the State

Clark Clifford and Earle Wheeler debating Vietnam at the White House. Wheeler and Westy wanted more troops; Clifford, the new SecDef, deplored their unending demands and their inability to terminate the war. (LBJ Library)

Department, the CIA, and the Joint Chiefs, that the war would last "maybe five years, maybe ten years." The American people, Dillon interjected, wouldn't stand for such a thing. Clark Clifford agreed. "Boys," he drawled to the group, "it's not there." By "it," he meant popular support, and any formula for victory.[42]

The Wise Men then sat down with LBJ and Vice President Humphrey. The majority opinion was summarized by the seventy-five-year-old Acheson. The war had become too costly in every area, and the attempt to create popular support for a South Vietnamese government had failed. If 500,000 American troops could not make "the enemy sue for peace, it won't happen—at least not in any time the American people will permit." It was time to "disengage."[43]

Mac Bundy quibbled some more, preferring "deescalate" to "disengage," and LBJ's face darkened as he went around the table. "Those establishment bastards have bailed out," he muttered during a break outside the Cabinet Room. The walls were closing in on the incumbent president. His plan to offer Americans "the Churchill peace, not the Chamberlain peace," as he put it, would strain to meet even the Chamberlain standard. His polling for the Wisconsin primary, just a week away, looked terrible, and yet, as Clark Clifford observed, all of the old PR tricks had lost their magic: "One thing seems sure—the old slogan that success is just around the corner won't work."[44]

The Wise Men, working with Clifford, Nitze, Warnke, and other senior officials, rejected out of hand major troop increases, reserve call-ups, more bombing, and incursions into North Vietnam, Laos, or Cambodia. LBJ noted that the Senate would almost certainly filibuster any White House attempt to expand the war. All Clifford would concede to the chiefs and Westmoreland was an additional 24,500 troops—six combat battalions on an "emergency basis," raising the force level in Vietnam to 549,500, a number that, due to the lags in programming, would never actually be reached.[45]

What stood out about the Army-led strategic debate after Tet was its dishonesty. Privately, Wheeler and Westmoreland agreed between themselves to ask for 206,000 new troops in three "force increments." Only the first of the three increments—108,000 troops by May 1, 1968—would be guaranteed for Vietnam. It would furnish Westy with a theater reserve of two divisions plus support units. Wheeler planned to prep the next two force increments—43,000 and 55,000, respectively—for deployment to Vietnam in October and December only "if all the worst contingencies materialized." He knew that they almost certainly would not, and he would then send those troops not to Vietnam but to other theaters or to the strategic reserve. In early March 1968, Clifford's task force met with Wheeler to drill deeper on the rationale for a 206,000-troop increase. Wheeler made no mention of his parsing of the manpower into fungible increments, or Westmoreland's proposed offensive strategy, and instead passed the question along to Westy in Saigon for a more detailed answer.[46]

Westmoreland continued to prevaricate, giving no hint of a new strategy other than this: "Be prepared for contingency operations if required." His forces, he said, were "postured" to seal South Vietnam's borders against further infiltration. More troops would "add flexibility and punch." It was time to launch "a general offensive," to "carry the attack to the enemy," as if that had not been the essence of search and destroy all along.

Wheeler pressed LBJ to stay the course: "It is not timely to consider fundamental changes in strategy when we are fully committed in what could be the decisive battle of the war." Army briefers in Saigon hinted darkly but vaguely at new commitments. Asked directly by a reporter on March 20 if more US troops were needed in Vietnam, one replied with masterful obfuscation. It all depended, he said, on the "desired rate of concentration." He concluded with a puzzling epigram, from which only the most perceptive listeners might have inferred invasions of Laos, Cambodia, and North Vietnam: "You can defeat the iceberg on the surface of the water, but if it continues to form, that is not a decisive victory." In what the briefer must have regarded as helpful elucidation, he then uttered an even more confounding sentence: "By no means does this make a case for why what we have is sufficient to conclude it."

Those who claimed then and subsequently that the United States could have won the war with more aggressive methods must first explain the coquettish reticence of the Joint Chiefs and Westmoreland. How could the president be expected to adopt more aggressive methods if his field commander and military advisers spoke to him in riddles?[47]

Strategically, there was nothing new at "Pentagon East"—just more inconclusive flailing against an enemy who was weirdly becoming stronger, now equipping even his local forces with AK-47s and RPGs. Despite "losing" the Tet battle, the communists had succeeded in tearing away 40 percent of the hamlets that CORDS had certified as secure. After its Tet "victory," the Saigon government found itself in control of only 4,500 of the country's 13,984 hamlets. The communists were pushing into that vacuum as hungrily as all of the new refugees crowding into threadbare government camps and the pestilential slums around the cities. Saigon by 1968 was no longer a model of American-fostered development. It now led the world's major cities in cholera, smallpox, bubonic plague, and typhoid.[48]

Evaluating the deceptive approach that Wheeler and Westmoreland considered cunning, Assistant Secretary of Defense Paul Warnke judged it just plain stupid. Asking for 206,000 more troops to do "more of the same"—search and destroy in unpopulated areas—struck Warnke and the others as dead on arrival. They could discern in it "no military plan for attaining victory in Vietnam." And yet, Warnke added, "if it was thought that giving Westy the 206,000 would lead in fact to the invasion of Laos, Cambodia, or North Vietnam, a lot of people who *supported* the troop request would have *withdrawn* their support."[49]

Nor was there money to *pay* for a bigger war in an American economy that was already overheated and pushing the limits of American power. The war as it stood was costing over $25 billion a year. Tet and Khe Sanh alone added $5 billion in costs due to the increased tempo, additional deployments, and the need to overhaul or replace so much damaged or expended infrastructure and equipment. In Washington, liberal senators put that massive supplemental appropriation request in context. It alone would pay for interstate highways, school lunches, Head Start, the VISTA program, federal grants to universities, mortgage subsidies, veterans' benefits, environmental protection, and many other national priorities.[50]

Confronted with Westmoreland's call for reinforcements, Treasury Secretary Henry Fowler quailed at the price tag. These troops and their supporting elements would cost another $12.5 billion in 1968 and 1969. McNamara put their true cost at $15 billion, nearly doubling the war's annual cost. Even without that new spending, the budget deficit hit $23 billion in fiscal 1968.

"Inflation," one economist observed, "followed as the night the day." And the problem with inflation—6 percent in 1968—was that it alone, without any additional combat operations, drove the price of the war to alarming new heights. The only way to reduce inflation's effect—and to keep America's defense spending within feasible limits—was to wind the war down. Vietnam-era inflation also converted an American trade surplus into a trade deficit, as inflation eroded the competitiveness of US exports, increased the budget deficit at home, and forced LBJ to slam shut the US Treasury's "gold window" as foreign banks, panicked by America's reckless spending, began to convert billions of dollars to bullion.

Some have argued since the 1970s that, had the president only heeded Westmoreland's advice—tentative, cloaked, political, and inscrutable as it was—America could have won the war. It could not. The war was too costly, inflationary, unpopular, unfocused, and open-ended. Even Walt Rostow allowed that Vietnam by now represented "a gross overcommitment of U.S. military resources" given that North Vietnam's level of effort was unlimited and America's sharply limited by dwindling support and competing commitments. Dean Acheson put it this way in March 1968, words that prodded Johnson to relinquish the presidency: "We can no longer accomplish what we have set out to do in the time we have left and the time has come to disengage."[51]

Chapter 15

KHE SANH

In 1968, "disengaging" was only a dream. The United States had built to a strength of seven Army and two Marine divisions sprawled across South Vietnam, providing most of the security for the quarreling government and its floundering armed forces.

Despite the Tet "victory" and half a million American troops on the ground, no one seemed hopeful. Despite their "defeat" in Tet, the VC appeared to be in control everywhere, and they worked cleverly to win the peace being dangled by LBJ. Their "liberation forces" had failed to trigger a "general uprising." Now they tacked back to a more political line, sponsoring what they called an "Alliance of Democratic, National, and Peace Forces." Their symbol was a white dove on a blue field—sure to be popular with the South Vietnamese people, who had been scourged by American firepower for the past three years.[1]

In March 1968, the battered people of I Corps were given yet another reason to fear the trigger-happy Americans at least as much as the communists. Three platoons of the Americal Division's 11th Brigade, commanded by Captain Ernest Medina, air-assaulted into Song My, a VC-controlled village near Quang Ngai. The hamlets of Song My, situated inland from the VC-held Batangan Peninsula, were such a hive of communist activity that the Americans called the whole area "Pinkville."

Like many such places along the coastal plain in I Corps, the region had been declared a free-fire zone. All inhabitants had been ordered to move to refugee camps so that any activity in the sector could be fired on. And yet many villagers had elected not to leave, preferring the risks of a free-fire zone to the squalor of the camps. Tim O'Brien, author of one of the great memoirs of the war, *The Things They Carried*, was a grunt in the Americal. "We were really hated," he recalled of his tour around Quang Ngai. "You could see the hostility in everybody's eyes."[2]

During the day, there were no military-aged men around, only women, children, and the elderly. The Americal, ordered to root out a VC local-force battalion known to be in the area, had already been to Song My twice in the last thirty days, taking casualties from mines, booby traps, and snipers each time. In this third search and destroy mission through "Pinkville," the grunts were in an ugly mood. They had been in the field for forty days without relief. One recalled that in the past two ops, they had passed safely through hamlets only to be sniped in the back by hidden VC: "Every time we got hit it was from the rear. So the third time in there the order came down to go in and make sure no one was behind."[3]

Those orders came down the chain of command, from the brigade commander to the company commander, Captain Medina, and then to the platoon leaders: "Go in there aggressively, close with the enemy, and wipe out for good." Medina ordered his company to kill everything that was "walking, crawling, or growling," burn the huts, and poison the wells.

Medina's three platoons surrounded a hamlet called My Lai 4. Two of them wrapped around it in a horseshoe formation, and the other—twenty-five-year-old William Calley's 1st Platoon—walked through the open end of the horseshoe to search the hamlet for VC and weapons. The whole op, a combat assault preceded by artillery, lasted three or four hours. There was heavy firing, and then the platoons moved on, Captain Medina radioing his infantry in My Lai—"The party's over, that's enough shooting for today"—and reporting a VC body count of 128.[4]

One of Lieutenant Calley's sergeants, Michael Bernhardt, followed 1st Platoon into My Lai 4 and immediately noticed that all of the fire he was hearing was outgoing, none incoming. Calley's grunts were entering the huts and shooting anyone inside, or setting the huts on fire and shooting the people when they ran outside. They were gathering villagers in groups and gunning them down. It was, Sergeant Bernhardt said, "point-blank murder," and it was captured on film by an Army photographer named Ronald

Haeberle, who had hitched a ride with the seventy-man company to pho-
tograph the operation. There were no military-aged men among the 500 or
so victims; they were all women, children, and old men. One hundred and
twenty of them were kids under the age of five. More would have died had
Hugh Thompson, a helicopter pilot from another outfit, not seen the massacre from above, landed, and ordered Medina's company to cease firing.[5]

Twenty-two-year-old Paul Meadlo later testified that Lieutenant Calley
had assembled a group of forty or fifty civilians in the middle of My Lai 4 and
ordered Meadlo to kill them: "Get with it," Calley said. "I want them dead."
Calley, Bernhardt recalled, "was rotten to the core, pure evil," a loser who
had flunked out of junior college, qualified for officer training only because
the Army was so desperate for men willing to go to Vietnam, and did not
miss the opportunity to rape villagers when he could, usually with his .45
pistol pressed to their heads. Calley, Meadlo, and others machine-gunned
that group, then pushed another terrified clump of peasants into a drainage
ditch and shot them as they lay helpless. Lieutenant Stephen Brooks, who
commanded Medina's 2nd Platoon in My Lai, proved as odious as Calley.
He "lost control," a grunt recalled, and let the platoon "run berserk" in his
eagerness to be accepted as "one of the boys."[6]

Michael Terry, a grunt in Medina's Charlie Company, saw villagers
being lined up along the edge of a ditch and mowed down. "It was," he said,
"just like a Nazi-type thing." Some of the grunts refused to carry out the
orders. Terry saw one soldier throw down his weapon and walk away. But
Bernhardt estimated that 90 percent of the men in the company joined in
the shootings. Meadlo recalled that Captain Medina was present for much
of the massacre. "He and Calley passed each other quite a few times that
morning, but didn't say anything. Medina could have put a stop to it anytime he wanted." Medina didn't want to stop it. Hovering over the hamlet in
his helicopter, Hugh Thompson watched the captain walk up to a wounded
girl, kick her, and then shoot her in the head.[7]

News of My Lai and the massacre of at least ninety more civilians by
a company of the 4th Battalion of the 3rd Infantry Regiment at the nearby
hamlet of My Khe spread through the US forces. Atrocities were common
enough—grunts raping, abusing, or killing villagers they encountered—and
word of them was usually suppressed by higher-ups, but this was on a grand
scale, too big to suppress. An officer in Saigon recalled that he heard about

the "Pinkville Massacre" almost immediately and was "amazed" that the Army was able to hush it up for over a year.

LBJ would not hear of My Lai until after he left office. It would not emerge as an issue until late 1969, when Ron Ridenhour, a grunt in the Americal who had heard about the slaughter from Terry and Bernhardt, exposed the ongoing cover-up. In March 1969, a year after the massacre, Ridenhour wrote a three-page letter describing the atrocity and copied thirty US officials, including the chief of staff of the Army and several senators. It was that letter that forced the Army to reopen the investigation thirteen months later.[8]

For now, MACV turned a blind eye to My Lai, for Westmoreland was fixated on Khe Sanh. In one of the many ironies of the terrible and wasteful war, LBJ's decision to seek peace and disengage from the conflict coincided with the onset of its bloodiest battle in the hills around the Marine combat base.

The president's remarks to Dean Rusk when the battle began captured his mood of defeat: "It appears to be the judgment of our enemies that we are sufficiently weak and uncertain at home, sufficiently stretched in our military dispositions abroad, and sufficiently anxious to end the war in Vietnam that we are likely to accept, if not defeat, at least a degree of humiliation." He then pointed to increased North Korean aggression, Pyongyang's seizure of the USS *Pueblo*, Hanoi's brazen descent on Khe Sanh with 40,000 men, and the surging VC attacks against airfields, cities, and towns all over South Vietnam as indisputable evidence that the enemy believed that America was beaten. LBJ clearly thought so too. He saw no way out of the dead end other than more spending, new taxes, bigger drafts, extended tours of duty, and "greater unity" at home. The chances of getting those things, or even most of them, were nil.[9]

The NVA's siege of Khe Sanh, begun on January 21, 1968, intensified in the weeks that followed, heavier NVA bombardments of the base coinciding with the Clifford review and the president's decision to end the war. This futility of effort and waste of good lives is what gave the battle such an enduring stench. With heavy rains blinding and grounding American aircraft, the NVA was able to isolate this far western end of the DMZ, cut Route 9, and begin surrounding Khe Sanh. And yet, Michael Herr observed on a visit to the Marine combat base, "on the higher levels of Command, the

Khe Sanh situation was being regarded with great optimism, the kind that had seen us through Tet, smiling in the shambles."[10]

To prevent Khe Sanh from becoming another Dien Bien Phu, the daily obsession of President Johnson, the Marines clung to the hilltop outposts, making it harder for the NVA to encircle and pulverize the combat base. The Marine outposts on four critical hills, all identified by their elevation, would make the difference in the siege. The NVA had taken Hill 881N, but its view of the combat base was blocked by the Marine-held hills in between. Those hills—881S, 861, 861A, and 558, a long blue ridge hulking over the base—were exposed, dangerous, and adrift on a spreading sea of NVA manpower and artillery.

About 3,000 Marines held the hills at any given time during the siege while another 3,000 Marines and 600 ARVN Rangers held the combat base. The Marines in the hills waited in trenches, with runway matting stretched over the top and piled with eight layers of sandbags plus a layer of rocks or 105 mm shell casings. That was enough—maybe—to stop a mortar round, but it would collapse under 152 mm artillery or the 122 mm rockets fired from launch sites on Hill 881N. The daily struggle for the hills was a key feature of the siege. If the NVA pushed the Marines off the summits, they would be able to "fire right down the throats of the base defenders and make their position untenable," a Marine captain wrote.[11]

The combat base itself, two square miles of red dirt, was safer only because there were more Marines and ARVN gathered there in better defenses. Bunkers for the expanded garrison were scraped from the red soil of the plateau. These dugouts, a few still intact and scattered around the old combat base today, would be home for the Marines. They were wretched holes in the ground, eight feet long and eight feet wide. Their only real requirement was that they withstand the blast of an 82 mm mortar round. A log in each corner supported layers of planks, runway matting, and 5,000 sandbags, with loose dirt poured in between the two or three sandbag layers. Another log rose from the center of the dugout, further confining the Marines inside, who would hug their legs and tuck their chins whenever the NVA guns fired. The whole sodden scene seemed designed to confirm the old Army jest: "Marines know how to die."[12]

A reporter who spent a night in one of those bunkers was most impressed by the stench: "the smell of urine, of old, old sweat, C-ration decay, moldy canvas and private crud." Trenches were dug around the perimeter and more runway matting, piled high with sandbags, was placed at intervals along the trench so that Marines standing guard in the trenches could dive under cover whenever enemy rounds fell. Besieged by two NVA divisions, the Marines sent daily patrols a quarter mile beyond the fence to give early warning of any enemy assaults that might be creeping forward in the fog.[13]

In the first week of February, while the combat still raged in Hue and Saigon and Wheeler and Westy were cooking up their plan to dupe the president about force levels, two battalions of the NVA 304th Division, supported by twelve tanks, overran the Lang Vei Special Forces camp, which overlooked the border with Laos just three miles southwest of Khe Sanh. The Green Berets at Lang Vei had moved there from Khe Sanh in 1966, when the combat base, just six miles from the Ho Chi Minh Trail, had been expanded and entrusted to the Marines. The tanks, the first used by the communists inside South Vietnam, cut through the good defenses at Lang Vei and spearheaded the rout of the garrison.

Flushed from their bunkers by flamethrowers and satchel charges, the 24 Green Berets and 400 Montagnard troops at Lang Vei fought for their lives. The Green Beret commander called in air strikes and artillery on his own position. Half of his men were killed or captured; the survivors fled in the night toward the gates of the Khe Sanh combat base, where 100 stragglers turned up early on February 7 pleading to be let inside.

Colonel David Lownds, who commanded the 26th Marine Regiment and the combat base, felt certain that the Lang Vei attack was intended to lure him outside and into an ambush. He rebuffed Army calls to send Marines to relieve the garrison at Lang Vei, leading to a bitter fight between the services that was resolved only when Westy personally ordered Marine helicopters to fly Army Green Berets into the Special Forces camp to rescue any survivors.

Having overrun Lang Vei in the night, the NVA took control of Route 9 on both sides of Khe Sanh. Next, the NVA committed an entire battalion of the 325C Division to overrun Hill 861A. Khe Sanh could not be besieged forever. Major reinforcements, reliably clear skies, and unrestricted American airpower would eventually force the big NVA units to scatter and abandon the siege.

The communists doubled down, moving their antiaircraft guns under the cover of fog, rain, and darkness closer to the Khe Sanh airstrip, which was the base's only lifeline. They also began digging siege works like the ones they had used to strangle Dien Bien Phu.

The Marines first detected them in late February: trenches and supply bunkers dug toward the Khe Sanh perimeter, branching off to run parallel to the Marine lines as they got closer to the fence. Every inch the NVA sapped forward made it harder to bomb them. The rule of thumb for safe bombing around friendly troops was one yard from friendlies for every pound of ordnance delivered. For a 500-pound bomb, the enemy had to be at least 500 yards away. For B-52 strikes, the enemy had to be 3,000 yards away. Even the Marine decision to narrow that "safe" envelope to just 1,100 yards would give little protection against a foe who dug to within a half mile of the base. On CBS, Walter Cronkite, already alarmed by the loss of Lang Vei to NVA tanks, warned that "Khe Sanh could well fall with the terrible loss of American lives, prestige, and morale." Contemplating the role of LBJ and Westy, Cronkite added: "And this is a tragedy of our stubbornness there."[14]

If the NVA got close enough to launch infantry attacks, defense of the combat base would hinge on artillery and tactical air strikes. Colonel Lownds said at the start of the siege that "the side which can keep its artillery intact will win the battle." Khe Sanh's artillery had two critical missions: defensive fire plans to keep the enemy away from Khe Sanh's hilltop outposts and perimeter, and final protective fires to destroy the enemy if and when he massed his strength for an all-out assault on the combat base.

The French artillery at Dien Bien Phu had undertaken the same missions but had been crushed by the Viet Minh batteries, leaving Dien Bien Phu all but defenseless. The Marines did better, holding the most critical high ground throughout the siege and losing only three guns in the entire course of it. They placed their howitzers in sandbagged revetments, where only a direct hit could knock the gun out, and stored their shells in twelve-foot-deep berms accessed by trucks that darted between the batteries.

Well supplied by Westy's airlift, the motto of the Marine artillery at Khe Sanh was "Be Generous." They had forty-six guns in five batteries at Khe Sanh and were supported by four Army batteries of 175 mm artillery, one at the Rockpile, nine miles northeast of Khe Sanh, and the others at

Camp Carroll, thirteen miles to the northeast. In the course of the siege, they would fire over 100,000 rounds, which was about 1,500 rounds a day. The fire of these guns, near and far, was controlled by the Fire Support Coordination Center inside the combat base as well as the Direct Air Support Center, which had to make sure that barrages of artillery did not collide with US aircraft.[15]

Artillery played an even larger role in Khe Sanh's defense than usual because Westy's air campaign to defend the isolated base was hampered by the foul weather, described by the 3rd Marine Division commander as "the worst I've ever seen for combat purposes."

Helicopters needed a minimum 1,500-foot ceiling to shoot an overhead approach into LZs on the hills or the combat base. Yet on the cloudy Khe Sanh plateau, a notch in the high mountains dividing Vietnam and Laos, visibility for fixed-wing and helicopter pilots was "below minimum" about 40 percent of the time—even in the dry season.

The cargo planes that flew essential supplies to Khe Sanh had to contend both with NVA antiaircraft guns, which fired at the sound of the incoming planes, and with heavy mortar and rocket fire, which struck Khe Sanh's airstrip whenever the planes touched down. The Marines called these C-130s and C-123s "mortar magnets," and the pilots acted accordingly, diving steeply into the base, unloading, taking on passengers and wounded, and then taking off again, all in three minutes or less, as mortar and rocket rounds detonated along their path. They would touch down, shove pallets of supplies and ammo out the doors, and load running passengers and stretcher-bearers as the pilot turned around on the short runway, never stopping. Under these conditions, more than half of the supplies for the base had to be dropped in by parachute.[16]

The most dangerous job of all was resupplying the hilltop outposts, which, with enemy trenches dug between the base and the hills, could only be done by CH-46 Sea Knight cargo helicopters, the smaller, lighter Marine equivalent of the Army's Chinook. Those pilots had to contend with blistering machine gun and RPG fire whenever they came in or out, and mortar fire when they touched down. On an average day, the Marines might lose three of these big choppers as they struggled to land on the hills.

To keep the approach lanes open and the hills in American hands, the Marine Air Group at Chu Lai introduced the "super gaggle," yet another example of American ingenuity in this unforgiving war. The "super gaggles," which sharply reduced helicopter losses over the hills, teamed the cargo helicopters with attack aircraft and gunships. Twelve A-4 Skyhawks would streak over the hills as the cargo helicopters, lumbering forward with 4,000-pound external loads, neared the hills. Four Skyhawks would hit the enemy gun positions with bombs and napalm. Two other Skyhawks would drench those positions with tear gas. Forty seconds before the final run-in by the helicopters, two more Skyhawks would lay a smoke screen all along the lines of approach while four others swarmed over the enemy positions hitting them with cluster bomblets, rockets, and 20 mm cannon fire. The gunships came in last, to add to the suppressive fire and rescue any downed cargo pilots.[17]

All of this was part of Operation Niagara, the great air umbrella deployed by Westmoreland to prevent the fall of Khe Sanh. "No regiment in history ever had such an overwhelming amount of firepower at their disposal," one awed Marine wrote. Westmoreland spared no expense to prevent the NVA from achieving what he called "a battlefield spectacular." By now, there were millions of eyeballs on Khe Sanh. In the United States, it was the most heavily reported story of the war. Reporters shuttled in and out of the Marine combat base, and the networks devoted most of their film reports to it.[18]

Between January and April 1968, Khe Sanh was the busiest airspace in Vietnam, with an average of 184 attack sorties every twenty-four hours. For Marines on the hills and in the base, the howl of jet engines became just another note in the background noise of thunder, rain, and artillery. Marine, Navy, and Air Force strike fighters stacked themselves up to a height of 35,000 feet over the combat base in tight, circular holding patterns. As the planes at the base of the stack delivered their bombs against NVA targets and scooted for home, the flights above them, guided by air or ground controllers, augured down through the clouds and fog to find holes in the overcast, snake through, and drop their bombs. Besides enemy fire, they had to contend with dust and haze when there wasn't fog and rain, as well as camouflaged helicopters and Cessna spotter planes, which were easy to miss in a jet hurtling at the speed of sound.[19]

More damage to the NVA was done by the B-52 Stratofortress. Flying out of Guam and Thailand, three- or six-plane "packages" hit the NVA forces around Khe Sanh every two or three hours for sixty-six days. Each B-52 lugged a twenty-seven-ton payload of 108 bombs, a mix of 500- and 750-pounders. In the course of the siege, the B-52s flew 2,602 sorties over Khe Sanh and dropped 75,631 tons of bombs, twice the sorties and tonnage employed in all other areas of South Vietnam and the DMZ combined. The NVA, which had massed in bunker complexes around Khe Sanh, were easy targets. The Air Force programmed the enemy coordinates into the B-52 onboard computers, which released the bombs from altitudes above 30,000 feet.[20]

The pilots never saw the bombs hit and the North Vietnamese troops on the ground never heard them coming. They would be abruptly caught in the maelstrom, the terrain ripped up around them, trees hewn down, the ground shaking from the blasts. Many of the enemy died from the concussion alone, or from internal hemorrhaging. Communist soldiers would wander around aimlessly after the strikes, blood pouring from their noses, mouths, and ears.

An NVA diary entry from February 18 read: "The B-52 explosions are so strong that our lungs hurt." The Marines learned to put massed artillery fire into every target area fifteen minutes after the bombers departed to kill the dazed survivors, who would just be digging themselves out to emerge aboveground. A veteran recalled his first sight of ground pounded by the Buffs: "Trees eighty to one hundred feet tall were stacked up like matchsticks on the edges of the craters. The craters were thirty to forty feet across, and deep enough to hold a basement for the average two-story house in America."[21]

The communists never seriously threatened Khe Sanh. The NVA general staff had hoped that rain and fog would nullify American firepower, but American technology, ingenuity, and largesse prevailed. On an average winter day at Khe Sanh, there were 350 American fighter-bombers and 60 B-52s dropping 1,800 tons of bombs around the combat base. In their 22,000 sorties, they dropped 100,000 tons of bombs, which worked out to five tons of bombs for *each* of the 20,000 NVA troops committed to the siege. NVA troops moving or digging at night would be hit by cluster bomb and napalm strikes that showered them with grenade-sized bomblets and flaming sheets of jellied gasoline. The Marine and Army artillery used ground and aerial observers, photo reconnaissance, infrared imagery, signals intelligence, and strings of hundreds of acoustic and seismic sensors, dropped by Navy patrol bombers into the NVA positions and all around the combat base, to fire accurately in all conditions.[22]

The sensors, part of a larger program code-named Muscle Shoals, were supposed to give early warning of enemy concentrations or movements but were as problematic here as they were on the short-lived McNamara Line. They were frequently activated by friendly bombs and shells, by passing Montagnards, or by wild animals prowling around them. Nevertheless, they detected every major NVA attempt to attack Khe Sanh. A quiet area would suddenly buzz with activity as troops gathered and convoys moved. The Marine artillery would fire "boxes" of shells around the seismic activity, working them in and out like pistons, and air strikes would saturate the area with bombs and napalm, breaking up any major offensive before it could launch.[23]

American logistics delivered so much ammunition to Khe Sanh that the Marines, despite their isolation, fired fourteen shells for every one received in the siege. They endured a total of 11,000 incoming rounds and fired 159,000 back at the enemy. They were so amply supplied with ammo that by March 1968, two months into the siege, they had accumulated more shells than their storage berms could hold—a single data point that perfectly depicted the futility of Hanoi's attempt to strangle the combat base.[24]

Both of these tools—artillery and airpower—had their severest test during the night of February 29, when the NVA launched their biggest assault on the base. The sensors strung along Route 9 lit up as elements of the NVA 304th Division advanced toward the eastern perimeter of the combat base, which was defended by the ARVN Rangers. Unable to capture the critical hills around the base, the NVA was trying to take Khe Sanh by storm, launching three attacks that night and into the predawn hours of March 1.

The first attack came at 9:30 p.m. and the last at 3:15 in the morning, which was enough time for B-52s to be diverted to Khe Sanh to join in the slaughter wrought by massed artillery and waves of tac air strikes. The next day, the Marines found dozens of dead NVA sappers crouched in trenches near the perimeter, killed by airbursts. Behind them, other assault formations and reserves had been obliterated by concentrated fire after they tripped the electronic sensors. The B-52s had carpeted every line of retreat with high explosive. The tentativeness of the attack and the haste with which the NVA broke it off confirmed that they were not willing to pay an unlimited price for Khe Sanh.[25]

President Johnson apparently was. The cost of defending Khe Sanh, a base that would shortly be abandoned, was astronomical. The price of the Scotland and Niagara operations, added to the costs of Tet, made 1968 the costliest and bloodiest year of the war for the United States. Nearly 17,000 Americans would be killed in 1968, over 87,000 wounded, and another $27 billion flushed down the drain. The war's costs—over $2 billion every month—would shortly eclipse all of the money that had been spent on higher education, mortgage subsidies, and police protection in the entire history of the United States. These were shocking numbers for a domestic-reform president like LBJ.[26]

While the siege progressed, Secretary of Defense Clark Clifford finished his review. He called it "a whole new look at the whole situation," the first really strategic review of a war that had grown gradually, massively, and unthinkingly.

To Westmoreland's call for troops, Clifford answered: "We can no longer rely just on the field commander. He can want troops and want troops and want troops, but we must look at the overall impact on *us*." The new SecDef cited the antiwar movement, inflation, the alienation of allies, the still "bleak" negotiations track, and the crushing opportunity cost of pouring so much into a lost cause. "I am not sure we can ever find our way out if we continue to shovel men into Vietnam."

Johnson heard the findings and sadly decided that the war had killed his presidency. He had narrowly defeated antiwar candidate Eugene McCarthy in New Hampshire's primary on March 12, and took another hit four days later when Robert F. Kennedy announced that he too would challenge Johnson for the nomination that summer. "All of you," LBJ berated his senior advisers, "have counseled, advised, consulted and then—as usual—placed the monkey on my back again." The Vietnam monkey now reached around to throttle the president and Westmoreland. Hanoi had failed to collapse South Vietnam, but it had succeeded in one of its aims: "to break America's will to war."[27]

Clifford concluded that no amount of American reinforcements—"not 206,000, or double or triple that quantity"—could win the war in view of the Saigon government's unpopularity, the continuing weakness of the

ARVN, and Hanoi's determination to prevail. It was no longer feasible, Clifford said, to achieve even America's minimum war aim, which he defined as "a viable South Vietnam which can live in peace."[28]

On March 24, 1968, the *New York Times* broke the news that LBJ had made the decision to sack Westmoreland and bring him back to Washington as Army chief of staff that summer. On March 31, even as 18,000 troopers of the Cav "saddled up" and prepared to fly to the relief of the Marines at Khe Sanh, President Johnson went on television at 9:00 p.m. to announce a bombing halt in North Vietnam and his appointment of Averell Harriman to be his personal representative at peace talks in Paris.

Johnson then read lines that shocked the nation: "I will not seek, nor will I accept, the nomination of my party for another term as your president." The United States, LBJ asserted, had been torn apart by the war. "The unity of our people," he said, "must not now be lost in suspicion, distrust, selfishness, and politics." To bind up America's wounds, the president would "deescalate the conflict...and move immediately toward peace through negotiations." Johnson offered to pause most of the Rolling Thunder air strikes without conditions "to permit the contending forces to move closer to a political settlement."[29]

This was a pivotal moment in the war. The American president was publicly announcing that the search for a military solution was over and the quest for a nonmilitary, negotiated solution was on. Thousands of lives and billions of dollars had been wasted, as three years earlier, in January 1965, Johnson had rejected precisely the course he now adopted: "Deploy all of our resources along a track of negotiation aimed at salvaging what little can be preserved."[30]

He was giving away for free the bombing halt that he had tried to sell for major concessions in 1965 and 1967. Republican presidential candidate Richard Nixon, who was campaigning against LBJ's military "gradualism," called Johnson's latest move "camouflaged surrender." More than any other single event, this capitulation by one of the fiercest and most ambitious politicians in American history proved that Hanoi's Tet Offensive had achieved its purpose—turning the American press, public, and political establishment irrevocably against the war.[31]

In his last meetings before the decision, LBJ had seen no viable path forward. Westmoreland's troop surge would cost at least $20 billion. Four thousand American troops had been killed in the last weeks alone, and yet MACV had no solutions other than relentless escalation, Westy writing the president on March 28 that "the enemy has no predesignated point for his main effort, no timetable, only a constant opportunism" fueled by a largely unimpeded flow of new VC recruits and NVA infiltrators, who had little to fear from the ARVN and the ruff-puffs, who had vanished back into their sandbagged posts after Tet. No one seemed to be in charge, with the ARVN reporting a shortage of 5,000 officers in the ranks between captain and colonel. The shortage was owed more to desertion than casualties. Over the past two years, the US Marines, with one-seventh as many troops in Vietnam as the ARVN, had lost seven times more majors and lieutenant colonels in action than the skittish ARVN. American casualties had soared 500 percent even as ARVN casualties were static.[32]

Westy's deputy and imminent replacement, General Creighton Abrams, pulled his staff together and told them what they would soon be facing from Washington when he took command of MACV: "You might be asked, 'what should you do?' Suppose you answer, 'we'll just keep on doing what we're doing.' And the next question would be, 'how long is that going to take?' Then, 'what's that going to do? What's the price tag on that? How many lives are you talking about? Another 30,000? I mean, where is this going to wind up?'" Abrams paused, glanced around the room, and concluded: "It could be quite a problem."[33]

Brought to the White House in March 1968 to supply answers to the very questions he had anticipated, Abrams was not nearly as venturesome in the Family Dining Room as he had been in the briefing he'd given his staff at "Pentagon East." When asked directly and beseechingly by LBJ, "Is there *anything* we should be doing that we aren't doing?" Abrams sat quietly while General Wheeler recited the party line: "Our basic strategy is sound; we can't fight a war on the defensive and win, so Westmoreland is on the tactical offense." LBJ had heard all of this before.

The president turned hopefully to Abrams, and got the same party line: "I don't feel we need to change strategy, we need to be more flexible tactically inside South Vietnam." What did *that* mean? And what time, effort, and loss did it entail? Probably Abrams was displaying loyalty to Westmoreland by not showing his hand prematurely, but he was denying the president critical advice that he so clearly needed. Abrams refused to elaborate, and the Army continued to speak in riddles. Politically, Johnson felt totally isolated as he implemented what he called "strategy change." "Everybody," he groaned to his advisers, "is recommending surrender." Everyone around him was "gloomy and doomy," except the generals, who remained full of hope but gave him no solutions.[34]

March 31, the day Johnson announced a halt to the bombing of most of North Vietnam as well as his decision not to run for reelection, was also the end of the Marines' ordeal at Khe Sanh. With reliably clear skies, the Army and Marines terminated Operation Scotland and launched Operation Pegasus on April 1, moving those 18,000 troops of the Cav to a river valley eleven miles northeast of Khe Sanh, just beyond the range of the NVA artillery in Laos that had been pummeling the Marine combat base. There the Cav cut LZ Stud out of the wilderness—"a forward operating base that looked better than most permanent installations in I Corps," a reporter observed. Marine engineers moved along Route 9, fixing bridges, removing mines, and meeting no real resistance. The Marines had suffered 205 killed and 1,670 wounded during the siege. They found only 1,602 NVA dead around their perimeter but estimated that the total might be as high as 15,000.[35]

Creighton Abrams meeting in the White House with LBJ in March 1968. No less than Westy, Abrams spoke in riddles, exasperating the war-weary president. (LBJ Library)

Westmoreland was leaving Vietnam because of the shock of Tet and his own ineffectual performance as field commander. Internal Army surveys revealed what may have been his greatest "strategic failure"—that over 70 percent of the generals he commanded were never sure what he was trying to accomplish with all of his flailing operations.

Nevertheless, Westy treated Khe Sanh like a lap of honor, boasting to *Time* magazine in April 1968 of a 75:1 kill ratio and great strategic gains. In fact, the kill ratio was probably closer to 5:1, less than half of what was considered remarkable in American military circles. If you counted all of the Marine, Army, Navy, and Air Force personnel killed in Operations Scotland, Pegasus, and Scotland II—the Marine accompaniment to Pegasus—American KIAs were 1,000, not 200. And if you subjected Westy's NVA body count to a more scrupulous analysis, it was closer to 5,000 than 15,000. MACV's own numbers—never published by Westmoreland, because they made him look bad—indicated that 5,500 NVA had probably died at Khe Sanh: 3,500 from air and artillery, 2,000 in ground attacks. In that secret internal analysis, MACV concluded that the North Vietnamese decision *not* to launch a major ground assault against the combat base spared them the many thousands of additional casualties that Westmoreland counted anyway.[36]

Chapter 16

MINI-TET

In his nationally televised address on March 31, 1968, when President Johnson announced that he would not seek reelection, he also declared a unilateral bombing halt in North Vietnam above the 20th parallel. This concession diminished the leverage of bombing. Only 10 percent of North Vietnam's population lived south of the 20th parallel. Relatively few would be inconvenienced (or killed) by bombs dropped there.[1]

One who was vastly inconvenienced by the partial bombing halt was Hubert Humphrey. With Johnson bowing out, the vice president hungered for the presidency, but he would have to fight his way through a pack of contenders that included instant front-runner Robert F. Kennedy, peace candidate Eugene McCarthy, segregationist George Wallace, and, quite possibly, a resurgent LBJ, who, if successful in his bid for peace, might be drafted by the Democratic National Convention in August to run again. Bobby Kennedy stated his opposition to the war plainly: "It is time to face the reality that a military victory is not in sight, and that it probably never will come."

Vice President Humphrey wallowed in no-man's-land. Privately, he lamented his past support for the war, now allowing that the United States was "throwing lives and money down a corrupt rat-hole in South Vietnam." Publicly, he did not dare break with LBJ, who was still commanding the war as well as the Democratic Party campaign funds that Humphrey would need if nominated. The bestselling novelist Saul Bellow, who knew Humphrey from his days as a professor at the University of Minnesota, had planned to write an admiring piece about the vice president, but he put his pen down, "anticipating," as he put it, "no pleasure in writing about poor Hubert's misery as LBJ's captive."[2]

Hanoi was subject to none of these doubts and course changes. Lieutenant Commander John McCain III, who had been shot down and imprisoned in Hanoi six months earlier, recalled the elation expressed by his guards after Tet and Johnson's bombing halt: "They thought they had the war won." None of the guards and prison officials were surprised by the bombing halt. One of them had told McCain it was going to happen a month before it did. "They were convinced that they had wrecked Johnson's chances for re-election. And they thought they had the majority of the American people on their side."

John McCain was visited in his cell by two North Vietnamese generals, who boasted that the NVA was just getting started: "After we liberate South Vietnam we're going to liberate Cambodia. And after Cambodia we're going to liberate Laos, and after we liberate Laos we're going to liberate Thailand. And after we liberate Thailand we're going to liberate Malaysia, and then Burma. We're going to liberate all of Southeast Asia."[3]

For now, the NVA used the bombing halt to reinforce and resupply its units in South Vietnam. MACV's weekly situation reports described an enemy army of at least 200,000 inside South Vietnam. VC losses during Tet had been offset by 229,000 fresh troops infiltrated into South Vietnam during and after the offensive, more than enough to replace casualties in the NVA divisions and put 14,000 "fillers" into the decimated VC units.[4]

The supply surge enabled by Johnson's bombing halt was dramatic, from a weekly average of 1,300 North Vietnamese trucks moving down the Ho Chi Minh Trail in Laos to 2,300 trucks every week in April. And these were just trucks sighted from the air; there were many others unseen as they crawled under jungle canopy and through the dark of night.

In Cambodia, freighters carrying tons of Chinese-made weapons docked at Sihanoukville. Their cargos were sent along the coast to the Mekong Delta or distributed among Cambodian Chinese trucking companies and driven through Phnom Penh—under the protection of the royal family—and all the way north to Bo Kheo, where the Cambodians were met by VC drivers, who moved the cargo onto their trucks and drove into South Vietnam's Central Highlands.

To handle these big shipments, the communists repaired their essential roads in I and II Corps and extended their critical routes in the A Shau and Plei Tran Valleys, treating South Vietnamese territory as their own. It was clear to MACV that the enemy had reduced offensive action not as a deescalation measure to secure the bombing halt but rather to rebuild units that had been cut to pieces in the Tet Offensive.[5]

By 1968, the A Shau Valley in I Corps was a major artery of the Ho Chi Minh Trail. The NVA troops who had attacked Hue during Tet had come from here, as had their reinforcements. Before Tet, Westmoreland had planned to assault and seize the A Shau in one of his "war-winning" offensives against the communist sanctuaries—this one *inside* the borders of South Vietnam. It was an NVA fortress crammed with truck parks, supply bunkers, regimental headquarters, and hospitals, and it was stirring again.

Looking at the growing NVA and VC numbers as well as the rising volume of supplies bumping down the Ho Chi Minh Trail, the CIA saw phase two of Hanoi's Tet Offensive taking shape. CIA analysts warned that a "second general offensive" was imminent, whether on May Day, May 7 (the date Dien Bien Phu fell), or May 11 or 19 (the birthdays of Buddha and Ho Chi Minh, respectively).[6]

Westmoreland took the offensive, launching Operation Delaware on April 19, 1968, with brigades of the 101st Airborne Division and the Cav, who had just lifted the siege of Khe Sanh. The Cav flew into the northwest end of the A Shau Valley, while the 101st Airborne approached from the east to seize a key piece of the Ho Chi Minh Trail. Westy felt confident; with 20,000 troops and 450 helicopters, the Cav and the 101st Airborne had the resources to move, fight, and win. Or so he thought, with the obduracy that was his trademark.[7]

The weather did not cooperate. April was supposed to be dry in the valley, but this one was wet. With the high peaks flanking the A Shau Valley cloaked in rain, clouds, and fog, the Cav ran into the heaviest weather and antiaircraft fire of the war. Slicks with troops and Chinooks with sling-loaded artillery were shot down in previously unimaginable numbers. Ten helicopters were lost and twenty-three badly damaged on the first day alone.[8]

The brave men of the Cav, who would suffer the highest casualties of any American division in Vietnam, slopped along the valley for three weeks under torrential rains that washed away airstrips and left the grunts reliant on airdrops of food and ammo from C-130s flying at great risk just above the valley floor. The brigade of the 101st Airborne, trying to work in from the east to take the A Shau defenders between two fires, never broke through the NVA bunker lines guarding that flank.

Westmoreland terminated the op after twenty-eight days, published a long list of captured enemy matériel, and judged Delaware a "major success." It was anything but. The Army and Marines had avoided the A Shau Valley for three years because all of their manpower in I Corps was tied up along the DMZ and in the coastal plain. There was nothing to spare for the A Shau. There still wasn't. The Cav and the B-52s blasted the valley for four weeks, killed 739 of the enemy, and then left, ending the op, as Michael Herr put it, "like a speech cut at mid-sentence."[9]

Most of the NVA forces in the A Shau had slipped across the border to Laos during the operation. A rear guard had remained behind to fight from networks of bunkers carved into the wooded peaks flanking the only road through the valley. The moment the Cav and the Airborne withdrew, the NVA crossed back into the valley from Laos, replacing the matériel they had lost to Operation Delaware with new deliveries along the uninterrupted Ho Chi Minh Trail. The Cav's after-action assertion that it had demonstrated to the enemy "that he has no sanctuaries" was laughable on its face. By this date, half of the US combat troops in Vietnam were up here in I Corps—thirty Army and twenty-four Marine maneuver battalions—and yet the enemy continued to move and operate freely everywhere, most of all in the A Shau.[10]

The Americans lost 142 dead and 530 wounded in Operation Delaware. Twenty-seven helicopters were destroyed, with thirty-five others badly damaged. Westmoreland's claims of victory, Michael Herr observed, "were made for once without much enthusiasm, indicating that even the Command had to acknowledge the inviolability of the place."[11]

Westmoreland had vowed to "break the NVA stranglehold" on the valley, and failed. Operation Delaware proved again the hollowness of the argument that had the Americans only attacked the cross-border sanctuaries they could have won the war. The A Shau Valley was a sanctuary *inside*

South Vietnam, a major hub of the Ho Chi Minh Trail, with a more or less permanent garrison of 20,000 NVA troops rotating in and out of combat. The Army and Marines—stretched to the breaking point elsewhere in I Corps—couldn't even take and hold *this* sanctuary. How would they have taken and controlled the much larger sanctuaries in Cambodia and Laos with a total strength in South Vietnam that never exceeded nine US infantry divisions and couldn't be increased beyond that number?

As the Cav sank into the mud of the A Shau Valley, Hanoi's Second General Offensive or "Mini-Tet," as it came to be called, exploded at midnight on May 4, 1968. It was not "mini" at all. It lasted for a week, during which more Americans were killed than in any other week of the war. It flickered out, and then resumed for three more weeks at the end of May.

The fighting coincided with the start of LBJ's long-sought peace talks at the Hotel Majestic in Paris in the second week of May. The American delegation, led by seventy-six-year-old Averell Harriman, had just taken their seats when the whole conference had to be suspended because of a general strike and student riots in Paris against the Vietnam War and the conservative government of President Charles de Gaulle.

Wincing from tear gas and the cries of rioters and riot police, the peacemakers may have wished that they had chosen one of the other candidate cities for the conference—Warsaw or Phnom Penh. But wherever they located, there would be delays. No progress would be made for the next six *months*, as the North Vietnamese delegation, steered by Le Duan's deputy Le Duc Tho, haggled over everything—whether to admit South Vietnamese negotiators, whether to cease their attacks in the South, and on what terms to convert the partial bombing halt to a full bombing halt. The delays were deliberate, "talks about talks" to divide Washington and Saigon, tie American hands, and mollify Mao Zedong, who opposed *any* negotiations.[12]

There were no delays of Mini-Tet. Determined to keep the pressure on, provoke the general uprising that had not materialized during Tet, and hasten the American withdrawal, the communists attacked again all across South Vietnam, hitting 129 military bases, provincial capitals, and district towns. Again they were driven off, but the CIA concluded that the fury of this May 1968 offensive, added to that of Tet, succeeded in driving a permanent wedge between the South Vietnamese people and their government. Everywhere, the CIA reported, communists "are intimidating or convincing people to support the VC and destroy government mechanisms." Security, the CIA added, was more "precarious" than ever, with the Viet Cong free to recruit, tax, and propagandize.[13]

Mini-Tet also confirmed to Americans that the war was hopeless. MACV was in the midst of Operation Complete Victory in the Saigon Circle when the communist offensive erupted. Every US and ARVN combat unit in III Corps had already been fighting for a month. Five hundred and sixty-four Americans and nearly 800 ARVN had been killed in yet another unsuccessful effort to destroy the same communist units that now moved into Saigon for the second time in four months.

With elements of the US 9th and 25th Infantry Divisions and the 199th Light Infantry Brigade forced to fight in the streets of Saigon against fanatical VC resistance, US casualties in May 1968 were the highest of the war: 2,169 Americans killed in a single month, a figure that was even more

With American troops forced to fight in the streets of Saigon, US casualties in May 1968 were the highest the war. Here grunts of the 9th ID move cautiously through a ruined Saigon neighborhood. (National Archives)

distressing to Americans when they learned that it outnumbered South Vietnamese KIAs of 2,054. Also disturbing was the discovery that the casualty rate in American maneuver battalions in the first half of 1968 was *four times higher* than the World War II average for all theaters. By 1968 there were twenty-three American hospitals in South Vietnam, and their 5,300 beds were full. Most voters had to agree with Richard Nixon's latest campaign ad: "Never has so much military, economic, and diplomatic power been used so ineffectively as in Vietnam."[14]

The communist attacks on Saigon in May 1968—dubbed the "Second Wave"—were even more demoralizing than those of Tet's first-wave attacks. Once again—three months after the unlearned lesson of Tet—VC troops slipped into the capital with surprising ease. Faced with the prospect of prying them out in bloody house-to-house combat, the Americans and ARVN chose to bomb and shell them instead, with the predicted result. They destroyed another 30,000 homes and created another 155,000 refugees in Saigon in the effort to uproot small teams of VC infiltrators during the four-week battle. "The Viet Cong has no air force of his own," Saigon's police chief joked to a reporter. "So he uses *ours*."[15]

American and ARVN aircraft flew 500 sorties against Saigon and Cholon, dropping 500- and 750-pound fragmentation bombs as well as large quantities of napalm into city streets and lanes to destroy enemy foxholes, bunkers, and tunnels that had been dug under the concrete slabs of civilian homes and apartment buildings. Fixed-wing gunships fired 74,000 rounds into Saigon, and American and ARVN firebases shelled the city center out to a radius of five miles. A thousand B-52 strikes were flown on the outskirts of the city, just twenty-five miles from downtown, to hit the base camps and supply points of the VC 5th and 9th Divisions, which were shunting enemy troops into the capital.[16]

Artillery and airpower saved American and ARVN lives, but bombing South Vietnamese neighborhoods to kill small units of VC ensured that any allied victory in this war would be Pyrrhic. American intelligence had ample evidence by this stage that these suicidal VC forays were part of a larger communist strategy to disgust the American and South Vietnamese citizenry with the war being waged in their name and to fracture the allied war effort. As strategic theorist Herman Kahn tartly observed in 1968, American firepower created "empathy and support for the heroic little man in black pajamas and antagonism toward the white man in the B-52."[17]

General Nguyen Ngoc Loan, who still commanded Saigon's National Police, was nearly killed in a firefight at the start of Mini-Tet. This made him the first and only South Vietnamese general wounded in ground combat in the entire war. As the injury to Loan's shattered right leg worsened, American doctors were rushed in to replace his Vietnamese surgeons.

Vice President Ky was especially solicitous, for among the 100,000 lucky men of the National Police, many of whom paid bribes to avoid military service, were the spies and informers who were Ky's eyes and ears. "As long as Ky remains in power I will remain in power," Loan liked to say, always adding: "And as long as I remain in power, Ky will remain in power." The general was saved, but not for long. He was transferred to Walter Reed Hospital in Washington in order to save the leg, and this gave Thieu a pretext to replace him a month later with one of his own cronies—ARVN Ranger commander Colonel Tran Van Hai. It was yet another demoralizing outburst of musical chairs, Loan's removal provoking gun battles between factions of police loyal to him and others loyal to the new chief.[18]

America's rescue of South Vietnam during Tet and Mini-Tet was not received gratefully. The bruising attacks of Mini-Tet coincided with conflict between the idled delegations in Paris. Thieu suspected (correctly) that the Americans would make massive concessions to exit the war. Secretary of Defense Clifford had already sketched the future—what he called the "long pull-out" of American forces and their replacement with South Vietnamese conscripts. The Americans might even permit Hanoi to leave NVA troops inside South Vietnam, and invite the Viet Cong to join the government in Saigon. Or they might just leave, Clifford contending in White House meetings that if the North and South could not agree on terms to terminate the war, then the United States should terminate it by departing.

Before talks even began, Xuan Thuy, who chaired Hanoi's delegation, peremptorily refused to pull NVA troops out of South Vietnam or even to recognize Thieu's government. Thieu became frantic, all the more so because the forty-one-year-old Viet Cong delegate Nguyen Thi Binh remained in Paris, demanding a seat at the table for her VC political wing. The talks, so hopefully begun, stalled for months as the opposing delegations argued over first principles. Ambassador Ellsworth Bunker warned

LBJ that "Thieu's sudden intransigence" might scupper any prospect of peace.[19]

In Saigon, peace was nowhere in sight. Of the air and artillery strikes that flattened and burned so much of Saigon in May and June, a rather obtuse MACV staff officer wrote: "The news media assigns the bulk of the destruction to air strikes, artillery, and fires. This creates controversy over whether the military success of the fire support compensated for the inevitable anger generated in the civilian populace." The "controversy" was plainly confined to the halls of MACV. Saigon's inhabitants saw no "military success" in the flattening of their homes and city.[20]

Only President Thieu seemed to have benefited from all of the fratricide and collateral damage. He had been busy since Tet using his presidential powers to remove or demote as many of Vice President Ky's men as he could. He had replaced Ky's appointees at the airport, customs office, and wharves, cutting into the vice president's income from narcotics and smuggling.

Then, on June 2, 1968, when Ky's brother-in-law, the police chiefs of Saigon and Cholon, and several other Ky appointees gathered to witness the destruction of the last VC units holding out in the South Vietnamese capital, an American helicopter gunship fired a short round that killed the brother-in-law, the police chiefs, and four other officials. The fallout from this "Cholon helicopter incident" was more acrimonious than usual because most of the casualties were Ky protégés, which ignited rumors that the Americans had deliberately targeted the group to strengthen Thieu. This paranoia fit with all of the other demoralizing rumors percolating now that LBJ was intensifying his efforts to make peace and end the war.[21]

On the North Vietnamese side, the Mini-Tet attacks, after the failure of the Tet attacks, seemed irrational in military terms, but they were perfectly rational politically. With LBJ seeking peace, the politburo was determined to create the impression of chaos, weakness, and hopelessness in South Vietnam, increase international pressure on American "immorality," and hasten Johnson's run for the exits. For this reason, Le Duan and his generals accepted yet another massacre at American hands: an estimated 26,000 communists killed and captured in battles that flared through and around the DMZ, Hue, Da Nang, Kontum City, the central coast, and Saigon. For Le Duan, it was worth it, to further divide South Vietnam and frustrate any remaining American hopes.[22]

One major change after Tet was the Phoenix Program. Its history was long and checkered, a perfect encapsulation of the key problems of South Vietnam. The CIA-run Phoenix Program was an outgrowth of another CIA program from the early 1960s called Census Grievance.

Census Grievance had been devised by Tran Ngoc Chau, a South Vietnamese officer who had been appointed province chief of Kien Hoa in the Mekong Delta in 1962 by Diem. Lieutenant Colonel Chau, who lived and worked in Kien Hoa from 1962 to 1965, was one of the few South Vietnamese officers praised by Lieutenant Colonel John Paul Vann during his time in the Delta. Chau was imaginative and energetic, recognizing that rural people were being alienated by the ARVN's "shoot first, ask questions later" policy and that the intelligence that government forces acquired on the VC was all but useless, usually the product of paid informants who fed the government stale or fake information.[23]

Needing actionable intelligence from the peasants themselves, who were too fearful of VC reprisals to give it, Chau came at them diagonally, sending teams into the hamlets to ask innocuous, census-type questions that nevertheless produced intelligence: "Have you noticed any changes here? Anything new? What can the government do to help you? How do the local government and security forces function?" The teams also constructed a map of family ties, wealth, property ownership, religious affiliation, and local travel, allowing them to identify interlopers and mobilize families, parishes, and hamlets against communist agents.

Gradually, a picture of the hidden Viet Cong and the most abusive local officials emerged, and Chau's counterinsurgency performance in Kien Hoa proved remarkably effective—a clear contrast with the failing record everywhere else. He created "counterterror teams" to go into VC-controlled hamlets and kill or capture Viet Cong leaders. Daniel Ellsberg, the RAND Corporation analyst who had spent two years in Vietnam working on rural security for the State Department, called Chau "the leading Vietnamese expert on the pacification process."

In 1965, Chau was made head of a new counterinsurgency training program, with the brief to expand his Kien Hoa program into every threatened area. But, this being South Vietnam, Chau's remarkably effective program quickly snagged on the many ineffective prongs of the South Vietnamese bureaucracy. He provoked jealousy and infighting, and in 1967, just as the

Phoenix Program, his own redesign of counterinsurgency, was set to launch, Chau resigned his commission and ran for a seat in the South Vietnamese National Assembly. Disillusioned by his battle with the bureaucracy, he now campaigned for a compromise peace with the communists. President Thieu ordered Chau arrested and detained for the rest of the war.[24]

The Phoenix Program took flight anyway. Without Chau, it was dominated by the Americans, and it was certainly less effective than it would have been otherwise. Phoenix, called Phung Hoang in Vietnamese, used the same methods as Census Grievance to acquire intelligence and sent the same counterterror teams, now called Provincial Reconnaissance Units (PRUs), after the VC cadres inside South Vietnam.

Chau had acknowledged the likelihood of self-defeating abuse—that jealous officials, merchants, or farmers might denounce rivals to get them killed or arrested—and had employed inspectors to authorize controversial assassinations or arrests, ensuring that his program would not become yet another arrow in the quiver of Thieu, Ky, and their minions. But Phoenix was less discriminating than Chau would have liked. It emphasized "capture or kill" over accuracy. Chau had wanted to enlist the Vietnamese people on the side of the government. Phoenix was more focused on killing the enemy, even if innocents were killed in the process.[25]

Phoenix was just one of the myriad programs set back by the Tet and Mini-Tet offensives. The Provincial Reconnaissance Units were pulled from their "capture or kill" missions and deployed in static positions in the provincial capitals to fill the void left by ARVN, ruff-puff, and police desertions.

The Census Grievance program broke down when the government lost control of roads, rivers, and hamlets, the key fonts of intelligence. Worse, when the government clawed back the lost ground and roads, they found peasants focused entirely on financial restitution—the part of the program that was supposed to cloak the intelligence-gathering component, not replace it. Now the peasants talked only of their terrible losses from battle damage and the need for recompense.

In some provinces, the painstakingly assembled databases of peasant families and VC activity were captured and destroyed by the communists in the first attacks. MACV noted a "significant degradation of ruff-puff capability" in twenty of South Vietnam's forty-four provinces. Men deserted, weapons were lost, and facilities were abandoned to the enemy. Nearly 500 outposts were destroyed. Ninety-six Regional Force companies and 388 Popular Force platoons either vanished completely or had to be withdrawn for "reorganization."[26]

In the meantime, their assigned "pacification areas" were surrendered to the communists. MACV predicted that it would take all of 1968 just to get the ruff-puffs back to where they had been at the end of 1967. "The clear-cut gain of the VC is *this*," General Fred Weyand's operations chief reported. With their bold offensives, "they have frightened the population." Grisly stories of ruff-puff "collaborators" shot in the head by "VC penetrators" circulated broadly. Viet Cong "strategic terrorism" was galloping to victory on the back of the VC's tactical defeat.[27]

MACV briefers, who relied on statistics to color their reports, struggled to find ways to account for the surge in VC prestige despite the high communist casualties during Tet and Mini-Tet. They reverted to lies and blather: There had been no "pattern of collapse or failure" among the South Vietnamese; the communists had paid a steep price; neither the ARVN nor the economy had been shattered; pacification had not been derailed. The VC, Lieutenant Colonel David Hughes assured the Saigon press pool, had had "no lasting effect in the country in tangible terms." And yet, he wanly concluded, "perhaps this war is not being fought on tangible terms."

That was to miss the point entirely. Heavy VC casualties had not been decisive or even crippling because of the *tangible* resources of the communist war effort, which ensured that VC losses could be made good by recruitment and infiltration.

New American surveillance techniques along the Ho Chi Minh Trail showed that infiltrators and supplies, whose numbers had previously been guessed at, could now be calculated with some precision. In 1968, for example, Hanoi infiltrated 229,000 troops, more than enough to replace the estimated 161,000 communist troops killed that year. When American bombing in Laos destroyed critical convoys of food and weapons, the communist forces subsisted on fewer calories, paused their major offensive operations, and shifted convoys to Cambodia, where there was no bombing. As General Fred Weyand put it: "There was no single element of the enemy's organization that, if attacked, would cause the collapse of his force structure or the reduction of his will to resist."[28]

Kien Hoa itself, which Chau had tried to make the model province for counterinsurgency, slumped wretchedly back to old habits. In the weeks and months after Tet and Mini-Tet, all of the friction that Chau had identified as the source of VC popularity returned. Five thousand homes had been destroyed in the province during Tet, filling makeshift camps with 40,000 more refugees. The official sent by the Ministry of Social Welfare to manage the crisis was accused by the American advisory teams of "indifference and incompetence" as well as the theft of USAID commodities intended for the refugees. The province chief, who had been cut in on the theft, naturally took the official's side in the dispute and refused to act.

In other provinces where more ethical officials tried to intervene, they were usually recalled to Saigon after protests from the province chiefs, who didn't tolerate scrutiny of their rackets. ARVN troops hungrily eyed food aid sent for the refugees and ate it. "Work on resettlement centers," one American official wrote, "has not been halted for the simple reason that it was never begun."[29]

Lieutenant Colonel Chau had viewed clean, efficient government as the most durable defense against communism, and had tried to make Kien Hoa a model for what might be achieved. But, as Neil Sheehan put it, "the system he served did not permit him to follow through in deed." His bold changes were erased in less than a year by the venal politics of South Vietnam. The province chief who succeeded Chau, and all of his subordinates, would be indicted for corruption in December 1968.[30]

British diplomats in Hanoi took the temperature of North Vietnam after the losses of 1968 and were surprised to find it unchanged. True to form, Westmoreland had asserted in February that Hanoi had spent "all of their military chips" and "gone for broke." An unusually hopeful CIA report had stated that Rolling Thunder and Tet had so weakened North Vietnam that they might not continue the war. None of this was true. North Vietnam kept going, refusing to die or surrender. A North Vietnamese man drafted in June 1968 recalled that of the many men conscripted from his village, fifty miles south of Hanoi, not a single one had returned from the war or even posted a letter home. His father had been too sad to say goodbye, leaving the formality to his mother, who said: "You must go, I know that, but try to come back."[31]

The resolve of the NVA and VC remained a fact of life. More than half a million North Vietnamese troops had come down the Ho Chi Minh Trail since 1965, accepting their lot: that most of them would never return home alive or intact. That they would never get leave, or even a letter. That they would subsist for weeks at a time on nothing more than a handful of rice and roasted salt, and be subjected to cataclysmal artillery and airpower when they were not battling malaria, dysentery, crushing fatigue, festering wounds, and hunger. Life in straitened North Vietnam would have seemed easy by comparison.

A British official living in Hanoi dismissed Westmoreland's assertion that Tet had been a final, desperate communist fling: "Were there the slightest evidence of a will to compromise in Hanoi I would take the 'final fling thesis' more seriously. I can find none. The DRV [Democratic Republic of Vietnam] are ready to settle down to a long war." He detected "no evidence of a fundamental DRV change of mood," reporting that the "people of Hanoi were in good spirits before Tet and are greatly encouraged thereafter."[32]

Le Monde correspondent Jacques Decornoy reported from Hanoi in March 1968 that—despite US bombing—the city's appearance was largely unchanged and that "the sturdy national spirit remains the same." He then traveled for two weeks in the North Vietnamese countryside, reporting that "morale, clothing, food, distribution, and supply had not deteriorated." The rural population was dispersed and better fed than the residents of Hanoi. Everywhere the Frenchman went he found "the will to fight remains unimpaired."

Before LBJ announced his bombing halt, which he had hoped to trade for a war-ending truce, Decornoy had correctly predicted that the Americans would have to halt the bombing *without* conditions: "There is no slackening of the determination to fight on as long as necessary to achieve DRV and NLF [National Liberation Front] objectives." Le Duan's politburo seemed unbothered by their immense losses, as well as by their broken promises—that 10,000 Americans would be killed, that the South Vietnamese would rise up, that the war would end. Undaunted, they continued the war, certain that they were close to defeating the Americans and unifying Vietnam under communist rule.[33]

Chapter 17

A BETTER WAR?

In his last act before being removed as field commander in Vietnam, Westmoreland abandoned Khe Sanh in June 1968. It was a fitting end to his war of futility. He had spent hundreds of lives and billions of dollars defending the combat base, and now he let it go. With 50,000 troops of the Marines, the Cav, the Americal, and the 101st Airborne Division based in I Corps, Westy breezily explained, there was no longer a need "to keep five battalions buttoned up at Khe Sanh." Why they had *ever* been buttoned up there under daily bombardment remained a question that has never been persuasively answered. Why the troops at Khe Sanh were *still* being bombarded by four regiments of NVA infantry, which had returned to the hills around the combat base after the Cav had moved from Khe Sanh to the A Shau Valley, was a fact too embarrassing to be mentioned. The McNamara Line of fencing and sensors, intended to link fortified hubs like Dak To, Khe Sanh, and Con Thien, was also quietly abandoned. "*Sic transit gloria mundi*," a Marine chaplain scribbled as he watched bulldozers scrape the Khe Sanh combat base and fill in its trenches.[1]

Westmoreland was leaving Vietnam almost four years to the day after replacing Paul Harkins. Westy's tenure was a disaster: four wasted years chasing an elusive enemy through the boonies while the VC spread its influence into South Vietnam's most densely populated areas against a faltering ARVN, and a pacification program that hid negative facts on the ground with positive statistics and briefings. Veteran Tim O'Brien summarized search and destroy this way: "A bunch of dumb Cub Scouts chasing phantoms, with no sense of place or direction, probing for an enemy that nobody could see."[2]

The grunts had been ground down as much by Westy's hyperactivity as anything else. American infantry in Vietnam endured an average of 240 days of combat every year, compared with just 40 for the GIs of World War II. They lugged sixty pounds of weapons and gear through stifling heat and humidity, slept on the ground, patrolled by day, ambushed by night, and battled ringworm, hookworm, malaria, dysentery, and trench foot as grimly as they hunted the elusive enemy. "Respite," a Marine reminded posterity, "was rotating back to the mud-filled regimental combat base for four or five days, where rocket and mortar attacks were frequent and troops manned defensive bunkers at night." Casualties among these hard-pressed American troops, just five per thousand in 1965, had soared to seventy-three per thousand in 1968. They pressed numbly on, intoning the nihilistic mantra of the grunt in Vietnam: "It don't mean nothin'."[3]

No, it really didn't. Most of the effort and bloodshed was entirely in vain. A CIA study of Westmoreland's operations in 1967–1968 made the startling discovery that less than 1 percent of 2 *million* US and ARVN small-unit operations resulted in contact with the enemy. And combining numbers for the two armies made them look better, if that were possible. The numbers for the ARVN alone were far worse: only one-tenth of 1 percent of *their* operations contacted the enemy. Hanoi's strategy was obvious: compel the Americans to increase their effort and spending to the point of congressional and public rejection of the war, and wait for the day when the communist forces could array themselves against the ARVN alone.[4]

Even during unusual periods like Tet and Mini-Tet, when intense contact *was* made, the communists had suffered heavy casualties with no lasting impact on their war effort. An NSC study of North Vietnamese manpower after Tet found that 120,000 physically fit males reached draft age every year in North Vietnam, and that, despite the high kill ratios and body counts trumpeted by Westmoreland, the North Vietnamese were only using about 45 percent of their military-aged males in 1968. Westy had assumed that he was gnawing his way through North Vietnam's 1 million military-aged males, but by making more age groups eligible for the draft, Hanoi had turned 1 million military-aged males into 2.3 million. Even if communist casualties remained high, "it would take 13 years to exhaust the pool" of eighteen-to-thirty-four-year-old men in North Vietnam. "Attrition," the NSC report concluded, "will not work."[5]

Westmoreland busied himself in his final days drafting apologias for his own blundering conduct of the war. "Any American commander who took the same vast losses as Giap would have been sacked overnight," he grumbled, confirming that he still misunderstood the nature of the war he had led. Westy's zeal to clean up his reputation was inexhaustible. Later, he would write the foreword to the Marine Corps history of Khe Sanh and fill it with self-serving nonsense about the value of the operation, his law-yerly edits revealing a fervid effort to cover his tracks after being duped by the North Vietnamese: "Please revise to say *not* that I took forces from 'less critical' areas but from areas under 'less pressure.'" In Westy's mind, semantics like these were significant. He had not stripped the critical areas of Vietnam of troops and aircraft to chase uselessly through the wilderness and orbit Khe Sanh. No, he had merely levitated from a low-pressure area to a high-pressure one, like the drifting feather that was his war effort.[6]

Westmoreland was succeeded by his deputy, fifty-three-year-old General Creighton Abrams. "Abe" Abrams was a real star. In World War II, he had spearheaded the relief of Bastogne, and George S. Patton had called him "the best tank commander in the Army." In Korea, Abrams had served as chief of staff to three different corps, and President Johnson had given him a fourth star in 1964 so that he could bring his talents to bear on the war in Vietnam. Abrams had worked out his "one-war" concept in 1966—the idea that military operations and pacification were two sides of the same coin.[7]

Abrams now acknowledged that the dire situation in South Vietnam had been exacerbated by his predecessor's stubborn focus on Khe Sanh and I Corps. The siege had moved scarce US forces north, permitting massive communist infiltration in II, III, and IV Corps. Abrams agreed with Clark Clifford's review, which demanded a change of strategy—"from one of pro-tecting real estate to protecting people, from a geographic approach of Viet-nam strategy to a demographic approach."[8]

Superficially, Abrams did as he was told. He changed concept. His first Strategic Objectives Plan as MACV commander confessed the useless-ness of Westmoreland's search and destroy strategy: "In single-mindedly attempting to achieve the destruction of the VC/NVA forces, we have failed to do what was urgently required: steadily provide genuine security to increasingly large numbers of people."

Abrams noted that in fiscal 1968 Washington had spent $14 billion on bombing and offensive ground operations and only $850 million on pacification and aid programs. In that single year, the United States had spent five times more on bombing and search and destroy operations than it had spent on economic aid to South Vietnam over the past *seven* years. Abrams contrasted that blunderbuss approach with the enemy's "one-war" approach: "He knows there's no such thing as a war of big battalions, a war of pacification, or a war of territorial security," and "that this is just one, repeat one, war."[9]

The problem was one of priorities and effects. Westmoreland's bombing, shelling, and sweeps were, as *New York Times* reporter Malcolm Browne put it, "like a sledgehammer landing on a floating cork. Somehow the cork refused to stay down." Militarily ineffective, search and destroy had been politically disastrous, hurting civilians as much as the enemy, and making pacification even harder than it would have been otherwise.

Westy had carelessly subcontracted pacification to the South Vietnamese and scorned the Marines' combined action platoons (CAPs). Abrams now gave the CAP program a second look. He ditched the term "search and destroy" and instead spoke of "clear and hold" operations. Success on Abrams' watch would be measured not by ops launched and body count but by the number of hamlets, villages, and towns brought under Saigon government control. There would be nothing glorious or dramatic about any of this, he warned his staff: "It's just a lot of damn drudgery."[10]

The South Vietnamese armed forces squirmed uncomfortably between the poles of big-unit operations and small-unit pacification. Abrams' efforts in 1967 to hasten the training of the ARVN looked good on paper—rising numbers of ARVN and ruff-puff units declared capable—but they still relied entirely on American air, artillery, supply, and lift.

"It is impossible," one American officer reported in mid-1968, "to write a timetable for *any* plan to put South Vietnamese into combat jobs the U.S. is now doing." General Melvin Zais, who had commanded the US 1st Infantry Division in 1966 and now returned to Vietnam in 1968 to command the 101st Airborne Division, looked in vain for evidence of real ARVN improvement in the year he had been away. "We should be working ourselves out of a job, but we're not. We're not coaching a team. We're like five college football players who have come down to coach a high-school team and have inserted ourselves into the lineup."[11]

Hanoi's 1968 offensives hastened the shift in Washington toward disengagement from Vietnam. Westmoreland and the chiefs had failed to devise a strategy or even make a convincing case for the war they were fighting. In a secret nineteen-page memo titled "Neo-Isolationism," the British ambassador to the United States, Patrick Dean, warned his government in July 1968 that big changes were coming. Dean described a "climate of depression, self-criticism, frustration, and lack of self-confidence" spreading across the United States, "the most widespread and profound questioning of the basic tenets of foreign and domestic policy since the 1860s."

The country had been rocked in quick succession by the assassinations of civil rights leader Martin Luther King Jr. in April and then Democratic presidential candidate Robert F. Kennedy in June, race riots in sixty cities, urban decay, inflation, a weakening dollar, and soaring deficits. All of the major candidates running in 1968—Democrat Hubert Humphrey and the two leading Republicans, Richard Nixon and Nelson Rockefeller—focused on the country's domestic problems and commented as little as possible about the war in Vietnam other than to say that they would wage it more effectively than LBJ. "Ending the war and winning the peace" was Nixon's campaign promise.[12]

By now, polls consistently showed that more Americans opposed the war than supported it. "The answer to failure is not simply more of the same," Nixon hazarded. He had a "secret plan," he said, "to end the war and win the peace in the Pacific." But the Republican candidate was deliberately vague, promising more military pressure to some audiences, "nonmilitary steps toward peace" to others. Only the independent candidate, George Wallace, dared say that he would escalate the war until America won on the battlefield. Wallace chose as his running mate retired Air Force general Curtis LeMay—the same man who had urged LBJ to bomb North Vietnam "into the Stone Age" four years earlier. "The Bombsy Twins," as Wallace and LeMay were known, demanded "the military defeat of the Viet Cong and North Vietnam"—a truly terrifying prospect to anyone briefed on the long war's realities.[13]

That particular danger would be averted, but there were others. America's Cold War strategy, to create regional alliances such as NATO and SEATO that would secure their own first-line defense with distant American backing, looked increasingly naive. Instead of reducing US defense requirements, the alliances had *increased* them. The war in Vietnam was a perfect example of this. Rather than loitering in the background, the US military found itself everywhere on the front line. One hundred billion dollars of US aid to the developing world had also failed to pay dividends, with many of the recipients exhibiting more hostility than gratitude to the United States.

Walt Rostow, one of the last hawks around LBJ, worried that the patience of American voters had run out. Americans no longer wanted "to fill the various vacuums created by World War II," such as Vietnam. To them, "Fortress America" looked like a wiser strategy than global engagement.[14]

Johnson, meanwhile, rolled up his sleeves and worked for peace as he had promised on March 31. To hasten the process, he abandoned his old tactic of bluster to coerce concessions from Hanoi and instead gave away just about everything before the negotiations even began. He turned a deaf ear to those who argued that a hard line was essential in dealing with communists. He finally understood that North Vietnam's politburo, backed by Moscow and Beijing, was going to keep going until they won, and would not sit down for peace talks unless *their* conditions were met.

And so LBJ conceded up front most of what Hanoi wanted. He agreed to the unilateral withdrawal of American forces rather than the mutual withdrawal of US and NVA troops. He halted the bombing of North Vietnam everywhere except the southern panhandle adjacent to the DMZ, sparing 90 percent of the North Vietnamese population and 75 percent of their territory. By November 1968, he would move to a total bombing halt.

Johnson accepted a VC presence at the peace talks in the form of an NLF delegation headed by Nguyen Thi Binh. The president declared himself willing to accept a nonaligned South Vietnam. He offered American aid dollars to repair and develop *both* Vietnams after the war. The only concessions LBJ extracted from the North Vietnamese were what he called "the three facts of life": Hanoi must agree to admit the Saigon government to the peace talks, must respect the DMZ, and must stop shelling the cities of

South Vietnam. It was basically the same climbdown he had once laughingly dismissed as "you disarm, while we pistol-whip you."[15]

Captured NVA and VC documents in Vietnam around this time confirmed that, unable to defeat the Americans in battle, the enemy had made "negotiations his main arena." And why not? For Hanoi, the sputtering talks in Paris yielded priceless intangibles. They were stunningly effective at widening the rift between Saigon and Washington and energizing the American and global antiwar movements while conveying an image of communist strength and imperturbability.[16]

And the talks were profitable for Hanoi, yielding peace marches and protests, the bombing pauses and halts, and the admission of the VC to the Paris talks, with no obligation to withdraw the 120,000 NVA troops solidly established inside South Vietnam in late 1968. Unable to win on the battlefield, Hanoi was using diplomacy to saw away at the American objective: a viable noncommunist South Vietnam. This was exactly the kind of "false peace" that Thieu and Ky had been denouncing since before they even took up residence in the presidential palace.

But Johnson, his political career ruined by the war and its 30,000 American dead, feared the Saigon government no more. He was a man with nothing to lose politically and everything to gain. He might salvage his legacy by ending the war in the months before the presidential election in November. Peace talks, begun in May 1968 and immediately stalled by basic disagreements, were unlocked by Johnson's broad concessions. After a long delay, negotiations had resumed and were moving toward a settlement.[17]

They were "moving" mainly on the North Vietnamese and American ends of the table. The South Vietnamese rejected any thought of a "peace government" for South Vietnam that might include communists from the Viet Cong's political wing. Thieu warned the Americans that his people would rise against him, or his generals would overthrow him in a coup, if he accepted a coalition government with the VC. The US embassy, meeting constantly with Thieu, despaired over the lack of any progress: "No sense of urgency is detectable."[18]

The reason for the lack of urgency was a forty-five-year-old member of President Johnson's delegation in Paris named Henry Kissinger. The Thieu government was already alarmed by the prospect of a deal between

Washington and Hanoi to end the war in a hurry, and Kissinger, a wily and ambitious Harvard professor serving as an informal diplomat for Dean Rusk, resolved to exploit that alarm for his own ends.[19]

Kissinger hatched the idea of sabotaging Johnson's peace effort to prevent an "October surprise" peace deal. Nixon in the summer of 1968 was leading in the polls in large part because of American frustration with the war and deep suspicion of the flip-flopping Humphrey. If Johnson ended the war at the last minute, Humphrey might surge in the polls and overtake the Republican front-runner. Nixon, confident until now, was suddenly beset with worry. Johnson "wants to play the peacemaker," he fretted. "Can he do it? We don't know what moves have been made *off* the board."[20]

Kissinger first had to maneuver himself into Nixon's confidence. Kissinger, a professor of government, had advised Nixon's rival, Nelson Rockefeller, in the past three presidential campaigns and as recently as July 1968 had called Nixon "the most dangerous, of all the men running, to have as president." To make amends, Kissinger now lied to Johnson's chief negotiator, Averell Harriman, that he had broken with the G.O.P. "My dear Averell," Kissinger wrote. "I am through with Republican politics; the party is hopeless and unfit to govern." Kissinger then turned around and offered his services to Nixon as a mole inside Johnson's peace delegation.

A peace deal was coming together, Kissinger warned Nixon's campaign in September and October 1968. Le Duan had poured everything he had into the three 1968 offensives—Tet, Mini-Tet, and a third round of attacks in August—and they had all been broken by American and ARVN counterattacks. Communist casualties were staggering at a time when the Americans still had half a million troops in-country and the ranks of the ARVN were swelling with recruits from Thieu's new mobilization law. Le Duan now ordered Le Duc Tho to negotiate seriously in Paris and to accept the participation of the Thieu government if Thieu would accept a VC delegation.

Harriman, Kissinger whispered, was so confident of a deal that he had "broken open the champagne." Hanoi's "unconditional" posture was being softened by Soviet pressure. The Russians, with an eye on Nixon's lead over Humphrey in the polls and their own heavy expenditure on the long war in Vietnam, wanted Hanoi to make some basic concessions to give peace and the more dovish Humphrey a chance, and to prevent North Vietnam falling deeper into China's embrace.[21]

A Soviet diplomat in London confided to his American counterpart that Moscow would not object to a US military presence in South Vietnam after the war because "we face a common enemy there"—Mao's China. Suddenly Le Duc Tho pronounced himself willing to admit Thieu's "puppet government" to the negotiations, removing the obstacle that had blocked all progress for six months.

On October 27, 1968, the North Vietnamese delegation finally did what LBJ had been craving for his entire presidency: they dropped all outstanding demands and agreed that if bombing stopped on October 30, final negotiations could commence on November 3. That was the reason for Kissinger's alarm and Harriman's chilling of the champagne.

Nixon, a mere candidate, had no leverage over LBJ, Moscow, or Hanoi. But if he could persuade President Thieu to wreck the peace process by refusing to send a delegation to join the talks in Paris, he could then portray it as yet another failure of the Johnson-Humphrey administration and fend off an "October surprise."[22]

Candidate Nixon had lost to John F. Kennedy by a narrow margin in 1960 in an election marred by allegations of voter fraud. He feared another defeat in 1968, and decided to throw a wrench into LBJ's peace negotiations. He activated Anna Chennault, the forty-five-year-old, Chinese-born widow of General Claire Chennault. Claire Chennault had commanded the Flying Tigers in World War II and organized Chiang Kai-shek's air force in his war against the Japanese and Mao's communists.[23]

Anna Chennault, a glamorous stalwart of Washington's China Lobby who lived in a luxury apartment in the Watergate complex, agreed to carry secret messages between the Nixon campaign and the South Vietnamese government. In early 1968, she had met with Nixon and the South Vietnamese ambassador, Bui Diem, at the Pierre Hotel in New York, creating the circuit through which secret communications would flow between the Nixon team and President Thieu. Thieu needed no prodding to cooperate with Nixon. He considered Humphrey too willing to cut a deal with the VC, and Johnson too eager to sign a peace treaty. Nixon, Thieu smiled, will give me "more rope to play with."[24]

Clearly these campaign machinations were a gross violation of the "one-president-at-a-time" tradition and probably of the Logan Act of 1799, which deemed "treasonous" all efforts by American citizens to interfere in the foreign policy negotiations of the United States government. They also threatened to prolong the terrible war to serve the personal ambitions of Nixon and Kissinger.[25]

Nixon's plot came as no surprise to Johnson, who was wiretapping the South Vietnamese embassy as well as Thieu's presidential office. The president phoned Senate minority leader Everett Dirksen and told him about Nixon's meddling: "We could stop the killing out there, but they've got this new formula put in there—namely wait on Nixon. They're killing four or five hundred [Americans] a day waiting on Nixon." LBJ confronted Nixon directly, but the Republican candidate lied with his usual lubricity: "I would *never* do anything to encourage South Vietnam not to come to the table."[26]

Humphrey, meanwhile, struggled to gain traction. He was loathed by antiwar liberals, who had watched him wobble and grovel to gain Johnson's trust. Young voters called him "Johnson's War Salesman." He was, Norman Mailer wrote, the "high shaman and excruciated warlock of the old Democratic party." Robert F. Kennedy, who had supported a coalition government in Saigon and a prompt end to the war, had been the great hope of the new Democrats. RFK had been tied with Humphrey in the polls and would have pulled ahead after winning the California primary had he not been assassinated in June in Los Angeles on the night of his victory.[27]

The Democratic National Convention in Chicago two months after Bobby Kennedy's assassination was the scene of riotous "Dump the Hump" demonstrations against the vice president's nomination, and a violent police assault on the demonstrators. The thousands of protesters expressed, as Mailer put it, "all the fury of the beatings and the tear-gassings, all the bitter disappointments of that recently elapsed bright spring when the only critical problem was who would make a better president, Kennedy or McCarthy."

Instead, they now confronted "hundreds of police in sky-blue shirts and sky-blue crash helmets" and "all the dread of a future with Humphrey or Nixon." Johnson speechwriter Richard Goodwin watched the horrifying police assault on the protesters. The police waded into the unarmed crowd swinging their nightsticks, brutally beating and kicking the young men and women. Over 300 people were admitted to local hospitals with cracked skulls, broken bones, and contusions. Goodwin worried that this was just the start, not the climax, of war-related political violence in the United States: "There'll be four years of this."

Protesters were already chanting "McCarthy is not enough," a reference to the antiwar candidate Senator Eugene McCarthy of Minnesota. What *would* be enough? Certainly not Humphrey or Nixon. LBJ continued to hold Humphrey in a vise, cautioning the nominee to do or say nothing that might weaken the president's hand at the Paris peace talks. He even sent his most trusted fixer to Humphrey's convention headquarters to make sure that the vice president stayed on message.[28]

Campaigning on what Humphrey risibly called "a politics of joy" at a time when the nation was split by the war, race riots, and youth culture, the Hump seemed doomed until he ever so cautiously announced a slight break with LBJ on September 30—pledging that, if elected, he would halt *all* bombing of North Vietnam as "an acceptable risk for peace."[29]

Nixon's back channel to Thieu remained hidden from the public. With the Republican nominee *seeming* to support Johnson's war policy, the more pacific Humphrey began to climb in the polls just a month before the election. It now appeared that a presidential "October surprise," a diplomatic breakthrough in Paris, might put Humphrey over the top.[30]

Nixon panicked. The smoking gun linking Nixon to the interference did not emerge until 2012, when Nixon biographer John Farrell found White House chief of staff Bob Haldeman's notes containing Nixon's explicit order to "monkey wrench" LBJ's negotiations and "keep Anna Chennault working on SVN [South Vietnam]." Nixon also directed Haldeman to activate oil executive Louis Kung, another China Lobby partisan, who was the nephew of Madame Chiang Kai-shek.

Nixon instructed Kung to tell "Thieu to hold firm" and *not* agree to any peace deal proffered by President Johnson. Nixon reached out to Chiang Kai-shek as well—involving the Taiwanese president in the scheme—and told his vice presidential candidate, Spiro Agnew, to threaten the CIA director Richard Helms. "Tell him we want the truth" about the peace talks, Nixon instructed Agnew. If Helms didn't tell Nixon how close LBJ was to a peace deal, he wouldn't be kept on as CIA director in a new Republican administration.[31]

The stuttering Paris talks and Nixon's devious conduct played out against a darkening background in South Vietnam. Westmoreland's removal and Abrams' appointment in June had accelerated the process of "Vietnamization," shifting responsibility for all aspects of the war to the South Vietnamese.

LBJ had begun the program in early 1968 as what Clark Clifford called the only feasible means to exit Vietnam if Hanoi rebuffed every peace offer. It was given the nickname "I&M"—short for "improvement and modernization." The ARVN and the ruff-puffs would be provided with the same mobility, communications, and firepower that made American forces so lethal. Polls showed that "de-Americanization" of the war was by now the only popular feature of the conflict. Abrams ordered commanders in Vietnam to give it "top priority."[32]

But the I&M program was not going well. Abrams realigned US forces in Vietnam to form a shield—the 3rd Marine Division stretched horizontally across the DMZ, the 4th ID extended vertically along South Vietnam's western border, the other eight divisions concentrated around Saigon and the major population centers.

Wheeler and the Joint Chiefs predicted that "several years" would be needed to get the ARVN ready to come out from behind the shield. American taxpayers kept funding increases to Saigon's "military space ceiling"— the maximum number of troops paid for by the United States—and the force barely budged upward. How could it? Twenty of every 1,000 ARVN and ruff-puff soldiers deserted every month in 1968, prompting indignant cables from CINCPAC to MACV: cut South Vietnam's monthly desertion rate by 50 percent, or else.

Or else what? To get the desertion rate down, the United States would have to furnish South Vietnam with a burning patriotism, and with more dollars to improve ARVN pay, housing, and subsidies for dependents. But with de-Americanization under way, budgets were getting squeezed, not expanded, and no amount of aid was going to forge patriotism.[33]

This was the whole problem with the war. The United States had no leverage over its indispensable ally, and the ally knew it. The leverage was even weaker once "Vietnamization" officially began and the United States found itself having to grant more than a billion dollars a year to "modernize" a corrupt and ineffective military just to keep it going while America disengaged. An early MACV commentary on Vietnamization made clear that the Johnson administration, like the Nixon administration after it, knew in advance that it was wasting time, effort, money, and lives in this hopeless endeavor: "Confusion and corruption will be the result. But making the South Vietnamese responsible for the program *could* have a healthy effect."[34]

It probably couldn't, and everyone knew it—no one more than those closest to the action. With the South Vietnamese military wallowing like a leaky boat from its desertion and morale problem, there were still not enough troops to go around, even though the United States was paying for 800,000 South Vietnamese troops in 1968, would pay for 850,000 in 1969, and would raise the total to a million in 1970. And those were just the regular ARVN troops—American taxpayers were also on the hook for 2 million ruff-puffs by 1969. The South Vietnamese military had more than 3 million men but never seemed sufficient for even the most basic missions. NVA and VC attacks in August 1968—timed to coincide with the Democratic National Convention in Chicago—briefly penetrated Hue, Chu Lai, and Tay Ninh before receding under allied fire. "Security in every corps area continues to deteriorate," the CIA reported.[35]

Operation Complete Victory, which had aimed to clean out the Saigon Circle and secure the capital region in April 1968, had not achieved its purpose and cost 1,400 allied lives, including nearly 600 Americans. Naturally, it was followed by Operation Complete Victory II in June 1968, which was intended to do what the first operation had failed to do. Even more American troops were thrust into the III Corps battle space—five American divisions and four ARVN divisions in all—maneuvering to secure (again) a space that had supposedly been cleaned out at the cost of 300 American KIAs during Operation Junction City the previous year. Eighteen hundred more Americans were killed in the seven-month operation, and that was followed by Operation Complete Victory III, which worked over the same ground in 1969, killing the enemy, capturing more rice and weapons, and killing another 1,533 Americans. And yet somehow, despite astonishing enemy body counts—8,000 in the first operation, 26,000 in the second, and 41,000 in the third—"complete victory," or any victory at all, seemed no closer than it had been at the outset of more than a year of combat on the outskirts of Saigon that killed 4,000 American soldiers.[36]

To be sure, the enemy suffered mightily from the three big operations. They lost troops, and some of the pre-positioned logistics "noses" that Abrams was gunning for: tons of rice, millions of rounds of rifle and machine gun ammunition, thousands of grenades and mortar rounds, hundreds of rockets, and large quantities of penicillin, quinine, and plasma. With 80 percent of the B-52 strikes in South Vietnam aimed at them, VC and NVA prisoners in the Saigon Circle spoke of slumping morale under relentless attack. Enemy battalions were reduced to a dozen men.[37]

Whole enemy divisions suffered famine and critical shortages of cash, medicine, and ammo. Even light wounds would result in death or permanent disability in a communist force severely weakened by chronic anemia, malaria, and dysentery. VC organizations were "disintegrated" by the constant harrying. Communist countersweep operations and road interdiction declined sharply. One journalist noted that these achievements led the Americans, with their insistence that every report show progress, to believe that the communists were finished, when, in fact, it was the communist method "to look for problems, identify the trouble, and then solve it."[38]

The communists were far from finished. Despite heavy American, ARVN, and communist losses in the campaign to destroy the supply caches, little changed on the ground. The communists created a "shadow supply system" that was harder to interdict. Food and weapons were moved in sampans, or in logging or fuel trucks with false compartments. They would unload by the side of the road in wilderness areas, and VC porters would carry everything on their backs to hidden units.

Hanoi introduced new *bon tap* tactics to reduce their exposure to the American fire that they knew was strong but waning. Attack units would no longer approach an area with normal marches and rests. They would descend on their objective in a single forced march from a distant assembly area, attack, and then immediately scatter and withdraw.

A squad leader in the US 4th Infantry Division saw no quit in the enemy despite the heavy casualties: "They were doing their best to make us pay a price in blood for every cache we found and every one of their men we killed." An NVA deserter summed up the mood of the battered, hungry communist troops: "The other men in my unit will not desert because they feel that the war will soon be over" when the Americans withdrew. The 1st ID's Grumman Mohawk surveillance planes, which constantly circled III Corps with airborne radar and infrared systems, detected *increasing*, not decreasing, enemy infiltration.[39]

Faced with this communist resiliency, Clark Clifford in the Pentagon read Abrams' demands for escalation of the war and an invasion of the neutral sanctuaries in disbelief. It was all "garbage," Clifford fumed. "MACV keeps sending accounts of new offensives and other crap none of which are accurate or mean anything." Indeed, Abrams' "better war" was not proving any more effective or economical in lives or treasure than Westmoreland's. It seemed to do little more than substitute one unreliable metric for another. Instead of measuring success by body count, Abrams focused on "caches seized"—tons of weapons, vehicles, ammo, medicine, salt, and rice. More often than not, US troops searched for weeks or months on end and found next to nothing. Two battalions of the 4th ID, ordered to destroy a massive base area that had been reestablished in the An Lao Valley (the same ground "cleared" by Operation White Wing in 1966), never found the hidden caches. "We never broke into that area and destroyed it," a squad leader wrote, "because we never figured out where it was."[40]

On October 30, 1968, at the end of a month in which 942 Americans had been killed fighting to seize rice and weapons caches in the space between the Cambodian border and Saigon, the "monkey wrench" Nixon had thrown into the Paris talks finally did its work. Prodded by Kissinger, Thieu thwarted LBJ's "October surprise" with his own "November surprise." He announced that he was withdrawing from the peace talks on the eve of the American presidential election because he objected to the seating arrangements. Thieu wanted the Viet Cong delegation seated with the North Vietnamese. Hanoi insisted that the VC sit separately, to uphold the fiction that they were a separate movement and a fourth party to the negotiations.

Ultimately, there's no way to know if Averell Harriman would have secured a peace deal without Nixon and Kissinger's interference. One of his colleagues considered his optimism "wishful thinking," based on Harriman's assumption that "if we were nice to them, the North Vietnamese would respond," a view the colleague dismissed as "a lot of horseshit." Still, Harriman was offering the same deal that Nixon and Kissinger would later offer and that Hanoi would accept. Le Duan probably would have accepted it in 1968 even more eagerly than in 1973.

What we know with certainty is that Nixon and Kissinger violated constitutional and diplomatic norms to block the path to peace at a time when hundreds of Americans were dying every month in a war of acknowledged futility. They assuaged their consciences by assuring themselves that what they were doing was better for America: a better peace, a better deal, a better outcome. They claimed that the issue for them was less Vietnam than American credibility. A military and diplomatic defeat at the hands of Hanoi ("a third-class Communist peasant state") would weaken "the future world position of the United States" and "demoralize" Asian allies from Japan and South Korea to the Philippines and Australia. Without muscular American leadership, those nations might drift into the Chinese or Soviet orbit.[41]

Nixon and Kissinger felt certain that *they* would extract better outcomes from North Vietnam than LBJ would have done had they not thwarted his "October surprise." In the event, they would be disappointed on all counts. They would fight on for four more years, condemn 28,000 more American soldiers to death, and end up getting the same deal that Johnson was about to get when Nixon and Kissinger dropped their monkey wrench into the peace process.[42]

Furious at Nixon's interference, Johnson had to assume that another reason Thieu backed out was Humphrey's call for a total bombing halt, or perhaps Thieu's awareness of the souring mood in the White House, where Clark Clifford warned that Thieu's government "did not want the war to end—not while it was protected by a half million troops and a golden flow of money." Everyone knew by this point that Saigon feared the Democratic Party's eagerness to jettison the war and wanted Nixon elected.[43]

From Thieu's perspective, it was fair to use his leverage to prevent a "false peace" before election day on November 5, 1968. Peace under LBJ's permissive conditions would have massively undercut Thieu. President Johnson was angry and frustrated—with Thieu, Nixon, *and* Humphrey. There was loose talk of removing Thieu with another coup, but no appetite for it. Out of options, LBJ decided himself to halt all bombing on October 31. And why not? *Foreign Affairs* had just reported that Operation Rolling Thunder had cost $6 billion and hundreds of aircrew to destroy just $340 million worth of North Vietnamese targets.[44]

In the last days before American voters went to the polls, LBJ agonized over whether or not to reveal Nixon's conspiracy to the public. The president decided in the end to stay silent. He had no concrete proof of Nixon's direct involvement, and knew that to out Nixon would be to out his own surveillance of his South Vietnamese ally and a number of American citizens as well. None of these revelations would smooth the path to peace. And so LBJ went to his grave with the secret, leaving behind a complete dossier—the "X File"—with all of the details of the Chennault Affair. It would remain classified in the Johnson presidential library until 2011.[45]

Nixon won in November 1968 with the smallest plurality of any American president-elect since 1912, winning handily in the Electoral College but squeaking past Humphrey by just 500,000 votes in an election in which 73 million votes were cast. Walt Rostow, whom LBJ entrusted with the "X File" when the thirty-sixth president died in 1973, wrote a memo that year that linked the Chennault affair to the Watergate scandal that had just begun to emerge. Nixon got away with encouraging "Thieu's recalcitrance" in 1968, Rostow recalled, effectively putting him over the top in a close election by nullifying the good news of LBJ's bombing halt and fruitful peace talks.[46]

The Chennault affair, Rostow wrote, had been "the margin of victory" in 1968. And it encouraged Nixon to hazard more dirty tricks in 1972—tricks that would be his undoing. The break-in at the Watergate by Nixon's "plumbers" had its roots in the Chennault affair, Nixon nervous until his death that his successful effort to prolong the Vietnam War in 1968 to serve his own ambitions would be exposed by the Democrats. He sent the burglars into Democratic headquarters to look for compromising material not just on presidential candidate George McGovern but also on himself.[47]

All of that lay in the future. For now, the president-elect's chief concern had to be ending the unpopular war. In its review of Bob Hope's Christmas Tour in 1968, *Variety* captured the mood in Vietnam: "What a boon he is to the sinking spirits of the men who defend our way of life." This was Bob Hope's fifth Christmas Tour through South Vietnam, and the jokes were beginning to wear thin. Americans eagerly watched his Christmas specials, always aired in January of the new year and featuring highlights of the Vietnam tour, but this time the military audiences, mired in a hopeless struggle for what Nixon was calling "peace with honor," were not the usual festive crowd. Another 14,958 Americans had been killed and 95,798 wounded in 1968, to no good effect. "Where There's Death, There's Hope," the troops at the Christmas shows joked.[48]

Chapter 18

HAMBURGER HILL

Richard Nixon, who took office in January 1969, had run in 1968 on another fib—that he had a "secret plan" to end the war. "I'm going to stop the war, fast," he had promised. He would "break with the policies and mistakes of the past." The "secret plan," such as it was, combined several policies: major concessions in Paris, summit meetings in Moscow and Beijing to weaken the link between Hanoi and its patrons, troop reductions to mollify the American public, a massive expansion of the South Vietnamese armed forces, attacks into Cambodia and Laos to destroy communist sanctuaries, and a resumption of bombing in North Vietnam to bludgeon Hanoi into ending the war. "I call it the Madman Theory," Nixon confided to White House chief of staff Bob Haldeman. "I want the North Vietnamese to believe I've reached the point where I might do *anything* to stop the war." Just hint that I might "have my hand on the nuclear button," Nixon chuckled, "and Ho Chi Minh himself will be in Paris in two days begging for peace."[1]

In their private conversations, it was clear that Nixon and his national security adviser, Henry Kissinger, had no actionable plan for peace. They would prop up South Vietnam with deliveries of aid and weapons and kill as many communist forces as they could with the American troops still in-country in the hope that the Saigon regime would survive an American pullout just long enough—Kissinger spoke of a "decent interval"—to shield Nixon from any accusation of losing the war or abandoning an ally.

Kissinger's view was this: For better or worse, the United States had committed 500,000 troops to Vietnam. To admit defeat after investing so much would damage American credibility. The withdrawal, Kissinger explained, must be made to look like "an expression of policy, not a collapse." The inevitable defeat must accrue to South Vietnam, not America.[2]

Above all, Nixon and Kissinger agreed that Johnson's policy of "graduated pressure" had been an absurdity, combining meekness and ferocity. They would discard LBJ's meekness and hit with nothing but ferocity, proving, as Kissinger put it, "that Hanoi is simply unable to defeat us militarily." They assumed that they could quiet the antiwar protests that had made LBJ's presidency so raucous by swiftly turning the tide in Southeast Asia and then handing the war over to the South Vietnamese through a policy of "military Vietnamization." While doing all of this, they would link the war in Vietnam to a diplomatic revolution. The United States would exploit the Sino-Soviet split by pursuing détente with *both* communist powers,

Nixon, Thieu, Kissinger, Ky, and Ambassador Bunker descend the stairs of the presidential palace during Nixon's visit to South Vietnam in July 1969. (National Archives)

reducing their financial and material support to North Vietnam. Nixon called all of this "the big play."[3]

Joe McGinniss, author of *The Selling of the President 1968*, summarized Nixon's campaign strategy on Vietnam this way: "The war was not bad because of insane suffering and death. The war was bad because it was *ineffective*." Nixon vowed to make it effective, right out of the gate. "A change of policy toward Cambodia should be one of the priorities when we get in," he wrote Kissinger in January 1969. Like LBJ, Nixon regarded forty-six-year-old Prince Norodom Sihanouk as a shill of Hanoi. Nearly 22,000 tons of Soviet and Chinese supplies had landed on Cambodian docks over the past two years for delivery to VC and NVA units in the Mekong Delta and the border sanctuaries. Johnson had refused to expand the war over the border, where it might tip all of Cambodia into crisis and a communist takeover.

General Creighton Abrams, who commanded MACV after Westmoreland's return to Washington, sought broad authority to strike into Cambodia. Nixon was willing. Sihanouk's cousin, fifty-five-year-old Sisowath Siri Matak, would be Nixon's man in Phnom Penh. Siri Matak rejected Sihanouk's "extreme neutrality" and argued so ardently for action against the NVA and VC sanctuaries that Sihanouk had sent him abroad as an ambassador in the 1960s to keep him as far from the levers of power as possible. By 1969, Siri Matak was back in Phnom Penh, and his star was rising. Sihanouk's prime minister, General Lon Nol, made Siri Matak his deputy, and, encouraged by the Nixon administration, the two men began to sideline Sihanouk and move against the communist sanctuaries and supply lines. Unfortunately, the military impact of this new line proved disastrous for all but the NVA, VC, and the Cambodian communists known as the Khmer Rouge.[4]

In March 1969, Nixon launched Operation Menu, which was a secret air campaign against the NVA sanctuaries in eastern Cambodia. Abrams said that a single B-52 strike would be enough to wipe out the Central Office for South Vietnam—the "VC Pentagon"—but 4,000 sorties were flown against six target areas and COSVN was never hit or even located.

The impact of the raids on Cambodia was more consequential. Instead of solving the problem of sanctuaries, the air raids made it worse. To escape the bombing, the VC and NVA forces, aided by Pol Pot's Khmer Rouge guerrillas, moved westward, deeper into Cambodia, scattering Lon Nol's weak government forces and threatening the general's grip on power. Nixon had pledged that "no Cambodians lived" in the six target areas, but that was just another lie. At least 4,200 civilians lived in the bombed areas, and they fled or died in the Operation Menu raids, creating a scandal inside Cambodia and new recruits for the Khmer Rouge.[5]

Operation Menu pounded Cambodia for fourteen months and was capped by a coup in Phnom Penh, when General Lon Nol, supported by Nixon, ousted Sihanouk in March 1970. Infuriated by the coup, Sihanouk would make his way to Beijing and strike an alliance with the Khmer Rouge to "liberate our motherland." Until the secret bombing and the Lon Nol coup, the Khmer Rouge had been a fringe group. When Sihanouk embraced them, their membership soared among the rural peasantry. Sihanouk and the Khmer Rouge created a parallel government in Beijing and the "liberated areas" of Cambodia, which is what they rather daringly called the NVA sanctuaries. They called themselves GRUNK—a French acronym for Royal Government of the National Union of Kampuchea. GRUNK began to fight FANK (National Khmer Armed Forces), Lon Nol's American-backed military. Here in a nutshell was why LBJ had never invaded Cambodia—his certainty that such an invasion would make Cambodia a failed state, or communist.[6]

In South Vietnam, Nixon kept on with B-52 raids, tac air strikes, and "herbicide operations"—dumping poison on South Vietnam's paddy fields, roadsides, and forests. He went at maximum capacity, resisting congressional calls for a "phasedown." His new field commander, Abe Abrams, did not seem all that different from Westmoreland. When LBJ had halted all bombing of North Vietnam on November 1, 1968, he instructed Abrams to "maintain maximum pressure" on the NVA and VC in South Vietnam to give Washington and Saigon some leverage at the Paris peace talks.

Nixon initially did nothing to change this. At a press conference in April 1969, he said as much: "I have not ordered nor do I intend to order any reduction of our activity. We will do what is necessary to defend our position and to maintain the strength of our bargaining position in the Paris peace talks." But Hanoi's 1969 offensive, launched in February, had killed another 1,300 Americans by the time Nixon stepped before the cameras in April. The president abruptly pulled back on the reins, reminding Abrams that "American public opinion is in a highly critical condition." Nixon had been president for only a few months and he was already confessing his inability to deploy the ferocity he considered necessary to terminate the war. Abrams grudgingly pivoted away from attrition strategy, deciding instead to emphasize clear and hold operations around populated areas that would buy time for pacification and "institutional rebuilding in South Vietnam" after the destruction of 1968. Instead of hunting for the communist main-force units, Abrams would try to thwart NVA offensives into the populated areas by destroying their base areas and logistics.[7]

This *sounded* like a big difference, characterized this way by a reporter: "Westmoreland was a search-and-destroy and count-the-bodies man. Abrams proved to be an interdict-and-weigh-the-rice man." But, in practice, there was little difference between the Westmoreland and Abrams methods, the latter defined by Abrams himself as "stay on top of them and smash every move they try to make."

Whereas Westmoreland had tended to slow the pace during lulls in enemy offensive activity, Abrams pushed his troops to keep attacking even during the lulls, indeed especially during the lulls, when the enemy was digging his bunkers and tunnels and pre-positioning supplies for the next offensive. "The military machine runs best at full throttle," Abrams explained. "That's about where we have it and where I intend to keep it." Abrams called this restless activity "working against the *whole* system."[8]

Unfortunately, attacking the whole communist system was at least as dangerous as attacking parts of it. A sergeant in the 4th ID, operating in the Central Highlands in 1969, put it this way: "Major Dixon described what we did as 'Search and Clearing Operations,' but from our perspective it was basic search-and-destroy stuff: two opposing groups of men searching for and destroying each other." American efforts to find caches and the troops guarding them inevitably attracted additional enemy combat units, who fought fiercely to defend their guns and butter.[9]

The Battle of Hamburger Hill in May 1969 was the most notorious example of this superficially reformed American strategy, defined by Abrams as "all out with all we have." Hill 937 overlooked the A Shau Valley, which ran along the Laotian border, just a mile inside South Vietnam. The valley had been an avenue for communist infiltration since the French ruled Indochina and had been the scene of Operation Delaware a year earlier, when the Cav and the 101st Airborne had suffered 672 casualties with little to show for it. They had seized communist trucks and supplies, but nothing more.

The whole area remained a logistics "nose," stocked with everything the NVA needed to launch combat operations toward the principal cities of I Corps: Quang Tri, Hue, and Da Nang. American bombers had struck the valley for years, but few had been foolish enough to try to occupy this strip of South Vietnam, for the fate of the A Shau Valley was no different from the fate of every other French and then American "border surveillance outpost" in I Corps. Most of the CIDG camps set up in the days of the Kennedy administration, when it was believed that intrepid Green Berets embedded with local Montagnards could hold the line against communist infiltration, had been rolled up one by one: Khe Sanh, Lang Vei, A Shau, and Kham Duc. Their droll welcome signs—"If you kill for money you're a mercenary. If you kill for pleasure you're a sadist. If you kill for both you're a Green Beret"— had long since been torn down and split into kindling. By 1969, those camps and several others were all in communist hands, part of a network of NVA base areas that shuttled men and supplies down the Ho Chi Minh Trail and deep into South Vietnam.[10]

The fall of Kham Duc, the last surviving CIDG camp in I Corps during Mini-Tet, had demonstrated the futility of trying to cling to these little islands in a communist sea. Kham Duc, site of President Diem's old hunting lodge, had been reinforced during Mini-Tet with several companies of American infantry and a battery of field artillery, but it had been surrounded and subjected to such a heavy bombardment that MACV had been compelled, after airlifting in 1,500 troops of the Americal Division, five howitzers, and 400 tons of supplies, to airlift it all out again. Observing the rout from Saigon, General Abrams had judged Kham Duc "a minor disaster." It had been a major one, and the press had missed it only because they had all been in Saigon reporting on the street fighting there.[11]

Nearly 200 Americans were killed or wounded in Kham Duc, many of them blown to bits by their own artillery and air strikes, which had to be called in on their own positions. Thirty-one more grunts were seized by the enemy, joining a lengthening list of MIAs. Two hundred South Vietnamese dependents and their American aircrew died when their C-130 struggled to take off from Kham Duc and crashed under communist fire. The Montagnards left behind were gutted by the war, losing about 250,000 people—a quarter of their prewar population—to the combat and reprisals that swept through their villages.[12]

Communist strength along the Ho Chi Minh Trail had increased with every American troop surge. In 1965, Hanoi had managed to send 400 tons of supplies down the trail every week. By 1969, they were sending 10,000 tons a week. Five thousand NVA troops had moved south along the trail in 1965. By 1969, hundreds of thousands of NVA troops were projected to move south in a single year. To stanch this flood, Nixon and Abrams resolved to put a finger in the dike.

Here was another tragedy of the Vietnam War. To give as many American officers as possible a "combat tour," the US military rotated officers out of their front-line assignments every six months. Due to these quick rotations, there was always a tendency to forget even recent experience, and there was always a new roster of officers eager to make a name for themselves. Eye Corps was now dominated by one such go-getter, General Dick Stillwell, Westmoreland's old deputy, who had left the offices of MACV to assume command of XXIV Corps, which was beginning to shoulder the Marines out of I Corps. Putting the Americal, the Cav, and the 101st Airborne Division into I Corps to reinforce the two Marine divisions had made the III Marine Amphibious Force one of the biggest commands in Marine Corps history—more of a field army than a corps. Within a year, the Marines would have to yield command to the Army.

They were already doing so. Dick Stillwell ordered up Operation Apache Snow in May 1969 to find NVA Base Area 611 and destroy its "nose" of supplies in the A Shau Valley. Operation Delaware had come this way in 1968 and failed for many reasons—the foul mountain weather, the lack of an all-weather road to supply troops overland when aerial resupply was impossible, and the strong enemy fortifications and antiaircraft defenses in the valley that had inflicted the heaviest losses on American helicopters and crews of the entire war.[13]

To secure the A Shau Valley, Dick Stillwell now decided to build a hard road from the 101st Airborne Division headquarters at Camp Eagle, three miles southeast of Hue, through the mountains and into the A Shau. The road progressed easily enough into the foothills of the A Shau, but when the engineers reached the high peaks overlooking the valley, they met furious resistance.

Earlier battles at Khiem Duc and Polei Kleng had shown the great risk of moving into these border areas, which had been converted by the enemy into natural fortresses of interlocked caves and bunkers. Here in the A Shau, the Marines had just wrapped up their own bloody, two-month Operation Dewey Canyon, in which 130 Marines had been killed and 932 wounded to push out the defenders and destroy a logistics "nose" containing 220,000 pounds of rice and 800,000 rounds of ammunition. Abe Abrams applauded the operation. Those captured ammo rounds, he ventured, might save the Americans "what? Five—six thousand casualties." Maybe, but they had undeniably cost over 1,000 Marines killed or wounded to seize them.[14]

Apache Snow would be the Army's second operation of a three-phase attack on the A Shau Valley to drive out the NVA and finish the road from Camp Eagle. The first phase, Operation Massachusetts Striker, had been an assault by the 101st Airborne's 2nd Brigade into the southern end of the A Shau Valley. Massachusetts Striker in March and April 1969 had "succeeded" in that it had unearthed 100 tons of enemy supplies, but 76 more Americans had been killed and 259 wounded to destroy signals equipment, medicine, and munitions. And the enemy remained as stubborn as before, dug into the sides of the mountains, all but willing the Americans to continue their bloody advance. On the western edge of the valley, the NVA 29th Regiment took up positions on the jungle-covered peak that would shortly be given the name "Hamburger Hill." They and every other communist unit in South Vietnam were under orders to improve Hanoi's position in the stuttering Paris peace talks through "a process of continuous attacks and uprisings—to be urgently carried out, every hour, every day."[15]

With only 39 percent of Americans supporting the war in Vietnam by early 1969, grinding operations like this latest foray into the A Shau Valley risked what little support remained. A new MACV Objectives Plan unveiled by Abrams in March 1969 stated that the war was being handed over to the South Vietnamese and that US forces should focus on village security and rapid training of the territorial forces. But it was plainly not being handed over to the South Vietnamese *here*. Costly American ground attacks on enemy base areas set back NVA planning, but for how long? The wharves in Haiphong were crammed with replacements for everything lost in the A Shau and Plei Trap Valleys. Was it rational or moral to continue trading

American lives for sacks of rice, vials of Russian penicillin, and crates of ammunition—even as the war was being terminated?

Analysts were also aware of an eerie quiet in South Vietnam. The rice harvest in 1969 was the best in five years. Road and bridge security was better than in the past. Land was being distributed to peasants, and refugees were being settled in better housing. When Abrams sent troops into communist base areas, he provoked battles. But elsewhere in South Vietnam, the NVA and VC were sitting on their hands—waiting for American troop withdrawals, when they would emerge to intensify the war against the ARVN alone. How long would American grunts (and voters) support an operation like this, spilling more American blood merely to "level the playing field" or to "buy time" for the Saigon regime?[16]

Such fundamental questions do not seem to have disturbed Abrams and Stillwell. The Marines had used a regiment in the A Shau. Stillwell would use the equivalent of two divisions—although most of the fighting would be done by five battalions of the 101st Airborne's 3rd Brigade. Abrams, Stillwell, and the commander of the 101st Airborne Division, fifty-three-year-old General Melvin Zais, looked over the plans and okayed everything, including the decision by Zais' most aggressive battalion commander, thirty-eight-year-old Lieutenant Colonel Weldon Honeycutt, to assault Hill 937, the 3,100-foot Ap Bia Mountain, which overlooked the A Shau Valley and was riddled with the bunkers and tunnels of the NVA 29th Regiment.

Hill 937 was just the sort of place where the enemy would stand and fight. The bunkers were flush to the ground, protected with overhead cover, hidden by jungle foliage, and connected by tunnels, so enemy troops could slip from one to the other without exposing themselves to American bombs and artillery.

Operation Apache Snow was pitched as a "reconnaissance in force," an op designed to uncover supply caches and kill any NVA troops in the A Shau Valley, which curled southeast from Laos and funneled communist troops and matériel toward the big coastal cities of I Corps. Eighteen hundred Airborne troops along with two battalions of the ARVN 1st Infantry Division were supposed to air-assault into the valley, flush whatever enemy they found from cover, and use their airmobility to trap and destroy the communist forces if they tried to run for Laos. The allied troops would then turn their attention to completing the all-weather road from Camp Eagle into the A Shau Valley and destroying enemy supplies. It was part of Abrams' last gasp: "maximum pressure" on the communists to weaken their hand in the Paris talks before the war was entirely "Vietnamized."

Hill 937 was in the sector assigned to Lieutenant Colonel Honeycutt's 3rd Battalion of the 187th Airborne Regiment. These were the "Rakkasans," so named because their regiment had jumped into Okinawa at the end of World War II, and the Japanese had called them *rakkasan*s, their word for "parachute." On May 10, Honeycutt ordered his three companies to search around the base of the mountain, and on the following day he ordered them to climb its north face to the summit. Honeycutt, a Westmoreland protégé, was itching for contact. His nickname was "Tiger." He spread his three companies wide, and each of them met stiff resistance from the NVA 29th Regiment, which used rifle pits and bunkers to slow the advance of the Airborne infantry.[17]

Bravo Company battled to within 1,000 yards of the summit, but the fighting was vicious—700 Americans firing blindly into dense jungle and being hit with aimed fire from the invisible communist bunkers dug into the steep slopes. One paratrooper who scrambled forward to retrieve the dead and wounded of his company could not recognize any of them: "Their faces were completely gone; that memory will haunt me forever."

Five friendly-fire incidents added to their agonies. In the first of them, on May 11, a Cobra gunship mistakenly shot up Honeycutt's command post, wounding the commander and thirty-four others and killing two. Whatever momentum Bravo Company had gained melted away instantly as the leaderless battalion reeled back down the slope. Watching the mangled dead and wounded pile up, the Airborne troops began calling the peak "Hamburger Hill."[18]

Honeycutt had assumed that the mountain was held by no more than a company and that his three companies could maneuver up the hill to encircle and destroy the NVA on the summit. Three days into the battle he grasped that there were at least 900 troops of the NVA 29th Regiment dug in above and around him. These were crack troops, nicknamed the "Pride of Ho Chi Minh." They had fought the Marines in Hue during Tet.

Honeycutt's efforts to "concentrate" his three scattered companies for a coordinated assault on the hill took two full days—May 12 and 13—with the troops slithering down steep, muddy ravines, or hacking through dense jungle to find each other and usually finding artfully concealed enemy machine gun nests instead. Delta Company needed five hours to move 500 yards, without finding Honeycutt. The commander of the 3rd Brigade, Colonel Joseph Conmy, ordered a second Airborne battalion—the "Currahees," the 1st Battalion of the 506th—to march two and a half miles from its sector south of the mountain to reinforce Honeycutt. Conmy assumed that the maneuver would take a day, but it ended up taking nearly a *week*, rough terrain and dense jungle slowing the movement to a crawl and giving new meaning to the unit's Cherokee nickname, which meant "Stand Alone." In a single forty-hour period, the isolated battalion moved just 1,500 yards. Ordered to march on May 13, the Currahees would not get into a position to support the Rakkasans until May 19.

In the meantime, Tiger Honeycutt decided to storm Hamburger Hill on his own on May 14. He sent Bravo Company again up the main ridge with Delta Company on its left and Charlie Company on its right. The three companies, funneled into steep, muddy jungle paths, collided with enemy bunker positions, machine guns, RPGs, and claymore mines that piled up more American casualties. There were no LZs for medevacs or resupply, and any helicopters that tried to hover overhead and winch the casualties out were shot down or driven off by antiaircraft fire. Charlie Company, just south of Bravo, lost two of three platoon leaders, the company's executive officer, every senior NCO, and forty enlisted men. Honeycutt was unmoved. "Damn it, get those men moving," he berated a subordinate over the radio. "You are being paid to *fight* this war, not discuss it."[19]

Honeycutt's outfit reported twelve KIAs and eighty wounded that day. All of them, the quick and the dead, would have been amused to learn that they had been cut down on the very day that Nixon went on television to announce his "first comprehensive peace plan." It called for a total withdrawal of US and North Vietnamese forces in South Vietnam within twelve months. It was a nonstarter for Hanoi, and no help to the Rakkasans.

On May 15, Honeycutt ordered his Alpha and Bravo Companies to renew the frontal assault toward the summit. They closed to within 150 yards of their objective but were stopped by enemy fire and more friendly fire, this time from a Cobra gunship that rocketed Bravo's command post in error. "I'll take a court martial before I go up again," one nineteen-year-old grunt told a reporter. "It's suicide."[20]

With both companies reduced by 50 percent casualties and Bravo's company commander wounded in the latest friendly-fire incident, the grunts retreated down the slope to less exposed night positions. There would be five documented friendly-fire incidents like this in the battle; they killed seven Americans and wounded fifty-three. By luring the Rakkasans onto Hamburger Hill, whose slopes were hidden beneath thick jungle, the NVA had deprived them of their chief advantage—the ability to focus artillery fire and air strikes on the enemy.

In this battle, the NVA, continually reinforced from Laos, fought on equal terms with the Americans. Each time the Americans pulled back to create a safe envelope for bombing, shelling, or napalm, the NVA would sink into their trenches and bunkers until the Americans resumed their stumbling advance. They would then emerge to continue the infantry fight, cutting down every American push with cross fire from mortars, machine guns, and RPGs.

Honeycutt planned to renew the attack on May 15 but was ordered by Colonel Conmy to wait for the Currahees, who were struggling to reach the southern face of Hamburger Hill. By now, curious reporters had arrived on the scene to pose awkward questions: Why were American infantry forces being used in close combat instead of bombers and artillery? Why were the two ARVN battalions attached to the operation not doing anything? The Associated Press reporter Jay Sharbutt flew into the A Shau Valley, and his account of what he witnessed on Hamburger Hill ran in newspapers all over America: "The paratroopers came down the mountain, their green shirts darkened with sweat, their weapons gone, their bandages stained brown and red—with mud and blood." Lieutenant Colonel Honeycutt's radio call sign was "Blackjack." It was well known to the grunts, who had heard the battalion commander's impatient calls for more assaults crackling over the platoon radios. One paratrooper told Sharbutt: "That damn Blackjack won't stop until he kills every one of us."

Sharbutt's reporting shocked Americans, who had supposed that battles like this were a thing of the past, certainly not a part of President Nixon's "secret plan" or General Abrams' "better war." When four Airborne battalions finally took the height on May 20, there was little to celebrate.

The green mountain had been shaved clean of its trees by ten batteries of artillery and 500 tons of bombs and napalm. But what had been gained? Seventy-two more Americans had been killed and 400 wounded in eleven assaults on a height that was attacked with obsessive zeal and then promptly abandoned.

General Zais justified what had been done with the search and destroy bravado of the Westmoreland era: "The hill had no military value whatsoever. We found the enemy on Hill 937 and that's where we fought him." And yet 472 Americans had been killed or wounded for an enemy body count of 630. It was not a good trade for anyone but Hanoi.[21]

The Nixon White House was as dismayed as the American public by the brutish tactics employed by the 101st Airborne Division on Hamburger Hill. Nixon, Kissinger, and Secretary of Defense Melvin Laird saw that their "secret plan" to raise the level of pain in North Vietnam and quickly persuade Hanoi to end the war was not merely failing; it was backfiring.

Hanoi was not deterred by casualties that were no worse than in previous years. The antiwar protests in the United States were sharpened, not weakened, by operations such as Hamburger Hill. In a piece titled "U.S. Battle Losses Stir Nixon Aides" that ran two days after the op ended, *New York Times* reporter Hedrick Smith noted that during the week of Hamburger Hill, a total of 430 Americans had been killed in Vietnam. Supposedly committed to more cautious tactics under Abrams, the Army appeared out of control despite all of the hopeful talk of deescalation. "We are fighting a limited war," a Nixon aide told Smith. "Now clearly the greatest limitation is the reaction of the American public. They react to the casualty lists. I don't understand why the military doesn't get the picture. The military is defeating the very thing it most wants—more time to gain a stronger hand."[22]

Asked by reporters to explain his casualties, General Melvin Zais answered cavalierly: "I've never received orders to hold down casualties. If they wanted to hold down casualties then I'd be told not to fight." At the Pentagon, Westmoreland praised "the gallant operation." Anger at this obstinacy spread to the United States Senate, where Senator Edward Kennedy excoriated the Army's blimpish insistence that the battle made sense: "It is both senseless and irresponsible to keep sending our young men to their deaths to capture hills and positions that have no relation to ending this conflict." The costly tactical thrust had no strategic value. "How then can we justify sending our boys against a hill a dozen times or more, until soldiers themselves question the madness of the action?" Kennedy continued. "The assault on 'Hamburger Hill' is only symptomatic of a mentality and a policy that requires immediate attention. American boys are too valuable to be sacrificed for a false sense of military pride."[23]

The "American boys" in the maneuver companies knew this better than anyone. They began "bounty hunting" in 1969, offering rewards for the assassination of officers and NCOs, such as Honeycutt, deemed dangerous to the lives of the grunts. Incensed by Tiger Honeycutt's methods, the Army underground newspaper *GI Says* offered a $10,000 bounty on the lieutenant colonel, the money usually pooled by men in the affected unit. Several attempts were made on Honeycutt's life, or so the grunts alleged.

Bounty hunting would evolve into "fragging," killing troublesome superiors with a hand grenade. The Army began keeping statistics on fragging for the first time in 1969 when there were ninety-six incidents that killed thirty-seven officers. This restiveness forced Abrams to curtail major ops after Hamburger Hill. Zais remained obtuse and unrepentant to the end. Gunning for the third star and corps command that he would shortly receive, Zais boorishly insisted that he did not "consider casualties on Hill 937 high at all" and that Hamburger Hill was really "a tremendous, gallant victory, and people are acting as if it were a catastrophe."[24]

A month after the controversial battle in the A Shau, *Life* magazine published its most famous cover story of the war: "Faces of the American Dead in Vietnam: One Week's Toll, June 1969." Of the 241 servicemen killed that week, only seven were casualties from Hamburger Hill. (The others had perished earlier.) But many Americans, stunned by the reporting from the A Shau Valley, assumed that they were *all* victims of Hamburger Hill.[25]

Nixon, who had given Abrams broad discretion in his conduct of the war, pulled back hard on the reins. His "secret plan" was not working. Thirty thousand Americans had already died in Vietnam when he and Kissinger sabotaged Johnson's peace talks in 1968. Seven thousand more had died in the meantime. Another 21,000 would die in the next three years. The American public, still unaware of Nixon's election-year chicanery, was in no mood for more prevarication, or for escalation. The chairman of the Joint Chiefs of Staff, General Earle Wheeler, considered the war an absurdity by this point. "It's a very curious, almost a phenomenal situation," he groused.

Nixon "is practically apologizing for our position in Vietnam." Any gains the military made could not be exploited or reinforced because of public, media, and congressional resistance to the war. "We're hanging on over here by the teeth, barely able to stay in the stadium," Wheeler complained.[26]

Even as he said this, Nixon was beginning to empty the stadium. Feeling the heat emanating from "victories" like Hamburger Hill, Nixon hastened to announce the first troop withdrawals from Vietnam—25,000 men—and ordered MACV to minimize casualties going forward. Creighton Abrams' "maximum pressure" campaign ended on the sour note of Hamburger Hill. From now on, Abrams would only authorize "protective reaction." US forces would not go looking for logistics "noses" or anything else. They would risk battle only to preempt an impending attack on themselves. There would be no more "compressed contact" with the enemy.

The tactical victory of Hamburger Hill did allow Abrams to drive the all-weather road from Camp Eagle through the mountains overlooking the A Shau and into the valley, but it was too little too late. Abrams had planned to build a permanent base and airfield in the A Shau Valley to control it, but he was overtaken by Nixon's accelerating troop withdrawals, which subtracted not only maneuver battalions but helicopters, howitzers, and tac air sorties as well. That summer, Nixon announced the withdrawal of 60,000 troops from Vietnam, including the entire 3rd Marine Division. This meant that the 101st Airborne Division had to abandon the A Shau and the new road in August 1969 and move back to the coastal plain and the DMZ to fill in behind the departing Marines.[27]

Here was just the latest example of the war's futility. The United States never deployed enough force, will, or follow-through to win—if winning were even possible. A quiet mutiny began to spread among American troops, who could see that they were being sacrificed like pawns on a chessboard to improve Nixon's hand in the Paris negotiations. Somehow this had never occurred to Nixon and Kissinger—that their phased plan to terminate the war would make the troops still there reluctant to risk their lives in a cause acknowledged to be lost.

Pressed during his first year in office to reveal his "secret plan" to end the war, Nixon had performed a kind of striptease in news conferences and speeches, slowly revealing a plan almost calculated to make the grunts stop fighting. He abandoned "military victory" as the objective of the war.

The new goal would be South Vietnamese "self-determination" and an "honorable peace." He curtailed but did not end US military operations—permitting battles such as Hamburger Hill before condemning them—and announced major troop withdrawals. He suggested that the war might never end formally. It might just "fade out" without a political settlement whenever a South Vietnamese government became strong enough to survive an American withdrawal. These objectives were narrower than Johnson's but no less demoralizing to the troops.[28]

Chapter 19

SEARCH AND AVOID

The South Vietnamese would have to carry the ball from now on. But would they? The communists launched an Autumn Campaign in August 1969 that ripped through all four corps areas. The fighting, aimed at "disrupting pacification" everywhere, was even bloodier than usual, for it was augmented by massive deliveries of Chinese and Soviet weapons to the VC.[1]

South Vietnam's Regional and Popular Forces had added 500,000 men in 1969 to meet these attacks, but the ruff-puffs wilted under them instead. "As soldiers the ARVN were useless," a grunt in the Americal observed, but "the Ruff-and-Puffs were outright dangerous." They "bled weapons" to the enemy everywhere, an adviser reported, surrendering M-16s, M-79 grenade launchers, 60 mm mortars, and PRC-10 radios. The regular ARVN divisions, which had enjoyed favorable kill ratios when fighting alongside the Americans, now routinely lost as many men as the communists in battle, despite air and artillery superiority. With Nixon accelerating US troop withdrawals—reducing the total number in-country to 363,000 in June 1969—ARVN commanders expressed "fear about the ability of Vietnamese units to replace U.S. units." Morale continued to plummet, most of the ARVN and ruff-puff casualties being MIAs, not KIAs or wounded—men, in other words, who had run away or surrendered rather than fight the communists to the bitter end. A senior US officer charged with evaluating ARVN improvement called it "painfully slow," adding: "If you want to be discouraged, *this* is the place to settle down."[2]

Another piece of Nixon's "secret plan" was forcing Thieu to accept the same peace deal that Nixon and Kissinger had instructed him *not* to accept from Lyndon Johnson. This Nixon gambit was immediately complicated by the president's decision in January 1969 to admit the Viet Cong to the peace talks in Paris, breaking the promise he'd made to Thieu during the Chennault affair. Now it was the turn of Nixon and Kissinger to be met with the full force of South Vietnamese recalcitrance. After Nixon's election, Thieu proposed sending a group to Paris not to negotiate peace but to make "preliminary contacts." The only major step Thieu took was to appoint Vice President Ky "delegation spokesman"—to remove his most threatening rival from Saigon. Thieu was fearless, for Nixon's conspiracy with Anna Chennault had provided the South Vietnamese president with blackmail material. If Nixon tried to cut and run from Vietnam, he had to worry that Thieu might expose his sabotage of LBJ's peace plan before the Democrats did.[3]

Nevertheless, it was clear that Nixon would get out of Vietnam as quickly as he could. The primary American aim now softened. Instead of destroying the communist armies and forcing negotiations on Hanoi, the aim became preventing the resurgence of the decimated VC, pulling up their political infrastructure, and installing a viable South Vietnamese administration in the beleaguered country's cities and villages. But such a mission, at this stage of the war when American force and patience were running out, seemed as hopeless as search and destroy. Militarily, it was probably not going to work for all of the reasons it had not worked so far, and for a new one: the combat effectiveness of American troops was plummeting as the grunts came to understand that they were pawns in a purposeless war. "President Nixon may claim credit for phasing down the war," Fred Gardner wrote in the *New York Times*. "Congress may debate a timetable for pulling out, but the fact is that rank-and-file GIs are ending the fighting on their own," refusing to fight with the old tenacity, practicing "search and avoid" rather than "search and clear."[4]

In September 1969, US forces captured the notebook of the NVA commander in I Corps. It contained a number of insights, including this: "Peace will be signed by the end of 1969, but our activity will continue until Vietnam is reunified under a communist regime." The "peace with honor" sought by Nixon and Kissinger would be nothing more than a theatrical pause for the thirty-seventh president to wash his hands of a war he had cynically prolonged. The captured NVA notebook, which was copied to CINCPAC and all relevant departments in Washington, made clear that "the enemy was preparing to exploit any peace settlement" to resume the war on *his* terms. The moment the Americans left, the NVA would finish off South Vietnam.[5]

To prepare South Vietnam for that day of reckoning, US advisory groups worked to ready the ARVN for life without the Americans. Unfortunately, the ARVN continued to struggle with basic operations. Their command and supply systems still tethered them to fixed bases, where they were easily avoided by the enemy. ARVN operations still averaged five days—not enough to contact the enemy, let alone defeat him. (American ops lasted thirty days or more in the field.) AWOLs and desertions hollowed out the all-important South Vietnamese maneuver units, and the intelligence gathering of ARVN units was still, as one senior adviser put it, "grossly inadequate." ARVN leadership, despite two decades of combat, remained "woefully inadequate." In combat units, officers down to the battalion level were named by the Joint General Staff in Saigon, and even the worst of them could not be removed by a corps, division, or brigade commander without several months of appeals and paperwork.[6]

The ARVN units hardly fought, preferring static defense of large towns, which they would begrudgingly leave for "walks in the sun" one or two klicks outside of town before hurrying back to the safety of their bunkers. The South Vietnamese Air Force continued to withhold its helicopters from the ARVN, and their strike aircraft continued to fly with little connection to friendly infantry on the ground. They had no radar-equipped aircraft and relied entirely on Americans for their air traffic control, target acquisition, and intelligence. In battle, ARVN infantry still depended on American helicopters for lift, medevacs, and emergency resupply.[7]

The ruff-puffs, critical to pacification because they were the stay-behind units in every village, were another recipient of American largesse. Abrams gave them priority for M-16s over the ARVN. LBJ had already begun an "omnibus action program" to pull the Regional Forces and Popular Forces together and give them a proper "management system." Nixon continued the charade, announcing and meeting "management targets" that had little

A Cav adviser training ruff-puffs at Camp Evans near Hue. (National Archives)

military effect, certainly not enough to justify the soaring cost of the program to American taxpayers. An American adviser who made a surprise visit to a Popular Force outpost in late 1969 found no one patrolling or even ready for action. The abashed militiamen ran off in search of their M-16s and ammo belts, then carefully picked up their steel helmets, which they had laid out to collect rainwater, and poured the contents into a barrel. They had not fired in anger at an enemy in two years.[8]

These ruff-puff reforms were tied to a new Hamlet Evaluation System managed by CORDS. This was just another of the screeching anomalies of Vietnamization. If you were turning the war over to the South Vietnamese, you would think the first thing you would turn over would be village security. But no—it was acknowledged in 1969 that the South Vietnamese government could not be trusted with it. For too many years, Saigon had routinely placed corrupt and abusive colonels in charge of the provinces, and so the Americans found themselves in the absurd position of having to measure and monitor everything at the local level—hamlet rosters, hamlet boundaries, VC activity, ruff-puff efficacy, the number of radios and televisions in every hamlet, school attendance, and whether or not hamlet chiefs actually slept in their hamlets or somewhere else where they (but certainly not their charges) were safe from VC assassins—even as they disengaged.[9]

Bob Komer had left CORDS in 1968, his fiery zeal for the war smothered by the 90,000 pages of hamlet evaluations generated every *month* by his staff. Blowtorch Bob was replaced by forty-eight-year-old William Colby, who had been CIA chief of station in Saigon. Colby took stock of the situation in 1969. After the three communist offensives in 1968, the VC had shifted their attacks to South Vietnam's pacification and Phoenix programs, aiming to weaken and destroy them both with targeted assassinations.

With the VC picking off his officials, Bill Colby decided to pick off theirs. In 1969, the Americans tightened their control of Phoenix, acknowledging that the program—established in 1968 to penetrate and eliminate the VC infrastructure (VCI)—had been too opaque and too readily abused by infighting South Vietnamese officials, who, as one analyst put it, viewed Phoenix "as yet another U.S. requirement that they will fulfill to the minimum degree while availing themselves of the maximum financial benefits of the program."[10]

Yet another opportunity, in short, had been missed. The VCI—crucial, shrouded, and hard to reach—was the linchpin of the war. The term referred to members of the People's Revolutionary Party, who were the true believers controlling the South Vietnamese population through the VC's administrative and military elements. They were hard targets, protected at all times by a squad or platoon of hamlet guerrillas, and they coordinated military operations, propaganda, recruiting, tax collection, communications, security, logistics, liaison, and reconnaissance for the VC and NVA main-force units. The VCI were the eyes, ears, and local muscle of Hanoi inside South Vietnam. They connected the communist armies as well as an estimated 70,000 South Vietnamese citizens actively working for Hanoi. If you penetrated or eliminated the VCI, you would take a long step toward defeating the communist movement in South Vietnam.[11]

Only the South Vietnamese could pull this off, but they shrank from the task. In the first place, digging up the VCI carried the risk of self-incrimination. As a US corps commander in Vietnam noted, "People are reluctant to participate in Phoenix because many members of their immediate families—sons, daughters, husbands—have worked with the VC. If the program succeeds, many of them will be dead or in jail." Then there was the fear of reprisals. The ceaseless activity of the VC in South Vietnam cowed people into silence. The low quality of South Vietnam's province and district officials—many on their second or third job after being fired from the previous ones for corruption, abuse, or incompetence—added to the difficulties. It took six to eight months to fire even the worst officials. "The problems are recognized, but solutions have not been found," an American adviser wanly explained.

This meant that yet another crucial area that should have been Vietnamized under Saigon's National Police or the ARVN's Military Security Service (MSS) had to be dragged back into CORDS under American control. A reformed Phoenix school at Vung Tau was taught in 1969 by Vietnamese "with U.S. advisers providing the impetus," the spirit of which was summarized by Colonel Werner Michel, MACV's special assistant for VCI intelligence: "Keep pressing! Indoctrinate! Suggest! Help! Keep records of progress!"[12]

Unfortunately, in this field as in so many others, progress was hard to discern. With the drawdown, the US military was shifting back to the advisory model that had prevailed before the introduction of American combat troops in 1965. The advisers in this improvement and modernization program found little of either. American efforts to make the ARVN MSS more daring—more willing to launch "penetration operations" that would put agents at risk but gather critical human intelligence—foundered again on the ARVN's risk-averse nature.

The South Vietnamese preferred to compile "blacklists" of names divulged by defectors or in National Police interrogations, and then kill the people on the lists. They would kill over 26,000 South Vietnamese in the course of the program, many of whom were not actually VC—just a name coughed up during a rough interrogation or in a fit of pique. The killing was done by 4,000 PRUs, described by an American adviser as "extortion and assassination team[s] run directly by the CIA and composed mostly of criminals, deserters, and former Viet Cong." The deliverables of this refashioned Phoenix program were always scanty. No more than 7 percent of VC casualties were caused by Phoenix, and that figure was padded with large numbers of innocents. The Americans wanted the South Vietnamese to kill less and focus more on recruiting agents, penetrating the VCI, and collecting actionable intelligence instead of murdering it.[13]

In this too, the Americans were continually disappointed. In 1969, MACV labeled the ARVN's province-level Phoenix committees "an untouched pool of leads." The VC had five distinct intelligence organizations working at different echelons: hamlet, village, district, province, and central government. They were collecting and countering the Saigon government's intelligence at every turn. And yet try as they might—"Keep pressing! Suggest! Help!"—the Americans could not induce the ARVN Military Security Service to collect intelligence. The operatives considered that far too dangerous. They only did counterintelligence—usually assassinating VC suspects—because that was safer.[14]

No ARVN officer in his right mind wanted to volunteer for a "penetration operation" that might be disclosed to the enemy (by a VC agent inside the MSS) or converted into a PRU "neutralization operation" while the penetrator was still among the soon-to-be-neutralized. And so nothing much happened. The ARVN's Military Security Service refused to coordinate with other government agencies to widen their net, leaving officers and clerks sitting in their offices stacking up index cards with the names and aliases of VCI suspects. The MSS evinced no regret or determination to do better.[15]

And yet with General Abrams shifting more emphasis to population security and pacification, the Phoenix (Phung Hoang) Program was more important than ever. Those five levels of VC intelligence that kept a watch over every inch of South Vietnam, from the presidential palace down to the meanest hamlet, had to be decisively met and countered if the Saigon government had any hope of turning back the communist tide. MACV and the CIA challenged the South Vietnamese to avail themselves of yet more financial and logistical support in return for a commitment to destroy 5 percent of the VCI in every province every month—yet another statistical measure of progress all but begging to be abused.[16]

In March 1969, an American team toured Kien Tuong province in IV Corps to see how the beefed-up, reenergized Phoenix program was functioning. It wasn't. They debriefed the departing US Phoenix adviser and learned that in meetings of the province's Phung Hoang Committee, the South Vietnamese Phoenix director had no official authority over anything and slammed into "a wall of passivity" whenever he requested anything. The province's Phoenix Program was pathetic: twenty index cards with the names of twenty VC suspects, none with photos, physical descriptions, or any operational data. "No collation or analysis takes place here," the American reported. "The South Vietnamese just re-type reports and re-disseminate them to other offices." Spycatchers they were not.[17]

The Americans had advised the ARVN to name Phoenix coordinators at the province and district levels, individuals who would get the first crack at every piece of intelligence gleaned in the towns and villages. That way they could move swiftly against VC suspects. Coordinators had been assigned for new Provincial Intelligence and Operation Coordinating Centers (PIOCCs) and District Intelligence and Operation Coordinating Centers (DIOCCs), two more exotic blooms of the flourishing bureaucracy that employed so many South Vietnamese and Americans. But none of the existing agencies sent these new PIOCCs and DIOCCs information. They just continued to send their scraps of intelligence to whomever they were used to sending them to. The DIOCCs in the province, the Americans remarked, were nothing more than "paper entities," indifferently shuffled by whichever junior officer the province chief assigned the task. "Their files are sparse or non-existent, with no distinction made between VCI and ordinary VC guerrillas." They routinely reported civilian KIAs as VCI to "meet monthly neutralization quotas." None of the districts had ever produced a single targeted neutralization.[18]

With reigning apathy like this, there was no need for wary South Vietnamese to actually obstruct the work of Phoenix—total indifference would do nicely. Once again, American efforts to impose their priorities on the South Vietnamese failed, a fact glumly admitted by the MSS' ranking Phoenix adviser: "Since pursuit of VCI must necessarily rest in Vietnamese hands, we need forceful leadership at all levels, but there is little hope for improvement because there is no production of useful intelligence and no reaction to that intelligence."[19]

To bolster the South Vietnamese, Abrams instructed US units fighting in Vietnam to make the anti-VCI campaign a "top priority." VCI, Abrams explained, was more important to the enemy than his main-force units. "It's the part he can't let go down the drain." Unfortunately, the Americans did as badly at this as the South Vietnamese. In January 1969, Major Marcel

Wiedmaier led a military intelligence team on a tour of I Corps to verify that all US units there were giving their "total support" to operations against the Viet Cong infrastructure. The Marines were all in, but the Army, which now dominated I Corps, showed no interest.

"Phoenix people handle anti-VCI" was a common refrain in Army units and headquarters, usually followed by "We have no specific tasking on that." At a two-hour roundtable in Da Nang, attended by every Army and Marine senior officer involved in military intelligence, Wiedmaier was most struck by the zeal of the Marines—"We've given the anti-VCI campaign our top priority and total support"—and the indifference of the Army. "Lieutenant Colonel Dunkelberger, representing the 525th Military Intelligence Group, sat silently until he was asked what he is doing in anti-VCI. He replied: 'I've got no specific tasking on that, we do orders of battle and lines of communication. The Phoenix people handle VCI.'" This was astonishing. The brigade-strength 525th Military Intelligence Group was MACV's principal intelligence arm. It was headquartered at Tan Son Nhut Airport, near MACV headquarters, yet had somehow contrived to ignore Abrams' new priority.[20]

Buck-passing was everywhere on display. Wiedmaier and his team visited the Americal Division's interrogation center at Cape Batangan. If any Army unit was going to show interest in the VCI, it should have been the Americal. They were now the biggest US division in Vietnam and had just joined with the Marines in Operation Russell Beach, seizing the VC-fortified Batangan Peninsula in a three-week battle for the sandy cape honeycombed with bunkers and tunnels. Sixty Americans had died and 12,000 civilians had been evacuated for screening, the peninsula's fishing villages having been under VC control for twenty years. Wiedmaier's team met with a captain from Americal's military intelligence staff to observe the screening and interrogation of VCI suspects seized during Operation Russell Beach. "We don't get into VCI," the captain told Wiedmaier, who must have wondered if they weren't all reading from the same script. "Phoenix handles that. We just do order of battle stuff." When Wiedmaier then asked where the Phoenix people were, the captain shrugged—he had no idea.

Wiedmaier's team returned to Americal Division headquarters at Chu Lai to present their findings to the division's intelligence chief and his deputy. The two, a colonel and a major, listened and conferred, and then the

major said: "Nobody here really understands what is and what is not VCI."
Wiedmaier interrupted: "That's all spelled out in Big Mack and the VCI
Newsletters." Those were intelligence products that routed information on
VCI suspects from corps to division to province, and then stopped there,
which was one reason—but certainly not the only one—that the DIOCCs
were so ineffectual.

The two officers drew a blank, finally dispatching a sergeant to see if
either of them was on the distribution list for Big Mack and the VCI Newsletter. Both of them were. The Americal colonel abashedly explained that
"commanders here are really only interested in weapons and body count.
VCI is of no interest to them." There were 108 men in the division's military intelligence shop, but none of them were pursuing VCI in an area that
had been governed by the VC since the French colonial period. Wiedmaier
pressed: were they not aware of Abrams' emphasis on VCI and his message
to that effect of September 28, 1968? Yes, the colonel sighed, they were, but
since *everything* from Saigon came in over Abrams' signature, *everything*
had to have top priority.

In this haphazard way the US Army took the all-important hunt for
VCI about as seriously as the ARVN did, which was to say not seriously at
all. There were exceptions that showed what could be done and how the war
could have been waged more effectively. The Marines, with their small-war
emphasis and aptitude for fighting "among the people," embraced the
anti-VCI campaign. The Marines exhibited all of the patience and competence in this campaign that the Army lacked. During their ops they would
screen, say, 500 VCI suspects and come away with just four confirmed VCI.
But those were real VCI, and their capture was a real blow to the communist
organization.[21]

Wiedmaier and his team finished their tour of I Corps with a visit to
Thua Thien, the scarred region around Hue, where more American troops
died in the war than in any other province of South Vietnam. They met
there with the province's Phoenix coordinator and his two military deputies. Phoenix, the coordinator confessed, was bedeviled by "the problem
of inflated and unrealistic neutralization stats." The Army's body count
scam had been extended to its reporting on VCI neutralization. Units were
reporting neutralizations without knowing what job (if any) the target did
within the VCI, or even the full name of the victim. The South Vietnamese

routinely generated fake VCI lists to mollify Abrams and his staff. Later arguments by apologists for the American failure in Vietnam—that Phoenix "neutralized" as many as 60,000 communist agents, for example—were based on the cooked numbers of MACV, the ARVN, and the CIA, not reality.[22]

Viet Cong pressure on the South Vietnamese people tightened as Saigon's vigilance and authority slipped. In all four corps areas, VC cadres and security section chiefs organized the population to join the fight and "annihilate all tyrants." There was nothing voluntary about it. Peasants were ordered to contribute the maximum in labor and taxes. In a typical hamlet, that meant between $10 and $100 per person as well as in-kind contributions of rice. Word was passed to peasants who had fled to refugee camps in government-controlled areas to return, or their homes and property would be confiscated. The VC dispatched villagers to the markets to buy rice, salt, and fish for the communist forces, and ordered other villagers to dig the spike pits and plant the mines and booby traps that took such a bloody toll on allied forces. Others were pressed into service as porters, lugging food and ammo to the hidden main-force units. The communists were in a hurry because they assumed that any peace deal in Paris would freeze the military situation where it stood whenever a cease-fire was announced. They wanted to bring as much territory as they could under their control as rapidly as possible.[23]

Abrams responded with his own "Accelerated Pacification Program"— what his aides called a "land rush." He too wanted to snatch back as much territory as he could from the VC before a cease-fire intervened. Both sides expected an armistice to be agreed in Paris by the end of 1969. CORDS, now in the hands of Bill Colby, estimated that the VC still controlled half of the South Vietnamese population and was bidding for more, pushing "liberation committees" into government-controlled hamlets. Colby sold Abrams on a plan to bring 1,000 contested or communist-controlled hamlets under firm government control within ninety days, starting in November 1968.[24]

As always, IV Corps, the watery Mekong Delta region, remained an intractable hub of VC activity, threatening Saigon and the food supply, and serving as a land bridge between the communist sanctuaries in Cambodia, the Saigon Circle, and the lush Delta, where 6 million South Vietnamese lived and worked. The ARVN had three entire divisions in IV Corps, but they remained as gun-shy as ever. Observing an ARVN battalion "sweeping" the ground around Sa Dec—a river port on the Mekong heavily trafficked by the VC—Peter Kann of the *Wall Street Journal* shook his head in disbelief. It was midafternoon, not night, and here were "three companies of ARVN soldiers, accompanied by armored personnel carriers, marching down the middle of the road—hardly the place to locate and engage enemy forces." This was search and avoid on a grand scale. The enemy forces, of course, would be swinging in their hammocks at this hour, resting for their nighttime exertions, when those ARVN companies would be back in their sandbagged bunkers. No one having discovered a way to fight and defeat the communists in IV Corps—it had been the source of John Paul Vann's complaints as far back as 1962—Abrams decided to approve what became one of the most notorious operations of the war: General Julien Ewell's Operation Speedy Express.[25]

Chapter 20

"I WILL NOT BE
THE FIRST PRESIDENT
TO LOSE A WAR"

Kien Hoa province in IV Corps was close to Saigon, home to the big towns of My Tho and Ben Tre. It had been under informal VC control since at least 1960, despite the presence there of the ARVN 7th Division and large numbers of ruff-puffs, US aircraft, and advisers. The province, girt by two arms of the Mekong River and crisscrossed by canals, had seen fierce combat during Tet, when US air strikes and artillery had flattened Ben Tre and a major of the US 9th Infantry Division had famously told reporter Peter Arnett that "it became necessary to destroy the town to save it." In the predictable way of the Vietnam War, the VC had flowed back in as the Americans flowed out after Tet, and so Kien Hoa, dominated again by the VC, became a prime target of Abe Abrams' "land rush" and Julien Ewell's Operation Speedy Express.

The Army would later investigate and cover up General Ewell's conduct, which was barbaric. In his eagerness to submit a "record-breaking" body count of 10,889 dead VC, Ewell and the 8,000 men of the 9th ID killed thousands of civilians between December 1968 and May 1969, when the grisly operation was finally terminated. Conservative estimates submitted by the Army's own inspector general put the likely number of noncombatant deaths included in Ewell's 10,889 body count somewhere between 5,000 and 7,000.[1]

In Kien Hoa, the fifty-three-year-old Ewell ran into the same problems American officers were encountering everywhere else in Vietnam. It was hard to *find* the communists. They sidestepped the big daytime sweeps and operated at night to maintain their control over the local people and the economy. Ewell's division psychiatrist worried about the outfit's morale, with the men dealing every day "with the same old thing": base camp life in soggy, unlit tents, with everyone on bunker guard or thirty-minute alert, or life in the field, where "you walk all day and ambush at night, either sleeping in the trees or on the dikes, or just curling up in the mud with the snakes, mosquitoes, and leeches."[2]

These problems were magnified by the dense population of the Mekong Delta, which made it harder than anywhere else to use the firepower central to the American approach. Six million people were crammed into less than 15,000 square miles. The US embassy in Saigon had pressed the Army to stay out of the Delta for fear that it would end up killing too many civilians. But in the "land rush" of 1969, Ewell's 9th ID, which earlier had operated as a "Mobile Riverine Force," attacking the VC in the streams and marshes of the Delta, was authorized to carry the fight into the cluttered towns and villages. Of Abrams' "one-war" concept, Ewell commented: "Like most powerful ideas it was very simple. Also, like most ideas in Vietnam it was difficult in execution."[3]

Especially, he might have added, when executed his way. The result was exactly the carnage the State Department had feared. In Operation Speedy Express, Ewell took the 1st Brigade of the 9th ID into Kien Hoa and let them rip. He used fifty howitzers, fifty gunships, and 3,400 tactical air strikes to desolate the province in four months of mayhem, relying on sudden air assaults to take on the small VC units where they appeared—"barreling in at 120 knots, the skids only a few feet above the rice, then slamming to a hovering halt with a pounding flapping of rotor blades."[4]

Pitched battles were rare. Normally the division smashed down villages and farms, machine-gunned and rocketed peasants from the air, and burned fields, orchards, and hamlets. Among the claimed body count of 10,889, Ewell produced only 748 captured weapons. The 76:1 "kill ratio" that the general trumpeted as evidence of his prowess was ten to fifteen times the norm. Would not so many dead VC have taken more Americans with them? Hospital admissions in the province were overwhelmingly attributed to careless American fire. In Ben Tre, 76 percent of civilians admitted to the hospital during the operation had wounds from American munitions.[5]

Ewell and his chief of staff, Colonel Ira Hunt, defended what they did. "We took the night away from the enemy," Hunt boasted. "They just totally unraveled in the Delta." Hunt commanded Ewell's 1st Brigade during Speedy Express. He equipped gunship pilots and door gunners with night-vision equipment, and instructed his troops and pilots to assume that anything moving in the dark was VC. Hunt named these night flights the "Phantom III hunter-killer program."

Louis Janowski, a US adviser in the Delta who ended up summoning medevacs for civilians wounded by Phantom III, called the program "non-selective terrorism." He confirmed that the vast majority of Phantom III's victims were not VC. He personally witnessed ops in which fewer than one in ten of the victims was VC. The killing, in other words, was entirely indiscriminate, just mowing down the general population to hike the body count. "Air sports" was how one jacked-up gunship pilot described his work: there was "nothing finer, you're up there at two thousand, you're God, just open up the flexies and watch it pee, nail those slime to the paddy wall, nothing finer, double back and get the caribou."[6]

Colonel Hunt also expanded the use of snipers. A sniper team was attached to each of the 1st Brigade's four battalions and basically told to shoot anyone who appeared in their sights. Two veterans of the 9th ID's operations in the Delta, future senator Chuck Hagel and David "Hack" Hackworth, had an entirely negative view of the operation. Hackworth, who commanded Hunt's best infantry battalion, called the colonel a "liar" and judged Hunt's "victory" in Speedy Express "as make-believe as a paper moon."[7]

Other officers reported that they were inserted into the field and told to stay there till they had increased their body counts. R&R allocations, stand-downs, and medals were made contingent on high body counts. The eagerness of the grunts to escape the misery of the Delta for one of MACV's stand-down R&R centers, such as the "Tay Ninh Holiday Inn" or "Waikiki East" in Cu Chi, appears to have made them more willing to shoot civilians and add them to the body count. "Free-fire zones," where anyone could be judged an enemy and killed, were liberally granted. Artillery, tac air, gunships, snipers, and even B-52s attacked without restraint in these areas. Air strikes and artillery were routinely fired into populated areas. Hackworth noted that Ewell's 9th ID took credit for 20,000 VC dead in 1968–1969, yet produced only 2,000 weapons for all of those KIAs. "How much of the 'body count' consisted of civilians?" Hackworth asked.[8]

Commanders like Ewell and Hunt were reacting to their frustration with the way the enemy operated. Sampans, the motorized fishing boats that plied the rivers and canals, were often stocked with goods for communist forces—ammo, rice, fish sauce, sugar, milk, water purification tablets, hammocks, mosquito netting, and all of the other things the guerrillas needed to operate in the marshy wilderness. In most cases, the sampans were owned by an entrepreneur who would buy goods in a market and then sell them to the VC at 400 percent markups. Was such a person a civilian or a combatant? It was hard to say. The sampans would be unloaded by hired laborers, who would lug the cargo to cache points, where, at night, VC troops would appear to carry the items to their jungle hideouts. Were the laborers civilians or combatants? In any event, there were simply more sampans and trawlers moving around on any given day than could be inspected. The Mobile Riverine Force inspected about 70,000 a year, which hinted at the sheer volume. Ewell and Hunt decided to shoot first and ask questions later, if at all.[9]

A year after the operation ended, a 9th ID whistleblower sent anonymous letters to General Westmoreland, the Army chief of staff in Washington, alleging that civilians had been slaughtered with the full knowledge and complicity of commanders—to drive up the body count. The whistleblower, who signed the letters "Concerned Sergeant," revealed that the 9th ID under General Ewell had perpetrated "a My Lai each month for over a year" in the Delta and had gotten away with it. Ewell had acquired a nickname—"the Butcher of the Delta"—which he seemed to enjoy, joking that his peers considered him more ruthless than Attila the Hun.[10]

Abrams refused interview requests on the subject and referred reporters to his MACV spokesmen, who feigned ignorance of the Speedy Express rules of engagement and determinedly hushed up the controversy, proclaiming the operation a resounding success. Abrams dismissed VC reports of atrocities in the Mekong Delta as "propaganda." He called Ewell's Speedy

Express performance "magnificent" and promoted Ewell to the corps command of II Field Force, which defended III Corps.

In Washington, Westmoreland's office identified the "Concerned Sergeant" as George Lewis, who had served in the Delta with the 9th ID from June 1968 to May 1969 and received a Purple Heart. Lewis had served in Hunt's brigade and Hackworth's battalion as a radio operator. As such, he had overheard Ewell's "cussing and screaming" and Hack's radio calls. They contained none of the compassion or principled opposition that Hackworth took credit for in his memoirs. Hack, Lewis wrote, would say things like "I don't give a shit, shoot them anyway, women or not." Reading these allegations, Westmoreland made no effort to contact Lewis, and he and Abrams stamped out efforts by the secretary of the Army's general counsel to investigate the alleged atrocities. Coming on the heels of My Lai, it would have been too embarrassing for the Army, not least because all of the principals—Westmoreland, Abrams, Ewell, and Hunt—were West Point graduates. Their failures were the Army's failures.[11]

In 2002, journalist Nick Turse did some digging in the National Archives of the United States and discovered files that converted 1969's allegations of atrocity into fact. It was Ewell's own senior officer debriefing report, submitted in September 1969, that kindled Turse's suspicion, the general allowing that in many areas where "discriminate and selective use of firepower was not feasible, the countryside looked like the Verdun battlefields." That reference to the desolated moonscape of 1916, where more than fifty French villages had been permanently erased from the map in World War I's most notorious battle, persuaded Turse to investigate further.

He found George Lewis' ten-page letter to Westmoreland of May 1970, and two others, which the Army had also suppressed. The letters described orders and policies within the 9th ID that made civilian massacres inevitable. "Sir," Lewis opened the first letter, "the 9th Division did nothing to prevent the killing, and by pushing the body count so hard, we were 'told' to kill many times more Vietnamese than at My Lai, and very few per cent of them did we know were enemy."

Sergeant Lewis then listed his evidence: "In case you don't think I mean lots of Vietnamese got killed this way, I can give you some idea how many. A battalion would kill maybe 15 to 20 a day. With 4 battalions in the Brigade that would be maybe 40 to 50 a day or 1,200 to 1,500 a month, easy. (One battalion claimed almost 1000 body counts one month!) If I am only 10% right, and believe me it's lots more, then I am trying to tell you about 120–150 murders, or a My Lai each month for over a year." The sniper teams, Lewis wrote, never rested, and they made no distinction between VC and civilians. "The snipers would get 5 or 10 a day, and I think all 4 battalions had sniper teams. That's 20 a day or at least 600 each month." The snipers alone, Lewis surmised, probably killed as many civilians as had been slaughtered at My Lai.[12]

The "number-one killer" of civilians during Operation Speedy Express was the 1st Brigade's policy of shooting anyone who ran. If a peasant ran from the approach of a US platoon or helicopter—and who wouldn't, with the "Butcher of the Delta" afield?—he or she would be treated as VC and killed. "Helicopters would hover over a guy in a field till he got scared and run and they'd zap him," Lewis wrote.

Snipers were encouraged to shoot civilians even if they didn't run, to pad a body count that was relentlessly driven upward. "The General in charge and all the commanders were riding us all the time to get a big body count." Lewis noted that all commanders were embarrassed by their failure to find weapons among all of the fallen "VC," and so lies were offered instead—saying, for example, that they had captured weapons but destroyed them by dropping them into streams, canals, and paddies. They said this even during dry season in the Delta, when the streams, canals, and paddies were dusty flats. "The General," Lewis wrote, "must have known this was made up."[13]

Colonel Ira Hunt, presiding in his command and control helicopter, drove the killing to insane heights. He later denied it all in postwar interviews, but Lewis, pilots who flew Hunt around, and other dissidents such as General Robert Gard, who commanded the 9th ID's five artillery battalions during Speedy Express, confirmed it. Gard recalled that Hunt cherished his nickname and call sign, "Rice-Paddy Daddy." The colonel, Gard said, was even more "berserk" than Ewell in the quest for corpses. A pilot who flew Hunt's command and control chopper described Hunt ordering his door gunner to shoot anyone on the ground in black pajamas. "Well sir, I thought workers in the fields wore black pajamas," the pilot protested. "No, not around here," Hunt replied. "Black pajamas are Viet Cong."

Sergeant Lewis described patrols where "Hunt used to holler and curse over the radio and talk about the goddamn gooks and tell the gunships to shoot the sonsofbitches, because this is a free-fire zone." If they were unarmed women, it made no difference to Hunt. When artillery forward observers (FOs) refused to fire on populated areas, battalion and company commanders—intimidated by Hunt—would order the guns to fire anyway. "The FO would tell my company commander that he couldn't shoot in the village because it was in the population overlay." Hearing this, the battalion commander "would get mad and cuss over the radio at my company commander and declare a contact [with the enemy] so the FO would shoot anyway." Not warning shots—high explosive, right into the houses, right away. Abrams and his staff *must* have spotted the anomaly that the 9th ID had the highest kill ratio in Vietnam but the lowest weapons-captured-to-enemy-killed ratio.

John Paul Vann returned to the Delta in February 1969 as civilian director of pacification efforts in IV Corps. He was appalled by everything he saw. As a civilian CORDS adviser when Ewell's year of command was running out, Vann described the Phantom III and daylight "hunter-killer" missions as especially harmful: "The U.S. is on very shaky ground. Literally hundreds of examples have been documented by irate advisers, both military and civilian." Vann went along on many of the raids and reported that no effort was made to distinguish between civilians and VC. The pilots and gunners were ordered to kill every living being they saw on the ground, including farm animals.[14]

Ultimately, there was method to the madness of Ewell and Hunt. They were trying to solve two problems quickly. Militarily, they wanted to overcome the problem that hampered every operation in Vietnam—the inability to find and kill a stealthy enemy. Seven out of every eight operations in 1968–1969 made no contact with the enemy. Ewell and Hunt introduced "night raids," using Cobra gunships and heliborne infantry to hit villages suspected of harboring VC. This flushed some VC, who had come into the villages to eat, rest, and proselytize, but killed far more civilians. When Abrams called their performance "magnificent" and "unparalleled and unequaled," knowing full well that the body count was faked, Ewell and Hunt can be forgiven for assuming that they had solved the first problem, however cruelly and immorally. After all, with no firm rules of engagement in force, *all* of Ewell's operations "made contact with the enemy." It looked like progress, the rarest glimmer of good news.[15]

The second problem was more political. Ewell and Hunt were instruments in Abrams' "land rush"—to claw territory out of VC hands before an armistice was struck in Paris. They successfully "liberated" 120,000 inhabitants of the Delta and pushed the communists away from the big towns. Before Speedy Express, the VC had controlled 45 percent of the Delta's population. After the ferocious operation, they controlled just 24 percent. Some point to operations like this as proof of the success of Abrams' "better war." But what a "liberation" it was. Thousands of innocents were slaughtered, villages and towns destroyed, livestock, schools, and clinics liquidated. And those 120,000 who were successfully "pacified" were anything but. They flowed into more wretched refugee centers to contemplate all that they had lost and to hear the increasingly attractive entreaties of the Viet Cong, who worked the refugee camps and urban shantytowns as assiduously as the hamlets. Abe Abrams' determination to "exploit superior firepower and mobility" was nothing new, and it had the same effect as Westy's airmobile operations: it killed civilians.[16]

When *Newsweek* reporter Kevin Buckley toured the Delta two years later, he discovered that Operation Speedy Express had touched the lives of literally everyone there, and not for the better: "In each of the many places where I went, the testimony was the same: 100 killed here, 200 killed there. One old man summed up all the stories: 'The Americans killed some VC, but not many. But of the civilians, there were a large number killed.'"[17]

Jeffrey Record, a twenty-five-year-old graduate student at Johns Hopkins University, spent a year as a civilian adviser for psyops in Bac Lieu province, which bordered Kien Hoa. Record was in the Delta during Operation Speedy Express and was struck by the speed with which the rule of "modest restraint" when it came to the use of firepower in densely populated areas was replaced by the Ewell-Hunt practice of unrestrained firepower. Until Operation Speedy Express, provinces like Bac Lieu and Kien Hoa had been off-limits to naval bombardments, B-52 strikes, and even .50-caliber machine guns, whose range and velocity made them difficult to confine. Air strikes by gunships or fighters could be summoned from the IV Corps air base in Can Tho in a pinch, but, given the nature of the war in the Delta, they were rarely needed or even suitable. It would take thirty minutes for friendly aircraft to arrive overhead. By then, the enemy would be gone.[18]

Restraint in the use of firepower, however, had always been opposed, Record observed, "by older officers, many close to retirement, for whom Vietnam provided their first and last chance to see real combat." Such men, Record recalled, "found the idea of restraint incompatible with war" and never ceased agitating against it. Record, who went on to teach strategy at the Air War College in Montgomery, Alabama, noted that officials in favor of "modest restraint"—the province and district chiefs and the US advisers attached to their headquarters—would marshal three arguments against these trigger-happy officers: the moral argument that innocents would die, the political argument that neutrals would be converted to VC, and the military argument that there were few if any targets to warrant the massive application of artillery and air strikes in the Mekong Delta, where full-time, hard-core VC were constantly moving and hidden.

To the moral argument, the firepower advocates answered: "War is hell." To the political argument, they answered that by driving the people into refugee camps, they would at least put the civilians under government control and deny their resources to the VC. The military argument they "dismissed out of hand." If there were no targets, they mulishly insisted, what was the harm in strafing fields, woods, and streams?

Record made another important observation, too often overlooked in discussions of the war. Mowing down civilians and their huts came to serve a crucial *bureaucratic* purpose. In Bac Lieu province, there were an estimated 3,000 VC opposed by 20,000 government troops—elements of the ARVN 21st Division plus ruff-puffs and the new Popular Self-Defense Force (PSDF) organized by Vice President Ky. In the entire province, there were only three small "free-fire zones," where locals had been evacuated and airpower and artillery could be used freely. Everywhere else, the people were densely packed around the hamlets and canals.

The only feasible way to defeat the VC in this environment was to pry them out one by one, using police methods and intelligence. But when Ewell made Cobra gunships widely available to every province in IV Corps for Phantom III raids in October 1968, Record noted that the pressure from higher headquarters to use them was too powerful to resist. Record's province, Bac Lieu, would get them on Mondays and Thursdays. In theory, they were meant to destroy enemy personnel and installations and generally "harass and terrorize" the VC. This ignored the problem that no one knew where the VC and their "installations" were. If they did, those 20,000 South Vietnamese troops and thousands more police would have been sufficient to round them up.

But no one focused on *that* problem. They focused on another: the *programmatic* need to find a use for Bell Helicopter's new Cobra gunship, which was a technological marvel and a killing machine whose airspeed (170 miles per hour) and rate of fire from its flex guns was so high that it was inevitably underutilized in the crowded Delta. The Cobra, recently introduced to the war, was an armored attack helicopter built to survive antiaircraft fire around hot LZs and to give withering fire support to embattled troops on the ground. It had a crew of two—pilot and gunner—and its only load was ammunition for its guns: two rocket pods on stub wings with fifty-two 70 mm rockets, and either a chin-mounted turret mini gun that fired 100 rounds a *second* or twin 40 mm grenade launchers that pumped out 400 grenades a minute.

MACV pressured the province chiefs and their senior American advisers to welcome the Phantom III missions and find a use for the Cobras. The pressure was not subtle. If the Cobras were not fully utilized—if they did not generate body count and devastation that could be relayed to Saigon and Washington as "indispensable achievements"—then the Cobras would be sent to other theaters, or face program cuts in Congress.

To avoid this fate, IV Corps headquarters cut the Delta into slices and sent Phantom III missions of two or three Cobras on a fixed schedule over every slice every week. No effort was expended to figure out which slice needed Cobras more than another. They all got Cobras twice a week and were expected to submit impressive results. The VC in every province immediately figured out what days were Phantom III days and laid low, especially in the "free-fire zones," which the Cobras rocketed with thousands of dollars of wasted ordnance. Of the few unscheduled missions, Record noted that the VC received advance warning of them from their network of informers in every ARVN and provincial headquarters.

Had that been the extent of the waste, it would have been manageable. But it wasn't. There was constant organizational pressure to claim more enemy "killed by air" and "structures destroyed," none being available in the desolated free-fire zones. And so the Phantom III missions began attacking populated areas and classifying the dead and wounded there as Viet Cong. Record, who interviewed VC defectors in the province, was told that the Cobras were shooting up the canals and sweeping over fields to mow down the peasants and their water buffalo. An American working in Bac Lieu's hospital told him that, despite a decrease in combat operations, more and more civilians were being admitted with wounds from Cobra rockets, mini guns, and grenades. Most of them were women and children.

Record took this information to the American officers in Bac Lieu's Tactical Operations Center (TOC), where he was told: "We don't shoot individuals on the ground unless they run away when the Cobras approach. People that run must be VC. Why else would they run unless they had something to hide?" Record shared his findings with the province senior adviser, who told him that official pressure to use the Cobras was now irresistible and that he would do his best to restrain the Phantom III missions in the same way that he had tried to restrain the use of artillery and tac air in the province. "He failed to grasp," Record later wrote, "that the problem lay not in their *indiscriminate* use but in the very nature of the gunships themselves. *Any* use of Cobras in a densely populated province having only a small enemy presence would be indiscriminate."[19]

Record asked to ride along in the command and control helicopter of a Phantom III mission. He said he wanted to scatter psyops leaflets, but his real purpose was to see for himself what was going on. He was stunned by what he observed from the air: "Returning from my first mission I witnessed the machinegunning of an entire herd of water buffalo along with the six or seven buffalo boys who were tending the herd. No command had been given. The Cobras simply broke formation and began their deadly dives. Within seconds the still waters of the rice paddy in which the buffalos and their little friends had been resting was transformed into a bloody ooze littered with bits of mangled flesh. The dead boys and the water buffalo were added to the official body count of the Viet Cong."

Once back on the ground in Bac Lieu, Record went to the TOC and demanded—"as a human being and a Psychological Operations Adviser"— that the Cobra pilots be punished. He got the runaround: "They're not under our command," "Can Tho has jurisdiction," and so on. "What had started out as a program to hamper Viet Cong operations," Record concluded, "had become an unmanageable and monstrous terror directed against the entire rural population." Scruples and conscience availed nothing against the measures of success required by Abrams and Ewell. "Pilots had become mesmerized by the familiar litany of aerial warfare in Vietnam—'kills by air, sampans sunk, enemy structures destroyed.' The Phantom program had increased by twofold the enemy body count demanded every month by insatiable computers in Saigon."[20]

As the Operation Speedy Express "land rush" petered out in June 1969, Nixon flew west and Thieu flew east to convene on Midway Island. Nixon had wanted to hold the summit in California, but he worried that it might be marred by antiwar protests, to say nothing of Thieu's intransigence. Midway, whose only inhabitants were a few thousand well-behaved US government employees, was chosen instead. The peace talks that had resumed in Paris after Nixon's inauguration were still going nowhere. The communist demands for a total US withdrawal, the resignation of Thieu and his ministers, and a vote by the South Vietnamese people for a Provisional Revolutionary Government molded by Hanoi collided with Thieu's "Four No's": no recognition of the VC, no neutralization of South Vietnam, no coalition government, and no surrender of territory.[21]

In Hanoi, the politburo was absorbing the heavy, painful losses of 1968–1969 and adjusting. They officially abandoned the "quick military victory" scheme that had powered Tet and Mini-Tet, and opted instead in mid-1969 for a policy of "partial victories during the period of U.S. withdrawal." Their team in Paris would delay American negotiators while giving every appearance of cooperation. They called this revised strategy "talk and fight." With President Thieu carping about American faithlessness, Nixon assured him at the Midway Conference on June 8 that Washington would back Saigon to the hilt and insist on the allied country's "self-determination without interference" by the hordes of NVA and VC troops camped in South Vietnam and the sanctuaries.[22]

How Nixon would insist on *anything* was hard to see. The chief takeaway of the Midway Conference was that the Americans were leaving as quickly as they could. MACV's mission statement was quietly amended. The old one had called for the defeat and removal of the NVA from South Vietnam. The new one pledged nothing more than "maximum assistance" to Saigon and a rapid expansion of the ARVN and the territorial forces.

Nixon officially terminated the Johnson administration policies of escalation and attrition at Midway and announced his own intention to withdraw 115,000 American troops over the next seven months.

The force of 543,000 American troops present in Vietnam when Nixon was sworn in would be leaving as fast as they could be moved to the exits. More funds would be earmarked for "improvement and modernization" to permit the replacement of Americans with South Vietnamese. The Big Red One, which had been holding the Iron Triangle since 1965, would be replaced by the ARVN 5th Division. The US 4th Infantry Division, which had fought so many battles in the Central Highlands since 1966, would be replaced by the ARVN 22nd Division. The US 9th Infantry Division, which had been in the Delta since 1967, would be replaced by the ARVN 7th Division. Nixon's "Midway Package" pledged to offset these American "redeployments" by increasing the South Vietnamese regular armed forces to a million troops in 1970 and the irregular ruff-puff and self-defense forces to 2.5 million troops or more.[23]

Nixon's Midway Package also called for an "accelerated pacification program" that had the usual ring of fakery—intended more to check boxes and peddle statistics than solve problems on the ground. The aim was to rapidly bring *all* of South Vietnam's population under government control, as if that had not already been tried many times by many programs.[24]

The Saigon government remained unreformed, its pillars the same as they were under Diem: the army, the uniformed province and district chiefs, the religious communities, and, lastly, the political parties. All American and South Vietnamese hopes now resided in President Thieu, who had been funded and shielded by the Americans and increasingly enjoyed an unassailable position. But for what exactly? Thieu's network of power owed everything to the Americans and would collapse if anything happened to Thieu. Like the weak and powerless parties, Thieu's network was not institutionalized, and it was relatively old and graying. Young people gave up on it and turned to the Viet Cong. The best that could be hoped for, sympathetic foreign observers noted, was an authoritarian regime with local democracy at the village level and a moderate president in charge of a well-led and contented army. But even those modest goals looked far out of reach.[25]

In Paris, the negotiations had been deadlocked for fifteen months. In South Vietnam, Hanoi's "neo-revolutionary guerrilla war," announced in

April 1969, was proving far more potent than in the past thanks to all of the new Soviet and Chinese weaponry that had been passed down the Ho Chi Minh Trail in the meantime. Marine and Army records in 1969 became a dismal catalog of grunts maimed and killed by booby traps, command-detonated mines, ambushes, and regular mortar and rocket attacks on fuel and ammo dumps, airfields, and ports. US aircraft had to make short runs and steep climbs out of air bases all over the country to offer the smallest possible target to VC with shoulder-fired rockets assumed to be hidden just beyond the perimeter of every allied airfield and helipad. Returning to base, these same aircraft "crash dived," dropping onto their runways like a stone.

The Defense Intelligence Agency began enumerating new measures of failure—"aircraft destroyed on the ground" and "bridges damaged and destroyed." Both categories showed rising weekly losses in all corps areas in 1969. An analyst was called before the Senate to estimate the future cost of death pensions and disability payments for the tens of thousands of Americans killed and the 160,000 Americans severely wounded in the war. He confirmed that those items would end up costing more than the war itself. Pressed to say exactly how much, he threw up his arms in frustration: "The impact of Vietnam is so gigantic and diffuse that no adequate calculation can be made at this time."[26]

In the course of 1969, more South Vietnamese were brought back under government control. By year-end, Saigon claimed that it controlled 92 percent of the population, as compared with 67 percent two years earlier on the eve of Tet. Much of this "control" was owed not to Saigon's prowess but to the American creation of refugees, so many that a population that had been 80 percent rural ten years earlier was now half rural and half urban. For the communists, the urban population was harder to reach and exploit. This explained Hanoi's strategic shift in 1969 back to "protracted warfare," to "take back the cities, countryside, and the mountains" and defeat Abrams' pacification program and strategy of clear and hold.[27]

Hanoi had a clear view of Nixon's plan and what they needed to do to thwart it. Their own planning documents stressed the need to attack US forces, inflict casualties, demoralize the Americans, and stop them from "exiting the war from a position of strength." The United States had to be driven out swiftly and completely, so that they could not "deescalate gradually" and take the time to modernize the ARVN. The communists planned to "neutralize and disintegrate" the largely unimproved South Vietnamese military so that it could never "clear and hold" the country and successfully "Vietnamize" the war.[28]

Nixon and Kissinger, who had deliberately prolonged this senseless war to get into office, now struggled to terminate it. They would not announce the first troop withdrawals until June 1969, but they knew that they had no mandate to escalate the war. Hanoi knew this too. With Hanoi refusing to recognize the Thieu government in the Paris talks and upbraiding Nixon for "demoting" the peace talks in his effort to gain military leverage, the negotiations stalled for months at a time. Nixon impatiently looked for ways to force Le Duan back to the table. Wheeler and Abrams recommended that he target the communist sanctuaries in Cambodia, which fueled the war in III and IV Corps. The president could blockade the port of Sihanoukville, or he could strike across the border with American troops. *That* would get Hanoi's attention.[29]

Prince Sihanouk had pursued his policy of "extreme neutrality" until this point. In practice, this meant cozying up to China and tolerating NVA and VC sanctuaries along Cambodia's border with South Vietnam. The Cambodians had no love for the South Vietnamese, but even if they had, their population was so small and their military so weak that Sihanouk felt that he had no choice but to permit Hanoi to use his territory, especially with the Americans so obviously losing the war in South Vietnam.

But parliamentary elections in 1966 had returned a conservative, nationalist majority, determined to erase the North Vietnamese sanctuaries and restore Cambodian sovereignty. General Lon Nol, who had served the French until 1954, had been named prime minister of a new Government of National Salvation. Two years later, in August 1968, Cambodia and the United States had resumed diplomatic relations. Prince Sihanouk had begun tacking back to the right. He feared the implications of Mao Zedong's Cultural Revolution, the spreading power of Hanoi on his territory, and the rising threat of Pol Pot's Khmer Rouge.[30]

To exploit this thaw in the Cambodian-American relationship, Nixon, Wheeler, and Abrams had decided to bomb the sanctuaries in Cambodia shortly after Nixon took office in 1969. Wheeler and Abrams deemed those Operation Menu raids "a prerequisite" to clean out the sanctuaries before

US forces began withdrawing so that the ARVN could battle the communists on more favorable terms. Nixon also wanted to show his teeth. With Hanoi refusing to concede Nixon's chief demand in Paris, which was that North Vietnam accept the Thieu government as a legitimate partner for peace, Nixon was desperate to up the ante—to, as Kissinger put it, land a "savage, punishing blow against this third-rate power." Nixon's "madman theory" held that enemies needed to fear that the president might use *any* amount of force to achieve his objective.[31]

Nixon, who had been Eisenhower's vice president in 1953, believed that the Chinese had agreed to end the Korean War only because they had feared that Ike might use nuclear weapons against them if they did not. Nixon was now trying to re-create that dynamic in Southeast Asia by increasing strategic bombing. "Must use the great power of the office *to do something*," he mused. "Now is the time to go for broke."

Nixon would start with the Cambodian sanctuaries, then hit the ones in Laos, and persuade Hanoi that he might just continue up the ladder to resume bombing North Vietnam with conventional and even nuclear weapons. The president ordered up a plan for this in 1969 and called it Operation Duck Hook. If Hanoi refused to bend in Paris, Nixon would bomb the Red River dikes (drowning the North Vietnamese population and food supply), carpet-bomb the country, mine the harbors, and, if the politburo still refused to yield, drop nuclear bombs around Hanoi and Haiphong. "I will not be the first president of the United States to lose a war," Nixon growled.[32]

Nixon's gambit would begin in Cambodia. This was hugely problematic, for Cambodia was a neutral nation. Bombing there could not precede a congressional declaration of war, yet Congress, eager to quit the war, would never even consider such a declaration. Secretary of Defense Melvin Laird, Secretary of State William Rogers, and even Kissinger, Nixon's national security adviser, had opposed the "secret bombing" for this reason—that it would not remain secret, and that it would incite lawmakers and the public to still greater opposition to the war. It would also derail or further delay the already faltering peace talks in Paris.

Nixon, however, was adamant. He authorized Operation Menu, an air campaign so secret that special arrangements had to be made to conceal it from the Air Force chief of staff and secretary, as well as everyone else outside a narrow inner circle. American B-52s pounded the Cambodian base areas for over a year—from March 1969 until May 1970.[33]

The first Menu raid—Operation Breakfast—was carried out by sixty B-52s flying from Guam. The aircrews dumped their bombs on Base Area 353, the region of Cambodia known to Americans as the "Fishhook," which was considered the likely headquarters of Pham Hung's COSVN. The devastation was as expected: each of the eight-engined B-52s released its thirty tons of bombs along an axis that was 1,000 feet wide and four miles long. But efforts by a ground team to discover what they actually hit were driven off by unsubdued North Vietnamese troops. A second Special Forces team sent to resume the search and "mop up" COSVN mutinied rather than march to a certain death. "We've done nothing more than poke a beehive with a stick," a Green Beret sneered. B-52s were no more than a palliative. The enemy still held the contested ground.[34]

But Nixon understood that airpower was the only power he had left—the only lever he had to shift Hanoi. Abrams, who saw his lever of ground troops shrinking, agreed and provided coordinates and ground controllers for new Menu missions stretching into 1970. Operation Lunch hit Base Area 609; Operation Snack hit Base Area 351; Operation Dinner hit Base Area 352; Operation Supper hit Base Area 740, and Operation Dessert hit Base Area 350. Four thousand sorties rained 104,000 tons of bombs on the NVA sanctuaries.

The secrecy of this "secret bombing" was maintained by subterfuge. Commands were relayed inside a tight circle, essentially the president, Wheeler, Laird, Abrams, General Bruce Holloway, who led the Strategic Air Command, and Admiral John McCain Jr., who was the CINCPAC in Honolulu. Once bombers were aloft, with targets inside South Vietnam, ground computers would switch their targets to new ones inside Cambodia. Only the pilots and navigators, who were sworn to secrecy, knew that the targets were in neutral Cambodia.[35]

All of this effort inconvenienced but did not dissuade the NVA, who simply moved things around to continue the war. They learned to disperse their shelters and supplies in such a way that they would not all be hit by the linear pattern of the B-52s. The communists moved critical infrastructure deeper into Cambodia, further destabilizing Sihanouk's regime.

The NVA May Offensive in 1969 was no less potent than that of the previous year, proof that supplies and troops were still moving smoothly through the sanctuaries. And Nixon's "secret" did not last long. In May 1969, William Beecher revealed it in the *New York Times*, setting off a desperate hunt inside the Nixon administration for the source of the leak. Kissinger aide Morton Halperin was illegally wiretapped for twenty-one months— another precursor, like the Chennault affair, of the dirty tricks that would lead to Watergate.[36]

The fury Nixon felt about his inability to terminate the war could only be directed inward, not outward. With the budget and dollar under continuous pressure, and the Senate in June 1969 demanding a greater voice in "national commitments" abroad, the White House announced a new Nixon Doctrine in July 1969 that made clear that the United States would share the burden of global defense with willing "proxies" such as South Vietnam, Israel, and Iran while reducing US troop deployments and easing tensions with China and the Soviet Union. America, Nixon said, had "a full plate" of commitments and would undertake no new ones "unless our national interests are very vitally involved." Countries under threat, from the NATO allies to South Korea and South Vietnam, would have to provide the manpower for their own defense. "Self-help" was the new mantra.[37]

But time was needed to "Vietnamize" South Vietnam and prepare it for its front-line role, and time was running out, for the communist plan to force the Americans out of the war was working. Nixon's support was softening. Students were restive. The press was critical. In June the Senate's National Commitments Resolution had passed overwhelmingly. It defined what a "national commitment" like the war in Vietnam was, and insisted that all future commitments be subject to legislative approval. Nixon's room for maneuver continued to shrink.

Nixon had campaigned and won on his plan to end the war, but there was no apparent plan or progress. Negotiations had resumed in Paris on January 16, 1969, but nothing had been achieved other than agreement on the shape of the conference table. It would be two separate tables with a smaller one inserted in between, so that the VC could pretend that they were sitting alongside the South Vietnamese government and the South Vietnamese could pretend that they were not. In April, American deaths in Vietnam reached 33,630, nearly 10,000 more than when Johnson had left office, and more than had died in the Korean War.

In May, the VC delegation in Paris had demanded a unilateral American withdrawal from Vietnam as the essential first step to peace. Nixon had responded with his first public plan to end the war. It was a fantasy, vowing to re-create the conditions of 1954: withdrawal of all foreign forces, implementation of the Geneva Accords, and internationally supervised elections. Nixon and Kissinger naively assumed that they could make Hanoi withdraw its forces from South Vietnam or, at the very least, permit the Americans to remove their forces in unhurried increments as ARVN forces were improved and modernized.

Hanoi demurred, demanding instead that they immediately be given a fixed timetable for the removal of all American troops. Either way, the communist forces would keep killing Americans until Nixon quailed. Internally, the NVA characterized their 1969 spring offensive as "a significant tactical and a great strategic victory, for we killed more Americans than we did in the 1968 spring offensive." Hanoi approvingly noted the political effect in the United States: "The anti-war movement flared up again strongly demanding the withdrawal of U.S. troops." In early August 1969, an increasingly frantic Nixon instructed Kissinger to hand an ultimatum to Le Duc Tho in Paris. Hanoi had until November 1 "to make major progress toward a solution." If there was no progress, Nixon would unleash "measures of the greatest consequence," by which he meant Operation Duck Hook.[38]

Opposition to the war took another ugly turn. "Give us six months," Kissinger had confidently told critics of the war when the new administration had taken office. Six months had passed with nothing to show for it. The Weathermen, a violent faction of the antiwar Students for a Democratic Society (SDS), vowed to "bring the war home," to expose Americans to the violence that was being heaped on Southeast Asia.

On October 8, 1969, the Weathermen launched the "Days of Rage" demonstrations in Chicago. Several hundred demonstrators trashed four blocks of Chicago's Gold Coast neighborhood, smashing windows, setting cars alight, and drawing a massive police reaction. The next day, 2,000 SDS protesters marched through Chicago, this time peacefully. The following day, 300 Weathermen returned, this time to the Loop, where they smashed more cars and storefronts. On October 15, 1969, more than a million

Americans—alarmed by the "secret bombing" and the slow pace of Nixon's promised withdrawal from Vietnam—marched in massive, synchronized demonstrations and held peace vigils in Washington, DC, New York, Boston, Chicago, Detroit, Denver, Miami, Los Angeles, and many other cities. These marches, the first nationwide protests against Nixon's conduct of the war, were collectively named the Moratorium to End the War in Vietnam. The honeymoon Nixon had enjoyed as a new president was over.[39]

Nixon was rattled. Polls showed that 55 percent of Americans now called themselves "doves." The number of self-described "hawks" had fallen to 31 percent, from 44 percent a year earlier. Support for the war dropped in every poll. The Moratorium was the first time that politically moderate middle-class families had come out to protest, and they did it peacefully, less in anger than in sadness at the mounting losses and destruction in Vietnam, as well as Nixon's "token pullout" of just 25,000 troops.[40]

"You don't need a weatherman to know which way the wind blows," Bob Dylan had sung—giving the radicals their name—and the wind was blowing harder than ever against Nixon's efforts to end the war on his terms. The Moratorium movement posed great danger to Nixon. It planned to organize more "national shutdowns" like the one on October 15 to oppose the horrors of the war and hold at least one "peace day" a month to stress the war's economic cost: 19 cents of every American tax dollar being spent in Vietnam, 54 cents of every tax dollar being spent on the US military. The Moratorium leaders hoped at the very least to provoke a taxpayer revolt. For their part, the Weather Underground mocked these moderates of the Moratorium movement. They were, the terrorists scoffed, "Johnny-come-latelies, Kennedy liberals responsible for the Vietnam War—45,000 dead later they come out against the war."[41]

These splits in the antiwar movement were cold comfort for the Nixon administration, which agonized over the rising tide of opposition. First Nixon tried mockery against these threats, dispatching Vice President Spiro Agnew to blast the spirit of "national masochism encouraged by an effete corps of impudent snobs who characterize themselves as intellectuals." Nixon vowed that he would not be swayed by "anarchy in the streets," but that so mischaracterized what had happened during the Moratorium that he went on television on November 3, just a year after his election, to plead for more time and patience.[42]

Nixon appealed to America's "great silent majority," pledging that "anything is negotiable except the right of the people of South Vietnam to determine their own future." He concluded with a swing at the antiwar movement: "Let us be united against defeat. North Vietnam cannot defeat or humiliate the United States. Only Americans can do that." After briefly jumping in the polls, he exulted in the Oval Office: "We've got those liberal bastards on the run, and we're going to keep them on the run now." It was false bravado. The public was more excited by Nixon's pledge in the speech to "Vietnamize" the war completely and to enact a "timetable" for complete American withdrawal than by anything else in it.[43]

Two days before the speech, Nixon had been compelled, as he himself put it, "to face the fact that the raging anti-war controversy had probably destroyed the credibility of my ultimatum to Hanoi." His own cabinet was deeply split, with Laird and Rogers wanting to accelerate US withdrawal from South Vietnam and only Agnew, Kissinger, and Attorney General John Mitchell supporting escalation.

The public was more restive than ever. Five hundred thousand pro-testers were descending on Washington for a second Moratorium in mid-November—a three-day March Against Death. It would snake from Arlington National Cemetery past the White House to Capitol Hill and would be the biggest demonstration in the capital since the civil rights March on Washington in 1963. Demonstrators formed up by their state of birth or residence and paraded past the White House carrying signs with the names of men from their states killed in the war. Others carried signs with the names of Vietnamese villages wiped off the map by American bombing.

The optics could not have been worse for Nixon as he weighed esca-lation. Secretary of Defense Laird quietly informed Abrams that Nixon's original plan for Vietnamization—to prepare the ARVN and ruff-puffs to defeat the VC, with US support forces lingering to fight the NVA—had been amended. Now *all* US forces would be out by mid-1973, if not sooner. The South Vietnamese would have to fight entirely alone. Operation Duck Hook was quietly shelved, Kissinger's threat to Hanoi of "measures of the greatest consequence" revealed to be another empty threat. Nixon's "secret plan" to end the war had relied on the president's willingness, as Kissinger put it, "to find Hanoi's breaking point." But both Nixon and Kissinger shrank from doing just that. The grunts would have none of it, and the domestic and international fallout would be too great.[44]

On November 13, 1969, investigative reporter Seymour Hersh broke the most scandalous story of the war, not in the *New York Times* or the *Washington Post*, but below the fold on the front page of the *St. Louis Post-Dispatch*: "Lieutenant Accused of Murdering 109 Civilians." The My Lai massacre, which the Army had covered up in March 1968, now inconveniently burst into the open.

Hersh's scoop coincided with the massive Moratorium march in Washington, DC, as well as one in San Francisco, where 250,000 protesters appeared. Nixon again vowed that he would not be "affected" by the protests, even when groups that had never before joined the protesters turned out to demand an end to the war. The Moratorium marked a new peak in domestic opposition to the war. Demonstrations spread beyond the major cities. "Thirty people meeting in a church basement in Peoria to protest the war for the first time may be infinitely more important than 30,000 people converging on Washington," one organizer noted. Nixon felt pushed by this intensifying pressure to accelerate the troop withdrawals. He promised to withdraw another 50,000 troops by April 15, 1970. He planned to have nothing but a "residual force" or no troops at all in South Vietnam by the time he ran for reelection in 1972.[45]

Hersh's My Lai story, picked up by every news outlet in the country, was just the sort of news Nixon did not want as he tried to wind down the war and dampen protest. On December 5, 1969, *Life* magazine published gory photos of the massacre—hundreds of murdered men, women, and children piled in the ditches and fields of My Lai. The Army and the State Department were instructed to "relativize" the scandal by providing data on "offsetting" VC terror, as if My Lai could be excused because the VC killed civilians too. Westmoreland ordered the Army's chief of military history to write "a brief history of war crimes" that would place the massacre in what Westy hoped would be an exonerating context. Westmoreland then commissioned a white paper on the massacre for public release on December 7, 1969. As he had done in Vietnam, he put a thumb on the scale: "Relate the attacks on discipline in American society over the past several years to the impact on discipline in the Army."[46]

Ho Chi Minh missed this latest American donnybrook. He had died from a heart condition in September 1969 at the age of seventy-nine. Le Duan now consolidated his power. He published Ho's last will and testament, which insisted that "whatever happens, we must keep firm our resolve to fight the U.S. aggressors till total victory." Le Duan icily reminded his colleagues that "the party is an army which in combat must act as one man." Politburo consensus, maintained by Le Duan's grip on the secret police, would hold Moscow and Beijing onside and "keep options open." No cracks would be allowed to appear in the façade. Le Duan launched a new round of preemptive purges against "wreckers, deviationists, and saboteurs," labels affixed to anyone willing to end the awful war now.[47]

Few of the battered North Vietnamese people were prepared to "wreck" or "deviate" anyway. Conditioned by an intrusive police state to take a "passive attitude to the war," they may have privately opposed the conflict and its colossal waste of lives and resources, but they did not dare raise their voices against it for a simple reason adduced by the British embassy: "There is no way for popular discontent to make itself felt." The politburo wielded all power in North Vietnam, and whatever popular discontent existed was, an analyst in Hanoi observed, "allied to an absolute political inertia."[48]

By late 1969, there were a quarter of a million communist troops in South Vietnam and about 84,000 VCI cadres. They were operating from eight divisional headquarters, with 57 regiments, 271 combat battalions, and 58 combat support battalions. The days of fighting with cast-off World War II weapons were over. These communist units all had AK-47 assault rifles, light and heavy machine guns, B-40 and B-41 RPGs, mortars, and 60 mm and 120 mm recoilless rifles, as well as the latest Soviet and Chinese tactical radios. Their ability to kill Americans and "disintegrate" the ARVN was better than ever. For the first time in the war, NVA regulars appeared in the Mekong Delta to replace all of the VC killed in the reckless offensives of 1968–1969. With the US 9th Infantry Division pulling out—one of the first American troop withdrawals—two NVA regiments crossed from Cambodia into the flat ricelands and swamp areas of the Delta. Everything gained by Operation Speedy Express would shortly be taken back.[49]

On his 1969 Christmas Tour of Vietnam, Bob Hope dropped in on the 1st Infantry Division at their base camp at Lai Khe, thirty-seven miles northwest of Saigon. Despite regular allied sweeps, the enemy was as entrenched here as ever. Lai Khe was known as "Rocket City" for the frequency of mortar and rocket attacks. Bob Hope joked to 10,000 personnel of the Big Red One and other units that the enemy was so close that "we had to give the Viet Cong half the tickets." In the first years of the war, Hope had been warmly received by the troops. This time was different. When he told the troops that Nixon had "a plan to end the war," he was showered with boos. When TV cameras panned across the crowd, viewers could see the troops standing, hissing, throwing trash at the stage, giving Hope the finger, or flexing Black Power salutes. Dozens of MPs had to form a perimeter around the stage while Hope was hurriedly evacuated. Ron Kovic, who served two tours before being paralyzed in combat, attended the show and summed up the feelings of the troops: "People didn't laugh at his jokes. The war wasn't funny anymore, and a hundred Bob Hopes wouldn't have made any difference."[50]

Chapter 21

"CAMBODIA IS
A MAN'S JOB"

In 1970, there was lull in the big-unit war. Nixon's troop drawdowns continued, with the ARVN 1st Division replacing the Marines along the DMZ, and the ARVN 2nd Division taking over much of the Americal Division's Delaware-sized AO south of it. This was the "Vietnamization" of the war promised by Nixon in 1968. The ARVN greeted it everywhere with panic. In III Corps, when General Nguyen Van Hieu's ARVN 5th Division was ordered to move into the departing US 1st Division's AO along Route 13, linking Saigon with the Cambodian border, General Hieu attempted to resign his command. He explained that without American support his division would be unable even to *move*, let alone fight the VC.

Fortunately for the ARVN, the South Vietnamese Joint General Staff and MACV agreed that the enemy had also been lulled into inactivity. They predicted that the communists, gutted by their casualties over the past two years, would wait until at least 1972 to rebuild their combat units before hazarding another major offensive. By then, US personnel would be down to 250,000 or fewer, and NVA reinforcements would be trained and combat-ready.[1]

Hanoi had correctly judged that Nixon's political need to withdraw American troops "was the greatest weak point" of the free-world position.

The more troops came out, the weaker the Thieu regime would be. For now, the Americans continued to seize enemy logistics caches—some of the biggest seizures of the war. These operations, conceived as a last service to President Thieu, continued to kill and wound large numbers of Americans, who ran over mines and tripped booby traps of increasing force and sophistication. Medical officers reported a five-fold increase in multiple amputees among US combat troops in 1970.[2]

Fighting continued sporadically through the rural areas, where the NVA and VC were determined to defeat Saigon's ruff-puff and self-defense forces, stymie pacification, replace VC infrastructure lost to the Phoenix Program, and grab back as much of the peasant population as they could as prelude to yet another general offensive and uprising. These fights were brutal, usually involving ruff-puff units overrun or ambushed, and occasionally reinforced by ARVN troops and American air and artillery. Kill ratios that had always favored the ARVN—when the Americans were fully engaged—were now neutral or negative, the ARVN and the territorial forces losing as many or more troops as the communists. As yet, there was no drawdown in American bombing. The B-52 sortie rate inside South Vietnam continued at 1,800 every month, raining bombs on any area suspected of harboring communist troops and supplies.[3]

Like everything else, CORDS was finally Vietnamized in 1970. The handover went so badly that American personnel in CORDS soared that year, instead of declining. The official explanation for this was that all of those extra Americans were needed to "stimulate the GVN to do more." Bill Colby, who had replaced Bob Komer as director of CORDS, made a tour of the four corps areas to assess the effectiveness of these American stimulants and was disappointed everywhere he went. In I Corps, the Army officers he met could not agree on whether they were succeeding or failing. They claimed to have eliminated 400 VCI in 1969, but then sheepishly admitted that the VC had replaced those 400 cadres with 1,500 new ones. And so it went in every corps area. "It will be many years," Colby dejectedly concluded, "before the VCI will feel the effect of the Phoenix Program."[4]

As for "population security," the other great strut of Abrams' "better war," it too seemed to be failing. Creighton Abrams had briefed his commanders in April 1970 on "the changing nature of the war" and made clear that everything now hinged not on "military operations" but on the "political contest" between the Thieu government and the communists. And yet in all four corps areas Bill Colby observed a total lack of ambition in that vital contest. He was told that "consolidation," not expansion, was the goal for 1970, and that government-controlled areas would only remain so if growing numbers of ruff-puff, National Police, and self-defense force units were funded, armed, and trained by the United States and then deployed around the edges of secure "population envelopes." Colby interjected that at this stage of the war, such ever-increasing American allocations for the territorial forces could not be relied on. "The Vietnamese," he declared, "must learn to cooperate with each other and become self-sufficient."[5]

That wasn't happening. Meetings between the Americans and the ARVN about the militia forces broke down in mutual recriminations, the ARVN bemoaning the "lack of leadership and logistics" in ruff-puff and PSDF units and demanding that Nixon slow down his troop withdrawals to buy *more* time to train and field the South Vietnamese forces. *Esquire* reporter Michael Herr judged Abrams' pacification program no better than Westmoreland's: "psychotic vaudeville, a swollen, computerized tit being forced upon an already violated population, a costly, valueless program that worked only in press conferences."[6]

This was true, and it got to the heart of the eternal problem in Vietnam: How do you know if you're winning? Statistics such as body count had been devalued but certainly not abandoned. New metrics, such as population security measured by mathematical scoring systems, were no more helpful than the old ones, replacing one misleading routine with another. Bob Komer had summed them up this way: "They run the whole gamut from overconfidence to despair." Abrams was blunter: "Yeah, and that comes from another sickness, and that is the worship of *charts*. It finally gets to the point where that's really the whole war—fucking *charts*. Somehow the chart itself becomes the whole damn war, instead of the *people*, and the *real* things."[7]

Nixon had thwarted the peace process in 1968 to get himself elected. He had justified what he did by assuring himself that he, better than LBJ, could coerce Hanoi into ending the war on terms favorable to the United States. In 1969, however, the thirty-seventh president had failed even to *start* the peace negotiations that he had promised voters. The envoys who had finally taken their seats in January 1969 had made no progress twelve months later, prompting the chief American negotiators, Henry Cabot Lodge Jr. and Lawrence Walsh, to resign in December. The obduracy of the North Vietnamese in Paris—clearly playing for time, for the day when *all* US forces would leave Vietnam—had begun to make Nixon look gullible.

The backlash after Hamburger Hill reminded Nixon that he had little leverage. Even minor casualties upset Congress and the public. By year-end 1969, over 40,000 Americans had been killed in action in Vietnam, with more than 9,000 of them in Nixon's first year in office. With over 300,000 killed and wounded in the war, the United States had now suffered as many casualties in Vietnam as it had lost in the trenches of World War I.

Nixon boasted that he had increased the proportion of South Vietnamese territory under government control from 79 to 90 percent in 1969, a typical piece of Vietnam legerdemain that, even if true, was almost certainly untenable against a future communist onslaught. American escalation—Nixon's trump card—was off the table, and the enemy knew it, for Nixon, who had vowed to batter the communists until they agreed to peace terms that favored Saigon and Washington, kept *subtracting* troops from the force he had in Vietnam to appease critics and reduce the cost of the war.[8]

On December 15, 1969, Nixon had announced another major troop withdrawal: 50,000 more men would come out by April 1970, reducing the troops in-country to 434,000. A year earlier he had inherited an army of 543,000. That had been insufficient to coerce Hanoi. Why would a smaller force prove any more coercive? In 1970, Nixon began reassessing his war strategy. He had taken over every element of Johnson's war in Vietnam, including the promise to remove US forces as well as the "bombing halt," which had deprived the president of most of the leverage he had with Hanoi—his ability to bomb North Vietnamese territory.[9]

Nixon's assumption of LBJ's war had included another self-denying ordinance—Johnson's refusal to attack the communist sanctuaries in Laos and Cambodia. They remained bastions of power and recuperation just beyond the reach of free-world forces. In 1970, Nixon, who needed to find a way out of the unpopular war before the elections in 1972, struggled to claw back some leverage, to find ways to hurt the North Vietnamese and make them negotiate in earnest. In February 1970, Le Duan reiterated that the war could go on forever as far as Hanoi was concerned. Protracted war, he said, was the Viet Cong's "strategic principle." The long war, as hard as it was, was "modifying the balance of forces in our favor." "The longer the war lasts," Le Duan concluded, "the weaker the enemy becomes."[10]

To prod negotiations along, Nixon sidestepped the formal peace process and authorized Kissinger to open secret negotiations with Le Duc Tho on the sidelines of the Paris peace talks on February 21, 1970. Unfortunately, Le Duc Tho stipulated the same terms that Hanoi's official delegation was demanding: that the United States withdraw all troops from Vietnam and agree to place the VC's PRP inside a South Vietnamese coalition government shorn of Thieu and Ky.

To Nixon's chagrin, the North Vietnamese government betrayed no sign of war weariness or demoralization. All members of the politburo, tamed and terrified by Le Duan's security apparatus, now agreed that the war must be won without political concessions to the Americans or Saigon. Hopes that a battered North Vietnamese population would pressure the politburo to compromise were also disappointed. Fifteen years of war had made Hanoi's internal security machine stronger, not weaker. The communist party wielded power unchallenged. Poorly fed and housed workers who wanted more were advised to "overcome capitalist thinking" and submit to their "collective masters." In sum, the British embassy in Hanoi concluded, the energies and capacity for resistance of most North Vietnamese were spent entirely "in staying alive and beating the system while appearing to acquiesce in it."[11]

This being the situation, Nixon and Kissinger looked desperately for ways to gain *some* leverage in negotiations. They decided that they would hit the NVA sanctuaries with air and ground forces. Only in this way, they reasoned, could they persuade Hanoi that America would go the extra mile in securing what Nixon called a "just peace, with honor."

Cambodia beckoned again. Communist fighters in I Corps and II Corps were supplied by the Ho Chi Minh Trail through Laos. Abrams' failure to take and hold the A Shau Valley in 1968–1969 meant that Laos was essentially unassailable. One hundred thousand NVA and Pathet Lao troops controlled northern Laos and the Mekong Valley. American bombing in Laos never interrupted the flow of communist supplies.

To Nixon, Kissinger, and Abrams, Cambodia seemed more promising. The VC and NVA units in III and IV Corps were heavily supplied by the Sihanouk Trail, which wended up from the port of Sihanoukville on the

Gulf of Thailand. Many of the Soviet and Chinese rockets, mortars, and bullets fired into US forces came through Cambodia. Ironically, they reached their end users in South Vietnam via the Friendship Highway, which the United States had built in the 1950s at a cost of $34 million to connect Sihanoukville, Phnom Penh, and the eastern border areas.[12]

The growing army of communists in IV Corps was entirely supplied through Cambodia. The Army had intensified its hunt for enemy supply caches inside South Vietnam in early 1970 and made record seizures. "We're as busy as a one-legged man at an ass-kicking contest," one officer reported. In February alone, they had captured 500 tons of matériel: small arms ammo, machine guns, rockets, mortars, recoilless rifles, RPGs, flame-throwers, blocks of explosive, detonator cords, mines, and tactical radios. The biggest caches were in III Corps, and all of their contents had been carried into South Vietnam from Cambodia for use in future offensives. Captured enemy troops spoke of NVA plans to strike from Cambodia to seize the ARVN IV Corps headquarters, base camp, and air base at Can Tho—to rip the Mekong Delta from the hands of the demoralized ARVN, which was being steadily reduced by booby traps and mines brought from Cambodia.[13]

Kissinger's military aide, forty-six-year-old General Alexander Haig, had risen from battalion to brigade command in Vietnam four years earlier. Haig now argued that the internal security situation in South Vietnam was all but irrelevant if the main threat resided in the sanctuaries of Laos and Cambodia, where the NVA was free to build up overwhelming force. Kissinger made the same point, and another: so long as the NVA enjoyed strategic depth and impunity in Cambodia and Laos, the United States would never be able to Vietnamize the war. The most ardent advocate of escalation was the CINCPAC—Admiral John McCain Jr., commander in chief of US forces in the Pacific. The fifty-nine-year-old McCain, whose son had been shot down over Hanoi in 1967, was notorious for his rambling briefings and scare-mongering. In the Pentagon, they called him the "Big Red Arrow Man" for the way he enlivened his briefings with maps of East Asia depicting lurid red arrows sprouting from China to threaten every American interest in the Indo-Pacific.

Admiral McCain now took up the cause of Cambodia. It *had* to be invaded and rid of NVA base camps if Vietnamization was to succeed.

When General Lon Nol launched a coup against Prince Sihanouk in March 1970, Nixon decided to take the plunge into Cambodia.[14]

A whole animal-crackers nomenclature had emerged at MACV to describe the kinks and bulges in the frontier separating South Vietnam and Cambodia. The Americans had given them names such as Crow's Nest, Parrot's Beak, Elephant's Foot, Angel's Wing, Dog's Head, and Fishhook. They contained fourteen known communist sanctuaries and base areas, threatening the two-thirds of the South Vietnamese population who lived in the III and IV Corps areas. Three entire NVA divisions were known to be sheltering along the border in this zone, along with the VC 9th and 5th Divisions. Pham Hung's COSVN was also there. The threat these sanctuaries presented was magnified by their nearness to Saigon. The Fishhook, believed to be the home of COSVN, lay forty-eight miles north of Saigon. The Parrot's Beak was just twenty-four miles west of Saigon.[15]

Nixon had continued the "secret bombing" of the Cambodian sanctuaries begun in March 1969 into 1970. Three thousand sorties had been flown and 110,000 tons of bombs had been dropped on eastern Cambodia. In Washington, the administration falsified or destroyed every record of this illegal bombing of a neutral nation.

With Sihanouk in exile, Lon Nol and Siri Matak saw American bombing as the easiest way to compel North Vietnamese and VC units to abandon the Cambodian sanctuaries. If the Cambodians attacked the sanctuaries, they would incur NVA retaliation, which, given the small size and pathetic capabilities of the Cambodian military, had to be avoided at all costs.[16]

Having broken diplomatic relations with Cambodia in 1965 and only recently resumed them, the United States had scant information on Pol Pot's Khmer Rouge. In 1970, the CIA estimated that it numbered 5,000 or 6,000. In fact, it was over 100,000 strong. The number of NVA and VC troops in Cambodia was estimated to be 60,000. For Sihanouk, continued neutrality had been the only viable option. Hanoi kept the Khmer Rouge on a leash only so long as Phnom Penh continued the "extreme neutrality" that favored the NVA without a communist takeover of Cambodia.[17]

Nixon was bolder but shouldn't have been. The entire futility of what he was about to do, which came to be called the "Cambodian Incursion," was summed up by two of his own presidential acts in April 1970—the first on April 20, the second ten days later. On April 20, Nixon announced that he would withdraw 150,000 additional American troops from Vietnam over the next twelve months. By 1971, in other words, there would be half as many US troops in South Vietnam as had been there when Nixon took office. Militarily, this meant that the Americans would lack the manpower for major, sustained offensive operations *anywhere*, least of all Cambodia and Laos. The announcement was met with rapture on campuses but also in the Senate, where LBJ's old budget director went before Fulbright's Foreign Relations Committee and explained that troop withdrawals were the fastest way to shave about $5 billion from the $18.5 billion annual cost of the war.[18]

But they had to be enacted quickly, and without any "step-up in U.S. combat operations." The American sword, in other words, was disintegrating in its scabbard. On April 30, Nixon resolved to wield it before it was gone. He went on television to announce "U.S. operations against the communist sanctuaries in Cambodia." America, he scolded, must not "act like a pitiful helpless giant when the chips are down." This belligerent announcement was met with outrage. An American public and Congress that had been told the war was ending were confronted instead with its expansion.[19]

American voters didn't need to be reminded of the bargain Nixon had made with them in 1968. He would withdraw troops and end the war. If the South Vietnamese couldn't defend themselves, they would have to negotiate with the communists. With his decision to invade Cambodia, Nixon effectively suspended Vietnamization and sent American troops once again to fight for the Thieu-Ky regime.[20]

Nixon was hopeful, for Phnom Penh had been rocked by anti-Vietnamese riots, prompting Lon Nol to close the port of Sihanoukville, order all NVA and VC troops out of Cambodia within seventy-two hours, remove Sihanouk as head of state, and put himself in charge of a new Khmer Republic only too eager to tap into the same fountain of dollars that was sustaining Thieu. The coup, the CIA declared, "represents a reversal of the slow nibbling-away" at Cambodian sovereignty by Hanoi.[21]

But Nixon was desperate too. He may have said in that April 30 television address that he'd rather be a one-term president "than a two-term president at the cost of seeing America become a second-rate power," but he certainly didn't mean it. The Cambodian Incursion threatened his reelection, and he knew it.

Fundraising for Ed Muskie, George McGovern, and the thirteen other Democrats vying for the right to run against Nixon in 1972 took off after the president's speech announcing the invasion of Cambodia. Lon Nol was wobbly, his small army poorly armed and motivated. New formations equipped and trained by the Americans were not sent to fight the communists. They were kept in Phnom Penh as a palace guard. In February, America's "secret war" in Laos—begun by Kennedy and expanded to no good effect by LBJ and Nixon—had been exposed in the press and had resulted in an eleven-point drop in Nixon's poll numbers. Senate majority leader Mike Mansfield accused Nixon of secretly "re-involving" America in a war in Laos that had attained "disturbing proportions."[22]

That was putting it mildly. Laos, it now appeared, was the most heavily bombed country in the history of the world. Over 2 million tons of bombs had been dropped there by nearly 600,000 American sorties, killing somewhere between 30,000 and 100,000 Laotians and North Vietnamese. By this date, these were just more numbers to throw on the heap of grim statistics produced by the war.

All of that destruction checked but never stopped the flow of North Vietnamese troops and supplies down the trail—about 20,000 tons of matériel every month and an NVA troop presence in Laos that hovered around 100,000. What caused the drop in Nixon's poll numbers was not the pummeling of Laos or the meager effect of the bombing but the administration's admission that twenty-seven Americans had died there in the "secret war." A miscarriage in Cambodia could do far worse, and a miscarriage seemed inevitable.[23]

Even as Nixon planned the Cambodian Incursion, it was obvious that the operation would fail, and Nixon knew it. Secretary of Defense Laird and Secretary of State Rogers warned that any move into Cambodia would weaken Vietnamization by spreading scarce resources even thinner than they already were. CIA analysts predicted that an American strike into Cambodia would merely inconvenience the communists, not derail them.

MACV and the CIA had already reported the startling collapse of Lon Nol's army and the abrupt end of all attempts to coordinate joint ARVN and Cambodian operations against the communist sanctuaries in March 1970—at the time of the supposedly revivifying Lon Nol coup. On the Cambodian side, officers who had set up the joint operations were relieved. On the South Vietnamese side, officers were ordered to tell MACV nothing about arrangements for cooperation, lest the Americans insist on more of it. "Phnom Penh will do *nothing* against the NVA/VC," the CIA confirmed in early April.[24]

The Lon Nol government's bluster was just that: "They fear the growing communist threat and will only seek to *contain* the communist forces in their operating areas near the South Vietnamese borders." There would be no thought of attacking the 50,000 NVA and VC troops in Cambodia. Already additional NVA and VC battalions were moving from the Mekong Delta back into Cambodia to defend the sanctuaries, defeat Lon Nol's army, and seize control of half of Cambodia's seventeen provinces. Cambodian troops were observed defecting to the communists with their weapons. Lon Nol's minister of national defense was spotted berating his own troops in the field for their refusal to fight. "I have no confidence in their fighting abilities," he groused.[25]

Lon Nol, who had already delivered his own vote of no confidence by sending his family into exile in Singapore, now hit the brakes hard. On the South Vietnamese side, President Thieu was even less helpful. The ARVN, Thieu said, would do nothing more than "harass the border areas," to make it harder for the enemy to access his "enormous caches" of weapons and ammo. Thieu gave orders that ARVN units could advance no more than six miles into Cambodia, and only during daylight hours. They were required to return to Vietnamese territory before nightfall. There would be no war of annihilation, merely soft jabs to appease Nixon—jabs easily ducked or defeated by the communists.[26]

The feeble efforts actually undertaken by Lon Nol triggered a predictable backlash from the communist forces, who moved deeper into Cambodia to escape the American bombing, attack Lon Nol's troops, and punish the new regime, which had begun to intern, persecute, and even massacre the 400,000 ethnic Vietnamese living in Cambodia.

This threw an immediate wrench into Nixon's plan to unite the Cambodian and South Vietnamese military efforts. After watching tens of thousands of plundered Vietnamese flee into South Vietnam and inspecting the sites of massacres in Cambodia, the ARVN pronounced itself unwilling to coordinate with Lon Nol or *any* Cambodian regime. The ARVN paused during their own operations in Cambodia to loot every town or village they encountered, and then invoiced Lon Nol's government $6.5 million for the cost of their intervention.

"The Viet Cong came but left with nothing," a Cambodian officer told Peter Kann of the *Wall Street Journal*. "The South Vietnamese came and took *everything*." South Vietnamese air strikes in Cambodia made no distinction between civilian and military targets. To Kann, this splintered a key plank of the Nixon Doctrine—that anticommunist Asian regimes would assist each other and not rely entirely on the United States. "The fact is that most Asians don't much like other Asians," Kann remarked.[27]

Relations continued in the traditional vein, the Vietnamese regarding the Cambodians as weaklings who had tolerated the communist presence on their soil for too long, the Cambodians viewing the Vietnamese as haughty interlopers. Prince Sihanouk, who still enjoyed godlike status with the Cambodian peasantry, established a government-in-exile in Beijing that allied with Hanoi, the VC, the Khmer Rouge, and the Laotian Pathet Lao. The Americans, the prince fretted, "have turned the Vietnam War into an Indochina War." Urban enthusiasm for Lon Nol was offset by the hatred felt by Cambodia's more numerous peasantry, who interpreted Sihanouk's overthrow as sacrilege and rioted against the new regime. None of Nixon's gambits in Cambodia—Lon Nol, the secret bombing, the looming US incursion—would be worth the effort or lives expended if, as seemed likely, Lon Nol's government collapsed and the NVA or Khmer Rouge took over.[28]

If *that* happened, all of Cambodia, not just its eastern borderlands, would become a communist sanctuary. In the context of a popular war for a vital national interest, the incursion would have made perfect sense. In the context of Vietnam, it made no sense at all. America lacked the power to stay in Cambodia and police its vast space. Lon Nol stood no chance against the NVA, VC, and Khmer Rouge. This was already obvious. A month before Nixon invaded Cambodia, Lon Nol's army had been routed by the more professional NVA, who seized most of eastern Cambodia in an operation they named Campaign X. In mid-April 1970, Lon Nol told Nixon that his US-aligned Khmer Republic, only a year old, was about to perish from these communist attacks. Political cartoonists had a field day with this emerging fiasco, one depicting Kissinger gravely informing the president that "all we know about Lon Nol is that his name spelled backwards makes Lon Nol."[29]

People who knew Nixon worried that he was losing his mind. The president felt humiliated that his "secret plan" to end the war was a bust. Two of his picks for the Supreme Court had been rejected by the Senate. He was watching the film *Patton* over and over in this period, conflating himself with George C. Scott's muscular portrayal of Patton and steeling himself to do something brash and decisive, like the old tank general. "The liberals are waiting to see Nixon let Cambodia go down the drain just the way Eisenhower let Cuba go down the drain," he told Kissinger. "I'll show them who's tough." Withdrawing from Vietnam is "a boy's job," he sputtered to Bob Haldeman. "Cambodia is a man's job. It really needs to work." Spiro Agnew, Nixon's most hawkish enabler, exhorted the president to stop "pussyfooting" and go into Cambodia hard.[30]

The first American thrusts into Cambodia began on April 29, 1970, and Nixon went on television to address the American people the next day. Ten days earlier he had promised troop reductions. Now he was announcing the biggest battle of the war since 1967's Operation Junction City. This one, Operation Final Victory, sent 31,000 American troops into Cambodia, where 2,000 of them would be killed or wounded. Five years earlier, LBJ had said that "the lives of our sons are too great a price for national vanity." But not for Nixon. "This is not an invasion of Cambodia," the president assured the American people. "We take this action not for the purpose of expanding the war into Cambodia but for the purpose of ending the war in Vietnam and winning the just peace we all desire." In meetings with his inner circle, Nixon tried to sound Pattonesque: "Don't worry about divisiveness. Having drawn the sword, don't take it out. Stick it in hard. Hit 'em in the gut. No defensiveness."[31]

Invading Cambodia, Nixon told Americans, would buy more precious months to expand and train the ARVN. The president had just announced those four additional US troop withdrawals—totaling 150,000—to be brought home by April 1971, by which time only 240,000 US troops would remain. Nixon had ruled out a "precipitous" retreat from South Vietnam, vowing that he would tailor every withdrawal to the speed of ARVN improvement, progress in the Paris talks, and a verifiable decline in enemy activity, but in fact he was pulling out as precipitously as he could without verifying *any* of these things, so keen was he to secure his political flank before the 1972 elections. Privately, he called the troop withdrawal announcements "bombshells" that he could drop on the Democrats and the antiwar protesters. Militarily, there was nothing strategic about them.[32]

Abe Abrams warned Nixon that unless the NVA forces in Cambodia were significantly weakened, they would overrun South Vietnam before the American withdrawal was complete, which was to say *before* the 1972 elections. Army chief of staff Westmoreland gave more ammunition to those inclined to believe that, like the Bourbons, he had learned and forgotten nothing. Invading Cambodia, Westy wrote Abrams, "may be conducive to relaxation of some of the constraints under which we have been operating." He pressed Abrams to "take advantage of the opportunity."

But Abrams, unlike Westy, could face facts. With his army being cut in half over the next twelve months, small gains were all that could be expected. Abrams aimed at COSVN, which had eluded the B-52 raids. Nixon yearned for COSVN. He called it "the key control center" and expected to capture a "Bamboo Pentagon" staffed by 5,000 officers and technicians, with secret maps, code books, and hotlines to Hanoi, Beijing, and Moscow. Unfortunately, whatever facilities COSVN had, Pham Hung had moved them a month earlier in anticipation of the incursion, which, as usual, had been betrayed by high-placed communist spies in Saigon.[33]

COSVN did not have to go far to escape Nixon's incursion. MACV's rules of engagement allowed US forces to advance no more than eighteen miles into Cambodia, ARVN troops no more than thirty-one miles. In that narrow band of Cambodian territory along the border they found NVA training camps, hospital complexes, and headquarters—all mostly abandoned. They seized legendary enemy base areas with names like Shakey's Hill, Rock Island East, and The City. They scooped up 7,000 tons of rice, 1,700 tons of munitions, 20,000 weapons, 55 tons of medical supplies, 41 tons of explosives, and 3.5 million pages of documents. All that remained of COSVN, a reporter observed, "was a scattering of a few empty huts."[34]

Fifteen thousand troops of the Cav and the US 11th Armored Cavalry Regiment invaded the Fishhook and found it empty. There were caches but few enemy troops. Troopers of the Cav armored regiment took advantage of the respite to loot the Cambodian town of Snuol. The enemy and COSVN had fled westward, under orders "to conserve forces as much as we can."[35]

Eight thousand ARVN and 1,000 grunts of the US 25th Infantry Division plunged into the Parrot's Beak, which bulged to within twenty-four

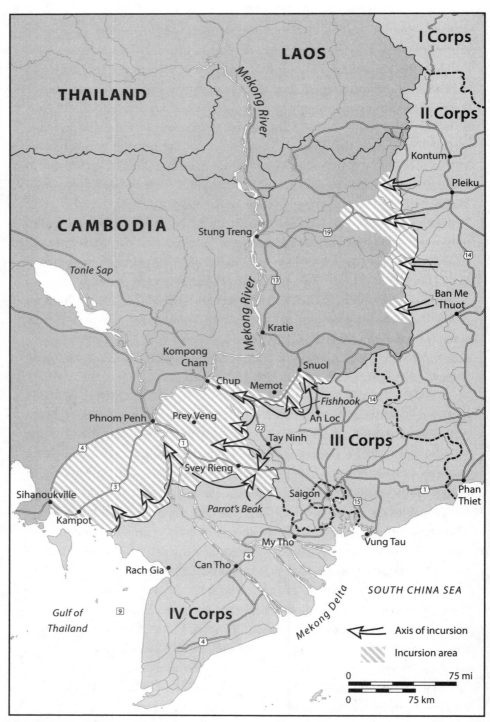

The Cambodian Incursion

miles of Saigon. In this early test of "Vietnamization," they fought a two-day battle against a communist rearguard that then fled deeper into Cambodia. Troops of the 101st Airborne and the 4th ID air-assaulted from Pleiku into the sanctuaries and found enemy base camps, bunkers, tunnels, and mortar positions, but only a smattering of communist troops. Tipped off about the operation, the NVA had retreated west across the Mekong River, which flowed parallel to the sanctuaries, just behind them. With the Americans leaving the war, they reasoned, why bother fighting them?[36]

In all, large pieces of four American divisions and three ARVN infantry-armor task forces struck into Cambodia. Denied the troops and authority to pursue the retreating enemy, they did little more than seize food and weapons caches—so much food that a company commander in the Cav recalled that during the operation starving communist troops trailed his platoons at a discreet distance "so they could eat our garbage, the stuff we'd throw away." The grunts found chicken and pig farms, mess halls, hospitals, firing ranges, bunkers, trucks, telephone switchboards, ammo, and food, but hardly any troops. They captured enough weapons to equip a 12,000-man enemy division and enough ammo to supply 126 communist battalions for four months of combat.

Secretary of Defense Laird's Systems Analysis Office in the Pentagon ran the numbers and estimated that the incursion had seized 25 percent of the NVA's supplies. But those items would be replaced, most within seventy-five days. British Conservative MP Enoch Powell, a fierce anticommunist, nevertheless ridiculed Nixon's incursion. "It is the futility of American policy that constitutes its culpability," Powell declaimed. "When the operation is over, the underlying facts of the situation will reassert themselves like the tide washing out footmarks in the sand."[37]

"Goddamn, goddamn," Abrams agreed. "We need another division, we need to go in deep. We need to go west from where we are, we need to go north and east from where we are. And we need to do it *now*." Abrams wasn't getting any of that, and he knew it. Secretary of Defense Melvin Laird had reluctantly consented to the incursion only because he took for granted that the communist troops would temporarily evacuate the sanctuaries—minimizing the chances of combat and casualties.[38]

Nixon flailed impotently. "Let's go blow the hell out of them," he shouted at Laird, Kissinger, and the chiefs in a Pentagon conclave. He then took the precaution of flying General Al Haig out to Saigon during the incursion to make sure that Abrams did *not* exceed White House limits: two months of duration and eighteen miles of penetration, not a day or an inch more. The last of the 19,300 US forces left Cambodia on June 30, leaving 29,000 ARVN to mop up and then follow them to the exits on July 22. General Abrams belatedly recognized the obvious: in dispatching the ARVN to "wander all over Cambodia," MACV had further undercut the job of pacification inside South Vietnam.[39]

Lon Nol's army, the FANK, was supposed to secure the "liberated" sanctuaries along the border. That was the key play in what Nixon called his "big game" in Cambodia. Instead, the FANK abandoned the sanctuaries to the enemy and retreated toward Phnom Penh. General Al Haig stopped in Phnom Penh to inform Lon Nol that US forces were returning to South Vietnam and handing the chaos they had created in Cambodia over to the FANK. Lon Nol burst into tears. He sobbed that his little army was powerless. His officers were corrupt and incompetent. Military training, conducted on Phnom Penh's golf course, was perfunctory, the equipment obsolete, and artillery and airpower nonexistent. Only the Americans could save Cambodia, the general wailed. Haig, in his starched fatigues, crossed the room, put his arm around Lon Nol, and pledged, through his interpreter, that America would do what it could.[40]

Hanoi's Cambodian strategy was now more easily implemented than ever against a weak opponent like the FANK, which its own commander derided as "less effective than the Paris police." Communist forces attacked Lon Nol's principal towns and supply lines, pinning down the entire FANK in defensive battles, while the NVA restored travel along the Ho Chi Minh Trail and brought the southern supply line from Sihanoukville back to life. Cambodia's rice and rubber production collapsed. Inflation spiked. Phnom Penh, a tidy city of 600,000, began to drown in a sea of refugees. Before long, it would look like Saigon, with 2 million displaced persons camped in its surrounding slums and shanties.[41]

Nixon now boasted that his Cambodian Incursion had showed Hanoi "the futility of expanded aggression." In a meeting with Laird and the Joint Chiefs he compared the incursion to "Teddy Roosevelt charging up San Juan Hill, a small event but dramatic, and people took notice."[42]

The wrong people, unfortunately. Nixon had kicked over a hornets' nest. Now the Khmer Rouge, backed by the NVA, seized larger tracts of territory and pressed Lon Nol's FANK into a narrow pocket around Phnom Penh. Lon Nol's hamlet chiefs and other officials were assassinated in their villages. ARVN troops roved around eastern Cambodia looting and pillaging. Lon Nol quarreled with Thieu about how to share the weapons captured in the NVA caches. Lon Nol wanted them all. Thieu wanted half. While they argued that point, 7,000 NVA troops took Siem Reap and camped in the ruins of Angkor Wat. Lon Nol begged the chairman of the South Vietnamese Joint General Staff to bomb the national treasure. Fortunately, General Cao Van Vien declined.[43]

It was not a pretty, edifying, or hopeful picture. Nixon nevertheless claimed victory in a televised address: "We have bought time for the South Vietnamese to strengthen themselves against the enemy." Three hundred and thirty-eight Americans had died and 1,525 had been wounded—many of them by the web of booby traps left by the communists. Others were killed or injured in the short, sharp battles around the captured caches.

Nixon continued to insist that the incursion had been undertaken to "save American lives" and to make clear that the United States was not "a pitiful, helpless giant." Grunt morale sank further. A sergeant who participated in the incursion recalled sharpened acrimony between "lifers"—career officers and NCOs—and their troops. "Lifers felt invading Cambodia was a strategic necessity. Conscripts saw it as an unnecessary risk of lives." One of the many American fatalities in Cambodia was twenty-four-year-old Captain Michael Davis O'Connell, who wrote the most famous poem of the war shortly before plummeting to his death in a helicopter crash. The poem's last verse evoked the futility and fickleness of the implacable war: "And in that time when men decide, and feel safe / to call the war insane, take one moment / to embrace these gentle heroes you left behind."[44]

Nixon's incursion with those gentle heroes had been premised on "cleaning out" the sanctuaries, but it left an even greater problem in its wake. Without US or ARVN forces to aid him, Lon Nol and the FANK were left alone against the North Vietnamese and the Khmer Rouge. Great plans for Cambodian military expansion had not been fulfilled. Lon Nol had imagined that Nixon would provide him the means to arm

1.5 million Cambodians. Instead, he found himself with a demoralized army of 140,000—only 100,000 of whom had weapons and ammunition.[45]

Within four months, Lon Nol, his army, and his government would be pushed into Phnom Penh, with the NVA, VC, and Khmer Rouge taking over everything else. The whole country—and certainly everything east of the Mekong River—was now a communist sanctuary subject to the worst savagery in the region: torture, mass executions, and the enslavement of an entire population to replenish the communist workforce and logistics lost to Nixon's incursion.[46]

The CIA reported that 50,000 NVA troops had responded to Nixon's pressure on the Sihanouk Trail by "cutting off the northern top of Cambodia to secure *new* lines of supply leading out of southeastern Laos." These were the disastrous strategic effects of the secret bombing, the Lon Nol coup, and Nixon's Cambodian Incursion. Sihanouk's despised neutrality looked like a win by comparison.[47]

There were more ramifications for Nixon. His secretary of state, William Rogers, had told the Senate Foreign Relations Committee just days before the incursion that the administration had no plans to invade Cambodia. Rogers had been kept in the dark. The incursion had been planned in secret by Nixon, Kissinger, Abrams, the Joint Chiefs, and a few other hard-liners. In June, an aggrieved Congress repealed the Tonkin Gulf Resolution, which had been the official basis for the war since 1964, and which Congress learned in 1968 had been based on fabricated or exaggerated incidents. Democratic senator Frank Church of Idaho and Republican John Cooper of Kentucky cosponsored and passed a bipartisan amendment to the Foreign Assistance Act of 1970 that curtailed support for American and South Vietnamese operations in Cambodia and Laos.

General Bruce Palmer, Westmoreland's vice chief of staff in Washington, considered the gains of the Cambodian Incursion trivial beside the "boomerang" political effect inside the United States. Almost overnight, a war that had merely been intensely unpopular became "proscribed." Funding would dry up faster than it would have otherwise.[48]

But the ease with which three American presidents had expanded the war in Vietnam was glimpsed again in the United States Senate's timid and halting attempt to snatch back its war and budget powers from the executive even *after* the Cambodian Incursion. There was a seven-week filibuster by hawks, and then amendments to the amendment. First, Republican senator Bob Dole of Kansas had a go at undoing the Cooper-Church Amendment by amending it to say that Nixon could ignore it so long as a single American POW was held in the cross-border sanctuaries.

Dole and Nixon thought they had a winner. What senator would cast a vote that seemed to abandon American prisoners to their fate? They were shocked when Dole's amendment was defeated 54–36. It was then the turn of Democratic senator Robert Byrd, another hawk, who successfully added language to the Cooper-Church Amendment that helped it pass both houses in December 1970 and left Nixon free to use military force "to protect the lives of U.S. armed forces wherever deployed." This was carte blanche, and Nixon would use it to expand the bombing in Cambodia, Laos, and North Vietnam in 1971–1972 without any congressional advice or consent. Two "end the war" amendments sponsored by Republican senator Mark Hatfield and Democratic senator George McGovern were defeated, giving Nixon yet more flexibility.[49]

But despite the narrow legislative wins, the president's ability to wring "peace with honor" from the dying war in Vietnam looked ever more hopeless. An American Congress that had always been more comfortable playing the hawk than the dove was being driven in a more dovish direction by polls, the media, and a spreading conviction that the country simply could not afford to keep spending billions of dollars on the war in South Vietnam.[50]

Nixon's war would cost US forces another 6,065 dead and 30,643 wounded in 1970. Senate majority leader Mike Mansfield was urging the administration to reduce its commitments around the world—even in NATO. Normally, the eighteen senators of the Armed Services Committee were a bastion of anticommunist containment. They were chaired by a Democrat, John Stennis of Mississippi, whose support for the war in Vietnam had been rock-solid. His fellow Democrats on the committee were no less ardent—hawks like Henry "Scoop" Jackson and Richard Russell—and the Republicans on the committee, such as John Tower, Strom Thurmond, and Barry Goldwater, were even more hawkish. None of them would have dared undercut the executive branch's position in previous years.

But Nixon's cavalier escalation of the war and its consequences at home finally moved even hawks to cut back support. Not, it must be said, because the hawks worried about Nixon's expansion of the war, but because they saw that expansion was eroding the preparedness of the US military elsewhere and even imperiling deployments to places such as South Korea, where Senate liberals now threatened to withdraw a division to help pay for Vietnam.

In 1970, the war was costing more than America's strategic missile force and was jeopardizing the $14 billion modernization of those missiles with multiple warheads and an anti-ballistic-missile system, neither of which looked affordable so long as the war in Southeast Asia continued. Stennis deplored these "austere" cuts and the postponement of critical R&D and weapons procurement. This was what seems to have aroused the moderate and conservative senators as much as anything else—a sense that the unwinnable war was eating the Pentagon's seed corn. Few of them agreed with Abe Abrams' witless insistence from Saigon that there was "no better place" to spend American defense dollars than in Vietnam.[51]

The new mood in Congress signaled by the Cooper-Church Amendment meant that even for operations *inside* South Vietnam, Nixon would have to justify every request for funds and troops. When the president had tried to block Cooper-Church, by leaning on his most livid partisans in Congress, the key Senate committees had threatened to go beyond reducing the foreign military sales that sustained the ARVN to cutting the US military's own funding as well. Nixon capitulated, cutting the 1971 budget for ARVN improvement and modernization nearly in half, from $575 million to $300 million. But he was running out of cards to play. Retired general James Gavin warned of the "dissipation" of American strength in Southeast Asia: "While we pursue one more tactical victory after another we lead the country down the road to strategic disaster."[52]

In the month of May 1970, over 4 million students came out to protest the Cambodian Incursion at 1,300 colleges and universities. One hundred thousand protesters assembled in Washington to protest the war. Nixon had to order National Guard and active-duty troops to garrison federal buildings to prevent them from being seized by protesters. Kissinger was forced to sleep in the White House basement because demonstrators had surrounded his apartment. The White House was ringed by a stockade of empty city buses, and troops of the 82nd Airborne Division bivouacked in the Executive Office Building to defend the president. Overseas, surveys by the USIS in Europe and Asia "showed a considerable decline in U.S. prestige as a result of the May–June operations in Cambodia."[53]

Kent State University in Ohio had been the site a decade earlier of a royal visit to America by none other than Prince Sihanouk, who had lectured the students about Cambodia's policy of neutrality and its need for peaceful development. The issue of Cambodia returned to Kent State on May 4, 1970, when nervous National Guard troops fired sixty-one live rounds into a crowd of student demonstrators, killing four and wounding eleven. Two days later, campus police at SUNY Buffalo shot and wounded several students. Three days after that, a rattled, sleepless Nixon made a bizarre appearance at the Lincoln Memorial at four o'clock in the morning, where he mingled with student protesters and tried to persuade them that he was a president of peace, as well as an expert on college football and surfing. On May 14, National Guardsmen in Mississippi stormed a dormitory at Jackson State and killed or wounded a dozen more students. The shootings at Kent State had been captured by student photographer Harold Walker. He published the shocking images, igniting yet another national scandal around the war.[54]

While Americans were protesting the Cambodian Incursion, the monsoon rains were slackening in I Corps. Incredible as it seemed under the circumstances prevailing in 1970, the US 101st Airborne Division launched yet another assault on the A Shau Valley: Operation Texas Star. It was the only major offensive launched by US forces inside South Vietnam in 1970, and the last of the war. Abrams callously ordered the op as a "final" assist to the ARVN, to destroy as many NVA troops and supplies as possible before the 101st Airborne was withdrawn.

This time, the role of the 101st Airborne would be more limited than during the battle for Hamburger Hill. In Operation Texas Star, Colonel Ben Harrison's 3rd Brigade would move back to the rim of the A Shau Valley to rebuild firebases abandoned after Hamburger Hill, chief among them FSB Ripcord. From these heights, the 101st Airborne would support Operation Chicago Peak by the ARVN 1st Division down in the valley. Not surprisingly, Operation Texas Star met fierce resistance as it tried to seize and fortify knobs and ridges overlooking the "Warehouse Area"—the camouflaged supply bunkers of the NVA 324B Division in the A Shau. It was a cautious, limited-liability operation from the start. Only two battalions were committed to it. Abrams was determined not to blunder into another Hamburger Hill. As it chanced, he would blunder into something even worse.

On July 1, 1970, having spent two months moving six battalions of the NVA 6th and 803rd Regiments into positions around FSB Ripcord, carefully hiding them from the American gunships and scout planes that orbited overhead when the skies were clear, the NVA attacked FSB Ripcord, which was the headquarters of the 2nd Battalion of the US 506th Infantry Regiment. The battalion, commanded by Lieutenant Colonel Andre Lucas, held on grimly through a three-week siege. The NVA occupied the hills flanking Ripcord and pummeled the firebase with heavy mortars, recoilless rifles, and RPGs. Lucas would send companies out on search and clear patrols only to see them mauled by the hidden, more numerous NVA.

When Colonel Harrison inserted his only reserve company to hold a key hill east of Ripcord, it too was encircled, mortared, and forced off the hill, leaving all of its dead behind. The survivors barely made it to a neighboring ridge where Hueys could dart in to extract the terrified paratroopers. The 2nd Battalion of the 506th, huddled inside Ripcord, watched things go from bad to worse. On the eighteenth day of the siege, a Chinook delivering artillery shells was shot down as it hovered over Ripcord's ammunition storage area. The flaming hulk, with sling loads of munitions beneath it, fell to the ground and detonated 2,200 howitzer rounds.[55]

Five days later, more Chinooks arrived to lift out the howitzers that had survived the blast and slicks flew in to extract the grunts who remained alive. Colonel Lucas was blown to bits by a 120 mm mortar round as he oversaw the hurried evacuation. In all, the 101st Airborne lost another 386 KIAs in Operation Texas Star. Seventy-five had died inside FSB Ripcord, the rest in the fighting around it. Without the supporting fires from Ripcord, the ARVN's Operation Chicago Peak achieved little besides friendly casualties. It shied away from the heavily defended Warehouse Area, briefly raided and patrolled around its edges, and then departed. By the fall of 1970, the ARVN 1st Division and the US 101st Airborne Division had surrendered the A Shau Valley (again) and retreated back to the foothills and the coastal plain. If any sentient American still believed that the war in Vietnam was winnable, the struggle for FSB Ripcord should have dispelled that illusion once and for all.[56]

Chapter 22

QUIET MUTINY

The pointlessness of Nixon's war in Vietnam made the draft increasingly controversial among *every* American demographic. A platoon leader freshly arrived in Vietnam in 1970 noticed immediately the "natural selection process" that had sifted the educated and privileged from his grunts and left "only those without skill, without schooling, and without friends." The draft pool of eligible American males was always so much greater than the numbers actually drafted that men with higher education secured deferments easily. "The radical young," Stewart Alsop wrote in *Newsweek* in June 1970, "talk as though they were a lost generation, condemned by the system to be hauled away to Vietnam, and killed or wounded." This "theme," Alsop continued, "is pure nonsense." In reality, the draft was an instrument of "class discrimination," in which young men who went to college quadrupled their chances of *not* being drafted.

In the entire course of the war, Alsop alleged, Yale, Harvard, and Princeton had together graduated precisely two students who were drafted and killed in action in Vietnam. College men amounted to only 10 percent of a typical draft, and they rarely saw any fighting because they were usually put into noncombat administrative jobs. It was the men with no more than a high school diploma who did the fighting. To avoid the draft, there was a sudden surge in college attendance in 1969, with 40 percent of male high school graduates choosing to go on to college as, among other things, a hedge against the draft.[1]

Over three-quarters of American troops who served in Vietnam were from working-class or lower-income families, while just 23 percent had parents in professional, managerial, or technical careers. Sons of the well-to-do could secure deferments by staying in school, feigning illness, or, like future president George W. Bush, magicking up an otherwise unattainable commission in their state National Guard to avoid service in Vietnam, as Bush did in May 1968, two weeks before he graduated from Yale and lost his student deferment. (Bush was joined that day by another grandee, the son of Texas senator Lloyd Bentsen, who wriggled into the same Air National Guard unit to escape the draft.)[2]

Nixon, like Johnson before him, loathed this burgeoning class of students, who protested the war from the safety of their dorms and quads. Unlike LBJ, Nixon did not fear overhauling the system and upsetting elites that he had always resented. He had pledged in his 1968 campaign to end the draft, and he now groped for ways to do that. With more scrutiny on the way men were drafted for Vietnam, he proposed a lottery system, where *every* young man would be at risk. Until now, men had appeared before local draft boards, which tended to defer white, middle-class males, whose futures were bright. Lower-income non-college whites and men of color were drafted instead.

College men, fearful of the draft, had historically been encouraged to volunteer for noncombat jobs to avoid the draft and assignment to Army specialty 11B (Eleven Bravo), which was the infantry, where people got killed and maimed in large numbers. This had actually worked out well for the Army, which had successfully frightened college men into volunteering (to avoid the infantry) while filling the combat arms with non-college draftees. Eighty-eight percent of the infantry in Vietnam in 1969 were draftees, as were 55 percent of the killed and wounded.[3]

When Nixon and Secretary of Defense Melvin Laird pressed the Army to give them a date beyond which no more draftees would be sent to Vietnam, the Army protested that historically the draft furnished only 30 percent of its manpower. Most soldiers "volunteered" in order to avoid combat. Without the menace of the draft, the Army protested, no one would volunteer for those essential noncombat support jobs.

But that message—abbreviated by a columnist to "leave the fighting to the peasants and the Walter Mittys"—raised yet more questions on

Capitol Hill and in the media. Infantry, artillery, and armor in Vietnam were manned by draftees. Stewart Alsop regarded the June 1969 *Life* magazine piece—"Faces of the American Dead in Vietnam: June 1969, One Week's Toll"—as a turning point. The 242 men killed in Vietnam that week "were not the kind of young men to whom it would have occurred to get a teaching job or to go to divinity school to avoid the draft." They had been plucked from their high schools, farms, or factories. They had not found ways to duck the draft or avoid combat. They were victims of class discrimination and a certain corruption of power.[4]

And yet such a jaundiced view ignored the whole concept of "selective service" as defined by its mandarin, seventy-six-year-old General Lewis Hershey, who had been directing the draft since 1936. Hershey, an early advocate of universal military training, viewed the draft as a compromise between the ideal of universal service and the chaos of general conscription, where everyone would be called but then, as happened in World War I, when selective service was born, exemptions for skilled labor and other "essential" functions had to be handed out piecemeal. This had complicated the process and kindled accusations of favoritism.[5]

Hershey's drafts, from World War II to Vietnam, had tried to steer a middle course that would maintain the armed forces in sufficient numbers without antagonizing powerful interests or wasting valuable human capital on the battlefield. In theory, this made perfect sense: exempt educated young men who would invent and apply the technology and techniques that would keep America rich and powerful, and draft the poorly educated to fight. Hershey called this the "club of induction." It could be used to "drive" young men into higher education for the nation's ultimate benefit. Those who showed no interest or aptitude could serve the nation in combat.

In the 1950s and 1960s, there was a nearly seven-fold increase in exemptions for men attending college or working in professional fields thanks to Hershey's "manpower channeling." In his World War II drafts, Hershey had exempted many farmers and industrial workers as "essential." The economic challenge posed by the Cold War—keeping the pipeline full of innovation—devalued the blue-collar worker and shifted exemptions overwhelmingly to university students and white-collar professionals.

McNamara's Pentagon, focused on the global struggle against communism, had eagerly embraced Hershey's methods and taken them a step further. High school dropouts, who historically were half as likely as graduates to complete enlistments, were taken in ever larger numbers. The Marines took the most—42 percent—but by 1969 dropouts furnished nearly a third of the men in all combat units. McNamara then set his sights on "Cat IVs"—men in Category IV of the Armed Forces Qualification Test. Category IV (of five) was the lowest acceptable for military service. In the 1960s, one-third of draft-age Americans fell into this category. These 600,000 men were generally poor and disproportionately Black. They hailed from urban slums and rural backwaters. They had difficulty following orders and performing complex tasks. They were rarely drafted, on the grounds that they might pose as much danger to themselves and their unit as to the enemy.

In 1966, McNamara had announced his intention to "salvage" these "rejectees" in a program he named "Project 100,000" and linked to LBJ's Great Society. Each fiscal year, 100,000 Cat IVs would be "rescued" from "squalid ghettos" and improved by military service, which, McNamara argued, would make these 100,000 men better earners, husbands, fathers, and citizens. LBJ, desperate for manpower but unwilling to revoke student deferments or call up the National Guard and reserves, eagerly embraced the use of these "second-class fellows," as he called them. He linked their induction to his War on Poverty. They would learn to "shave and bathe" in the Army, he said, and qualify for productive work after the war. The Cat IVs came with the added advantage that they could be shoveled, unresisting, into combat.[6]

The rejectees were renamed "New Standards Men," and 354,000 of them would join the military in the next five years. Forty percent of them were Black, at a time when Blacks were 11 percent of the population and 9 percent of active-duty personnel. The Pentagon brass never warmed to the program. They called the New Standards Men "McNamara's Moron Corps." Westmoreland, first as MACV commander and now as Army chief of staff, predicted that fewer than 10 percent of them would ever be molded into good soldiers. Many of them could not read, tie their boots, or even stand at attention. They often had low IQs, some in the 60s. One of McNamara's advisers reminded the SecDef that "wars are not won by using marginal manpower as cannon fodder, but by risking and sometimes losing the flower of a nation's youth."[7]

But, in the eyes of McNamara and LBJ, the New Standards Men had served a key function. Nearly all of them went to Vietnam, half of them as combat infantrymen, and they were killed at three times the rate of other grunts. New Standards Men furnished a quarter of all inductions and filled slots that otherwise would have been filled by better-off middle-class youth. They relieved pressure on the politicians.[8]

General Lewis Hershey, often compared with J. Edgar Hoover for his extreme longevity and broad influence, grasped and regretted the inherent "unfairness" of it all. "A deferment," he wrote, "is merely a term used to denote when one man goes in place of another." Didn't a machinist have as much right to a deferment as a college student? he grumbled during the Vietnam War as he watched the surge in student protests. But Hershey saw no better way to husband resources and accommodate the powerful lawmakers and interest groups who demanded deferments. He would have preferred a universal draft of all young men without fear or favor but knew that he would never get it. Johnson would no sooner have revoked student deferments as call up the reservists, whose numbers had ballooned during the war. Even the more daring Nixon, knowing how toxic the war had become, would not take those steps.[9]

But Nixon had to do *something*. He was running out of combat troops. Reenlistments and "replacement flow" were falling, and troops trying to change their military specialty from infantry, armor, engineers, or artillery in order to escape combat had to be told no—the policy had changed. Grunts they were and grunts they would remain. This too was hell on morale. Nixon hoped the lottery would give him more flexibility. But Hershey opposed the draft lottery put forward by Nixon as "blind chance." It would rob the nation of great minds and talents that would be better employed away from the battlefield. Hershey had tried a lottery system from 1940 to 1942, but only to establish the "order of call," at which point local draft boards had taken over to select and defer.[10]

Nixon now did something that no other president had dared to do. Hershey was an institution sustained by congressional support and gratitude for the way he had run the Selective Service since the New Deal. Nixon kicked Hershey upstairs, awarded him a fourth star, and then forced his retirement. Nixon then persuaded Congress to institute a true lottery system to "reduce inequities." At the same time, the president formed a commission to begin the transition to an all-volunteer military. Nixon had begun the campaign for a lottery just after his inauguration, and Congress approved the new system on November 26, 1969—just five days before the 1970 draft.

In that draft of 1970, many of the 850,000 young Americans born between 1944 and 1950 tuned to CBS and watched anxiously as Selective Service officials reached into a hopper at 9 p.m. Eastern Time on December 1 and pulled out plastic capsules, each containing a day of the year. If your birthday was pulled among the first 130 of the 366 dates, you would almost certainly be inducted.

A second lottery would follow. Officials would dip their hands into a jar with twenty-six capsules, each containing a letter of the alphabet. If they pulled, say, "W" first, then all men whose last names began with "W" would be the first to go within each inducted draft number. It certainly *seemed* fairer. For the first time, wealthy and educated boys of privilege—the "fortunate sons" excoriated by the band Creedence Clearwater Revival—found themselves on the chopping block. Most of them escaped. Donald Trump drew 356, Bill Clinton 311, Dan Quayle 211, and Rush Limbaugh 152. Ike's grandson David Eisenhower, a senior at Amherst College, drew number 10 but found safe haven in the Navy, where he attended Officer Candidate School and kept an apartment nearby for his wife, who was Nixon's daughter Julie. For those who *were* called, flat feet, bone spurs, heart murmurs, asthma, cysts, and a myriad of other conditions, certified by a compliant doctor, could still secure a deferment. National Guard and reserve units, barred to ordinary Americans and nearly every Black American, remained a safe haven for elite whites and professional athletes of all races.[11]

With the Nixon administration not actually pursuing *victory* in the war, massive morale problems arose in 1969–1970. "I don't want to get killed 'buying time' for the gooks," a grunt in the 1st ID grumbled. A platoon leader in the 25th ID observed that his men by now all had the same view of the war: "There just seemed to be no goal" other than fighting for Thieu and Ky, "who were no better than the guys we're fighting." The grunts, the roughly 80,000 combat troops left among the 400,000 total US military personnel in South Vietnam, knew that they were being sacrificed for lines on a map or to win a respite for the ARVN, neither of which seemed worth dying for. Their casualties, when they came, were horrific, inflicted by booby-trapped bombs and howitzer rounds, which tore off heads and limbs.[12]

Patrolling near Chu Lai in this phase of the war, a grunt of the Americal stepped on a booby-trapped 105 mm round that blew his remains into the upper branches of a tree. Two other grunts had to shinny up the tree and collect the body parts: "the white bone of an arm, pieces of skin, and something wet and yellow that must have been the intestines." One of the grunts sang Peter, Paul and Mary's "Lemon Tree" as he threw down the parts: "Lemon tree very pretty and the lemon flower is sweet / But the fruit of the poor lemon is impossible to eat." As that last ghoulish detail attested, these grunts were increasingly a weird and younger mix of Cat IVs, high school dropouts, and antiwar college boys injected by the lottery. The draft boards had tended to take men closer to twenty-six before their eligibility ran out. The lottery called nineteen-year-olds first.[13]

Love beads, peace signs, long hair, and the quiet mutiny. Troops in Vietnam changed after 1970, when the war was lost and Nixon's draft lottery injected more skeptics and college students into the armed forces. Here a squad leader of the 11th Light Infantry Brigade shouts instructions to his men near Chu Lai in January 1971. (National Archives)

John Pilger, a journalist sent to cover the war's "final act" in 1970, spent time in Saigon and on the Cambodian border at Fire Support Base Snuffy with a Cav squadron. He described life at FSB Snuffy this way: "No blood, no atrocities, just the rejection of the war by those sent here to fight it, just the quiet mutiny of the greatest army in history." The grunts were clearly fed up with the war. Even these formerly elite Cav troops, Pilger reported, were "slouching around with long hair and love beads, with peace signs on their helmets, muttering threats against any officer who might send them into action."

Two grunts described the demise of their company commander, a hated "lifer," who was shot in the back by his own men when he tried to coax a unit forward into enemy fire. All of this mocked the regimental slogan placarded over FSB Snuffy's main gate: "We Can, We Will." These Cav troopers of 1970, Pilger observed, "are a very different kind of American soldier, from a world mostly unknown to their commanders." They were "graduates of an American rebellion that stemmed from a war they were sent here to fight, and quietly but massively they have brought that rebellion with them here to Vietnam." The war was ending not because Nixon was changing strategy, Pilger concluded. "The war is ending because the grunt is taking no more bullshit."[14]

Nixon's increasingly panicky troop withdrawals—officially called "redeployments"—were organized as Operation Keystone. Kissinger opposed the withdrawals because they weakened his diplomatic hand in Paris. The North Vietnamese, he protested, did not need to concede anything in a situation where "we were on our way out of Vietnam by negotiation, if possible, by unilateral withdrawal if necessary." But Kissinger was largely alone in that protest. Against him were Secretary of Defense Laird, Secretary of State Rogers, and most Americans. They wanted a major drawdown and de-Americanization of the war before the 1972 elections.[15]

The first to depart was the US 9th Infantry Division, which left Vietnam in June 1969 in Operation Keystone Eagle. Forty-five thousand more troops came out in late 1969 in Operation Keystone Cardinal. Keystone Blue Jay followed in spring 1970, with 50,000 more troops heading home. In all, 115,000 pulled out in 1969 and 148,000 more followed in 1970, taking MACV's 543,000-man force down to 280,000 by year's end.[16]

Dark humor proliferated in the American ranks: "We are the Unwilling / Led by the Unqualified / Doing the Unnecessary / For the Ungrateful." That catchphrase, originally aimed at the Habsburgs by a Czech historian, now appeared on flak jackets, helmets, and cigarette lighters all over Vietnam. Army chief of staff Westmoreland stepped in to meddle with Abrams' arrangements and commit a final act of self-destructive mischief. To minimize the "turbulence" of the troop withdrawals, Abrams had wanted to send units home as units. No, Westy replied from Washington; the only fair system was to populate departing units with the troops who had served the longest in Vietnam, whether or not they were actually in the unit slated for withdrawal.

Westy got his way and set off a mad scramble among the grunts. The most experienced were plucked from every unit and sent home, to be replaced by inexperienced transfers from other outfits. Effective combat units were dissolved and reconstituted with strangers. Morale problems sharpened, as Abrams had predicted. Alcohol and drug use surged. Good whiskey sold in the PX for a dollar a bottle. Weed had always been available; heroin became widely available in 1970, when a Department of Defense study revealed that 60 percent of deployed personnel were smoking marijuana and 25 to 30 percent were using heroin, most of it smuggled into the firebases by Vietnamese "hooch maids." Convinced that the Army was covering up the issue, Nixon sent White House aide Egil "Bud" Krogh to Vietnam to investigate it. "You don't have a drug problem," Krogh reported. "You have a drug condition. It's available *everywhere*." During Operation Holly—Bob Hope's 1970 Christmas Tour of Vietnam—the jokes that landed best were all about drugs: "I hear you guys are into gardening here—growing your own grass." Or "I hear marijuana's as easy to get here as gum: Double your pleasure, double your fun."[17]

Four years earlier, when LBJ made a surprise visit to Cam Ranh Bay, Westmoreland had assured the president that "no Commander in Chief in our history has ever had finer troops than these." That was no longer the case. Draftees taken from a baby boom youth culture that had been watching the war on television increasingly spoke of a "generation gap" and questioned a system marred by race riots, political assassinations, and a war that gave every appearance of being prolonged for the benefit of politicians and

By 1970, US units in Vietnam had a serious drug problem. Here an MP of the 101st Airborne Division frisks a soldier for drugs at Camp Eagle near Hue. (National Archives)

special interests. "Never trust anyone over thirty" seemed like good advice when you studied the cynical moves of the Johnson and Nixon administrations. Peace signs were everywhere in Vietnam—drawn on bunkers, helmet covers, gun shields, trucks, tanks, and banners.[18]

Racial tensions had spiked after the assassination of Martin Luther King Jr. The self-segregation of Black and white troops in Southeast Asia became commonplace. Infantry companies extracted from the field and returned to base camp for stand-downs self-segregated, Blacks occupying one part of the camp, whites another. In the cities, there were separate bars, restaurants, massage parlors, and sex workers for whites and Blacks. Post offices and mess halls gathered Blacks in one area and whites in another. Whites would obstruct sidewalks so that Blacks would have to wait or walk around them, and vice versa. A half dozen Black soldiers standing in a walkway exchanging "daps" could block it for five minutes or more while the whites waited for the taps, pats, waves, shakes, slaps, snaps, and finger jives to end.[19]

Salutes, when rendered, were surly. Blacks expressed disgust for the "white man's war" in Vietnam, a feeling shared by the whites themselves.

An Air Force pilot recalled mandatory "race-relations training" introduced around this time to teach troops "the nuances of offensive language and actions." It worked too well, "broadening the means of insulting someone." Troops who had gone to Vietnam without knowing the racial and ethnic slurs in use in other parts of the United States were now handed "a much wider vocabulary," which they "brought to bear with great precision."[20]

Desertion and AWOL rates spiked. Nearly half of US personnel in Vietnam went AWOL in 1970–1971. Nearly one-fifth of combat troops deserted. These were higher percentages than in Korea or World War II. A secret Army study in 1970 concluded that senior officers in Vietnam had replaced the ethic of "duty, honor, and country" with "me, my ass, and my career." They were "fearful of personal failure," utterly unmoved by "the sweat and frustration of their subordinates," and "engulfed in producing statistical results."[21]

With leadership like this, a blank nihilism descended on the grunts, abetted by the music of the era, some of which, like the Animals' "We Gotta Get Out of This Place," had to be banned on Armed Forces Radio. Asked to compile an "info sheet" on Cam Ranh Bay, home to the US Army's biggest military seaport and two Air Force wings, the inhabitants responded to the survey in this way: "Any famous landmarks? None. Animals? None. Vegetation of locality? Sand. Weather? Wet. Any special native habits? None. Prices? Too high. Any special items to be bought? Charcoal."[22]

The incidence of "fragging"—murdering one's own officers and NCOs—doubled in 1970. The weapon of choice was usually a fragmentation grenade, which was issued to grunts without a serial number and conveniently burst into 2,000 frags that flayed everything inside a thirty-three-foot radius. There had been 96 attacks on officers in 1969, and there were 209 in 1970, numbers that were probably just 10 percent of the real totals because they counted only cases that were adjudicated. But there was no question that formerly gung-ho officers and NCOs were easing up to appease the grunts and avoid reprisals. The US forces in Vietnam frayed most noticeably among the "paper soldiers" in the rear, where there was more opportunity for slacking.[23]

A Pentagon review board warned of "black frustration and anger." An Army report spoke of "the polarization of the races" in Vietnam and concluded that Black soldiers "had lost faith in the Army system." In the field, some African American grunts formed into "Ju Ju" and "Mau Mau" groups to oppose unreasonable orders from whites, variously called "Chucks," "beasts," or "foreigners." African Americans flew black flags on their vehicles and scowled at all of the Confederate flags flapping from barracks and trucks or emblazoned on the shoulder patches of many of the helicopter pilots who flew Black grunts in and out of ops. In the platoons, Black soldiers complained that they, more than whites, were made to carry the heavy M-60 machine gun and its bandoliers of 7.62 mm cartridges.[24]

Westmoreland's deputy in the Pentagon estimated that in December 1970 morale and standards of leadership had plunged to just 30 percent of what they had been in 1967. The Army's greatest fear at this point was that the NVA might overrun one or more of these demoralized units in the field or at a firebase and defeat them with "very high casualties," which would only increase the pressure on Nixon to quit the war. As it was, Nixon's withdrawals were not shrewdly or tactically calculated but were acts of desperation, to get this rotting army out of Vietnam before it disintegrated.[25]

General Arthur S. Collins Jr., who had commanded the 4th ID in Vietnam in 1966 and returned to command I Field Force in 1970, noted a sharp deterioration of morale, discipline, and standards in the time between his two tours. Eye Field Force was the American corps command in II Corps. In his travels around the massive AO—the biggest in South Vietnam—Collins questioned the whole American way of war in Vietnam. Sprawling ports, airfields, base camps, and other structures had "turned into a burden," leaching away the Army's "foxhole strength" to staff the huge facilities. "We have too much of everything—too many containers, too much wire, too many vehicles, too much ammo." There was little appreciation "of the unchanging and harsh demands of the combat environment."

Grunts were whisked to and from increasingly perfunctory ops and, even in the forward area, provided with "paper plates, hot meals, ice cream, and mountains of beer and soft drinks." The troops had become soft and querulous, putting on bizarre uniforms, declining to wear shirts and helmets in combat, shooting their peers accidentally (or deliberately), and using drugs day and night. Their relations with their Vietnamese ally were poor if the regular complaints from the ARVN, the ruff-puffs, and civilians were to be believed. US vehicles, always driving too fast to avoid ambushes, made the roads a constant hazard, even more so when they took potshots at South Vietnamese along the roads or heaved cans and bottles at them. These acts were always ignored or forgiven by American officers—put down to "horseplay" or "boys being boys." Collins could not tell if softening American discipline was the cause or effect of these daily affronts. "How far," Collins wrote, "can we travel on this road and still perform our mission effectively?"[26]

Collins scoffed at an Army that had become accustomed to patting itself on the back and would later protest that, had it only been given more of everything, it could have won the war. There never had been a plan to win and there still wasn't. Firepower was everywhere carried to extremes. "I'll use any amount of supporting fire to save even one American soldier," officers said self-righteously, but this had proven counterproductive, even disastrous. Forward supply points and firing positions contained too much ammo, which was routinely targeted by enemy mortars and recoilless rifles, resulting in massive conflagrations.

More friendly casualties were generated loading, unloading, transporting, and guarding all of these munitions. Friendly fire, usually due to "shooting too much," killed and maimed a steady stream of allied forces. These, and all wounded, became a drag on every operation. When he investigated why his maneuver battalions were reporting poor results in their contacts with the enemy in 1970, Collins found that the mania for instant medical evacuation by helicopter meant that even a single casualty could halt a platoon in its tracks, "with platoon leaders and sergeants tied up on the radio calling for medevac and providing security for the incoming chopper." While the platoon halted to dust off the casualty, the enemy would regroup or slip away to safety.[27]

The war's cost ballooned because of "unbridled firepower," defined by Collins as the routine summoning of artillery, gunships, and tac air to engage even one or two Viet Cong. This, he added, "has not made us a better or more effective army." On the contrary, American infantry were losing the ability to close with the enemy in small units, using their rifles, M-79s, machine guns, and grenades as they walked behind a barrage of artillery fire. Instead, they increasingly remained at a safe distance from the enemy while "the gunship, tac airstrike, and battery concentration routine" was employed. It killed some of the enemy, but, being a "routine" as opposed to a surprise, it allowed most of the enemy to escape. The Army's use of firepower in Vietnam, Collins concluded, was "wasteful, inefficient, and lacking the stamp of the true professional."[28]

Life magazine ran a shocking piece by John Saar in October 1970 titled "You Just Can't Hand Out Orders." It told the story of Captain Brian Utermahlen, West Point '68, who had suspended normal discipline in his Cav company in order to hold it together. By 1970, even the Cav "seethed with problems," chiefly leadership's need, as Saar put it, to forge an altogether new relationship with grunts who were increasingly "liberated, educated, and aware." Fifty percent of the men in Alpha Company had college time under their belts. Troops smoking pot weren't punished. Troops who refused to fight weren't court-martialed.[29]

Utermahlen's company, with Saar along for the ride, went on a seventeen-day op without generating any body count or an adverse report. "The draftees," Saar observed, evinced "a frank disinterest in anything that might cost an American life." Grunt logic, Saar wrote, was simple: If Nixon had decided not to win this war, why should they die in it? That logic multiplied by every American platoon still in Vietnam meant that the Army was no longer the efficient, responsive instrument of the early years of the war. Grunts, led by squad leaders who were also draftees, were flatly refusing to go into combat, and officers and NCOs had little choice but to "work it out" with them. Taking it all in, the formerly hawkish *Newsweek* columnist Stewart Alsop implored Nixon to get the Army out of Vietnam before it imploded: "It's time to take these bitter draftees in our crumbling Army out of Vietnam—and the sooner the better."[30]

Seventeen thousand new draftees would go to Vietnam in 1971, and the Army brass struggled to segregate this "new meat"—as the draftees were called—from the demoralized mass already in-country, which Alsop judged "a non-fighting army." The Army was winding down to just two full-strength US divisions in Vietnam: the Americal and the 101st Airborne. And yet since the My Lai massacre, the Americal had become a byword for dysfunction. Lieutenant Calley's atrocity had been followed by the case of an Americal brigade commander charged with machine-gunning civilians from his helicopter. Then Americal's commanding general had been relieved after one of his firebases, defended by 250 grunts, had been overrun by just 50 VC, who killed or wounded 115 Americans in the raid. The hallowed 101st Airborne Division, which had defended Bastogne in 1944 and fought valiantly in this war since its arrival in 1965, was now known as the "one-oh-*worst*," with as much drug use, fragging, racial strife, and aversion to combat as any other outfit. Visiting it in the field and in its base camps, a reporter concluded: "The problem of motivation is so overwhelming as to defy rational 'solutions' and 'programs' other than withdrawal."[31]

In November 1970, Lieutenant William Calley's court-martial finally began at Fort Benning, Georgia, by which time US forces in Vietnam were down to 280,000. A four-monthlong review, led by General William Peers, had recommended charges against twenty-eight officers, for the evidence proved even more damning than expected. That number was now whittled down to fourteen. Only five would actually be tried, and only one convicted. Ninety-one witnesses appeared, depositions were taken, documents and photographs were scrutinized. Peers considered the Americal Division's cover-up of the massacre as troubling as the atrocity itself. General Sam Koster and his staff and unit commanders had lied to investigators and destroyed all incriminating logs and reports.

Calley's platoon had slaughtered babies, infants, women, and old men, broken for lunch, and then resumed the massacre. The lunch break during the massacre was a detail that Army chief of staff Westmoreland considered especially "diabolical." Charges against thirteen officers were dropped for lack of conclusive evidence. Lieutenant Calley had no such luck. Charged with the murder of 109 civilians in My Lai, he was convicted of slaying twenty-nine of them himself. (He'd been observed reloading his M-16 more than a dozen times during the massacre.) In March 1971, Calley was handed a life sentence with hard labor for those twenty-nine counts of premeditated murder.[32]

Nixon treated the trial as just another PR problem to be gamed. "Most people don't give a shit" about Calley, he smirked to Kissinger. He was right. A Gallup poll in April 1971 showed that 69 percent of Americans believed that Calley was a scapegoat, thrown in jail to spare his superiors, and commissioned only because so many privileged college boys had avoided military service. In the red states, Calley was a hero. Country music stations played songs like "Set Lt. Calley Free" and "Battle Hymn of Lieutenant Calley." The latter sold 2 million records. It shifted blame from Calley to the antiwar movement:

While we're fighting in the jungles, they were marching in the street
While we're dying in the rice fields, they were helping our defeat
While we're facing VC bullets, they were sounding a retreat.

General Peers watched Calley's bizarre rehabilitation in horror. "And now, he's practically a hero. It's a tragedy," Peers despaired. Nixon saw it differently—as just another lever to rouse his conservative base. He quietly freed Calley from the Fort Benning stockade and put him under house arrest in luxury quarters while the lieutenant's (successful) appeals went forward. With spectacularly bad taste, *Esquire* put a grinning Calley on its cover, flanked by four Vietnamese children. General Koster lost a star and his post as superintendent of West Point, but nothing else. The men and officers of Bravo Company, 4th Battalion, 3rd Infantry, who had slaughtered ninety civilians at My Khe while Medina's company was murdering the inhabitants of My Lai, were quietly exonerated so as not to muddy the Pentagon message that My Lai was a singular atrocity, not part of a pattern of lawlessness. Records of that second massacre were classified top secret and buried. When reporters pressed for details on the massacre at My Khe, Pentagon briefers lied that it had been perpetrated by the ARVN. "Westmoreland covered his ass," an Army colonel involved in the investigation observed. "He did what he had to do to preserve the system." Pressed by the Senate to get his troops under control, Abrams sounded unhinged. Those senators, he brayed, "must be having champagne parties and celebrations—I don't know, parades over the disarray in our country."[33]

"War is bad, so we've got to avoid more bad wars" was Nixon's comment on the matter. "Lieutenant Calley should not be treated like [Charles] Manson." Calley, who had behaved with exceptional cowardice and cruelty, would be released from confinement in 1974. In the meantime, My Lai's chief impact on the war effort was to snarl American operations in even stricter rules of engagement. Westmoreland worried that he himself might be put on trial for failing to prevent atrocities by his troops—a proposal actually floated on the *Dick Cavett Show* by none other than retired General Telford Taylor, who had served as chief counsel for the prosecution at the Nuremberg trials. Westy now raced to implement what he called "an elaborate system of checks and clearances to insure the safety of civilians." AOs would be divided into free-fire, restricted, and no-fire zones. If a VC fired at you from an inhabited area, you would never receive clearance to return fire. "This was not like the John Wayne movies that I had watched growing up," one warrant officer commented.[34]

The split among Americans over the war was profound. The Vietnam Veterans Against the War led the "Winter Soldier Investigation" in February 1971, in which speakers were invited to describe the misconduct and crimes they had observed during their service in Vietnam. In April, a group of veterans threw the medals they had earned in Vietnam onto the Capitol steps. They called it Operation Dewey Canyon III. Navy lieutenant John Kerry testified before the Senate Foreign Relations Committee that April. He posed the question on every grunt's mind: "How do you ask a man to be the last man to die in Vietnam... To die for a mistake?"[35]

But arrayed against these pro-peace forces were the "hard hats," the conservative, pro-war working class, as well as much of Middle America. "Middle America," a term coined by columnist Joseph Kraft in 1967, referred to the roughly 100 million Americans of all classes who were socially conservative and hostile to the youth culture of the 1960s. *Time* magazine had made "Middle Americans" its "Man of the Year" in 1970, finding solace in the resistance of ordinary Americans to "the liberals, the radicals, the defiant young, and a [media] that they often believed was lying to them." Middle America's bumper stickers read "Honor America" or "Spiro Is My Hero," not "Make Love Not War." In 1971, 60 percent of Americans polled by Gallup called the war a "mistake," but 30 percent still supported it, and 10 percent expressed "no opinion."

Nixon had been elected by appealing to these hawkish and indifferent constituencies—the "forgotten Americans," as he called them—and hiving off as many Wallace votes as he could. All of Nixon's campaign ads on Vietnam had been painstakingly edited: Black soldiers were removed from photo montages, helmet covers were scrubbed of antiwar messages ("it reminds Midwest voters of hippies," a consultant warned), and images of American casualties were banned for having "too dovish an impact." Nixon cultivated George Meany, president of the AFL-CIO, to make sure that white-ethnic union workers supported the war in Vietnam.[36]

Public reaction to the Kent State massacre seemed to validate Nixon's insight that the only thing more unpopular than the war was the antiwar youth movement. A *Newsweek* poll in mid-May revealed that 50 percent of

Americans approved of the Cambodian Incursion. The *Washington Post*, given first crack at photographer Harold Walker's searing images of the killings at Kent State University, refused to run them on the grounds that they might be "faked." Ohio governor James Rhodes called the protesters at Kent State "the worst type of people we have in America."[37]

Bestselling novelist James Michener, who wrote an account of the Kent State shootings, noted that for several *weeks* after Ohio's National Guard troops had killed or wounded fifteen students, the town of Kent's daily newspaper had felt compelled to reserve a full page for "one of the most virulent outpourings of community hatred in recent decades"—not against the trigger-happy Guard unit that had fired on the students with live ammunition, but against the student victims, who were denigrated as punks, creeps, subversives, vandals, and crybabies. "Live ammunition! Well, really, what did they expect? Spitballs?" was a typical comment by a Ravenna, Ohio, resident. "The National Guard made only one mistake," another reader wrote, "they should have fired sooner and longer."[38]

Studying those daily broadsides, Michener wrote that "they give a portrait of Middle America at the beginning of the 1970s that is frightening." Middle America feared the virulence of the antiwar protests and handed Nixon an unexpected bounce in his approval rating. By the spring of 1970, it had crept up to 59 percent. "How easily everyone crumbles," Nixon gloated. The hard hats now set out to crumble the antiwar movement. On May 8, 1970, 500 hard hats paraded in New York in support of Nixon's war policy and Cambodian Incursion. They were also motivated by racism. They were white workers in white unions doggedly refusing to open up their union rolls to Blacks and Puerto Ricans. Many of them had moved from the South and the Midwest to work construction jobs in Manhattan. "America—love it or leave it," they chanted. "Hard hats put all college kids in one category," a construction worker explained. "They're all pot smokers, rabble-rousers, or faggots, and they deserve to be beaten up."[39]

The hard hats were aided by the firms that employed them—who shut down job sites like the twin towers of the World Trade Center so that the hard hats could march—and by the police, who let the hard hats pass through cordons unhindered to attack the war protesters with fists, hammers, wrenches, and wire cutters. The hard hats stormed City Hall, where Republican mayor John V. Lindsay had lowered flags to half-staff in memory of the four students killed at Kent State. Chanting "Lindsay's a Red" and "Kill the hippies, kill the traitors," the hard hats got into City Hall, savagely beating seventy people, and raised the flag back to its summit, ordering the cowed police to "get your helmets off," which they did. The newspapers called it "Bloody Friday."[40]

The construction union that conspired in the demonstration claimed that it was flooded with laudatory messages from all over the country that ran twenty to one in favor of the hard hats "for their patriotism." The hard hats marched again on May 20, shutting down every major construction project in Manhattan and rallying 100,000 New Yorkers around City Hall, waving signs that read "National Guard 4, Kent 0" and "Lindsay Sucks." Nixon invited the union leaders to the White House for a meeting in the Cabinet Room, where he thanked them for their "tremendous outpouring of support" for himself and for "our men fighting for peace in Southeast Asia." The delighted union bosses presented the president with a hard hat.[41]

More hard hats were to be found in both houses of Congress. Some Republican politicians appeared wearing hard hats decorated with Nixon stickers or flag decals to show their solidarity with these vigilantes. They aligned themselves with Nixon's effort to construct a new GOP base of Republicans, conservative Democrats, hard hats, southern whites, and, as Nixon put it, "Poles, Italians, Elks, Rotarians, and Catholics." In a sequence of close votes in 1971, the Senate tried and narrowly failed to put a fixed deadline on US participation in the war and to confine all military spending in Vietnam to troop withdrawals, not combat. Despite being the first president since Zachary Taylor in 1849 to take office without control of either congressional chamber, Nixon could still rally half of the Senate in favor of continuing the war, and—even in 1971—had little to fear from the House of Representatives, whose assent was required to cut funding for the war. Two hundred and eighteen representatives were needed for a majority in the 435-person House, yet such were the politics of national security that there were always 220 to 255 reliable votes to "support the troops"—so to speak—and prolong the war.[42]

General Arthur S. Collins Jr. was busy winding down I Field Force, which would shortly be deactivated as more and more American grunts withdrew from II Corps. In January 1971, Collins submitted his take on the year 1970. The central problem, he said, continued to be the 400,000-man

ARVN. For fifteen years, Collins wrote, the Americans had run training programs in this country, but they just kept "making excuses for the
ARVN." The South Vietnamese remained reluctant to do basic things such
as locating forward division command posts in the field or leaving troops
in the field overnight. Thieu's "promotion of incompetents" to maintain his
political machine wrecked the ARVN from within. Even terrible and corrupt generals were "not marked and removed from positions of responsibility." Collins found it incomprehensible that "for a country where survival is
at stake" there was "such a long delay in getting better leadership."[43]

In the meantime, VC penetration agents were increasingly active and
successful coaxing desertions from ARVN regiments. In January 1971, captured VC documents revealed that there were thirty-three agents inside the
ARVN 18th Division. Other divisions were assumed to be as vulnerable, not
least because the ARVN had begun drafting VC defectors into the army.
(Of the ARVN 18th Division's obviously inattentive commander, General
Abrams had this to say: "Not only the worst general in the Vietnamese
army, but the worst general in any army.")[44]

The ruff-puffs and self-defense forces were now the mainstay of South
Vietnam's defense, described by Saigon's Joint General Staff in March
1970 as "the saviors of Vietnam—in time." "Saviors" because they had the
numbers—a paper strength of millions—to defend South Vietnam's vast
embattled territory. "In time" because the militia units remained weak in
leadership, morale, training, and equipment. They were more likely to run
away than to fight.

The ARVN Joint General Staff's inspection reports of ruff-puff units in
1971 found the same problems everywhere: appalling leadership, officers
stealing from the troops, rampant desertion, begrimed and rusted weapons, careless construction of defensive works, perimeters overgrown with
high grass, and a near total failure to find the enemy whenever on patrol.
So few of their patrols and ambushes made contact with the enemy that it
was obvious from a glance at the numbers alone that the militiamen were
trying *not* to make contact. A typical report read, "3,400 patrols, 23 contacts." Instead of living in the villages and aggressively patrolling, the territorial forces usually chose static hilltop positions and remained in them.
At night, the ruff-puffs and self-defense forces were bypassed or overrun,
for they all went to sleep. "Every disaster we investigated," General Collins

summarized, "resulted from that one failing—sleeping—no one on alert." As yet, Vice President Ky's provincial self-defense force was no threat to anyone. In I Corps in 1970, the 500,000 men of the PSDF shared 82,000 weapons.[45]

Taking it all in, Collins concluded that it was past time for America to shake off the dust of Vietnam. "The Nixon drawdown," Collins concluded in January 1971, "is the right program." The US level of effort, he found, was "much too large," and the South Vietnamese would not do things for themselves until convinced that the Americans were really leaving. Until then, they would depend on the Americans for everything: tac air, gunships, firebases, medevac, and logistics. Collins recommended drastic cuts to the military adviser program as well: "To provide adviser teams to commanders who have been fighting for ten years no longer makes sense." The ARVN, he noted, had gotten materially stronger, while the NVA, assailed on the three fronts of Laos, Cambodia, and South Vietnam, was severely "stretched," yet still striving for victory. For its part, Saigon showed no evidence of "a will and desire to win." Clausewitz had famously said that resistance increases as either the will or the means to resist increase. And yet increased means in South Vietnam never translated into increased will or resistance.[46]

Confronted with reports like these and the unceasing demands of Thieu and Ky for yet *more* money for military expansion, Secretary of Defense Laird belatedly drew the line. Foes in Congress were beginning to call Vietnamization a "semantic hoax," just the latest version of the old LBJ policy of dragging the war out indefinitely. Washington had already agreed to pay for 12 South Vietnamese infantry divisions, 50 air squadrons, 1,200 naval ships, logistics, artillery, and over 2 million territorial forces, none of which were performing brilliantly. More increases, Laird growled, would only lead to more of these "troublesome effects," by which he meant bureaucracy, graft, and a general aversion to combat. First, Laird demanded, they had to fix what they already had.[47]

Chapter 23

"THE HEAVIEST DEFEAT EVER FOR NIXON & COMPANY"

Hanoi had expected a "Laotian Incursion" to follow the one in Cambodia like a one-two punch. Nixon's attack into Cambodia in 1970 had disrupted the sanctuaries and pushed communist units there away from the South Vietnamese border. For the United States and Saigon, the war-widening impact on Cambodia outweighed short-term benefits that wouldn't last. But there was no question that the communists had temporarily lost ground, caches, and supply lines in their prime sanctuaries, forcing them to postpone major offensive operations and make up the shortfall in Cambodia by moving more supplies south through Laos. Now, Abe Abrams hungered for a thrust into Laos to crimp that line of supply as well.[1]

Roads were so scarce in Laos that a second American punch into the communist sanctuaries—a Laotian Incursion—would have to travel along Route 9, the northernmost east–west road in South Vietnam. It paralleled the DMZ and wound past every major American base in I Corps: Dong Ha, Con Thien, Camp Carroll, the Rockpile, Khe Sanh, and finally Lang Vei, the Special Forces border post that had been overrun by the

NVA during the siege of Khe Sanh. Westmoreland had fought for Khe Sanh in part because he had planned to base himself there for an invasion of Laos in 1969.

Westy had pitched that plan to Wheeler and the Joint Chiefs in 1967, but no one had dared bring it to LBJ because it would have required yet another troop surge, which Johnson would not have authorized. Nixon probably would have, but he had himself absorbed a one-two punch in the meantime: first public and media outrage at the Cambodian Incursion, and then the Cooper-Church Amendment in Congress, which barred American ground troops from participating in any new cross-border operations.

But Westy's dream of a mechanized, airmobile thrust along Route 9 to the Ho Chi Minh Trail junction of Xepon in Laos lingered on in MACV headquarters, and in the White House. Nixon knew that 1971 was, as he put it, his "last chance for any major positive action" in Southeast Asia. By 1972, there would not be enough American troops or aircraft to undertake any but the most minor military operations.

Prodded by Nixon, Abrams now pushed Thieu and the ARVN to make the incursion into Laos themselves. The Laotian town of Xepon, twenty-seven miles west of the South Vietnamese border, was as grim a place as could be found in Southeast Asia at the time. It straddled Base Area 604 on the Ho Chi Minh Trail, which was the NVA's first major staging area in Laos on the way to South Vietnam. It fed the six other Laotian base areas between the DMZ and the Cambodian border. Every summer Hanoi would pre-position supplies on the southern edge of North Vietnam and, when the monsoon-washed roads of Laos finally dried in October, those supplies would be pushed south in a great effort to move as many men and as much material as could be moved before the rains returned in June. This was the rhythm of the war: massive deliveries in January, February, and March, followed by peak communist combat activity in April and May before the monsoon returned to dump twenty inches of rain on the trail every month until September.[2]

Most troops and supplies for the communist war effort in South Vietnam passed through Xepon's Base Area 604 and then either forked east into I Corps or continued south for infiltration into Cambodia and the three other corps areas of South Vietnam. Xepon had already attracted more American bombs than had been dropped on any city in Germany during

World War II. The housing had been ground to dust, and the people who remained lived in caves. And yet the Ho Chi Minh Trail and its oil pipeline continued to wind through Xepon. Every night in the dry season, convoys of North Vietnamese trucks drove through the crossroads there to supply the combat in South Vietnam.

The ARVN Joint General Staff, pushed by Abrams, agreed to take up positions along the trail to "put a cap on it." Xepon was the obvious place. There the South Vietnamese would find massive supply dumps, and if they established themselves there, they could physically block the flow of men and matériel from the North. Abrams sketched out a four-phase operation that would last for three months.[3]

But the ARVN, urged by MACV to do *something*, made no plans to hold Xepon. They would merely take it, or perhaps not, and then abandon it, if it was ever taken. Britain's defense attaché in Washington asked General Bill DePuy, the Army's assistant vice chief of staff, what the ARVN concept for a Laotian incursion would be. DePuy answered: "There are no fixed objectives to be achieved at all costs."[4]

The duration of any incursion would be sharply limited by the requirements of the ARVN. It could not extend into monsoon season because nasty weather arriving in May would curtail the air operations the ARVN needed to sustain itself. It would not be prolonged if enemy resistance stiffened or friendly casualties rose. President Thieu feared the impact of casualties on his presidency. It was rumored that he had given secret orders to his I Corps commander, forty-two-year-old General Hoang Xuan Lam, to terminate the op the instant casualties mounted. The operation, in other words, was pointless. Whatever damage the ARVN inflicted would be rapidly repaired by the enemy.[5]

Taking no chances after Nixon's thrust into Cambodia, the NVA prepared for a massive follow-on attack against Xepon and Base Area 604. In the fall of 1970, they created a new corps headquarters for Xepon, garrisoned 11,000 troops there, and made plans to move 50,000 more into positions around Route 9 and Xepon at the first sign of trouble. MACV described a "logistics war" in southern Laos, where the communists, their supplies pinched by the Cambodian Incursion and Abrams' hunt for logistics "noses" in South Vietnam, would stand and fight to defend the Ho Chi Minh Trail and its most critical hubs such as Xepon.[6]

With five or six NVA divisions earmarked for Xepon, attacking Base Area 604 looked increasingly desperate. But Nixon and his generals were feeling desperate. MACV and the CIA worried about the military impact of US withdrawal. Congress was sawing away at funding for the war. The US Air Force by late 1970 was flying half as many monthly sorties as it had a year earlier. Total funding for the war had fallen off a cliff in 1970—from $26.5 billion in 1969 to just $12 billion budgeted for 1971. NVA and VC units that had been harried almost to extinction by American pursuit in 1970 were bouncing back in early 1971 as more and more US units withdrew from combat. An NVA prisoner captured near Da Nang told his captors that "after the American withdrawal in early 1971, morale rose, the fear of death dissipated, and the troops were now anxious to fight and believed victory was in sight."[7]

With American ground forces in retreat and legally prohibited by Congress from operating in Cambodia or Laos, the time seemed ripe—politically at least—to fight an all-ARVN battle and showcase the success of "Vietnamization." Nixon wanted to run on this achievement in 1972 to steal the thunder of Democratic antiwar candidates. Everyone who mattered was on board: Nixon, Laird, the CINCPAC, and the Joint Chiefs, who ordered Abrams, in the president's name, to get a Laotian incursion going. "The enemy's lack of mobility," the chiefs glibly assured Abrams, "should enable us to isolate the battlefield and ensure a South Vietnamese victory."

The communist preparations—the new corps area, and the plans to move five NVA divisions into the critical base area—were overlooked. MACV put the enemy force there at about 5,500 combat troops, with an equal number of laborers to operate the Ho Chi Minh Trail. In fact, there were about 20,000 combat troops of the NVA 304th, 308th, and 320th Divisions already there, with plans to move the rest of those divisions plus two more into southern Laos if the Americans or South Vietnamese invaded. That would yield a force of 60,000, who would probably make short work of the 17,000 ARVN troops assigned to the incursion.

For now, these grim tidings were cloaked in a fog of war and optimism. Fortified by lavish American aid and expanded conscription, the ARVN seemed stronger, on paper at least, than the NVA, which had suffered crushing losses of men and matériel over the past three years. With the Paris negotiators sitting down for their hundredth apparently futile session of talks, General Arthur Collins Jr. hazarded that now might be the moment to break the logjam once and for all. The ARVN could win the war in ninety days, he asserted, "if they really wanted to do it." They just needed that "will and desire to win. This we cannot give them. It is up to them."[8]

The Laotian Incursion was given a name: Operation Lam Son 719. It was conceived as an "extended raid" to disrupt NVA logistics along the Ho Chi Minh Trail in southern Laos. An attack on Laos, the Americans reasoned, would put the ARVN in a position to strangle the NVA war effort. With one boot on Cambodia's Sihanouk Trail, they would place the other across the Ho Chi Minh Trail at Xepon. Abrams called the operation "the decisive battle of the war."[9]

Unfortunately, everything would militate against ARVN success. In the first place, as in Cambodia, the results would almost certainly be transitory at best, not lasting. The operational area in Laos was mountainous and heavily forested. Its only access road—Route 9—was described by a reporter who traveled on it as "a long, narrow roller coaster of a road," alternately muddy and dusty, flanked by jungle and the Xepon River, and "just wide enough for one truck to squeeze by another."[10]

With the enemy avoiding the roads and using jungle tracks, Route 9 was mined, cut, and flanked by steep escarpments. Bridges along it had been dropped by bombing or sabotage. The smaller roads that branched off Route 9 were also mined. The weather, even in dry season, could not be relied on. Morning fog, rain, and cloud cover often clung to the hills until nightfall, making tac air and helicopter lifts exceedingly difficult, all the more so because the aircraft would be flying west into the afternoon sun and into the teeth of a powerful communist air defense system. In the fall of 1970, the NVA had moved twenty antiaircraft battalions into Laos to fend off allied aircraft and guard the Ho Chi Minh Trail.[11]

The vast majority of those ARVN aircraft would be flown by Americans. This latest tragedy was owed to House opposition to the Cooper-Church Amendment. The Senate version passed in June 1970 would have banned *all* American involvement in operations in Laos and Cambodia. The House version, adopted by both chambers in December 1970 and enacted in January 1971, permitted American *air* operations in both

Cambodia and Laos. Thanks to chickenhawks in the House, in other words, American aircrews would now have to face air defenses as deadly as those in the A Shau Valley, and the highest casualties and aircraft losses of the war.[12]

On the ground, the incursion itself would be managed by the South Vietnamese. "I hope Thieu understands," Kissinger cabled Ambassador Ellsworth Bunker, "that this may be his last crack at massive U.S. support." As things turned out, it would be. To placate public opinion, Nixon had pulled 100,000 more troops out of Vietnam in the last months of 1971, leaving just 175,000 in-country at the start of 1972.

Nixon had assured the nation in his "silent majority" speech that Vietnamization provided the means to end the war "regardless of what happens on the negotiating front," and it was clear that he was pushing the ARVN into the line of fire as quickly as he could to accelerate his exit from the politically toxic war. Lam Son 719 was nothing more than an elaborate stunt. An ARVN corporal, speaking to an American reporter as his unit prepared to move into Laos, ridiculed Abrams' plan to "cut" the Ho Chi Minh Trail at Xepon, or anywhere: "Do you think the NVA are all fools? I can tell you the Ho Chi Minh Trail is very complicated—you attack here, you attack there, but they will get through in other places."[13]

Of course they would. The enemy knew the incursion was coming, and everything about it—its size, objective, and duration. Operation Lam Son 719 had been betrayed to planners in Hanoi by planners in Saigon from the moment it was conceived four months earlier. By 1971, American analysts estimated that there were 30,000 South Vietnamese officials and other personnel working for Hanoi, entirely untroubled by any serious counterintelligence program.[14]

What details Hanoi didn't glean from informants in Saigon were leaked by the American press on the eve of the incursion. In the field, the NVA and VC had by now developed a sophisticated military intelligence group that used bilingual intercept teams to monitor ARVN and American radio transmissions in every combat zone. US advisers attached to the South Vietnamese units used in Lam Son 719 noted that they—not the South Vietnamese generals and staffs they advised—had total authority to move South Vietnamese brigades to their start lines near Laos because "we could not involve the Vietnamese, for security reasons."[15]

That fact alone was a stunning indictment of Thieu's government and armed forces. However, even had secrecy been maintained in Saigon, Lam Son 719 would have been betrayed by its own noisy preparations—long convoys of tanks, APCs, trucks, field artillery, and jeeps chugging along Route 9 to Khe Sanh, with hundreds of Army helicopters thudding overhead. And even if the element of surprise had been retained, the operation was not going to achieve anything significant. Like Westy's search and destroy battles, it would be episodically destructive but fleeting.

The South Vietnamese forces, unable to move quickly on Route 9, which was narrow and flanked by wooded hills, would depend almost entirely on helicopters and fixed-wing aircraft, which, in turn, depended entirely on good flying weather and LZs. When they could fly, they would dart in, destroy whatever they found (or be destroyed), and then dart out again (or not). Their access to LZs was always in doubt. The new NVA corps headquarters at Xepon had pre-positioned machine gun and mortar teams at every natural LZ and pickup zone in the area, ensuring that every airmobile maneuver—even single ship medevac or resupply flights—would have to fight its way in with gunship escorts to deliver supplies, dust off casualties, or rescue downed crews and aircraft. A pilot who flew in the operation recalled that in his thirty-ship company, "every one of our slicks would be shot down or shot up so bad that it would have to be taken out of service to be repaired." These were unprecedented losses.[16]

At best, Lam Son 719 would be just like the ARVN's equally harmless Operation Chicago Peak in 1970, when the ARVN had discarded the original plan—to "secure" the A Shau Valley—and dialed it back to a mere raid that had accomplished nothing lasting.

Thieu, no less than Nixon, used military operations to posture for upcoming elections. The South Vietnamese president was running for a second four-year term in 1971 and wanted to make a splash. But not a big one. Thieu privately resolved to abort the operation the moment casualties exceeded 3,000. He didn't dare risk a public outcry or the loss of his strategic reserve brigades, which he might need at any time to secure his regime in Saigon. Lam Son 719 was political theater, not war. Abrams, closer to the operation than Nixon and Kissinger, knew what he was dealing with. "We're pushing them too hard," he sighed on the eve of the attack. "We're going too far too fast."[17]

Thieu certainly had the haunted look of a man being pushed too far too fast. He waffled from the start, depressing expectations by announcing the operation over the radio on February 8 with the less than stirring caveat that "it was limited in time and space, with an open-ended option for withdrawal."[18]

These were not fighting words, and the ARVN responded as bidden. Until now, American leadership had papered over the failings of the ARVN officer corps. No longer. For the first time, Thieu committed the South Vietnamese Marine and Airborne divisions of his strategic reserve to a great battle. But their commanders sullenly refused to go. They outranked I Corps commander Lam on the seniority list and declined to travel to the front lest they be compelled to serve under his command—an unthinkable humiliation.

Both commanders—Le Nguyen Khang of the Marines and Du Quoc Dong of the Airborne—remained in their offices in Saigon to assert their privilege. They consented only to send subordinates to command the operation in Laos, and only later would they be shamed into going to the front themselves. Colonel Arthur Pence, US adviser to the ARVN Airborne Division, did not consider Dong's absence a catastrophe—"He lacks basic understanding of the mechanics of warfare"—but was not encouraged by what went to Laos in Dong's place. The two brigade commanders, Colonels Duong Xuan Luong and Tran Quoc Lich, were freelancers who routinely ignored orders. Luong "leaned heavily on his American adviser for moral support." Dong's aide-de-camp, Colonel Ho Truong Hau, was possessed of a "brilliant tactical mind" but was a heavy drinker publicly ridiculed by Dong.

Colonel Pence thought Hau possessed everything Dong lacked—a grasp of tactics and operations—but was held back by army politics: "It's not clear if he drinks because he's not promoted or if he's not promoted because he drinks." Lieutenant Colonel Be, Dong's military intelligence chief, "too often tells General Dong what he thinks General Dong wants to hear." Lieutenant Colonel Loung, Dong's operations director, would play an outsize role in the incursion with Dong kicking his heels in Saigon, but "Loung lacks authority, Dong doesn't have full confidence in him." The officer in charge of the division's transport and supplies, among the most important jobs in this airmobile operation, was Lieutenant Colonel Huy: "Huy is the least self-sufficient of the staff officers. He relies on the Americans to do his work." This being the state of the ARVN's elite division, what could reasonably be expected of the others?[19]

Not much. The Ranger battalions committed to the operation were notoriously fickle, often shutting off their radios to avoid hearing orders they did not want to hear. This partly explained their bad reputation in MACV, which characterized the ostensibly elite unit this way: "Commander: unaggressive. Leadership: extremely poor to good." Colonel Nguyen Trong Luat's Armored Task Force ("leadership and morale: fair to poor") would swerve between conflicting orders from Lam and Dong, fulfilling neither.

The ARVN's schism with the South Vietnamese Air Force was even more problematic because the VNAF controlled the tac air and helicopters that, in the US Army, were either on call or directly controlled by ground commanders. The VNAF was so unreliable that it had to be stiffened for this operation by the US 101st Aviation Group. South Vietnamese pilots had an ingrained habit of ignoring appeals from their infantry for lifts, supplies, and medevac with a by now familiar litany of excuses: weather, mechanical trouble, not enough fuel, or too much antiaircraft fire. That's why so many American helicopters would be shot down and so many American personnel would be killed and wounded in Laos in 1971. The 400 helicopters of the US 101st Aviation Group, augmented by 200 others scrounged for this operation from sundry outfits, had to take up the slack. They flew 100 sorties in Lam Son 719 for every one flown by the VNAF.[20]

None of the ARVN commanders had been briefed in advance on the operation for fear that they or their staffs would betray it to the enemy. As a result, *American* personnel and aircraft rather absurdly undertook the entire movement of the ARVN brigades, artillery, and support elements to the battlefield in an operation that had been conceived as a test of *South Vietnamese* capabilities. They did this for secrecy, but also because the deployment went forward during the Tet holiday week, when many of the vacationing South Vietnamese commanders could not be disturbed. Not surprisingly, D-Day came and went, and the first ARVN units did not venture across the frontier into Laos until D+8. Even then, General Lam hesitated and had to be shamed into action by the faraway Thieu.[21]

Lam then required another week to move a force of 10,000 troops twelve miles, pausing frequently to construct nearly a dozen fire support bases and

LZs on hilltops in the American style. Some of the LZs—blasted from thick jungle—were so difficult to access that the troops had to jump into them from a high hover. A company of the ARVN 1st Division suffered 60 percent casualties from broken legs while inserting in this way. The air insertion of the invasion force, meant to be secure and uneventful, ended up being a bloody gunfight for every LZ. Ships going into LZs were shot down by unnoticed air defenses or forced to abort their approaches. Half of the great 100-ship formations were told to fly back toward the South Vietnamese border to circle in holding patterns. Eventually they ran out of gas and had to return to Khe Sanh. The LZs, littered with wrecked American helicopters, had become unusable.[22]

By D+14, Lam's force had made it just halfway to Xepon, where, in the middle of the wilderness, for no apparent reason, it halted. This was not a blitzkrieg. On the road, Lam had an armored column with tanks, APCs, and combat engineers. North of the road, he had Airborne and Ranger units securing one flank. South of the road, he had the ARVN 1st Division securing the other flank. Speed was essential to the success of the stunt. Lam had to advance his entire strength of 17,000 into Laos, get them to Xepon, clean out the caches in the town and the hills and jungles around it, and then leapfrog back to Khe Sanh before the NVA, which had several divisions in the vicinity, could rush in overwhelming reinforcements.[23]

Thieu, always concerned about the safety of his palace guard, thought otherwise. He flew to Dong Ha to meet with Lam on February 12, 1971. The two men conferred, shared their pessimism, and agreed to prolong the halt on the road to Xepon. Thieu formally admonished Lam to limit his casualties to 3,000 or fewer and not to risk the Airborne and Marine divisions. The units north and south of Route 9 would patrol from their firebases in a search for enemy caches, and the armored column and engineers on the road would devote themselves to filling in the cuts dug by NVA saboteurs and repairing damaged bridges.[24]

The American advisers could hardly contain their impatience. A week later, with four NVA divisions filtering into positions around the ARVN firebases and along the heights commanding Route 9, Thieu returned to Dong Ha to meet again with Lam. Lam warned that resistance was stiffening—largely because Lam had not moved for seven days—and that a dash for Xepon now looked riskier than ever. "Take your time," Thieu advised. Lam should continue scouring the area he had already traversed and not risk any more advances. The ARVN had already stumbled upon a number of enemy caches. Why not "declare victory," cut losses, and get out?

Thus encouraged, the ARVN 1st Division spent more days searching through the jungle south of Route 9 for enemy supply dumps, warehouses, vehicle parks, and repair shops, which permitted more NVA troops to march up from the south to surround them with artillery and ambush positions.

Now the NVA commenced their counterattacks. First they rubbed out the Airborne and Ranger firebases holding and patrolling the northern flank of the operation in the third week of February. On the high ground south of Route 9, they began to attack the ARVN 1st Division, which had settled into its own firebases. The tactic was the same everywhere: convert the ARVN's hilltop fire support bases with helicopter LZs into liabilities. The tactic had not worked against the Americans, who had such a well-oiled network of responses: artillery, air strikes, aerial resupply, and fresh maneuver companies on slicks.[25]

But it worked well against the ARVN, whose firebases were poorly constructed and whose perimeters were razor thin—usually a single line of outposts, with no second line, fallback positions, or covering fire for that lonely outer perimeter. The NVA human-wave attacks would be delivered against that slender outer perimeter. The mortars would pulverize it and then a force of infantry calculated to be five times bigger than the garrison company would attack, crying, "Surrender, or you will all be killed!" These troops would punch through the outposts and "narrow the defensive position."

By closing fast to "hug" the firebase and its terrified occupants, the NVA attackers removed the garrison's last hope of salvation: artillery and tac air. With the enemy so near, the ARVN could not call in supporting fires or even medevacs. When an ARVN Airborne headquarters suffered a direct hit on February 21, severely wounding the battalion commander and his staff, all medevac requests to the South Vietnamese aviation group at Khe Sanh were denied "due to poor visibility." The sky was blue and cloudless. It was obvious that the South Vietnamese Air Force had no interest in flying to the relief of an army firebase bracketed by NVA mortars and antiaircraft guns. An American pilot overheard the panicky calls on his radio. The ARVN commander and his staff were severely burned and dying. He flew the mission himself and saved the four lives.[26]

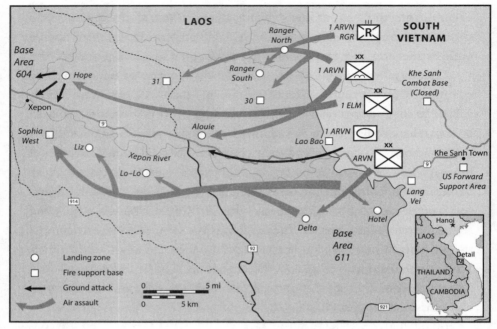

Lam Son 719

Each of the ARVN firebases became an Alamo. Any attempt by the ARVN garrison to medevac wounded or fly in supplies or reinforcements would be shattered by the enemy mortars, rockets, and antiaircraft guns pre-positioned around the firebase. With their battalion headquarters, howitzers, and LZs under attack, the other three companies of each ARVN battalion—usually poking around the jungle looking for caches—would race back to the threatened firebase. They would pass through NVA ambush units every 200 yards. Some would be cut off and destroyed by ambushes and tanks; others would be cut down by barrages of artillery along their routes of withdrawal. The lucky ones would make it inside the firebase, where they too would be taken under siege. In this way, what had been envisioned as a swift airmobile assault settled instead into a dreary battle of attrition, the NVA surrounding and destroying as many ARVN battalions as they could.[27]

ARVN combat leadership floundered everywhere, rare glimpses of quality overshadowed by all of the dross accumulated in Thieu's army. Six of the twenty-two ARVN battalions committed to the op were entirely wiped out or disintegrated by panic and collapse. They had never been briefed, and so, not knowing what exactly they were trying to accomplish, they never pressed their attacks with vigor or defended to the last.

Command was exercised by field commanders not actually on the field of battle. "Colonel Hau, you are to make no more tactical decisions," the Airborne commander General Dong was overheard yelling to his deputy commander over the radio. The deputy commander was actually in battle on the wooded heights north of Route 9, and the commander was in his headquarters—eighty miles away. No staff officers in this or any of the other divisions were asked for their recommendations, nor did they think to give them. Hundreds of ARVN wounded were left behind to be captured by the North Vietnamese or bombed by American B-52s.[28]

On Route 9 itself, the tanks and scout platoons of Colonel Luat's ARVN 1st Armored Brigade were supposed to "spearhead" the advance and secure Route 9 against enemy counterattacks. They now found themselves at the rear of the column—never the place for a spearhead. Ordered to get out in front, Luat blamed Lam's engineering battalion, which, in the view of its US adviser, was entirely blameworthy: "They had no leadership, and made no conscious effort to accomplish the mission." The ARVN engineers refused to work on some days and toiled only three or four hours on others. Seven hundred and fifty armor troopers were killed or wounded. Those who survived steered their vehicles off the road into old bomb craters, where they huddled fearfully.[29]

With this performative operation modeling more weakness than strength, Abrams met with General Jock Sutherland, who commanded US forces in the area, and vented his frustration at the slow pace and ineptitude: "The enemy is all over that goddamn area, and seems to be getting stronger, if anything." President Thieu, worried about his image and the mounting number of ARVN casualties, hurried Lam Son 719 to its end as abruptly as he had terminated Chicago Peak. No effort would be made to exploit tactical success or hold the NVA sanctuaries.

Abrams implored Thieu to commit his reserve division to Laos to "push the thing." Thieu refused. He had clung to a reserve division and never committed it throughout Lam Son 719, "judging," as US advisers put it, "that the political and military risks of this course were too great for him to take." In this way, Thieu's war mirrored MACV's—fast incursions followed by fast withdrawals, handing the briefly contested ground back to the communists. What was the point of such warfare? It destroyed lives and property for nothing.[30]

Thieu returned to Dong Ha at the end of February. He and Nixon needed some face-saving off-ramp, some way to recast defeat as victory. The ARVN had captured enemy caches of rice, fuel, and weapons along Route 9 but were in danger of being encircled by the NVA reinforcements, who were crushing the northern firebases and infiltrating the battlefield much faster and in greater numbers than MACV and the South Vietnamese Joint General Staff had predicted. Continuing at the glacial pace that Thieu had set for Lam was no longer an option.

But a hasty retreat would look like a defeat. Thieu decided to air-assault into the crossroads of Xepon, take it, and *then* retreat. He could then tell South Vietnam's press and voters that he had blocked the NVA's prime "resupply channel" (however briefly), stymied the spring invasion threat, and "taken Xepon." The last bit was a face-saving stunt that should never have been authorized by Abrams, who controlled the helicopters and their American crews. But by now both allies were invested in making Vietnamization look successful. A stunt was needed.

The rewritten plan called for the ARVN 1st Division, with the Vietnamese Marines in reserve, to air-assault into four LZs around Xepon between March 3 and March 7, secure the commanding heights, descend on the town itself, take it, and then withdraw back along Route 9 to South Vietnam. "You go in there just long enough to take a piss and then leave quickly," Thieu instructed Lam.[31]

The requirements for the assault on Xepon were out of all proportion to any benefit the op would deliver. As American planners organized the lifts, they discovered that they would require more helicopters for this single episode than had been used in *any* combat assault in history. Men who saw the lift of ARVN infantry from Khe Sanh to Xepon never forgot the sight: "120 Hueys in a single-ship trail formation, with birds spaced thirty seconds apart in one long column stretching across the horizon." The 240 American pilots of the 120 Hueys in that majestic formation would be flying into the heaviest antiaircraft fire of the entire war.[32]

For three days, the ARVN fought for the landing zones around Xepon with heavy casualties. On the first day, fifty-five helicopters were shot down or damaged. One US pilot noted that five hours of preparatory air strikes with B-52s, tac air, and gunships had little effect on the entrenched NVA antiaircraft battalions. The air commanders had been assured that the LZs were secure, that it was a "piece-of-cake mission," but when "we went in, it sounded like a million people opened up on us."[33]

On the second day, nearly as many helicopters were destroyed or damaged. Hueys descending to their LZs were met with barrages of RPGs and gunfire that smashed their windshields and shot out their engines, tail rotors, and hydraulics. ARVN infantry could be seen spilling out of spinning Hueys and tumbling 100 feet to the ground. One pilot, crouching near the wreckage of his machine, watched another Huey plummet down to the LZ in flames. Everyone got out safely except the copilot, twenty-four-year-old Lieutenant Charles Anderson of Newark, Delaware, who did not duck low enough to avoid the spinning main rotor blade.

On March 7, two battalions of the ARVN 1st Division took the fourth LZ, closer to Xepon, and advanced into the town, which they briefly held and then abandoned. There were now 17,000 ARVN troops sprawled across the great battlefield, confronted by more than twice that number of enemy infantry, with artillery, two tank regiments, and nineteen antiaircraft battalions. While Lam had been focused on the Xepon caper, many of those NVA troops had ranged themselves along Route 9. Originally construed as an "offensive operations corridor," the road had now become the ARVN's only overland line of retreat.[34]

A rout ensued. The NVA force, which had been rapidly reinforced to a strength of 50,000 men in five divisions, now hit the ARVN ground forces as they began their withdrawal. The ARVN did everything wrong. They had little air cover, reconnaissance, flank protection, or rear guards. They blundered blindly backward through phased ambushes. Aerial resupply was driven off by unsuppressed antiaircraft fire. Even the US Army's Cobra gunships, whose speed and skinny fuselage made them more survivable than the Hueys, were shot down or scared off. "I kept thinking to myself how absurd all of this was," one American pilot recalled as the losses and the rout accelerated.[35]

Meeting with Thieu, Vien, and Lam on March 9, Abrams and Bunker urged the South Vietnamese to double down, halt their blundering retreat, reinforce it, and fight to the finish. Thieu refused. He did not dare risk even the Airborne Division, let alone the ARVN 2nd Division, which Abrams wanted him to rush into action from Quang Ngai province. Abrams never forgave Thieu for this timidity, but it was just as well. The battle was entirely lost.

The last ARVN firebases were overrun and silenced by NVA attacks. General Lam lost an estimated 6,100 killed or wounded and 2,500 missing in action—50 percent of the force he had pushed into Laos. "We can't figure out a way to fight back against the North Vietnamese," a wounded ARVN Ranger told a reporter during the battle. "They don't fear air strikes or artillery." Probably because air strikes and artillery were so rare, and the Rangers and the Airborne—mobile assault units with light weapons and no training in the control of US air assets—were unsuited for defending static positions such as the firebases. "It was a case of having all or having nothing at all," one US adviser remarked. Usually, he added, "it was a very small piece of nothing."[36]

With his squadrons chewed up by enemy antiaircraft fire and the extra maintenance demanded by the high tempo, General Jock Sutherland, the US XXIV Corps commander tasked with supporting Lam Son 719, failed to keep his full complement of helicopters in service. How could he? There was a pilot shortage owing to Nixon's drawdown, and the pilots who remained were flying eight-to-ten-hour days over Laos for over a month. There was no slack in the system. Lam, alarmed by this rare glimpse of American fallibility, took to rebuffing most requests for air and artillery support or even medevacs with the explanation that "priority was with another unit." General Fred Weyand, Abrams' deputy, blamed Sutherland, who was an armor officer: "You've got a corps commander up there who's supposed to be keeping track of every fucking bird. . . . He just doesn't know what the hell's going on." Abrams seethed, reminding Jock Sutherland that all of their heads were on the block: "The entire national strategic concept is at stake here!"[37]

The "strategic concept" was revealed to be a fraud. "*Vietnamization* really meant *Americanization*," an ARVN officer observed. MACV loaded the South Vietnamese up with American technology and concepts but neglected the animating spirit, staffs, and training. The façade was impressive, but the foundation was rotten, not least because Thieu and his generals made no adjustments to *their* doctrine or training to compensate for the withdrawal of American capabilities. No one seems to have heeded the warning of the first modern adviser, T. E. Lawrence: "Better they do it imperfectly than that you do it perfectly, for it is their country, their war, and your time is limited."

Nixon snarled that *his* time had become even more limited thanks to ARVN bungling. Lam and Thieu had "broken the thin thread" binding public faith in Vietnamization. In Saigon, the CIA's chief strategy analyst was brutally candid: "Lam Son 719 told us everything we needed to know about where Vietnamization had really got to—and it told Hanoi the same things."[38]

The ARVN, which had been bleeding a monthly average of 12,000 deserters before the battle, showed little pluck. They abandoned 54 tanks, 80 M-113 armored personnel carriers, 300 trucks, 96 howitzers, 3,500 gallons of fuel, and 2,500 tons of ammo—the equivalent of four tank companies, five artillery battalions, and all of their gas and munitions. The communists captured many of these vehicles intact with keys in the ignition, engines running. The ARVN engineering battalion abandoned everything it took into Laos—trucks, trailers, graders, and bulldozers.

Healthy soldiers of every ARVN branch were observed jumping on board medevac helicopters or hanging from their skids to escape the fighting. The ARVN 1st Division, unable to move on Route 9, tried its southern branch, Route 92, and found it even worse. The enemy had placed two regiments in five successive defense lines across it, each of which mowed down and enveloped the retreating ARVN. In a single night, March 18, one of the ARVN 1st Division's regiments lost 732 killed, wounded, or missing.[39]

American-piloted Hueys flew 160,000 sorties into Laos—far and away the greatest expenditure of airmobile support on any one operation of the entire war. "It was a battle like no other ever seen in helicopter warfare," one awed participant recalled. Mainly for its self-destructiveness: 750 helicopters were committed to the operation, and 726 of them were destroyed or damaged. Of the American aircrews, 270 were killed and 1,580 were wounded. Thirty-one-year-old Captain Keith Brandt was one of the dead, remembered for his last radio call as he plummeted to the jungle floor: "I've lost my engine and my transmission is breaking up. Goodbye. Send my love to my family. I'm dead."[40]

Radio Hanoi jeered that Lam Son 719 "was the heaviest defeat ever for Nixon & Company." The NVA committed eleven regiments of infantry, four artillery regiments, and 100 tanks to the operation. MACV estimated that thirteen of the enemy battalions were rendered "operationally ineffective." Two enemy divisions had been nearly destroyed. But the losses were inflicted more by thousands of American air sorties than by the ARVN, who gave ground everywhere.[41]

ARVN morale collapsed during Lam Son 719, despite Saigon's spurious claims of victory. The "open-ended" invasion had been terminated after two humiliating weeks under a storm of dispiriting excuses: bad weather, inadequate air support, superior enemy artillery, poor artillery counterfire, too many leaked secrets, and insufficient reinforcement, medevacs, and supply. "It's a jolt to their confidence," one of the American advisers wrote—more failure than success, and all the more galling because every problem that emerged had been foreseen by the Americans and by the South Vietnamese themselves.

The commander, General Lam, was Thieu's political boss in Hue, not a fighting general and not a leader. The South Vietnamese divisions engaged in the operation neither trusted nor cooperated with each other. They remained "political clans," the Airborne, Marines, Rangers, and armored units refusing to take orders from generals such as Lam, who had risen through the numbered ARVN divisions, which were regarded by the strategic reserve units as inferior. Lam was not the man to unify the clans. Of him, it was said: "Lam considers the Rangers first cousins, the Airborne distant cousins, and the ARVN 1st Division the son."[42]

American advisers noted the obvious. The slicks, medevacs, and "nonorganic" firepower (artillery, gunships, and tac air) that were always available to American grunts were usually unavailable to the ARVN. They had these things; they just did not use them. "Phases of the battle were not tied together," an adviser noted. "There was no integrated effort." Pressed by the Americans to fight from an airmobile posture, Lam did not even consider it. The only thing Lam or his corps could manage was what he called the "fixed-base concept": crawling slowly forward, pausing to construct firebases, and congratulating himself that he was performing "overwatch" in Laos.

In fact, Lam was merely supplying fat, stationary targets for the NVA, who enveloped and destroyed the ARVN with tanks, artillery, and infantry wherever they lingered. Despite all of the costly "improvement and

An ARVN Ranger company commander and his radio operator cautiously advance. The South Vietnamese divisions involved in Lam Son 719 were political clans that hesitated to cooperate and fled from the more powerful NVA. (National Archives)

modernization," the ARVN continued to demonstrate no aptitude for combined-arms warfare and essential staff work. Nothing could be delegated because the ARVN commanders usually remained at headquarters in a defensive crouch, or went forward theatrically, without their staffs. When the American advisers urged ARVN leaders to attack—to use their helicopters and armor, to maneuver, to drop paratroops onto the high ground, to move their firebases every three days, to go beyond their self-imposed "limits of advance"—they were rebuffed. "Every excuse was used to berate the lack of U.S. support," one adviser noted.[43]

In the end, the only area in which the ARVN matched the Americans was their ability to conjure numbers and charades to create the illusion of victory. Nixon started the bidding on the day the last ARVN unit crossed back into South Vietnam. "Tonight," the president announced on national television, "I can report that Vietnamization has succeeded." At MACV, General Weyand deemed the operation "worth it—I think it's going to prove terribly decisive." The pell-mell retreat was not a rout; it was "mobile maneuvering." Not to be outdone, President Thieu judged Lam Son 719 "the greatest victory *ever*—a moral, political, and psychological Dien Bien Phu."[44]

General Cao Van Vien, the chief of the Joint General Staff, assured Thieu that Lam Son 719 must be regarded not as a humiliating rout but as a successful withdrawal using "empty area tactics." In fact, Vien insisted, it was really a kind of triumph: Lam's corps had put seventeen of thirty-three enemy battalions out of action, captured enough rice to feed 140 NVA battalions for thirty days, and "disrupted" NVA plans to attack inside South Vietnam for several months.

General Vien publicly claimed a body count of 13,000 dead communists and many times that number of wounded, but the real number was closer to 8,000 killed or wounded, half of them from American air strikes and artillery. With at least 8,000 casualties of their own—half the force they'd marched into Laos—this was not a satisfactory kill ratio for the better-equipped and more mobile ARVN. Nearly 2,000 Americans had been killed or wounded in the operation—nearly all of them from the anti-aircraft fire that had wrecked or damaged 726 helicopters and shot down six strike fighters.[45]

Privately, General Vien questioned the accuracy of the body counts and cache weights that he was transmitting to Thieu as indicators of victory. The quantity of stores captured by his divisions seemed grossly inflated—2,000 vehicles, 90,000 gallons of fuel, and 170,000 tons of munitions, plus rice, weapons, and even a handful of tanks and artillery. How could an army that had spent most of the operation fighting for its life have seized and disposed of so much material? The body counts had been inflated by the usual dodges learned from the Americans. Few of the reported supply caches were ever documented with photographs.[46]

With all of this in mind, General Vien warned Thieu that the ARVN certainly could not afford any more "victories" like this one. Lam Son 719 had exposed the inability of the South Vietnamese to prolong operations for more than a few days. Any future campaigns in Laos or Cambodia would encounter the same problems of resupply and fire support against a determined enemy with better control of the battlefield. The best the ARVN could do would be "hit and run, heliborne assaults on enemy storage and installations, and then a swift withdrawal, after no more than seven days." Anything longer would result in certain defeat.[47]

The "great irony" of Lam Son 719, the South Vietnamese Joint General Staff abashedly observed, was that it had entirely flipped the war's script. Now, the American-designed South Vietnamese military looked like the "ragtag guerrilla army"—ever short of ammo and everything else, only able to move safely at night or under jungle canopy—whereas the NVA had become the confident, "superior" conventional army, capable of shaping the battlefield as they pleased, day or night. For the first time in the war, the NVA had fired more artillery rounds in the battle than the ARVN and the Americans. Nixon and Thieu agreed to call Lam Son 719 a victory anyway—Thieu to forestall criticism, Nixon to justify another great round of withdrawals. In April 1971, Nixon announced that he would withdraw 100,000 more American troops.[48]

The ARVN failure in Laos hammered yet another nail into the coffin—their own, and that of American advocates of a wider war. The argument that the war might have been won had the United States or the ARVN only been more aggressive in challenging NVA control of Laos and wresting away the Ho Chi Minh Trail was revealed again to be an absurdity by facts on the ground. MACV had already pronounced the NVA "masters of Laos" in early 1970 when an estimated 100,000 communist troops had cut the country in two, taking total control of northern Laos and the Mekong Valley and pressing pro-American forces back to the capital, Vientiane, where China's embassy confidently predicted that "in view of its other commitments, the U.S. was unlikely to involve itself further in Laos."[49]

Qiao Guanha, a confidant of Zhou Enlai and a senior foreign ministry official who would shortly coordinate China's takeover of Taiwan's UN seat, now threatened that any further "adventurist policies" in Laos by US forces or even ARVN forces alone would be met by Chinese intervention in the war. "If Dr. Kissinger and the Pentagon cry out for some other spectacular move to assist American disengagement from Vietnam," Qiao warned, China "would not remain inactive." Reviewing the threat of Chinese intervention—conveyed to the Americans by Norway's ambassador in Beijing—the British chargé in the Chinese capital noted: "The Chinese may be overstating their position to make American flesh creep, but not by much."[50]

Chapter 24

"WE'VE MADE THE WAR
TOO MUCH OF
A GOOD THING"

L am Son 719 had certainly made ARVN flesh creep. It was their first
corps-level campaign with multiple divisions from different services
in rough terrain and weather, and it had been a disaster. MACV's chief
of military intelligence said that what it really proved was that the Vietnamization "concept [was] years, probably *decades*, away." The ARVN
remained "completely dependent" on US forces. South Vietnamese leadership failed utterly.

Lam, who commanded the ARVN corps under Thieu's distant direction, revealed all of his massive shortcomings as a field commander.
When it became apparent that the firebases along the route of advance
were untenable, he refused to evacuate them. They became living hells,
encircled by enemy guns, mortars, and rockets in defilade positions on
the steep slopes around the firebases. He gave his two Marine brigades
orders variously described by their US adviser as "absurd" and "ludicrous." He belatedly offered them supporting fires from howitzers that
were obviously out of range, and querulously demanded that the Marines
remove their own howitzers to safety, even though they lacked the means

to do it. When the Americans offered to bomb around the South Vietnamese Marine perimeter with B-52s, Lam refused the offer: "Now the Marines will *have* to fight," he scowled.[1]

Over a thousand Vietnamese Marines were killed, wounded, or captured in that particular fracas south of Route 9 at FSB Delta, which was just one of many fiascos. NVA observation posts had spotted every ARVN maneuver and crushed it immediately under instant, accurate, concentrated artillery fire—volleys of 100 to 200 rounds from all directions. Under such conditions, counter-battery fire from the small number of guns in the ARVN firebases was ineffective.

The cream of the ARVN officer and NCO corps was exterminated in the battle. The Airborne Division lost 40 percent of its officers—153 killed and wounded—as well as 284 NCOs and 2,100 paratroopers. One of the survivors confessed that it would take at least six months for his men to get over the trauma. They "would prefer to desert or risk jail rather than go into such a battle again." Every Ranger battalion inserted north of Route 9 lost at least half of its men and officers. The ARVN 1st Division lost three of five battalion commanders and most of its field and company-grade officers and NCOs. In an army that had difficulty finding even one cohort of capable officers, how would these men *ever* be replaced?[2]

Abandoned by fire support elements that had materialized automatically when the Americans were in charge, the ARVN had been cut to pieces by the more fluid NVA. Gloria Emerson, who interviewed survivors of the battle as they were extracted, described them as "shattered." And these were troops of the most elite South Vietnamese units—the ARVN 1st Infantry Division, the Rangers, the Airborne Division, and the Marines. Many had piled onto American helicopters to be extracted without combat packs, helmets, or even weapons. "Nothing mattered," they muttered, "except getting out."[3]

By March 25, 1971, forty-five days after the launch of Lam Son 719, the last ARVN units straggled back across the border into South Vietnam. Somehow, the flacks at MACV made a triumph out of this wretched defeat. MACV asserted that the war was nearly won. B-52s were pounding the Ho Chi Minh Trail. Allied naval patrols were denying South Vietnam's coastline to the enemy, and American bombers, flying freely inside "neutral" Cambodia, had shut down the Sihanouk Trail. Lam Son 719 had nearly starved the NVA, whose units in I Corps suffered "famine" as a result of all of the rice seized in Laos. Communist morale was "plunging." Though the operation might *seem* to have failed to the layman, MACV alleged, what it revealed to the military expert was a much bolder, scrappier ARVN with the ability to commit six of twelve infantry divisions to cross-border operations. Surely, the briefers concluded, this *proved* that "the South Vietnamese are ready to assume responsibility for the war effort."[4]

Surely, they were not. Privately, the White House raged and MACV wept. "I wouldn't believe a word Abrams says anymore," Kissinger counseled the president. Nixon was itching to fire the MACV commander. "Get on the first available plane and fly to Saigon," Nixon barked to Kissinger's military assistant, General Al Haig. "You're taking command." Nixon's contempt for Creighton Abrams—the general's complaints, leaks, and lack of imagination—was sharpening. The president was particularly aggrieved that Abrams had never left his headquarters in Saigon to supervise Lam. The Laotian Incursion had not polled well. Nixon's approval rating fell to an all-time low. Seventy percent of Americans surveyed by Gallup in March thought the president was deceiving them about events in Laos and Vietnam. The president and Kissinger blamed Abrams for letting the half-baked operation blunder into life, conveniently forgetting that they had ardently pushed the incursion.[5]

Lam Son 719 had exposed the continuing weakness of the ARVN, strengthened Hanoi's hand in the Paris talks, and even threatened Nixon's reelection. "We can't have South Vietnam knocked over brutally *before* the election," Kissinger warned. "That's right," Nixon agreed. If it was, Nixon might lose in 1972. To the problem of a war that was costing $66 million a day had to be added a weakening dollar, a slumping stock market, and rising inflation, unemployment, and budget deficits. Americans were fed up.[6]

The essential problem was this: the ARVN was only superficially modern. In reality, it was an unworkable mess wrought from Nixon's political and budgetary requirements. "Basically, we've retained a system that was built for the *old* system," a senior US adviser confessed. And yet this new system could not function without the ingredients of the old system—all of which were being rapidly withdrawn by Nixon. Lam had technically commanded Operation Lam Son 719 from Dong Ha and Khe Sanh, but, practically speaking, he had relied entirely on his senior US adviser in Quang

Tri City and General Jock Sutherland's US XXIV Corps staff in Da Nang for nearly all aviation and logistics. The division and brigade commanders beneath Lam had relied entirely on their US advisers, none of whom were permitted to enter Laos, to summon those US assets. Under such conditions, the summons was usually late and only partially fulfilled.

The elements of the new system, which were supposed to take over from the old system, proved entirely incompetent. The South Vietnamese, MACV concluded in April 1971, exhibited "a total lack of coordination in the use of artillery, tactical air, and helicopter support." ARVN commanders everywhere became "overburdened with frantic communications and crises." Nothing could be delegated because staffs were "as inexperienced as the senior commanders themselves."

The chief effect of "military Vietnamization," in short, was entirely negative. It had not coaxed the ARVN from dependence to independence. It had not made the South Vietnamese armed forces flexible and adaptable to meet changing tactical situations. Instead, Vietnamization tied everything in bureaucratic knots while quietly snipping the connection between ARVN divisions and US assets to make Nixon's troop and aircraft withdrawals easier.[7]

Vietnamization, in short, was all hardware and no software. Without US staffs and advisers, the ARVN flopped like a beached whale, with "no grasp of the overall tactical situation or assets" and no facility in the key tasks of this war: command and control, reconnaissance, firepower, close air support, troop lift, heavy lift, and supply. The ARVN was an absurdity, really—a tech-heavy army built in the American image, with no ability to thrive or even exist when detached from the mother ship. And even the mother ship had been unable to save it during the modest incursion into Laos. If Vietnamization was the future, the future looked entirely bleak.[8]

In Cambodia, the other key front in the war against the sanctuaries, things were going no better. Thieu combined his Laotian incursion with a second Cambodian incursion that began in January 1971 and culminated in April and May. This incursion, called Operation Toan Thang 171, ended as wretchedly as Lam Son 719.

Lon Nol had promoted himself in the meantime to the rank of field marshal. Nixon hoped that he would display a field marshal's confidence. He didn't. With the Khmer Rouge multiplying, the NVA and VC expanding their sanctuaries, the Americans withdrawing, and the ARVN in retreat, the marshal—as Lon Nol now styled himself—suffered a debilitating stroke and then holed up in his capital, ceding most of Cambodia, apart from a few provincial capitals and Kompong Som (the renamed port of Sihanoukville), to the communists.

Lon Nol submitted to examination by a US Army psychiatrist, who found the head of state more "vague and unstructured" than he had been before the stroke. An American general sent to organize Cambodian military training noted that Lon Nol had surrounded himself with yes-men and had no functioning chain of command. The FANK was more a political organization than a military one. A spirit of "drift and futility" enveloped the country. The marshal had become a mad little island in a sea of chaos.[9]

Nixon and Kissinger stubbornly insisted that Lon Nol was "the key to stability" in Southeast Asia. Yet, as many had predicted, Nixon's Cambodian Incursion had converted the entire country, not just the border strips, into an NVA sanctuary. ARVN units sent across the border to join the fight and secure the key road between Phnom Penh and Kompong Som were thrown back again. The ARVN fled across the border, leaving yet more trucks, APCs, howitzers, generators, and radio-relay units to the enemy.[10]

In Laos, Thieu's incursion had the same effect that Nixon's had on Cambodia. Now more, not less, of Laos fell under communist control. The NVA had built a new road through Xepon and captured the Bolovens Plateau, the Sekong Valley, and Route 16 as "alternate supply routes" should Thieu decide to invade Laos again. The Pathet Lao, goaded by NVA advisers, had driven government forces out of the area northwest of Luang Prabang. Aerial imagery revealed a massive expansion of Chinese air defense and radar facilities along Route 46, the "Chinese Road" connecting southern China and northern Laos. All of this communist activity had a single object in mind: fortify the Ho Chi Minh Trail and the corridor to South Vietnam. The best that Laotian prime minister Souvanna Phouma could do after Lam Son 719 was "close his eyes to continuing NVA use of his territory." How could he do otherwise? The Pathet Lao, buttressed by the NVA and China, held all of the cards in the critical border regions. They moved supplies and ammunition without resistance from a weak and corrupt Laotian military.[11]

By April 1971, the Ho Chi Minh Trail and Base Area 604 were back to running at full capacity. Infiltrators, weapons, and ammo were moving down the trail as if the hiccup of Lam Son 719 had never happened. The only achievement of the allied activity in Cambodia and Laos was that it had briefly shifted the war to those places. With the enemy putting a massive effort into rebuilding the supply centers torn up by the cross-border incursions, a welcome calm descended on South Vietnam. But everyone knew that it wouldn't last. What the enemy was doing, the CIA reported, was "creating the capability to fight in South Vietnam over the long haul." They were subduing the last flickers of sovereign government resistance in Cambodia and Laos and restocking their sanctuaries. American troops in South Vietnam were projected to fall to 140,000 in January 1972 and to just 70,000 by Easter. The ARVN, reduced by 200,000 KIAs in the years since 1965, would soon be standing alone. The NVA planned to demolish it in battle.[12]

While allied forces in South Vietnam braced for that final onslaught, the Nixon White House struggled with the *New York Times*. On Sunday, June 23, 1971, the venerable "newspaper of record" began publishing the Pentagon Papers, a daily series of articles culled from a 7,000-page secret study commissioned by McNamara four years earlier to understand how the agonizing war had begun and escalated. Together, these classified Pentagon documents showed just how political and futile the conflict had been from the start—how it had been kept going with lies and hyperbole to guard the political flanks of one president after another.

Nixon, elated by the White House wedding of his daughter Tricia on Saturday, was overcome with wrath as he read the Sunday *Times*. The leaked Pentagon study, officially titled *U.S. Decision-Making in Vietnam, 1945–68*, ran only to the end of the Johnson administration. But Nixon could not bear the thought of leakers standing ready to reveal *his* secrets. He also understood that a key finding of the Pentagon Papers was that America had not been nobly and tragically sucked into Vietnam; it had deliberately gone in, just as Nixon was deliberately prolonging the war. A second edition, brought up to date, might reveal his own sins: the Chennault affair, the "secret bombing," the not-so-"better war," the Lon Nol coup, and so on.

The worried president phoned Kissinger: "This is a treasonable action.... And people have got to be put to the torch for this sort of thing." The leaker was tracked down and revealed to be forty-year-old Daniel Ellsberg. The former Marine officer had worked in Vietnam as a civilian and then returned to Washington to help compile the Pentagon Papers. His unmasking and indictment were not enough for Nixon. The president pulled together a "special investigations unit," nicknamed "the plumbers," to plug leaks from the White House, and instructed them to break into the office of Ellsberg's psychiatrist to steal embarrassing material from the RAND analyst's medical file. They also broke into the Brookings Institution think tank, looking for any Vietnam documents that might embarrass Nixon. A year later these same plumbers would break into the offices of the Democratic National Committee in the Watergate building to steal material on George McGovern, Ted Kennedy, and other Democrats.[13]

That summer of 1971 saw monthly American deaths in Vietnam fall below 100 for the first time since US entry into the war in 1965. Decreased casualties reflected sharply decreased activity. The grunts were leaving, and those forced to remain were laying down their tools in protest against the pointless war. The once reliable Cav mutinied in one of its firebases on the Cambodian border in October 1971, refusing to go on night ambushes or daylight patrols. These "temporary combat refusals" had become commonplace. When Secretary of Defense Laird insisted that despite Vietnamization the grunts must keep fighting—"it should be clear to all that there will still be action by American military units"—the troops scoffed. They were, they complained, "forgotten men," increasingly dedicated to "keeping their heads down." This confluence of American demoralization and shoddy Vietnamization encouraged Hanoi to plan a war-winning general offensive—their fifth attempt since Tet. Just after Labor Day, CIA director Dick Helms briefed Nixon's NSC that the NVA appeared to be preparing a massive 1972 offensive through the DMZ and the Central Highlands.[14]

Everything now hinged on the durability of Thieu's regime and military in the face of the expected onslaught. In October 1971, Thieu was reelected president of South Vietnam. He ran unopposed after passing criteria for candidacy through the National Assembly that were so stringent that not even Vice President Ky could qualify. Ky returned to the air force and suffered a further humiliation. Thieu sidelined or retired Ky loyalists in the armed forces and replaced them with his own. The reelected president improbably claimed that 88 percent of his citizens had voted and that he had garnered 94 percent of their votes.[15]

The Americans, embarrassed by this latest rigged election, now awak-ened to the fact that *they* had made Thieu invincible. They fought the war for him, guarded him against coups, gave his soldiers and civil servants a pay raise on the eve of every election, and poured *billions* into the South Vietnamese government and economy. With pork like that to dole out, it was easy to see how Thieu had smothered the rise of any national politi-cal parties or leaders in the years since the Diem coup. Thieu's network of loyalties in the armed forces and in government at every level from Saigon down to the villages made him unassailable. Or nearly unassailable. Nixon and Kissinger might have terminated the war several months earlier if they had accepted Hanoi's condition that they persuade Thieu not to run again, and back a candidate committed to negotiation with the VC. They hadn't dared, both men fearing that twisting Thieu's arm would look like a modern-day Diem coup and "destroy South Vietnam's political fabric."[16]

The fabric was awfully thin. By this stage of the war, the VC had shorn off Thieu's support in the cities no less than the countryside. The commu-nists had fueled a protest movement of students, workers, intellectuals, journalists, and Buddhists. They were all committed to VC goals: overthrow of the Thieu regime, total withdrawal of US forces, better living conditions, and a coalition government. Economically, VC agents had already begun purchasing farms and ranches inside South Vietnam to free themselves from reliance on the Ho Chi Minh Trail and to position themselves for eco-nomic dominance after the war.[17]

With no popular base, Thieu relied on a narrowing and selfish band of elites. Business consultant Eliot Janeway appeared before Fulbright's foreign relations committee to detail how the South Vietnamese (and Cambodian) elites were diverting the cheap, subsidized dollars given them by American taxpayers. Instead of modernizing their countries, they were creating an Asian offshore dollar market for their own personal profit. "What we are developing is not a new lease on economic life...not catalyzing undevel-oped feudalism into modern economic society...but, instead, creating an old loan-shark's racket, profiteering, and, adding insult to injury, the loan sharks we are financing are profiteering not merely at the expense of their own people but at the expense of ours." American subsidies made it cheaper to borrow dollars in Saigon than in Seattle.

Given these perverse incentives, Janeway explained, Thieu, Ky, Lon Nol, and their oligarchs were in no hurry to end the war. This explained their foot-dragging in every peace parley, and Thieu's peace-obstructing policy of "Four No's": no coalition, no neutralization, no territorial concessions, and no communist forces in South Vietnam. "We have permitted the war to be made so much of a good thing all through Southeastern Asia that those doing well out of it there are not likely to share our desire for a cooling off of hostilities and a political stabilization of the crisis there," Janeway concluded.[18]

Nixon wasn't dragging *his* feet. Thieu's rigged reelection in October 1971 had soured even Senate hawks on Vietnam. Washington senator Scoop Jackson—the reliably pugnacious "senator from Boeing"—was actually threatening a cutoff of aid to Thieu. Other Senate Democrats were calling for a total troop pullout within six months. Their only condition would be the return of American POWs. Thieu could go hang as far as they were concerned. Nixon's plan to present American voters with tangible achievements by election day 1972 was unraveling. Having made the 600 American POWs in North Vietnam a major issue to rally public support, the president was now unable to get any of them out, the North Vietnamese insisting that these "stakes in a bigger game" would be freed only when the United States withdrew its last soldier from Vietnam.

Nixon began to blame Kissinger for "playing Bismarck" and investing too much in the diplomatic merry-go-round. Kissinger pressed Nixon to stick with the negotiations. Nixon believed that they made him look weak, as they had made LBJ look weak. He considered walking away from the Paris negotiations, pausing only to bomb North Vietnam so heavily that it would require many months—the desired "decent interval"—to resume its attack on South Vietnam. Kissinger cautioned Nixon that such a move would "swing us from post–World War II predominance to post-Vietnam abdication."[19]

In October 1971, Kissinger presented Hanoi with yet another peace proposal. He felt confident that Nixon's plan to visit Moscow and Beijing in early 1972 would deter Hanoi from launching another offensive. And yet Soviet and Chinese deliveries of military and economic aid to North Vietnam were at an all-time high in 1971–1972, facilitating the very offensive that Kissinger believed he was thwarting. Outwardly hopeful, Nixon boiled inside with frustration, humiliation, and vindictiveness. Even if he lost reelection, he growled to Kissinger (a year before the polls opened), he was going to "pop" North Vietnam hard after the votes were counted. He would reinforce the Seventh Fleet in the South China Sea and add more B-52s to the air bases in Guam and Thailand. "The day after the election we will bomb the bejesus out of them," Nixon vowed on November 20, 1971.[20]

Dick Helms had warned in September that Hanoi appeared to be preparing a major offensive across the DMZ and through the Central Highlands. Nixon's refusal to move against Thieu before South Vietnam's 1971 presidential election had made the offensive inevitable. Removal of the uncompromising "Thieu clique" and its replacement with a coalition government was a prime communist demand. Thieu's reelection, accomplished with American bribes and subsidies, meant that Hanoi would have to march on Saigon and remove Thieu by force.

In the winter of 1971, 20,000 NVA troops set off down the Ho Chi Minh Trail. Over the next four months, 63,000 more would follow. American aerial reconnaissance spotted bigger concentrations of NVA tanks than ever seen before. For the first time, North Vietnamese fighter jets moved into air bases on the country's border with South Vietnam. They had never dared to venture that close to the DMZ, knowing they would be wiped out by American bombs. They seemed to be writing off the American threat, but they also took measures to thwart it. Twenty-four NVA SAM missile battalions deployed on the trails through the DMZ.[21]

This North Vietnamese deployment coincided with the ongoing, hurried US drawdown. Nixon had withdrawn 179,000 American troops in 1971 alone. Even the long-suffering 101st Airborne Division pulled out that year. It was replaced by thirty-seven-year-old General Vu Van Giai's ARVN 3rd Division, which took over the hazardous strip of territory facing the DMZ.

By January 1972, there were only 156,000 US troops left, and, to mollify Congress and the public, Nixon was increasing the withdrawal rate from 10,000 a month to 23,300 a month, boasting that he'd have the US presence down to just 69,000 noncombat troops by July 1972. There would be only 12,000 left by election day. Nixon had begun his first term with over half a million troops in-country. He'd removed 65,000 in 1969, 50,000 in 1970, and 250,000 in 1971. Secretary of Defense Melvin Laird nevertheless projected calm, assuring a press conference that there was nothing to worry about. True, US troop numbers were down 87 percent since Nixon's inauguration, and air sorties down 67 percent, but Laird expressed "confidence that the Vietnamization program has moved forward with sufficient vigor and progress that the South Vietnamese are in a position where they can provide for the security responsibilities in-country which are theirs."[22]

Abrams and the Joint Chiefs didn't share Laird's serenity. They were alarmed by the NVA buildup and the shifting balance of power. Hanoi was very deliberately planning to give Nixon a black eye on the eve of the 1972 presidential elections. The president took notice. In early polls, he had already fallen behind Democratic front-runner Senator Edmund Muskie of Maine, who had been Humphrey's running mate in 1968. Muskie mocked the interminable negotiations of Kissinger—trying "to win at the conference table what we have not won and cannot win on the battlefield."

In place of Kissinger's eight-point plan, Ed Muskie offered a simple two-point plan that the North Vietnamese would certainly accept: promptly withdraw all US forces in exchange for the POWs and instruct Thieu to come to terms with the VC or forfeit all American aid. Nixon had hoped that by divulging Kissinger's heretofore secret negotiations with Le Duc Tho to the American people in January 1972 he would buy himself some time and gratitude. He hadn't. Muskie's plan highlighted Nixon's great vulnerability at this stage—that he was continuing the terrible war and sacrificing American lives "to save Thieu," a man regarded by most Americans as not worth saving.[23]

On January 4, 1972, Abrams warned Nixon to expect the great NVA offensive soon—as early as the following month. In the White House, the president chaired a frank discussion about ARVN capabilities and how much US combat support could be provided by jets, artillery, and armor. Nixon waffled, his desire to smash the NVA while they assembled tempered by the need to do nothing provocative before his February trip to Beijing. On January 20, Abrams requested heavier air strikes against the NVA trails and sanctuaries, chiefly in Laos. Nixon assented. On January 25, Nixon went on television to warn of the impending communist offensive and to take credit for his peace negotiations with the North Vietnamese as well as the peace deal he had offered them in October. If the deal is rejected, he glowered, he would be forced to take military action to defend the Americans still in Vietnam.[24]

Whatever Nixon had in mind would be sharply limited, and everyone knew it. There were not enough troops, and what troops there were refused to fight. There was an added urgency—if any were needed. Nixon was offering Moscow détente, a relaxation of the arms race, if they would lean on Hanoi to sign a peace treaty. The president then went to China in February 1972. Part of his agenda there was to trade huge American concessions—withdrawal from Vietnam, disengagement from Taiwan, and diplomatic recognition of Mao's Chinese Communist Party—for Chinese pressure on Hanoi to end the war. The Chinese, worried by the increasingly close cooperation between Hanoi and Moscow, might just make the trade.[25]

Conditions in North Vietnam had worsened in 1970, and again in 1971, as the economy crumbled and support for the war thinned alarmingly. With most of the healthy young men in the NVA, the workforce was largely female, constantly hungry, and entirely exhausted by an economy increasingly dominated by black markets, hoarding, and speculation. Le Duan's regime would have to increase its already draconian repressive measures against "pessimists" and "reactionaries" to stifle dissent now that even Mao Zedong leaned toward reducing support for Hanoi in return for a thaw in US-China relations.

"We must annihilate as much of the United States and its puppet's potential as possible," the politburo resolved. Mao, Le Duan complained, had thrown a lifeline to a "drowning" Nixon, and might "sell out" Hanoi again as he had done in 1954 when the Chinese leader had agreed to two Vietnamese states. Making matters worse, the Soviets might abandon Hanoi to get a deal on Berlin or arms control, or to forestall a complete Sino-American rapprochement. To win before any of these diplomatic defeats materialized, the NVA planned a massive coordinated offensive by main-force divisions. In 1972, they would slash across the DMZ and the Laotian and Cambodian borders to combine with VC regional and local forces in South Vietnam. The plan was to crush the ARVN in the field and take Saigon by May 19—Ho Chi Minh's birthday.[26]

Chapter 25

"DEFEAT IS NOT AN OPTION"

The Soviets and Chinese had reequipped the NVA in the years since Nixon's inauguration with heavy field artillery, tanks, and the latest in antitank and antiaircraft missiles, including Soviet wire-guided AT-3 Saggers and SAM-7 shoulder-fired rockets. Nixon's visits to Beijing and Moscow—intended to reduce their support to Hanoi—had done nothing of the sort. Deliveries of critical war matériel had continued to flow across the Chinese land border and into the port of Haiphong. In 1971–1972, the Soviets sent MiG-21 jet fighters, SAM antiaircraft missiles, T-54 tanks, and artillery of all calibers.[1]

To find the manpower for a last great push, Hanoi expanded the age limits of their draft law, formerly eighteen to thirty-two years of age, to between seventeen and forty. They did away with exemptions for men with critical skills and, for the first time, drafted Catholics and women into front-line units. In villages where every eligible man had already been drafted or killed, boys as young as fifteen were conscripted, often in the middle of a school term. Rushing to reinforce their weakened divisions in time for a spring offensive in 1972, the NVA cut its nine-month basic training course to just three months.[2]

Fresh manpower and capabilities meant that the NVA could now fight for the first time with multiple corps commanding multidivision forces with armor and artillery in South Vietnam. Springtime promised optimal weather—dry roads to move the NVA tanks, supplies, and motorized infantry, and low ceilings to minimize the effect of South Vietnamese and American tactical aircraft. Nixon's panicky troop withdrawals had catastrophically thinned the number of free-world forces defending South Vietnam. In 1969, there had been fifty-six allied maneuver battalions in northern I Corps—thirty-seven American and nineteen ARVN—with 400 guns. By 1972, there were just thirty ARVN battalions with 160 guns. Declines of 50 to 60 percent in troops and artillery were the norm in all four corps areas.

This sharp drop in South Vietnamese military power encouraged Hanoi to go all in. Le Duan gave command of the looming Easter Offensive to General Van Tien Tung. Le Duan conceived it as a reprise of the 1968 Tet Offensive. It would smash the ARVN, provoke a general uprising against Thieu, and deliver total victory. The general uprising having fizzled in 1968, Le Duan coordinated with Pham Hung's COSVN to make sure it worked this time.[3]

Amazingly, in view of all of the American intelligence capabilities that were still in-country, the North Vietnamese Easter Offensive launched on March 30, 1972, would take the ARVN and Americans by surprise. The MACV commander, his chief of military intelligence, and the US ambassador would all be visiting their wives out of country. Nixon's secretary of defense would be on a plane to Puerto Rico to play golf. The CIA's estimate of enemy intentions for 1972 had assured those decision-makers that "Hanoi cannot launch a nationwide military offensive on anything approaching the scale of Tet 1968."[4]

In early March 1972, the NVA 324B Division moved into the A Shau Valley, where it was joined by two additional NVA regiments. Two more NVA regiments moved along the DMZ to threaten Route 1, the main north–south highway in South Vietnam. Captured COSVN documents spoke of an impending NVA/VC spring offensive.[5]

American command elements—Westmoreland in Washington, Abrams in Saigon, and Fritz Kroesen in Da Nang—continued to believe that there would be no major offensive, despite the massing of fourteen NVA divisions with supporting armor and artillery. Their view was shared by the South Vietnamese commander of Military Region 1 (MR 1), which was the new name given I Corps during Vietnamization.[6]

The MR 1 commander was none other than General Hoang Xuan Lam, the same man who had stumbled through the disastrous Laotian Incursion a year earlier. He had not been replaced in the meantime because Thieu regarded him as an indispensable crony. In private conversations with Americans, Thieu confessed that few of his generals—including himself—could command more than a division, and fewer still could do even that well. But with the ARVN controlling the country's central government and provinces and the Americans pulling out, he had to rely on these underperforming generals for his political survival. There were no viable alternatives. General Fritz Kroesen, leading the First Regional Assistance Command, which was all that remained of XXIV Corps, was expected to stiffen Lam.[7]

The NVA buildup of tanks, artillery, aircraft, SAMs, and infantry along the DMZ was so obvious by February 1972 that Abrams and the Joint Chiefs sought Nixon's permission to launch naval, artillery, and air strikes against the massing forces. "Each time we were told 'no,'" Admiral Thomas Moorer, the chairman of the Joint Chiefs, recalled. Straining as desperately as LBJ had done to score a face-saving peace deal in Paris, Nixon and Kissinger did not dare upset Hanoi with preemptive strikes in North Vietnamese territory.[8]

If the NVA struck, Abrams and the South Vietnamese would have to wait until they moved across the DMZ to engage the ARVN forces. Unfortunately, the ARVN remained weak, despite the accelerated improvement and modernization program. The ARVN 3rd Division was a shoddy outfit comprising two new regiments of "deserters and malcontents," the 56th and 57th, and buttressed by one good regiment—the 2nd, which had been stripped from the ARVN 1st Division. Somehow this was the division selected to defend the long line of the DMZ in the event of an NVA invasion. As the division's regiments trudged to new firebases around Camp Carroll, the most critical artillery support location in MR 1, they were hit with a devastating cannonade on March 30. Thirty thousand NVA troops with 200 Soviet T-54 tanks swarmed across the DMZ. They were under orders to "gain decisive victory in 1972" and "totally change the face of the war in South Vietnam."[9]

Within forty-eight hours, General Vu Van Giai—known to his colleagues as "the unlucky commander of the division that nobody wanted"—had moved his ARVN 3rd Division headquarters back to Quang Tri City. On April 2, Camp Carroll, the most powerful DMZ firebase, with the ARVN's heaviest guns and all of the Vietnamese Marines' artillery, surrendered to onrushing columns of NVA troops. Camp Carroll had been entrusted to the ARVN 56th Regiment, that catch basin for deserters and mutineers. The entire outfit—1,500 troops with twenty-two howitzers—surrendered without a fight. Their US advisers barely escaped in a helicopter. The communists then raced ahead to capture the vital bridge across the Cua Viet River near Camp Carroll.[10]

General Giai now ordered a retreat behind the Cua Viet River. In effect, he abandoned the country around Camp Carroll and the Rockpile to shelter behind the river, which protected Quang Tri, the northernmost South Vietnamese city. Giai's tactical withdrawal touched off the battle for Dong Ha, a town of 30,000, where Route 1 crossed the river. Fighting spread along the river to a second bridge built by the French. These two bridges plus the one at Camp Carroll would give the NVA a broad, open path to Quang Tri City, Hue, and Da Nang. It was left to US advisers to blow the bridge across Route 1 on April 2, slowing the momentum of the communist advance.[11]

Fritz Kroesen and MR 1 commander Hoang Xuan Lam were unaccountably surprised by all of this. Now forty-four, Lam—"an amiable, round-faced officer who favored a swagger stick and a tanker's black beret"—had expected the attack to come from Laos, not across the DMZ. He and Giai had moved their best regiment, the ARVN 2nd Infantry, out of the DMZ and into positions west of Hue. By April 2, Easter Sunday, all ARVN firebases north of the Cam Lo River were in enemy hands. These included storied places like the Rockpile, Con Thien, and Camp Carroll, as well as eleven others. President Thieu's boast from Quang Tri on the eve of the invasion—"let them come and we will finish the war right here"—was revealed to be just another of his grand and dangerous illusions.[12]

The Cam Lo River, which ran along Route 9, the road connecting the northern firebases to the coast, delimited what used to be called "Leatherneck Square," a free-fire zone extending from the river's southern bank up to the DMZ and its firebases. It had been successfully defended by the Americans for six years. It now fell in four days. Throughout, Lam remained in his headquarters at Da Nang assuring the press gathered there that "the situation is serious, but not critical." Lam did not set up a forward command post at Hue, and he made rare visits to units at the front, zipping in and out of Hue in an American-piloted helicopter, always returning to Da Nang for lunch and dinner.[13]

The fall of Camp Carroll, fortified with the heavy artillery that had saved Khe Sanh in 1968, was a scandal. ARVN Lieutenant Colonel Phan Van Dinh radioed the NVA 304th Division and offered to surrender Camp Carroll and its garrison without a fight, an offer the NVA 24th Regiment hastened to accept. The next day Lieutenant Colonel Dinh went on Radio Hanoi to announce the surrender of his ARVN 56th Regiment and to entreat the rest of the ARVN to lay down their arms. The war, he said, was lost.[14]

Fritz Kroesen, like Westmoreland before him, struggled to cover up the debacle. He circulated the lie that the ARVN 56th Regiment had fought bravely and had lost two battalions and three batteries in the fight. In fact, the entire regiment had surrendered without resistance. They handed over a battery of four 175 mm guns, a 155 mm howitzer battery, two 105 mm batteries, and numerous quad .50s and twin .40s. None were destroyed. They were all delivered intact to the enemy along with their bunkers of carefully stacked shells. It was more than a humiliation. It represented the loss of all land-based indirect fire support in MR 1.[15]

US pilots were now the only thing that stood between the ARVN and defeat. "I doubt the fabric of this thing can be held together without U.S. air," Abrams told his commanders. But Nixon's troop withdrawals had reduced American airpower in Vietnam as sharply as everything else. Nixon had pledged to support Thieu if Hanoi launched a major offensive, but with what? Most of his bombers and strike fighters had been withdrawn. Air Force, Navy, and Marine aircraft now had to rush back to the theater—in most cases all the way from the United States.

The Navy had two carriers on station when the NVA struck on March 30. Thirty days later, they had six carriers off the coast of Vietnam. The Marines flew in squadrons of F-4s. Air Force F-105s and F-4s streaked around the world from bases in New Mexico, Kansas, North Carolina, and Florida. One hundred and twenty B-52s flew into Guam and Thailand, along with eighty-four aerial refueling tankers. In April and May 1972, the Air Force increased its number of strike aircraft in South Vietnam from 375

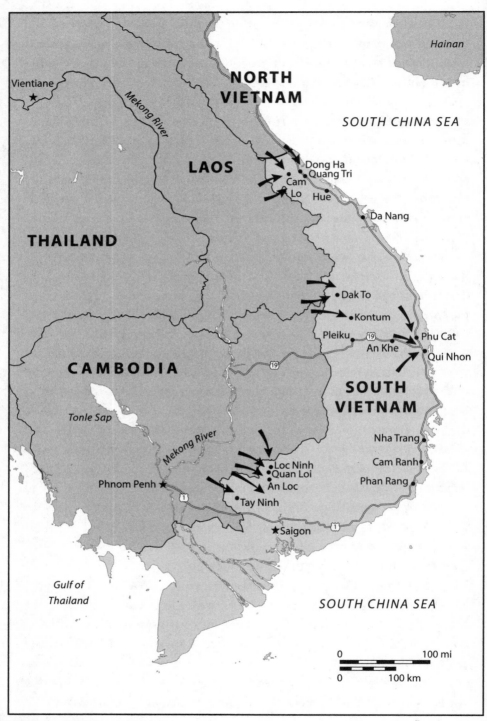

The Easter Offensive

to 625. By July, the number was up to 900. "Defeat is not an option," Nixon railed. It was an election year. If South Vietnam collapsed after so much investment in combat and Vietnamization, the Republican president would have to shoulder the blame.[16]

Lam's predicament in MR 1 was just one of three massive threats to the ARVN in 1972. The NVA offensive with tanks and artillery was three-pronged: south across the DMZ in the direction of Hue, east through the Central Highlands to Pleiku and Kontum City, and east from Cambodia, through the crossroads of An Loc, to Saigon. The thrust from Cambodia toward Saigon with three NVA divisions revealed just how ephemeral the "brilliant success" of Nixon's Cambodian Incursion had been.[17]

Three more NVA divisions—20,000 infantry with tanks and artillery—pushed toward Kontum City in MR 2, which was defended by the ARVN 22nd and 23rd Divisions. These were the army's weakest. When the ARVN 22nd Division fell apart, Thieu chipped in one of his Airborne brigades to strengthen the defense. The notebook of an NVA political officer involved in the attack on Kontum City showed how difficult it was to keep driving the communist divisions into the fire. The majority of NVA troops on this front were the new and inexperienced draftees of 1971. Many were passive and sloppy, others terrified. The NVA solution was to place every soldier into a category—"progressive" or "backward"—and target the latter for "enhanced indoctrination" by the political cadre. "Each unit," the political officer commanded, "must control the thought of all soldiers and eliminate all illusions of peace, fear of sacrifice, and liberalism." They must be forced to "carry out the last will of Uncle Ho."[18]

John Paul Vann had moved to MR 2 as a civilian adviser. Vann persuaded Abrams to press Thieu to send a second brigade of Airborne troops to defend the Central Highlands. The Airborne troops joined the fight for "Rocket Ridge," which overlooked Route 14, the north–south road serving the Central Highlands.

If the NVA took Rocket Ridge, they would be able to sever Kontum City from Dak To and Tan Canh, the northern outposts of MR 2. In the days after April 3, the NVA seized the ARVN firebases on Rocket Ridge one after the other. Among the victims were the fifteen Americans assigned as advisers to the ARVN 22nd Division: four killed, one wounded, and ten dragged away by the communist troops.

The senior adviser, Colonel Phillip Kaplan, later described the conduct of the ARVN 22nd Division commander, Colonel Le Duc Dat: "Dat was really demoralized." Even as the battle raged, the colonel said to Kaplan: "We're going to lose, we're going to be overrun, we will all be killed and captured." He wasn't wrong. Having seized intact the entire ARVN artillery on Rocket Ridge—twenty-six howitzers and 16,000 shells—the communists then cut across Route 19, which connected MR 2's coastal ports with the highland towns. In the face of these escalating attacks, Thieu yanked the Airborne brigades out and replaced them with the exhausted ARVN 6th Ranger Group, which had been fighting in Quang Tri without a rest.[19]

General Van Tien Dung, the NVA chief of staff, had planned to deliver his knockout punch in MR 3, the old III Corps space between Saigon and the Cambodian border. This was the shortest path to the capital and contained most of South Vietnam's resources and population. But it was downgraded at the last moment to a secondary thrust due to the difficulty of supplying and reinforcing troops so far from North Vietnam.

Still, Dung hoped to do more with less. On April 2, NVA General Tran Van Tra led three divisions from the sanctuaries around Snuol, site of a major ARVN defeat in 1971, into Binh Long province north of Tay Ninh. The NVA 7th Division took control of Route 13—the main road up from Saigon and Long Binh—while other units advanced on Saigon. Colonel William H. Miller, the US adviser to General Le Van Hung's ARVN 5th Division, implored the general to counterattack this enemy thrust through Binh Long province. The US 1st Infantry Division and 11th Armored Cavalry Regiment had stood on this exact spot three years earlier to halt an NVA advance on Saigon.

Unfortunately, Hung's ARVN 5th Division did not repeat the feat. They fled. "Hung choked," the general's American advisers noted. "He just didn't do a damn thing for a long time." American forward air controllers looked down and saw NVA T-54 tanks bashing through the wire around Loc Ninh airfield while enemy human wave attacks swarmed into the position. The FACs saw the same story play out at every other ARVN firebase in the area, and summarized it this way: "Friendlies calling in fire on their own positions. All personnel fleeing."[20]

Loc Ninh fell on April 7, furnishing Le Duan with a sixty-fifth-birthday present. US Army gunships and Navy and Air Force strike fighters had to be summoned to attack the NVA columns, which now closed on An Loc, just sixty miles from Saigon. For the first time in the long war, President Thieu disturbed the regional languor of his regular divisions by ordering parts of them actually to move to where the fighting was. Thieu shifted the ARVN 21st Division and part of the ARVN 9th Division from the Mekong Delta to Route 13 and An Loc, with orders to hold the road to Saigon at all costs.[21]

In Washington, an interagency group was convened on April 10 to consider the question: "If the NVA pull back, do the South Vietnamese have the capability to pursue them?" The answer was no. General Lam, who commanded South Vietnamese forces in MR 1, was not a fighting general and never would be. Thieu had promoted him to ever more powerful posts since Lam had intervened with the generals in 1967 to ensure that Thieu, not Ky, headed the presidential ticket. Lam had theatrically ripped the general's stars off his uniform that day, slapped them on the table, and vowed to resign if Ky were chosen over Thieu. Ever since, Thieu had protected Lam.

But Lam was completely out of his depth in a shooting war, as the Laotian Incursion had amply demonstrated. So were most of the South Vietnamese generals. They had done little since 1969 but sweep familiar countryside and keep tabs on the Viet Cong. Suddenly they found themselves in a major war of movement, forced, as an onlooker put it, to "fend off North Vietnamese divisions, shift battalions, coordinate with other units, and get the choppers, the artillery, and the air strikes, all with Saigon on your neck 24 hours a day."

Until now, the Americans had done all of this. Peter Braestrup, the *Washington Post* bureau chief in Saigon, noted that the Easter Offensive exposed as never before the weakness of the Thieu-Ky system, where military commanders were chosen for political not professional reasons, to ward off the coups and countercoups that had been a feature of South Vietnamese life until 1967. Thieu now had to clean house while this existential battle raged. He replaced two of his four regional commanders, three of thirteen division commanders, and a dozen of his forty-four military province chiefs. American officials looking over his shoulder pronounced this only a "modest improvement."[22]

Until now, the Americans had run the big-unit war, leaving the South Vietnamese generals to tag along or dabble in pacification and politics. What talent existed was spread thin. With ARVN officers already staffing four corps areas, 44 provinces, 220 districts, and six cities, they suddenly found themselves with total operational responsibility for a million-man regular army—the fourth biggest army in the world in 1972. Failure was certain. Abrams spoke the obvious: there were simply not enough good, experienced leaders to promote. "The Americans brought equipment here," a South Vietnamese official told the *New York Times*. "But one thing the Americans cannot bring here is leadership—they cannot bring that in from their arsenal."[23]

The ARVN counteroffensive in MR 1 failed, prompting the NVA to resume the attack there on April 23 with 40,000 men grouped in four divisions. On that date Kissinger was in Moscow, pressing Brezhnev to order Hanoi to halt the offensive. Brezhnev declined, infuriating Nixon, who could see that he was receiving nothing in return for his controversial "opening" to China and his offers of détente to Moscow.

NVA columns took Dong Ha on April 28 and Quang Tri City on April 29. The retreating ARVN looted Dong Ha as they fled. Body count, which had been so hard to manufacture earlier, was now everywhere in plain sight, with the NVA forced to march and fight in big formations in the open. An American reporter saw a squad of dead NVA at Quang Tri—"strewn over the edges of their foxholes like the petals of a spent bloom, heads blown open like eggshells."[24]

The road south from these places was packed with South Vietnamese refugees, "fugitive people," the same reporter wrote, "not *going* anywhere, but fleeing *from*." Route 1 itself was lined and layered with "mounds of cartridge brass, motorcycles, and bikes flattened as neatly as pressed flowers by passing tanks." The ditches on either side of the road were filled with army litter and bloated corpses. Cloud cover prevented US air strikes and, in a coda to the indiscipline that had been gripping American forces in South Vietnam for over two years, a company of the Americal Division, deployed in a firebase southwest of Hue, refused to take the field against the NVA. After a two-hour harangue by their commanding officer, they finally agreed to leave the safety of their bunkers, but made clear that they would fight only to protect themselves or other Americans, not the South Vietnamese.[25]

Nixon told White House chief of staff Bob Haldeman on May 1 that the war would be over by August—"because either we will have broken them or they will have broken us." To avert breakdown, Thieu replaced the once highly regarded General Giai with Nguyen Duy Hinh, and then had Giai tried by a military tribunal and jailed. As ARVN 3rd Division commander, Giai had suffered a nervous breakdown during the fast-moving battle.

Having dispatched part of the ARVN 2nd Division from the plain south of Da Nang to Hue, Thieu now shifted his strategic reserve to the defense of Hue, leaving Saigon defended only by its police, ruff-puffs, and regular divisions of draftees. Lam, whom Thieu had coddled till now, was finally sacked and replaced as commander of MR 1 with forty-three-year-old General Ngo Quang Truong.[26]

Truong, who had ably commanded the ARVN 1st Division in I Corps in 1968 and then gone on to command IV Corps in the Delta, now returned to his old headquarters in Hue to lead the faltering counterattack. Lam slouched away to his new assignment: leading yet another anticorruption campaign in Saigon's Ministry of Defense. Truong was regarded as the ARVN's best field commander and the only division commander who took seriously training, staff work, and the selection of subordinate commanders. The general was stunned by what he had just inherited, including a river of civilians flowing from Quang Tri City down Route 1 toward Hue. "The disorder and panic among these refugees were contagious," he observed. The NVA swept the road with fire, callously slaughtering everything on it—soldiers and civilians.[27]

General Truong, trying to rebuild the ARVN 3rd Division after its debacle at Camp Carroll, dug in along the My Chanh River, halfway between Quang Tri City and Hue. The NVA was losing momentum as it advanced and strained its supply lines, but it was still potent enough to defeat (again) the ARVN 3rd Division, which yielded the river line, pulled back to Quang Tri City, and dug in there.

More defeats followed, the American advisers noting time and again that the meshing of infantry and fire support that the Americans had made look easy was not easy at all for the inexperienced officers and staffs of the ARVN. Ineffective fire, friendly fire, or no fire at all demoralized the South Vietnamese troops. On May 2, the entire 10,000-man ARVN 3rd Division plus 1,000 ARVN Rangers ran from Quang Tri City down Route 1 toward Hue, forty miles to the south. *New York Times* reporter Sydney Schanberg watched as troops and officers alike "commandeered civilian vehicles, feigned nonexistent injuries, carried away C-rations but not their ammunition, and threw rocks at Western news photographers taking pictures of their flight."[28]

Most of the ARVN troops did not even pause to regroup at Hue. Those who did looted and ransacked the city, setting fire to the central market. They could be heard shouting, "Let's burn the whole city." Schanberg witnessed the rampage on May 3: "Runaways from the scattered Third Division were roaming through Hue today like armed gangsters—looting, intimidating, and firing on those who displeased them." The rest bowled past Hue, heading for Da Nang, fifty miles farther south, the troops clinging to their vehicles and leveling their rifles at anyone who tried to slow them. Others paused just long enough to commandeer more cars, buses, trucks, and motorbikes. "With horns blaring and headlights glowing in the midday sun, they raced down the center of the road, pushing other vehicles out of the way."[29]

It was among the most ignominious episodes of a war rife with such episodes, the ARVN 3rd Division elbowing 150,000 refugees off the road to speed their flight. Only America's "expeditionary airpower," rushed out to South Vietnam in the first days of April, succeeded in halting this northern thrust. In three days, US attack aircraft dropped 45 bridges connecting the NVA forces advancing on Hue with their supply lines. They screamed over the NVA columns on the roads between Quang Tri City and Hue, destroying 130 mm artillery, tanks, and trucks—a task complicated by North Vietnamese SAMs south of the DMZ, but facilitated by America's first combat use of laser-guided bombs. The northern prong of the NVA offensive stalled as April turned to May.[30]

In MR 2, the ARVN garrisons of Tan Canh and Dak To surrendered on April 24, exposing Kontum City, which lay just twenty-five miles down the road. "There was a lot of cowardice," an American adviser reported. "The troops' morale was just broken. Some broke and ran and didn't know where to go. Some deserted to the VC. They just didn't know what to do, and that was because of their lack of leadership in any depth."[31]

The NVA thrust toward Saigon culminated at An Loc. There President Thieu reinforced General Le Van Hung's ARVN 5th Division with the ARVN 1st Airborne Brigade and the ARVN 3rd Ranger Group. These 15,000 men were promptly surrounded and cut off. The siege of An Loc would last from April 12 until June 1, with the ARVN troops supplied from the air while the NVA pounded them with 50,000 artillery rounds.

This third prong of the communist offensive needed An Loc. In possession of it, the communists could control Route 13 as far as the big ARVN base camp at Lai Khe. If they could take *that*, the road to Saigon would be wide open. Over 100 civilians, mostly women and children, were killed by the communist bombardment of An Loc. An American adviser there told a reporter in late April that "things are getting worse and worse and the Vietnamese just aren't doing anything." The ARVN troops looted the town until there was nothing left to loot, and then they fought each other for possession of the airdrops that fell inside their siege lines.[32]

On May 1, Nixon lost patience with the unfolding catastrophe and told Kissinger that he wanted to "go for broke." He put aside his earlier fear of antagonizing Le Duan and scuttling the peace talks, and authorized Operation Linebacker I. All of North Vietnam would be made available for bombing—including Hanoi and Haiphong. In April, US airpower had focused on interdicting NVA supply lines and close air support for the ARVN. LBJ had halted the bombing of North Vietnam four years earlier on the condition that the NVA not strike across the DMZ. Now that they had, Nixon vowed to retaliate: "The bastards have never been bombed like they're going to be bombed this time," the president growled.[33]

Nixon's decision to resume bombing North Vietnam was opposed by his secretary of state, who pointed out the obvious—that in an endgame focused on the retrieval of hundreds of American POWs, it would merely provide Hanoi with more of them. Abrams and Laird opposed it too, arguing that every available aircraft was needed over places in South Vietnam like Quang Tri City and An Loc. We shouldn't "be away hunting rabbits when the backyard is filled with lions," Abrams admonished. Laird added that there were no worthy targets in North Vietnam anyway. Hanoi's bases of supply were in China and the Soviet Union. The president countered that he would no longer permit North Vietnam to be treated as a sanctuary. The North Vietnamese had invaded. Now they would be bombed. "What distinguishes me from Johnson," Nixon boasted, "is that I have the will in spades."[34]

On May 9, 1972, the president unleashed Operation Linebacker I. For the first time since 1968, B-52s struck North Vietnam in a broad five-month air campaign against strategic targets—ports, military bases, airfields, air defenses, roads, bridges, warehouses, pipelines, and fuel depots. In Hanoi, the miserable American POWs felt stirrings of hope. Their cells quaked and chunks of plaster fell from the walls and ceilings, but they felt "seen" for the first time in three and a half years. "Pressure," one captive pilot recalled, "was being placed on the North Vietnamese and maybe victory would come soon."[35]

Nixon was following through on his pledge to hit North Vietnam if they continued to attack South Vietnam. He mined Haiphong harbor and bombed closer than ever before to population centers. The air attacks crushed North Vietnam's transportation network, closed Haiphong harbor for the first time in the war, and reduced North Vietnam's imports by 80 percent. Headed to Moscow at the end of May to sign an arms reduction treaty, Nixon launched the air campaign partly to reassure hawks in Congress that he was not going soft on communism. "We can't go to the summit while Russian tanks and guns are kicking the shit out of us in Vietnam," Nixon told Kissinger.[36]

On May 12, Abrams ordered B-52 strikes around Kontum City, which was by now under siege and, like An Loc, could be supplied only from the air. John Paul Vann, like the other 5,300 US advisers still in-country, helped direct these American air strikes against the NVA attacks in the Central Highlands, inflicting 40,000 casualties on the communists in MR 2. For twenty-four hours, three B-52 sorties hit the enemy positions every 55 minutes. With the B-52s bombing more heavily than ever inside South Vietnam, Abrams rejoiced that the "brutality is the highest it's been in the whole war." In the clinch, Abe seemed as indifferent as Westmoreland to the social and political effects of such brutality.[37]

Vann marveled at the destructiveness of American airpower, which made short work of even entrenched communist troops. "Wherever you dropped bombs you scattered bodies," Vann recalled. Vann's picaresque life would be terminated on June 9, 1972, when the adviser's Kiowa helicopter, piloted by an inexperienced lieutenant, flew into a tree near the last NVA positions. Had Vann lived, he would have noticed that the ARVN failed to counterattack and retake Tan Canh and Dak To. The NVA would garrison those places for the rest of the war.[38]

On May 11, the NVA briefly seized An Loc. It was the worst day of the battle, with the NVA hitting the little town, which could be crossed on foot in ten minutes, with 7,000 rounds of artillery, mortar, and rocket fire. Abrams ordered B-52 strikes on the town itself, dropping 2.6 million pounds of bombs in one twenty-four-hour period. The ARVN retook the rubble after big battles on May 14 and May 20, but here too they failed to pursue the retreating enemy, not even attempting to recapture the 333 square miles of the Loc Ninh district, which would become another de facto province of the NVA inside South Vietnam.[39]

At Lai Khe, which had housed a brigade of the Big Red One until 1970 and had recently been turned over to the ARVN 5th Division, a reporter detected none of the activity that would have been common during the American presence, especially with a battle like this raging all around. "Lai Khe was at a standstill for a two-hour lunch. No rushing trucks with badly needed ammo, no bustling staff officers with pressing plans—just the broiling 100-degree heat in the open, and the gentle swinging of the hammocks in the beguiling shade of the rubber trees."[40]

The ARVN lost 2,700 dead and 2,700 wounded at An Loc. Many of the wounded languished in filthy bunkers for a month, their Vietnamese medevacs refusing to land on the strip of Route 13 that was their LZ. They would hover for a few seconds, push any supplies or troops on board off, and then zoom away, "leaving the gathered wounded with a new layer of red Binh Long dirt in their wounds and another two hours to wait," a reporter observed. US advisers reported that every man in the ARVN 5th Division was a casualty. Those who lived had multiple wounds. The NVA lost an estimated 25,000 dead in the inferno. American advisers agreed that at An Loc, as at Kontum City, the NVA generals had erred. By cutting all the roads out of those places, they "left the ARVN no alternative but to fight." Had they left roads open, the ARVN would have run away and the B-52s would not have had the dense targets they found in the siege lines around An Loc.[41]

Thieu, a late and opportunistic convert to Catholicism, flew into An Loc on July 7 to kneel and pray before a crucifix that had withstood the bombing. By now, Thieu was reviled by most of his citizens. They considered him "another Diem" without any of Diem's redeeming qualities. The few reforms Thieu initiated were always late, incomplete, or unfulfilled. He had handed the country over to the thieving ARVN generals and to the Americans, who dully accepted the South Vietnamese corruption, or actively profited from it. By the summer of 1972, the number of Americans involved in black-market trading, currency fraud, and drug smuggling in Vietnam was conservatively estimated to be 15,000.[42]

In June 1972, Abe Abrams met the same fate as Westmoreland. He was kicked upstairs to replace Westy in Washington as US Army chief of staff. By the end, Nixon despised Abrams: "He's had it. Look, he's fat, he's drinking too much, and he's not able to do the job." Nixon believed that Abrams had failed in 1972 to counter the NVA ground attacks and had slowed the delivery of air attacks against North Vietnam. And these were just the latest failings. Nixon had wrestled throughout his first term with Abrams, whom he considered stolid, unimaginative, and insubordinate. As fearful of that insubordination as any of his predecessors, Nixon fobbed Abrams off with command of the United States Army from the Pentagon. But he did so with extreme reluctance, sourly observing that Abrams was "just a clod" and that his leadership in Vietnam constituted "a sad chapter in the proud military history of this country." Abrams departed Vietnam in June, like a thief in the night, without fanfare or ceremony. He would be dead in two years, killed by stress, ulcers, and cancer.[43]

By this date, there were only 47,000 US troops remaining in Vietnam. General Fred Weyand became the last MACV commander in Vietnam, formally replacing Abrams two weeks after five men were arrested for breaking into the Democratic National Committee headquarters at the Watergate building in Washington, and two weeks after General Truong presented a plan to retake Quang Tri City. ARVN troops had battled back to the outskirts of the city by July 4. The grueling urban battle, to which Thieu committed Airborne and Marine troops, lasted until September 15, when the ARVN evicted the last invaders. Ten thousand NVA troops died in Quang Tri City, along with 5,000 ARVN.[44]

It was hard for anyone on either side to take comfort from any of these events. Ultimately, the Americans had crushed Hanoi's Easter Offensive with airpower. American gunships, fighters, and bombers destroyed the NVA thrust from the DMZ with 18,000 sorties flown between April and June. In all, American aircraft had combined with the ARVN to inflict 100,000 communist casualties. American ships and cargo planes had shuttled in and out of Da Nang to replace even the heaviest ARVN losses of tanks, vehicles, howitzers, and ammo.

American advisers had braced wavering ARVN commanders on every battlefield, and provided "ground truth"—a precise description of what exactly was happening in every fight—for the American air commanders. When members of Fulbright's Senate Foreign Relations Committee traveled to Vietnam after the repulse of the Easter Offensive, they asked their MACV briefer what would have happened had American advisers and airpower not been made available. "We would be meeting in some other place today," the briefer answered.[45]

But American airpower had only softened the blow. Forty thousand more ARVN troops had been killed, wounded, or gone missing; another 25,000 South Vietnamese civilians had been killed, and a million more refugees created. AP photographer Nick Ut's searing photo of the nine-year-old "Napalm Girl" fleeing from an air strike and screaming with pain from her burns captured for Americans the sheer horror of a war that by now had killed nearly 1 million civilians in Indochina.

And Hanoi's revolutionary warfare did not require a complete victory. This partial one would do nicely. It placed more South Vietnamese territory under Hanoi's control, disrupted pacification *again*, and further demoralized South Vietnam and the United States. John Saar, reporting on the Easter Offensive for *Life*, found in it "a perpetual war formula": the North Vietnamese "grinding on through the blood of their youth and the Vietnamized forces of the South brought to parity by U.S. air power." And yet Le Duan could see that a short-war formula was more likely. US airpower would depart, and the South would fall.[46]

That probability was cold comfort in Hanoi, where the politburo and the NVA leadership were stunned by their own 100,000 casualties and the loss of half of their artillery and nearly all of their tanks—over 450 of them. Some NVA divisions were 100 percent destroyed. In Hanoi, General Van Tien Dung considered the casualties so catastrophic as to rule out any new offensives for "three to five years."

Nixon's intensive bombing of North Vietnam, nothing like LBJ's surgical strikes, had wiped out industrial production, the country's oil supply, the electric grid, as well as other key infrastructure and communications systems. In Cambodia, Marshal Lon Nol had been "reelected" that summer in a rigged election that Hanoi had to assume was prelude to more American military support for the anticommunist regime and more pressure on its Cambodian sanctuaries.[47]

NVA performance in South Vietnam was abysmal. Fourteen divisions were frittered away in those multiple pincers that should have been reduced to two. Successes could not be reinforced. Thieu was able to shift reserves to threatened units before they could be annihilated. Communist tanks were not massed for shock effect. They were expended as mobile artillery for the infantry. Time and troops were wasted besieging places like Kontum City and An Loc that should have been bypassed. NVA field commanders consumed supplies and reserves without decisive effect.[48]

Thousands of NVA infantry were squandered in human-wave attacks that were easy meat for free-world artillery, tac air, naval gunfire, and B-52s. One-third of the NVA was killed or wounded in the offensive. Summoned to Moscow to account for all the wasted lives and matériel, NVA general Tran Van Quang, the deputy chief of the general staff, explained that in their rapid buildup and modernization, the communist army had neglected to refine their system of command and control, or even assure the competence of field commanders: "There is a lack of high-quality tactical training and combat experience."[49]

North Vietnamese morale *had* to be waning after a rebuff like this one. An unposted letter, written by a North Vietnamese soldier and discovered by South Vietnamese troops near Saigon, described the sheer terror of American bombing: "I would like to jump straight up for thousands of miles to get away from here, from this killing....I feel death very near whenever I see an airplane coming through the clouds." Not only had the NVA not broken through to Saigon, but once again Hanoi had failed to trigger a general uprising.[50]

Nixon desperately sought a peace deal before the November 1972 presidential election. There had been five antiwar roll-call votes in Congress in 1969. In 1972, there were thirty-five. In July 1972, actress Jane Fonda had traveled to North Vietnam, where she broadcast an antiwar message on Radio Hanoi and allowed herself to be filmed sitting astride an antiaircraft gun. The Senate confirmation of Abrams as Army chief of staff ran into immediate trouble when senators learned of Abrams' clandestine authorization of B-52 strikes in proscribed areas. In August, the Senate voted 49–47 to end the war by December. If all US POWs were released, the Senate resolved, all US funding and troops for the war would be terminated by year-end. As usual, the hawkish House refused its assent, but all of this legislative pushback showed Nixon how much his room for maneuver had narrowed.[51]

Ed Muskie, the early Democratic front-runner, had washed out, but the Democratic presidential nominee, South Dakota senator George McGovern, was a World War II combat veteran who mocked the president's floundering. "Nixon can put a man on the moon," McGovern told a jeering crowd, "but he can't put an end to the Vietnam War!" The Democrats *would* end it. McGovern pledged to cut off support to the Thieu regime, bring the POWs home, and end the war within ninety days of his inauguration. Nixon called this "peace by surrender." He vowed not to "impose a communist government" on Saigon. Congress was not ready to shut off funding for Thieu and the ARVN, but it certainly would have balked had Nixon reversed the troop withdrawals or ordered Americans back into battle. Time and patience were exhausted.[52]

In October 1972, Hanoi's chief negotiator in Paris, Le Duc Tho, finally agreed that President Thieu could remain in power in the South after a cease-fire. It was a major concession—offered to make the Linebacker I bombing stop, but also a recognition by Hanoi that pressure from Beijing and Moscow to end the war was materializing. The two powers had stopped sending offensive weapons during the Easter Offensive and were only equipping the NVA with defensive ones. Privately, they were girding for communist victory. "Negotiate a coalition government with Thieu," Zhou Enlai had instructed Prime Minister Pham Van Dong with a wink that summer. "If it does not work out, fight again. The Americans will not return."[53]

Nixon had revoked LBJ's bombing halt and rules of engagement over North Vietnam with Linebacker I—hitting areas previously held off limits, permitting effective strikes against airfields, SAM sites, and letting the B-52s operate in force. Following the progress of the peace talks as closely as he could from prison cells in North Vietnam, Lieutenant Commander John McCain III, now in his fifth year of captivity, observed that "the only reason the North Vietnamese began negotiating in October 1972 was because they could read the polls as well as you and I can and they knew that Nixon was going to have an overwhelming victory in his reelection bid and wanted to negotiate a cease-fire *before* the elections."[54]

But Nixon had to make his own major concessions: that 125,000 NVA troops could remain *inside* the borders of South Vietnam after a cease-fire, and that a VC Provisional Revolutionary Government would be given official standing in the Paris negotiations and, once the shooting stopped, in a South Vietnamese electoral commission. Thieu and his negotiators cried foul, perhaps remembering that when LBJ had offered the same deal four years earlier Kissinger had sneered that it made "as much sense as to attempt to overcome the problems of Mississippi through a coalition of the SDS [Students for a Democratic Society] and the Ku Klux Klan." But Kissinger had lost his earlier confidence in his ability to thread the needle in Paris. "Thieu is right," Kissinger confided to Nixon. "Our terms will eventually destroy him."[55]

In a bid to deliver an "October surprise" of his own to defeat George McGovern, Kissinger had signaled on October 26, 1972, that "peace is at hand." Washington and Hanoi were in "substantial agreement" on a nine-point peace settlement. This last-minute flurry seemed to credit Hunter Thompson's quip that Nixon had not been lying when he had campaigned four years earlier on a "secret plan" to end the war. "Which was true," Thompson wrote. "The plan was to end the war just in time to get himself re-elected in 1972."[56]

But Nixon and Kissinger did not reckon with Saigon. On November 1, Thieu stiff-armed Nixon as he had stiff-armed Johnson four years earlier. He had watched Nixon's opening to China with fear and loathing: "America has been looking for a better mistress and now Nixon has discovered China," he sneered to his aides. South Vietnam had become "the old and ugly mistress." Thieu denounced the draft agreement as "a surrender of the South Vietnamese people to the Communists" and declared that he would never sign it. Nixon, Thieu sulked, had offered them "to the Communists on a golden platter."

He certainly had. Kissinger's draft agreement did not reestablish the DMZ, and it legitimized vast NVA-controlled enclaves inside South Vietnam, referring to them as a third Vietnamese "entity." Washington's *real* aim, Kissinger confided to Nixon, was simply to equip South Vietnam well enough for it to survive for a year or two. Its inevitable fall must appear to be "the result of South Vietnamese incompetence." Thieu spat defiance, insisting that the United States must defend every square mile of South Vietnam no less fervently than it defended the territory of West Germany and South Korea. The talks stalled again while Nixon scrambled to placate Thieu and buy him off with Operation Enhance Plus—massive additional deliveries of American tanks, aircraft, missiles, and artillery.[57]

Nixon sent Kissinger, Abrams, and Haig to Saigon to, as the president put it, "cram [the agreement] down [Thieu's] throat." Nixon made expansive promises that he knew would not be kept: American aircraft would remain in Thailand and Guam to police the peace; the Seventh Fleet would loiter indefinitely off the coast of Vietnam; CINCPAC would "react vigorously" to any serious violation of the cease-fire by North Vietnam; American economic and military aid would flow to Saigon as long as needed.

Kissinger, aware that his plans had all come to naught, sulkily lashed out at everyone but himself. "It is a fact," he said to Thieu, "that in the United States all the press, the media and intellectuals have a vested interest in our defeat." He castigated Thieu for his ingratitude, confessing that he, Nixon, and their predecessors had "mortgaged everything for the defense of one country," South Vietnam. He also blamed the North Vietnamese, calling them "tawdry, filthy shits"; to Nixon, he fulminated, "They never do anything that isn't tawdry." He recommended that Nixon "start bombing the bejesus out of them"—again.[58]

Having trounced McGovern on November 7, Nixon authorized Operation Linebacker II. It began on December 19, 1972, and lasted eleven days. This "Christmas bombing"—3,420 sorties strewing 20,000 tons of bombs over Hanoi and Haiphong—was the heaviest air raid by any power since World War II. The bombers hit supply depots, power plants, radio and television transmitters, bridges, ports, airfields, and SAM sites. Four thousand North Vietnamese civilians were killed or wounded. With Congress in recess, Haldeman summarized Nixon's view on this collateral damage: "Don't worry about killing civilians, go ahead and kill 'em."[59]

The official aim of the Linebacker raids was to force Hanoi to make concessions and sign a peace agreement. Nixon's White House taping system captured his unofficial aim in a meeting with Kissinger and Vice President Spiro Agnew on December 16. Nixon wanted to show Thieu, with this wave of murder and destruction, that his pledge to use "massive retaliation" against North Vietnam was not an empty threat. He would do it again if Thieu was threatened again. Thieu should take comfort in that, and stop obstructing Kissinger's talks.[60]

Hanoi anticipated Operation Linebacker II, for it was the only card Nixon could play. General Van Tien Dung had an air defense plan ready by December 3 and took the added precaution of evacuating half of Hanoi's civilian population to the countryside.[61]

Allied governments deplored "Nixon's Christmas deluge of death." The pope denounced "the sudden resumption of harsh and massive war actions." In the Kremlin, Brezhnev angrily insisted that Nixon terminate the war at once. In Beijing, the Chinese Communist Party organized the largest anti-American demonstration of the war. Even in the United States, there was scant support for the Christmas bombing, even less when the heavy American losses were tallied: twenty-eight planes shot down by North Vietnamese SAMs, forty-three US airmen killed, and forty-nine captured. An Air Force pilot in Thailand recalled the malaise affecting personnel there. The American squadrons were all in the process of being merged or deactivated as part of the drawdown, and they had watched a presidential campaign in which both candidates had battled "about who was going to end the war more quickly." No one, he hardly needed to add, "wanted to be the last person to die in a losing cause."[62]

Secretary of Defense Laird opposed Linebacker II on the grounds that it was an unsuitable use of the B-52, which was needed to deter the Soviets and the Chinese in the Cold War. As it was, 207 B-52s, half of America's manned bomber force, were in Southeast Asia. Any additional losses in this already lost war could not be made good, for production lines for the B-52 had been shut down years earlier. General Al Haig, the Army's vice chief of staff and a Kissinger adviser, later divulged that Nixon stopped the Christmas bombing because the cabinet would not support it and because Congress threatened impeachment if it continued. The press called it "war by tantrum" and "Stone Age barbarism."[63]

But in their Hanoi prison, Lieutenant Commander John McCain III and the other inmates welcomed the tantrum: "Our morale skyrocketed.... We were cheering and hollering.... [W]e had sat there for three-and-a-half years with no bombing going on and were fully aware that the only way we were ever going to get out was for our Government to turn the screws on Hanoi." Outside the walls of McCain's prison, Joan Baez roamed the streets, kicking the rubble of Hanoi's Bach Mai Hospital and damning Nixon and the war. The United States, torn by massive protests in 1970 and 1971, was quieter this time, probably because Congress was adjourned, college students were home for Christmas, and people were focused on holiday parties and shopping.[64]

Bob Hope's 1972 Christmas Tour, always an expansive affair with troupes of 100 or more, ten tons of cargo, celebrities, athletes, and bands, was severely cut back. The Army drawdown in 1972 had been so rapid that there was just strength and logistic support for a single show, and it could only be secured in the heart of Saigon at Tan Son Nhut Airport. When Hope asked the Air Force if they would host (and secure) a second show at Da Nang Airbase, they demurred. Due to the constant threat of mortar and rocket attacks, it would be unsafe to fill an amphitheater there: "We can no longer have large numbers of spectators in one place." They suggested that Hope ask the Navy to host a show offshore on a carrier of the Seventh Fleet. By this stage of the war, "offshore" was the safest place in Vietnam.[65]

Chapter 26

THE FALL

Nixon's intensified bombing campaign had its desired effect. Linebacker II forced all sides back to the table. President Thieu's frantic resistance to the "false peace" being crafted by Kissinger in Paris was finally broken by a threat from Nixon: "You must decide now whether you wish to continue our alliance or whether you want me to seek a settlement with the enemy which serves U.S. interests alone." Thieu had a last stab at defiance, insisting that "the invaded must cease to be invaded and the aggressor must go home." Safely reelected, Nixon rolled his eyes. Once a great booster of South Vietnamese "sovereignty and independence," Nixon reminded Thieu of Saigon's abject dependency. He admonished Thieu to join him "in concluding a satisfactory agreement, or I will proceed at whatever cost."[1]

With Thieu reluctantly onboard, Nixon halted the Linebacker II bombing on December 30, 1972, and Hanoi agreed to resume talks. Both Moscow and Beijing pressed Le Duan to sign the peace agreement to get the United States out of Southeast Asia. The goal, Mao scolded, was peace, not "to fight for another 100 years." Zhou Enlai concurred: "The most important thing is to let the Americans leave." In "six months to a year," he roguishly added, "the situation will change."[2]

Le Duan, who had always regarded "puppet collapse" as the essential preliminary to American withdrawal, finally understood, after the failed general offensives of 1968, 1969, and 1972, that he would have to negotiate the Americans out of the war entirely, and only *then* go after the puppet.

Nixon's bombers and relaxed rules of engagement had pulverized North Vietnam's air defenses and left them exposed to far greater destruction. Douglas Pike, America's foremost analyst on the VC and the NVA, called the Linebacker raids the politburo's first experience of "all-out strategic air war." It shattered them, he concluded, "causing them to reverse virtually overnight their bargaining position at the Paris talks." The North Vietnamese disputed that view, later insisting that they returned to the peace table only because they knew that Americans, their allies, and Congress were all demanding that Nixon produce a final settlement, which they were eager to accept to get the United States out of the picture.[3]

Had President Johnson's Operation Rolling Thunder proceeded in the brutal vein of Linebacker II, LBJ might have rid himself of the war years earlier and still been president. Nixon remarked that he wished he'd done it in 1969 and not waited three years. Hanoi, its economy shattered and alliances weakened, feared an even bigger pounding. But it was too little too late. Nixon, whose approval rating dropped amid the savagery of the Christmas bombing, could see congressional support and appropriations shutting down as quickly as public support.[4]

Both houses of Congress passed legislation in early January 1973 that would stop all funding of the war in Vietnam upon the return of American POWs. Western allies were horrified by the eleven-day air campaign and its thousands of civilian casualties. Kissinger, who had flown to Paris after Linebacker II ended, finally brought the war to a kind of end with the signature of the Paris Peace Accords on January 27, which terminated US military involvement. Announcing this grandly named "Agreement on Ending the War and Restoring Peace in Vietnam" on January 23, 1973, Nixon boasted that it was a settlement to "end the war and bring peace with honor to Vietnam and Southeast Asia."[5]

On the appointed day, there was no evidence of celebration around the vast baize-covered tables where the four parties to the accords had been jousting for five years through 250 meetings. Instead, there were two separate signing ceremonies, described by a witness as "cold and gloomy," as "glum as the drizzly, gray Paris sky outside." The second ceremony had been convened so that the United States and North Vietnam could sign documents referencing the Viet Cong Provisional Revolutionary Government that the South Vietnamese refused to sign on what Kissinger called "theological" grounds.[6]

Secretary of State William Rogers called January 27, 1973, "a great day, a milestone in achieving peace." It was anything but that. Only the Americans and North Vietnamese benefited. The 25,000 American troops still in Vietnam would come home along with the 591 American POWs held in North Vietnamese prisons. For the South Vietnamese, the Paris agreement was a catastrophe, a "standstill" cease-fire that left 160,000 NVA combat troops inside the borders of South Vietnam. It merely enjoined Hanoi to remove its troops from South Vietnam, cease its support for the Viet Cong, and stop using the sanctuaries in Laos and Cambodia. Why would Hanoi stop this behavior under no threat when it had been doing these things for eleven years under heavy threat?

The communists accepted these American words on the page because they knew that they had the upper hand. If they did not win through negotiations, they were poised to resume the war at any time. Truong Nhu Tang, a senior VC official, noted the obvious: "Complete American withdrawal and the permanent emplacement of the North Vietnamese army [inside South Vietnam] assured the eventual destruction of the South Vietnamese regime."[7]

By the terms of the agreement, Thieu would have to enter into a "joint military commission" with the Viet Cong to create a National Council of Reconciliation and Concord that would lay the groundwork for new elections in South Vietnam. Thieu had tried to kill the joint commission but had succeeded only in changing other words on the page—his negotiations with the Viet Cong were redefined as "advisory," not "administrative." For the South Vietnamese, this may have been the only tangible impact on the Paris talks of Nixon's ferocious Christmas bombing.

The agreement also created a four-party joint military commission—American, North and South Vietnamese, and VC—to arrange the removal of the NVA troops inside South Vietnam, which would probably never happen because the agreement did not even define the border between the two countries. South Vietnamese efforts to make the DMZ the border had been rebuffed.

Vagueness on national frontiers suited the communists, who held the initiative. Overall, the January 1973 peace agreement was a scarcely changed version of the October 1972 draft, prompting Kissinger aide John Negroponte to quip: "We bombed the North Vietnamese into accepting our concessions." In truth, it was a scarcely changed version of LBJ's peace plan, which Nixon had wrecked more than four years earlier, when he had rationalized his devious conduct thus: "I considered it unthinkable that we would fight a bitter war for four years, lose 30,000 men, and spend tens of billions of dollars for the goal of getting our POWs back."[8]

In the end, Nixon had forced the nation to fight for four *more* years, lose 28,000 *more* men, and spend *more* tens of billions of dollars to get the POWs back. Nixon was only too aware of this hideous fact. Before Kissinger went before the cameras to announce the peace, Nixon forbade his national security adviser "to get into the intricacies of the settlement." They were far too embarrassing for the administration. Thieu, who had tried to scuttle the negotiations, had been forced to sign or else face a coup, a cutoff of American aid, and no promise of American airpower in the future. "We were doomed to failure, but we could not do otherwise," he sighed.[9]

A journalist mingling with ARVN troops and refugees near Saigon at the hour of the cease-fire reported that the "'peace' may have been hailed in the rest of the world but was greeted in Vietnam with wary uncertainty." Local VC had fought all night to take as many hamlets as they could before the cease-fire at 8 a.m., when Thieu's voice could be heard everywhere in South Vietnam over the distant thumping of artillery. It crackled through transistor radios and village loudspeakers announcing the peace but urging the South Vietnamese to remain vigilant against communist violations. "The president can say anything," an ARVN sergeant scoffed, "but this war will never end."[10]

The last American troops in South Vietnam left on March 29, 1973. The American POWs had been released, and most of the 2,300 MIAs, their fates unknown, had been summarily deemed KIA/BNR—"killed in action/body not recovered" to finalize Nixon's peace accords. At 1 p.m. on March 29, General Fred Weyand formally deactivated MACV in a dreary ceremony at "Pentagon East," the sprawling headquarters building that had opened six years earlier when the great battlefields of the war—Khe Sanh, Con Thien, Dak To, Ia Drang, and the Iron Triangle—had been behind American and

ARVN lines. As Weyand folded MACV's colors for the last time, those places, and many more like them, found themselves behind NVA lines, despite being well inside the borders of South Vietnam.

"Certain war has yielded to an uncertain peace in Vietnam," Kissinger declared in his Nobel Peace Prize acceptance speech in December 1973. "Uncertain" was putting it mildly. Neither side was comfortable with the 1973 peace accords. Thieu wanted to reconquer the communist enclaves inside South Vietnam. Le Duan wanted to unify both Vietnams under communist rule. Already in 1973, the NVA was preparing a new offensive, but the politburo remained wary of Nixon, for the president had pledged to reenter the war if North Vietnam violated the accords.

Although Nixon had taken the B-52s, 4,500 of 5,000 helicopters, and most of America's tactical air home to the United States, he *might* send it all back to South Vietnam if Hanoi rolled the dice again. Thieu had assumed that, having lost 58,000 American lives and spent $168 billion in Vietnam (about $1.5 trillion today), the Americans would not let the country fall. But Nixon's authority waned as the Watergate scandal ripened. In April 1973, White House counsel John Dean began cooperating with Watergate prosecutors and the Senate created a committee to investigate "presidential campaign activities and the Watergate break-in."[11]

Nixon's peace agreement had put soothing words on the page about Cambodia and Laos too. There all foreign troops would be withdrawn, sanctuaries emptied, and the national governments' independence and sovereignty respected. But no deadline was specified, and everyone knew that the NVA had no intention of withdrawing from the sanctuaries in either country until South Vietnam was defeated.

Pol Pot's Khmer Rouge went their own way after the Paris accords and attacked Marshal Lon Nol's Cambodian Republic. In 1973, they surrounded Phnom Penh. Nixon sent the B-52s again to blast the Khmer Rouge back from the capital. Thousands of peasants were slaughtered in these raids, which were plotted with scant concern for collateral damage. "It was justified," a US embassy official breezily concluded, "to save them from a much greater slaughter at the hands of the Communists."[12]

In all of 1972, American B-52s had dropped 37,000 tons of bombs in Cambodia. In 1973, they dropped that quantity on Cambodia every *month*. But the deluge of American bombs hardly checked Lon Nol's slide into irrelevance. The Khmer Rouge began bombarding Phnom Penh with rockets and artillery. Thousands were killed, and 100,000 homes were flattened. Lon Nol declared a state of siege. Nixon flew in ammunition and rice for the marshal, but nothing more.[13]

When Nixon submitted a supplemental appropriations bill in May 1973 to pay for continuing US bombing in Cambodia and Laos, Congress, for the first time in the entire war, refused to fund it. In June, Congress passed the Case-Church Amendment, which banned all military action in Laos, Cambodia, and Vietnam. Nixon reluctantly agreed to halt all bombing by August 15, 1973.[14]

On that date, US Air Force auditors were startled to discover that in the four years since 1969 they had dropped 539,000 tons of bombs on Cambodia, which was more than three times the weight of bombs dropped on Japan in World War II. Half of those bombs had been dropped on Cambodia in the first half of 1973 alone, to slow the Khmer Rouge drive on the capital.

The impact on the land and the people was cataclysmal. An estimated 150,000 Cambodian civilians were blown to bits. Villages were wiped from the map. Dams and dikes were flattened, releasing catastrophic floods. Eighty percent of the country's rice fields were lost to bombs and flood waters. Hundreds of thousands of refugees slopped along muddy roads, gazing fearfully at the skies. Nixon publicly defended the bombing as akin to General Eisenhower's decision to bomb German-occupied France in 1944. Privately, he and Kissinger agreed that they had caused "the collapse of Cambodia."[15]

US Air Force planners, who controlled these B-52 raids from bases in Thailand, congratulated themselves that "in defiance of the conventional wisdom that 'air cannot take ground or hold it,' we have done it." No, they most certainly hadn't. The seventy-five Khmer Rouge battalions committed to the battle for Phnom Penh continued their bloody advance, "going on," as journalist William Shawcross put it, "in thinner ranks through a landscape that would have seemed lunar had it not been under water."[16]

His "big play" in Cambodia having failed wretchedly, Nixon now struggled even to fulfill that other obligation of the 1973 peace accords: Saigon's "right to unlimited military replacement aid" and "unlimited economic aid." On Capitol Hill, where such aid had to originate, there was no appetite to fulfill Nixon's pledges. Congress cut Nixon's request for $1.6 billion in military aid to Saigon in 1974 to $1.1 billion. They would slash the 1975 package to just $700 million. This would have happened with or without Watergate. Public support for aid to Vietnam had sunk to just 15 percent, and Nixon himself lost all interest in Vietnam after the peace accords. Kissinger's staff observed that "there are hardly any of us around anymore to prod the ARVN and the GVN to high levels of performance."[17]

The ARVN now struggled to attain even low levels of performance. Vietnamization had been premised on giving the ARVN the ability to "move, shoot, and communicate," but tumbling levels of American aid voided that premise. The mountain of matériel given to Saigon by Operation Enhance Plus—a billion dollars' worth of tanks, artillery, ships, and aircraft—was recognized even at the time as being all but useless because the South Vietnamese lacked the pilots, crews, mechanics, and other personnel needed to operate and maintain all of that hardware. "What we're leaving behind," a US major confided to a reporter, "is a well-equipped military corpse."[18]

The slackening of US aid and the rising price of fuel in the wake of OPEC's 1973 oil embargo meant that what aircraft and vehicles the South Vietnamese *could* operate flew and drove less. Flight time had to be strictly rationed. Spare parts ran out. Ships, aircraft, and vehicles were mothballed. Pilots in the world's fourth-biggest air force were converted to infantrymen. Desertion spiked again as inflation eroded soldier pay, and the ARVN ran low on ammunition.[19]

Thieu had tried to reduce the number of South Vietnamese under arms in 1973 to stimulate economic growth, but he was now forced to try to get back to 1.1 million troops, with little success. Fewer than half of the 450,000 troops in the ARVN were in combat units. Most sought refuge in the army's long administrative and logistical tail. Others became *linh bong*—"flower soldiers," who paid their commanders to look the other way while they shirked active duty.

South Vietnamese casualties were undiminished by the American peace accords in Paris. There were 28,000 ARVN deaths in 1973, and 31,000 more in 1974. Desertion continued at an even faster clip than usual. This forced the Thieu regime to depend entirely on the 200,000 boys who turned eighteen each year, only a third of whom could be dragooned into the armed forces in any given year. Senior officials became more corrupt than ever, trying to secure their fortunes before the fall.

Thieu's staff informed him in 1974 that over two-thirds of ARVN generals and colonels were involved in illegal rackets, and that lower command echelons were busy selling US-provided weapons and equipment on the black market. VNAF helicopter pilots were observed demanding payment from wounded ARVN soldiers before they would medevac them. A RAND Corporation survey of morale heard this from a South Vietnamese officer: "You're a squad leader with your squad, and you get the order to defend a hill to the death. And you look to Saigon, where the rich have food, liquor, they have money, they relax, they have a good time. Why fight to the death? For whom?"[20]

Thieu's presidency swerved into authoritarianism after 1972, when the already unpopular president declared martial law, closed opposition newspapers, jailed journalists, and replaced elected village officials with his own men. Clans and factions battled for control of every important office. The people of this nation of 18 million had no more stomach for war. Every family had at least one or two members on active duty. Farmers had been driven into squalid refugee camps. Unemployment stood at 20 percent, inflation at over 100 percent. Everyone yearned for an end to the war. A Vietnamese resident of Saigon said to an American visitor: "What you have done here is create a monkey climate. The only Vietnamese you really know—the ones you have dealt with—are monkeys. Why don't you at least help us get rid of the monkeys before you go."[21]

On April 16, 1974, Thieu suspended his military and political talks with the VC, blaming the "increasing number of truce violations by the Communists." The thirteen NVA divisions permitted to remain inside the borders of South Vietnam by the terms of Nixon's peace accords had been busy grabbing more land and population. Licensed to move freely across the old DMZ, the North Vietnamese had marched another 40,000 troops into South Vietnam, as well as large numbers of tanks and artillery. Everywhere Thieu was losing ground. When he appealed to Nixon for more aid for what he called a "Third Indochina War" against these emboldened communists, Nixon's latest secretary of defense, James Schlesinger, advised the president to deny the request. All aid should be "terminated," Schlesinger said, because Thieu's armed forces were "fully capable." The improvement and modernization program was deemed complete. Congress went along with the joke, cutting Saigon's aid package by a third.[22]

In December 1974, four months after Watergate had forced Nixon to resign the presidency, Soviet general Viktor Kulikov flew to Hanoi to meet with Le Duan and the politburo. The last time a Russian officer this senior had visited Hanoi was late 1971, on the eve of the Easter Offensive. In the weeks after Kulikov's visit, Soviet deliveries of weapons to Haiphong harbor rose four-fold. Enough matériel landed in the port to replace everything lost in 1972 and equip a sixth general offensive. The ARVN, in contrast, saw its ammo supply rates plummet as US aid receded. ARVN infantry received just 1.6 rounds a day by late 1974, ARVN howitzers just 6 rounds a day.[23]

North Vietnam got stronger in other ways. With no more American bombing or mining, Hanoi paved sections of the Ho Chi Minh Trail and ran an oil pipeline alongside it. They then ran another pipeline into South Vietnam, terminating at Loc Ninh, just seventy-five miles from Saigon. Between January 1974 and April 1975, the NVA transported more supplies into South Vietnam than they had moved over the past thirteen years. Convoys of hundreds of NVA trucks moved entire combat units into South Vietnam with impunity.

All of the North Vietnamese divisions were restored to full strength, with more weapons, ammo, food, and fuel than in the past. Three hundred thousand communist troops and agents spread into the space around Saigon, Da Nang, and the central coast, agitating for what Hanoi unctuously called a "war to preserve peace." The NVA "enclaves" in South Vietnam had expanded to comprise nearly half of Saigon's territory.

To correct the tactical mistakes of 1972, the NVA reorganized their main-force divisions and grouped them in new corps headquarters to facilitate broad, synchronized combined-arms operations. They spent most of 1974 testing these new arrangements while repelling Thieu's attacks on their enclaves and bleeding the ARVN. When Graham Martin, America's last ambassador to South Vietnam, appeared before Congress in the summer of 1974 spouting the usual line that all was well and that Thieu was "stronger than ever," Representative Patricia Schroeder of Colorado stated what must have been on everyone's mind: "I have a feeling you believe in the Tooth Fairy."[24]

In October 1974, the North Vietnamese leadership met to discuss how to finish off their toothless adversary. Le Duan argued that Nixon's resignation in August 1974 all but guaranteed that US forces would not return to Southeast Asia. The South Vietnamese would have to fight alone. Others in the politburo worried that the NVA's preparations and logistics were not yet complete and that Nixon's successor as president, sixty-one-year-old Gerald Ford, *might* fight back. The House had cast its first decisive vote against the Vietnam War in June 1973, joining the Senate in forbidding all US combat activity in Indochina after August 15, 1973. But Congress was still providing $1.1 billion of aid in 1974 and $700 million in 1975, in line with Nixon's promises to Thieu "to provide adequate economic and military assistance" after the peace.[25]

Nixon had also promised "vigorous" American action against any North Vietnamese violations of the peace accords. Despite American exhaustion with the conflict, there was a chance that Jerry Ford might use emergency powers to save the ARVN again. The politburo decided after long debate that in December 1974 a trial offensive would be launched from Cambodia into the hill towns of Phuoc Long province, just seventy-five miles northwest of Saigon. If President Ford declined to react, the NVA would proceed to a massive, war-winning offensive.[26]

US military intelligence forces had departed South Vietnam after the Paris accords were signed in January 1973, leaving small numbers of personnel from the defense attaché's office and the CIA station to collect intelligence and coordinate with Thieu's government and the ARVN. To smooth relations between the two countries, all "political," "controversial," or "sensitive" collection was forbidden.

Critiques of Thieu or allegations of corruption and incompetence never reached Washington. When the lone Defense Intelligence Agency (DIA) analyst working full-time on the ARVN in 1974 sought detailed information on its capabilities from the US defense attaché's office in Saigon, he was told that "this information is not available." A war that had begun a decade earlier with deliberate American obfuscation about its brittle ally was crawling to its end in the same way. Politically, it would be more expedient to appear "surprised" by South Vietnamese defeats than prepared for them.[27]

Hanoi by now had penetrated Thieu's inner circle and had agents turning over South Vietnamese plans and preparations the moment they were conceived. When Thieu launched his last offensives of the war, a sequence of attacks between January and June 1974 to beat the communists back from Saigon and the Mekong Delta, each thrust was parried by the communists.

The NVA counterattacked all summer, grabbing more territory around Hue and Da Nang. General John Murray, the American defense attaché in Saigon, stuck to the script that had served MACV so well in Vietnam: make everything a question of numbers. "You can roughly equate cuts in support to loss of real estate," he ventured. The ARVN, he continued, might hold with annual aid of $1.3 billion, but it would be unable even to defend itself with the $750 million promised for 1975. Somehow, half a million dollars would make all the difference in an ugly war that had already consumed $168 *billion* to no good effect.

Staffers dispatched to Saigon by the Senate Foreign Relations Committee in June ridiculed the embassy there and General Murray's reporting, noting that concealment of inconvenient facts was still their stock-in-trade. The embassy's "reputation for close identification with the policies of the South Vietnamese government and selective reporting" persisted despite defeat and humiliation: "These tendencies are still apparent today."[28]

Saigon had no assets inside the politburo and was surprised by the Phuoc Long Offensive, which launched on December 12, 1974. This was Hanoi's probe to test whether or not the Ford administration would intervene to save the ARVN. General Tran Van Tra, who had led the NVA attacks on Loc Ninh and An Loc in 1972, drove south from the Cambodian border area toward Phuoc Binh City with two NVA divisions, a tank battalion, and an artillery regiment.

Phuoc Binh City was the province capital, a tidy town of 25,000 on a bend of the Song Be River. By New Year's Day, Tra's troops had pressed about 3,000 ARVN troops inside the city, which they now subjected to heavy shelling. VNAF strike fighters hesitated to join the fight. First, they blamed thick clouds and low ceilings. Then they refused to dive below 12,000 feet, citing the NVA air defenses. This failure made it difficult for VNAF helicopters to fly in with supplies and reinforcements. Thieu was able to reinforce Phuoc Binh's ruff-puffs with an ARVN battalion and two companies of

ARVN Rangers, but with 3,000 shells a day detonating in their midst, they surrendered on January 6, 1975.

Of the 5,000 ARVN troops committed to the battle, only 850 escaped. With no victories on the ground and no American B-52s flying to the rescue, President Thieu urged the nation to seek solace in Christ and Buddha: "I appeal to the entire population to reserve three days to pray." He then vowed to retake the city, but how? Phuoc Binh City had fallen in just two days. The VNAF appeared only after NVA troops had secured the town and retired to bunkers on its outskirts. They dropped their bombs onto its smoldering ruins, finishing off many of the 1,500 dead and missing South Vietnamese soldiers and civilians in the town.

The fall of Phuoc Binh, just seventy-five miles from Saigon, was ominous. "Its fall showed that the central government in Saigon is quite weak," a State Department analyst noted. "A year ago, they would have gone in to defend or recover the place." Thieu, of course, had always hoped that the United States would save his bacon. That explained his otherwise inexplicable "hold everywhere" strategy. Even though the South Vietnamese armed forces had burned through most of their fuel and ammo in the course of 1974, Thieu still expected his troops to defend the entire country with a mobility and firepower that they all too obviously lacked.

Thieu's Joint General Staff was no help. An American who knew the generals summed up their contribution to the strategic debate: "Weak and cowed by Thieu, passivity and prayer were their recipe." But this time the Americans didn't leap into action as they had two years earlier. Democrats had expanded their control of both houses of Congress in the November 1974 midterms and now moved, as Senator Edward Kennedy put it, to stop "the endless support for the endless war."

With no congressional support, President Ford agreed only to put the 3rd Marine Division in Okinawa on alert and move the USS *Enterprise* closer to Vietnam. In his State of the Union address on January 15, 1975, Ford made no mention of South Vietnam. At a press conference a week later, President Ford made American nonintervention plain: "I can see *no* circumstances under which the United States will reenter the war."[29]

The NVA commander, fifty-seven-year-old General Van Tien Dung, had planned a final NVA offensive in 1976. Pushed by Le Duan—"Never have we had military and political conditions so perfect as we have now"—the general tried another local offensive in March 1975 to test ARVN capabilities as American aid petered out. North Vietnamese forces, buttressed by a record stockpile of supplies, were the strongest they had ever been. There seemed no reason to wait until 1976. A Viet Minh general in the old days, Dung had been the NVA chief of staff for the past two decades. He now took aim at another weakly defended provincial capital, Ban Me Thuot—the largest city in the Central Highlands.[30]

Ban Me Thuot sat on an 1,800-foot height overlooking roads north to Pleiku and east to Cam Ranh Bay. Coffee and tea grew on the high ground, rice and rubber in the valleys. The town, a critical crossroads, was garrisoned by an ARVN regiment, a Ranger group, and ruff-puffs. Here the continuing failure of the ARVN to detect NVA movements proved fatal. Three entire NVA divisions appeared unobserved around Ban Me Thuot, allowing the enemy to achieve a five-to-one manpower advantage before they struck and seized the town in a week of fighting in early March.

Thieu airlifted two ARVN regiments to Phuoc An, twenty miles east of Ban Me Thuot. He ordered them to retake the province's capital. They dissolved instead. And who could blame them? With the Joint General Staff's chronic inefficiency and the cuts in American aid, everything was in short supply and many of the troops were not being armed, paid, or even fed. The ARVN, one of its generals dolefully recalled, found it "hard to adjust to the shift from extreme wealth to extreme poverty within a very short time."[31]

With the ARVN buckling, Thieu decided to abandon the Central Highlands and most of northern South Vietnam. He would cling to the coastal strips, the Mekong Delta, and key strongpoints like Da Nang, Cam Ranh Bay, and the Saigon Circle. The decision was entirely his. "Hold our prosperous and populated areas" and cut loose the rest, he told an astonished Joint General Staff, which had not been consulted. Thieu knew that the thirteen divisions of the ARVN were not enough to defend the whole country. He planned to reconstitute South Vietnam as a much smaller country that would nevertheless enclose most of the nation's rice, rubber, and industry, newly discovered offshore oil deposits, and the great capital of Saigon.[32]

On March 13, 1975, the ARVN began withdrawing from eight provinces that comprised 40 percent of South Vietnam's territory. Thieu planned to pull back to a more defensible line from Tay Ninh on the Cambodian

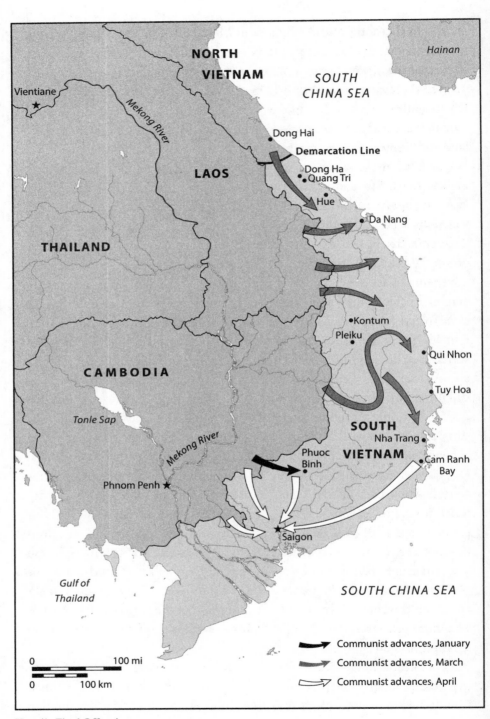

NORTH
VIETNAM

SOUTH
CHINA SEA

Hainan

Vientiane

Mekong River

LAOS

Dong Hai

Demarcation Line

Dong Ha
Quang Tri

Hue

Da Nang

THAILAND

Kontum
Pleiku

Qui Nhon

Tuy Hoa

CAMBODIA

Tonle Sap

Mekong River

Phnom Penh ★

Phuoc
Binh

SOUTH

Nha Trang

VIETNAM

Cam Ranh
Bay

Saigon

*Gulf of
Thailand*

SOUTH CHINA SEA

0   100 mi

0   100 km

Communist advances, January

Communist advances, March

Communist advances, April

Hanoi's Final Offensives

border to the coast at Cam Ranh Bay. South of this line sat most of South Vietnam's population and resources. But the impulsive and unheralded retreat of the armed forces without first evacuating the civilian population triggered mass panic and refugee flight.[33]

Withdrawing in good order to the new defense line could not be done under these anarchic conditions. The ARVN general commanding MR 2 and the Central Highlands, forty-eight-year-old General Pham Van Phu, was told to abandon Kontum City and Pleiku and withdraw to Tuy Hoa on the coast. Tuy Hoa, just north of Cam Ranh Bay, was a major air base built by the Americans in 1966 and turned over to the VNAF in 1972. General Phu, who had fought for the French and been captured at Dien Bien Phu, now discovered that the only open road to the coast was Provincial Route 7B, a narrow logging road. Fiasco ensued. What was meant to be a disciplined "redeployment" became a rout. Commanders abandoned their troops, who had to struggle through a twenty-mile-long swarm of refugees and military dependents filling the road, or trek cross-country through the jungle. "I saw old people and babies fall down on the road and tanks and trucks would go over them," an ARVN colonel recalled.[34]

By March 27, the stragglers of General Phu's ARVN corps reached Tuy Hoa, but two-thirds of the 60,000-man corps had disappeared. Scores of aircraft, hundreds of vehicles, and 18,000 tons of ammunition had been abandoned to the enemy. Of the collapse, Air Marshal Ky smirked: "Everywhere, commanding officers ran first."[35]

Farther north, ARVN units ordered into new positions also disintegrated. MR 1 commander General Ngo Quang Truong, who had replaced Lam during the Easter Offensive, was told to hold Da Nang with its port and air base at all costs. NVA columns seized Quang Tri City on March 19. Route 1, the coastal highway connecting Quang Tri, Hue, Da Nang, and Saigon, filled again with panicked refugees. This was the "Column of Sorrow" referenced by so many reporters.

Even the chief of the South Vietnamese Joint General Staff called this *sauve qui peut* what it was: "a rout of strategic proportions." Hue fell to the communists on March 25 without a fight. Da Nang became a circle of hell, with 2 million refugees crowding into a city built for 300,000 only to find General Truong evacuating the city's well-armed defenders from the beach. Ten thousand ARVN troops waded into the South China Sea on March 29 to slither onto boats that would take them south. The refugees stared in shock, fury, and disbelief. Da Nang, with all of its critical infrastructure and armaments, fell on March 30.[36]

Paul Vogle, a stringer with United Press International, hitched a ride on a Boeing 727 from Tan Son Nhut Airport in Saigon to Da Nang on March 29. The flight had been arranged by World Airways president Ed Daly to carry as many South Vietnamese women and children as the plane could fit to safety. Vogle and Daly landed to find "a mob in motion," over a thousand people surging across the runway toward the lowered tail ramp, "speeded by sheer desperation and panic."

Also present on the runway was the Hac Bao (Black Panther) Company—the elite rapid reaction force of the ARVN 1st Division. They now reacted more rapidly than ever, cutting through the mob with knives and lowered rifles and bulling their way on to the plane to take every seat. Vogle saw one of the soldiers kick an elderly woman in the face to get aboard. The woman toppled backward and Vogle glimpsed her for an instant: "lying flat on the tarmac, seeing hope, seeing life itself, just off the end of her fingertips and rolling the other way."

With communist rockets bursting all around the airfield, the 727 taxied to take off. Other ARVN troops, angry at being left behind, fired at the plane. One threw a grenade that burst, jamming the flaps full open and the wheels fully extended. As the jet lumbered aloft, the legs of fugitives in the wheel wells could be seen dangling from the undercarriage. One of them lost his grip and plummeted into the South China Sea. Vogle walked up the aisle and counted 265 ARVN troops and only three civilians—two women and a baby. The ARVN soldiers "said nothing. They didn't talk to each other or us. They looked at the floor."[37]

Da Nang was 370 miles northeast of Saigon. Halfway down the coast was Cam Ranh Bay, which had been developed after 1965 as America's principal deepwater port and logistics base in Vietnam and now housed the headquarters of MR 2, which had been hastily moved here from Pleiku. Visiting Cam Ranh on April 1, 1975, Le Kim Dinh, a former ARVN conscript now working for the *New York Times* Saigon bureau, found it "a hell on earth," teeming with more than 100,000 refugees, many of whom had paid over 1 million piasters—about $1,200—to sail from Da Nang to Saigon. The Saigon authorities, however, had ordered the ships to halt at Cam Ranh Bay, where everyone was "waiting and listening for the approaching rumble of North Vietnamese tanks."

While they waited, they watched skirmishes around the naval base and airfield between South Vietnamese troops: Marines and Rangers, who had escaped here from Da Nang, and troops sent from Saigon to secure the regional headquarters. Military discipline evaporated as the ARVN troops, instructed by Thieu to fight "a poor man's war" now that American aid had dried up, instead fought each other for the spoils under their noses—the piasters, dollars, gold, jewels, and family treasures that could be looted from all of these defenseless refugees.

The official reason given by the South Vietnamese navy for the halting of the ships at Cam Ranh Bay was that the Saigon authorities did not want a flood of new refugees to aggravate their own worsening situation. Unofficially, word went around that "it was just a question of money." If the refugees, who had been at sea for two days or more and were suffering from hunger, thirst, and the scorching sun, could come up with *more* money, they might continue their journey. "When they are willing to pay another 1 million piasters per person, then those ships will set sail for Saigon," a soldier informed Dinh.[38]

As these events unfolded, Secretary of Defense James Schlesinger discovered that the ARVN had abandoned $1 billion of US-supplied equipment in a single month of half-hearted combat. That was a lot. Schlesinger noted that the South Vietnamese military had been given $3 or $4 billion worth of equipment during Vietnamization. In other words, in just thirty days they had surrendered between a quarter and a third of everything they had been given for improvement and modernization: jets, helicopters, tanks, APCs, trucks, artillery, communications equipment, fuel, and munitions.[39]

Informed of this, Congress brusquely rejected Ford's request in early April 1975 for a billion dollars of emergency aid to Saigon. Congress killed the aid request in committee, agreeing only to fund the evacuation of personnel from Saigon and some refugee relief. But South Vietnam was collapsing so quickly that the money would not have helped anyway. It was probably a performative gesture by Ford—to show that he had *tried* to do something.[40]

On April 2, CIA director Bill Colby warned that the balance of forces in South Vietnam had shifted "decisively" in favor of the NVA. The next day,

Ford received an interagency intelligence assessment that predicted a South Vietnamese military collapse "within months, if not weeks." Only Ambassador Graham Martin was still bullish on Saigon, insisting that the NVA had shot its bolt and that Thieu, if helped by the United States, could claw back the lost ground.

Le Duan ordered General Dung to capture Saigon before the monsoon season started in May. "We must race against time, make use of every day," Le Duan exhorted. He believed that Beijing preferred two Vietnams to one and would take the opportunity to recognize the VC provisional government in Saigon to keep Vietnam divided, weak, and dependent. The NVA had to finish the job at once. There was reason for optimism. The trial offensives alone had nearly collapsed South Vietnam. The ARVN had retreated to a defensive ring around Saigon, defending the five main roads into the capital. One final push might topple the regime. On April 8, General Fred Weyand, now the Army chief of staff after Abrams' death from lung cancer, flew to Saigon and, after meetings with the bizarrely optimistic ambassador, assured President Ford that South Vietnam "still has the spirit and capability to defeat the North Vietnamese." Weyand urged them to keep battling, but they kept retreating. The general sheepishly revised his first take, warning Ford: "The South Vietnamese are on the brink of total military defeat."[41]

The collapse in South Vietnam was mirrored in Cambodia. The Khmer Rouge, who had nearly taken the capital in 1973, had been held on the outskirts for over a year by a massively reequipped FANK. But, like the ARVN, the FANK had no answers after its lavish budget was halved by Congress. With Nixon gone, Congress was no longer willing to pay the entire cost of Marshal Lon Nol's corrupt and inefficient state. On April Fool's Day, Lon Nol resigned and fled the country.

With the Khmer Rouge barbarians closing around the city, President Ford implemented Operation Eagle Pull, which yanked US nationals and select Cambodians out of Phnom Penh and onto US Navy ships in the Gulf of Thailand. The last Americans and the lucky few Cambodians got out just in time. On April 17, 1975, the Khmer Rouge broadcast that "we are entering the city by force of arms."[42]

As Lon Nol's northern defense line collapsed, Cambodian soldiers and refugees poured into Phnom Penh. Soldiers removed their uniforms and put on civilian clothes. Office workers pulled on the black pajamas that were the Indochinese communist uniform. By 9 a.m., the first Khmer Rouge troops entered the city, coming straight down Monivong Boulevard from the north. A witness described them as "dripping with arms like overladen fruit trees—grenades, pistols, rifles, rockets."

The guerrillas began immediately to empty the city, roving through the streets, commanding people to leave their homes. That day, Khmer Rouge troops ordered 2 million Cambodians to leave Phnom Penh for the country-side. The city dwellers were told that they had to leave for their own safety, that the US Air Force planned to bomb Phnom Penh, that they could return later. It was all a lie. Every other Cambodian city and town was emptied too, as 4 million people—of a population of 7 million—were force-marched deep into the countryside to till the soil.

Those in Phnom Penh marched at least sixty-five miles under a scald-ing sun. In Washington, Cambodia's ambassador vented his anger, more at the Americans than the Khmer Rouge: "Let's face it, you took advantage of us. You are much cleverer than we are. If the United States had respected our neutrality then the fighting, the killing and things might not have happened."[43]

Forty-one-year-old Sydney Schanberg was in Phnom Penh reporting for the *New York Times*. His Cambodian coverage would win a Pulitzer Prize and be the basis of the 1984 film *The Killing Fields*. "Two million people," Schanberg wrote, "suddenly moved out of the city in stunned silence— walking, bicycling, pushing cars that had run out of fuel, covering the roads like a human carpet." Sick and wounded in the city's hospitals were forced out too, "right down to the last patient. They went—limping, crawling, on crutches, carried on relatives' backs, wheeled on their hospital beds."[44]

This was all part of a plan by forty-nine-year-old Pol Pot, the Khmer Rouge leader, to create a new Cambodia, which he named Democratic Kam-puchea. Pol Pot despised what he called the "new people"—urbanized, edu-cated, or mixed-ethnicity Cambodians. He vaunted the pure-race Khmer peasantry and pronounced 1975 "Year Zero" of a national revival.

As revivals went, it got off to a self-destructive start. Pol Pot shuttered schools, factories, shops, banks, and even hospitals to eradicate all vestiges of modern civilization. Cars were junked, money banned, and religion out-lawed. Children were taken from their parents to be indoctrinated. Among the maxims in Pol Pot's little red book was this: "He who protests is an enemy and he who opposes is a corpse." Between 2 and 3 million Cambodians would be starved, worked to death, or murdered by the vicious Khmer Rouge government. In the regime's mass graves alone, there are 1.4 million corpses.[45]

Schanberg, who holed up in the French embassy for thirteen days before being evacuated to Thailand, observed the Khmer Rouge occupation of Phnom Penh through the windows of the embassy. He remembered the Khmer Rouge troops—"peasant boys, pure and simple—darker skinned than their city brethren, with gold in their front teeth." They looted the shops, robbed the refugees, and slid into the abandoned cars and beat on them with their rifle butts when they refused to start. They would then settle down to honking the horns for hours on end or switching the headlights on and off until the car batteries died. They would then move on, "as children might."[46]

Schanberg went to Cambodia's Information Ministry, where a thirty-five-year-old Khmer Rouge general had installed himself and ordered all high officials of the Lon Nol regime to assemble. Fifty had already complied. They stood outside the building—"very nervous but trying to appear untroubled." Lon Non, the younger brother of Lon Nol, was there. Schanberg also recognized several generals and cabinet ministers as well as one of the "seven traitors" marked for immediate execution: Premier Long Boret, whose offer of surrender with conditions had been contemptuously rejected the previous day.

The next day another of the "seven traitors" was pulled from his refuge in the French embassy—Sisowath Siri Matak. The French, who were sheltering Phnom Penh's entire foreign colony, surrendered Siri Matak along with 500 other Cambodians so as not to "compromise" the safety of the remaining 800 fugitives. The sixty-one-year-old general and prime minister, who had sat beside Nixon in the White House Cabinet Room in better days, was now hauled away in the back of a garbage truck.

The Khmer Rouge had simply refused to recognize the embassy compound as sovereign French territory. They insisted that it was nothing more than a refugee "regroupment center" under *their* control. Prince Sihanouk had been deposed by Lon Nol and Siri Matak in 1970 and had lived in exile in Beijing ever since, calling himself the Khmer Rouge head of state.

Schanberg reported that "none of the soldiers we talked with brought up his name."[47]

Cambodia's collapse made as little impression on South Vietnam as the simultaneous collapse in Laos. For all of its flailing, violence, free-world rhetoric, and investment in anticommunist forces, the American war effort in Indochina died with barely a whimper. "You people are worse than the French," a Cambodian agent of the CIA sneered over the radio to her American handler in Saigon as she heard her door being broken down by Khmer Rouge guerrillas and desperately called for help that never came.[48]

While the Khmer Rouge took control of Cambodia, the Pathet Lao communists forced Laos' King Savang Vatthana to abdicate, abolished the monarchy, and packed the king and the royal family off to reeducation camps. They were all dead within twelve months. The Lao People's Democratic Republic that took their place immediately signed a treaty with Hanoi granting the NVA the right to station forces in Laos. They then declared war on "American collaborators." The Hmong people, who had taken American subsidies to follow General Vang Pao in a war against the Pathet Lao and the NVA base areas, fled into Thailand. Most of Laos' educated elite fled as well. Ten percent of the Laotian population left the country in 1975.[49]

All of this was background noise to the great symphony beating to its dismal close in Vietnam. General Van Tien Dung, having unexpectedly cleared most of South Vietnam of ARVN forces in a month of combat and pursuit, was now joined in his headquarters by Pham Hung and Le Duc Tho to plan the endgame. With Thieu massing his remaining forces in the Saigon Circle, vowing to "fight to the last bullet, the last grain of rice," Dung took aim at Xuan Loc.[50]

The town sat on the northeastern face of the ARVN defense ring, on Route 1, forty miles above Saigon. As a defensive bastion, Xuan Loc shielded the critical facilities at Bien Hoa and Long Binh and guarded the road into Saigon. It was a keystone of the defense, held by the ARVN 18th Division. The commander, forty-two-year-old General Le Minh Dao, vowed to hold the line: "I don't care how many divisions the other side sends against me, I will smash them all." He was immediately assailed by the three infantry divisions, tanks, and artillery of the NVA IV Corps.[51]

The two-week battle for Xuan Loc began on April 9. President Thieu, who had already shipped his personal fortune and household effects to

Taiwan and Canada, loftily ordered the town held at all costs. While Thieu focused his efforts on trying to move the sixteen tons of gold in Saigon's treasury to Switzerland, he paused to order his 1st Airborne Brigade to fly into Xuan Loc to reinforce Dao. But with the NVA II Corps pressing down from the north on Route 1, breaking through Thieu's line at Cam Ranh Bay, and joining the advance on Saigon, Dao and the "supermen" of the ARVN 18th Division, who had fought heroically for two weeks, were forced to yield Xuan Loc.[52]

They were about to be outflanked, and the NVA bombardment of Bien Hoa Airbase prevented any tac air from flying to support Dao's beleaguered troops. Dao's ARVN 18th Division retreated toward Saigon, reduced by two-thirds. They halted only to bulldoze President Thieu's ancestral grave site. Thieu, an ARVN general observed, had become "the most hated man in Vietnam." For Dung and the NVA, the road into the South Vietnamese capital lay wide open.[53]

President Thieu regarded Xuan Loc as the end. Seven NVA divisions were encircling Saigon and eight more were closing in, yet only four intact ARVN divisions remained to defend the capital. Philip Caputo, who had commanded a Marine platoon in 1965–1966, had returned to Vietnam as a correspondent for the *Chicago Tribune*. He now found himself at Long Binh on Route 1 as the ARVN retreated on the entire forty-mile front between Xuan Loc and Bien Hoa. Route 1 was the old French *rue sans joie*, and "today," Caputo wrote, "it is living up to that name." He felt certain that he was witnessing "one of the great tragedies of modern times." The bridge over the Dong Hai River was shivering under the impact of the NVA shells and rockets that had laid waste the Bien Hoa Airbase and were now grazing along Route 1.

The road was jammed with a twenty-mile-long column of refugees and beaten ARVN troops—"a stream of flesh and blood and bone, of exhausted, frightened faces, of crushed hopes and loss." They were fleeing the battles all around them, but many of them had retreated from as far away as Hue and Da Nang. They filed past, "their heads hunched down against the driving monsoon rain." Caputo described the sounds—the shuffling of sandaled feet, the wails of crying children, the bellowing of water buffalo, and the throb of idling engines. Cars, trucks, buses, and scooters were piled with crates, luggage, and bundles and were hardly moving. When the rain stopped, the road "shimmered in the heat, like an asphalt river upon which floated old shell casings, fragments of barbed wire coils, empty canvas bandoliers—the junk of war."[54]

On April 21, 1975, Thieu delivered a rancorous farewell address and resigned as president of South Vietnam. "The United States has not respected its promises. It is unfair. It is inhumane. It is not trustworthy. It is irresponsible," the two-term president raged. Nixon, Thieu asserted, had promised him that the United States would *always* stand ready to aid South Vietnam if the communists violated the 1973 peace accord. "I won a solid pledge," Thieu ranted, "that when and if North Vietnam renewed its aggression, the United States would actively and strongly intervene." Four days later, the beaten man slouched off to Taiwan, then on to London. In the 1990s, he would move to the United States, where he settled in Foxborough, Massachusetts, grumbling to all who would listen that "the United States led the South Vietnamese people to their death."[55]

Vice President Tran Van Huong took over and immediately called for a cease-fire and negotiations to end the war in line with the terms of the Paris Accords. Huong had hoped that Thieu's resignation would persuade Hanoi to set up a coalition government with him, an act of chutzpah that the communists coldly rejected. The United States, Hanoi replied, must "abandon the Nguyen Van Thieu clique and not just the person of Nguyen Van Thieu" for there to be a political settlement in South Vietnam.[56]

President Ford blamed Congress for his failure to support Thieu as the regime collapsed. The day Thieu resigned, Ford complained to CBS that by cutting aid to Saigon, Congress "took away from the President the power to move in a military way to enforce the agreements that were signed in Paris." The thirty-eighth president then flew to New Orleans to speak at Tulane University on April 23. The speech, delivered as Thieu seethed in Saigon and packed for his London exile, made clear that Jerry Ford was secretly delighted that Congress had snatched the war from his hands. The president treated Vietnam as a dead letter, ancient history, something to move on from—the sooner the better. "I ask tonight that we stop refighting the battles and recriminations of the past," Ford said. He called for "a great national reconciliation" and for a new effort to regain "the sense of pride that existed *before* Vietnam." The war, he bluntly stated, "is *finished* as far as America is concerned."[57]

It was nearly finished in Vietnam too. General Dung ordered the final attack on Saigon on April 26. NVA troops ringed the capital and blocked all of the roads in and out. NVA artillery and rockets began hitting Saigon on April 27. The next day, in a case of tragedy repeating itself as farce, the now fifty-nine-year-old General Duong Van Minh replaced Huong as president. The retired general and eternal presidential aspirant had finally found a way back from exile and into the presidential palace.[58]

Big Minh had always leaned left in his politics, boasted of his contacts in Hanoi, and now hoped to reach a peace with the communists as a "third force" seeking unification on the basis of shared nationalism. Like Le Duan, he knew that China was seeking to bypass Hanoi and recognize a VC government in Saigon. He called for a cease-fire and a coalition "government of reconciliation" that would, of course, include him. The NVA answered this parley with more volleys of artillery plus air strikes on Tan Son Nhut Airport flown by captured VNAF jets. "It is obvious," a communist communiqué sneered, "that this clique continues to prolong the war to maintain American neocolonialism." The NVA offensive would continue "until all of Saigon's troops have laid down their arms and all of America's warships have left South Vietnamese waters."[59]

The United States seemed as startled as anyone by the speed of the collapse. A million-man army fitted with $5 billion of American weapons and gear had disintegrated in just fifty-five days. With five forsaken ARVN divisions still fighting on the roads into Saigon and pleading for close air support, American officers at Tan Son Nhut were startled by the appearance in their compound of the VNAF commander, General Tran Van Minh, and thirty of his most senior air force officers. They demanded immediate evacuation, signaling the end of all serious resistance. At the US Embassy, the Marine guards were no less startled by the arrival of South Vietnam's chairman of the Joint General Staff, General Cao Van Vien. He eagerly stripped off his uniform, put on civvies, strode out to the embassy tennis courts, and boarded a helicopter out of the country. "The army was leaderless," the CIA hardly needed to add.[60]

Secret American plans to evacuate American citizens and 50,000 Vietnamese "whose lives would be endangered if they stayed behind" rolled out slowly, and without the urgency needed to coordinate and protect flights and ships. US ambassador Graham Martin thought it would demoralize the

South Vietnamese if the Americans left too soon or precipitously. Twenty thousand South Vietnamese had been flown to safety on Guam and Wake Islands, but there were at least 30,000 more requiring an evacuation that Martin kept postponing until it was too late. After the fall of Xuan Loc and Thieu's resignation, it was clear to everyone but Graham Martin that the evacuation had to speed forward.[61]

Fortunately, General Dung was under orders to proceed slowly to allow the Americans to finish their evacuation. Even so, the evacuation was a needlessly hurried operation. Ambassador Martin had limited flights out of Saigon and even the burning of classified material so as not to alarm Thieu. Everything now had to be done in a panicky rush. On April 29, with fixed-wing flights out of Tan Son Nhut Airport impossible, Martin belatedly authorized Operation Frequent Wind, which was the final removal by helicopters. Fifteen hundred Americans and 5,500 South Vietnamese evacuated in choppers from Saigon on April 29 and 30. Seventy thousand more left by sea in private boats and naval ships. In all, 130,000 South Vietnamese fled the country as it fell. Five hundred thousand more would leave in the following weeks, most in overcrowded pleasure craft and fishing boats. Those who could paid $5,000 to $10,000 per family member for space on a barge.[62]

Ambassador Martin departed on April 30. A few hours later, the NVA occupation of the city began. Keyes Beech, reporting from Saigon for the Chicago *Daily News*, was nearly stranded that day. Tan Son Nhut Airport was closed to all flights just as his bus filled with evacuees pulled up to the gate. Beech and the others then drove to the port area through crowds of bewildered people, the soldiers in the streets angrily firing their rifles in the air.

In the port, there was no sign of life or welcome aboard the few sandbagged South Vietnamese ships tied up along the docks. Beech's group returned to the bus and drove to the US embassy, where they had to climb over the ten-foot wall of the embassy compound amid "a seething mass" of frantic South Vietnamese. Together with several other reporters, the sixty-one-year-old Beech scratched, clawed, and punched his way up the wall. "Now," he later recalled thinking, "I know what it's like to be a Vietnamese, but if I could get over the wall I would be an American again."

The Marines on the wall pulled the Americans to safety. Beech was on one of the last helicopters out that evening, fuming at Ambassador Martin:

"He gambled with American lives, including mine, by dragging his heels on the evacuation." The reporter's last view of Saigon was through the tail door of the Marine helicopter as they lifted off the embassy roof. "Tan Son Nhut was burning. So was Bien Hoa. Then the door closed—closed on the most humiliating chapter in American history."[63]

Beech had been observed by his bureau chief, Bob Tamarkin, who had preceded Beech over the wall, requiring ninety minutes to climb three feet through masses of Vietnamese gathered at the wall and pleading to be let through the only entrance, a three-foot gap in the barbed wire on the top of the wall, where the Marines had pushed the wire aside and now pulled some people through and pushed others back down. The gates into the compound could not be opened, because there were thousands of Vietnamese pressed against each of them and there were only 140 Marines in the embassy to provide security.

NVA tank columns were already through Bien Hoa, just fifteen miles away, and racing for Saigon. "From now on, I and the commanding generals will be among you day and night," General Vinh Loc, the last chief of the Joint General Staff, announced to his quavering troops late on April 30. He ordered them to stop "running away like mice" and to stand and fight. The general then boarded an American helicopter and flew away to safety. More helicopters lifted off from the embassy roof, red lights blinking, and wheeled out to sea, where ships of the Seventh Fleet awaited them.[64]

Smoke belched from the US embassy's chimney as the last remaining staff hurried to burn classified material. CH-53 Jolly Green Giants, rated to carry fifty people, were jammed with ninety. The helicopters would struggle upward and then turn away from Saigon to waiting US carriers in the South China Sea. Four US Marines were killed in this final evacuation. Tamarkin remembered the sight of French embassy personnel standing on the walls of their nearby compound watching the riot unfold. Many of the terrified Vietnamese ran over to the French, waving their papers and cards, but "the French ignored them." Thirty years of war, Tamarkin thought, was about to end. Tamarkin boarded one of the last helicopters to leave—at 5:30 a.m. The sight he never forgot was hundreds of Vietnamese gathered in the US embassy courtyard, people who had been admitted to the compound and promised evacuation. They were peering up at his helicopter, waiting for the next one. "It never came."[65]

NVA tanks drove into the city, and one of them smashed through the gates of the presidential palace. George Esper, the AP bureau chief in Saigon, recorded that with this act "a century of Western influence came to an end." Big Minh went on the radio to order all South Vietnamese troops to surrender at 10:24 a.m. Minh, waiting inside the presidential palace to surrender formally, was informed that power had already passed to the people's revolution and that he could not surrender what he did not possess.

While the South Vietnamese flag was lowered and replaced with the Viet Cong flag, Big Minh was arrested and forced to make a second broadcast. This one announced the "liberation" of Saigon and the South Vietnamese government's "unconditional surrender." General Tran Van Tra, deputy commander of the NVA forces, seated himself as "area commander" in Saigon. In their first official act, the Viet Cong Provisional Revolutionary Government changed the name of Saigon to Ho Chi Minh City. When the victorious communist forces paraded through the renamed southern capital, the VC troops were pointedly placed in the rear, not the front, of the long column of NVA tanks, vehicles, and soldiers.[66]

The war had killed 58,000 Americans, 250,000 ARVNs, half a million South Vietnamese civilians, and 1.4 million NVA and Viet Cong. Four million Vietnamese—10 percent of the combined population of the two countries—had been killed or wounded. But even now it was not over. In their rushed evacuation, the Americans left behind important files, including the names of 30,000 Vietnamese who had worked in the Phoenix Program. These people were among the first to be rounded up, tortured, and killed by their "liberators." Two and a half million South Vietnamese were placed under arrest as *nguy*—"puppets." Anyone affiliated with the old regime was sent without trial to one of 300 "thought-reform" camps in rural areas. An estimated 165,000 of these political prisoners died of neglect and maltreatment in these brutal labor camps. Like the Khmer Rouge, the North Vietnamese communists lied to their victims, assuring them in 1975 that they would be detained for just ten days of reeducation. Ninety to ninety-five percent of their victims fell for the lie and were imprisoned for three, five, ten, or fifteen years in starvation conditions. "All we could think about was food, food, food," a former ARVN Ranger recalled. "I saw university professors fighting each other for a piece of corn or some burnt rice."[67]

The "boat people" struggled to escape this fate. One hundred and thirty thousand of them took to the sea in the last months of war. By 1995, 2 million had fled by that route. They went in overloaded small boats, and 50 to 70 percent of them died at sea. Nonetheless, it was easy to understand why they ran so many risks to leave. Officers, functionaries, professionals, and other "collaborators" of the Saigon regime were first jailed and then, when released, denied education and suitable employment, as were most of their relatives and progeny. "We've been worse than Pol Pot," a North Vietnamese official snickered, "but the outside world knows nothing."[68]

CONCLUSION

As communist purges loomed and hundreds of thousands of South Vietnamese sought frantically for ways out of their defeated country, Republican president Gerald Ford's eagerness to wash his hands of the Vietnam War sat uneasily with his career-long advocacy of it. Ford had been the hawkish House minority leader constantly pressing LBJ to escalate the war: to bomb more, to put in more troops, to, in LBJ's phrase, "nail more coonskins to the wall." Now Jerry Ford, like every other hawk, broke up with South Vietnam—without a backward glance.[1]

And so it went across the United States government. The great love object of American policy was hurled away in a fit of disgust. But the disgust was feigned. All of South Vietnam's flaws—the corruption, the inefficiency, the unequal society, the military weakness—had been on display from the beginning. What changed?

The politics. Vietnam was above all else a political war. It was a luxury that only a phenomenally rich great power like the United States could afford. The threat to Southeast Asia could have been managed without resort to a massive military intervention.

Eisenhower, Kennedy, and Johnson escalated the war because they could, and to avoid appearing "weak" or "soft" on communism. They agreed with McGeorge Bundy's rationale for the war, that it was founded "upon rocks that were put in place at the time of Franklin Roosevelt," when "the United States became inescapably drawn to difficulty and to responsibility all over the world." The media, Congress, the public, and allied governments around the world largely supported this vision of American power, despite the obvious futility of the Vietnam War from

531

the very *beginning*, when Senator John F. Kennedy, after a tour of French Indochina during the Truman administration, declared that "no amount of military assistance can conquer an enemy which is everywhere and at the same time nowhere, an 'enemy of the people' which has the sympathy and covert support of the people."[2]

The rather lazy American consensus on the war would disintegrate by 1969, when Nixon tried a new dodge. He would escalate the war and play the "madman." He was checked by different politics—enormous antiwar demonstrations, sharpening media attacks, and the first stirrings of congressional resistance.

Nixon's Vietnamization of the war, pitched as a deliberate act of strategy, was in fact a panicked political improvisation that fit perfectly with Kissinger's admission—long before the defeat—that what the Nixon administration really sought in Vietnam was a "decent interval" during which Saigon would hold on just long enough for the United States to escape the war, if not its effects.

Kennedy had treated Vietnam with the circumspection it required. He understood that Saigon and its faltering regimes comprised a cluster of problems that Washington could never fix. But with influential hawks calling Vietnam "an Asian version of Berlin," a test of American mettle, Kennedy didn't dare cut and run, so he kept the mission going to secure reelection.

Cut down in Dallas in 1963, JFK never ran for reelection. Lyndon Baines Johnson did, and he shared Kennedy's fear that retreat from Vietnam would be interpreted by American voters, the media, congressional allies, and political opponents as a capitulation to communism. Yet LBJ won the presidential election of 1964 because the public supported Johnson's domestic reforms—civil rights, the Great Society, the War on Poverty—and feared that the extremist Goldwater would take the nation to war in Vietnam, and elsewhere.

And so LBJ tried to thread the needle, to contain communism without alarming the public with a big war. He fashioned what critics called a "no-win war." He knew what it would take to win. The Pentagon had played war games in 1964 with escalating levels of violence and had concluded that only an unflinching attack on North Vietnam's cities, ports, and infrastructure, with no regard for civilian casualties, *might* bring victory against such a proud, determined, and disciplined people. Johnson flinched, knowing that such a brutal attack would alienate Western allies, large numbers of American voters, and quite possibly trigger Chinese or Soviet intervention in the war.

A war begun for political reasons was then prosecuted as a political exercise, the councils of war conducted by Mac Bundy, Walt Rostow, and Bob McNamara bearing no resemblance to actual war. Clausewitz famously said that war is a continuation of policy by other means, but he certainly did not mean in *this* way. The Prussian theorist meant that violent war would be waged to achieve political objectives that could not be obtained diplomatically. He did not mean that war should be waged in a wishy-washy political way to achieve wishy-washy political objectives.

The ultraviolence inflicted on South Vietnam was not wishy-washy. The country was ripped to pieces. A bitter South Vietnamese official described "cratered rice fields and defoliated forests, devastated by an alien air force that seems at war with the very land of Vietnam." Half of the rural population was forced into refugee camps and urban slums; "their choices," a US Marine recalled, "ranged from horrible to hopeless." Hundreds of thousands were killed or wounded. The precise number will never be known, but we do know that at least 40 percent of the dead in the Vietnam War were civilians. Most of this killing was inflicted in South Vietnam. Johnson never tested the limits in *North* Vietnam or its sanctuaries. He feared the escalating costs of the war as well as the likelihood of foreign intervention. All of his operations in Vietnam were limited: the bombing of the North, the refusal to invade the trails and sanctuaries in Laos and Cambodia, the strict rules of engagement, and the hard ceiling on manpower levels in South Vietnam.[3]

From 1964 until he left office in 1969, LBJ was constantly pleading with Hanoi to make peace, making clear to them who had the upper hand. The "war for peace"—the phrase was used in Hanoi and Washington—was an absurdity. For Hanoi, it cloaked their real aim—the conquest and regimentation of South Vietnam. For Washington, whose real aim *was* peace, inflicting a punishing war on Southeast Asia was the absolute worst way to get it.

And the US military was the absolute worst instrument. In the first place, they exerted natural momentum for a war that *no one* really wanted. Kennedy had acknowledged this and taken pains to keep the generals on the sidelines. David Halberstam said this of the American brass during the war: "Their particular power with the Hill and with hawkish journalists, their stronger hold on patriotic-*machismo* arguments, their particular certitude, made them far more powerful players than men raising doubts." Failure seldom stuck to the US military, for they always had ready excuses—not enough troops, not enough money, not enough targets. With their already fathomless budget of $50 billion a year in the early 1960s, the service chiefs were like this on everything—Vietnam, but also missiles, bombers, ships, tanks, and troops for NATO and other theaters. They exerted unstoppable energy for escalation.[4]

Once embarked on the Vietnam War, the US military waged it with a stunning lack of effectiveness. The efficiency of the military in Vietnam was impressive. They solved technical problems and coordinated and deconflicted air, artillery, and ground missions with a practiced ease that was laudable, if utterly demoralizing to their South Vietnamese ally, who knew that, as a poor country, they would never attain such levels of professional competence.

But that should not have mattered. From 1965 to 1969 the war was entirely Americanized. Westmoreland's theory of victory held that he would annihilate the NVA "bully boys" and leave the Viet Cong "termites" to the more numerous but less capable South Vietnamese. This plan was never more than a conceit. The two wars—the one against the bully boys and the one against the termites—could not be separated. This explained the running, rancorous battle between the Army and the Marines in Vietnam. Leave the NVA out in the boonies, the Marines argued, and focus American troops on securing the population. No, Westmoreland countered; that would be too passive, and it would permit unlimited infiltration.

In fact, Westy was just doing what he knew how to do—maneuver and fight. His airmobile operations *seemed* impressive, but the vast majority of them made no contact with the enemy. Four years were wasted in this way, raising the cost of the war to unsustainable heights. Not making significant contact with the enemy did not diminish fuel and ammo consumption and did not reduce the number of American troops, vehicles, and aircraft destroyed by accidents, mortar attacks, mines, booby traps, opportunistic ambushes, and antiaircraft fire. As the human and material costs of the war ticked relentlessly upward, with no end in sight, American patience naturally ran out. Running for reelection in 1968, LBJ enlisted Westmoreland in the political campaign to plead for yet more patience. He brought the MACV commander to New York and Washington to assure voters, Congress, and the media that "the end was coming into view," that the US military had "turned the corner" in Vietnam.

That's why the Tet Offensive of 1968 was so devastating to the American war effort. Televised scenes of the US embassy in Saigon under VC attack and of the two-weeklong battle for Hue, where the US Marines suffered one casualty for every yard of the city they retook from the communists, demolished any lingering faith Americans had in LBJ's leadership of the war. MACV's insistence that Tet was a "tactical victory" cut no ice with a public that increasingly hewed to Walter Cronkite's view that "it now seems more certain than ever that the bloody experience of Vietnam is to end in stalemate."[5]

Tet persuaded LBJ to stop seeking "victory" or an "honorable peace" in South Vietnam and to pour all of his efforts into securing *any* kind of peace. Johnson's war had been waged on McNamara's assurance that the United States could "convert the contest from one of will to one of physical capability." The war proved that will has a force-multiplying capability all its own against which the Americans and South Vietnamese were helpless. The North Vietnamese were no more inclined after Tet to make concessions than they had been before. Johnson dropped most of his earlier demands. He gave away everything: a bombing halt, a communist military presence in South Vietnam after a cease-fire, and a coalition government and national elections that would almost certainly make Vietnam a communist state. This was a deal that the communists, scourged by three years of American bombing and firepower, would take. Lyndon Johnson's decision after Tet to relinquish the presidency and spend his last months in office negotiating an end to the war was nearly crowned with success. The Vietnam War, begun in 1965, would have ended in 1968 with a peace deal and 30,000 American dead.[6]

Nixon had always played politics with national security. Jingoism and dirty tricks were his brand, from the day he got elected to the Senate from California in 1950 by calling his opponent "the Pink Lady—pink right down to her underwear" and insinuating that her Jewish husband could never be considered a loyal American. Nixon had lost the presidency to Kennedy in

1960 and lost in his run for governor of California in 1962. In 1968, Nixon led in the polls for most of the presidential campaign. But when Democratic nominee Hubert Humphrey appeared poised to overtake him at the finish line thanks to LBJ's "October surprise," an emerging peace treaty with North Vietnam, Nixon sprang into action. He covertly derailed the peace talks and prolonged a war that most Americans considered a dreadful mistake.

He and Kissinger justified their conspiracy with lofty strategic arguments, chiefly that they would fight a better war and achieve a better peace that better served American interests. In this way, the Vietnam War became twice as long, twice as bloody, and no less futile than it would have been if terminated by LBJ in 1968 without Nixon's sabotage. And Nixon's war was only superficially different from Johnson's. How was Abrams' "better war" any better than Westmoreland's? Abrams' Operation Speedy Express in the Mekong Delta was a scandal—thousands of civilians were killed to produce "record body counts" that achieved their objective of "population security" only in the ancient Roman sense of "making a desert and calling it peace."

Elsewhere, Abrams' pursuit of enemy logistics "noses" instead of body count was a distinction without a difference. Abrams' bloody operations in the A Shau Valley, culminating in Hamburger Hill, were no different from the airmobile assaults ordered by Westmoreland. Abrams would have continued in that vein had Nixon, alarmed by the disgust of the American people, media, and Congress, not forced him to relent and stop attacking. In truth, Abrams' war was as callous and ineffectual as Westmoreland's. Its chief effect was to prolong a war that was as unwinnable when Abrams left as it had been when he arrived.[7]

Nixon's Cambodian Incursion of 1970, intended to crush the communist sanctuaries, was a tentative, restricted campaign that achieved nothing lasting, destabilized Cambodia, and set off another round of antiwar protest in America. The Laotian Incursion of 1971 was intended to showcase the success of Vietnamization but instead revealed its failure.

Nixon's apocalyptic bombing of Cambodia in 1973 to deny its sanctuaries to the communists delivered the entire country to the Khmer Rouge, the NVA, and the VC. Unlike Westmoreland, Abrams at least had a keen eye for the absurdity of the Vietnam War, its "worship of charts," as he put it. The "fucking chart," Abrams exclaimed, "becomes the whole damn war, instead of the people, and *real* things." But the war of charts and statistics begun by Harkins and expanded by Westmoreland was still going strong when Abrams returned to Washington in 1972, full of hope and forward-facing optimism and somehow convinced that Vietnam was still the optimal place to spend American defense dollars. Abrams' defenders, some of whom think the war was winnable, oddly rely on the very charts maligned by the general himself to prove his success: caches seized, villages secured, VC neutralized, ARVN trained, militias armed, and so on. As this book demonstrates, none of those charts mattered in the end, and most of them didn't even matter at the time, for they were no less fake under Abrams than they had been under Westmoreland and Harkins. They substituted fungible numbers for truth.

Nixon's one act of boldness that seems to have achieved a concrete result was his resumption of the bombing of North Vietnam in 1972. But the result achieved was the same result that LBJ had nearly achieved four years earlier. When Kissinger aide John Negroponte quipped that Nixon had "bombed Hanoi into accepting our concessions," he could as well have added, "and into accepting the peace deal offered by Averell Harriman in 1968."

A war begun and expanded to secure political careers crawled to its wretched end in the same way, Nixon flailing and bombing to win the war before the 1972 elections so that he could proclaim the success of his "secret plan." Mac Bundy had set the dangerously insouciant tone for administration hawks that persisted under Rostow and Kissinger: Casualties were terrible, Bundy had written in 1966, "but the danger to one man's life, as such, is not a worthy guide." No, Bundy had insisted from the safety of Pennsylvania Avenue, "the casualties and costs are to be accepted if the basic questions of interest, right, and power are answered."[8]

Below this shielded elite of political and military egos were the grunts, the ARVN *binh chi*, the peasants, the students, the Buddhists—all of the millions of Americans and Vietnamese gripped by the war. The courage of the grunts, sent out on patrol in a hostile land rigged with booby traps, mines, mortars, and ambushes, is all the more engrossing because of the mordant humor they voiced throughout. Bob Hope's questionnaires, sent to the troops before his Christmas tours to gather material, are a delicious catalogue of the black humor they applied to a war that they all knew to be, as they put it, "bullshit."

The South Vietnamese can hardly be faulted for fighting less effectively than the Viet Cong and the North Vietnamese. People need a cause to fight for, and South Vietnam never made a case for itself. Senior officials and generals who escaped to the United States as Saigon fell admitted in surveys that the entire regime had been corrupt. South Vietnamese officials entered government or military service not to save democracy but to profit from connections, rackets, bribery, and kickbacks. Kennedy and Johnson agonized over this. Kennedy reluctantly okayed the Diem coup in 1963 in the hope that a junta of dynamic generals would rally the South Vietnamese. Johnson's White House tapes and transcripts are salted with queries such as "Why don't *our* Vietnamese fight as hard as *their* Vietnamese?" The failure of the American war in Vietnam cannot be separated from the chronic failure of the Saigon regime to perform the basic functions of good government despite massive infusions of American money and aid. And yet Washington rushed into this with eyes wide open, Maxwell Taylor opining in 1961, four years before the first American troops were introduced, that "we should not get in the position of fighting for a country that wouldn't fight for itself."[9]

North Vietnam, with its heroic Viet Minh legacy, had all of the legitimacy in the political struggle for South Vietnam. South Vietnam was an entirely artificial state. Thieu's rise through the juntas to the presidency in 1967, which he held until the fall of the regime in 1975, was a juggling act, in which he traded commands, ministerial portfolios, and graft for political support, assuming that "Uncle Sugar," having sunk so many costs in Vietnam, would stick around forever to keep a "non-communist South Vietnam" alive. No one ever emerged in South Vietnam with the luster of a Ho Chi Minh. Men such as Thieu were former French officers who were easily caricatured by the communists as French puppets now dancing on an American string.

And so the South Vietnamese watched and waited, and waited some more. Their officials remained corrupt, the military and police unhelpful, and the communist government of the night far more daunting than Saigon's. Hanoi had begun the war with a functioning state and apparatus. Saigon had to create these things in the midst of war, with predictable results. The ARVN and the ruff-puffs could never fix their desertion problems because conditions, morale, and leadership were consistently bad. Villages were actively Viet Cong or noncommittal. Even the cities, the central government, and the Joint General Staff were penetrated by the communists. The historian cannot blame the South Vietnamese for fighting half-heartedly. The mistake was to make their war America's war, to Americanize it, warp it into something high-tech and Western, and then hand off parts of it, shorn of key ingredients, to the South Vietnamese before leaving in a hurry. Collapse was inevitable.

The great lesson of the war for Americans was how little all of that violence and expenditure of lives and treasure affected events on the ground in Southeast Asia. America's military failure coincided with South Vietnam's failure ever to organize its people and government. The ruthless Viet Minh movement that had been marching to victory when the United States launched Operation Rolling Thunder and sent the first Marines in 1965 was the same force that ten years later brushed Thieu aside, stepped over 58,000 American dead, took Saigon, and unified Vietnam. Was the lesson learned? Hardly. The long, fruitless "9/11 wars" in Iraq and Afghanistan would be as quixotic and wasteful, but the sobering lesson of Vietnam had been repressed long before that. Even as Saigon fell in 1975, Republican presidential hopeful Ronald Reagan went on the radio to denounce President Ford, Henry Kissinger, and Congress, growling that in their retreat from South Vietnam he heard "an echo of the hollow tapping of Neville Chamberlain's umbrella on the cobblestones of Munich."[10]

ACKNOWLEDGMENTS

This book is dedicated to Sherry Zhang, who has been my best friend, soulmate, and travel partner for many years now. She enlivened the field research by joining me for a tour of Cambodia before depositing me, well fed but hungry for more, on the border of Laos. Born and raised in Shanghai, Sherry likes to say that she has encouraged this "pivot to Asia" by her example, and indeed she has. She has taught me to be a little more careful and thoughtful in my analysis, and a lot more adventurous in restaurants. Above all, she has given me the love, care, and devotion that makes the relentless work that goes into a book such as this one tolerable. Beyond the book, she has made my life far better than it was before, and filled my heart with sun and spring.

As I write these acknowledgments, I pray that my mother, Judith Stoughton Wawro, now 100, will live to see this book in print. Each time I speak with her, she puts on her best Lyndon B. Johnson accent and asks: "How's the book on Veet-Nam coming?" Mum has propelled me all my life, and I can only hope that she'll propel me some more. She miraculously survived the car crash that killed my father and all other occupants of the vehicle when I was eighteen. I cannot imagine my fate had she perished as well.

Thanks to all of my siblings for their friendship and support, in particular my sister Jill, who has gently taken the reins of our big, sprawling family as they have slipped from my mother's grip. Jill is also the best sort of friend: kind, loyal, generous, and fun, always there when you need her.

As I described the fears and horrors in this book, I thought always of my two sons, Winslow and Matias, and of how precious they are to me. Every day that I write I have these sprightly, hard-charging young men in mind.

Thanks to Lara Heimert, publisher and editor at Basic Books, for making this whole process easier than it often is. More than a publisher,

ACKNOWLEDGMENTS

Lara is a friend, and a boon companion when time permits. I must also thank Tina Bennett for all of the encouragement she has given me over the years, and for connecting me with Lara after reading the first draft of this book (and my others).

Research time and funding for this book were provided by the University of North Texas, first with a research grant, and then a semester of faculty development leave to write. I am grateful for these gifts. Among my colleagues at UNT, I am beholden to my great friend Mike Leggiere, who has helped me build and direct the Military History Center over the years. Thanks also to Todd Smith for keeping my tennis game sharp and trudging around the golf course with me every week. When I needed an affordable long-term base in Washington, DC, to use the archives, my good friend Steve Connors found the solution, arranging for me to lease the magnificent house next door to him in Chevy Chase. (The house was more than magnificent; it was serendipitous; once installed in it I discovered that I was sleeping in the same bedroom and cooking in the same kitchen used by General Lyman Lemnitzer, the fourth chairman of the Joint Chiefs of Staff, who had given JFK advice on Vietnam.) My visits to the UK National Archives in Kew, the Parliamentary Archives, and the Liddell Hart Centre on the Strand all issued, as usual, from my old school chum David Noble's princely flat in Battersea. Thanks to David and Caroline and to Steve and Vicky for their hospitality in Washington, London, and Cheltenham.

I traveled extensively in Vietnam to research this book, and my visits to remote places such as Dien Bien Phu, the A Shau Valley, Hamburger Hill, the Rockpile, and Khe Sanh would have been much harder to arrange without the excellent guide services of Mr. Van Vu, who took me in hand, made sure I saw everything on my list, showed me things that I had never thought to ask to see, and enlivened the trip with anecdotes from his childhood as well as his father's experiences in the South Vietnamese army. He would be amused to know that what I remember most about our trip is how he would pass dozens of roadside stalls and restaurants and then abruptly stop at one that looked no different from the others. "Why this one?" I would ask. "Because they have the best rice," he would always say. The kindness of the Vietnamese people to me and the many other Americans traveling in their war-scarred country was surprising, and heartwarming.

SELECT BIBLIOGRAPHY

ARCHIVES

United States

College Park, MD
NARA   National Archives and Records Administration

United Kingdom

Kew
UKNA   UK National Archives

London
LHCMA   Liddell Hart Centre for Military Archives
UKPA   Houses of Parliament, UK Parliamentary Archives

PUBLISHED DOCUMENTS
Congressional Record
CQ Almanac
Foreign Relations of the United States series, https://history.state.gov
/historicaldocumentsPresidential Speeches, UVA Miller Center,
https://millercenter.org/the-presidency/presidential-speeches
U.S. Armed Forces in Vietnam 1954–1975, eight-volume study including many
declassified documents, prepared by BDM Corporation under contract with
the US Army, 1979–1980; consulted at LHCMA (see archives above)
Part One: Indochina Studies
Part Two: Vietnam: Lessons Learned
Part Three: Vietnam: Reports of U.S. Army Operations Archives
Part Four: Vietnam: U.S. Army Senior Debriefing Reports

PUBLISHED SOURCES
Adams, Sam. "Vietnam Cover-up: Playing War with Numbers." *Harper's*, May
1975, 41–73.

Addington, Larry H. *America's War in Vietnam: A Short Narrative History.* Bloomington: Indiana University Press, 2000.

Allen, George W. *None So Blind: A Personal Account of the Intelligence Failure in Vietnam.* New York: Ivan Dee, 2001.

Allison, William. "War for Sale: The Black Market, Currency Manipulation, and Corruption in the American War in Vietnam." *War and Society* 21, no. 2 (July 19, 2013): 135–164.

Altschuler, Bruce E. "Lyndon Johnson and the Public Polls." *Public Opinion Quarterly* 50, no. 3 (Autumn 1986): 285–299.

Appy, Christian. *Patriots: The Vietnam War Remembered from All Sides.* New York: Viking, 2003.

Asselin, Pierre. *Vietnam's American War: A History.* Cambridge: Cambridge University Press, 2018.

Barrett, David M., ed. *Lyndon B. Johnson's Vietnam Papers: A Documentary Collection.* College Station: Texas A&M University Press, 1997.

Barrett, David M. "The Mythology Surrounding Lyndon Johnson, His Advisers, and the 1965 Decision to Escalate the Vietnam War." *Political Science Quarterly* 103, no. 4 (Winter 1988–1989): 637–663.

Baskir, Lawrence M., and William A. Strauss. *Chance and Circumstance: The Draft, the War, and the Vietnam Generation.* New York: Knopf, 1978.

Baughman, James L. "Henry R. Luce and the Rise of the American News Media." *American Masters,* PBS, April 28, 2004.

Bergerud, Eric M. *The Dynamics of Defeat: The Vietnam War in Hau Nghia Province.* Boulder, CO: Westview, 1991.

Berman, Edgar. *Hubert.* New York: Putnam, 1979.

Berman, Larry. *Perfect Spy: The Incredible Double Life of Pham Xuan An,* Time *Magazine Reporter and Vietnamese Communist Agent.* New York: Harper Collins, 2009.

Beschloss, Michael. *Reaching for Glory: Lyndon Johnson's Secret White House Tapes 1964–1965.* New York: Simon & Schuster, 2001.

Beschloss, Michael. *Taking Charge: The Johnson White House Tapes 1963–1964.* New York: Simon & Schuster, 1997.

Bird, Kai. *The Color of Truth: McGeorge and William Bundy, Brothers in Arms.* New York: Simon & Schuster, 1998.

Boot, Max. *The Road Not Taken: Edward Lansdale and the American Tragedy in Vietnam.* New York: W. W. Norton, 2018.

Boylan, Kevin. *Losing Binh Dinh: The Failure of Pacification and Vietnamization, 1969–1971.* Lawrence: University Press of Kansas, 2016.

Bradley, Doug. *DEROS Vietnam: Dispatches from the Air-Conditioned Jungle.* New York: Warriors Publishing Group, 2012.

Bradley, Doug, and Craig Werner. *We Gotta Get Out of This Place: The Soundtrack of the Vietnam War.* Amherst: University of Massachusetts Press, 2015.

Brigham, Robert K. *Guerrilla Diplomacy: The NLF's Foreign Relations and the Viet Nam War*. Ithaca: Cornell University Press, 1999.

Brower, Charles F., IV. "Strategic Assessment in Vietnam: The Westmoreland 'Alternate Strategy' for 1967–1968." *Naval War College Review* 44, no. 2 (Spring 1991): 20–51.

Burr, William, and Jeffrey P. Kimball. *Nixon's Nuclear Specter: The Secret Alert of 1969, Madman Diplomacy, and the Vietnam War*. Lawrence: University Press of Kansas, 2015.

Buzzanco, Robert. *Masters of War: Military Dissent and Politics in the Vietnam Era*. Cambridge: Cambridge University Press, 1996.

Camp, Norman M. "U.S. Army Psychiatry in the Vietnam War." *U.S. Army Medical Department Journal*, April–June 2015.

Caputo, Philip. *A Rumor of War*. New York: Picador, 1977.

Caro, Robert A. *Master of the Senate*. New York: Knopf, 2002.

Caro, Robert A. *The Passage of Power: The Years of Lyndon Johnson*. New York: Knopf, 2012.

Clifford, Clark. "A Vietnam Reappraisal: A Personal History of One Man's View and How it Evolved." *Foreign Affairs* 47, no. 4 (July 1969): 601–622.

Clodfelter, Mark. *The Limits of Airpower: The American Bombing of North Vietnam*. New York: Free Press, 1989.

Colby, William. *Lost Victory: A Firsthand Account of America's Sixteen-Year Involvement in Vietnam*. Chicago: Contemporary Books, 1989.

Curry, Cecil B. *Victory at Any Cost: The Genius of Vietnam's General Vo Nguyen Giap*. Dulles, VA: Potomac Books, 2004.

Daddis, Gregory A. "Mired in a Quagmire: Popular Interpretations of the Vietnam War." *Orbis* 57 (2013): 532–548.

Daddis, Gregory A. *No Sure Victory: Measuring US Army Effectiveness and Progress in the Vietnam War*. New York: Oxford University Press, 2011.

Daddis, Gregory. "Out of Balance: Evaluating American Strategy in Vietnam, 1968–72." *War and Society* 32 (2013): 252–270.

Daddis, Gregory A. *Westmoreland's War: Reassessing American Strategy in Vietnam*. New York: Oxford University Press, 2014.

Daddis, Gregory. *Withdrawal: Reassessing America's Final Years in Vietnam*. New York: Oxford University Press, 2017.

Dallek, Robert. *An Unfinished Life: John F. Kennedy, 1917–1963*. Boston: Little, Brown, 2003.

Dastrup, Boyd L. *From Charts and Darts to Computers: Automating the U.S. Army's Field Artillery, 1945–2005*. Fort Sill, OK: US Army Field Artillery Center and School, 2005.

Davidson, Phillip B. *Vietnam at War: The History, 1946–1975*. Novato, CA: Presidio Press, 1988.

Downs, Frederick. *The Killing Zone: My Life in the Vietnam War*. New York: Norton, 2007.

Duiker, William J. *The Communist Road to Power in Vietnam*. Boulder, CO: Westview, 1981.

Elliott, David W. P. *The Vietnamese War: Revolution and Social Change in the Mekong Delta, 1930–1975*. London: Routledge, 2006.

Escobar, Gregory P. *A Strategy of Attrition: Why General Westmoreland Failed in 1967*. Ft. Leavenworth, KS: School of Advanced Military Studies, 2016.

Fall, Bernard B. *Anatomy of a Crisis: The Laotian Crisis of 1960–1961*. New York: Doubleday, 1969.

Fall, Bernard B. *Street Without Joy: The French Debacle in Indochina*. Orig. 1961. Lanham, MD: Stackpole Books, 2018.

Farrell, John A. *Richard Nixon: The Life*. New York: Doubleday, 2017.

Fitzgerald, Frances. *Fire in the Lake: The Vietnamese and the Americans in Vietnam*. Boston: Little, Brown, 1972.

Foster, Randy E. M. *Vietnam Firebases 1965–73: American and Australian Forces*. Oxford: Osprey, 2007.

Freedman, Lawrence. *Kennedy's Wars: Berlin, Cuba, Laos, and Vietnam*. New York: Oxford University Press, 2000.

Gillam, James T. *Life and Death in the Central Highlands: An American Sergeant in the Vietnam War, 1968–1970*. Denton: University of North Texas Press, 2010.

Goldstein, Gordon. *Lessons in Disaster: McGeorge Bundy and the Path to War in Vietnam*. New York: Henry Holt, 2008.

Goodwin, Doris Kearns. *Lyndon Johnson and the American Dream*. New York: St. Martin's, 1976.

Gravel, Mike. *The Pentagon Papers*. 4 vols. Boston: Beacon Press, 1971.

Gross, Chuck. *Rattler One-Seven: A Vietnam Helicopter Pilot's War Story*. Denton: University of North Texas Press, 2004.

Guan, Ang Cheng. "Decision-Making Leading to the Tet Offensive (1968)—The Vietnamese Communist Perspective." *Journal of Contemporary History* 33, no. 3 (1998): 341–353.

Guan, Ang Cheng. *Ending the Vietnam War: The Vietnamese Communists' Perspective*. London: Routledge, 2004.

Guan, Ang Cheng. *The Vietnam War from the Other Side: The Vietnamese Communists' Perspective*. London: Routledge, 2002.

Hackworth, David H. *Steel My Soldiers' Hearts: The Hopeless to Hardcore Transformation of U.S. Army 4th Battalion 39th Infantry, Vietnam*. New York: Rugged Land, 2002.

Halberstam, David. *The Best and the Brightest*. New York: Random House, 1972.

Hastings, Max. *Vietnam: An Epic Tragedy, 1945–1975*. New York: Harper Collins, 2018.

Haun, Phil, and Colin Jackson. "Breakers of Armies: Air Power in the Easter Offensive and the Myth of Linebacker I and II in the Vietnam War." *International Security* 40, no. 3 (2016): 139–178.

Haun, Phil. *Tactical Air Power and the Vietnam War: Explaining Effectiveness in Modern Air Warfare.* Cambridge: Cambridge University Press, 2024.

Hay, John H., Jr. *Vietnam Studies: Tactical and Materiel Innovations.* Washington, DC: Government Printing Office, 1974.

Head, William. "Hamburger Hill, May 10–20, 1969: The Beginning of the End of America's Commitment to the Republic of Vietnam." *Virginia Review of Asian Studies* 17 (2015): 93–112.

Helms, Richard, and William Hood. *A Look over My Shoulder: A Life in the Central Intelligence Agency.* New York: Random House, 2003.

Henry, John B., II. "February 1968." *Foreign Policy* 4 (1971): 3–34.

Herr, Michael. *Dispatches.* Orig. 1977. New York: Vintage, 1991.

Herring, George C. *The Secret Diplomacy of the Vietnam War: The Negotiating Volumes of the Pentagon Papers.* Austin: University of Texas Press, 1985.

Hoopes, Townsend. *The Limits of Intervention: The Inside Story of How the Johnson Policy of Escalation in Vietnam Was Reversed.* New York: D. McKay, 1969.

Hughes, Ken. *Chasing Shadows: The Nixon Tapes, the Chennault Affair, and the Origins of Watergate.* Charlottesville: University of Virginia Press, 2014.

Humphrey, Hubert. *The Education of a Public Man.* New York: Doubleday, 1976.

Hunt, Richard A. *Pacification: The American Struggle for Vietnam's Hearts and Minds.* London: Routledge, 1998.

Janis, Irving L. *Groupthink: Psychological Studies of Policy Decisions and Fiascoes.* 2d ed. Boston: Houghton Mifflin, 1983.

Johnson, Lyndon B. *The Vantage Point.* New York: Holt, Rinehart & Winston, 1971.

Kahin, George McTurnan. *Intervention: How America Became Involved in Vietnam.* New York: Knopf, 1986.

Kaiser, David. *American Tragedy: Kennedy, Johnson, and the Origins of the Vietnam War.* Cambridge, MA: Belknap Press of Harvard University Press, 2000.

Karnow, Stanley. *Vietnam: A History.* New York: Viking, 1983.

Ketwig, John. *And a Hard Rain Fell: A GI's True Story of the War in Vietnam.* Naperville, IL: Sourcebooks, 2002.

Kimball, Jeffrey. *Nixon's Vietnam War.* Lawrence: University Press of Kansas, 1998.

Kimball, Jeffrey. *The Vietnam War Files: Uncovering the Secret History of Nixon-Era Strategy.* Lawrence: University Press of Kansas, 2004.

Kissinger, Henry. *Ending the Vietnam War.* New York: Simon & Schuster, 2003.

Krepinevich, Andrew F. *The Army and Vietnam.* Baltimore: Johns Hopkins University Press, 1986.

Kreps, Sarah. *Taxing War: The American Way of War Finance and the Decline of Democracy.* New York: Oxford University Press, 2018.

Langguth, A. J. *Our Vietnam: The War, 1954–1975*. New York: Simon & Schuster, 2000.

Lewis, Norman. *A Dragon Apparent: Travels in Cambodia, Laos, and Vietnam*. Orig. 1951. London: Eland, 1982.

Lewy, Guenter. *America in Vietnam*. New York: Oxford University Press, 1978.

Logevall, Fredrik. *Choosing War: The Lost Chance for Peace and the Escalation of War in Vietnam*. Berkeley: University of California Press, 1999.

Logevall, Fredrik. *Embers of War: The Fall of an Empire and the Making of America's Vietnam*. New York: Random House, 2012.

Longley, Kyle. *LBJ's 1968: Power, Politics, and the Presidency in America's Year of Upheaval*. Cambridge: Cambridge University Press, 2018.

Marshall, Jonathan. "Dirty Wars: French and American Piaster Profiteering in Indochina, 1945–1975." *Asia-Pacific Journal* 12, iss. 32, no. 2 (August 19, 2014).

Mason, Robert. *Chickenhawk: A Shattering Personal Account of the Helicopter War in Vietnam*. New York: Viking, 1983.

McDonough, James R. *Platoon Leader*. Novato, CA: Presidio, 1985.

McGinniss, Joe. *The Selling of the President 1968*. New York: Simon & Schuster, 1969.

McMaster, H. R. *Dereliction of Duty: Lyndon Johnson, Robert McNamara, the Joint Chiefs of Staff and the Lies That Led to Vietnam*. New York: Harper Collins, 1997.

McNamara, Robert S. *In Retrospect: The Tragedy and Lessons of Vietnam*. New York: Crown, 1995.

Milam, Ron. *Not a Gentleman's War: An Inside View of Junior Officers in the Vietnam War*. Chapel Hill: University of North Carolina Press, 2009.

Moir, Nathaniel L. *Number One Realist: Bernard Fall and Vietnamese Revolutionary Warfare*. New York: Oxford University Press, 2021.

Moise, Edwin E. *Myths of Tet: The Most Misunderstood Event of the Vietnam War*. Lawrence: University Press of Kansas, 2017.

Moyar, Mark. *Triumph Forsaken: The Vietnam War, 1954–1965*. Cambridge: Cambridge University Press, 2006.

Nguyen, Lien-Hang T. *Hanoi's War: An International History of the War for Peace in Vietnam*. Chapel Hill: University of North Carolina Press, 2012.

Nguyen, Nathalie Huynh Chau. *South Vietnamese Soldiers: Memories of the Vietnam War and After*. Santa Barbara, CA: Praeger, 2016.

Nolan, Keith W. *Ripcord: Screaming Eagles Under Siege, Vietnam 1970*. Novato, CA: Presidio, 2003.

Norman, Lloyd. "No More Koreas." *Army* 15, no. 2 (May 1965): 22–29.

Oberdorfer, Don. *Tet!: The Turning Point in the Vietnam War*. Orig 1971. Baltimore: Johns Hopkins University Press, 2001.

O'Brien, Tim. *The Things They Carried*. New York: Penguin, 1990.

Palmer, Bruce, Jr. *The 25-Year War: America's Military Role in Vietnam*. Lexington: University of Kentucky Press, 1984.

Pape, Robert. *Bombing to Win: Air Power and Coercion in War*. Ithaca, NY: Cornell University Press, 1996.

Perlstein, Rick. *The Invisible Bridge: The Fall of Nixon and the Rise of Reagan*. New York: Simon & Schuster, 2014.

Perlstein, Rick. *Nixonland: The Rise of a President and the Fracturing of America*. New York: Scribner, 2008.

Phillips, Rufus. *Why Vietnam Matters: An Eyewitness Account of Lessons Not Learned*. Annapolis, MD: Naval Institute Press, 2008.

Pike, Douglas. *PAVN: People's Army of Vietnam*. Novato, CA: Presidio, 1986.

Porch, Douglas. *Counterinsurgency*. New York: Oxford University Press, 2010.

Preston, Andrew. *The War Council: McGeorge Bundy, the NSC, and Vietnam*. Cambridge, MA: Harvard University Press, 2006.

Quinn-Judge, Sophie. "The Ideological Debate in the DRV and the Significance of the Anti-Party Affair, 1967–68." *Cold War History* 5, no. 4 (November 2005).

Randolph, Stephen. *Powerful and Brutal Weapons: Nixon, Kissinger, and the Easter Offensive*. Cambridge, MA: Harvard University Press, 2007.

Rasimus, Ed. *Palace Cobra: A Fighter Pilot in the Vietnam War*. New York: St. Martin's, 2006.

Record, Jeffrey. *The Wrong War: Why We Lost in Vietnam*. Annapolis, MD: Naval Institute Press, 1998.

Reporting Vietnam: American Journalism 1959–1975. New York: Library of America, 1998.

Reporting Vietnam, Part One: American Journalism 1959–1969. New York: Library of America, 1998.

Reporting Vietnam, Part Two: American Journalism 1969–1975. New York: Library of America, 1998.

Ricks, Tom. *The Generals: American Military Command from World War II to Today*. New York: Penguin, 2012.

Rutenberg, Amy J. *Rough Draft: Cold War Military Manpower Policy and the Origins of the Vietnam-Era Draft Resistance*. Ithaca, NY: Cornell University Press, 2019.

Sallah, Michael, and Mitch Weiss. *Tiger Force: A True Story of Men and War*. Boston: Little, Brown, 2006.

Shapley, Deborah. *Promise and Power: The Life and Times of Robert McNamara*. Boston: Little, Brown, 1993.

Shaw, John M. *The Cambodian Campaign: The 1970 Offensive and America's Vietnam War*. Lawrence: University Press of Kansas, 2005.

Shawcross, William. *Sideshow: Nixon, Kissinger, and the Destruction of Cambodia*. New York: Simon & Schuster, 1979.

Sheehan, Neil. *A Bright Shining Lie: John Paul Vann and America in Vietnam*. New York: Vintage, 1989.

Shkurti, William J. *Soldiering On in a Dying War: The True Story of the Firebase Pace Incidents and the Vietnam Drawdown*. Lawrence: University Press of Kansas, 2011.

Smithsonian. *A Short History of the Vietnam War*. New York: DK Publishing, 2021.

Snepp, Frank. *Decent Interval: An Insider's Account of Saigon's Indecent End Told by the CIA's Chief Strategy Analyst in Vietnam*. Orig. 1977. Lawrence: University Press of Kansas, 2002.

Solberg, Carl. *Hubert Humphrey: A Biography*. New York: Norton, 1984.

Sorley, Lewis. *A Better War: The Unexamined Victories and Final Tragedy of America's Last Years in Vietnam*. Boston: Houghton Mifflin, 1999.

Sorley, Lewis, ed. *The Vietnam War: An Assessment by South Vietnam's Generals*. Lubbock: Texas Tech University Press, 2010.

Sorley, Lewis, ed. *Vietnam Chronicles: The Abrams Tapes, 1968–1972*. Lubbock: Texas Tech University Press, 2004.

Sorley, Lewis. *Westmoreland: The General Who Lost Vietnam*. Boston: Houghton Mifflin, 2011.

Spector, Ronald H. *After Tet: The Bloodiest Year in Vietnam*. New York: Free Press, 1993.

Summers, Harry G., Jr. *Historical Atlas of the Vietnam War*. Boston: Houghton Mifflin, 1995.

Summers, Harry G., Jr. *On Strategy: A Critical Analysis of the Vietnam War*. Novato, CA: Presidio Press, 1982.

Tang, Truong Nhu. *A Vietcong Memoir: An Inside Account of the Vietnam War and Its Aftermath*. New York: Vintage, 1986.

Taylor, Maxwell D. *The Uncertain Trumpet*. Orig. 1960. Westport, CT: Greenwood, 1974.

Terry, Wallace. *Bloods: An Oral History of the Vietnam War by Black Veterans*. New York: Random House, 1984.

Thayer, Thomas C. *A Systems Analysis View of the Vietnam War, 1965–1972*. 12 vols. Washington, DC: OASD, 1975.

Thi, Lam Quang. *Hell in An Loc: The 1972 Eastern Invasion and the Battle That Saved South Vietnam*. Denton: University of North Texas Press, 2012.

Trauschweizer, Ingo. *Maxwell Taylor's Cold War: From Berlin to Vietnam*. Lexington: University Press of Kentucky, 2019.

Trueheart, Charles. *Diplomats at War: Friendship and Betrayal on the Brink of the Vietnam Conflict*. Charlottesville: University of Virginia Press, 2024.

Truong, Ngo Quang. *The Vietnam War: An Assessment by South Vietnam's Generals*. Lubbock: Texas Tech University Press, 2010.

Turse, Nick. *Kill Anything That Moves: The Real American War in Vietnam*. New York: Metropolitan, 2013.

Udden, Richard. *21 Months, 24 Days: A Blue-Collar Kid's Journey to the Vietnam War and Back*. n.p.: CreateSpace, 2015.

US Marine Corps, History and Museums Division. *The Marines in Vietnam 1954–1973: An Anthology and Bibliography*. Washington, DC: Department of the Navy, 1974.

Valenti, Jack. *A Very Human President*. New York: Pocket Books, 1977.

VanDeMark, Brian. *Into the Quagmire: Lyndon Johnson and the Escalation of the Vietnam War*. New York: Oxford University Press, 1991.

Vandiver, Frank E. *Shadows of Vietnam: Lyndon Johnson's Wars*. College Station: Texas A&M University Press, 1997.

Veith, George J. *Black April: The Fall of South Vietnam 1973–1975*. New York: Encounter, 2012.

Walt, Lewis W. *Strange War, Strange Strategy: A General's Report on Vietnam*. New York: Funk & Wagnalls, 1970.

Ward, Geoffrey, and Ken Burns. *The Vietnam War: An Intimate History*. New York: Knopf, 2017.

Webb, James. *I Heard My Country Calling: A Memoir*. New York: Simon & Schuster, 2014.

Westmoreland, William C. *A Soldier Reports*. New York: Doubleday, 1976.

Wiest, Andrew, and Michael Doidge, *Triumph Revisited: Historians Battle for the Vietnam War*. New York: Routledge, 2010.

Wiest, Andrew. *Vietnam's Forgotten Army: Heroism and Betrayal in the ARVN*. New York: New York University Press, 2008.

Willbanks, James H. *Abandoning Vietnam: How America Left and South Vietnam Lost Its War*. Lawrence: University Press of Kansas, 2004.

Wolff, Tobias. *In Pharaoh's Army: Memories of a Lost War*. London: Bloomsbury, 1994.

Zoglin, Richard. *Hope: Entertainer of the Century*. New York: Simon & Schuster, 2014.

NOTES

INTRODUCTION

1. Charles Trueheart, *Diplomats at War* (Charlottesville: University of Virginia Press, 2024), 275.

2, "U.S. Viet Nam War Efforts," *CQ Almanac 1966*, 22nd ed. (Washington, DC: Congressional Quarterly, 1967), 378–389; "Viet Nam War Grows, Becomes Major Issue," *CQ Almanac 1965*, 21st ed. (Washington, DC: Congressional Quarterly, 1966), 449–457; H. R. McMaster, *Dereliction of Duty* (New York: Harper Collins, 1997), 289.

3. David Halberstam, *The Best and the Brightest* (New York: Random House, 1972), 512.

4. Robert Dallek, "JFK's Second Term," *The Atlantic*, June 2003.

5. Andrew F. Krepinevich Jr., *The Army in Vietnam* (Baltimore: Johns Hopkins University Press, 1986), 176, 197–198.

CHAPTER 1. Parody of High Strategy

1. Fredrik Logevall, *Embers of War* (New York: Random House, 2012), 464–465.

2. Charles Trueheart, *Diplomats at War* (Charlottesville: University of Virginia Press, 2024), 18–19.

3. Frances Fitzgerald, *Fire in the Lake* (Boston: Little, Brown, 1972), 88–90; Neil Sheehan, *A Bright Shining Lie* (New York: Vintage, 1989), 192.

4. National Archives and Records Administration (NARA), RG 472, MACV, TET Documents, Box 1, 24 May 68, MACV, J2, Sept. 1967, "Hanoi's Control and Direction of Enemy Efforts in South Vietnam"; Fitzgerald, 103; Sheehan, 187–188; Trueheart, 19.

5. Max Boot, *The Road Not Taken* (New York: Norton, 2018), 334; Trueheart, 10, 77.

6. Maxwell D. Taylor, *The Uncertain Trumpet* (1960; Westport, CT: Greenwood, 1974), 5–6, 97–99; Harry G. Summers Jr., *On Strategy* (Novato, CA: Presidio, 1982), 72–74; Ingo Trauschweizer, *Maxwell Taylor's Cold War* (Lexington: University Press of Kentucky, 2019), 69–73, 86–87, 97–100, 105–106.

7. Tom Ricks, *The Generals* (New York: Penguin, 2012), 228–230.

8. Eric M. Bergerud, *The Dynamics of Defeat* (Boulder, CO: Westview, 1991), 230; Sheehan, 74, 99–101, 115, 207–208, 331; Trueheart, 137–142.

9. Fredrik Logevall, *Choosing War* (Berkeley: University of California Press, 1999), xxi, 42, 52–53, 395–400; David Halberstam, *The Best and the Brightest* (New York: Random House, 1972), 283–285; Deborah Shapley, *Promise and Power* (Boston: Little, Brown, 1993), 149–151; Trueheart, 95–96.

10. Trauschweizer, 102–103, 107–108.

11. Sheehan, 300–304; Halberstam, 254–256; Trueheart, 85–86.

12. Shapley, 236–241, 265, 283–284, 413–415; Trueheart, 78.

13. Robert Dallek, *An Unfinished Life* (Boston: Little, Brown, 2003), 450–451; Jeff Greenfield, "Would JFK Have Lost Had He Lived?," *Politico*, Nov. 22, 2023.

14. James Webb, *I Heard My Country Calling* (New York: Simon & Schuster, 2014), 287–288.

15. Stanley Karnow, *Vietnam: A History* (New York: Viking, 1983), 248.

16. Marguerite Higgins, "The Diem Government, Pro and Con," in *Reporting Vietnam, Part One: American Journalism 1959–1969* (New York: Library of America, 1998), 88; H. R. McMaster, *Dereliction of Duty* (New York: Harper Collins, 1997), 38; Trueheart, 150–153, 201–206.

17. Malcolm W. Browne, "He Was Sitting in the Center of a Column of Flame," in *Reporting Vietnam: American Journalism 1959–1975* (New York: Library of America, 1998), 33; Boot, xxvi–xxvii; Trueheart, 157–161, 247.

18. David Kaiser, *American Tragedy* (Cambridge, MA: Belknap, 2000), 228–229; Fitzgerald, 247; Trueheart, 216–217; Trauschweizer, 133–134; Boot, xxix–xxxiv, 352; Shapley, 256–258; Homer Bigart, "Vietnam Victory Remote Despite U.S. Aid to Diem," in *Reporting Vietnam, Part One*, 61, 66; Higgins, "The Diem Government, Pro and Con," 89.

19. Higgins, "The Diem Government, Pro and Con," 87.

20. William Colby, *Lost Victory* (Chicago: Contemporary, 1989), 60.

21. Fitzgerald, 237.

22. Lawrence Freedman, *Kennedy's Wars* (New York: Oxford University Press, 2000), 392–397; Stanley Karnow, "The Fall of the House of Ngo Dinh," in *Reporting Vietnam*, 46–47; Trueheart, 264.

23. Karnow, "The Fall of the House of Ngo Dinh," 46–47; Boot, xxxii–xxxiii; McMaster, 41; Colby, 154.

24. Kai Bird, *The Color of Truth* (New York: Simon & Schuster, 1998), 220–222; Shapley, 262–263.

25. David M. Barrett, ed., *Lyndon B. Johnson's Vietnam Papers: A Documentary Collection* (College Station: Texas A&M University Press, 1997), 21, 26–28; Robert A. Caro, *The Passage of Power* (New York: Knopf, 2012), 402–403; Logevall, *Choosing War*, 78–79; Freedman, 403.

26. Barrett, ed., *LBJ's Vietnam Papers*, 25; Ronald H. Spector, *After Tet: The Bloodiest Year in Vietnam* (New York: Free Press, 1993), 184–188.

27. Neil Sheehan, "No Longer a Hawk: October 1966," in *Reporting Vietnam*, 172; William J. Duiker, *The Communist Road to Power in Vietnam* (Boulder, CO: Westview, 1981), 167–168, 195–199, 322–329; Spector, 186–187.

28. Logevall, *Choosing War*, 100–103, 111–112.

29. "Asian Turmoil," *New York Times*, Feb. 2, 1964.

30. NARA, RG 127, USMC Records of Units and Other Commands, Box 99, HQ MACV, Dec. 22, 1964, and Mar. 3, 1965, MG Richard G. Stillwell, "Lessons Learned Nos. 43 & 46"; Frank E. Vandiver, *Shadows of Vietnam* (College Station: Texas A&M University Press, 1997), 91; Logevall, *Choosing War*, 127–128.

31. McMaster, 52, 69–72.

32. Michael Beschloss, "LBJ's Secret War," *Washington Post*, Dec. 1, 2001.

33. Halberstam, 424.

34. Lien-Hang T. Nguyen, *Hanoi's War* (Chapel Hill: University of North Carolina Press, 2012), 67–69; McMaster, 79, 87–88.

35. McMaster, 79–86.

36. William C. Westmoreland, *A Soldier Reports* (New York: Doubleday, 1976), 112; Barrett, ed., *LBJ's Vietnam Papers*, 36–37.

37. McMaster, 96.

38. David M. Barrett, "The Mythology Surrounding Lyndon Johnson, His Advisers, and the 1965 Decision to Escalate the Vietnam War," *Political Science Quarterly* 103, no. 4 (Winter 1988–1989), 661.

39. Vandiver, 85; McMaster, 89–91.

40. Halberstam, 348, 355–357, 497–498; McMaster, 166–167.

CHAPTER 2. No-Win War
1. Kai Bird, *The Color of Truth* (New York: Simon & Schuster, 1998), 328–329, 336; Lawrence Freedman, *Kennedy's Wars* (New York: Oxford University Press, 2000), 36–37; H. R. McMaster, *Dereliction of Duty* (New York: Harper Collins, 1997), 88–89; David Halberstam, *The Best and the Brightest* (New York: Random House, 1972), 359–360.

2. Irving L. Janis, *Groupthink: Psychological Studies of Policy Decisions and Fiascoes*, 2d ed. (Boston: Houghton Mifflin, 1983), 108–109, 111–112, 174–175; Freedman, *Kennedy's Wars*, 399–400; Halberstam, 369–379, 392–394, 492–502; Fredrik Logevall, *Choosing War* (Berkeley: University of California Press, 1999), 78–80; Deborah Shapley, *Promise and Power* (Boston: Little, Brown, 1993), 332.

3. Halberstam, 367–368, 378.

4. Harry G. Summers Jr., *On Strategy* (Novato, CA: Presidio, 1982), 18.

5. Ingo Trauschweizer, *Maxwell Taylor's Cold War* (Lexington: University Press of Kentucky, 2019), 136; McMaster, 97–105.

6. Mark Moyar, *Triumph Forsaken* (Cambridge: Cambridge University Press, 2006), 293.

7. Gregory A. Daddis, *Westmoreland's War* (New York: Oxford University Press, 2014), 1; McMaster, 111.

8. Robert A. Caro, *The Passage of Power* (New York: Knopf, 2012), 402; McMaster, 112.

9. Tom Ricks, *The Generals* (New York: Penguin, 2012), 203–204, 231–235;

Lewis Sorley, *Westmoreland* (Boston: Houghton Mifflin, 2011), 67; Max Boot, *The Road Not Taken* (New York: Norton, 2018), 430–431; McMaster, 110; Halberstam, 560.

10. James Webb, *I Heard My Country Calling* (New York: Simon & Schuster, 2014), 268.

11. Lien-Hang T. Nguyen, *Hanoi's War* (Chapel Hill: University of North Carolina Press, 2012), 71–74; David M. Barrett, ed., *Lyndon B. Johnson's Vietnam Papers* (College Station: Texas A&M University Press, 1997), 59; McMaster, 112–117.

12. National Archives and Records Administration (NARA), RG 127, USMC Records, Box 99, HQ MACV, July 10, 1964, and Oct. 1964, MG Richard Stillwell, "Monthly Evaluations, June and September 1964"; Ronald H. Spector, *After Tet* (New York: Free Press, 1993), 108; William C. Westmoreland, *A Soldier Reports* (New York: Doubleday, 1976), 42.

13. NARA, RG 127, USMC Records, Box 99, HQ MACV, July 10, 1964, and Oct. 1964, MG Richard Stillwell, "Monthly Evaluations, June and September 1964"; Spector, 102–105.

14. McMaster, 116–119.

15. NARA, RG 127, USMC Records of Units and Other Commands, Box 99, HQ MACV, Dec. 22, 1964, MG Richard G. Stillwell, "Lessons Learned No. 43: Combat Tips I"; Jeffrey Kimball, *Nixon's Vietnam War* (Lawrence: University Press of Kansas, 1998), 29.

16. Barrett, ed., *LBJ's Vietnam Papers*, 47, 58–60; Halberstam, 404; McMaster, 95, 125.

17. McMaster, 119–121, 130.

18. Smithsonian, *A Short History of the Vietnam War* (New York: DK Publishing, 2021), 122–125.

19. Logevall, *Choosing War*, 196–203; Barrett, ed., *LBJ's Vietnam Papers*, 63–73.

20. Barrett, ed., *LBJ's Vietnam Papers*, 53; McMaster, 132; Halberstam, 407–415.

21. Barrett, ed., *LBJ's Vietnam Papers*, 47–48; McMaster, 130.

22. Shapley, 240; Barrett, ed., *LBJ's Vietnam Papers*, 74–78.

23. Logevall, *Choosing War*, 205; Barrett, ed., *LBJ's Vietnam Papers*, 53; McMaster, 133–137; Halberstam, 417–420.

24. Barrett, ed., *LBJ's Vietnam Papers*, 61.

25. McMaster, 128, 132, 156.

26. Trauschweizer, 128.

27. Susan Sheehan, "A Viet Cong," in *Reporting Vietnam, Part One: American Journalism 1959–1969* (New York: Library of America, 1998), 231; Halberstam, 460–464.

28. Frank E. Vandiver, *Shadows of Vietnam* (College Station: Texas A&M University Press, 1997), 85; Barrett, ed., *LBJ's Vietnam Papers*, 61; McMaster, 156–158.

29. Logevall, *Choosing War*, 92; Barrett, ed., *LBJ's Vietnam Papers*, 81.

30. McMaster, 157–162.

31. Ward S. Just, "Saigon and Other Syndromes," in *Reporting Vietnam, Part One*, 369; McMaster, 148–149, 168–171; Halberstam, 460–462.

32. McMaster, 139–140, 150–153, 229–230, 265; Halberstam, 465, 484–487.

33. Logevall, *Choosing War*, 287–288, 303–307, 360, 377.

34. Richard Zoglin, *Hope* (New York: Simon & Schuster, 2014), 370; McMaster, 172–175.

35. Trauschweizer, 154–155.

36. Westmoreland, 114; Nguyen, *Hanoi's War*, 50, 75.

37. Richard Helms, *A Look over My Shoulder* (New York: Random House, 2003), 316–317; Halberstam, 512.

CHAPTER 3. Eve of Destruction

1. Deborah Shapley, *Promise and Power* (Boston: Little, Brown, 1993), 278; Harry G. Summers Jr., *On Strategy* (Novato, CA: Presidio, 1982), 12.

2. David M. Barrett, ed., *LBJ's Vietnam Papers* (College Station: Texas A&M University Press, 1997), 88; H. R. McMaster, *Dereliction of Duty* (New York: Harper Collins, 1997), 153, 179–183, 319.

3. Richard Helms, *A Look over My Shoulder* (New York: Random House, 2003), 321–322.

4. "Viet Nam War Grows, Becomes Major Issue," *CQ Almanac 1965*, 21st ed. (Washington, DC: Congressional Quarterly, 1966), 449–457, http://library.cqpress.com/cqalmanac/cqal65-1259469; Max Boot, *The Road Not Taken* (New York: Norton, 2018), 449; Barrett, ed., *LBJ's Vietnam Papers*, 87–88, 96–99, 101–102, 136; David M. Barrett, "The Mythology Surrounding Lyndon Johnson, His Advisers, and the 1965 Decision to Escalate the Vietnam War," *Political Science Quarterly* 103, no. 4 (Winter 1988–1989): 650; Kai Bird, *The Color of Truth* (New York: Simon & Schuster, 1998), 339–340.

5. Fredrik Logevall, *Choosing War* (Berkeley: University of California Press, 1999), 356.

6. Michael Beschloss, "LBJ's Secret War," *Washington Post*, Dec. 1, 2001; David Halberstam, *The Best and the Brightest* (New York: Random House, 1972), 490, 501, 505–507, 528–531; Barrett, "Mythology," 646; Hubert Humphrey, *The Education of a Public Man* (New York: Doubleday, 1976), 320–325; Edgar Berman, *Hubert* (New York: Putnam, 1979), 88, 94; McMaster, 195, 202, 241–242; Barrett, ed., *LBJ's Vietnam Papers*, 137, 140, 370.

7. National Archives and Record Administration (NARA), RG 127, USMC Records, Box 99, HQ MACV, Mar. 1965, MG Richard Stillwell, "Monthly Evaluation Report, Feb. 1965."

8. William C. Westmoreland, *A Soldier Reports* (New York: Doubleday, 1976), 115.

9. Logevall, *Choosing War*, 324–327; McMaster, 206–207, 218–219; Halberstam, 508, 533–534.

10. Barrett, ed., *LBJ's Vietnam Papers*, 104–108; Lien-Hang T. Nguyen,

Hanoi's War (Chapel Hill: University of North Carolina Press, 2012), 41, 48, 57; Barrett, "Mythology," 650.

11. Logevall, *Choosing War*, 326.

12. "Vietnam Background: Congress and the War: Years of Support," *CQ Almanac 1975*, 31st ed. (Washington, DC: Congressional Quarterly, 1976), 296–299, http://library.cqpress.com/cqalmanac/cqal75-1213972; Halberstam, 521–522; Boot, 449; McMaster, 139, 220–222.

13. Westmoreland, 116–117; McMaster, 222–225.

14. George M. Kahin, *Intervention* (New York: Knopf, 1986), 232–235; McMaster, 227–228.

15. Lewis Sorley, ed., *The Vietnam War* (Lubbock: Texas Tech University Press, 2010), 7–8, 229; McMaster, 228.

16. Summers, *On Strategy*, 48.

17. NARA, RG 127, USMC Records, Box 99, HQ MACV, MG Richard Stillwell, "Monthly Evaluation Reports, Feb., March, and May 1965"; Barrett, ed., *LBJ's Vietnam Papers*, 119–126, 130; Kahin, 512.

18. Barrett, "Mythology," 644; McMaster, 206, 210, 228–230; "Viet Nam War Grows, Becomes Major Issue," 449–457.

19. Walter J. Boyne, "Route Pack 6," *Air and Space Forces Magazine*, Nov. 1, 1999; Barrett, ed., *LBJ's Vietnam Papers*, 122; Westmoreland, 117–118.

20. Jacob Van Staaveren, *Gradual Failure* (Washington, DC: Air Force History, 2002), 222; Harry G. Summers Jr., *Historical Atlas of the Vietnam War* (Boston: Houghton Mifflin, 1995), 96–97; Halberstam, 522; Smithsonian, 144; Boot, 449.

21. Robert A. Pape, *Bombing to Win* (Ithaca, NY: Cornell University Press, 1996), 176–181; Mark Clodfelter, *The Limits of Air Power* (New York: Free Press, 1989), 64–72.

22. Russell Baker, "Befuddled in Asia," in *Reporting Vietnam, Part One: American Journalism 1959–1969* (New York: Library of America, 1998), 138–139; McMaster, 219–220, 224–231, 266; Westmoreland, 119.

23. NARA, RG 127, USMC Records, Box 99, HQ MACV, MG Richard Stillwell, "Monthly Evaluation Reports, Feb. and May 1965"; McMaster, 212; Westmoreland, 84–85; Gregory A. Daddis, *Westmoreland's War* (New York: Oxford University Press, 2014), 124, 126.

24. Summers, *On Strategy*, 68–69.

25. Ingo Trauschweizer, *Maxwell Taylor's Cold War* (Lexington: University Press of Kentucky, 2019), 158, 161–163; Halberstam, 537–441, 545.

26. John Flynn, "Marines Get Flowers for a Tough Mission," in *Reporting Vietnam, Part One*, 140; McMaster, 203–204, 231–232.

27. "Memorandum from the Joint Chiefs to Secretary of Defense McNamara: Concept for Vietnam," Washington, DC, Aug. 27, 1965, https://history.state.gov/historicaldocuments; Boot, 450; Halberstam, 520, 542, 570; McMaster, 205, 300; Guenter Lewy, *America in Vietnam* (New York: Oxford University Press, 1978), 42–43.

28. Westmoreland, 125; Halberstam, 530; McMaster, 240, 244–245; Summers, *On Strategy*, 68–69.

29. McMaster, 265–266; Westmoreland, 134.

30. Westmoreland, 144.

31. Barrett, "Mythology," 647–649.

32. Ron Milam, *Not a Gentleman's War* (Chapel Hill: University of North Carolina Press, 2009), 98–102; Westmoreland, 155.

33. Roger Rapoport, "Protest, Learning, Heckling Spark Viet Rally," in *Reporting Vietnam, Part One*, 142–144; Tom Wolfe, "From *The Electric Kool-Aid Acid Test*," *Reporting Vietnam: Part One*, 198; McMaster, 259–260, 277.

34. Barrett, ed., *LBJs Vietnam Papers*, 138–139; McMaster, 259–260, 277; Frank E. Vandiver, *Shadows of Vietnam* (College Station: Texas A&M University Press, 1997), 95–96.

35. Vandiver, 103–105.

36. NARA, RG 127, USMC Records, Box 99, HQ MACV, July 1965, Col. L. M. Harris, "Monthly Evaluation Reports, June and Sept. 1965"; Halberstam, 582–583; Lewy, 48–49; McMaster, 287, 292; Barrett, ed., *LBJ's Vietnam Papers*, 162.

37. McMaster, 291, 295.

38. "Ky Is Said to Consider Hitler a Hero," *Washington Post*, July 10, 1965; "Viet Nam War Grows, Becomes Major Issue," 449–457; McMaster, 282–283.

39. Sean Fear, "Vietnam '67: The Feud That Sank Saigon," *New York Times*, Mar. 3, 2017; Robert Mason, *Chickenhawk* (New York: Viking, 1983), 70.

40. Neil Sheehan, "No Longer a Hawk: October 1966," in *Reporting Vietnam: American Journalism 1959–1975* (New York: Library of America, 1998), 172; Barrett, ed., *LBJ's Vietnam Papers*, 195–196.

41. McMaster, 289.

42. "U.S. Viet Nam War Efforts," *CQ Almanac 1966*, 22nd ed. (Washington, DC: Congressional Quarterly, 1967), 378–389, http://library.cqpress.com/cqalmanac /cqal66-1301628; "Viet Nam War Grows, Becomes Major Issue," 449–457.

43. Vandiver, 127–132; Halberstam, 596–601.

44. Barrett, ed., *LBJ's Vietnam Papers*, 196; Lyndon B. Johnson, *The Vantage Point* (New York: Holt, 1971), 153; Lewy, 50–51; Barrett, "Mythology," 651, 656, 658; Vandiver, 128–130.

45. Halberstam, 521.

46. Vandiver, 35–36; Halberstam, 525–526.

47. William Tuohy, "A Big 'Dirty Little War,'" in *Reporting Vietnam, Part One*, 188.

48. McMaster, 316–317, 320; Barrett, ed., *LBJ's Vietnam Papers*, 218.

49. Logevall, *Choosing War*, 331–334; Ronald H. Spector, *After Tet: The Bloodiest Year in Vietnam* (New York: Free Press, 1993), 27–28; Milam, 14–15.

50. Doris Kearns Goodwin, *Lyndon Johnson and the American Dream* (New York: St. Martin's, 1976), 251–252; Westmoreland, 143.

51. Barrett, ed., *LBJ's Vietnam Papers*, 253–255, 270, 272; Jeffrey Record, *The Wrong War* (Annapolis, MD: Naval Institute Press, 1998), 146; Bird, 339–340.

52. Halberstam, 604–610.

53. Barrett, ed., *LBJ's Vietnam Papers*, 226; Daddis, *Westmoreland's War*, 77.

CHAPTER 4. Strength Only for Defeat

1. David Halberstam, *The Best and the Brightest* (New York: Random House, 1972), 598.

2. "Presidential Speeches," July 28, 1965, Press Conference, https://millercenter.org/the-presidency/presidential-speeches.

3. Fredrik Logevall, *Choosing War* (Berkeley: University of California Press, 1999), 336.

4. Guenter Lewy, *America in Vietnam* (New York: Oxford University Press, 1978), 84; Halberstam, 619.

5. Frank E. Vandiver, *Shadows of Vietnam* (College Station: Texas A&M University Press, 1997), 133–134; Halberstam, 614–617.

6. Liddell Hart Centre for Military Archives (LHCMA), U.S. Armed Forces in Vietnam 1954–1975, MF 812, HQ I Field Force, Jan. 8, 1971, Lt. Gen. A. S. Collins Jr. to Commanding General, US Army Vietnam, Jan. 7, 1971, "Senior Officer's Debriefing Report, Inclusive Dates 15 Feb. 1970 Through 9 Jan. 1971"; Gregory A. Daddis, *Westmoreland's War* (New York: Oxford University Press, 2014), 72; Logevall, *Choosing War*, 373.

7. Ronald H. Spector, *After Tet* (New York: Free Press, 1993), 29–32.

8. Smithsonian, *A Short History of the Vietnam War* (New York: DK Publishing, 2021), 166, 195–196.

9. National Archives and Records Administration (NARA), RG 472, A1 38, Box 1, "Sphinx" Intelligence Summaries, MACV, INTSUM #93, Jan. 29, 1966; RG 472, MACV, Tet Documents, Box 1, Enemy Strategy Assess. 24 May 68, MACV, May 1, 1968, "Newsletter #4: Viet Cong Political Infrastructure," and May 24, 1968, BG Phillip B. Davidson Jr., J2, "Speech Data for Gen. Westmoreland as Chief of Staff: Myths of Vietnam"; Daddis, *Westmoreland's War*, 172.

10. "U.S. Viet Nam War Efforts," *CQ Almanac 1966*, 22nd ed. (Washington, DC: Congressional Quarterly, 1967), 378–389, http://library.cqpress.com/cqalmanac/cqal66-1301628; Harry G. Summers Jr., *Historical Atlas of the Vietnam War* (Boston: Houghton Mifflin, 1995), 98.

11. William C. Westmoreland, *A Soldier Reports* (New York: Doubleday, 1976), 185–188.

12. Robert Mason, *Chickenhawk* (New York: Viking, 1983), 64.

13. UK National Archives (UKNA), DEFE 68/808, Saigon, Nov. 29, 1966, Lt. Col. D. B. Wood, "Helicopter Operations"; NARA, RG 127, USMC Records, Box 99, HQ MACV, Dec. 31, 1965, Col. L. M. Harris, "Monthly Evaluation Report, Nov. 1965"; Mason, 23.

14. Daddis, *Westmoreland's War*, 93.

15. NARA, RG 127, USMC Records, Box 99, HQ MACV, Mar. 11, 1967, Capt. M. K. Wheeler, "Counterinsurgency Lessons Learned No. 62."

16. Mason, 142.

17. NARA, RG 472, P 1173, USARV/4th Infantry Division, ACOS, G-3, 26, Operation Junction City—1967, HQ 3d Brigade, May 12, 1967, 1Lt. Jerome Palmer, "Combat Operations After Action Report"; NARA, RG 472, P 1173, USARV/4th Infantry Division, ACOS, G-3, 23, Operation Sam Houston Critique Notes, 4th ID HQ, Apr. 27, 1967, Maj. Gen. W. R. Peers, "After Action Critique Notes"; LHCMA, MF 809, Reel 1/4, U.S. Armed Forces in Vietnam 1954–1975, Part Four: Vietnam: U.S. Army Senior Debriefing Reports, HQ U.S. Army Support Command, Saigon, Nov. 9, 1968, Brig. Gen. M. McD. Jones Jr., "Senior Officer Debriefing Report, July 1, 1967 to Nov. 9, 1968."

18. Ron Milam, *Not a Gentleman's War* (Chapel Hill: University of North Carolina Press, 2009), 68–69; NARA, RG 472, P 1173, USARV/4th Infantry Division, ACOS, G-3, 26, "Battle for Dak To, 25 Oct to 1 Dec 1967," HQ 4th ID, Jan. 3, 1968, Maj. Gen. W. R. Peers, "Combat Operations After Action Report: Battle for Dak To." (Sign posted at FSB Navel, home in Apr. 1970 to A Battery/4th Battalion/42d Artillery aka the Sandbaggers.)

19. NARA, RG 127, USMC Records, Box 99, HQ MACV, Mar. 11, 1967, Capt. M. K. Wheeler, "Counterinsurgency Lessons Learned No. 62"; James T. Gillam, *Life and Death in the Central Highlands* (Denton: University of North Texas Press, 2010), 119–120; Chuck Gross, *Rattler One-Seven* (Denton: University of North Texas Press, 2004), 25.

20. UKNA, DEFE 68/807, Saigon, Nov. 22, 1966, Lt. Col. D. B. Wood, "Casualty Statistics"; Kevin P. Buckley, "Pacification's Deadly Price," *Newsweek*, June 19, 1972, 42–43; James Sterba, "Scraps of Paper from Vietnam," in *Reporting Vietnam, Part Two: American Journalism 1969–1975* (New York: Library of America, 1998), 145–146, 151–152.

21. Matt Dietz, *Eagles Overhead* (Denton: University of North Texas Press, 2023), 103–105; Jonathan Schell, "From *The Military Half: An Account of the Destruction in Quang Ngai and Quang Tin*," in *Reporting Vietnam: American Journalism 1959–1975* (New York: Library of America, 1998), 216–217.

22. James Webb, *I Heard My Country Calling* (New York: Simon & Schuster, 2014), 259–262, 267.

23. John Saar, "A Frantic Night on the Edge of Laos," in *Reporting Vietnam, Part Two*, 181; Bernard B. Fall, "The Impersonal War: September 1965," in *Reporting Vietnam*, 116; Gross, 142; Gillam, 115.

24. NARA, RG 127, USMC Records, Box 99, HQ MACV, Mar. 11, 1967, Capt. M. K. Wheeler, "Counterinsurgency Lessons Learned No. 62"; UKNA, DEFE 68/767, Saigon, Sept. 19, 1967, Cdr. A. D. Levy, Lt. Col. K. A. Hill, Wing Cdr. A. T. Vacquier, "Application of Conventional Air Weapons"; LHCMA, MF 809, Reel 1/4, U.S. Armed Forces in Vietnam 1954–1975, Part Four: Vietnam: U.S. Army Senior Debriefing Reports, HQ U.S. Army Support Command, Saigon, Nov. 9, 1968, Brig. Gen. M. McD. Jones Jr., "Senior Officer Debriefing Report, July 1, 1967 to Nov. 9, 1968"; Smithsonian, 170–171.

25. Ingo Trauschweizer, *Maxwell Taylor's Cold War* (Lexington: University Press of Kentucky, 2019), 180.

26. NARA, RG 472, P 1173, 22, USARV/4th Infantry Division, ACOS, G-3, HQ 3d Brigade Task Force, 25th ID, Aug. 15, 1966, Brig. Gen. Glenn Walker, "Operational Report for Quarterly Period Ending 31 July 1966" and USARV/4th Infantry Division, ACOS, G-3, 26, "Battle for Dak To, 25 Oct to 1 Dec 1967," and HQ 4th ID, Jan. 3, 1968, Maj. Gen. W. R. Peers, "Combat Operations After Action Report: Battle for Dak To"; RG 127, USMC Records, Box 99, HQ MACV, Mar. 11, 1967, Capt. M. K. Wheeler, "Counterinsurgency Lessons Learned No. 62"; Robert Shaplen, "We Have Always Survived," in *Reporting Vietnam*, 564; Lewy, 49.

27. Max Boot, *The Road Not Taken* (New York: Norton, 2018), 412.

28. Bernard B. Fall, "Vietnam Blitz: A Report on the Impersonal War," in *Reporting Vietnam*, 106–117.

29. Fall, "Vietnam Blitz," 117.

30. Westmoreland, 145–146; Lewis Sorley, *A Better War* (Boston: Houghton Mifflin, 1999), 2.

31. NARA, RG 127, USMC Records, Box 99, MACV, CORDS, Reports and Analysis Directorate (RAD), June 1969, *Hamlet Evaluation System Handbook*; Susan Sheehan, "A Viet Cong," in *Reporting Vietnam, Part One: American Journalism 1959–1969* (New York: Library of America, 1998), 232–233; David Halberstam, "'An Endless, Relentless War,'" in *Reporting Vietnam, Part One*, 75; Daddis, *Westmoreland's War*, 78.

32. John H. Hay Jr., *Vietnam Studies: Tactical and Materiel Innovations* (Washington, DC: GPO, 1974), 172; Mason, 253.

33. Westmoreland, 100, 147; Andrew F. Krepinevich Jr., *The Army and Vietnam* (Baltimore: Johns Hopkins University Press, 1986), 194–195.

CHAPTER 5. Ia Drang

1. Fredrik Logevall, *Choosing War* (Berkeley: University of California Press, 1999), 366–367.

2. National Archives and Records Administration (NARA), RG 127, USMC Records, Box 99, HQ MACV, Dec. 31, 1965, Col. L. M. Harris, "Monthly Evaluation Report, Nov. 1965"; RG 472, MACV, Tet Documents, Box 1, Enemy Strategy Assess. 24 May 68, MACV, J2, Sept. 1967, "Hanoi's Control and Direction of Enemy Efforts in South Vietnam"; Guenter Lewy, *America in Vietnam* (New York: Oxford University Press, 1978), 38; David Halberstam, *The Best and the Brightest* (New York: Random House, 1972), 613.

3. NARA, RG 127, USMC Records, Box 99, HQ MACV, Oct. 1965, Col. L. M. Harris, "Monthly Evaluation Report, Sept. 1965"; RG 472, A1 38, Box 1, "Sphinx" Intelligence Summaries, MACV, INTSUM, Jan. 13, 1966; Fox Butterfield, "Who Was This Enemy?," in *Reporting Vietnam: American Journalism 1959–1975* (New York: Library of America, 1998), 654; Tim O'Brien, *The Things They Carried* (New York: Penguin, 1990), 103.

4. NARA, RG 127, USMC Records, Box 99, HQ MACV, Oct. 1965, Col. L. M. Harris, "Monthly Evaluation Report, Sept. 1965."

5. David M. Barrett, ed., *Lyndon B. Johnson's Vietnam Papers* (College Station: Texas A&M University Press, 1997), 307.

6. Norman Lewis, *A Dragon Apparent* (1951; London: Eland, 1982), 213–214.

7. NARA, RG 472, MACV, Tet Documents, Box 2, Press Briefings II, III, & IV CTZ, Apr. 17, 1968, "Press Briefing: 1968 Tet Offensive in II CTZ"; Frederick Downs, *The Killing Zone* (New York: Norton, 2007), 107.

8. Lewy, 50–53.

9. NARA, RG 472, MACV, Tet Documents, Box 1, Enemy Strategy Assess. 24 May 68, MACV, May 1, 1968, "Newsletter #4: Viet Cong Political Infrastructure."

10. Frank E. Vandiver, *Shadows of Vietnam* (College Station: Texas A&M University Press, 1997), 137; Robert Mason, *Chickenhawk* (New York: Viking, 1983), 35–36.

11. Mason, 40.

12. Mason, 82–83, 99.

13. NARA, RG 127, USMC Records, Box 99, HQ MACV, June 20, 1966, Maj. Wm. C. Carmichael, "Lessons Learned No. 58: Operation HAPPY VALLEY"; Lewis, 94–100.

14. NARA, RG 127, USMC Records, Box 99, HQ MACV, June 20, 1966, Maj. Wm. C. Carmichael, "Lessons Learned No. 58: Operation HAPPY VALLEY"; Mason, 82–83, 99; William Tuohy, "A Big 'Dirty Little War,'" in *Reporting Vietnam, Part One: American Journalism 1959–1969* (New York: Library of America, 1998), 195.

15. Specialist 4/C Jack P. Smith, "Death in the Ia Drang Valley," in *Reporting Vietnam*, 118.

16. Vandiver, 142–145.

17. Smith, "Death in the Ia Drang Valley," 119.

18. NARA, RG 127, USMC Records, Box 99, HQ MACV, Jan. 27, 1967, Maj. E. W. Gannon, "Counterinsurgency Lessons Learned No. 61."

19. UK National Archives (UKNA), DEFE 68/794, HQ 1st Bn 7th Cavalry, 1st Cav Div (Airmobile), Dec. 9, 1965, Col. Harold G. Moore, "After Action Report, Ia Drang Valley Operation, 1st Battalion, 7th Cavalry, 14–16 Nov. 1965"; NARA, RG 127, USMC Records, Box 99, HQ MACV, Dec. 31, 1965, Col. L. M. Harris, "Monthly Evaluation Report, Nov. 1965."

20. NARA, RG 127, USMC Records, Box 99, HQ MACV, Dec. 31, 1965, Col. L. M. Harris, "Monthly Evaluation Report, Nov. 1965"; Harry G. Summers Jr., *Historical Atlas of the Vietnam War* (Boston: Houghton Mifflin, 1995), 106; Gregory A. Daddis, *No Sure Victory* (New York: Oxford University Press, 2011), 80–83; William C. Westmoreland, *A Soldier Reports* (New York: Doubleday, 1976), 157; Mason, 147; Smith, "Death in the Ia Drang Valley," 125, 129, 132.

CHAPTER 6. "Nail the Coonskins to the Wall"

1. Andrew F. Krepinevich Jr., *The Army in Vietnam* (Baltimore: Johns Hopkins University Press, 1986), 169; Deborah Shapley, *Promise and Power* (Boston: Little, Brown, 1993), 356–357.

2. Gregory A. Daddis, *Westmoreland's War* (New York: Oxford University Press, 2014), 98; Kai Bird, *The Color of Truth* (New York: Simon & Schuster, 1998), 341; Shapley, 357–362.

3. Richard Helms, *A Look over My Shoulder* (New York: Random House, 2003); 311; Robert Mason, *Chickenhawk* (New York: Viking, 1983), 155, 169.

4. Ronald H. Spector, *After Tet* (New York: Free Press, 1993), 222–225.

5. National Archives and Records Administration (NARA), RG 472, MACV, Tet Documents, Box 2, "Battle for Khe Sanh by Capt. Moyers S. Shore, II, USMC," 12; Philip Caputo, *A Rumor of War* (New York: Picador, 1977), 192; Harry G. Summers Jr., *Historical Atlas of the Vietnam War* (Boston: Houghton Mifflin, 1995), 108–109.

6. NARA, RG 472, MACV, Tet Documents, Box 2, "Battle for Khe Sanh by Capt. Moyers S. Shore, II, USMC," 2–5.

7. NARA, RG 472, MACV, Tet Documents, Box 2, "Battle for Khe Sanh by Capt. Moyers S. Shore, II, USMC," 2–5.

8. Michael Herr, *Dispatches* (1977; New York: Vintage, 1991), 47–48.

9. NARA, RG 127, USMC Records, Box 99, HQ MACV, June 1965, MG Richard Stillwell, "Monthly Evaluation Report, May 1965," and Dec. 31, 1965, Col. L. M. Harris, "Monthly Evaluation Report, Nov. 1965"; Guenter Lewy, *America in Vietnam* (New York: Oxford University Press, 1978), 67; Summers, *Atlas*, 120–121; Spector, 222–223.

10. Frank E. Vandiver, *Shadows of Vietnam* (College Station: Texas A&M University Press, 1997), 145–147; Bird, 341.

11. David M. Barrett, ed., *Lyndon B. Johnson's Vietnam Papers* (College Station: Texas A&M University Press, 1997), 308–310; William C. Westmoreland, *A Soldier Reports* (New York: Doubleday, 1976), 179, 182; William Shawcross, *Sideshow* (New York: Simon & Schuster, 1979), 46–51, 60–64.

12. NARA, RG 472, A1 38, Box 1, "Sphinx" Intelligence Summaries, MACV, INTSUM, Jan. 4, 1966; Mason, 274; Westmoreland, 181, 184.

13. Bird, 357; Krepinevich, 188–189.

14. NARA, RG 127, USMC Records, Box 99, HQ MACV, Dec. 31, 1965, Col. L. M. Harris, "Monthly Evaluation Report, Nov. 1965"; David Halberstam, *The Best and the Brightest* (New York: Random House, 1972), 461; Daddis, *Westmoreland's War*, 100–101; Gregory A. Daddis, *No Sure Victory* (New York: Oxford University Press, 2011), 95; Barrett, ed., *LBJ's Vietnam Papers*, 319; Lewy, 83.

15. NARA, RG 127, USMC Records, Box 100, HQ MACV, Aug. 31, 1966, Col. E. D. Bryson, "Monthly Evaluation Report, July 1966"; Herr, 13; Lewy, 61–62.

16. NARA, RG 127, USMC Records, Box 99, HQ MACV, Dec. 31, 1965, Col. L. M. Harris, "Monthly Evaluation Report, Nov. 1965"; Mason, 176; Daddis, *Westmoreland's War*, 154.

17. NARA, RG 127, USMC Records, Box 99, HQ MACV, May 31, 1966, Col. E. D. Bryson, "Monthly Evaluation Report, April 1966."

18. NARA, RG 472, P 1173, 22, USARV/4th Infantry Division, ACOS, G-3, HQ 3d Brigade Task Force, 25th ID, Aug. 15, 1966, Brig. Gen. Glenn Walker,

"Operational Report for Quarterly Period Ending 31 July 1966," and June 6, 1967, Maj. Gilbert Reese, "After Action Report, Operation Fort Nisqually, 3d Brigade 4th Inf Division."

19. *The Pentagon Papers (New York Times Edition)* (New York: Bantam Books, 1971), 523; Walter J. Boyne, "Route Pack 6," *Air and Space Forces Magazine*, Nov. 1, 1999.

20. "U.S. Viet Nam War Efforts," *CQ Almanac 1966*, 22nd ed. (Washington, DC: Congressional Quarterly, 1967), 378–389, http://library.cqpress.com /cqalmanac/cqal66-1301628; Henry F. Graff, "Teach-In on Vietnam By...," in *Reporting Vietnam: American Journalism 1959–1975* (New York: Library of America, 1998), 135–136; Harrison E. Salisbury, "U.S. Raids Batter Two Towns; Supply Route Is Little Hurt," *New York Times*, Dec. 27, 1966; Tom Wolfe, "The Truest Sport: Jousting with Sam and Charlie," in *Reporting Vietnam, Part One: American Journalism 1959–1969* (New York: Library of America, 1998), 539–540; Stanley Karnow, *Vietnam: A History* (New York: Penguin, 1983), 489–490.

21. "U.S. Viet Nam War Efforts," 378–389; Lien-Hang T. Nguyen, *Hanoi's War* (Chapel Hill: University of North Carolina Press, 2012), 78.

22. Vandiver, 148, 161; Karnow, 481–483; Barrett, ed., *LBJ's Vietnam Papers*, 293–294.

23. "Viet Nam War Grows, Becomes Major Issue," *CQ Almanac 1965*, 21st ed. (Washington, DC: Congressional Quarterly, 1966), 449–457, http://library .cqpress.com/cqalmanac/cqal65-1259469; "U.S. Viet Nam War Efforts," 378–389; Graff, "Teach-In on Vietnam By...," 134, 147; Doris Kearns Goodwin, "From 'Who *Was* Lyndon Baines Johnson?,'" in *Reporting Vietnam*, 478.

24. Nick Turse, *Kill Anything That Moves* (New York: Metropolitan, 2013), 72–73.

25. Ron Milam, *Not a Gentleman's War* (Chapel Hill: University of North Carolina Press, 2009), 100–106; Caputo, 73–74; Max Boot, *The Road Not Taken* (New York: Norton, 2018), 486.

26. Neil Sheehan, "Not a Dove, but No Longer a Hawk," in *Reporting Vietnam*, 179.

27. Liddell Hart Centre for Military Archives (LHCMA), U.S. Armed Forces in Vietnam 1954–1975, MF 812, HQ I Field Force, Lt. Gen. A. S. Collins Jr. to Commanding General, US Army Vietnam, Jan. 7, 1971, "Senior Officer's Debriefing Report"; Dean Yates, "Vietnam Memorial Recalls Massacre by Korean Troops," Reuters, Jan. 20, 2000; Mason, 280–281; Lewis Sorley, *A Better War* (Boston: Houghton Mifflin, 1999), 175; Westmoreland, 257; Turse, 131–133.

28. Vandiver, 170–171.

29. "About the Vice President, Hubert H. Humphrey, 38th Vice President (1965–69)," www.senate.gov/about/officers-staff/vice-president/humphrey-hubert .htm; Boot, 451–452.

30. Ingo Trauschweizer, *Maxwell Taylor's Cold War* (Lexington: University Press of Kentucky, 2019), 178; Harry G. Summers Jr., *On Strategy* (Novato, CA: Presidio, 1982), 103–104.

31. Jeffrey Record, *The Wrong War* (Annapolis, MD: Naval Institute Press, 1998), 5.

32. "U.S. Viet Nam War Efforts," 378–389; Daddis, *No Sure Victory*, 89–90; Westmoreland, 160.

33. Westmoreland, 159.

34. John B. Henry II, "February, 1968," *Foreign Policy Quarterly*, Fall 1971, 18; "U.S. Viet Nam War Efforts," 378–389; Daddis, *Westmoreland's War*, 82; Vandiver, 166–168, 173; Westmoreland, 160–161.

35. Shapley, 367–375.

36. Joseph J. Thorndike, "Historical Perspective: Sacrifice and Surcharge," Dec. 5, 2004, taxhistory.org; Vandiver, 166–168, 197–200; Karnow, 486–487.

37. Henry, 28–29.

38. NARA, RG 127, USMC Records, Box 99, HQ MACV, Aug. 31, 1966, Col. E. D. Bryson, "Monthly Evaluation Report, July 1966"; Daddis, *Westmoreland's War*, 83, 127; Daddis, *No Sure Victory*, 92–93; Sorley, *Better War*, 2, 6.

39. Herr, 23–24.

40. UK National Archives (UKNA), DEFE 68/807, Saigon, Nov. 22, 1966, Lt. Col. D. B. Wood, "Casualty Statistics"; Sorley, *Better War*, 7.

41. NARA, RG 127, USMC Records, Box 99, HQ MACV, May 31, 1966, Col. E. D. Bryson, "Monthly Evaluation Report, April 1966"; Smithsonian, *A Short History of the Vietnam War* (New York: DK Publishing, 2021), 351–352; Sorley, *Better War*, 20; Lewy, 85.

42. Krepinevich, 165–168; Daddis, *No Sure Victory*, 93–94, 231; Daddis, *Westmoreland's War*, 79–80.

43. UKNA, DEFE 68/778, London, July 10, 1968, Maj. Gen. Richard Clutterbuck, "Report by Brigadier Clutterbuck on a Seminar on Vietnam Held at the Center for Strategic Studies, Washington, on 20th and 21st May 1968," www.historynet.com/marine-alternative-to-search-and-destroy.htm; Spector, 192–193.

44. Krepinevich, 172–177; Sorley, *Better War*, 20.

45. Westmoreland, 165–167.

46. Vandiver, 200–208; Westmoreland, 168–171.

47. Barrett, ed., *LBJ's Vietnam Papers*, 336–341, 359; Westmoreland, 176.

48. Andrew Wiest, *Vietnam's Forgotten Army* (New York: NYU Press, 2008), 57–59.

49. Rupert Cornwell, "William Bundy," *The Independent*, Oct. 12, 2000; "Address by Benjamin V. Cohen," *Congressional Record—Senate*, Aug. 22, 1967, 23563; Barrett, ed., *LBJ's Vietnam Papers*, 336–341.

50. Wiest, *Vietnam's Forgotten Army*, 59–63; Westmoreland, 170–172.

51. Robert H. Reid, "1966: Troops and Protests Increase Along with Strategy Concerns Against a Determined Enemy," *Stars and Stripes*, Nov. 10, 2016.

52. NARA, RG 127, USMC Records, Box 99, MACV Monthly Evaluation Reports, HQ MACV, May 31, 1966, and July 30, 1966, Col. E. D. Bryson, "Monthly Evaluation Reports, April and June 1966"; UKNA, FCO 15/482, May 8, 1967, D.

D. Hall, "MP's Tour of the North, 28 and 29 April"; "U.S. Viet Nam War Efforts," 378–389.

53. Mason, 298; Lewy, 62–63.

54. Spector, 193–195; Vandiver, 186–188.

55. UKNA, DEFE 68/778, London, July 10, 1968, Maj. Gen. Richard Clutterbuck, "Report by Brigadier Clutterbuck on a Seminar on Vietnam Held at the Center for Strategic Studies, Washington, on 20th and 21st May 1968"; Smithsonian, 216–219; Daddis, *Westmoreland's War*, 80; John Prados, "The Marines' Vietnam Commitment," *Naval History Magazine* 29, no. 2 (Apr. 2015); Gregory A. Daddis, *Withdrawal* (New York: Oxford University Press, 2017), 17–21.

CHAPTER 7. "The Country Is Behind You—50 Percent"

1. "U.S. Viet Nam War Efforts," *CQ Almanac 1966*, 22nd ed. (Washington, DC: Congressional Quarterly, 1967), 378–389, http://library.cqpress.com/cqalmanac/cqal66-1301628; Jonathan Marshall, "Dirty Wars: French and American Piaster Profiteering in Indochina, 1945–1975," *Asia-Pacific Journal* 12, no. 32 (Aug. 19, 2014); William C. Westmoreland, *A Soldier Reports* (New York: Doubleday, 1976), 182.

2. National Archives and Records Administration (NARA), RG 472, P 1173, 22, USARV/4th Infantry Division, ACOS, G-3, Jan. 28, 1967, "After Action Report Operation Paul Revere IV."

3. Ward S. Just, "Reconnaissance," in *Reporting Vietnam: American Journalism 1959–1975* (New York: Library of America, 1998), 152–153.

4. Just, "Reconnaissance," 152.

5. Robert Mason, *Chickenhawk* (New York: Viking, 1983), 295.

6. Just, "Reconnaissance," 165–168; Mason, 306.

7. NARA, RG 472, P 1173, 22, USARV/4th Infantry Division, ACOS, G-3, Jan. 28, 1967, "After Action Report Operation Paul Revere IV," and HQ 3d Brigade Task Force, Jan. 17, 1967, Col. James Shanahan, "After Action Report; Paul Revere IV," and HQ 4th ID, Apr. 27 and June 20, 1967, Maj. Gen. W. R. Peers, "Operation Sam Houston, 1967," and "After Action Critique Notes," and HQ 5th Bn (Airmobile), 7th Cav, 1st Air Cav Div, July 31, 1967, LTC John A. Wickham Jr., "Operational Report for Quarterly Period Ending 31 July 1967."

8. NARA, RG 472, P 1173, 22, USARV/4th Infantry Division, HQ 2d Brigade, Jan. 14, 1967, Major Frederick Neroni, "Combat After Action Report for Paul Revere IV," and 4th ID HQ, Apr. 27, 1967, Maj. Gen. W. R. Peers, "After Action Critique Notes" and "Operation Sam Houston Critique Notes," and HQ 3d Brigade Task Force, 25th ID, Aug. 15, 1966, Brig. Gen. Glenn Walker, "Operational Report for Quarterly Period Ending 31 July 1966," and USARV/4th Infantry Division, G-3, 1966–67, N.D., "Intelligence."

9. NARA, RG 472, P 1173, 22, USARV/4th Infantry Division, HQ 3d Brigade Task Force, 25th ID, Nov. 18, 1966, Col. James Shanahan, "Lessons Learned, 18 October to 18 November 1966 (Paul Revere IV)."

10. Frederick Downs, *The Killing Zone* (New York: Norton, 2007), 178–179.

11. NARA, RG 472, P1173, 22, USARV/4th Infantry Division, G-3, 1966–67, N.D., "Intelligence."

12. NARA, RG 472, P1173, 22, USARV/4th Infantry Division, G-3, 1966–67, N.D., "Intelligence."

13. NARA, RG 472, P 1173, 22, USARV/4th Infantry Division, HQ 2d Brigade, Jan. 14, 1967, Major Frederick Neroni, "Combat After Action Report for Paul Revere IV," and Jan. 28, 1967, "After Action Report Operation Paul Revere IV"; Downs, 108.

14. Robert H. Reid, "1966: Troops and Protests Increase Along with Strategy Concerns Against a Determined Enemy," *Stars and Stripes*, Nov. 10, 2016; David M. Barrett, ed., *Lyndon B. Johnson's Vietnam Papers* (College Station: Texas A&M University Press, 1997), 363–366, 372; Guenter Lewy, *American in Vietnam* (New York: Oxford University Press, 1978), 77–89; Lewis Sorley, *A Better War* (Boston: Houghton Mifflin, 1999), 21–22; Max Boot, *The Road Not Taken* (New York: Norton, 2018), 492; Deborah Shapley, *Promise and Power* (Boston: Little, Brown, 1993), 366–367.

15. Neil Sheehan, "Not a Dove, but No Longer a Hawk," in *Reporting Vietnam*, 180–181.

16. Nathalie Huynh Chau Nguyen, *South Vietnamese Soldiers* (Santa Barbara, CA: Praeger, 2016), 77.

17. Frank Harvey, "Only You Can Prevent Forests," in *Reporting Vietnam: Part One, American Journalism 1959–1969* (New York: Library of America, 1998), 282–285; James Sterba, "Scraps of Paper from Vietnam," in *Reporting Vietnam, Part Two: American Journalism 1969–1975* (New York: Library of America, 1998), 136–137.

18. NARA, RG 127, USMC Records, Box 100, HQ MACV, Oct. 24, 1966, Maj. E. W. Gannon, "Monthly Evaluation Report, Sept. 1966"; NARA, RG 472, P1173, 22, USARV/4th Infantry Division, G-3, 4 of 4 1966, 2/4th, "Inclosures"; Lien-Hang T. Nguyen, *Hanoi's War* (Chapel Hill: University of North Carolina Press, 2012), 78–79.

19. Sorley, *Better War*, 5, 405–406; Harry G. Summers Jr., *Historical Atlas of the Vietnam War* (Boston: Houghton Mifflin, 1995), 112.

20. NARA, RG 472, P1173, 22, USARV/4th Infantry Division, G-3, 1966–67, N.D., "Intelligence"; NARA, RG 127, USMC Records, Box 100, HQ MACV, Dec. 24, 1966, Capt. M. K. Wheeler, "Monthly Evaluation Report, Nov. 1966."

21. Tobias Wolff, *In Pharaoh's Army* (London: Bloomsbury, 1994), 72–73; Barrett, ed., *LBJ's Vietnam Papers*, 435.

22. NARA, RG 472, P1173, 22, USARV/4th Infantry Division, G-3, 3 of 4 1966–67, "Translation of Leaflet 1528, 1529"; UK National Archives (UKNA), FCO 15/482, Saigon, Jan. 4, 1967, Buxton to Waterstone, "Weekly Round-Up"; "U.S. Viet Nam War Efforts," 378–389; Richard Zoglin, *Hope* (New York: Simon & Schuster, 2014), 381.

CHAPTER 8. Jive at Five

1. "High Cost, Poor Results in Viet Nam War Stimulate Dissent; Congress Critical of Aims, Conduct and Impact on Economy," *CQ Almanac 1967*, 23rd ed. (Washington, DC: Congressional Quarterly, 1968), 07-917–07-925, http://library .cqpress.com/cqalmanac/cqal67-1313128; "U.S. Viet Nam War Efforts," *CQ Almanac 1966*, 22nd ed. (Washington, DC: Congressional Quarterly, 1 967), 378–389, http://library.cqpress.com/cqalmanac/cqal66-1301628; Amy J. Rutenberg, "How the Draft Reshaped America," *New York Times*, Oct. 6, 2017; David M. Barrett, ed., *Lyndon B. Johnson's Vietnam Papers* (College Station: Texas A&M University Press, 1997), 450.

2. Deborah Shapley, *Promise and Power* (Boston: Little, Brown, 1993), 367–376.

3. Charles F. Brower IV, "Strategic Assessment in Vietnam: The Westmoreland 'Alternate Strategy' for 1967–1968," *Naval War College Review* 44, no. 2 (Spring 1991): 23–24; "High Cost, Poor Results in Viet Nam War Stimulate Dissent."

4. Brower, 24–26; William C. Westmoreland, *A Soldier Reports* (New York: Doubleday, 1976), 252–253, 267, 285, 298–299, 355–358, 412–413, 466–467; "Vietnam Background: Congress and the War: Years of Support," *CQ Almanac 1975*, 31st ed. (Washington, DC: Congressional Quarterly, 1976), 296–299, http://library. cqpress.com/cqalmanac/cqal75-1213972; Gregory A. Daddis, *Westmoreland's War* (New York: Oxford University Press, 2014), 160; Barrett, ed., *LBJ's Vietnam Papers*, 391.

5. John B. Henry II, "February, 1968," *Foreign Policy Quarterly*, Fall 1971, 8–9; Barrett, ed., *LBJ's Vietnam Papers*, 391.

6. Henry, 16–18.

7. Barrett, ed., *LBJ's Vietnam Papers*, 412–415, 426–428; Lewis Sorley, *A Better War* (Boston: Houghton Mifflin, 1999), 5; Brower, 32.

8. R. W. Apple Jr., "Vietnam: The Signs of Stalemate," *New York Times*, Aug. 7, 1967.

9. Barrett, ed., *LBJ's Vietnam Papers*, 411; Michael Herr, *Dispatches* (1977; New York: Vintage, 1991), 47–48.

10. Sorley, *Better War*, 5–6.

11. Ward S. Just, "Saigon and Other Syndromes," in *Reporting Vietnam, Part One: American Journalism 1959–1969* (New York: Library of America, 1998), 357–360.

12. Sydney H. Schanberg, "The Saigon Follies, or, Trying to Head Them Off at Credibility Gap," in *Reporting Vietnam, Part Two: American Journalism 1969–1975* (New York: Library of America, 1998), 394, 405.

13. John E. Woodruff, "The Meo of Laos," in *Reporting Vietnam, Part Two*, 191–193.

14. National Archives and Records Administration (NARA), RG 472, MACV, Tet Documents, Box 1, Misc. Messages Jan–May 68, MACV, Feb. 5, 1968, "Cambodia"; Brower, 43–44; Westmoreland, 182.

15. Barrett, ed., *LBJ's Vietnam Papers*, 426; Brower, 27–30; Doris Kearns Goodwin, *Lyndon Johnson and the American Dream* (New York: St. Martin's, 1976), 251–252; Andrew Glass, "This Day in Politics: LBJ Asks Congress to Pass War Tax, Jan. 10, 1967," *Politico*, Jan. 10, 2019; Joseph J. Thorndike, "Historical Perspective: Sacrifice and Surcharge," Dec. 5, 2004, taxhistory.org.

16. Max Frankel, "Johnson Plans to Repeat Vietnam Strategy Parley," *New York Times*, Mar. 26, 1967, 1; Barrett, ed., *LBJ's Vietnam Papers*, 404; Vandiver, *Shadows of Vietnam* (College Station: Texas A&M University Press, 1997), 166–168, 228–232, 253.

17. Lien-Hang T. Nguyen, *Hanoi's War* (Chapel Hill: University of North Carolina Press, 2012), 80.

18. Bernard B. Fall, "The Impersonal War: September 1965," in *Reporting Vietnam: American Journalism 1959–1975* (New York: Library of America, 1998), 108; Henry F. Graff, "Teach-In on Vietnam By...," in *Reporting Vietnam*, 143–144.

19. Ang Cheng Guan, "Decision-Making Leading to the Tet Offensive (1968): The Vietnamese Communist Perspective," *Journal of Contemporary History* 33, no. 3 (July 1998): 343–344; Nguyen, *Hanoi's War*, 78–79; NARA, RG 472, MACV, DCSOPS, Summary of Operational Interest Messages, 14 Sept. 67 thru 31 May 68, Box 1, Oct. 22, 1967, Mar. 28, 30, Apr. 5, 1968, Col. Robert C. Hamilton; Vandiver, 150; Kyle Longley, "Vietnam '67: The Grunt's War," *New York Times*, Feb. 17, 2017.

20. NARA, RG 127, USMC Records, Box 100, HQ MACV, Feb. 25, 1967, Capt. M. K. Wheeler, "Monthly Evaluation Report, Jan. 1967."

21. "Address by Benjamin V. Cohen," *Congressional Record—Senate*, Aug. 22, 1967, 23563.

22. James R. McDonough, *Platoon Leader* (Novato, CA: Presidio, 1985), 68, 77, 104; Apple, "Vietnam: The Signs of Stalemate."

23. Apple, "Vietnam: The Signs of Stalemate."

24. Ronald H. Spector, *After Tet* (New York: Free Press, 1993), 279–282.

25. Westmoreland, 210–215; Gregory A. Daddis, *No Sure Victory* (New York: Oxford University Press, 2011), 13–15; Harry G. Summers Jr., *Historical Atlas of the Vietnam War* (Boston: Houghton Mifflin, 1995), 124–125.

26. "High Cost, Poor Results in Viet Nam War Stimulate Dissent"; Daddis, *Westmoreland's War*, 128–132; Barrett, ed., *LBJ's Vietnam Papers*, 402–403; William Colby, *Lost Victory* (Chicago: Contemporary, 1989), 190–191.

27. Sorley, *Better War*, 62–63.

28. Daddis, *Westmoreland's War*, 132–134.

29. UK National Archives (UKNA), DEFE 68/810, Saigon, Dec. 14, 1967, Lt. Col. D. B. Wood, "Pacification"; Guenter Lewy, *America in Vietnam* (New York: Oxford University Press, 1978), 65.

30. Daddis, *No Sure Victory*, 110–111; Bernard B. Fall, "Unrepentant, Unyielding," in *Reporting Vietnam*, 187–189, 199.

31. Christian G. Appy, *Patriots* (New York: Viking, 2003), 204.

32. Fall, "Unrepentant, Unyielding," 194.

33. Jonathan Schell, "The Village of Ben Suc," *New Yorker*, July 15, 1967.

34. Westmoreland, 205; Fall, "Unrepentant, Unyielding," 194.

35. UKNA, FCO 15/482, Saigon, Jan. 25, 1967, Thomas to Waterstone, "Weekly Round-Up"; Summers, *Atlas*, 116–117.

36. Westmoreland, 206.

37. Smithsonian, *A Short History of the Vietnam War* (New York: DK Publishing, 2021), 237, 248.

38. UKNA, FCO 15/482, Saigon, Apr. 20, 1967, Defence Attache, "Operation Junction City," and May 8, 1967, D. D. Hall, "MP's Tour of the North, 28 and 29 April."

39. R. W. Apple Jr., "Bernard Fall Killed in Vietnam by a Mine While with Marines," *New York Times*, Feb. 22, 1967; NARA, RG 127, USMC Records, Box 99, HQ MACV, Dec. 6, 1965, Capt. Howard Schulze, "Lessons Learned No. 53: VC Improvised Explosive Mines and Booby Traps," and Sept. 29, 1966, Maj. E. W. Gannon, "Counterinsurgency Lessons Learned No. 53 (Revised), and Jan. 27, 1967, Maj. E. W. Gannon, "Counterinsurgency Lessons Learned No. 61."

40. NARA, RG 472, P 1173, 25, USARV/4th Infantry Division, G-3, Operation Greeley Input 1 of 2, HQ 5th Bn (Airmobile), 7th Cav, 1st Air Cav Div, July 31, 1967, LTC John A. Wickham Jr., "Operational Report for Quarterly Period Ending 31 July 1967"; Chuck Gross, *Rattler One-Seven* (Denton: University of North Texas Press, 2004), 38–39.

41. William Comeau and Capt. Andrew Loflin, "The Battle of Suoi Tre," *Infantry*, Oct.–Dec. 2015, 5–9.

42. NARA, RG 472, P 1173, 26, USARV/4th Infantry Division, G-3, HQ 3d Brigade, May 12, 1967, 1Lt. Jerome Palmer, "Combat Operations After Action Report"; UKNA, FCO 15/482, Saigon, Apr. 20, 1967, Defence Attache, "Operation Junction City"; Maj. Gregory P. Escobar, *A Strategy of Attrition: Why General Westmoreland Failed in 1967* (Ft. Leavenworth, KS: School of Advanced Military Studies, 2016), 9–13; Just, "Saigon and Other Syndromes," 370.

43. UKNA, FCO 15/482, Saigon, Apr. 20, 1967, Defence Attache, Saigon, "Operation Junction City"; James H. Willbanks, *Abandoning Vietnam* (Lawrence: University Press of Kansas, 2004), 280.

44. NARA, RG 472, P 1173, 26, USARV/4th Infantry Division, G-3, HQ 3d Brigade, May 12, 1967, 1Lt. Jerome Palmer, "Combat Operations After Action Report."

45. UKNA, FCO 15/482, Saigon, Apr. 20, 1967, Defence Attache, "Operation Junction City"; NARA, RG 472, MACV, Tet Documents, Box 1, Enemy Strategy Assess. 24 May 68, MACV, J2, Oct. 1967, Maj. Reed, "Degree of Control Exerted in SVN by NVA and COSVN"; RG 472, Summary of Operational Interest Messages, MACV, Box 1, Feb. 28, Mar. 1, 2, 1968, Col. Robert C. Hamilton; Apple, "Vietnam: The Signs of Stalemate"; Escobar, 9–13.

CHAPTER 9. "We'll Just Go On Bleeding Them"

1. National Archives and Records Administration (NARA), RG 472, P 1173, 23, USARV/4th Infantry Division, G-3, Operation Sam Houston Working Papers 1 of 2, 1967, HQ 2nd Brigade, 4th ID, Apr. 20, 1967, Col. James B. Adamson, "Combat After Action Report for Sam Houston."

2. NARA, RG 472, P 1173, 22, USARV/4th Infantry Division, G-3, 22, Operation Sam Houston, 1967, HQ 4th ID, June 20, 1967, Maj. Gen. W. R. Peers, "Operation Sam Houston."

3. NARA, RG 472, P 1173, 22, USARV/4th Infantry Division, G-3, 22, Operation Sam Houston, 1967, HQ 4th ID, June 20, 1967, Maj. Gen. W. R. Peers, "Operation Sam Houston."

4. James T. Gillam, *Life and Death in the Central Highlands* (Denton: University of North Texas Press, 2010), 96–99.

5. Fox Butterfield, "Who Was This Enemy?," in *Reporting Vietnam: American Journalism 1959–1975* (New York: Library of America, 1998), 661–662.

6. UK National Archives (UKNA), DEFE 68/781, Saigon, Sept. 22, 1969, Lt. Col. H. P. Trueman, "Visit 22: Psychological and Political Warfare Staff and Units"; NARA, RG 127, USMC Records, Box 100, HQ MACV, Apr. 25, 1967, Maj. E. W. Gannon, "Monthly Evaluation Report, March 1967"; Charles F. Brower IV, "Strategic Assessment in Vietnam: The Westmoreland 'Alternate Strategy' for 1967–1968," *Naval War College Review* 44, no. 2 (Spring 1991): 21; David M. Barrett, ed., *Lyndon B. Johnson's Vietnam Papers* (College Station: Texas A&M University Press, 1997), 413.

7. "High Cost, Poor Results in Viet Nam War Stimulate Dissent," *CQ Almanac 1967*, 23rd ed. (Washington, DC: Congressional Quarterly, 1968), 07-917-07-925, http://library.cqpress.com/cqalmanac/cqal67-1313128; Guenter Lewy, *America in Vietnam* (New York: Oxford University Press, 1978), 73.

8. Barrett, ed., *LBJ's Vietnam Papers*, 414–418; Kai Bird, *The Color of Truth* (New York: Simon & Schuster, 1998), 360.

9. Bruce E. Altschuler, "Lyndon Johnson and the Public Polls," *Public Opinion Quarterly* 50, no. 3 (Autumn 1986): 288–291; Edwin L. Dale Jr., "What Vietnam Did to the American Economy," *New York Times*, Jan. 28, 1973; "Harris Poll Reports 55% in U.S. Favor Pressing the War," *New York Times*, Feb. 22, 1967.

10. John B. Henry II, "February 1968," *Foreign Policy Quarterly*, Fall 1971, 8–9; Barrett, ed., *LBJ's Vietnam Papers*, 414–415.

11. "High Cost, Poor Results in Viet Nam War Stimulate Dissent"; Brower, 32–34.

12. Brower, 33, 44.

13. NARA, RG 472, MACV, Tet Documents, Box 2, Combined Military Interrogation Center (CMIC) Interrogation Report, Mar. 25, 1967, "Tran Van Kiet Interrogation 8 March 1967: A VC's Opinion of the War in Vietnam."

14. Liddell Hart Centre for Military Archives (LHCMA), MF 809, Reel 1/4, U.S. Armed Forces in Vietnam 1954–1975, Part Four: Vietnam: U.S. Army Senior Debriefing Reports, HQ 9th ID, Feb. 25, 1968, Maj. Gen. George G. O'Connor, "Senior Officer's Debriefing Report: Analysis of 9th Division's Operations in the Delta"; William C. Westmoreland, *A Soldier Reports* (New York: Doubleday, 1976), 207–209.

15. LHCMA, MF 809, Reel 1/4, U.S. Armed Forces in Vietnam 1954–1975, Part Four: Vietnam: U.S. Army Senior Debriefing Reports, HQ 9th ID, Feb. 25,

1968, Maj. Gen. George G. O'Connor, "Senior Officer's Debriefing Report: Analysis of 9th Division's Operations in the Delta."

16. NARA, RG 127, USMC Records, Box 99, HQ MAAG, Oct. 19, 1963, BG Delk Oden, "Lessons Learned No. 32."

17. Gregory P. Escobar, *A Strategy of Attrition: Why General Westmoreland Failed in 1967* (Ft. Leavenworth, KS: School of Advanced Military Studies, 2016), 32–33.

18. NARA, RG 127, USMC Records, Box 99, HQ MACV, Oct. 1965, Col. L. M. Harris, "Monthly Evaluation Report, Sept. 1965."

19. Gregory A. Daddis, *Westmoreland's War* (New York: Oxford University Press, 2014), 87–88; Lewis Sorley, *A Better War* (Boston: Houghton Mifflin, 1999), 8; Frank E. Vandiver, *Shadows of Vietnam* (College Station: Texas A&M University Press, 1997), 224; Lewy, 83.

20. Barrett, ed., *LBJ's Vietnam Papers*, 400–402.

21. UKNA, FCO 15/482, May 8, 1967, D. D. Hall, "MP's Tour of the North, 28 and 29 April"; Barrett, ed., *LBJ's Vietnam Papers*, 400–402.

22. UKNA, FCO 15/482, May 8, 1967, D. D. Hall, "MP's Tour of the North, 28 and 29 April."

23. Martha Gellhorn, "'Suffer the Little Children...," in *Reporting Vietnam, Part One: American Journalism 1959–1969* (New York: Library of America, 1998), 290–293.

24. Robert Mason, *Chickenhawk* (New York: Viking, 1983), 171, 177, 179; UKNA, FCO 15/482, May 8, 1967, D. D. Hall, "MP's Tour of the North, 28 and 29 April."

25. NARA, RG 472, P 1173, 25, USARV/4th Infantry Division, G-3, Operation Greeley Input 1 of 2, STZ 24 Advisory Detachment, Oct. 27, 1967, Col. Eldeen H. Kauffman, Senior Advisor II Corps Tactical Zone to Commander U.S. MACV, "Combat After Action Report," and USARV/4th Infantry Division, G-3, Operation Greeley Input 1 of 2, HQ 5th Bn (Airmobile), 7th Cav, 1st Air Cav Div, July 31, 1967, LTC John A. Wickham Jr., "Operational Report for Quarterly Period Ending 31 July 1967," and USARV/4th Infantry Division, G-3, Operation Greeley Input 1 of 2, Senior Advisor Airborne Division Advisory Detachment (Airborne), Aug. 27, 1967, Maj. Fitzhugh H. Chandler, "Combat Operations After Action Report," www.virtualwall.org/units/hill830.htm.

26. Michael Herr, *Dispatches* (1977; New York: Vintage, 1991), 95–96.

27. Mason, 289.

28. UKNA, DEFE 68/767, Saigon, Sept. 19, 1967, Cdr. A. D. Levy, Lt. Col. K. A. Hill, Wing Cdr. A. T. Vacquier, "Application of Conventional Air Weapons."

29. UKNA, DEFE 68/767, Saigon, Sept. 19, 1967, Cdr. A. D. Levy, Lt. Col. K. A. Hill, Wing Cdr. A. T. Vacquier, "Application of Conventional Air Weapons"; LHCMA, MF 809, Reel 1/4, U.S. Armed Forces in Vietnam 1954–1975, Part Four: Vietnam: U.S. Army Senior Debriefing Reports, HQ U.S. Army Support Command, Saigon, Nov. 9, 1968, Brig. Gen. M. McD. Jones Jr., "Senior Officer

Debriefing Report, July 1, 1967 to Nov. 9, 1968"; Edwin L. Dale Jr., "What Vietnam Did to the American Economy," *New York Times*, Jan. 28, 1973.

30. NARA, RG 472, P 1173, 24, USARV/4th Infantry Division, G-3, Operation Francis Marion—Significant Actions, 1967, HQ 1st Bn, 12th Inf, 2d Brigade, 4th ID, July 28, 1967, LTC Corey Wright, "After Action Report."

31. Ron Milam, *Not a Gentleman's War* (Chapel Hill: University of North Carolina Press, 2009), 140–143; Ronald H. Spector, *After Tet* (New York: Free Press, 1993), 64–70.

32. NARA, RG 472, P 1173, 24, USARV/4th Infantry Division, G-3, Operation Francis Marion—Significant Actions, 1967, HQ 1st Bn, 12th Inf, 2d Brigade, 4th ID, July 28, 1967, LTC Corey Wright, "After Action Report"; Gillam, 28.

33. NARA, RG 472, P 1173, 24, USARV/4th Infantry Division, G-3, Operation Francis Marion—Significant Actions, 1967, HQ 1st Bn, 12th Inf, 2d Brigade, 4th ID, July 28, 1967, LTC Corey Wright, "After Action Report."

34. NARA, RG 472, P 1173, 24, USARV/4th Infantry Division, ACOS, G-3, 24, Operation Francis Marion—Significant Actions, 1967, HQ 1st Bn, 12th Inf, 2d Brigade, 4th ID, July 28, 1967, LTC Corey Wright, "After Action Report," https://redwarriors.us/Casualties_Pictures.htm.

35. Lien-Hang T. Nguyen, *Hanoi's War* (Chapel Hill: University of North Carolina Press, 2012), 94–95.

36. Ang Cheng Guan, "Decision-Making Leading to the Tet Offensive (1968): The Vietnamese Communist Perspective," *Journal of Contemporary History* 33, no. 3 (July 1998): 345–346, 349–350; Nguyen, *Hanoi's War*, 95–96.

37. UKNA, FCO 15/481, Oct. 12, 1967, Brian Stewart, "First Impressions of Hanoi—Oct. 1967."

38. UKNA, FCO 15/481, Zbigniew Soluba, "Two Thousand Kilometers Through Viet Nam," *Politkya* 31 (Aug. 5, 1967); Stanley Karnow, *Vietnam: A History* (New York: Viking, 1983), 454–455.

CHAPTER 10. "Victory Is Around the Corner"

1. Charles F. Brower IV, "Strategic Assessment in Vietnam: The Westmoreland 'Alternate Strategy' for 1967–1968," *Naval War College Review* 44, no. 2 (Spring 1991): 20–21; William C. Westmoreland, *A Soldier Reports* (New York: Doubleday, 1976), 223.

2. National Archives and Records Administration (NARA), RG 472, MACV, TET DOCUMENTS, Box 1, General Offensive and General Uprising (DIA Paper) 1968–69, DIA Working Paper, 10/23/70, "General Offensive and General Uprising (1968–1969)."

3. Deborah Shapley, *Promise and Power* (Boston: Little, Brown, 1993), 416–419, 425.

4. Westmoreland, 226–228.

5. Jeffrey Kimball, *Nixon's Vietnam War* (Lawrence: University Press of Kansas, 1998), 29; David M. Barrett, ed., *Lyndon B. Johnson's Vietnam Papers* (College Station: Texas A&M University Press, 1997), 445, 454, 460–461, 466, 479;

Frank E. Vandiver, *Shadows of Vietnam* (College Station: Texas A&M University Press, 1997), 251.

6. Ingo Trauschweizer, *Maxwell Taylor's Cold War* (Lexington: University Press of Kentucky, 2019), 184–185.

7. Barrett, ed., *LBJ's Vietnam Papers*, 454–455; Lewis Sorley, *A Better War* (Boston: Houghton Mifflin, 1999), 15–16; Brower, 20–51.

8. "High Cost, Poor Results in Viet Nam War Stimulate Dissent," *CQ Almanac 1967*, 23rd ed. (Washington, DC: Congressional Quarterly, 1968), 07-917–07-925, http://library.cqpress.com/cqalmanac/cqal67-1313128; Gregory A. Daddis, *Westmoreland's War* (New York: Oxford University Press, 2014), 88; Gregory A. Daddis, *No Sure Victory* (New York: Oxford University Press, 2011), 128–129.

9. Sean Fear, "Vietnam '67: The Feud That Sank Saigon," *New York Times*, Mar. 3, 2017; Max Boot, *The Road Not Taken* (New York: Norton, 2018), 510; "High Cost, Poor Results in Viet Nam War Stimulate Dissent"; Barrett, ed., *LBJ's Vietnam Papers*, 440, 445.

10. UK National Archives (UKNA), FCO 15/481, Hanoi, June 12, 1967, J. H. R. Colvin, "Power and Factions in the North Vietnamese Regime," and "External Influences on North Vietnamese Power"; Robert K. Brigham, *Guerrilla Diplomacy* (Ithaca, NY: Cornell University Press, 1999), 41–44, 60–61.

11. UKNA, FCO 15/481, Hanoi, Aug. 26, Sept. 8, 1967, John Colvin to Geo. Brown; Lien-Hang T. Nguyen, *Hanoi's War* (Chapel Hill: University of North Carolina Press, 2012), 96–99; Sophie Quinn-Judge, "The Ideological Debate in the DRV and the Significance of the Anti-Party Affair, 1967–68," *Cold War History* 5, no. 4 (Nov. 2005): 490; Ang Cheng Guan, *The Vietnam War from the Other Side* (London: Routledge, 2002), 115–119.

12. UKNA, FCO 15/481, Hanoi, Aug. 8, 1967, John Colvin to Geo. Brown, and London, Aug. 18, 1967, R. A. Fyjis-Walker, "Vietnam: Hanoi Despatch No. 7."

13. UKNA, FCO 15/481, Hanoi, Nov. 28, Dec. 8, 22, 29, 1967, Brian Stewart to Geo. Brown, "Hanoi Observations"; Nguyen, *Hanoi's War*, 98–107.

14. Gregory P. Escobar, *A Strategy of Attrition: Why General Westmoreland Failed in 1967* (Ft. Leavenworth, KS: School of Advanced Military Studies, 2016), 15.

15. UKNA, FCO 15/481, Hanoi, June 12, 1967, J. H. R. Colvin, "Power and Factions in the North Vietnamese Regime," and "External Influences on North Vietnamese Power"; NARA, RG 472, MACV, Tet Documents, Box 1, General Offensive and General Uprising (DIA Paper) 1968–69, DIA Working Paper, 10/23/70, "General Offensive and General Uprising (1968–1969); Nguyen, *Hanoi's War*, 98–109; A. J. Langguth, *Our Vietnam* (New York: Simon & Schuster, 2000), 439–440.

16. Guan, *The Vietnam War from the Other Side*, 120–124.

17. Quinn-Judge, "The Ideological Debate in the DRV," 482–486, 488; Nguyen, *Hanoi's War*, 101–105, 119.

18. UKNA, DEFE 68/758, Saigon, Mar. 14, 1967, Wing Commander A. T. Vacquier, "Communications—Further Details"; NARA, RG 472, P 1173, 25,

USARV/4th Infantry Division, G-3, Operation Greeley Input 1 of 2, HQ 5th Bn (Airmobile), 7th Cav, 1st Air Cav Div, July 31, 1967, LTC John A. Wickham Jr., "Operational Report for Quarterly Period Ending 31 July 1967"; Escobar, 26.

19. Liddell Hart Centre for Military Archives (LHCMA), MF 809, Reel 1/4, U.S. Armed Forces in Vietnam 1954–1975, Part Four: Vietnam: U.S. Army Senior Debriefing Reports, HQ U.S. Army Support Command, Saigon, Nov. 9, 1968, Brig. Gen. M. McD. Jones Jr., "Senior Officer Debriefing Report, July 1, 1967 to Nov. 9, 1968."

20. Andrew F. Krepinevich Jr., *The Army and Vietnam* (Baltimore: Johns Hopkins University Press, 1986), 176.

21. NARA, RG 127, USMC Records, Box 99, HQ MACV, Jan. 27, 1967, Maj. E. W. Gannon, "Counterinsurgency Lessons Learned No. 61"; RG 472, MACV, DCSOPS, Summary of Operational Interest Messages, 14 Sept. 67 thru 30 April 1969, Boxes 1 and 2, Dec. 6, 1967 and Dec. 22, 1968, Col. Robert C. Hamilton and Col. Paul Chmar.

22. "Congress Authorizes Supplemental Viet Nam Funds" and "High Cost, Poor Results in Viet Nam War Stimulate Dissent," *CQ Almanac 1967*, 23rd ed.; "350. Editorial Note," *Foreign Relations of the United States, 1964–1968*, Vol. V, Vietnam, 1967, https://history.state.gov/historicaldocuments/frus1964-68v05/d340.

23. "Address by Benjamin V. Cohen," *Congressional Record—Senate*, Aug. 22, 1967, 23563; NARA, RG 472, MACV, Tet Documents, Box 1, General Offensive and General Uprising (DIA Paper) 1968–69, DIA Working Paper, "General Offensive and General Uprising (1968–1969)."

24. Ronald H. Spector, *After Tet* (New York: Free Press, 1993), 100–102.

25. Shapley, 148.

26. NARA, RG 472, MACV, DCSOPS, Summary of Operational Interest Messages, 14 Sept. 67 thru 31 May 68, Box 1, Oct. 19, 1967, Col. Robert C. Hamilton; Daddis, *Westmoreland's War*, 86; John Ketwig, *And a Hard Rain Fell* (Naperville, IL: Sourcebooks, 2002), 109.

27. Tom Ricks, *The Generals* (New York: Penguin, 2012), 289; Stanley Karnow, *Vietnam: A History* (New York: Viking, 1983), 487–488; Joseph J. Thorndike, "Historical Perspective: Sacrifice and Surcharge," Dec. 5, 2004, taxhistory.org.

28. NARA, RG 472, MACV, DCSOPS, Summary of Operational Interest Messages, 14 Sept. 67 thru 31 May 68, Box 1, Oct. 19, 23, 28, Nov. 10, 15, 18, 20, 24, Dec. 19, 20, 29, 1967, and Mar. 8, May 26, 1968, Col. Robert C. Hamilton.

29. NARA, RG 472, P 1173, 23, USARV/4th Infantry Division, G-3, Operation Sam Houston Working Papers 1 of 2, 1967, HQ 1st Brigade, 4th ID, Apr. 23, 1967, Capt. Norman J. Melton, "Combat Operations After Action Report"; James Webb, *I Heard My Country Calling* (New York: Simon & Schuster, 2014), 264.

30. NARA, RG 127, USMC Records, Box 99, HQ MACV, Jan. 27 and Mar. 11, 1967, Maj. E. W. Gannon and Capt. M. K. Wheeler, "Counterinsurgency Lessons Learned Nos. 61 and 62"; Daddis, *Westmoreland's War*, 100; Escobar, 25.

31. Webb, 253–254, 268.

32. Westmoreland, 201; Gregory A. Daddis, *Withdrawal* (New York: Oxford University Press, 2017), 17–19.

33. Thomas C. Thayer, *A Systems Analysis View of the Vietnam War, 1965–1972* (Washington, DC: OASD, 1975), 8:147; Smithsonian, *A Short History of the Vietnam War* (New York: DK Publishing, 2021), 294.

34. LHCMA, MF 809, Reel 1/4, U.S. Armed Forces in Vietnam 1954–1975, Part Four: Vietnam: U.S. Army Senior Debriefing Reports, HQ Americal Division, June 2, 1968, Maj. Gen. S. W. Koster, "Senior Officer Debriefing Report, Sept 1967–June 1968"; Webb, 262.

35. Krepinevich, 200–201.

36. LHCMA, MF 809, Reel 1/4, U.S. Armed Forces in Vietnam 1954–1975, Part Four: Vietnam: U.S. Army Senior Debriefing Reports, HQ Americal Division, June 2, 1968, Maj. Gen. S. W. Koster, "Senior Officer Debriefing Report, Sept 1967–June 1968."

37. Webb, 280–281.

38. Frederick Downs, *The Killing Zone* (New York: Norton, 2007), 211, 249.

39. Michael Herr, *Dispatches* (1977; New York: Vintage, 1991), 51.

40. Boot, 443; Herr; 172; Norman M. Camp, "U.S. Army Psychiatry in the Vietnam War," *U.S. Army Medical Department Journal*, Apr.–June 2015, 20.

41. Smithsonian, 229.

42. NARA, RG 472, MACV, DCSOPS, Summary of Operational Interest Messages, 14 Sept. 67 thru 31 May 68, Box 1, Oct. 13, Dec. 17, 1967, Col. Robert C. Hamilton; NARA, RG 472, P1173, 22, USARV/4th Infantry Division, G-3, 4 of 4 1966, 2/4th, "Inclosures"; Escobar, 16–17; Guenter Lewy, *America in Vietnam* (New York: Oxford University Press, 1978), 70–73; Robert Mason, *Chickenhawk* (New York: Viking, 1983), 280–281; Ward S. Just, "Saigon and Other Syndromes," in *Reporting Vietnam, Part One: American Journalism 1959–1969* (New York: Library of America, 1998), 351.

43. Lewis Sorley, ed., *The Vietnam War* (Lubbock: Texas Tech University Press, 2010), 466–470.

44. Ang Cheng Guan, "Decision-Making Leading to the Tet Offensive (1968): The Vietnamese Communist Perspective," *Journal of Contemporary History* 33, no. 3 (July 1998): 345–346, 349–350; Jon M. Van Dyke, *North Vietnam's Strategy for Survival* (Palo Alto, CA: Pacific Books, 1972), 218–221; Nguyen, *Hanoi's War*, 90–93.

45. Nguyen, *Hanoi's War*, 90; Don Oberdorfer, *Tet* (1971; Baltimore: Johns Hopkins Univeresity Press, 2001), 42.

46. NARA, RG 472, MACV, Tet Documents, Box 2, Khe Sanh 1968, Apr. 17, 1968, L. R. Vasey and R. J. Hallenbeck, "Fact Sheet on Khe Sanh," and Box 1, General Offensive and General Uprising 1968–69, DIA Working Paper, "General Offensive and General Uprising (1968–1969)."

47. Herr, 48, 103, 105; "Interview with General Tran Van Tra" (1990), www.historynet.com/interview-with-nva-general-tran-van-tra.htm.

48. Jonathan Randal, "U.S. Marines Seize 3d Hill in Vietnam After 12-Day Push," in *Reporting Vietnam* (New York: Library of America, 1998), 201.

49. Westmoreland, 199–200.

50. Webb, 248.

51. NARA, RG 472, MACV, Tet Documents, Box 2, "Battle for Khe Sanh by Capt. Moyers S. Shore, II, USMC," 14; Harry G. Summers Jr., *Historical Atlas of the Vietnam War* (Boston: Houghton Mifflin, 1995), 126; Michael J. Arlen, "A Day in the Life," in *Reporting Vietnam*, 236; Herr, 57.

52. Don North, "Vietnam '67—A Little Piece of Hell," *New York Times*, July 4, 2017; Richard Harwood, "The War Just Doesn't Add Up," in *Reporting Vietnam, Part One*, 488.

53. Jonathan Schell, "A Reporter at Large: Quang Ngai and Quang Tin—I," *New Yorker*, Mar. 9, 1968, 37; Nick Turse, *Kill Anything That Moves* (New York: Metropolitan, 2013), 136–138.

54. NARA, RG 472, A1 60, Bob Hope Christmas Shows 1970–72, Oct. 31, 1970, Capt. Sherman, "Advance Information Sheets for Bob Hope Show."

55. Herr, 12.

56. LHCMA, MF 809, Reel 1/4, U.S. Armed Forces in Vietnam 1954–1975, Part Four: Vietnam: U.S. Army Senior Debriefing Reports, HQ Americal Division, June 2, 1968, Maj. Gen. S. W. Koster, "Senior Officer Debriefing Report, Sept 1967–June 1968"; NARA, RG 472, A1 60, Bob Hope Christmas Shows 1970–72, 1970, Oct. 31, 1970, Maj. Koestring, "Advance Information Sheets for Bob Hope Show"; Herr, 12.

57. David Halberstam, *The Best and the Brightest* (New York: Random House, 1972), 550.

CHAPTER 11. Zenith of Fatuity

1. National Archives and Records Administration (NARA), RG 472, MACV, Tet Documents, Box 2, Press Briefings II, III, & IV CTZ, Apr. 17, 1968, "Press Briefing: 1968 Tet Offensive in II CTZ"; William C. Westmoreland, *A Soldier Reports* (New York: Doubleday, 1976), 150.

2. Amy J. Rutenberg, "How the Draft Reshaped America," *New York Times*, Oct. 6, 2017; Smithsonian, *A Short History of the Vietnam War* (New York: DK Publishing, 2021), 253; David M. Barrett, ed., *Lyndon B. Johnson's Vietnam Papers* (College Station: Texas A&M University Press, 1997), 436, 514, 528.

3. Ron Milam, *Not a Gentleman's War* (Chapel Hill: University of North Carolina Press, 2009), 15–16; Barrett, ed., *LBJ's Vietnam Papers*, 675, 774–776.

4. Barrett, ed., *LBJ's Vietnam Papers*, 528, 553–557; Milam, 15–16.

5. NARA, RG 472, P 1173, 26, USARV/4th Infantry Division, G-3, HQ 4th ID, Jan. 3, 1968, Maj. Gen. W. R. Peers, "Combat Operations After Action Report: Battle for Dak To."

6. NARA, RG 472, P 1173, 26, USARV/4th Infantry Division, G-3, 26, HQ 173d Airborne Brigade (Separate) to 4th ID, Dec. 9, 1967, BG Leo H. Schweitzer, "Combat Operations After Action Report—The Battle of Dak To, Inclosure 7,

Civilian Press Coverage"; John Ketwig, *And a Hard Rain Fell* (Naperville, IL: Sourcebooks, 2002), 59–65.

7. NARA, RG 472, P 1173, 26, USARV/4th Infantry Division, G-3, HQ 4th ID, Jan. 3, 1968, Maj. Gen. W. R. Peers, "Combat Operations After Action Report: Battle for Dak To."

8. "Dak To 1967: '33 Days of Violent, Sustained Combat,'" www.ivydragoons .org/Files/DakTo/vfwdakto032006.pdf.

9. "Dak To 1967: '33 Days of Violent, Sustained Combat.'"

10. UK National Archives (UKNA), DEFE 68/774, Saigon, Feb. 27, 1968, Wing Commander D. Stewart, "Fighter Delivered Weapons and Their Effects in South Vietnam."

11. John Ismay, "At War: The Secret History of a Vietnam Airstrike Gone Terribly Wrong," *New York Times Magazine*, Jan. 31, 2019.

12. "Dak To 1967: '33 Days of Violent, Sustained Combat.'"

13. Peter Arnett, "Dak To: November 1967," in *Reporting Vietnam: American Journalism 1959–1975* (New York: Library of America, 1998), 267–268.

14. NARA, RG 472, P 1173, 26, USARV/4th Infantry Division, G-3, 26, HQ 173d Airborne Brigade (Separate) to 4th ID, Dec. 9, 1967, BG Leo H. Schweitzer, "Combat Operations After Action Report—The Battle of Dak To."

15. NARA, RG 472, P 1173, 26, USARV/4th Infantry Division, G-3, HQ 173d Airborne Brigade (Separate) to 4th ID, Dec. 9, 1967, BG Leo H. Schweitzer, "Combat Operations After Action Report—The Battle of Dak To."

16. NARA, RG 472, P 1173, 26, USARV/4th Infantry Division, G-3, HQ 4th ID, Jan. 3, 1968, Maj. Gen. W. R. Peers, "Combat Operations After Action Report: Battle for Dak To"; Westmoreland, 239, 313.

17. NARA, RG 472, P 1173, 24, USARV/4th Infantry Division, G-3, Operation Francis Marion—Significant Actions, 1967, "Significant Contacts," and HQ 4th ID, Aug. 16, 1967, Maj. Gen. W. R. Peers, "Unit After Action Report of Recent Contact"; "Dak To 1967: '33 Days of Violent, Sustained Combat.'"

18. NARA, RG 472, P 1173, 26, USARV/4th Infantry Division, G-3, HQ 4th ID, Jan. 3, 1968, Maj. Gen. W. R. Peers, "Combat Operations After Action Report: Battle for Dak To"; RG 472, MACV, Tet Documents, Box 1, Enemy Strategy Assess. 24 May 68, MACV, Mar. 20, 1968, Tet Offensive (Update); David Halberstam, "They Can Win a War if Someone Shows Them How," in *Reporting Vietnam*, 53; Stanley Karnow, "Giap Remembers," *New York Times*, June 24, 1990.

19. NARA, RG 472, P 1173, 26, USARV/4th Infantry Division, G-3, HQ 173d Airborne Brigade (Separate) to 4th ID, Dec. 10, 1967, 1Lt. W. L. Kvasnicka, "Combat Operations After Action Report—The Battle of Dak To"; Gregory A. Dadddis, *No Sure Victory* (New York: Oxford University Press, 2011), 229.

20. NARA, RG 472, MACV, Tet Documents, Box 1, Enemy Strategy Assess. 24 May 68, MACV, DOD SEA Analysis Report, Apr. 1968, "US Versus RVNAF Combat Deaths: Corrected Data"; Ketwig, 75.

21. Michael Herr, *Dispatches* (1977; New York: Vintage, 1991), 169.

22. "High Cost, Poor Results in Viet Nam War Stimulate Dissent," *CQ*

Almanac 1967, 23rd ed. (Washington, DC: Congressional Quarterly, 1968), 07-917–07-925, http://library.cqpress.com/cqalmanac/cqal67-1313128; NARA, RG 472, MACV, Summary of Operational Interest Messages, 14 Sept. 67 thru 31 May 68, Box 1, Oct. 12, Nov. 16, 1967, Jan. 25, Feb. 29, Mar. 7, 21, May 5, 30, June 23, Aug. 28, Oct. 31, 1968, Jan. 1, 1969, Col. Robert C. Hamilton, Col. Paul Chmar; Guenter Lewy, *America in Vietnam* (New York: Oxford University Press, 1978), 73; R. W. Apple Jr., "Vietnam: The Signs of Stalemate," *New York Times*, Aug. 7, 1967.

23. Stanley Karnow, *Vietnam: A History* (New York: Viking, 1983), 489–491.

24. UKNA, FCO 7/778, United States, July 16, 1968, Patrick Dean to Michael Stewart, "Neo-Isolationism."

25. Karnow, 488; Herr, 95.

26. Richard Harwood, "The War Just Doesn't Add Up," in *Reporting Vietnam, Part One: American Journalism 1959–1969* (New York: Library of America, 1998), 486–487; Geoffrey Ward and Ken Burns, *The Vietnam War* (New York: Knopf, 2017), 193.

27. Harry G. Summers Jr., *Historical Atlas of the Vietnam War* (Boston: Houghton Mifflin, 1995), 138.

28. NARA, RG 472, MACV, Summary of Operational Interest Messages, 14 Sept. 67 thru 31 May 68, Box 1, Jan. 2, 1968, Col. Robert C. Hamilton; Lewy, 66, 74–75.

29. "High Cost, Poor Results in Viet Nam War Stimulate Dissent."

30. Liddell Hart Centre for Military Archives (LHCMA), U.S. Armed Forces in Vietnam 1954–1975, MF 792, Reel 1, Brig. Gen. Tran Dinh Tho, *The Cambodian Incursion*, Indochina Monographs (Washington, DC: U.S. Army Center of Military History, 1979), preface, 10.

31. NARA, RG 472, MACV, DCSOPS, Summary of Operational Interest Messages, 14 Sept. 67 thru 31 May 68, Box 1, Dec. 31, 1967, Col. Robert C. Hamilton.

32. NARA, RG 472, MACV, Summary of Operational Interest Messages, 14 Sept. 67 thru 31 May 68, Box 1, Dec. 31, 1967, Feb. 29, Apr. 19, May 1, 3, 1968, Col. Robert C. Hamilton, and 1 June 68 thru 30 April 69, Box 2, Nov. 5, Dec. 5, 1968, Col. Paul Chmar; Lewy, 74.

33. Michell Owens, "Madame Nhu Almost Slept Here," *New York Times Magazine*, Jan. 12, 2003.

34. Apple, "Vietnam: The Signs of Stalemate"; "High Cost, Poor Results in Viet Nam War Stimulate Dissent."

35. Ronald H. Spector, *After Tet* (New York: Free Press, 1993), 197–198.

36. Gregory A. Daddis, *Westmoreland's War* (New York: Oxford University Press, 2017), 107–108.

37. Jonathan Schell, "From *The Military Half: An Account of the Destruction in Quang Ngai and Quang Tin*," in *Reporting Vietnam*, 204–207; "Vietnam War: Domestic Impact," *CQ Almanac 1970*, 26th ed. (Washington, DC: Congressional Quarterly, 1971), 04-962–04-964, http://library.cqpress.com/cqalmanac/cqal70 -1292128.

38. Spector, 215–216.

39. Ward S. Just, "Saigon and Other Syndromes," in *Reporting Vietnam, Part One*, 356; Jerry M. Silverman, "Vietnam: Official United States Reporting and the Credibility Gap," paper presented at the annual meeting of the American Political Science Association, Los Angeles, Sept. 8–12, 1970, 1; Lewy, 75; Max Boot, *The Road Not Taken* (New York: Norton, 2018), 474; Richard Harwood, "The War Just Doesn't Add Up," in *Reporting Vietnam, Part One*, 486.

40. Frederick Downs, *The Killing Zone* (New York: Norton, 2007), 202; Schell, "From *The Military Half*," 454; "Their Lions—Our Rabbits," *Newsweek*, Oct. 9, 1967, 44–50; James Landers, *The Weekly War: Newsmagazines and Vietnam* (Columbia: University of Missouri Press, 2004), 250–251; Spector, 100.

41. UKNA, FCO 15/482, Saigon, Nov. 6, 1967, Jenkin Thomas to David Waterstone, "Round-Up Letter."

42. Barrett, ed., *LBJ's Vietnam Papers*, 551; Daddis, *Westmoreland's War*, 159; Spector, 115–116.

43. NARA, RG 472, MACV, Tet Documents, Box 1, Enemy Strategy Assess. 24 May 68, MACV, DOD SEA Analysis Report, Apr. 1968, "RVNAF Status—CY 1967."

44. NARA, RG 472, MACV, Tet Documents, Box 1, Enemy Strategy Assess. 24 May 68, MACV, DOD SEA Analysis Report, Apr. 1968, "RVNAF Status—CY 1967"; NARA, RG 472, MACV, Tet Documents, Box 1, Enemy Strategy Assess. 24 May 68, MACV, DOD SEA Analysis Report, Apr. 1968, "US Versus RVNAF Combat Deaths: Corrected Data"; UKNA, FCO 15/482, Saigon, Nov. 6, 22, Dec. 6, 13, 1967, Jenkin Thomas to David Waterstone, "Round-Up Letter."

45. Herr, 46–47; Tom Wolfe, "The Truest Sport: Jousting with Sam and Charlie," in *Reporting Vietnam, Part One*, 533–538; Walter J. Boyne, "Route Pack 6," *Air and Space Forces Magazine*, Nov. 1, 1999; Ed Rasimus, *Palace Cobra* (New York: St. Martin's, 2006), 152; Lewis Sorley, *A Better War* (Boston: Houghton Mifflin, 1999), 196.

46. UKNA, FCO 15/482, Saigon, Mar. 20, 1968, Robert Cormack to P. Heap, "Round-Up Letter," and Saigon, Dec. 13, 20, 1967, Jenkin Thomas to David Waterstone, "Round-Up Letter."

47. UKNA, FCO 15/482, Saigon, Mar. 20, 1968, Robert Cormack to P. Heap, "Round-Up Letter," and Saigon, Dec. 13, 20, 1967, Jenkin Thomas to David Waterstone, "Round-Up Letter"; Sorley, *Better War*, 14–15.

48. NARA, RG 472, MACV, Summary of Operational Interest Messages, 14 Sept. 67 thru 31 May 68, Box 1, Mar. 20 and May 31, 1968, Col. Robert C. Hamilton and LTC Richard J. Uzee.

49. UKNA, FCO 15/482, Saigon, Jan. 4 and Feb. 1, 1967, Buxton and Thomas to Waterstone, "Weekly Round-Up"; Frank E. Vandiver, *Shadows of Vietnam* (College Station: Texas A&M University Press, 1997), 264.

50. Lien-Hang T. Nguyen, *Hanoi's War* (Chapel Hill: University of North Carolina Press, 2012), 107–108, 120.

51. Richard Helms, *A Look over My Shoulder* (New York: Random House,

2003), 331–332; UKNA, FCO 15/481, Saigon, Jan. 27, 1968, "Special Political Adviser, Brian Stewart, Visit to Hanoi, Jan. 9–20."

52. NARA, RG 472, MACV, Summary of Operational Interest Messages, 14 Sept. 67 thru 31 May 68, Box 1, Sept. 24, 26, Oct. 26, Dec. 5, 1967, Col. Robert C. Hamilton; Barrett, ed., *LBJ's Vietnam Papers*, 529–530; Richard A. Hunt, *Pacification* (London: Routledge, 1998), 70–71.

53. UKNA, FCO 15/482, Saigon, May 9, 1967, Thomas to Waterstone, "Round-Up Letter"; DEFE 68/810, Saigon, Dec. 14, 1967, Lt. Col. D. B. Wood, "Pacification"; LHMCA, MF 803, Reel 8/8, U.S. Armed Forces in Vietnam 1954–1975, Part Two, Vietnam: Lessons Learned, Vol. 6, "Conduct of the War" 141; "The CIA Report the President Doesn't Want You to Read: The Pike Papers, Highlights from the Suppressed House Intelligence Committee Report," *Village Voice*, Mar. 1, 2001; George W. Allen, *None So Blind* (New York: Ivan Dee, 2001); Kai Bird, *The Color of Truth* (New York: Simon & Schuster, 1998), 348.

54. Rudy Abramson, "Westmoreland to Drop Libel Suit Against CBS," *Los Angeles Times*, Feb. 18, 1985; Vandiver, 257–258.

55. LHMCA, MF 803, Reel 8/8, U.S. Armed Forces in Vietnam 1954–1975, Part Two, Vietnam: Lessons Learned, Vol. 6, "Conduct of the War," 81–83; Barrett, ed., *LBJ's Vietnam Papers*, 535–537, 552–554; Jeffrey Record, *The Wrong War* (Annapolis, MD: Naval Institute Press, 1998), 82–85; Bird, 363–364.

56. Helms, 324–328; William Colby, *Lost Victory* (Chicago: Contemporary, 1999), 184–185; Herr, 51–52; Gregory A. Daddis, *Withdrawal* (New York: Oxford University Press, 2017), 29–30.

57. NARA, RG 472, MACV, Tet Documents, Box 2, CIA Memo—Participating Communist Units, Feb. 1968, "Communist Units Participating in Attacks During the Tet Offensive, 30 January Through 13 February 1968"; Westmoreland, 230–235.

58. LHMCA, MF 803, Reel 8/8, U.S. Armed Forces in Vietnam 1954–1975, Part Two, Vietnam: Lessons Learned, Vol. 6, "Conduct of the War," 84; Vandiver, 261–262, 267; Tom Buckley, "Portrait of an Aging Despot," in *Reporting Vietnam*, 543; Barrett, ed., *LBJ's Vietnam Papers*, 541; Ketwig, 106.

59. Deborah Shapley, *Promise and Power* (Boston: Little, Brown, 1993), 408–409, 426–427.

60. Barrett, ed. *LBJ's Vietnam Papers*, 516, 526, 529, 531, 545–546, 554–556; John B. Henry II, "February, 1968," *Foreign Policy Quarterly*, Fall 1971, 31–32; Vandiver, 264; LHMCA, MF 803, Reel 8/8, U.S. Armed Forces in Vietnam 1954–1975, Part Two, Vietnam: Lessons Learned, Vol. 6, "Conduct of the War," 84; Ketwig, 106.

CHAPTER 12. Year of the Monkey

1. Ang Cheng Guan, *The Vietnam War from the Other Side* (London: Routledge, 2002), 120–126.

2. Ang Cheng Guan, "Decision-Making Leading to the Tet Offensive (1968): The Vietnamese Communist Perspective," *Journal of Contemporary History* 33, no. 3 (July 1998): 345–346, 349–351; National Archives and Records Administration

(NARA), RG 472, MACV, Tet Documents, Box 1, General Offensive and General Uprising (DIA Paper) 1968–69, DIASIS 33C-68, Feb. 2, 1968, "DIA Intelligence Summary"; Harry G. Summers Jr., *Historical Atlas of the Vietnam War* (Boston: Houghton Mifflin, 1995), 138; Smithsonian, *A Short History of the Vietnam War* (New York: DK Publishing, 2021), 262–263.

3. NARA, RG 472, MACV, Tet Documents, Box 2, AAR—Battle of Hue, 1st Cav Div., "Enemy Document Captured April 25, 1968."

4. Guan, "Decision-Making," 351; Stanley Karnow, "Giap Remembers," *New York Times*, June 24, 1990.

5. Karnow, "Giap Remembers"; James T. Gillam, *Life and Death in the Central Highlands* (Denton: University of North Texas Press, 2010), 2–4.

6. NARA, RG 472, A1 38, Box 1, "Sphinx" Intelligence Summaries, MACV, INTSUM, Jan. 4, 13, 15, 1966; RG 472, MACV, Tet Documents, Box 2, AAR—Battle of Hue, 1st Cav Div., Jan. 6, 1968, MACV, "Documents Captured on 23 December."

7. NARA, RG 472, MACV, Tet Documents, Box 2, AAR—Battle of Hue, 1st Cav Div., Jan. 2, 1968, JCS to CINCPAC, MACV.

8. William C. Westmoreland, *A Soldier Reports* (New York: Doubleday, 1976), 310; Norman Lewis, *A Dragon Apparent* (1951; London: Eland, 1982), 167.

9. NARA, RG 472, MACV, Tet Documents, Box 2, AAR—Battle of Hue, 1st Cav Div., Jan. 7, 17, 1968, CINCPAC to MACV and JCS, "TET Standown" and "TET Ceasefire"; David M. Barrett, ed., *Lyndon B. Johnson's Vietnam Papers* (College Station: Texas A&M University Press, 1997), 570.

10. NARA, RG 472, MACV, Tet Documents, Box 2, AAR—Battle of Hue, 1st Cav Div., "Enemy Document Captured April 25, 1968."

11. NARA, RG 472, MACV, Tet Documents, Box 1, General Offensive and General Uprising (DIA Paper) 1968–69, "DIA Working Paper."

12. NARA, RG 472, MACV, Tet Documents, Box 2, Order of Battle Feb. 68, OJCS, Jan. 25, 1968, "Combat Forces."

13. NARA, RG 472, MACV, Tet Documents, Box 2, "Battle for Khe Sanh by Capt. Moyers S. Shore, II, USMC," 31, 44; Summers, *Atlas*, 138.

14. Michael Herr, *Dispatches* (1977; New York: Vintage, 1991), 104; Barrett, ed., *LBJ's Vietnam Papers*, 570–571.

15. NARA, RG 472, MACV, Summary of Operational Interest Messages, 14 Sept. 67 thru 31 May 68, Box 1, Jan. 30, 1968, Col. Robert C. Hamilton; RG 472, MACV, Tet Documents, Box 2, II FFV, LTC David Hughes, "II Field Force, G-3 Briefing, 20 March 1968."

16. Barrett, ed., *LBJ's Vietnam Papers*, 576, 615.

17. Barrett, ed., *LBJ's Vietnam Papers*, 615; NARA, RG 472, MACV, Tet Documents, Box 2, "Battle for Khe Sanh by Capt. Moyers S. Shore, II, USMC," 56–59.

18. NARA, RG 472, MACV, Tet Documents, Box 2, "The Battle for Khe Sanh," Washington, DC, Mar. 29, 1969, Gen. W. C. Westmoreland (Army CS) to Gen. L. F. Chapman Jr. (Commandant, USMC); Ward S. Just, "Reconnaissance," in *Reporting Vietnam: American Journalism 1959-1975* (New York: Library of America, 1998),

150–151; Gregory A. Daddis, *Westmoreland's War* (New York: Oxford University Press, 2014), 122.

19. NARA, RG 472, MACV, Tet Documents, Box 2, "Battle for Khe Sanh by Capt. Moyers S. Shore, II, USMC," 34–35.

20. Wiliam A. Barry, "Air Power in the Siege of Khe Sanh," HistoryNet, Aug. 1, 2007, www.historynet.com/air-power-in-the-siege-of-khe-sanh.htm.

21. NARA, RG 472, MACV, Tet Documents, Box 2, Khe Sanh, Apr. 17, 1968, L. R. Vasey and R. J. Hallenbeck, "Fact Sheet on Khe Sanh," and "Battle for Khe Sanh by Capt. Moyers S. Shore, II, USMC," 67; Herr, 106; Frank E. Vandiver, *Shadows of Vietnam* (College Station: Texas A&M University Press, 1997), 270.

22. NARA, RG 472, MACV, Tet Documents, Box 2, CIA Memo—Participating Communist Units, Feb. 1968, "Communist Units Participating in Attacks During the Tet Offensive, 30 January Through 13 February 1968." The CIA released an interim report on Apr. 8, 1968, titled "Intelligence Warning of the Tet Offensive in South Vietnam": https://2001-2009.state.gov/r/pa/ho/frus/johnsonlb/vi/13689 .htm.

23. NARA, RG 472, MACV, Tet Documents, Box 2, AAR—Battle of Hue, 1st Cav Div., Jan. 2, 1968, MACV to NAVINTCOM, and American Division HQ, Apr. 5, 1968, Maj. Gen. Samuel W. Koster, "Combat Action Report"; NARA, RG 472, MACV, Summary of Operational Interest Messages, 14 Sept. 67 thru 31 May 68, Box 1, Oct. 28, 1967, Col. Robert C. Hamilton.

24. NARA, RG 472, MACV, Tet Documents, Box 2, CIA Memo, Feb. 1968, "Communist Units Participating in Attacks During the Tet Offensive, 30 January Through 13 February 1968."

25. Daddis, *Westmoreland's War*, 140.

26. NARA, RG 472, MACV, Tet Documents, Box 2, Defense of Saigon, Project CHECO [Contemporary Historical Evaluation of Combat Operations] Report, Dec. 14, 1968, Maj. A. W. Thompson, "The Defense of Saigon," 1; Summers, *Atlas*, 132.

27. NARA, RG 472, MACV, Summary of Operational Interest Messages, 14 Sept. 67 thru 31 May 68, Box 1, Jan. 30, 1968, Col. Robert C. Hamilton; Tom Glenn, "Vietnam '67: Was the Tet Offensive Really a Surprise?," *New York Times*, Nov. 3, 2017.

28. Neil Sheehan, *A Bright Shining Lie* (New York: Vintage, 1989), 703; David Halberstam, *The Best and the Brightest* (New York: Random House, 1972), 561.

29. Ronald H. Spector, *After Tet* (New York: Free Press, 1993), 159.

30. NARA, RG 472, MACV, Tet Documents, Box 2, Combined Military Interrogation Center (CMIC) Report, Feb. 25, 1968, "ARVN Interrogation Report of Tran Van An on 1 Feb. 1968," and II FF, LTC David Hughes, "II Field Force, G-3 Briefing, 20 March 1968."

31. NARA, RG 472, MACV, Tet Documents, Box 2, AAR—Battle of Hue, 1st Cav Div., "Enemy Document Captured April 25, 1968," and CIA Memo, Feb. 1968, "Communist Units Participating in Attacks During the Tet Offensive, 30 January

Through 13 February 1968"; Don Oberdorfer, *Tet!* (1971; Baltimore: Johns Hopkins University Press, 2001), 214.

32. Oberdorfer, 204.

33. NARA, RG 472, MACV, Tet Documents, Box 2, AAR—Battle of Hue, 1st Cav Div., "Enemy Document Captured April 25, 1968"; Daddis, *Westmoreland's War*, 140–141.

CHAPTER 13. Tet

1.   National Archives and Records Administration (NARA), RG 472, MACV, Tet Documents, Box 2, Press Briefings II, III, & IV CTZ, Apr. 17, 1968, "Press Briefing: 1968 Tet Offensive in II CTZ."

2.   John Ketwig, *And a Hard Rain Fell* (Naperville, IL: Sourcebooks, 2002), 100–102.

3.   NARA, RG 472, MACV, Tet Documents, Box 2, Army Aviation, HQ USARV, Long Binh, Apr. 17, 1968, LTC Charles D. Franklin, "Helicopter Gunships," and Apr. 17, 1968, "Press Briefing: 1968 Tet Offensive in II CTZ"; RG 472, MACV, Summary of Operational Interest Messages, 14 Sept. 67 thru 31 May 68, Box 1, Feb. 28, 1968, Mar. 1, 2, 1968, Col. Robert C. Hamilton; Don Oberdorfer, *Tet!* (1971; Baltimore: Johns Hopkins University Press, 2001), 129.

4.   NARA, RG 472, MACV, Tet Documents, Box 2, Press Briefings, II, III, & IV CTZ, Apr. 1968, "III CTZ TET Offensive Briefing—15 Minute Version," and Box 1, Misc. Messages Jan–May 68, MACV, Jan. 31, 1968, Amb. Bunker to Sec State, "Sitrep: I Corps."

5.   NARA, RG 472, MACV, Tet Documents, Box 1, Misc. Messages Jan–May 68, MACV, CIA to White House, etc., Mar. 17, 1968, "Assessment of Gen. Thang's Performance as IV Corps Commander."

6.   NARA, RG 472, MACV, Tet Documents, Box 2, Press Briefings II, III, & IV CTZ, HQ Advisory Team 96, Apr. 8, 1968, Capt. L. E. Lyons, "Historical Summary of VC Tet Offensive IV CTZ," and Box 1, RVNAF Performance During TET, MACV to JCS, CINCPAC, Mar. 21, 1968, "Assessment of RVNAF Status as of 29 Feb 68"; Ronald H. Spector, *After Tet* (New York: Free Press, 1993), 104, 145.

7.   NARA, RG 472, MACV, Tet Documents, Box 2, Press Briefings II, III, & IV CTZ, HQ Advisory Team 96, Apr. 8, 1968, Capt. L. E. Lyons, "Historical Summary of VC Tet Offensive IV CTZ."

8.   NARA, RG 472, MACV, Tet Documents, Box 2, II FFV, LTC David Hughes, "II Field Force, G-3 Briefing, 20 March 1968," and Box 2, Defense of Saigon, Project CHECO [Contemporary Historical Evaluation of Combat Operations] Report, Dec. 14, 1968, Maj. A. W. Thompson, "The Defense of Saigon," 2; William C. Westmoreland, *A Soldier Reports* (New York: Doubleday, 1976), 319, 323.

9.   NARA, RG 472, MACV, Tet Documents, Box 2, Press Briefings II, III, & IV CTZ, HQ Advisory Team 96, Apr. 8, 1968, Capt. L. E. Lyons, "Historical Summary of VC Tet Offensive IV CTZ," and Army Aviation, HQ USARV, Long Binh, Apr. 17, 1968, LTC Charles D. Franklin, "Helicopter Gunships"; RG 472, MACV, Summary

of Operational Interest Messages, 14 Sept. 67 thru 31 May 68, Box 1, Feb. 28, 1968, Mar. 1, 2, 1968, Col. Robert C. Hamilton.

10. Tom Ricks, *The Generals* (New York: Penguin, 2012), 287–288.

11. NARA, RG 472, MACV, Tet Documents, Box 2, Press Briefings II, III, & IV CTZ, Apr. 1968, "III CTZ: Tet Offensive Briefing."

12. NARA, RG 472, MACV, Tet Documents, Box 1, General Offensive and General Uprising (DIA Paper) 1968–69, MACV to Army Operations Center (AOC), Jan. 30–31, 1968, Maj. Marini; NARA, RG 472, MACV, Tet Documents, Box 2, II FFV, LTC David Hughes, "II Field Force, G-3 Briefing, 20 March 1968," and HQ 101st Airborne Division, Apr. 28, 1968, Maj. Gen. Olinto M. Barsanti, "Combat After Action Report."

13. David M. Barrett, ed., *Lyndon B. Johnson's Vietnam Papers* (College Station: Texas A&M University Press, 1997), 583.

14. NARA, RG 472, MACV, Tet Documents, Box 2, National Police, Saigon, Mar. 1, 1968, "Performance of Police in Saigon DURING ATTACK."

15. Tom Buckley, "Portrait of an Aging Despot," in *Reporting Vietnam: American Journalism 1959–1975* (New York: Library of America, 1998), 546–547.

16. NARA, RG 472, MACV, Tet Documents, Box 2, II FFV, LTC David Hughes, "II Field Force, G-3 Briefing, 20 March 1968," and HQ 101st Airborne Division, Apr. 28, 1968, Maj. Gen. Olinto M. Barsanti, "Combat After Action Report."

17. NARA, RG 472, MACV, Tet Documents, Box 2, Press Briefings II, III, & IV CTZ, Apr. 1968, "III CTZ: Tet Offensive Briefing"; Smithsonian, *A Short History of the Vietnam War* (New York: DK Publishing, 2021), 275.

18. NARA, RG 472, MACV, Tet Documents, Box 2, Army Aviation, HQ USARV, Long Binh, Apr. 17, 1968, LTC Charles D. Franklin, "Helicopter Gunships," and HQ 101st Airborne Division, Apr. 28, 1968, Maj. Gen, Olinto M. Barsanti, "Combat After Action Report," and COMUS MACV Field Visits, CG II IIFV, Feb. 9, 1968, "Visit of COMUSMACV."

19. NARA, RG 472, MACV, Tet Documents, Box 2, Phu Loi Base Camp Attack, HQ 1st ID, Feb. 11, 1968, Maj. Richard W. Wilmot, "Attack on Phu Loi Base Camp, 31 January to 7 February 1968."

20. NARA, RG 472, MACV, Tet Documents, Box 2, II FFV, LTC David Hughes, "II Field Force, G-3 Briefing, 20 March 1968."

21. NARA, RG 472, MACV, Tet Documents, Box 2, II FFV, LTC David Hughes, "II Field Force, G-3 Briefing, 20 March 1968."

22. NARA, RG 472, MACV, Tet Documents, Box 2, Defense of Saigon, Project CHECO [Contemporary Historical Evaluation of Combat Operations] Report, Dec. 14, 1968, Maj. A. W. Thompson, "The Defense of Saigon," 2–3, and HQ 101st Airborne Division, Apr. 28, 1968, Maj. Gen. Olinto M. Barsanti, "Combat After Action Report"; RG 472, MACV, Summary of Operational Interest Messages, 14 Sept. 67 thru 31 May 68, Box 1, Apr. 21, 1968, Col. Robert C. Hamilton.

23. NARA, RG 472, MACV, Tet Documents, Box 2, II FFV, LTC David Hughes,

"II Field Force, G-3 Briefing, 20 March 1968"; Gregory A. Daddis, *Westmoreland's War* (New York: Oxford University Press, 2014), 164.

24. Bernard B. Fall, "Vietnam Blitz: A Report on the Impersonal War," in *Reporting Vietnam*, 115; NARA, RG 472, MACV, Tet Documents, Box 2, HQ 1st ID, Feb. 11, 1968, Maj. Richard W. Wilmot, "Attack on Phu Loi Base Camp, 31 January to 7 February 1968"; John B. Henry II, "February 1968," *Foreign Policy*, Fall 1971, 3–7.

25. Barrett, ed., *LBJ's Vietnam Papers*, 598.

26. Don Oberdorfer, "From *Tet!*," in *Reporting Vietnam*, 305–306.

27. NARA, RG 472, MACV, Tet Documents, Box 2, AAR—Battle of Hue, 1st Cav Div, HQ Provisional Corps Vietnam, Aug. 1968, 31st Military History Detachment, Maj. Miles D. Waldron, "Historical Study 2-68: Operation Hue City."

28. NARA, RG 472, MACV, Tet Documents, Box 2, AAR—Battle of Hue, 1st Cav Div, HQ Provisional Corps Vietnam, Aug. 1968, 31st Military History Detachment, Maj. Miles D. Waldron, "Historical Study 2-68: Operation Hue City."

29. NARA, RG 472, MACV, Tet Documents, Box 2, AAR—Battle of Hue, 1st Cav Div, HQ Provisional Corps Vietnam, Aug. 1968, 31st Military History Detachment, Maj. Miles D. Waldron, "Historical Study 2-68: Operation Hue City."

30. Westmoreland, 329–331.

31. NARA, RG 472, MACV, Tet Documents, Box 2, AAR—Battle of Hue, 1st Cav Div, Mar. 10, 1968, 1st Cav Division (AM), 14th Military History Detachment, "The Battle of Hue, 2–26 February 1968," and II FFV, LTC David Hughes, "II Field Force, G-3 Briefing, 20 March 1968," and Defense of Saigon, Project CHECO [Contemporary Historical Evaluation of Combat Operations] Report, Dec. 14, 1968, Maj. A. W. Thompson, "The Defense of Saigon," 2.

32. Oberdorfer, 230–234.

33. NARA, RG 472, MACV, Tet Documents, Box 2, AAR—Battle of Hue, 1st Cav Div., Mar. 10 and Aug. 16, 1968, 1st Cav Division (AM), 14th Military History Detachment, "The Battle of Hue, 2–26 February 1968," and 1st Cav Div., "Enemy Document Captured April 25, 1968"; Oberdorfer, "From *Tet!*," 303, 311.

34. Oberdorfer, "From *Tet!*," 308–309.

35. Michael Herr, *Dispatches* (1977; New York: Vintage, 1991), 73.

36. Barrett, ed., *LBJ's Vietnam Papers*, 586–587, 601–605; Henry, 3–7.

37. NARA, RG 472, MACV, Tet Documents, Box 1, DIA Working Paper, "General Offensive and General Uprising (1968–1969)."

38. Herr, 78, 81.

39. NARA, RG 472, MACV, Tet Documents, Box 2, AAR—Battle of Hue, 1st Cav Div (AM), Mar. 10, 1968, 14th Military History Detachment, "The Battle of Hue, 2–26 February 1968."

40. Herr, 83.

41. NARA, RG 472, MACV, Tet Documents, Box 2, AAR—Battle of Hue, 1st Cav Div (AM), Mar. 10, 1968, 1st Cav Division, 14th Military History Detachment, "The Battle of Hue, 2–26 February 1968."

CHAPTER 14. "We Can Keep On Winning the War Forever"

1. National Archives and Records Administration (NARA), RG 472, MACV, Tet Documents, Box 1, Misc. Messages Jan–May 68, MACV, Feb. 25, 1968, CIA to White House, MACV, etc., "General Khang on Military/Political Situation."

2. David M. Barrett, ed., *Lyndon B. Johnson's Vietnam Papers* (College Station: Texas A&M University Press, 1997), 617–618.

3. Barrett, ed., *LBJ's Vietnam Papers*, 584, 600–601, 624–625; Sydney H. Schanberg, "The Saigon Follies, or, Trying to Head Them Off at Credibility Gap," in *Reporting Vietnam, Part Two: American Journalism 1969–1975* (New York: Library of America, 1998), 400; Smithsonian, *A Short History of the Vietnam War* (New York: DK Publishing, 2021), 263; Gregory A. Daddis, *Westmoreland's War* (New York: Oxford University Press, 2014), 141.

4. John B. Henry II, "February 1968," *Foreign Policy Quarterly*, Fall 1971, 12–13; Charles F. Brower IV, "Strategic Assessment in Vietnam: The Westmoreland 'Alternate Strategy' for 1967–1968," *Naval War College Review* 44, no. 2 (Spring 1991): 36–37.

5. William C. Westmoreland, *A Soldier Reports* (New York: Doubleday, 1976), 272; Henry, 12–13.

6. "A Creeping Doubt: Public Support for the Vietnam War in 1967," Roper Center, Aug. 16, 2017, https://ropercenter.cornell.edu/blog/creeping-doubt-public-support-vietnam-1967.

7. Tom Ricks, *The Generals* (New York: Penguin, 2012), 258.

8. Henry, 3–7.

9. Ricks, 257–258.

10. Barrett, ed., *LBJ's Vietnam Papers*, 612; Henry, 19; Westmoreland, 350–356.

11. Kyle Longley, *LBJ's 1968* (Cambridge: Cambridge University Press, 2018), 39–40.

12. Jeffrey Record, *The Wrong War* (Annapolis, MD: Naval Institute Press, 1998), 146; Brower, 33.

13. Barrett, ed., *LBJ's Vietnam Papers*, 610; Brower, 43–44.

14. Barrett, ed., *LBJ's Vietnam Papers*, 591–598, 612–613; Henry, 10–14.

15. Liddell Hart Centre for Military Archives (LHMCA), MF 803, Reel 8/8, U.S. Armed Forces in Vietnam 1954–1975, Part Two, Vietnam: Lessons Learned, Vol. 6, "Conduct of the War," 81–83.

16. NARA, RG 472, MACV, Tet Documents, Box 1, Enemy Strategy Assess. 24 May 68, MACV, Mar. 20, 1968, Tet Offensive (Update); NARA, RG 472, MACV, Tet Documents, Box 2, CIA Memo, Feb. 1968, "Communist Units Participating in Attacks During the Tet Offensive, 30 January Through 13 February 1968."

17. UK National Archives (UKNA), DEFE 68/807, Saigon, Nov. 22, 1966, Lt. Col. D. B. Wood, "Casualty Statistics"; NARA, RG 472, MACV, Tet Documents, Box 1, General Offensive and General Uprising (DIA Paper) 1968–69, DIASIS 34A-68, Feb. 3, 1968, "DIA Intelligence Summary"; Smithsonian, 249.

18. NARA, RG 472, MACV, Tet Documents, Box 2, Press Briefings II, III, & IV CTZ, Apr. 17, 1968, "Press Briefing: 1968 Tet Offensive in II CTZ," and II FFV, LTC David Hughes, "II Field Force, G-3 Briefing, 20 March 1968"; RG 472, MACV, Summary of Operational Interest Messages, 1 June 68 thru 30 April 69, Box 2, Dec. 8, 21, 1968, Jan. 6, Feb. 1, 1969, Col. Paul Chmar, LTC John Watkins Jr.

19. NARA, RG 472, MACV, Tet Documents, Box 1, Misc. Messages Jan–May 68, MACV, Feb. 2, 1968, CIA to White House, MACV, etc., "ARVN Officer on the Viet Cong Offensive"; Daddis, *Westmoreland's War*, 136; Robert Buzzanco, *Masters of War* (Cambridge: Cambridge University Press, 1996), 331; John Ketwig, *And a Hard Rain Fell* (Naperville, IL: Sourcebooks, 2002), 111.

20. NARA, RG 472, MACV, Tet Documents, Box 2, Press Briefings II, III, & IV CTZ, HQ Advisory Team 96, Apr. 8, 1968, Capt. L. E. Lyons, "Historical Summary of VC Tet Offensive IV CTZ."

21. NARA, RG 472, MACV, Tet Documents, Box 2, Press Briefings II, III, & IV CTZ, May 18, 1968, MACCORDS Fact Sheet, "Operation Recovery."

22. NARA, RG 472, MACV, Tet Documents, Box 2, Press Briefings II, III, & IV CTZ, May 18, 1968, MACCORDS Fact Sheet, "Operation Recovery," and HQ Advisory Team 96, Apr. 8, 1968, Capt. L.E. Lyons, "Historical Summary of VC Tet Offensive IV CTZ."

23. NARA, RG 472, MACV, Tet Documents, Box 2, Press Briefings II, III, & IV CTZ, May 18, 1968, MACCORDS Fact Sheet, "Operation Recovery"; RG 472, MACV, Tet Documents, Box 1, General Offensive and General Uprising (DIA Paper) 1968–69, "From: The Viet-Cong 'TET' Offensive (1968), Joint General Staff, RVNAF, July 1, 1969," and Misc. Messages, Feb. 25, 1968, CIA to White House, MACV, etc., "General Khang on Military/Political Situation."

24. Frank E. Vandiver, *Shadows of Vietnam* (College Station: Texas A&M University Press, 1997), 287.

25. Ricks, 290; Longley, 71–72.

26. Walter Cronkite, "We Are Mired in Stalemate...," in *Reporting Vietnam, Part One: American Journalism 1959–1969* (New York: Library of America, 1998), 581–582; NARA, RG 472, MACV, Tet Documents, Box 1, General Offensive and General Uprising (DIA Paper) 1968–69, DIASIS 34A-68, Feb. 3, 1968, "DIA Intelligence Summary"; Brower, 36; Smithsonian, 285.

27. Barrett, ed., *LBJ's Vietnam Papers*, 592–598.

28. John B. Henry II, "LBJ's Clashing Advisers," *New York Times*, Sept. 3, 1971; John B. Henry II, "February, 1968," *Foreign Policy Quarterly*, Fall 1971, 10–11, 20–21; Barrett, ed., *LBJ's Vietnam Papers*, 626–628; Longley, 67.

29. Buzzanco, 327–328; Barrett, ed., *LBJ's Vietnam Papers*, 591.

30. Barrett, ed., *LBJ's Vietnam Papers*, 591, 599, 604, 626–634; NARA, RG 472, MACV, Summary of Operational Interest Messages, 14 Sept. 67 thru 31 May 68, Box 1, Mar. 8, 31, Apr. 7, 11, 20, 1968, Col. Robert C. Hamilton; Henry, 20–25; Deborah Shapley, *Promise and Power* (Boston: Little, Brown, 1993), 374, 416.

31. Barrett, ed., *LBJ's Vietnam Papers*, 629–634, 667–668; Henry, 3–9, 14–18, 22–23; Brower, 40; Gregory A. Daddis, *No Sure Victory* (New York: Oxford University Press, 2011), 141–143.

32. Ronald H. Spector, *After Tet* (New York: Free Press, 1993), 9–11.

33. Vandiver, 288.

34. Barrett, ed., *LBJ's Vietnam Papers*, 629, 635–636; Henry, 22–23; Longley, 68–70.

35. Ingo Trauschweizer, *Maxwell Taylor's Cold War* (Lexington: Universty Press of Kentucky, 2019), 188–189; "What a 'War Tax' Means for the Global Economy," *The Economist*, May 23, 2023.

36. Longley, 72–73.

37. Westmoreland, 120; Henry, 27–30.

38. Henry, 28–29.

39. Barrett, ed., *LBJ's Vietnam Papers*, 749–752; Henry, 27–30.

40. Robert A. Pape, *Bombing to Win* (Ithaca, NY: Cornell University Press, 1996), 186–195; NARA, RG 472, MACV, Summary of Operational Interest Messages, 14 Sept. 67 thru 31 May 68, Box 1, Apr. 26, 1968, Col. Robert C. Hamilton.

41. *Congressional Record—Senate*, June 25, 1968, S7725–S7731; Walter J. Boyne, "Route Pack 6," *Air and Space Forces Magazine*, Nov. 1, 1999.

42. Don Oberdorfer, *Tet!* (1971; Baltimore: Johns Hopkins University Press, 2001), 308–315.

43. Longley, 80–83.

44. Richard Helms, *A Look over My Shoulder* (New York: Random House, 2003), 331–332; Longley, 80.

45. Clark M. Clifford, "A Vietnam Reappraisal: The Personal History of One Man's View and How It Evolved," *Foreign Affairs*, July 1969, 609–613; Don Oberdorfer, "An Ending of His Own," in *Reporting Vietnam, Part One*, 583–587; Henry, 24–26; Barrett, ed., *LBJ's Vietnam Papers*, 650.

46. Barrett, ed., *LBJ's Vietnam Papers*, 626–628, 632–634; Westmoreland, 357–358; Henry, 16–21; Daddis, *Westmoreland's War*, 142–143; Vandiver, 291–305.

47. NARA, RG 472, MACV, Tet Documents, Box 2, II FFV, LTC David Hughes, "II Field Force, G-3 Briefing, 20 March 1968"; Barrett, ed., *LBJ's Vietnam Papers*, 639–642, 661.

48. Spector, 158.

49. Brower, 40–42; Daddis, *Westmoreland's War*, 143.

50. *Congressional Record—Senate*, June 25, 1968, S7723.

51. Edwin L. Dale Jr., "What Vietnam Did to the American Economy," *New York Times*, Jan. 28, 1973; Barrett, ed., *LBJ's Vietnam Papers*, 642; Brower, 44; Buzzanco, 328–329.

CHAPTER 15. Khe Sanh

1. National Archives and Records Administration (NARA), RG 472, MACV, Tet Documents, Box 1, Misc. Messages Jan–May 68, MACV, Mar. 30, 1968, Amb. Bunker to Sec. State, "Political Developments in I Corps."

2. Christian Appy, *Patriots* (New York: Viking, 2003), 543.

3. Ron Milam, *Not a Gentleman's War* (Chapel Hill: University of North Carolina Press, 2009), 126–133.

4. "Calley's Trial Puts Emphasis on C.O.," *Bangor Daily News*, Dec. 21, 1970.

5. Appy, 346–353.

6. Milam, 129–131; Appy, 351.

7. Seymour M. Hersh, "The My Lai Massacre," in *Reporting Vietnam: American Journalism 1959–1975* (New York: Library of America, 1998), 418, 425–427; Appy, 347.

8. Daniel Lang, "Casualties of War," in *Reporting Vietnam, Part One: American Journalism 1959–1969* (New York: Library of America, 1998), 712–714; Hersh, "The My Lai Massacre," 421–422.

9. David M. Barrett, ed., *Lyndon B. Johnson's Vietnam Papers* (College Station: Texas A&M University Press, 1997), 578–579.

10. Michael Herr, *Dispatches* (1977; New York: Vintage, 1991), 143.

11. NARA, RG 472, MACV, Tet Documents, Box 2, "Battle for Khe Sanh by Capt. Moyers S. Shore, II, USMC," 41.

12. James Webb, *I Heard My Country Calling* (New York: Simon & Schuster, 2014), 262.

13. Herr, 128–129; John T. Wheeler, "Life in the V Ring," in *Reporting Vietnam*, 327.

14. Ronald H. Spector, *After Tet* (New York: Free Press, 1993), 122–123; NARA, RG 472, MACV, Tet Documents, Box 2, Khe Sanh, Apr. 17, 1968, L. R. Vasey and R. J. Hallenbeck, "Fact Sheet on Khe Sanh," and "Battle for Khe Sanh by Capt. Moyers S. Shore, II, USMC," 77.

15. William C. Westmoreland, *A Soldier Reports* (New York: Doubleday, 1976), 339–340.

16. Chuck Gross, *Rattler One-Seven* (Denton: University of North Texas Press, 2004), 125; NARA, RG 472, MACV, Tet Documents, Box 2, "Battle for Khe Sanh by Capt. Moyers S. Shore, II, USMC," 56–59.

17. NARA, RG 472, MACV, Tet Documents, Box 2, "Battle for Khe Sanh by Capt. Moyers S. Shore, II, USMC," 63, 67.

18. Spector, 122; Westmoreland, 196.

19. NARA, RG 472, MACV, Tet Documents, Box 2, Khe Sanh, Apr. 17, 1968, L. R. Vasey and R. J. Hallenbeck, "Fact Sheet on Khe Sanh."

20. Westmoreland, 340.

21. NARA, RG 472, MACV, Tet Documents, Box 2, Khe Sanh, Apr. 17, 1968, L. R. Vasey and R. J. Hallenbeck, "Fact Sheet on Khe Sanh."

22. NARA, RG 472, MACV, Tet Documents, Box 2, "Battle for Khe Sanh by Capt. Moyers S. Shore, II, USMC," 50.

23. Westmoreland, 340; NARA, RG 472, MACV, Tet Documents, Box 2, "Battle for Khe Sanh by Capt. Moyers S. Shore, II, USMC," 84–86.

24. NARA, RG 472, MACV, Tet Documents, Box 2, "Battle for Khe Sanh by Capt. Moyers S. Shore, II, USMC," 79–80.

25. NARA, RG 472, MACV, Tet Documents, Box 2, "Battle for Khe Sanh by Capt. Moyers S. Shore, II, USMC," 97–103; Dwight Jon Zimmermann, "The Guns of Khe Sanh, 1968," n.d., ARGunners, www.argunners.com/the-guns-at-khe-sanh-1968/.

26. "Vietnam Statistics—War Costs: Complete Picture Impossible," *CQ Almanac 1975*, 31st ed. (Washington, DC: Congressional Quarterly, 1976), 301–305, http://library.cqpress.com/cqalmanac/cqal75-1213988.

27. Robert Buzzanco, *Masters of War* (Cambridge: Cambridge University Press, 1996), 327, 332–333; Kyle Longley, *LBJ's 1968* (Cambridge: Cambridge University Press, 2018), 76–78.

28. Barrett, ed., *LBJ's Vietnam Papers*, 643–651, 658.

29. Longley, 100–101.

30. Max Boot, *The Road Not Taken* (New York: Norton, 2018), 449.

31. Jeffrey Kimball, *Nixon's Vietnam War* (Lawrence: University Press of Kansas, 1998), 55; Don Oberdorfer, "An Ending of His Own," in *Reporting Vietnam, Part One*, 596–597; Charles Mohr, "Departure of Westmoreland May Spur Shift in Strategy," *New York Times*, Mar. 24, 1968; Barrett, ed., *LBJ's Vietnam Papers*, 652–653.

32. Spector, 105; Barrett, ed., *LBJ's Vietnam Papers*, 768.

33. Lewis Sorley, *A Better War* (Boston: Houghton Mifflin, 1999), 112.

34. Barrett, ed., *LBJ's Vietnam Papers*, 654, 710; Sorley, *Better War*, 126–127; Buzzanco, 335–339.

35. Spector, 123–128; Herr, 155; NARA, RG 472, MACV, Tet Documents, Box 2, "Battle for Khe Sanh by Capt. Moyers S. Shore, II, USMC," 101–103.

36. Spector, 128–129; Peter Brush, "Recounting the Casualties at the Deadly Battle of Khe Sanh," HistoryNet, June 26, 2007, www.historynet.com/recounting-the-casualties-at-the-deadly-battle-of-khe-sanh.htm.

CHAPTER 16. Mini-Tet

1. *Congressional Record—Senate*, June 25, 1968, S7726, Sen. Proxmire; Lewis Sorley, *A Better War* (Boston: Houghton Mifflin, 1999), 123.

2. "About the Vice President, Hubert H. Humphrey, 38th Vice President (1965–69)," www.senate.gov/about/officers-staff/vice-president/humphrey-hubert.htm; Max Boot, *The Road Not Taken* (New York: Norton, 2018), 452; Gregory A. Daddis, *Westmoreland's War* (New York: Oxford University Press, 2014), 176.

3. John S. McCain III, "How the POWs Fought Back," in *Reporting Vietnam: American Journalism 1959–1975* (New York: Library of America, 1998), 695–696.

4. National Archives and Records Administration (NARA), RG 472, MACV, Tet Documents, Box 2, Press Briefings II, III, & IV CTZ, Apr. 1968, "The Tet Offensive—Unifying the South Vietnamese People (or the Backlash of Terror)."

5. NARA, RG 472, MACV, Tet Documents, Box 1, Misc. Messages Jan–May 68, MACV, Apr. 27, 1968, ADM Sharp, CINCPAC, to Gen. Wheeler, "Enemy Situation, SVN"; David M. Barrett, ed., *Lyndon B. Johnson's Vietnam Papers*

(College Station: Texas A&M University Press, 1997), 739–741; Sorley, *Better War*, 101–102.

6. NARA, RG 472, MACV, Tet Documents, Box 2, Defense of Saigon, Project CHECO [Contemporary Historical Evaluation of Combat Operations] Report, Dec. 14, 1968, Maj. A. W. Thompson, "The Defense of Saigon," 38–40; RG 472, MACV, Summary of Operational Interest Messages, 14 Sept. 67 thru 31 May 68, Box 1, May 2, 1968, Col. Robert C. Hamilton; William C. Westmoreland, *A Soldier Reports* (New York: Doubleday, 1976), 195.

7. Westmoreland, 347–349.

8. Ronald H. Spector, *After Tet* (New York: Free Press, 1993), 138–141.

9. Michael Herr, *Dispatches* (1977; New York: Vintage, 1991), 191–192.

10. Spector, 140, 147.

11. Keith Nolan, *Ripcord* (Novato, CA: Presidio, 2003), "Introduction"; Mike D. Shepherd, "A Valley Soaked in Rain & Blood," HistoryNet, June 30, 2015, www.historynet.com/a-valley-soaked-in-rain-blood/; Herr, 191–192.

12. Robert K. Brigham, *Guerrilla Diplomacy* (Ithaca, NY: Cornell University Press, 1999), 76–80; Lien-Hang T. Nguyen, *Hanoi's War* (Chapel Hill: University of North Carolina Press, 2012), 115, 118, 120–121; Frank E. Vandiver, *Shadows of Vietnam* (College Station: Texas A&M University Press, 1997), 33.

13. NARA, RG 472, MACV, Tet Documents, Box 1, DIA Working Paper, "General Offensive and General Uprising (1968–1969)."

14. NARA, RG 472, MACV, Summary of Operational Interest Messages, 14 Sept. 67 thru 31 May 68, Box 1, May 10, 1968, Col. William C. Wood, and Box 2, July 9, 1968, Col. Richard C. Hamilton; Herr, 230; Norman M. Camp, "U.S. Army Psychiatry in the Vietnam War," *U.S. Army Medical Department Journal*, Apr.–June 2015, 10, 15.

15. NARA, RG 472, MACV, Summary of Operational Interest Messages, 1 June 68 thru 30 April 69, Box 2, June 7, 1968, Col. Richard C. Hamilton; RG 472, MACV, Tet Documents, Box 2, Defense of Saigon, Project CHECO [Contemporary Historical Evaluation of Combat Operations] Report, Dec. 14, 1968, Maj. A. W. Thompson, "The Defense of Saigon," 46; Spector, 159, 162–163.

16. NARA, RG 472, MACV, Summary of Operational Interest Messages, 1 June 68 thru 30 April 69, Box 2, June 7, 1968, Col. Richard C. Hamilton.

17. NARA, RG 472, MACV, Tet Documents, Box 2, Defense of Saigon, Project CHECO [Contemporary Historical Evaluation of Combat Operations] Report, Dec. 14, 1968, Maj. A. W. Thompson, "The Defense of Saigon," 29–36; Boot, 524; Jeffrey Record, *The Wrong War* (Annapolis, MD: Naval Institute Press, 1998), 119.

18. Tom Buckley, "Portrait of an Aging Despot," in *Reporting Vietnam*, 541–542; NARA, RG 472, MACV, Summary of Operational Interest Messages, 14 Sept. 67 thru 31 May 68, Box 1, May 6, 10, June 9, 1968, Col. Robert C. Hamilton.

19. Barrett, ed., *LBJ's Vietnam Papers*, 733, 736; Smithsonian, *A Short History of the Vietnam War* (New York: DK Publishing, 2001), 314–317; Brigham, 83.

20. NARA, RG 472, MACV, Tet Documents, Box 2, Defense of Saigon, Project

CHECO [Contemporary Historical Evaluation of Combat Operations] Report, Dec. 14, 1968, Maj. A. W. Thompson, "The Defense of Saigon," 34.

21. NARA, RG 472, MACV, Tet Documents, Box 2, Defense of Saigon, Project CHECO [Contemporary Historical Evaluation of Combat Operations] Report, Dec. 14, 1968, Maj. A. W. Thompson, "The Defense of Saigon," 35–36; RG 472, MACV, Summary of Operational Interest Messages, 1 June 68 thru 30 Apr. 69, Box 2, June 7, 1968, Col. Richard C. Hamilton; Sean Fear, "Vietnam '67: The Feud That Sank Saigon," *New York Times*, Mar. 3, 2017.

22. NARA, RG 472, MACV, Summary of Operational Interest Messages, 1 June 68 thru 30 April 69, Box 2, July 7, Oct. 30, 1968, Col. Richard C. Hamilton, Col. Paul Chmar.

23. William Colby, *Lost Victory* (Chicago: Contemporary, 1989), 187–188.

24. Edward Miller, "Behind the Phoenix Program," *New York Times*, Dec. 29, 2017.

25. NARA, RG 472, MACV, Summary of Operational Interest Messages, 1 June 68 thru 30 April 69, Box 2, July 23, 1968, Col. Paul Chmar; Miller, "Behind the Phoenix Program."

26. NARA, RG 472, MACV, Tet Documents, Box 2, Press Briefings, HQ Advisory Team 96, Apr. 8, 1968, Capt. L. E. Lyons, "Historical Summary of VC Tet Offensive IV CTZ."

27. NARA, RG 472, MACV, Tet Documents, Box 1, RVNAF Performance During TET, MACV to JCS, CINCPAC, Mar. 21, 1968, "Assessment of RVNAF Status as of 29 Feb 68."

28. NARA, RG 472, MACV, Tet Documents, Box 2, II FFV, LTC David Hughes, "II Field Force, G-3 Briefing, 20 March 1968"; Daddis, *Westmoreland's War*, 174; Sorley, *Better War*, 50–53, 57, 59–60, 94, 97.

29. NARA, RG 472, MACV, Summary of Operational Interest Messages, 1 June 68 thru 30 April 69, Box 2, Dec. 14, 1968, Col. Paul Chmar.

30. Neil Sheehan, *A Bright Shining Lie* (New York: Vintage, 1989), 609; NARA, RG 472, MACV, Tet Documents, Box 2, Press Briefings, HQ Advisory Team 96, Apr. 8, 1968, Capt. L. E. Lyons, "Historical Summary of VC Tet Offensive IV CTZ."

31. NARA, RG 472, MACV, Summary of Operational Interest Messages, 14 Sept. 67 thru 31 May 68, Box 1, Jan. 31, 1968, Col. Robert C. Hamilton; John B. Henry II, "February, 1968," *Foreign Policy Quarterly*, Fall 1971, 12–13.

32. UK National Archives (UKNA), FCO 15/481, Saigon, Feb. 13, 1968, "Mood in Hanoi," D. Watson; Fox Butterfield, "Who Was This Enemy?," in *Reporting Vietnam*, 654–655; Gloria Emerson, "We Are All 'Bui Doi,'" in *Reporting Vietnam, Part Two: American Journalism 1969–1975* (New York: Library of America, 1998), 254.

33. UKNA, FCO 15/481, Hanoi, Mar. 8 and 26, 1968, "Hanoi After One More Year of War (March 1968)," B. T. W. Stewart to Brown; NARA, RG 472, MACV, Tet Documents, Box 1, Enemy Strategy Assessment, MACV, Mar. 20, 1968, Tet Offensive (May 1968 Update).

CHAPTER 17. A Better War?

1.   National Archives and Records Administration (NARA), RG 472, MACV, Tet Documents, Box 2, "Battle for Khe Sanh by Capt. Moyers S. Shore, II, USMC," 118–119; Ronald H. Spector, *After Tet* (New York: Free Press, 1993), 128–129, 140–141, 228–231.

2.   Tim O'Brien, *The Things They Carried* (New York: Penguin, 1990), 249.

3.   James Webb, *I Heard My Country Calling* (New York: Simon & Schuster, 2014), 269; Smithsonian, *A Short History of the Vietnam War* (New York: DK Publishing, 2021), 246.

4.   Norman M. Camp, "U.S. Army Psychiatry in the Vietnam War," *U.S. Army Medical Dept. Journal*, Apr.–June 2015, 10; Guenter Lewy, *America in Vietnam* (New York: Oxford University Press, 1978), 83; James T. Gillam, *Life and Death in the Central Highlands* (Denton: University of North Texas Press, 2010), 131.

5.   NARA, RG 472, MACV, Tet Documents, Box 1, Enemy Strategy Assess., 24 May 68, Saigon, May 9, 1968, "Controlled American Source, Vietnam: Rallier's Assessment of Possible Impact of Paris Talks on Viet Cong Morale," and May 18, 1968, LTC Tighe, "VC Strategy, Plans and Capabilities—Col. Dac"; RG 472, MACV, Summary of Operational Interest Messages, 1 June 68 thru 30 April 69, Box 2, Oct. 19, 21, Nov. 8, 1969, LTC John B. Watkins Jr.; "Changing of the Guard," *Time*, Apr. 19, 1968, 25–32; Lewy, 84.

6.   NARA, RG 472, MACV, Tet Documents, Box 2, Washington, DC, July 15, 1969, Gen. W. C. Westmoreland (Army CS) to Gen. L. F. Chapman Jr. (Commandant, USMC); Stanley Karnow, "Giap Remembers," *New York Times*, June 24, 1990; William C. Westmoreland, *A Soldier Reports* (New York: Doubleday, 1976), 251–252, 336–341.

7.   Spector, 213–214.

8.   David M. Barrett, ed., *Lyndon B. Johnson's Vietnam Papers* (College Station: Texas A&M University Press, 1997), 643–651; Robert Buzzanco, *Masters of War* (Cambridge: Cambridge University Press, 1996), 335.

9.   Lewis Sorley, *A Better War* (Boston: Houghton Mifflin, 1999), 18; Lewy, 78, 89–93.

10. Gregory A. Daddis, *Westmoreland's War* (New York: Oxford University Press, 2014), 118–119; Smithsonian, 352–353; Lewy, 90; Sorley, *Better War*, 22–23, 36.

11. Daddis, *Westmoreland's War*, 166–167.

12. John A. Farrell, *Richard Nixon* (New York: Doubleday, 2017), 360.

13. Jeffrey Kimball, *Nixon's Vietnam War* (Lawrence: University Press of Kansas, 1998), 40–42; Don Oberdorfer, "An Ending of His Own," in *Reporting Vietnam, Part One: American Journalism 1959–1969* (New York: Library of America, 1998), 593; William Shawcross, *Sideshow* (New York: Simon & Schuster, 1979), 86; Rick Perlstein, *Nixonland* (New York: Scribner, 2008), 353–354; Richard Helms, *A Look over My Shoulder* (New York: Random House, 2003), 334; Farrell, *Richard Nixon*, 340–341.

14. UK National Archives (UKNA), FCO 7/778, United States, July 16, 1968, Sir Patrick Dean to Mr. Michael Stewart, "Neo-Isolationism."

15. Barrett, ed., *LBJ's Vietnam Papers*, 704–705, 731.

16. Sorley, *Better War*, 110, 114, 154–157.

17. UKNA, DEFE 68/778, London, July 10, 1968, Maj. Gen. Richard Clutterbuck, "Report by Brigadier Clutterbuck on a Seminar on Vietnam Held at the Center for Strategic Studies, Washington, on 20th and 21st May 1968."

18. NARA, RG 472, MACV, Summary of Operational Interest Messages, 1 June 68 thru 30 Apr. 69, Box 2, July 10, Nov. 3, 5, 13, Dec. 3, 7, 12, 19,20, 31, 1968, Jan. 3, 28, 1969, Col. Paul Chmar, LTC John Watkins Jr.

19. Farrell, *Richard Nixon*, 341–344.

20. Kimball, *Nixon's Vietnam War*, 55; Barrett, ed. *LBJ's Vietnam Papers*, 476–479, 498–508, 769–770; NARA, RG 472, MACV, Summary of Operational Interest Messages, 1 June 68 thru 30 Apr. 69, Box 2, July 10, 1968, Col. Richard C. Hamilton.

21. Ang Cheng Guan, *Ending the Vietnam War* (London: Routledge, 2004), 13–16.

22. NARA, RG 472, MACV, Summary of Operational Interest Messages, 1 June 68 thru 30 Apr. 69, Box 2, Aug. 6, 7, Oct. 29, 31, Nov. 9, 15, 1968, Col. Paul Chmar; Lien-Hang T. Nguyen, *Hanoi's War* (Chapel Hill: University of North Carolina Press, 2012), 127–128; Barrett, ed., *LBJ's Vietnam Papers*, 778, 794–795, 806–813; Frank E. Vandiver, *Shadows of Vietnam* (College Station: Texas A&M University Press, 1997), 336–337; Shawcross, 79; A. J. Langguth, *Our Vietnam* (New York: Simon & Schuster, 2000), 523.

23. Perlstein, *Nixonland*, 350–351.

24. Barrett, ed., *LBJ's Vietnam Papers*, 771–772; Kimball, *Nixon's Vietnam War*, 56–57; Vandiver, 337–338.

25. Kyle Longley, *LBJ's 1968* (Cambridge: Cambridge University Press, 2018), 234–255.

26. John A. Farrell, "When a Candidate Conspired with a Foreign Power to Win an Election," *Politico*, Aug. 6, 2017.

27. Longley, 210–213.

28. Longley, 230–231.

29. Spector, 296.

30. Norman Mailer, "From *The Siege of Chicago*," in *Reporting Vietnam, Part One*, 628–630, 634, 638; "About the Vice President, Hubert H. Humphrey, 38th Vice President (1965–69)," www.senate.gov/about/officers-staff/vice-president /humphrey-hubert.htm.

31. Farrell, *Richard Nixon*, 342; John A. Farrell, "Nixon's Vietnam Treachery," *New York Times*, Dec. 31, 2016; Peter Baker, "Nixon Tried to Spoil Johnson's Vietnam Peace Talks, Notes Show," *New York Times*, Jan. 2, 2017; Kimball, *Nixon's Vietnam War*, 60.

32. Kimball, *Nixon's Vietnam War*, 42; Sorley, *Better War*, 113–117, 164–166.

33. NARA, RG 472, MACV, Summary of Operational Interest Messages,

1 June 68 thru 30 April 69, Box 2, Sept. 1, 16, Oct. 21, Nov. 25, Dec. 4, 22, 1968, Jan. 14, 1969, Col. Paul Chmar, LTC John B. Watkins Jr.; "War, Defense Commitments Dominate Foreign Affairs," *CQ Almanac 1969*, 25th ed. (Washington, DC: Congressional Quarterly, 1970), 997–1007, http://library.cqpress.com/cqalmanac /cqal69-871-26652-1245891; Kimball, *Nixon's Vietnam War*, 42; Sorley, *Better War*, 43–44; Barrett, ed., *LBJ's Vietnam Papers*, 736–739.

34. "War, Defense Commitments Dominate Foreign Affairs," 997–1007; NARA, RG 472, MACV, Summary of Operational Interest Messages, 1 June 68 thru 30 April 69, Box 2, June 7, 1968, Col. Richard C. Hamilton.

35. NARA, RG 472, MACV, Summary of Operational Interest Messages, 1 June 68 thru 30 April 69, Box 2, June 11, 27, Aug. 6, 7, Oct. 4, 5, 29, 31, Nov. 9, 15, Dec. 8, 13, 1968, Jan. 2, 1969, Col. Richard C. Hamilton, Col. Paul Chmar, LTC John B. Watkins Jr.; RG 472, MACV, Tet Documents, Box 1, DIA Working Paper, "General Offensive and General Uprising (1968–1969)"; Peter Braestrup, "The South Vietnamese Army," in *Reporting Vietnam: American Journalism 1959–1975* (New York: Library of America, 1998), 617.

36. NARA, RG 472, MACV, Tet Documents, Box 1, General Offensive and General Uprising (DIA Paper) 1968–69, Feb. 24, 1969, LTC Cook, Talking Paper, "Ground Operations, South Vietnam, 16–23 February 1969."

37. Gregory A. Daddis, *Withdrawal* (New York: Oxford University Press, 2017), 42–43.

38. NARA, RG 472, MACV, Summary of Operational Interest Messages, 1 June 68 thru 30 April 69, Box 2, Mar. 15, 1969, LTC John B. Watkins Jr.; RG 472, MACV, A1 168, MACV, Weekly Assessment of Military Position, August 68 thru Dec. 70, Box 1, Aug. 16, 1969, COMUSMACV to CJCS, AMEMB SAIGON, CINCPAC, AMEMB PARIS, "Weekly Assessment of Military Position"; Fox Butterfield, "Who Was This Enemy?," in *Reporting Vietnam*, 663.

39. NARA, RG 472, MACV, Summary of Operational Interest Messages, 1 June 68 thru 30 April 69, Box 2, Jan. 5, 1969, LTC John B. Watkins Jr.; NARA, RG 472, A1 38, Box 1, "Sphinx" Intelligence Summaries, MACV, Jan. 6, Feb. 2, 3, Mar. 6, 1969, Feb. 27, 1970; Gillam, 121.

40. NARA, RG 472, MACV, A1 168, MACV, Weekly Assessment of Military Position, August 68 thru Dec. 70, Box 1, Feb. 14, 1970, COMUSMACV to CJCS, AMEMB SAIGON, CINCPAC, AMEMB PARIS. RG 472, A1 1158, USARV/1st Infantry Division, Intelligence Reports, Lai Khe, June 10, 16, Oct. 26, 1968, G-2 Deskis; RG 472, MACV, Tet Documents, Box 1, General Offensive and General Uprising (DIA Paper) 1968–69, Feb. 24, 1969, LTC Cook, Talking Paper, "Ground Operations, South Vietnam, 16–23 February 1969"; Daddis, *Withdrawal*, xii, 6–10, 37–42, 45; Daddis, *Westmoreland's War*, 170–171; Gillam, 78.

41. Farrell, 350–351.

42. Barrett, ed., *LBJ's Vietnam Papers*, 814–826; Sorley, *Better War*, 151–152; Shawcross, 87–91.

43. Spector, 299.

44. Barrett, ed., *LBJ's Vietnam Papers*, 812, 827, 837–842; Mary McCarthy,

"Hanoi—March 1968," in *Reporting Vietnam*, 343; Farrell, "Nixon's Vietnam Treachery"; Baker, "Nixon Tried to Spoil Johnson's Vietnam Peace Talks."

45. "LBJ's 'X' File on Nixon, the Bombing Halt, Anna Chennault, and the 1968 Election," History in Pieces, n.d., https://historyinpieces.com/research/documents/lbjs-files-nixon-bombing-halt-1968-election.

46. Longley, 252–254.

47. Kimball, *Nixon's Vietnam War*, 60–61; Farrell, "When a Candidate Conspired with a Foreign Power."

48. Richard Zoglin, *Hope* (New York: Simon & Schuster, 2014), 391.

CHAPTER 18. Hamburger Hill

1. William Shawcross, *Sideshow* (New York: Simon & Schuster, 1979), 86–90; Smithsonian, *A Short History of the Vietnam War* (New York: DK Publishing, 2021), 341.

2. Jeffrey Kimball, *Nixon's Vietnam War* (Lawrence: University Press of Kansas, 1998), 72–73, 76–77; John A. Farrell, *Richard Nixon* (New York: Doubleday, 2017), 361–363; Shawcross, 77, 86–91.

3. Jeffrey Record, *The Wrong War* (Annapolis, MD: Naval Institute Press, 1998), xv; Gregory A. Daddis, *No Sure Victory* (New York: Oxford University Press, 2011), 158.

4. Joe McGinniss, "From *The Selling of the President 1968*," in *Reporting Vietnam, Part One: American Journalism 1959–1969* (New York: Library of America, 1998), 658–659; Lewis Sorley, *A Better War* (Boston: Houghton Mifflin, 1999), 117–120; William C. Westmoreland, *A Soldier Reports* (New York: Doubleday, 1976), 182.

5. Kimball, *Nixon's Vietnam War*, 131–133; Smithsonian, 382–385.

6. National Archives and Records Administration (NARA), RG 472, MACV, Summary of Operational Interest Messages, 1 June 68 thru 30 April 69, Box 2, June 29–Sept. 13, 1969, LTC John B. Watkins Jr.; Shawcross, 246–251.

7. Eric M. Bergerud, *The Dynamics of Defeat* (Boulder, CO: Westview, 1991), 244–247; Kimball, *Nixon's Vietnam War*, 73; Gregory A. Daddis, *Withdrawal* (New York: Oxford University Press, 2017), 46–47.

8. Daddis, *No Sure Victory*, 152–153, 157, 202; Daddis, *Withdrawal*, 46–47.

9. Sorley, *Better War*, 21; James T. Gillam, *Life and Death in the Central Highlands* (Denton: University of North Texas Press, 2010), 63.

10. Michael Herr, *Dispatches* (1977; New York: Vintage, 1991), 257.

11. Ronald H. Spector, *After Tet* (New York: Free Press, 1993), 166–175.

12. Smithsonian, 103.

13. UK National Archives (UKNA), DEFE 11/696, Washington, Apr. 9, 1971, Col. A. G. H. Jukes to Min of Defence, "South Vietnamese Operations in Laos" and "Operation Lam Son 719: A Preliminary Assessment as at 2 Apr 71."

14. Sorley, *Better War*, 138–139.

15. UKNA, DEFE 11/696, Hanoi, May 26, 1970, Daphne Park, "Collective Leadership and the Collective Masters in North Vietnam"; NARA, RG 472, A1

1158, USARV/1st Infantry Division, Intelligence Reports, Lai Khe, RVN, July 27, 1968, G-2 Benedict; NARA, RG 472, MACV, Summary of Operational Interest Messages, 14 Sept. 67 thru 31 May 68, Box 1, May 18, 28, 1968, Col. William C. Wood and Col. Robert C. Hamilton, and Box 2, July 2, Aug. 6, 7, Oct. 29, 31, Nov. 9, 15, 1968, Col. Richard C. Hamilton, Col. Paul Chmar.

16. NARA, RG 472, MACV, Tet Documents, Box 1, General Offensive and General Uprising (DIA Paper) 1968–69, Feb. 24, 1969, LTC Cook, Talking Paper, "Ground Operations, South Vietnam, 16–23 February 1969"; Smithsonian, 349; Sorley, *Better War*, 123–124, 162.

17. Westmoreland, 151.

18. Capt. Justin Wright, "How a 76-Year-Old Vietnam Veteran Was Able to Carry a Fallen Friend to the Top of Hamburger Hill," Defense Visual Information Distribution Service, July 17, 2020, www.dvidshub.net/news/374108/76-year-old -vietnam-veteran-able-carry-fallen-friend-top-hamburger-hill.

19. Daddis, *Withdrawal*, 65.

20. Kimball, *Nixon's Vietnam War*, 147; Smithsonian, 366.

21. William Head, "Hamburger Hill, May 10–20, 1969: The Beginning of the End of America's Commitment to the Republic of Vietnam," *Virginia Review of Asian Studies* 17 (2015): 93–112.

22. Hedrick Smith, "U.S. Battle Losses Stir Nixon Aides," *New York Times*, May 23, 1969.

23. Sen. Edward Kennedy, "Hamburger Hill Speech," May 20, 1969, www .tedkennedy.org; David Hoffman, "Hamburger Hill: The Army's Rationale," in *Reporting Vietnam, Part One*, 700; Daddis, *No Sure Victory*, 166–168.

24. Hoffman, "Hamburger Hill: The Army's Rationale," 700; Peter Brush, "The Hard Truth About Fragging," HistoryNet, July 28, 2010, www.historynet .com/the-hard-truth-about-fragging/.

25. Ben Cosgrove, "Faces of the American Dead in Vietnam: One Week's Toll, June 1969," *Life*, June 27, 1969.

26. Sorley, *Better War*, 157–158, 160–162.

27. Daddis, *No Sure Victory*, 167–168.

28. "High Cost, Poor Results in Viet Nam War Stimulate Dissent; Congress Critical of Aims, Conduct and Impact on Economy," *CQ Almanac 1967*, 23rd ed. (Washington, DC: Congressional Quarterly, 1968), 07-917–07-925, http://library .cqpress.com/cqalmanac/cqal67-1313128; Kimball, *Nixon's Vietnam War*, 97–100; Daddis, *Withdrawal*, 62–63.

CHAPTER 19. Search and Avoid

1. National Archives and Records Administration (NARA), RG 472, MACV, Summary of Operational Interest Messages, 1 June 68 thru 30 April 69, Box 2, Aug. 18, Sept. 17, Oct. 7, 1969, LTC John B. Watkins Jr.; Ang Cheng Guan, *Ending the Vietnam War* (London: Routledge, 2004), 32–34.

2. NARA, RG 472, MACV, Summary of Operational Interest Messages, 1 June 68 thru 30 April 69, Box 2, June 29, Oct. 19, 21, Nov. 8, 1969, LTC John B.

Watkins Jr.; Gregory A. Daddis, *No Sure Victory* (New York: Oxford University Press, 2011), 172–173; Tim O'Brien, *The Things They Carried* (New York: Penguin, 1990), 103.

3. NARA, RG 472, MACV, Summary of Operational Interest Messages, 1 June 68 thru 30 April 69, Box 2, Nov. 3, 5, 13, Dec. 3, 7, 12, 19, 20, 31, 1968, Jan. 3, 10, 16, 28, 1969, Mar. 14, 26, Sept. 24, 1969, Col. Paul Chmar, LTC John B. Watkins Jr.

4. UK National Archives (UKNA), DEFE 68/778, London, July 10, 1968, Maj. Gen. Richard Clutterbuck, "Report by Brigadier Clutterbuck on a Seminar on Vietnam Held at the Center for Strategic Studies, Washington, on 20th and 21st May 1968"; Fred Gardner, "War and GI Morale," *New York Times*, Nov. 21, 1970.

5. NARA, RG 472, MACV, Tet Documents, Box 1, VC Terror, DIA to AIG, et al., Sept. 20, 1969, "Far East Summary."

6. Liddell Hart Centre for Military Archives (LHCMA), U.S. Armed Forces in Vietnam 1954–1975, Part 4, Vietnam: Senior Officer Debriefing Reports, MF 812, Reel 4/4, HQ I Field Force, Jan. 8, 1971, Lt. Gen. A. S. Collins Jr. to Commanding General, US Army Vietnam, Jan. 7, 1971, "Senior Officer's Debriefing Report, Inclusive Dates 15 Feb. 1970 Through 9 Jan. 1971."

7. LHCMA, U.S. Armed Forces in Vietnam 1954–1975, Part 4, Vietnam: U.S. Army Senior Debriefing Reports, MF 809, Reel 1/4, HQ U.S. Army Advisory Group, II Corps Tactical Zone, Dec. 15, 1968, Brig. Gen. John W. Barnes, Dep. Senior Adviser, "Debrief Report, Nov. 18, 1967 to Dec. 15, 1968"; NARA, RG 472, MACV, A1 182, Operations Plans 1967–69, Box 1, MACV, Mar. 24, 1969, Col. Edwin C. Gibson, "Visit to IV Corps, 22 and 23 March 1968."

8. NARA, RG 472, MACV, Summary of Operational Interest Messages, 1 June 68 thru 30 April 69, Box 2, June 12, 1968, Col. Richard C. Hamilton; Lewis Sorley, *A Better War* (Boston: Houghton Mifflin, 1999), 72–73; Peter R. Kann, "A Long, Leisurely Drive Through Mekong Delta Tells Much of the War," in *Reporting Vietnam: American Journalism 1959–1975* (New York: Library of America, 1998), 404–405.

9. NARA, RG 127, USMC Records, Box 99, MACV, CORDS, Reports and Analysis Directorate (RAD), June 1969, *Hamlet Evaluation System Handbook*.

10. NARA, RG 472, A1 63, MACV, J2 VCI Intelligence, Staff Visit Files, Box 1, Mar. 16, 1969, Col. Werner E. Michel to Col. Roberts, "Field Trip to G2, HQ II FFV"; Gregory A. Daddis, *Westmoreland's War* (New York: Oxford University Press, 2014), 136.

11. Smithsonian, *A Short History of the Vietnam War* (New York: DK Publishing, 2021), 326–327.

12. LHCMA, U.S. Armed Forces in Vietnam 1954–1975, MF 812, HQ I Field Force, Jan. 8, 1971, Lt. Gen. A. S. Collins Jr. to Commanding General, US Army Vietnam, Jan. 7, 1971, "Senior Officer's Debriefing Report, Inclusive Dates 15 Feb. 1970 Through 9 Jan. 1971"; NARA, RG 472, A1 63, MACV, J2 VCI Intelligence, Staff Visit Files, Box 1, Mar. 16, 1969, Col. Werner E. Michel to Col. Roberts, "Field Trip to G2, HQ II FFV."

13. Ronald H. Spector, *After Tet* (New York: Free Press, 1993), 287–288; Jeffrey

Record, "Maximizing Cobra Utilization," *Washington Monthly*, Apr. 1971, 8; Nick Turse, *Kill Anything That Moves* (New York: Metropolitan, 2013), 190–191.

14. Gregory A. Daddis, *Withdrawal* (New York: Oxford University Press, 2017), 96–98.

15. NARA, RG 472, A1 63, MACV, J2 VCI Intelligence, Staff Visit Files, Box 1, HQ 3d Bn, 525th MI Gp, Sept. 15, 1968, LTC Paul Langford, Commanding 3d Bn (Prov), 525th MI Group, and LTC Nguyen Van Khuyen, Commander, III CTZ MSS, "Joint Letter of Instruction," and Feb. 1, 1969, LTC Paul Langford to Commanding General II FFV, Attn: G2, "Mission of the ARVN Military Security Service (MSS) in the III CTZ."

16. Richard Helms, *A Look over My Shoulder* (New York: Random House, 2003), 336–339.

17. NARA, RG 472, A1 63, MACV, J2 VCI Intelligence, Staff Visit Files, Box 1, Dec. 27, 1968, Henry M. Robertson, Kien Tuong Province Phoenix Advisor, "Status of Phoenix Program in Kien Tuong Province."

18. NARA, RG 472, A1 63, MACV, J2 VCI Intelligence, Staff Visit Files, Box 1, Feb. 5, 1969, Maj. Marcel Wiedmaier, USAF to Col. Michel, "Trip Report to Vinh Long Province," and Mar. 4, 1969, Col. Werner Michel to Gen. Davidson, "Maj. Rosen Trip Report IV CTZ—An Giang Province and Thot Not District," and Dec. 27, 1968, Henry M. Robertson, Kien Tuong Province Phoenix Advisor, "Status of Phoenix Program in Kien Tuong Province."

19. NARA, RG 472, A1 63, MACV, J2 VCI Intelligence, Staff Visit Files, Box 1, Dec. 27, 1968, Henry M. Robertson, Kien Tuong Province Phoenix Advisor, "Status of Phoenix Program in Kien Tuong Province."

20. NARA, RG 472, A1 63, MACV, J2 VCI Intelligence, Staff Visit Files, Box 1, Jan. 31, 1969, Maj. Marcel Wiedmaier, USAF to Col. Michel, "Trip Report to I CTZ/III MAF"; Sorley, *Better War*, 77.

21. NARA, RG 472, A1 63, MACV, J2 VCI Intelligence, Staff Visit Files, Box 1, Jan. 31, 1969, Maj. Marcel Wiedmaier, USAF to Col. Michel, "Trip Report to I CTZ/III MAF," Attachment: "1st Marine Division—Anti-VCI Operation 29 Dec. 68 to 25 Jan. 69."

22. NARA, RG 472, A1 63, MACV, J2 VCI Intelligence, Staff Visit Files, Box 1, Jan. 31, 1969, Maj. Marcel Wiedmaier, USAF to Col. Michel, "Trip Report to I CTZ/III MAF," and Feb. 5, 1969, Maj. Marcel Wiedmaier, USAF to Col. Michel, "Trip Report to Vinh Long Province"; Kai Bird, *The Color of Truth* (New York: Simon & Schuster, 1998), 356–357.

23. NARA, RG 472, MACV, Tet Documents, Box 1, Misc. Messages Jan–May 68, MACV, Mar. 11, 1968, "I Corps Situation Report," and Mar. 3, 1968, CIA to White House Situation Room, "Situation in Quang Tri, Quang Tin, and Quang Ngai Provinces of I Corps."

24. NARA, RG 472, MACV, Tet Documents, Box 1, VC Terror, DIA to AIG, et al., Sept. 20, 1969, "Far East Summary"; Sorley, *Better War*, 64–66.

25. Kann, "A Long Leisurely Drive," 411.

CHAPTER 20. "I Will Not Be the First President to Lose a War"

1. Gregory A. Daddis, *No Sure Victory* (New York: Oxford University Press, 2011), 164–166.

2. Norman M. Camp, "U.S. Army Psychiatry in the Vietnam War," *U.S. Army Medical Department Journal*, Apr.–June 2015, 19.

3. Lewis Sorley, *A Better War* (Boston: Houghton Mifflin, 1999), 18; Nick Turse, *Kill Anything That Moves* (New York: Metropolitan, 2013), 204–205.

4. Philip A. McCombs, "Scars of Delta Savagery," in *Reporting Vietnam, Part Two: American Journalism 1969–1975* (New York: Library of America, 1998), 474.

5. McCombs, "Scars of Delta Savagery," 474.

6. Michael Herr, *Dispatches* (1977; New York: Vintage, 1991), 62; Turse, 90.

7. David Hackworth, *Steel My Soldiers' Hearts* (New York: Rugged Land, 2002), 350; Turse, 206–210.

8. Jeffrey Record, "Maximizing Cobra Utilization," *Washington Monthly*, Apr. 1971, 8–12; Hackworth, 350.

9. National Archives and Records Administration (NARA), RG 472, A1 1158, 1, USARV/1st Infantry Division, Intelligence Reports, Lai Khe, RVN, Nov. 11, Dec. 26, 1968, G-2 Deskis; Smithsonian, *A Short History of the Vietnam War* (New York: DK Publishing, 2021), 223; Daddis, *No Sure Victory*, 166.

10. Turse, 214–220.

11. Patricia Sullivan, "Julian J. Ewell, 93, Dies; Decorated General Led Forces in Vietnam," *Washington Post*, Aug. 5, 2009; Kevin P. Buckley, "Pacification's Deadly Price," *Newsweek*, June 19, 1972, 42–43; Turse, 214–217, 220.

12. Turse, 214–220.

13. Turse, 216–217.

14. Turse, 210–211.

15. "Maj. Gen. Ira Hunt, Ret., Recounts the U.S. Army's 9th Infantry Division's Operations in the Mekong Delta," C-SPAN, Oct. 10, 2010, www.c-span .org/video/?296486-2/the-9th-infantry-division-vietnam.

16. Gregory A. Daddis, *Withdrawal* (New York: Oxford University Press, 2017), 47.

17. Kevin P. Buckley, "Pacification's Deadly Price," *Newsweek*, June 19, 1972, 42–43; Turse, 248–258.

18. Jeffrey Record, *The Wrong War* (Annapolis, MD: Naval Institute Press, 1998), 87–91.

19. Record, "Maximizing Cobra Utilization," 8–12.

20. Record, "Maximizing Cobra Utilization"; Turse, 210–211.

21. Liddell Hart Centre for Military Archives (LHCMA), U.S. Armed Forces in Vietnam 1954–1975, MF 792, Reel 1, Brig. Gen. Tran Dinh Tho, *The Cambodian Incursion*, Indochina Monographs (Washington, DC: US Army Center of Military History, 1979), 6–8; Jeffrey Kimball, *Nixon's Vietnam War* (Lawrence: University Press of Kansas, 1998), 149.

22. Lien-Hang T. Nguyen, *Hanoi's War* (Chapel Hill: University of North

Carolina Press, 2012), 141; James H. Willbanks, *Abandoning Vietnam* (Lawrence: University Press of Kansas, 2004), 67–68.

23. UK National Archives (UKNA), DEFE 11/696, Washington, Dec. 29, 1970, Air Marshal Sir John Lapsley to Marshal of the RAF Sir Charles Elworthy, Chief of the Defence Staff, "US Army Morale and Its Effect on Military Activities in South Vietnam," and Washington, Jan. 20, 1972, Jukes to Stanbridge, "U.S. Withdrawals from Vietnam"; Kimball, *Nixon's Vietnam War*, 150–151; Sorley, *Better War*, 166; Daddis, *Withdrawal*, 69–70.

24. Daddis, *Withdrawal*, 91–96.

25. UKNA, DEFE 11/696, Saigon, Aug. 24, 1970, Amb. J. O. Moreton, "Government and Opposition Under President Thieu"; LHCMA, U.S. Armed Forces in Vietnam 1954–1975, MF 792, Reel 1, Brig. Gen. Tran Dinh Tho, *The Cambodian Incursion*, 2–4; Robert Shaplen, "We Have Always Survived," in *Reporting Vietnam: American Journalism 1959–1975* (New York: Library of America, 1998), 567; Sorley, *Better War*, 167, 184–185.

26. "Vietnam Statistics—War Costs: Complete Picture Impossible," *CQ Almanac 1975*, 31st ed. (Washington, DC: Congressional Quarterly, 1976), 301–305, http://library.cqpress.com/cqalmanac/cqal75-1213988; NARA, RG 472, MACV, Summary of Operational Interest Messages, 1 June 68 thru 30 April 69, Box 2, Nov. 20, 24, Dec. 22, 27, 29, 1969, LTC John B. Watkins Jr.

27. Shaplen, "We Have Always Survived," 586–587.

28. LHCMA, U.S. Armed Forces in Vietnam 1954–1975, MF 792, Reel 1, Brig. Gen. Tran Dinh Tho, *The Cambodian Incursion*, 3–9.

29. Nguyen, *Hanoi's War*, 161; Sorley, *Better War*, 200–202; Daddis, *Withdrawal*, 118–121.

30. William Shawcross, *Sideshow* (New York: Simon & Schuster, 1979), 113–114.

31. Daddis, *Withdrawal*, 118–121; Shawcross, 108–111.

32. William Burr and Jeffrey Kimball, *Nixon's Nuclear Specter: The Secret Alert of 1969, Madman Diplomacy, and the Vietnam War* (Lawrence: University Press of Kansas, 2015); Kimball, *Nixon's Vietnam War*, 160–163; Nguyen, *Hanoi's War*, 145; Willbanks, *Abandoning*, 61.

33. Shawcross, 92–95.

34. Kimball, *Nixon's Vietnam War*, 135; Shawcross, 25–26.

35. Sorley, *Better War*, 117–122; Shawcross, 21–32.

36. William Beecher, "Raids in Cambodia by U.S. Unprotested," *New York Times*, May 9, 1969; Shawcross, 33–35, 105–108, 112–114.

37. Nguyen, *Hanoi's War*, 159–160; Kimball, *Nixon's Vietnam War*, 154–155.

38. "War, Defense Commitments Dominate Foreign Affairs," 997–1007; Kimball, *Nixon's Vietnam War*, 157; Shawcross, 108–109.

39. Willbanks, *Abandoning*, 61–63.

40. Daddis, *Withdrawal*, 116–118.

41. Francine du Plessix Gray, "The Moratorium and the New Mobe," in

Reporting Vietnam, Part Two, 40–41, 48–49; Kimball, *Nixon's Vietnam War*, 165–166.

42. Rick Perlstein, *Nixonland* (New York: Scribner, 2008), 277–278, 430–435; Ang Cheng Guan, *Ending the Vietnam War* (London: Routledge, 2004), 35.

43. John A. Farrell, *Richard Nixon* (New York: Doubleday, 2017), 333–334, 369–370; Stanley Karnow, *Vietnam: A History* (New York: Penguin, 1983), 600–601; Willbanks, *Abandoning*, 64–65.

44. Kimball, *Nixon's Vietnam War*, 169–173; Sorley, *Better War*, 166; Willbanks, *Abandoning*, 65; Shawcross, 108–111.

45. Seymour M. Hersh, "The My Lai Massacre," in *Reporting Vietnam*, 413–417; UKNA, DEFE 11/696, Washington, Dec. 29, 1970, Air Marshal Sir John Lapsley to Marshal of the RAF Sir Charles Elworthy, Chief of the Defence Staff, "US Army Morale and Its Effect on Military Activities in South Vietnam"; NARA, RG 472, MACV, Summary of Operational Interest Messages, 1 June 68 thru 30 April 69, Box 2, Nov. 22, 1969, LTC John B. Watkins Jr.; "War, Defense Commitments Dominate Foreign Affairs," 997–1007.

46. NARA, RG 472, MACV, Tet Documents, Box 2, Atrocities (DCSOPS REQ), Dec. 4, 1969, LTC Jared B. Schopper, General Staff, "Memo for Record: My Lai Incident—Preparation of a White Paper"; Tom Ricks, *The Generals* (New York: Penguin, 2012), 292–303; Perlstein, *Nixonland*, 441–443.

47. Guan, *Ending the Vietnam War*, 20–22, 29, 53–54.

48. UKNA, DEFE 11/696, Hanoi, May 26, 1970, Daphne Park, "Collective Leadership and the Collective Masters in North Vietnam"; Joseph Kraft, "Letter from Hanoi," in *Reporting Vietnam*, 635.

49. LHCMA, U.S. Armed Forces in Vietnam 1954–1975, MF 792, Reel 1, Brig. Gen. Tran Dinh Tho, *The Cambodian Incursion*, 9–10; Peter R. Kann, "A Long, Leisurely Drive Through Mekong Delta Tells Much of the War," in *Reporting Vietnam: American Journalism 1959–1975* (New York: Library of America, 1998), 405.

50. Richard Zoglin, *Hope* (New York: Simon & Schuster, 2014), 394–397.

CHAPTER 21. "Cambodia Is a Man's Job"

1. National Archives and Records Administration (NARA), RG 472, MACV, A1 168, MACV, Weekly Assessment of Military Position, August 68 thru Dec. 70, Box 1, Jan. 3 and Feb. 14, 1970, COMUSMACV to CJCS, AMEMB SAIGON, CINCPAC, AMEMB PARIS, "Weekly Assessment of Military Position"; Harry G. Summers Jr., *On Strategy* (Novato, CA: Presidio, 1982), 89–90.

2. Jeffrey Kimball, *Nixon's Vietnam War* (Lawrence: University Press of Kansas, 1998), 113.

3. NARA, RG 472, MACV, A1 168, MACV, Weekly Assessment of Military Position, August 68 thru Dec. 70, Box 1, Jan. 3 and Feb. 14, 1970, COMUSMACV to CJCS, AMEMB SAIGON, CINCPAC, AMEMB PARIS, "Weekly Assessment of Military Position"; RG 472, MACV, 1 June 68 thru 30 April 69, Box 2, June 29, 1969, and 1 Sept. 69 thru 30 Sept. 70, Box 3, Jan. 31, Feb. 1, Feb. 24, 25, Mar. 10, 16, 17, May 2, 1970, LTC John B. Watkins Jr., and May 22, July 3, Nov. 23, 1970, Col. G.

Procter Jr.; James Sterba, "Scraps of Paper from Vietnam," in *Reporting Vietnam, Part Two: American Journalism 1969–1975* (New York: Library of America, 1998), 145.

4. NARA, RG 472, A1 485, MACV, Box 1, June 1972, "Vietnamization of CORDS Briefing."

5. Lewis Sorley, *A Better War* (Boston: Houghton Mifflin, 1999), 192.

6. Michael Herr, *Dispatches* (1977; New York: Vintage, 1991), 215.

7. NARA, RG 472, A1 63, MACV, J2 VCI Intelligence, Staff Visit Files, Box 1, Nov. 17, 1969, LTC Fletcher A. K. Aleong, "Trip Report, I CTZ," and Nov. 19, 1969, LTC Fletcher A. K. Aleong, "Trip Report, II CTZ," and Nov. 20, 1969, LTC Fletcher A. K. Aleong, "Trip Report III CTZ," and Nov. 26, 1969, LTC Fletcher A. K. Aleong, "Trip Report, IV CTZ"; RG 472, MACV, Summary of Operational Interest Messages, 1 June 68 thru 30 April 69, Box 2, Mar. 5, 6, 1970, LTC John B. Watkins Jr.; Gregory A. Daddis, *No Sure Victory* (New York: Oxford University Press, 2011), 202–206; Sorley, *Better War*, 195.

8. "War, Defense Commitments Dominate Foreign Affairs," *CQ Almanac 1969*, 25th ed. (Washington, DC: Congressional Quarterly, 1970), 997–1007, http://library.cqpress.com/cqalmanac/cqal69-871-26652-1245891.

9. "War, Defense Commitments Dominate Foreign Affairs," 997–1007.

10. UK National Archives (UKNA), DEFE 11/696, Hanoi, May 26, 1970, Daphne Park, "Collective Leadership and the Collective Masters in North Vietnam."

11. UKNA, DEFE 11/696, Hanoi, May 26, 1970, Daphne Park, "Collective Leadership and the Collective Masters in North Vietnam"; Kimball, *Nixon's Vietnam War*, 187–188.

12. NARA, RG 472, MACV, Summary of Operational Interest Messages, 1 Sept. 69 thru 30 Sept. 70, Box 3, Jan. 29, Feb. 28, Mar. 25, 30, Apr. 2, 1970, LTC John B. Watkins Jr.; Liddell Hart Centre for Military Archives (LHMCA), MF 803, Reel 8/8, U.S. Armed Forces in Vietnam 1954–1975, Part Two, Vietnam: Lessons Learned, Vol. 6, "Conduct of the War," 88; Sorley, *Better War*, 198; James H. Willbanks, *Abandoning Vietnam* (Lawrence: University Press of Kansas, 2004), 70–72; William Shawcross, *Sideshow* (New York: Simon & Schuster, 1979), 64.

13. NARA, RG 472, MACV, 1 Sept. 69 thru 30 Sept. 70, Box 3, Jan. 30, Feb. 24, 25, Mar. 10, May 2, 1970, LTC John B. Watkins Jr.; RG 472, A1 38, Box 1, "Sphinx" Intelligence Summaries, MACV, DISUM, Jan. 11, 1970; Eric Bergerud, *The Dynamics of Defeat* (Boulder, CO: Westview, 1991), 241–254; Gregory A. Daddis, *Withdrawal* (New York: Oxford University Press, 2017), 118–123.

14. Daddis, *No Sure Victory*, 209; Sorley, *Better War*, 177, 200–202; Shawcross, 136.

15. NARA, RG 472, A1 1158, 1, USARV/1st Infantry Division, Intelligence Reports, Lai Khe, RVN, Nov. 11, 26, Dec. 26, 1968, G-2 Deskis; Sorley, *Better War*, 202.

16. Shawcross, 114–117.

17. Lien-Hang T. Nguyen, *Hanoi's War* (Chapel Hill: University of North Carolina Press, 2012), 165–166; Shawcross, 116.

18. "Vietnam War: Domestic Impact," *CQ Almanac 1970*, 26th ed. (Washington, DC: Congressional Quarterly, 1971), 04-962–04-964, http://library.cqpress.com/cqalmanac/cqal70-1292128.

19. John A. Farrell, *Richard Nixon* (New York: Doubleday, 2017), 403–404.

20. "Vietnam War: Domestic Impact"; Sorley, *Better War*, 124–125; Willbanks, *Abandoning*, 78; Shawcross, 130, 136–139; Anthony Lewis, "Why Are We in Vietnam?," *New York Times*, May 9, 1970.

21. Nguyen, *Hanoi's War*, 166; Shawcross, 117–123, 132.

22. Shawcross, 130–131, 147, 152.

23. NARA, RG 472, MACV, Summary of Operational Interest Messages, 1 Sept. 69 thru 30 Sept. 70, Box 3, Feb. 28, Mar. 25, 30, Apr. 2, 3, 4, 20, 21, 24, 28, May 3, 4, 9, 12, 13, 14, 16, LTC John B. Watkins Jr., and Aug. 3, 31, 1970, Col. G. Procter Jr.; "War, Defense Commitments Dominate Foreign Affairs," 997–1007; Smithsonian, *A Short History of the Vietnam War* (New York: DK Publishing, 2021), 93, 214–215; Kimball, *Nixon's Vietnam War*, 193–196.

24. Shawcross, 137–141.

25. NARA, RG 472, MACV, Summary of Operational Interest Messages, 1 Sept. 69 thru 30 Sept. 70, Box 3, Mar. 25, 30, Apr. 2, 3, 4, 20, 21, 24, 28, 1970, LTC John B. Watkins Jr.

26. NARA, RG 472, MACV, Summary of Operational Interest Messages, 1 Sept. 69 thru 30 Sept. 70, Box 3, Mar. 25, 30, Apr. 2, 3, 4, 20, 21, 24, 28, 1970, LTC John B. Watkins Jr.; James T. Gillam, *Life and Death in the Central Highlands* (Denton: University of North Texas Press, 2010), 184.

27. Nguyen, *Hanoi's War*, 175–177.

28. Peter R. Kann, "Vietnamese Alienate Cambodians in Fight Against Mutual Enemy," in *Reporting Vietnam, Part Two*, 124–125; Sorley, *Better War*, 208; Nguyen, *Hanoi's War*, 169; Shawcross, 125–127, 132–133.

29. Rick Perlstein, *Nixonland* (New York: Scribner, 2008), 472–473, 476–479.

30. Kimball, *Nixon's Vietnam War*, 198–199; Peter R. Kann, "Vietnamese Alienate Cambodians in Fight Against Mutual Enemy," in *Reporting Vietnam, Part Two*, 123; Smithsonian, 390; Kimball, *Nixon's Vietnam War*, 202–204; Shawcross, 118–123, 128, 134–135.

31. "Viet Nam War Grows, Becomes Major Issue," *CQ Almanac 1965*, 21st ed. (Washington, DC: Congressional Quarterly, 1966), 449–457, http://library.cqpress.com/cqalmanac/cqal65-1259469; Shawcross, 152–153.

32. "War, Defense Commitments Dominate Foreign Affairs," 997–1007; Willbanks, *Abandoning*, 68.

33. Shawcross, 19–20, 138–140, 150; Willbanks, *Abandoning*, 72–76.

34. NARA, RG 472, MACV, Summary of Operational Interest Messages, 1 Sept. 69 thru 30 Sept. 70, Box 3, May 22, 1970, LTC John B. Watkins Jr., and July 3, 1970, Col. G. Procter Jr.; LHCMA, U.S. Armed Forces in Vietnam 1954–1975,

MF 792, Reel 1, Brig. Gen. Tran Dinh Tho, *The Cambodian Incursion*, 9–10, and MF 803, Reel 8/8, U.S. Armed Forces in Vietnam 1954–1975, Part Two, Vietnam: Lessons Learned, Vol. 6, "Conduct of the War," 88; Sorley, *Better War*, 203; Smithsonian, 393; Gillam, 206.

35. Daddis, *Withdrawal*, 123–128.

36. Daddis, *No Sure Victory*, 210–211; Sorley, *Better War*, 203; Willbanks, *Abandoning*, 79–80.

37. Anthony Lewis, "Why Are We in Vietnam?," *New York Times*, May 9, 1970; Shawcross, 173.

38. Daddis, *Withdrawal*, 129–130.

39. Wallace Terry, *Bloods* (New York: Random House, 1984), 232; Sorley, *Better War*, 203–205, 210; Willbanks, *Abandoning*, 79–84; Shawcross, 147, 152.

40. Shawcross, 163–165.

41. Kimball, *Nixon's Vietnam War*, 224; Sorley, *Better War*, 203–205; Shawcross, 68, 183–185, 220–222.

42. William C. Westmoreland, *A Soldier Reports* (New York: Doubleday, 1976), 388; Shawcross, 174–175; Kimball, *Nixon's Vietnam War*, 223.

43. NARA, RG 472, MACV, Summary of Operational Interest Messages, 1 Oct. 70 thru 31 July 72, Box 4, Mar. 22, 1972, Col. John F. C. Kenney Jr.

44. NARA, RG 472, MACV, Summary of Operational Interest Messages, 1 Sept. 69 thru 30 Sept. 70, Box 3, June 1, 2, 4, 8, 9, 10, 11, 1970, LTC John B. Watkins Jr.; Gillam, 194; Kimball, *Nixon's Vietnam War*, 210–212.

45. Daddis, *Withdrawal*, 130–131.

46. Lewis Sorley, ed., *The Vietnam War* (Lubbock: Texas Tech University Press, 2010), 548.

47. William J. Duiker, *The Communist Road to Power in Vietnam* (Boulder, CO: Westview, 1981), 283–289.

48. Willbanks, *Abandoning*, 85.

49. John W. Finney, "Senator Byrd's Loophole," *New York Times*, June 24, 1970.

50. "War, Defense Commitments Dominate Foreign Affairs," 997–1007; Perlstein, *Nixonland*, 472; Daddis, *Withdrawal*, 166.

51. "Vietnam War: Domestic Impact"; Richard Halloran, "Ban Sought on Troops for Cambodia," *New York Times*, Apr. 12, 1970; John W. Finney, "Congress Urged by Nixon's Aides to Kill War Curb," *New York Times*, July 16, 1970; Gloria Emerson, "We Are All 'Bui Doi,'" in *Reporting Vietnam, Part Two*, 258; Sorley, *Better War*, 176.

52. "Vietnam War: Domestic Impact"; Sorley, *Better War*, 176.

53. Willbanks, *Abandoning*, 85–86.

54. Finney, "Congress Urged by Nixon's Aides to Kill War Curb"; Edwin L. Dale Jr., "What Vietnam Did to the American Economy," *New York Times*, Jan. 28, 1973; Kimball, *Nixon's Vietnam War*, 215–218; Shawcross, 153; Daddis, *Withdrawal*, 128–131.

55. Daddis, *Withdrawal*, 133–134.

56. Keith W. Nolan, *Ripcord* (Novato, CA: Presidio, 2003), 171–174; Andrew Wiest, *Vietnam's Forgotten Army* (New York: NYU Press, 2008), 186–190.

CHAPTER 22. Quiet Mutiny

1. James R. McDonough, *Platoon Leader* (Novato, CA: Presidio, 1985), 63; Stewart Alsop, "The American Class System," in *Reporting Vietnam: American Journalism 1959–1975* (New York: Library of America, 1998), 463.

2. George Lardner Jr. and Lois Romano, "At Height of Vietnam, Bush Picks Guard," *Washington Post*, July 28, 1999; David Halbfinger and Steven Holmes, "A Nation at War: The Troops," *New York Times*, Mar. 30, 2003.

3. James T. Gillam, *Life and Death in the Central Highlands* (Denton: University of North Texas Press, 2010), 17; Lewis Sorley, *A Better War* (Boston: Houghton Mifflin, 1999), 301–304.

4. Alsop, "The American Class System," 463–465.

5. Ronald H. Spector, *After Tet* (New York: Free Press, 1993), 29–32.

6. Deborah Shapley, *Promise and Power* (Boston: Little, Brown, 1993), 384–387.

7. Amy J. Rutenberg, "How the Draft Reshaped America," *New York Times*, Oct. 6, 2017.

8. John T. Correll, "When the Draft Calls Ended," *Air Force Magazine*, Apr. 1, 2008; Gregory A. Daddis, *No Sure Victory* (New York: Oxford University Press, 2011), 185–187, 194–195.

9. Jordan A. Schwarz, "Hershey's Draft," *Reviews in American History* 14, no. 1 (Mar. 1986): 136; Hamilton Gregory, "How a Plan to Salvage Military Rejects for Vietnam War Service Ended Disastrously," HistoryNet, June 15, 2018, www. historynet.com/mcnamaras-boys/.

10. James Sterba, "Scraps of Paper from Vietnam," in *Reporting Vietnam, Part Two: American Journalism 1969–1975* (New York: Library of America, 1998), 139–140.

11. Blake Stillwell, "11 Ways People Dodged the Draft During the Vietnam War," *Business Insider*, Jan. 5, 2020; Spector, 28.

12. Eric M. Bergerud, *The Dynamics of Defeat* (Boulder, CO: Westview, 1991), 231; Ron Milam, *Not a Gentleman's War* (Chapel Hill: University of North Carolina Press, 2009), 89–92; William C. Westmoreland, *A Soldier Reports* (New York: Doubleday, 1976), 296; Daddis, *No Sure Victory*, 189.

13. Tim O'Brien, *The Things They Carried* (New York: Penguin, 1990), 89.

14. John Pilger, "The Quiet Mutiny," *World in Action*, 1970, YouTube (posted September 10, 2011, by yeoldbasser), www.youtube.com/watch?v=krcNTkAgRrA.

15. Jeffrey Kimball, *Nixon's Vietnam War* (Lawrence: University Press of Kansas, 1998), 111.

16. James H. Willbanks, *Abandoning Vietnam* (Lawrence: University Press of Kansas, 2004), 46–47; Smithsonian, *A Short History of the Vietnam War* (New York: DK Publishing, 2021), 358–359.

17. "Hope Brings Laughter to DMZ," *Bangkok Post*, Dec. 23, 1970; Norman M. Camp, "U.S. Army Psychiatry in the Vietnam War," *U.S. Army Medical Dept. Journal*, Apr.–June 2015, 19; Kimball, *Nixon's Vietnam War*, 155; Sorley, *Better War*, 129–130, 289–293, 298; Milam, 146–149; Spector, 273–278.

18. Westmoreland, 192.

19. Milam, 151–154; Spector, 249–252.

20. Ed Rasimus, *Palace Cobra* (New York: St. Martin's, 2006), 146–147.

21. Tom Ricks, *The Generals* (New York: Penguin, 2012), 309–314.

22. National Archives and Records Administration (NARA), RG 472, A1 60, Bob Hope Christmas Shows 1970–72, 1970, Oct. 31, 1970, Maj. Davis, GS, Project Officer, "Advance Information Sheets for Bob Hope Show"; Camp, 19, 26.

23. NARA, RG 472, A1 60, Bob Hope Christmas Shows 1970–72, 1970, Oct. 31, 1970, Capt. Sherman, GS, Project Officer, "Advance Information Sheets for Bob Hope Show"; Milam, 157–161; Peter Brush, "The Hard Truth About Fragging," HistoryNet, July 28, 2010, www.historynet.com/the-hard-truth-about-fragging/.

24. Wallace Terry, "Black Power in Viet Nam," in *Reporting Vietnam*, 397–398; Milam, 154–157; Gregory A. Daddis, *Withdrawal* (New York: Oxford University Press, 2017), 150–156; Spector, 244–247.

25. UK National Archives (UKNA), DEFE 11/696, Washington, Dec. 29, 1970, Air Marshal Sir John Lapsley to Marshal of the RAF Sir Charles Elworthy, Chief of the Defence Staff, "US Army Morale and Its Effect on Military Activities in South Vietnam."

26. Liddell Hart Centre for Military Archives (LHCMA), U.S. Armed Forces in Vietnam 1954–1975, MF 812, HQ I Field Force, Jan. 8, 1971, Lt. Gen. A. S. Collins Jr. to Commanding General, US Army Vietnam, Jan. 7, 1971, "Senior Officer's Debriefing Report, Inclusive Dates 15 Feb. 1970 Through 9 Jan. 1971."

27. LHCMA, U.S. Armed Forces in Vietnam 1954–1975, MF 812, HQ I Field Force, Jan. 8, 1971, Lt. Gen. A. S. Collins Jr. to Commanding General, US Army Vietnam, Jan. 7, 1971, "Senior Officer's Debriefing Report, Inclusive Dates 15 Feb. 1970 Through 9 Jan. 1971."

28. LHCMA, U.S. Armed Forces in Vietnam 1954–1975, MF 812, HQ I Field Force, Jan. 8, 1971, Lt. Gen. A. S. Collins Jr. to Commanding General, US Army Vietnam, Jan. 7, 1971, "Senior Officer's Debriefing Report, Inclusive Dates 15 Feb. 1970 Through 9 Jan. 1971"; Andrew F. Krepinevich Jr., *The Army and Vietnam* (Baltimore: Johns Hopkins University Press, 1986), 196–202.

29. John Saar, "You Can't Just Hand Out Orders," *Life*, Nov. 9, 1970, 30–37.

30. Daddis, *Withdrawal*, 146–149; Stewart Alsop, "Vietnam: Out Faster," *Newsweek*, Dec. 7, 1970; Robert Shaplen, "We Have Always Survived," in *Reporting Vietnam*, 558; Daddis, *No Sure Victory*, 188.

31. Westmoreland, 368; Donald Kirk, "Who Wants to Be the Last American Killed in Vietnam," in *Reporting Vietnam*, 526, 538.

32. Westmoreland, 377–378; Milam, 164–165.

33. Nick Turse, *Kill Anything That Moves* (New York: Metropolitan, 2013),

228–230, 242–243; Rick Perlstein, *Nixonland* (New York: Scribner, 2008), 441–442, 554–557; Ricks, 300–307; Daddis, *Withdrawal*, 129–130.

34. Chuck Gross, *Rattler One-Seven* (Denton: University of North Texas PressPress, 2004), 46; Turse, 231–233; James E. Wright, "Nixon's Leniency After My Lai Hurt Veterans," Dec. 15, 2019, Defense One, www.defenseone.com/ideas/2019/12/nixons-leniency-after-my-lai-hurt-veterans-trumps-will-too/161905/.

35. Kimball, *Nixon's Vietnam War*, 251–252.

36. "Man and Woman of the Year: The Middle Americans," *Time*, Jan. 5, 1970; Camp, 23; Kimball, *Nixon's Vietnam War*, 250; Joe McGinniss, "From *The Selling of the President 1968*," in *Reporting Vietnam, Part One: American Journalism 1959–1969* (New York: Library of America, 1998), 659.

37. Perlstein, *Nixonland*, 484–489.

38. William Shawcross, *Sideshow* (New York: Simon & Schuster, 1979), 153; Willbanks, *Abandoning*, 86.

39. James A. Michener, "From *Kent State: What Happened and Why*," in *Reporting Vietnam*, 451–453; Kimball, *Nixon's Vietnam War*, 219.

40. Perlstein, *Nixonland*, 493–495.

41. Fred J. Cook, "Hard-Hats: The Rampaging Patriots," in *Reporting Vietnam, Part Two*, 100, 104–110.

42. "Vietnam Background: Congress and the War: Years of Support," *CQ Almanac 1975*, 31st ed. (Washington, DC: Congressional Quarterly, 1976), 296–299, http://library.cqpress.com/cqalmanac/cqal75-1213972.

43. Lewis Sorley, ed., *The Vietnam War* (Lubbock: Texas Tech University Press, 2010), 52.

44. LHCMA, U.S. Armed Forces in Vietnam 1954–1975, MF 812, HQ I Field Force, Jan. 8, 1971, Lt. Gen. A. S. Collins Jr. to Commanding General, US Army Vietnam, Jan. 7, 1971, "Senior Officer's Debriefing Report, Inclusive Dates 15 Feb. 1970 Through 9 Jan. 1971"; NARA, RG 472, MACV, Summary of Operational Interest Messages, 1 Sept. 69 thru 30 Sept. 70, Box 3, Jan. 29, Mar. 6, May 19, 1970, LTC John B. Watkins Jr., and 1 Oct. 70 thru 31 July 72, Box 4, Nov. 21, 1971, LTC Robert A. Mountel; RG 472, A1 38, Box 1, "Sphinx" Intelligence Summaries, MACV, DISUM, Mar. 30, 1970, Feb. 5, 9, 14, Mar. 20, 1971; Sorley, *Better War*, 378. (The general in question was Do Ke Giai.)

45. NARA, RG 472, A1 127, MACV, Province Inspection Reports 1971, "Darlac, An Giang, Gia Dinh, Pleiku, Quang Nam," etc.; LHCMA, U.S. Armed Forces in Vietnam 1954–1975, MF 812, HQ I Field Force, Jan. 8, 1971, Lt. Gen. A. S. Collins Jr. to Commanding General, US Army Vietnam, Jan. 7, 1971, "Senior Officer's Debriefing Report, Inclusive Dates 15 Feb. 1970 Through 9 Jan. 1971"; Spector, 283–284.

46. LHCMA, U.S. Armed Forces in Vietnam 1954–1975, MF 812, HQ I Field Force, Jan. 8, 1971, Lt. Gen. A. S. Collins Jr. to Commanding General, US Army Vietnam, Jan. 7, 1971, "Senior Officer's Debriefing Report, Inclusive Dates 15 Feb. 1970 Through 9 Jan. 1971."

47. NARA, RG 472, A1 127, MACV, Province Inspection Reports 1971,

Translations, "Inspection of Pleiku Sector, 20–25 Sept. 1971," and "Inspection of An Giang Sector, 25–29 Oct. 1971," and "Inspection of Darlac Sector, 18–20 Oct. 1971," and "Inspection of Gia Dinh Sector, 30 Aug. to 4 Sept. 1971," and "Inspection of Binh Long Sector, 11–16 Oct. 1971," and "Inspection of Quang Nam Sector, 1–6 Nov. 1971," and "Inspection of Quang Tri Sector, 3–12 Aug. 1971"; RG 472, MACV, Summary of Operational Interest Messages, 1 Sept. 69 thru 30 Sept. 70, Box 3, May 21, 1970, LTC John B. Watkins Jr.; Sorley, *Better War*, 214–215; Willbanks, *Abandoning*, 90.

CHAPTER 23. "The Heaviest Defeat Ever for Nixon & Company"

1. Andrew Wiest, *Vietnam's Forgotten Army* (New York: New York University Press, 2008), 197–199.

2. Jeffrey Kimball, *Nixon's Vietnam War* (Lawrence: University Press of Kansas, 1998), 245; Lewis Sorley, *A Better War* (Boston: Houghton Mifflin, 1999), 230–234; James H. Willbanks, *Abandoning Vietnam* (Lawrence: University Press of Kansas, 2004), 95.

3. Smithsonian, *A Short History of the Vietnam War* (New York: DK Publishing, 2021), 408–409; Sorley, *Better War*, 178, 198, 235–236.

4. UK National Archives (UKNA), DEFE 11/696, Washington, Apr. 9, 1971, Col. A. G. H. Jukes to Min of Defence, "South Vietnamese Operations in Laos" and "Operation Lam Son 719: A Preliminary Assessment as at 2 Apr 71."

5. National Archives and Records Administration (NARA), RG 472, A1 128, Lessons Learned from Operation Lam Son 719, MACV J3 #30–#41, [1971], "Lam Son 719 Briefing."

6. Sorley, *Better War*, 232–233; Willbanks, *Abandoning*, 95–96.

7. Lien-Hang T. Nguyen, *Hanoi's War* (Chapel Hill: University of North Carolina Press, 2012), 202.

8. LHCMA, U.S. Armed Forces in Vietnam 1954–1975, MF 812, HQ I Field Force, Jan. 8, 1971, Lt. Gen. A. S. Collins Jr. to Commanding General, US Army Vietnam, Jan. 7, 1971, "Senior Officer's Debriefing Report, Inclusive Dates 15 Feb. 1970 Through 9 Jan. 1971."

9. Gregory A. Daddis, *Withdrawal* (New York: Oxford University Press, 2017), 174.

10. Gloria Emerson, "A Border Crossing into Laos, the Litter of Troops and History," in *Reporting Vietnam, Part Two: American Journalism 1969–1975* (New York: Library of America, 1998), 186.

11. Willbanks, *Abandoning*, 94–98.

12. William Shawcross, *Sideshow* (New York: Simon & Schuster, 1979), 214.

13. "War, Defense Commitments Dominate Foreign Affairs," *CQ Almanac 1969*, 25th ed. (Washington, DC: Congressional Quarterly, 1970), 997–1007, http://library.cqpress.com/cqalmanac/cqal69-871-26652-1245891; Nguyen, *Hanoi's War*, 201–202; Emerson, "A Border Crossing into Laos," 187–188; Smithsonian, 411.

14. NARA, RG 472, A1 38, Box 1, "Sphinx" Intelligence Summaries, MACV, DISUM, Jan. 14, 1970; Daddis, *Withdrawal*, 168–176.

15. NARA, RG 472, A1 128, Lessons Learned from Operation Lam Son 719, Apr. 1, 1971, Col. Arthur W. Pence, "After-Action Report: Lamson 719," and MACV J3, n.d., "Lessons Learned from Operation Lam Son 719," and "Lam Son 719 Briefing"; Nguyen, *Hanoi's War*, 203; Jeffrey Record, *The Wrong War* (Annapolis, MD: Naval Institute Press, 1998), 138.

16. Chuck Gross, *Rattler One-Seven* (Denton: University of North Texas Press, 2004), 134.

17. NARA, RG 472, A1 128, Lessons Learned from Operation Lam Son 719, HQ 101st Airborne Division (Airmobile), Mar. 20, 1971, BG Sidney Berry, "Memorandum for Record: Airmobile Operations in Support of Operation Lam Son 719"; Max Hastings, *Vietnam* (New York: Harper Collins, 2018), 497.

18. UKNA, DEFE 11/696, Washington, Apr. 9, 1971, Col. A. G. H. Jukes to Min of Defence, "South Vietnamese Operations in Laos" and "Operation Lam Son 719: A Preliminary Assessment as at 2 Apr 71"; NARA, RG 472, A1 128, Lessons Learned from Operation Lam Son 719, MACV J3 #30–#41, [1971], "Lam Son 719 Briefing."

19. NARA, RG 472, A1 128, Lessons Learned from Operation Lam Son 719, Apr. 1, 1971, Col. Arthur W. Pence, "After-Action Report: Lamson 719"; Sorley, *Better War*, 257–258.

20. NARA, RG 472, A1 128, Lessons Learned from Operation Lam Son 719, MACV J3 #19–#29, "Lamson 719 Daily Air Support," and MACV to CINCPAC, Apr. 26, 1971, "Request for Data," and Apr. 1, 1971, Col. Arthur W. Pence, "After-Action Report: Lamson 719."

21. Willbanks, *Abandoning*, 101–102; Wiest, *Vietnam's Forgotten Army*, 203–206.

22. Gross, 136–137.

23. NARA, RG 472, A1 128, Lessons Learned from Operation Lam Son 719, MACV J3 #1–#15, May 15, 1971, BG John Q. Henion, Director, MACT, "Lessons Learned Data from the 1st ARVN Division"; Willbanks, *Abandoning*, 105–106.

24. Sorley, *Better War*, 247–248; Wiest, *Vietnam's Forgotten Army*, 210–211.

25. NARA, RG 472, A1 128, Lessons Learned from Operation Lam Son 719, MACV J3 #1–#15, Saigon, July 25, 1971, MACV translation, JGS/RVNAF, "Battlefield Experience Report—1st ARVN Division, X Regt, from 17 to 26 Feb. 71."

26. NARA, RG 472, A1 128, Lessons Learned from Operation Lam Son 719, Apr. 1, 1971, Col. Arthur W. Pence, "After-Action Report: Lamson 719."

27. NARA, RG 472, A1 128, Lessons Learned from Operation Lam Son 719, MACV J3 #1–#15, Saigon, July 30, 1971, MACV translation, J3/JGS, "Combat Experience—Operation Lam Son 719."

28. NARA, RG 472, A1 128, Lessons Learned from Operation Lam Son 719, MACV J3 #30–#41, MACJ3-05, n.d., "Observations of Tank-Infantry Combined Arms Coordination," and May 22, 1971, Col. Raymond Battreall, Armor, Senior Advisor, "Performance of 1st Armor Brigade in Operation Lam Son 719," and Apr. 13, 1971, LCDR Richard Morgan, "Lessons Learned in PSYOP During Lam Son

719," and "Lessons Learned from Operation Lam Son 719," and Apr. 1, 1971, Col. Arthur W. Pence, "After-Action Report: Lamson 719."

29. NARA, RG 472, A1 128, Lessons Learned from Operation Lam Son 719, MACV J3 #19–#29, Mar. 30, 1971, Col. James B. Vaught, Infantry, Senior Advisor, "Significant Lessons Learned."

30. UKNA, DEFE 11/696, Washington, Apr. 9, 1971, Col. A. G. H. Jukes to Min of Defence, "South Vietnamese Operations in Laos" and "Operation Lam Son 719: A Preliminary Assessment as at 2 Apr 71"; NARA, RG 472, A1 128, Lessons Learned from Operation Lam Son 719, MACV J3 #30–#41, [1971], "Lam Son 719 Briefing"; Sorley, *Better War*, 255.

31. Gross, 110–111.

32. Kimball, *Nixon's Vietnam War*, 245–246.

33. Gross, 148–149.

34. NARA, RG 472, A1 128, Lessons Learned from Operation Lam Son 719, HQ 101st Airborne Division (Airmobile), Mar. 20, 1971, BG Sidney Berry, "Memorandum for Record: Airmobile Operations in Support of Operation Lam Son 719," and MACV J3 #19–#29, Mar. 30, 1971, Col. James B. Vaught, Infantry, Senior Advisor, "Significant Lessons Learned," and MACJ3–05, n.d., "Observations of Tank-Infantry Combined Arms Coordination," and Apr. 1, 1971, Col. Arthur W. Pence, "After-Action Report: Lamson 719," and May 22, 1971, Col. Raymond Battreall, Armor, Senior Advisor, "Performance of 1st Armor Brigade in Operation Lam Son 719," and Apr. 13, 1971, LCDR Richard Morgan, "Lessons Learned in PSYOP During Lam Son 719"; James H. Willbanks, "Lam Son 719: South Vietnam Invades Laos, 1971," HistoryNet, Apr. 13, 2017, www.historynet .com/south-vietnam-invades-laos-1971/.

35. Gross, 162.

36. Gross, 145; Willbanks, *Abandoning*, 109–110.

37. NARA, RG 472, A1 128, Lessons Learned from Operation Lam Son 719, MACV J3 #19–#29, May 22, 1971, Col. Raymond Battreall, Armor, Senior Advisor, "Performance of 1st Armor Brigade in Operation Lam Son 719," and MACAG translation, n.d., "Attack against Hill 583 Base Occupied by the Ranger Battalion B During Operation Lam Son 719," and MACJ3–05, n.d., "Working Paper—Evaluation of Unit Combat Effectiveness—Lam Son 719"; Hastings, 498–499; Sorley, *Better War*, 250–252.

38. Harry G. Summers Jr., *On Strategy* (Novato, CA: Presidio, 1982), 176; Willbanks, *Abandoning*, 281–283, 288; Kimball, *Nixon's Vietnam War*, 247.

39. NARA, RG 472, A1 128, Lessons Learned from Operation Lam Son 719, MACV J3, Saigon, July 26, 1971, MACV translation, JGS/RVNAF, "Battlefield Experience Report—1st ARVN Division Attack upon Cua-Viet in Lower Laos from 13 to 21 March 71," and May 15, 1971, BG John Q. Henion, Director, MACT, "Lessons Learned Data from the 1st ARVN Division," and Saigon, Apr. 11, 1971, Col. Tran Dinh Tho, J3, JGS, "Total Friendly and Enemy Losses in Operation Lam Son 719"; Willbanks, *Abandoning*, 108.

40. William C. Westmoreland, *A Soldier Reports* (New York: Doubleday, 1976), 391.

41. NARA, RG 472, A1 128, Lessons Learned from Operation Lam Son 719, MACV J3, Mar. 30, 1971, Col. James B. Vaught, Infantry, Senior Advisor, "Significant Lessons Learned"; Sorley, *Better War*, 256–257.

42. NARA, RG 472, A1 128, Lessons Learned from Operation Lam Son 719, MACV J3, Saigon, July 30, 1971, MACV translation, J3/JGS, "Combat Experience—Operation Lam Son 719," and Apr. 13, 1971, LCDR Richard Morgan, "Lessons Learned in PSYOP During Lam Son 719"; Sorley, *Better War*, 184–185.

43. NARA, RG 472, A1 128, Lessons Learned from Operation Lam Son 719, Apr. 1, 1971, Col. Arthur W. Pence, "After-Action Report: Lamson 719."

44. Willbanks, "Lam Son 719: South Vietnam Invades Laos, 1971"; Sorley, *Better War*, 262; Willbanks, *Abandoning*, 111, 115.

45. NARA, RG 472, A1 128, Lessons Learned from Operation Lam Son 719, MACV J3, Saigon, Apr. 2, 1971, Gen. Cao Van Vien, "Operations in Cambodia and Laos," and July 30, 1971, MACV translation, J3/JGS, "Combat Experience—Operation Lam Son 719"; Lewis Sorley, ed., *The Vietnam War* (Lubbock: Texas Tech University Press, 2010), 593–594.

46. NARA, RG 472, A1 128, Lessons Learned from Operation Lam Son 719, MACV J3, Saigon, Apr. 15, 1971, Gen. Cao Van Vien, "Reporting of Friendly and Enemy Casualties During Operations."

47. NARA, RG 472, A1 128, Lessons Learned from Operation Lam Son 719, MACV J3, Saigon, Apr. 2, 1971, Gen. Cao Van Vien, "Operations in Cambodia and Laos," and July 25, 1971, MACV translation, JGS/RVNAF, "Battlefield Experience Report—1st ARVN Division, X Regt, from 17 to 26 Feb. 71, and July 26, 1971, MACV translation, JGS/RVNAF, "Battlefield Experience Report—1st ARVN Division Attack upon Cua-Viet in Lower Laos from 13 to 21 March 71."

48. NARA, RG 472, A1 128, Lessons Learned from Operation Lam Son 719, MACV J3, Saigon, July 30, 1971, MACV translation, J3/JGS, "Combat Experience—Operation Lam Son 719," and n.d., "Observations of Tank-Infantry Combined Arms Coordination"; UKNA, DEFE 11/696, Washington, Apr. 9, 1971, Col. A. G. H. Jukes to Min of Defence, "South Vietnamese Operations in Laos" and "Operation Lam Son 719: A Preliminary Assessment as at 2 Apr 71," and NATO Military Committee, May 1971, Gen. B. E. Spivy, "Transcript of Admiral Moorer's Remarks on Lam Son 719"; Gloria Emerson, "Copters Return from Laos with the Dead," in *Reporting Vietnam: American Journalism 1959–1975* (New York: Library of America, 1998), 511; Peter Braestrup, "The South Vietnamese Army," in *Reporting Vietnam*, 620–621.

49. Summers, *On Strategy*, 104.

50. UKNA, DEFE 11/696, Peking, Mar. 2, 1971, John Denson to FCO, "Confidential-Eclipse"; NARA, RG 472, MACV, Summary of Operational Interest Messages, 1 Sept. 69 thru 30 Sept. 70, Box 3, Feb. 28, Mar. 25, 30, Apr. 2, 1970, LTC John B. Watkins Jr.; Nguyen, *Hanoi's War*, 204–207.

CHAPTER 24. "We've Made the War Too Much of a Good Thing"

1. National Archives and Records Administration (NARA), RG 472, A1 128, Lessons Learned from Operation Lam Son 719, Mar. 21, 1971, Senior Marine Advisor, "Combat Operations After Action Report Lam Son 719."

2. NARA, RG 472, A1 128, Lessons Learned from Operation Lam Son 719, MACV to CINCPAC, Apr. 26, 1971, "Request for Data," and MACJ3-05, n.d., "Working Paper—Evaluation of Unit Combat Effectiveness—Lam Son 719."

3. Gloria Emerson, "Spirit of Saigon's Army Shaken in Laos," in *Reporting Vietnam: American Journalism 1959–1975* (New York: Library of America, 1998), 512–513.

4. NARA, RG 472, A1 128, Lessons Learned from Operation Lam Son 719, MACV J3 #30–#41, [1971], "Lam Son 719 Briefing"; RG 472, A1 38, Box 2, "Sphinx" Intelligence Summaries, MACV, DISUM, June 27, 1971; William Shawcross, *Sideshow* (New York: Simon & Schuster, 1979), 218.

5. Gregory A. Daddis, *Withdrawal* (New York: Oxford University Press, 2017), 174–175.

6. James H. Willbanks, *Abandoning Vietnam* (Lawrence: University Press of Kansas, 2004), 118; Max Hastings, *Vietnam* (New York: Harper Collins, 2018), 502–503; Lewis Sorley, *A Better War* (Boston: Houghton Mifflin, 1999), 262–264.

7. Andrew Wiest, *Vietnam's Forgotten Army* (New York: New York University Press, 2008), 194, 230–233.

8. NARA, RG 472, A1 128, Lessons Learned from Operation Lam Son 719, MACV J3, Apr. 29, 1971, Maj. Moore, "Combat Service Support Missions," and MACV J3, n.d., "Observations of Tank-Infantry Combined Arms Coordination," and Apr. 1, 1971, Col. Arthur W. Pence, "After-Action Report: Lamson 719"; Hastings, 502.

9. Shawcross, 200, 208, 231.

10. NARA, RG 472, A1 128, Lessons Learned from Operation Lam Son 719, undated, untitled, unsigned 22-page MACV briefing on "Lessons Learned and Experiences Gained from RVN and US Sources on Operation Lam Son 719 and Operation Snuol"; Shawcross, 233.

11. NARA, RG 472, MACV, Summary of Operational Interest Messages, 1 Sept. 69 thru 30 Sept. 70, Box 3, Mar. 13, May 26, 28, Aug. 15, 25, Oct. 1, 1970, LTC John B. Watkins Jr., and Col. G. Procter Jr., and 1 Oct. 70 thru 31 July 72, Box 4, Oct. 1, Nov. 27, Dec. 26, 1970, Sept. 27, 1971, LTC Robert A. Mountel.

12. NARA, RG 472, A1 38, Box 2, "Sphinx" Intelligence Summaries, MACV, DISUM, June 9, 1971; RG 472, MACV, Summary of Operational Interest Messages, 1 Oct. 70 thru 31 July 72, Box 4, Nov. 22, 27, 1970, Col. G. Procter Jr.; Smithsonian, *A Short History of the Vietnam War* (New York: DK Publishing, 2021), 357; Lewis Sorley, ed., *The Vietnam War* (Lubbock: Texas Tech University Press, 2010), 610–611.

13. John A. Farrell, *Richard Nixon* (New York: Doubleday, 2017), 493; Rick Perlstein, *Nixonland* (New York: Scribner, 2008), 580–581; Jeffrey Kimball, *Nixon's*

Vietnam War (Lawrence: University Press of Kansas, 1998), 253–255; Daddis, *Withdrawal*, 159.

14. William J. Shkurti, *Soldiering On in a Dying War* (Lawrence: University Press of Kansas, 2011), 91–94, 177–178; Donald Kirk, "Who Wants to Be the Last American Killed in Vietnam," in *Reporting Vietnam*, 524.

15. Lien-Hang T. Nguyen, *Hanoi's War* (Chapel Hill: University of North Carolina Press, 2012), 219–221; Daddis, *Withdrawal*, 181–182.

16. UK National Archives (UKNA), DEFE 11/696, Saigon, Aug. 24, 1970, Amb. J. O. Moreton, "Government and Opposition Under President Thieu"; NARA, RG 472, MACV, Summary of Operational Interest Messages, 1 Sept. 69 thru 30 Sept. 70, Box 3, June 16, 1970, LTC John B. Watkins Jr., and Aug. 26, 1970, Col. G. Procter Jr.; Kimball, *Nixon's Vietnam War*, 270–276; Sorley, *Better War*, 280–281.

17. NARA, RG 472, A1 38, Box 1, "Sphinx" Intelligence Summaries, MACV, DISUM, Feb. 5, Mar. 17, 1971; UKNA, DEFE 11/696, Saigon, Aug. 24, 1970, Amb. J. O. Moreton, "Government and Opposition Under President Thieu"; Smithsonian, 411.

18. "Vietnam War: Domestic Impact," *CQ Almanac 1970*, 26th ed. (Washington, DC: Congressional Quarterly, 1971), 04-962–04-964, http://library.cqpress.com/cqalmanac/cqal70-1292128.

19. Kimball, *Nixon's Vietnam War*, 279.

20. Kimball, *Nixon's Vietnam War*, 278–285.

21. Kimball, *Nixon's Vietnam War*, 276–278.

22. UKNA, DEFE 11/696, Washington, Jan. 20, 1972, Jukes to Stanbridge, "U.S. Withdrawals from Vietnam"; Kimball, *Nixon's Vietnam War*, 289; Nguyen, *Hanoi's War*, 221–222; Willbanks, *Abandoning*, 46–49.

23. James M. Naughton, "Muskie Peace Plan Bids Saigon Settle or Lose Aid," *New York Times*, Feb. 3, 1972; Willbanks, *Abandoning*, 121.

24. UKNA, DEFE 11/696, Washington, Jan. 20, 1972, Jukes to Stanbridge, "U.S. Withdrawals from Vietnam"; Kimball, *Nixon's Vietnam War*, 264.

25. Morris Janowitz, "Volunteer Armed Forces and Military Purpose," *Foreign Affairs*, Apr. 1972, 428; Nguyen, *Hanoi's War*, 189; Kimball, *Nixon's Vietnam War*, 261–263.

26. Ang Cheng Guan, *Ending the Vietnam War* (London: Routledge, 2004), 107–108; Nguyen, *Hanoi's War*, 195–196, 241–242, 262; Kimball, *Nixon's Vietnam War*, 119–120; Smithsonian, 419.

CHAPTER 25. "Defeat Is Not an Option"

1. Lien-Hang T. Nguyen, *Hanoi's War* (Chapel Hill: University of North Carolina Press, 2012), 195, 214, 216; James H. Willbanks, *Abandoning Vietnam* (Lawrence: University Press of Kansas, 2004), 126.

2. Fox Butterfield, "Who Was This Enemy?," in *Reporting Vietnam: American Journalism 1959–1975* (New York: Library of America, 1998), 664.

3. Willbanks, *Abandoning*, 124–126; Lewis Sorley, ed., *The Vietnam War* (Lubbock: Texas Tech University Press, 2010), 756–757; Nguyen, *Hanoi's War*, 233–235, 240.

4. Willbanks, *Abandoning*, 129.

5. Thomas H. Lee, "Military Intelligence Operations and the Easter Offensive," U.S. Army Center of Military History, Sept. 6, 1990, 25–32; W. R. Baker, "HUMINT: A Continuing Crisis," *Small Wars Journal*, May 8, 2017; Willbanks, *Abandoning*, 123.

6. Gregory A. Daddis, *Withdrawal* (New York: Oxford University Press, 2017), 183–185.

7. Lewis Sorley, *A Better War* (Boston: Houghton Mifflin, 1999), 184–186.

8. Andrew Wiest, *Vietnam's Forgotten Army* (New York: New York University Press, 2008), 242–244; Sorley, *Better War*, 314–316.

9. Wiest, *Vietnam's Forgotten Army*, 235–238; Sorley, ed., *The Vietnam War*, 616; Sorley, *Better War*, 321.

10. National Archives and Records Administration (NARA), RG 472, MACV, Summary of Operational Interest Messages, 1 Oct. 70 thru 31 July 72, Box 4, Apr. 2, 1972, Col. John F. C. Kenney Jr.; Sorley, ed., *The Vietnam War*, 619.

11. Willbanks, *Abandoning*, 142–143; Chuck Gross, *Rattler One-Seven* (Denton: University of North Texas Press, 2004), 112.

12. Wiest, *Vietnam's Forgotten Army*, 254; Peter Braestrup, "The South Vietnamese Army," in *Reporting Vietnam*, 614.

13. Braestrup, "The South Vietnamese Army," 614.

14. Wiest, *Vietnam's Forgotten Army*, 260–262; Baker, "HUMINT: A Continuing Crisis"; Willbanks, *Abandoning*, 133.

15. UK National Archives (UKNA), DEFE 11/696, Washington, Jan. 20, 1972, Jukes to Stanbridge, "U.S. Withdrawals from Vietnam"; Baker, "HUMINT: A Continuing Crisis."

16. John A. Farrell, *Richard Nixon* (New York: Doubleday, 2017), 490–492; Rebecca Grant, "Linebacker I," *Air Force Magazine*, June 1, 2012; Jeffrey Kimball, *Nixon's Vietnam War* (Lawrence: University Press of Kansas, 1998), 295; Sorley, *Better War*, 316–317, 325–326; Willbanks, *Abandoning*, 134.

17. William Shawcross, *Sideshow* (New York: Simon & Schuster, 1979), 218.

18. Butterfield, "Who Was This Enemy?," 662.

19. NARA, RG 472, MACV, Summary of Operational Interest Messages, 1 Oct. 70 thru 31 July 72, Box 4, Apr. 25, 1972, Col. John F. C. Kenney Jr.; Willbanks, *Abandoning*, 141.

20. NARA, RG 472, MACV, Summary of Operational Interest Messages, 1 Oct. 70 thru 31 July 72, Box 4, Apr. 8, 1972, Col. John F . C. Kenney Jr.; Willbanks, *Abandoning*, 155.

21. NARA, RG 472, MACV, Summary of Operational Interest Messages, 1 Oct. 70 thru 31 July 72, Box 4, Apr. 8, 1972, Col. John F. C. Kenney Jr.; Willbanks, *Abandoning*, 137–139.

22. Braestrup, "The South Vietnamese Army," 613, 619.

23. Willbanks, *Abandoning*, 155–156; Braestrup, "The South Vietnamese Army," 615; Smithsonian, *A Short History of the Vietnam War* (New York: DK Publishing, 2021), 441.

24. John Saar, "Report from the Inferno," in *Reporting Vietnam*, 607–608.

25. Nguyen, *Hanoi's War*, 247–248; Saar, "Report from the Inferno," 611–612.

26. Sorley, *Better War*, 331; Sorley, ed., *The Vietnam War*, 633–634.

27. Nguyen, *Hanoi's War*, 259; Braestrup, "The South Vietnamese Army," 616, 622; Willbanks, *Abandoning*, 148–149.

28. Sydney H. Schanberg, "The South Vietnamese Retreat,'" in *Reporting Vietnam, Part Two: American Journalism 1969–1975* (New York: Library of America, 1998), 342–347; Willbanks, *Abandoning*, 157.

29. Willbanks, *Abandoning*, 157.

30. NARA, RG 472, MACV, Summary of Operational Interest Messages, 1 Oct. 70 thru 31 July 72, Box 4, Mar. 26, 27, 29, 30, 1972, Col. John F. C. Kenney Jr.; Schanberg, "The South Vietnamese Retreat," 342–347.

31. Willbanks, *Abandoning*, 155–156; Butterfield, "Who Was This Enemy?," 660.

32. NARA, RG 472, MACV, Summary of Operational Interest Messages, 1 Oct. 70 thru 31 July 72, Box 4, Apr. 15, 1972, Col. John F. C. Kenney Jr.; Saar, "Report from the Inferno," 612; Willbanks, *Abandoning*, 157.

33. Robert A. Pape, *Bombing to Win* (Ithaca, NY: Cornell University Press, 1996), 198–202; Grant, "Linebacker I."

34. Rick Perlstein, *Nixonland* (New York: Scribner, 2008), 656–657; Kimball, *Nixon's Vietnam War*, 304–305, 311, 315; Sorley, *Better War*, 327; Daddis, *Withdrawal*, 187.

35. Mark Clodfelter, *The Limits of Air Power* (New York: Free Press, 1989), 150–163; Ed Rasimus, *Palace Cobra* (New York: St. Martin's, 2006), 149–150; Daddis, *Withdrawal*, 187.

36. Farrell, *Richard Nixon*, 490–491; Pape, 200–205; Sorley, *Better War*, 327.

37. Daddis, *Withdrawal*, 188.

38. Max Boot, *The Road Not Taken* (New York: Norton, 2018), 553–554; Smithsonian, 424–427, 432–435; Sorley, *Better War*, 334, 338, 344.

39. Daddis, *Withdrawal*, 189.

40. Robert Shaplen, "We Have Always Survived," in *Reporting Vietnam*, 558.

41. Willbanks, *Abandoning*, 151, 155–156.

42. Ronald H. Spector, *After Tet* (New York: Free Press, 1993), 290–294; Shaplen, "We Have Always Survived," 565.

43. Daddis, *Withdrawal*, 187–191.

44. Willbanks, *Abandoning*, 150.

45. Willbanks, *Abandoning*, 158–160.

46. Sorley, ed., *The Vietnam War*, 633; Willbanks, *Abandoning*, 151–152.

47. Clodfelter, 166–172; Shawcross, 232–235; Willbanks, *Abandoning*, 158–159.

48. Ang Cheng Guan, *Ending the Vietnam War* (London: Routledge, 2004), 100–102.

49. Willbanks, *Abandoning*, 154, 158–159.

50. Butterfield, "Who Was This Enemy?," 665; Saar, "Report from the Inferno," 606; Grant, "Linebacker I"; Daddis, *No Sure Victory* (New York: Oxford University Press, 2011), 217; Sorley, *Better War*, 341–342; Nguyen, *Hanoi's War*, 259; Willbanks, *Abandoning*, 152–153.

51. "Vietnam Background: Congress and the War: Years of Support," *CQ Almanac 1975*, 31st ed. (Washington, DC: Congressional Quarterly, 1976), 296–299, http://library.cqpress.com/cqalmanac/cqal75-1213972; Daddis, *Withdrawal*, 108–109, 190–191.

52. LCDR John S. McCain III, "How the POWs Fought Back," in *Reporting Vietnam*, 698; Willbanks, *Abandoning*, 163–164.

53. Nguyen, *Hanoi's War*, 261, 263–264.

54. Walter J. Boyne, "Route Pack 6," *Air & Space Forces Magazine*, Nov. 1, 1999; McCain, "How the POWs Fought Back," 694–695.

55. Daddis, *No Sure Victory*, 218; Smithsonian, 479; Shawcross, 88.

56. Hunter S. Thompson, "From *Fear and Loathing on the Campaign Trail '72*," in *Reporting Vietnam*, 653.

57. Nguyen, *Hanoi's War*, 204–205, 267–268, 279, 284; Willbanks, *Abandoning*, 170; Daddis, *Withdrawal*, 191.

58. "Vietnam Statistics—War Costs: Complete Picture Impossible," *CQ Almanac 1975*, 31st ed. (Washington, DC: Congressional Quarterly, 1976), 301–305, http://library.cqpress.com/cqalmanac/cqal75-1213988; Kimball, *Nixon's Vietnam War*, 330–337, 360; Sorley, *Better War*, 343, 349, 358–359; Sorley, ed., *The Vietnam War*, 770–773, 787–791; Willbanks, *Abandoning*, 167–168.

59. Farrell, *Richard Nixon*, 492–493, 499–500.

60. Clodfelter, 194–202; Kimball, *Nixon's Vietnam War*, 364–365; Smithsonian, 461.

61. Guan, *Ending the Vietnam War*, 119–120.

62. Robert K. Brigham, *Guerrilla Diplomacy* (Ithaca, NY: Cornell University Press, 1999), 111; McCain, "How the POWs Fought Back," 694; Rasimus, 121; Sorley, *Better War*, 354–356; Daddis, *Withdrawal*, 194–195.

63. Liddell Hart Centre for Military Archives (LHCMA), MF 803, Reel 8/8, U.S. Armed Forces in Vietnam 1954–1975, Part Two, Vietnam: Lessons Learned, Vol. 6, "Conduct of the War," 92–94; Daddis, *No Sure Victory*, 218; Willbanks, *Abandoning*, 182.

64. McCain, "How the POWs Fought Back," 694, 696; Nguyen, *Hanoi's War*, 296; Clodfelter, 195.

65. NARA, RG 472, A1 60, Bob Hope Christmas Shows 1970–72, Bob Hope Christmas Show 1972, Sept. 1, 1972, Col. John Von Der Bruegge Jr. to Director

of Personnel, MACV, "Bob Hope Christmas Show," and n.d., Maj Gen. W. W. Marshall, USAF, Vice Commander to MACV/CS, "Bob Hope Christmas Show."

CHAPTER 26. The Fall

1. Henry Kissinger, *Ending the Vietnam War* (New York: Simon & Schuster, 2003), 418, 426–428; Mark Clodfelter, *The Limits of Air Power* (New York: Free Press, 1989), 183–184, 200–201; James H. Willbanks, *Abandoning Vietnam* (Lawrence: University Press of Kansas, 2004), 178, 182–183.

2. Lien-Hang T. Nguyen, *Hanoi's War* (Chapel Hill: University of North Carolina Press, 2012), 295–297.

3. Robert A. Pape, *Bombing to Win* (Ithaca, NY: Cornell University Press, 1996), 202–210; Robert K. Brigham, *Guerrilla Diplomacy* (Ithaca, NY: Cornell University Press, 1999), 111; Nguyen, *Hanoi's War*, 295–297.

4. Gregory A. Daddis, *Withdrawal* (New York: Oxford University Press, 2017), 196–197.

5. "Vietnam Background: Congress and the War: Years of Support," *CQ Almanac 1975*, 31st ed. (Washington, DC: Congressional Quarterly, 1976), 296–299, http://library.cqpress.com/cqalmanac/cqal75-1213972; Lewis Sorley, *A Better War* (Boston: Houghton Mifflin, 1999), 355, 360; Jeffrey Kimball, *Nixon's Vietnam War* (Lawrence: University Press of Kansas, 1998), 337; William Colby, *Lost Victory* (Chicago: Contemporary, 1989), 341; Nguyen, *Hanoi's War*, 270, 295–298; Willbanks, *Abandoning*, 181–182.

6. Kissinger, 422–423.

7. Jeffrey Record, *The Wrong War* (Annapolis, MD: Naval Institute Press, 1998), xiii.

8. Ang Cheng Guan, *Ending the Vietnam War* (London: Routledge, 2004), 122–123.

9. John A. Farrell, *Richard Nixon* (New York: Doubleday, 2017), 500–501; Kissinger, 497; Sorley, *Better War*, 351–353, 360; Max Boot, *The Road Not Taken* (New York: Norton, 2018), 561–562; Flora Lewis, "Vietnam Peace Pacts Signed; America's Longest War Halts," in *Reporting Vietnam, Part Two: American Journalism 1969–1975* (New York: Library of America, 1998), 420–424; Smithsonian, *A Short History of the Vietnam War* (New York: DK Publishing, 2021), 467; Brigham, 111–112.

10. Arnold R. Isaacs, "War Lingers in Hamlets as Cease-Fire Hour Passes," in *Reporting Vietnam: American Journalism 1959–1975* (New York: Library of America, 1998), 667.

11. Lewis Sorley, ed., *The Vietnam War* (Lubbock: Texas Tech University Press, 2010), 756–760, 780; Smithsonian, 477.

12. Kissinger, 577.

13. William Shawcross, *Sideshow* (New York: Simon & Schuster, 1979), 261–262, 266–267, 271–278.

14. Shawcross, 284–285.

15. Farrell, *Richard Nixon*, 364; Nick Turse, "Henry Kissinger's Bloody Legacy," *Intercepted*, May 25, 2023; Kissinger, 478–479, 567–572; Daddis, *Withdrawal*, 206.

16. Shawcross, 296–269, 317.

17. "Vietnam Background: Congress and the War: Years of Support," 296–299; Smithsonian, 477; Farrell, *Richard Nixon*, 539–540; Kimball, *Nixon's Vietnam War*, 370–371; Sorley, *Better War*, 364; Rick Perlstein, *The Invisible Bridge* (New York: Simon & Schuster, 2014), 423, 426.

18. Daddis, *Withdrawal*, 177, 197.

19. Willbanks, *Abandoning*, 174–175, 202.

20. Shawcross, 259; Willbanks, *Abandoning*, 189–190, 204–206.

21. Robert Shaplen, "We Have Always Survived," in *Reporting Vietnam*, 605; Sorley, *Better War*, 367–370; Sorley, ed., *The Vietnam War*, 14, 64–65, 738, 775; Willbanks, *Abandoning*, 206–207.

22. "Vietnam Statistics—War Costs: Complete Picture Impossible," *CQ Almanac 1975*, 31st ed. (Washington, DC: Congressional Quarterly, 1976), 301–305, http://library.cqpress.com/cqalmanac/cqal75-1213988; Willbanks, *Abandoning*, 192–193, 195.

23. Liddell Hart Centre for Military Archives (LHCMA), MF 803, Reel 8/8, U.S. Armed Forces in Vietnam 1954–1975, Part Two, Vietnam: Lessons Learned, Vol. 6, "Conduct of the War," 96–97; Sorley, *Better War*, 370; Willbanks, *Abandoning*, 203.

24. Sorley, *Better War*, 370–371; Sorley, ed., *The Vietnam War*, 93, 770–773, 776; Smithsonian, 482; Willbanks, *Abandoning*, 171, 208–214, 220–222.

25. Guan, *Ending the Vietnam War*, 150–153; Brigham, 122–125.

26. "Vietnam Background: Congress and the War: Years of Support," 296–299.

27. LHCMA, MF 803, Reel 8/8, U.S. Armed Forces in Vietnam 1954–1975, Part Two, Vietnam: Lessons Learned, Vol. 6, "Conduct of the War," 92–94.

28. George J. Veith and Bernard Gwertzman, "Report Criticizes Embassy in Saigon," *New York Times*, Aug. 6, 1974.

29. Willbanks, *Abandoning*, 206, 215–218, 220, 227; Smithsonian, 484–485.

30. LHCMA, MF 803, Reel 8/8, U.S. Armed Forces in Vietnam 1954–1975, Part Two, Vietnam: Lessons Learned, Vol. 6, "Conduct of the War," 98, 104; Sorley, *Better War*, 340.

31. Sorley, ed., *The Vietnam War*, 776–777, 779; Willbanks, *Abandoning*, 228, 233–238.

32. William C. Westmoreland, *A Soldier Reports* (New York: Doubleday, 1976), 397–398; Willbanks, *Abandoning*, 235–237.

33. Sorley, ed., *The Vietnam War*, 91–93, 785, 801; Willbanks, *Abandoning*, 238–246.

34. Perlstein, *The Invisible Bridge*, 420–423.

35. Westmoreland, 400–401; Smithsonian, 488–489; Willbanks, *Abandoning*, 242–245.

36. Sorley, *Better War*, 377; Sorley, ed., *The Vietnam War*, 816; Willbanks, *Abandoning*, 252–255.

37. Paul Vogle, "A Flight into Hell," in *Reporting Vietnam*, 706–709.

38. Le Kim Dinh, "For Those Who Flee, Life Is 'Hell on Earth,'" in *Reporting Vietnam*, 710–712; Sorley, ed., *The Vietnam War*, 93.

39. "Vietnam Statistics—War Costs: Complete Picture Impossible," 301–305.

40. "Indochina War Ends; North Vietnam Victorious," *CQ Almanac 1975*, 31st ed. (Washington, DC: Congressional Quarterly, 1976), 295, http://library.cqpress.com/cqalmanac/cqal75-1213970.

41. LHCMA, MF 803, Reel 8/8, U.S. Armed Forces in Vietnam 1954–1975, Part Two, Vietnam: Lessons Learned, Vol. 6, "Conduct of the War," 98, 104; "Vietnam Statistics—War Costs: Complete Picture Impossible," 301–305; Sorley, *Better War*, 377–378; Willbanks, *Abandoning*, 258–259; Perlstein, *The Invisible Bridge*, 423; Guan, *Ending the Vietnam War*, 164–165.

42. Shawcross, 312–317, 340, 361–363.

43. Shawcross, 363.

44. Sydney H. Schanberg, "The Fall of Phnom Penh," in *Reporting Vietnam*, 713–715.

45. Smithsonian, 504–505, 524–525; Shawcross, 367.

46. Schanberg, "The Fall of Phnom Penh," 724.

47. Schanberg, "The Fall of Phnom Penh," 720–721.

48. Shawcross, 372.

49. Shawcross, 372.

50. Frank Snepp, *Decent Interval* (1977; Lawrence: University Press of Kansas, 2002), 399–401, 450; Richard Pearson, "Nyugen Van Thieu Dies," *Washington Post*, Oct. 1, 2001.

51. Smithsonian, 492–493.

52. Snepp, 379.

53. Willbanks, *Abandoning*, 268.

54. Philip Caputo, "Running Again—the Last Retreat," in *Reporting Vietnam*, 736–739; Philip Caputo, "The Battle of Xuan Loc," in *Reporting Vietnam, Part Two*, 500; Sorley, *Better War*, 379.

55. Daddis, *Withdrawal*, 198; Willbanks, *Abandoning*, 269–270; Pearson, "Nyugen Van Thieu Dies."

56. "Vietnam Statistics—War Costs: Complete Picture Impossible," 301–305.

57. "Indochina War Ends; North Vietnam Victorious," 295.

58. Snepp, 399–401.

59. Guan, *Ending the Vietnam War*, 164–165; Stanley Karnow, *Vietnam: A History* (New York: Viking, 1983), 666–671; Willbanks, *Abandoning*, 273–274; Sorley, ed., *The Vietnam War*, 822.

60. Snepp, 454–455; Willbanks, *Abandoning*, 275, 277.

61. Snepp, 452; Sorley, ed., *The Vietnam War*, 822–824.

62. Snepp, 402–413, 451, 543; Willbanks, *Abandoning*, 275–276.

63. Keyes Beech, "We Clawed for Our Lives," in *Reporting Vietnam*, 740–755; Bob Tamarkin, "Diary of S. Viet's Last Hours," in *Reporting Vietnam*, 747; Colby, 9.

64. Snepp, 515–516; Willbanks, *Abandoning*, 276.

65. Tamarkin, "Diary of S. Viet's Last Hours," 749, 753.

66. George Esper, "Communists Enter Saigon," in *Reporting Vietnam, Part Two*, 498–499; Sorley, *Better War*, 14.

67. Nathalie Huynh Chau Nguyen, *South Vietnamese Soldiers* (Santa Barbara, CA: Praeger, 2016), 81–82; James Webb, *I Heard My Country Calling* (New York: Simon & Schuster, 2014), 286.

68. Smithsonian, 516–518.

Conclusion

1. Deborah Shapley, *Promise and Power* (Boston: Little, Brown, 1993), 374.

2. Kai Bird, *The Color of Truth* (New York: Simon & Schuster, 1998), 326; Fredrik Logevall, *Choosing War* (Berkeley: University of California Press, 1999), 376–378, 388–395, 400–404; Charles Trueheart, *Diplomats at War* (Charlottesville: University of Virginia Press, 2024), 16.

3. Gregory A. Daddis, *Withdrawal* (New York: Oxford University Press, 2017), 188; James Webb, *I Heard My Country Calling* (New York: Simon & Schuster, 2014), 278; Greiner Bernd, "The March 1968 Massacre in My Lai 4 and My Khe 4," Sciences Po, Oct. 5, 2009, www.sciencespo.fr/mass-violence-war-massacre-resistance/fr/document/march-1968-massacre-my-lai-4-and-my-khe-4.html.

4. David Halberstam, *The Best and the Brightest* (New York: Random House, 1972), 178–179.

5. Frank E. Vandiver, *Shadows of Vietnam* (College Station: Texas A&M University Press, 1997), 287.

6. Shapley, 363.

7. Daddis, *Withdrawal*, 204–207.

8. Bird, 346–347.

9. Ingo Trauschweizer, *Maxwell Taylor's Cold War* (Lexington: University Press of Kentucky, 2019), 138; Ronald H. Spector, *After Tet* (New York: Free Press, 1993), 104.

10. Rick Perlstein, *The Invisible Bridge* (New York: Simon & Schuster, 2014), 432.

INDEX

A-4 Skyhawks, 309

Abrams, Creighton
  Accelerated Pacification Program, 375
  as Army Vice Chief of Staff,
    122–124, 196
  "better war" strategy, 345, 360, 384,
    402–403, 536
  bombing campaigns, 491–493, 497
  clear and hold operations, 334, 353–354
  death of, 520
  escalation demands, 345
  Korean War service, 333
  land rush, 378, 384, 388
  Laotian Incursion, 445, 448–449,
    457–460, 469
  as MACV commander, 314–315,
    315(photo), 351, 393, 413, 438, 442,
    451, 480
  maximum pressure strategy, 358, 363
  "one-war" concept, 333, 378
  on Operation Speedy Express, 380–381
  pacification program, 403
  sacking of, 494
  troop withdrawals, 431
  warnings of NVA offensives, 477–478
  as Westmoreland's deputy, 156, 223,
    230, 278
  World War II service, 333

Acheson, Dean, 296, 297, 300

Adams, Eddie, 268

African Americans, 75, 426, 428,
    432–434, 439

Agent Orange, 4, 213–214

Agnew, Spiro, 341, 396, 397, 412, 499

air ambulances, 77, 83

airfields, 77, 83–84

airmobile operations, 77, 78(photo), 79, 83,
    99, 109, 200, 534

Albany LZ, 107, 109

alcohol use by deployed soldiers, 431, 434

Ali, Muhammad, 222

Allen, George, 243

Allen, Terry D., 208–209

Alliance of Democratic, National, and
    Peace Forces, 301

Alsop, Stewart, 423, 425, 436

ambushes, 207–208

ammunition supply points, 81

Anderson, Charles, 459

Angkor Wat, 417

An Loc, 490–491, 493, 496

Ann-Margaret, 143(photo)

anti-war protests, 8, 62, 65–66, 153, 222,
    222(photo), 284, 350, 361, 395–398,
    420–421, 439–440, 501

Armed Forces Council, 56

Armed Forces Qualification Test,
    Category IV, 426

Army of the Republic of Vietnam (ARVN)
  1st Armored Brigade, 457
  1st Division, 258, 272–273, 278–279, 357, 401, 422, 454, 458–462, 468, 518
  2nd Division, 401, 482, 489
  3rd Division, 476, 481, 489–490
  3rd Ranger Group, 490
  3rd Regiment, 273
  5th Division, 389, 401, 486, 490, 493
  6th Ranger Group, 486
  7th Division, 377, 389
  9th Division, 487
  18th Division, 523–524
  21st Division, 487
  22nd Division, 118, 389, 485–486
  23rd Division, 485
  56th Regiment, 481, 482
  57th Regiment, 481
  Airborne battalions, 273, 283
  Cambodia operations, 410–411
  capabilities tested by NVA, 513–515
  casualties, 56, 322, 365, 453, 464, 468, 485, 493, 495, 509–510, 529
  civil war, 125–126
  desertions, 64, 238, 342, 365, 367, 442, 490, 538
  failures of, 37, 57, 175, 515, 517–518
  faking of operations by, 20
  financial aid to, 185, 513, 519
  generals, 22–23
  Hac Bao Company, 518
  I&M program, 342
  intelligence weaknesses, 88–89
  Joint General Staff, 193, 442, 458, 465, 514, 528, 539
  lack of improvement in, 19(photo), 334–335, 367–375, 403, 441–443, 470
  Laotian Incursion, 446–465, 456(fig.), 467–470
  Military Security Service, 370–372
  mobilization law, 238–240
  morale problems, 489–490, 510
  officers, 203–204
  political warfare training, 126
  Ranger battalions, 453, 462, 463(photo)
  rules of engagement, 413
  supply rates, 511
  surrender of, 529
  Tet Offensive failures, 263–265, 271
  troop numbers, 59, 233, 343, 509–510
  US assistance to, 15–18
  Westmoreland's PR campaign, 238
Arnett, Peter, 223, 227, 377
The Arrogance of Power (Fulbright), 161
artillery
  dud rounds, 163, 211
  fire support bases (FSBs), 80–82, 99, 134–135
  flying, 82–83, 99
  wasteful use of, 435–436
Art of War (Sun Tzu), 29
ARVN. *See* Army of the Republic of Vietnam
A Shau Valley, 148, 319–321, 353–357, 363, 405, 421–422, 451, 536
Australian troops in Vietnam, 75, 141, 205, 250
AWOL rates, 170, 433

B-52 Stratofortress, 84, 99, 163, 204, 254, 309–311, 393, 492, 500, 507
Baez, Joan, 501

Baker, Russell, 59

Ball, George, 20, 30, 32, 45, 47, 54, 56, 66, 222, 296

Ban Me Thuot, 515

Bao Dai, 12, 281

"Battle Hymn of Lieutenant Calley" (song), 437–438

Beech, Keyes, 527–528

Beecher, William, 394

Bell Helicopter, 77, 82

Bellow, Saul, 318

Bentsen, Lloyd, 424

Bernhardt, Michael, 302–304

Bien Hoa Air Base, 47, 49, 53, 60–61, 77, 85, 256, 268, 269, 524

Binh, Nguyen Thi, 324, 336

bird dogs (prop planes), 84

boat people, 530

body counts

American, 53, 83, 105–107, 115, 117, 119, 123, 145, 167, 170, 181, 194, 202, 204, 207, 209, 216, 226–227, 229–231, 263, 279, 287, 321, 322–323, 343, 345, 361, 395, 404, 464, 500, 529

ARVN, 56, 322, 365, 453, 464, 468, 493, 495, 509–510, 529

civilian casualties, 28, 45, 119, 180, 220, 377–378, 491, 495, 499, 529, 533

enemy, 115, 119, 165–166, 167, 170, 172, 179, 181, 184, 229, 263, 279, 323, 325, 343, 377, 378–379, 464, 493, 494, 529

inflation of, 178, 213, 232, 316, 374, 382–383, 464

minimization of, 54

bombing campaigns

Cambodia, 351–352, 392–393, 407, 411, 508

Johnson's halt to, 313–315, 317–318, 330, 336, 346

Laos, 409, 508

North Vietnam, 28–29, 40–41, 43–46, 54–55, 58–59, 116–117, 198, 294–295, 491–492, 495, 499–501, 537

Operation Rolling Thunder, 28–29, 58–59, 60, 62, 91, 116–117, 139, 191, 198, 238, 241, 294–296, 346

South Vietnam, 84, 185, 225(photo), 225–226, 235, 270, 296, 307, 309–311, 323, 402

booby traps, 163–164, 211, 212, 302, 402, 429

Boret, Long, 522

bounty hunting, 362

Bradley, Omar, 296

Braestrup, Peter, 487

Brandt, Keith, 461

Brezhnev, Leonid, 48, 488, 500

A Bright Shining Lie (Sheehan), 17

Brink Hotel bombing, 48, 160

Britain

aid for troops offer to, 75

on Cambodian Incursion, 415

on cost effectiveness, 185

defense analysis by, 79

defense budget cuts, 205

Brooks, Stephen, 303

Browne, Malcolm, 334

Buchwald, Art, 293

Buckley, Kevin, 384

Buckley, Tom, 244, 268

INDEX

Buddhism, Buddhists, 537
  anti-American protests, 56
  in communist front organizations, 275
  Struggle Movement, 21–22, 125–127
Bundy, McGeorge, 45–46, 66, 148, 175, 195,
  282, 296, 297, 533
  on air strikes, 59
  on casualties, 537
  coup cable to Lodge, 23
  graduated pressure strategy, 3–4, 28, 30,
    31, 56, 239–240
  in Kennedy administration, 16–17, 22
  rationale for war, 531
  support for escalation, 52, 67–69, 74–75
  Vietnam tours, 53–54
Bundy, William, 21, 32, 43, 52, 54–55,
  85, 126
Bunker, Ellsworth, 193, 197, 324–325,
  350(photo), 450
Busby, Horace, 71
Bush, George W., 424
Byrd, Robert, 267, 419

C-47 transport aircraft, 83
C-123 Providers, 140, 308
C-130 Hercules, 81(photo), 202, 308,
  320, 354
Calley, William, 302–303, 436–438
Cambodia
  air strikes against, 351–352, 392–394,
    407, 411, 508
  bombing halted in, 508
  communist sanctuaries in, 407, 408,
    410, 418
  coups, 351, 408
  elections, 391, 495–496

  extreme neutrality policy, 113, 233–234,
    391, 407
  French loss of control in, 92–93
  Ho Chi Minh Trail, 3, 6, 37, 48, 76, 92
  Incursion, 8, 407–422, 414(fig.), 445,
    470–471, 536–537
  Khmer Rouge, 11, 113, 234, 351–352,
    391, 407, 417–418, 507–508,
    520–523, 536
  Nixon's secret bombing campaign in,
    392–394
  NVA in, 113, 407, 409
  operations restricted near border of,
    138–139
  Phnom Penh occupation, 521–523
  relationship with United States, 391–392,
    407, 411
  Royal General Staff, 233
  supply surge into, 318–319
  technical neutrality of, 3, 93
  Vietnamese living in, 410
  Westmoreland's plan to strike into,
    147–148, 194, 245, 283
  Year Zero, 521–522
Cam Lo River, 482–483
Campaign X, 411
Camp Carroll, 111, 481–483, 489
Camp David, 66
Camp Eagle, 355–356, 363
Camp Holloway, 53–54, 181
Cam Ranh Bay, 431, 433, 517–519
Caputo, Philip, 111, 524
Carpenter, Bill, 132–133
Carroll, Lewis, 89
Case-Church Amendment, 508
Cates, William, 228

Catholics, Catholicism
 drafted by NVA, 479
 Greater Unity Force, 241
 priests killed in Tet Offensive, 275
 in South Vietnam, 12, 22
 Thieu's conversion, 23, 64, 493
 treatment of Buddhist troops, 17
CBS Evening News, 290
CBS News, 243
cease-fires, 249–250, 506, 525, 526
Census Grievance program, 156, 326–327
Central Intelligence Agency (CIA), 18, 31,
 34, 42, 49, 52, 56, 272
 Census Grievance program, 156,
 326–327
 enemy forces counts, 243–244, 254, 418
 findings on Westmoreland's
 operations, 332
 Khang's views on Thieu and Ky to, 281
 Khmer Rouge estimates, 407
 on Mini-Tet, 321–322
 Office of Current Intelligence, 242
 opposition to escalation, 54
 pacification, 242–243
 Phoenix Program, 326, 327, 369–374,
 402, 529
 on Thieu, 57
 warnings of NVA offensives, 473, 480
Central Office for South Vietnam
 (COSVN), 35, 141, 161, 167, 214–215,
 250, 255, 393, 407, 413, 480
CH-46 Sea Knight helicopters, 308
CH-47 Chinook helicopters, 79, 81(photo),
 99, 134–135, 159, 422
CH-53 Jolly Green Giant helicopters, 528
CH-54 Skycrane helicopters, 79, 159

Chamberlain, Neville, 297, 539
charts and statistics, 403, 536–537
Chau, Tran Ngoc, 326, 329
Chennault, Anna, 339, 341, 347, 366
Chennault, Claire, 339
Chiang Kai-shek, 3, 339, 341
Chicago Tribune (periodical), 524
Chieu Hoi (Open Arms) amnesty program,
 89, 156, 170, 172
China
 aid to North Vietnam, 189–190, 214
 anti-American protests, 500
 backing of NVA by, 113–114,
 139, 479
 Cultural Revolution, 190, 391
 "forest armies," 11
 Nixon's trip to, 478, 479
 pressure to end war by, 497
 risks of intervention by, 58, 61, 465
 Sino-Soviet rift, 189–190, 199
 thermonuclear bomb testing, 285
China Lobby, 3
Chinese Communist Party, 500
Chinook helicopters, 79, 81(photo), 99,
 134–135, 159, 422
Cholon helicopter incident, 325
Christmas shows. *See* Vietnam
 Christmas Tour
Chu Lai operation, 209–213, 219
Church, Frank, 418
CINCPAC, 35, 233–234, 367, 393, 448, 499
civic action, 98
civilian casualties, 28, 45, 119, 180, 220,
 377–378, 491, 495, 499, 529, 533
civilian irregular defense group (CIDG)
 camps, 97, 354

Civil Operations and Revolutionary Development Support (CORDS), 155–157, 219, 242, 255, 368–370, 375, 402

Civil Rights Bill (1964), 41

Clausewitz, Carl von, 180, 443, 533

Clifford, Clark, 64, 66–67, 70(photo), 195, 245, 276, 282, 284–286, 293–298, 297(photo), 312–313, 324, 342, 345

Clinton, Bill, 428

Coalition Front for Peace, 275

Cobra gunships, 82–83, 385–387, 459

Colby, William, 369, 375, 402–403, 519

Cold War, 9, 58, 75, 336, 425

collateral damage, 87, 140, 499

college campus protests, 222, 284, 420–421, 424, 439–440

Collins, Arthur S., Jr., 434–435, 441–443, 449

Column of Sorrow, 517

Colvin, John, 197

communism

    Democrats on, 2

    "Denunciation of Communists Campaign," 15–16

    financial costs of fighting, 52

    front organizations, 275

    as a national organization in Vietnam, 26

    Red Scare, 3

    Republicans on, 2

Conmy, Joseph, 359–360

Constellation, USS, 282

Con Thien offensive, 215, 217–218

Cook, Jon Wambi, 226

Cooper, John, 418

Cooper-Church Amendment, 418–420, 446, 449–450

CORDS. *See* Civil Operations and Revolutionary Development Support

Corson, William, 128

COSVN. *See* Central Office for South Vietnam

counterinsurgency measures, 37–38, 57, 61, 326–327

coups, 22–27, 56, 59, 64, 351, 408, 538

covert operations, 39–40

Cronkite, Walter, 290(photo), 290–291, 307, 535

Cuban missile crisis, 43

Currahees, 359

Cushman, Robert, 251–252, 278

Dak Seang Special Forces camp, 182

Dak To, Battle of, 170, 215, 221, 223–230, 232, 257

Dak To Special Forces camp, 182

Daly, Ed, 518

Da Nang, 517–519

Da Nang Air Base, 263

Dao, Le Minh, 523–524

Dat, Le Duc, 486

Dean, Arthur, 296

Dean, John, 507

Dean, Patrick, 335

Declaration of Honolulu, 121, 126

Decornoy, Jacques, 330

Defense Intelligence Agency, 203, 390, 512

De Gaulle, Charles, 27

demilitarized zone (DMZ), 37, 110–112, 217–218, 221, 476

Democratic National Committee, 473, 494

Democratic National Convention, 317, 340–341, 343

Democratic Republic of Vietnam (DRV), 330

Democrats, on communism, 2

Department of Defense, 203

DePuy, Bill, 76, 128, 447

DEROS policy, 187–188, 188(photo), 200

desertions, 64, 238, 342, 365, 367, 433, 442, 509

Dick Cavett Show (TV show), 438

Diem, Bui, 339

Diem, Ngo Dinh
  assassination of, 24
  coup against, 22–25, 538
  "Denunciation of Communists Campaign," 15–16
  elections cancelled by, 12
  in exile, 15
  human rights abuses, 21–22
  presidency, 12
  presidential palace, 234
  Struggle Movement against, 21–22
  US visit, 13, 13(photo)

Dien Bien Phu, 12

Dien Bien Phu, Battle of, 84, 307, 517

Dillon, Douglas, 296

Dinh, Le Kim, 518

Dinh, Ton That, 23, 24

Dirksen, Everett, 340

District Intelligence and Operation Coordinating Centers (DIOCCs), 372, 374

Doctor Strangelove (film), 43

Dole, Bob, 419

"domino theory," 1

Don, Tran Van, 23, 25

Dong, Du Quoc, 452–453, 457

Dong, Pham Von, 197, 497

Dong Ha, 488

Dong Hai River, 524

Dong Tam Base Camp, 175–176

draft
  calls, 222
  class discrimination and, 8, 423–425
  deferments, 423–424, 427, 428
  exemptions, 425
  increasing calls, 73, 145
  lottery system, 9, 427–428
  Nixon's pledge to end, 424
  NVA, 479
  Selective Service Act (1948), 75
  Thieu's conscription law, 238–240
  World War II, 425

drug smuggling, 64

drug use, 8, 431, 432(photo), 437

Duan, Le
  consolidation of power, 399
  determination to win, 29
  Easter Offensive, 478, 480, 486, 491, 495
  escalations by, 141, 197–199, 221, 325
  orders to capture Saigon, 520
  peace talks, 503–504
  peace talks rejections, 63, 146, 191, 345
  protracted war strategy, 404–405
  resistance to, 215
  Soviet and Chinese support for, 49, 189
  Tet Offensive planning, 247–248, 271, 338
  "theory of two mistakes," 28, 241–242
  VC reorganization, 35

Duc, Thich Quang, 21

Dulles, John Foster, 13(photo)

Dung, Van Tien, 199, 221, 250, 251, 486, 495, 500, 514–515, 523–524, 526–527

Dylan, Bob, 396

Easter Offensive, 480–495, 484(fig)

Eisenhower, David, 428

Eisenhower, Dwight
    aid to South Vietnam, 12–13, 15
    communism fears, 1, 3, 12
    Diem's US trip, 13(photo)
    Korean War, 2
    MACV establishment, 17
    meeting with Johnson, 57
    Nixon as vice president of, 392
    "no land wars in Asia" precept, 11–12
    nuclear retaliation strategy, 29
    reasons for escalation, 531–532

Ellsberg, Daniel, 73, 326, 472–473

Emerson, Gloria, 468

enemy invisibility, 111–116

English, Lowell, 253

Enlai, Zhou, 465, 497, 503

enlistment demographics, 425–427

Enterprise, USS, 514

Enthoven, Alain, 20, 178–179, 194

Esper, George, 529

Esquire (periodical), 184, 438

Ewell, Julien, 376, 377–388

"Eve of Destruction" (McGuire), 65

F-4C Phantom, 83, 165

F-100 Super Sabre, 83, 204

Falcon LZ, 99, 102, 104

Fall, Bernard, 86–87, 153, 159–160, 163, 271–272

FANK, 351, 416–417, 471, 520

Farrell, John, 341

fighter bombers, 83

fire support bases (FSBs), 80–82, 99, 134–135

first lift, 99–100, 100(photo)

Fonda, Jane, 496

Ford, Gerald
    denounced by Reagan, 539
    House minority leadership, 55
    nonintervention plan, 512, 514
    Saigon aid request, 519
    Tulane University speech, 525
    Weyand's warnings to, 520

Foreign Assistance Act (1970), 418

Forrestal, Mike, 32

Fortas, Abe, 296

Fort Benning, 78

forward air controllers (FACs), 82, 84

Fowler, Henry, 300

fragging, 8, 362, 433, 437

French Indochina, 11, 532

friendly fire, 106, 132, 180, 181, 226, 358, 435

Friendship Highway, 406

Fulbright, J. William, 41–42, 57–58, 118–120, 122, 161, 231, 241, 243, 282, 408, 474

Fulton, William, 178

Galbraith, John Kenneth, 25, 204

Garcia, Richard, 131–132

Gard, Robert, 382

Gardner, Fred, 366

Garvin, James, 420

Gellhorn, Martha, 180

INDEX

Geneva Treaty (1954), 241

Giai, Vu Van, 476, 482, 489

Giap, Vo Nguyen, 111, 141, 152, 197–200, 221, 227, 229, 248, 250, 271

GI Says (periodical), 362

Gold FSB, 165–166

Goldwater, Barry, 1, 20, 27–28, 33, 38, 42, 47, 419, 532

Goodwin, Doris Kearns, 69

Goodwin, Richard, 340–341

Greater Unity Force, 241

Great Society programs, 2, 47, 51–52, 61, 68–69, 122, 532

Greek Civil War, 52

Green Berets, 306, 354

Greene, Graham, 16

Greene, Wallace, 27, 46, 61

Greenway, Hugh, 223

"groupthink," 31–32, 33, 38, 54

Gruening, Ernest, 42

Grumman Mohawk surveillance planes, 344

GRUNK, 351

Guanha, Qiao, 465

Gulf of Tonkin, 39–41

gunships, 77, 82–83, 269, 385–387, 459

Hac Bao (Black Panther) Company, 518

Hackworth, David, 130–134, 379, 381

Haeberle, Ronald, 302–303

Hagel, Chuck, 379

Hai, Tran Van, 324

Haig, Alexander, 406, 415, 469, 499, 500

Haiphong harbor, 2

Halberstam, David, 18, 534

Haldeman, Bob, 341, 349, 412, 488, 499

Halperin, Morton, 394

Hamburger Hill, Battle of, 8, 353–354, 356–364, 404, 421, 536

hard hats demonstrations, 440–441

Harkins, Paul, 17–20, 22, 34, 60, 237, 331, 537

Harriman, Averell, 22, 32, 34, 313, 321, 338–339, 345, 537

Harris, Lou, 47–48

Harrison, Ben, 421–422

Hatfield, Mark, 419

Hau, Ho Truong, 452, 457

Hay, John, 206–207, 209

helicopters, 78(photo), 81(photo), 227
    Army's air-assault division, 78–79
    gunships, 82–83
    in Korean War, 77
    in Laotian Incursion, 458–461
    NVA tracking of, 135
    "super gaggles," 308–309
    visibility requirements, 308

Helms, Richard, 244, 283, 341, 473, 476

Herr, Michael, 115, 123, 184, 212–213, 219, 230, 240, 244, 276, 278, 304–305, 321, 403

Herrick, John, 40

Hersey, John, 160

Hersh, Seymour, 398

Hershey, Lewis, 425, 427

Hieu, Nguyen Van, 401

Higgins, Marguerite, 23

Higinbotham, Lew, 131–132

Hilsman, Roger, 22, 32

Hinh, Nguyen Duy, 489

"Hiroshima" (Hersey), 160

Hmong, 151, 523

INDEX

Ho Chi Minh City, 529

Ho Chi Minh Trail, 3, 6, 37, 48, 76, 112, 147, 193, 233, 328, 355, 446, 471–472, 476, 511

Holloway, Bruce, 393

Honeycutt, Weldon, 357–364

Honolulu summit, 63, 120–121, 126

Hoover, J. Edgar, 427

Hope, Bob, 48, 143, 160, 347, 399–400, 431, 501, 537

House Ways and Means Committee, 70, 152

howitzers, 80–82, 81(photo), 165

Huey Firebird helicopters, 82

Huey helicopters (UH-1s), 77–78, 82, 104, 135, 185, 204, 458–461

Hughes, David, 328

Humphrey, Hubert, 7
  call for bombing halt, 346
  "duality," 119–120
  election campaigns, 335, 338, 340–341, 347, 477, 536
  excluded by Johnson, 53, 54, 119–120
  opposition to escalation, 52–53
  public support for Johnson, 317–318
  Saigon trip, 221–222

Hung, Le Van, 486

Hung, Pham, 215, 250, 407, 413, 480, 523

Hunt, Ira, 379–388

Huong, Tran Van, 525

Ia Drang, Battle of, 98–107, 109

Ia Drang Valley, 91, 94–96, 186

Imperial Citadel, Hue, 273–279

improvement and modernization (I&M) program, 342

Indochina, 14(fig.)

inflation, 7, 70, 173, 205, 300

Iron Triangle, 158–161, 168

irregulars, 211–212

Israel, 199

Jackson, Henry, 419, 475

Janeway, Eliot, 474–475

Janis, Irving, 31

Jarai people, 97

Javits, Jacob, 42

jingoism, 58

Johnson, Harold "H.K.," 46, 49, 69, 109, 115, 122–125, 235

Johnson, Lady Bird, 53

Johnson, Lyndon B., 8, 26, 49, 70(photo), 232, 315(photo)
  air strike authorization, 55–56, 58–59, 62, 91, 116–117, 504
  approval ratings, 125, 173
  bombing halted by, 313–315, 317–318, 330, 336, 346
  credibility gap, 69–70
  cross-border operations plan, 112
  desire for secrecy about war, 68–69
  doubts about the war, 27
  election campaigns, 27–28, 42–43, 47, 51, 53, 532
  exclusion of Humphrey, 53, 54, 119–120
  fears of, 27, 281–283, 285–286, 291–293
  foreign aid promises, 62–63
  graduated pressure strategy, 3–4, 29, 33, 56, 116–117, 350
  Great Society programs, 2, 47, 51–52, 68–69, 122, 532
  Guam meeting, 152

"hold-until-November" strategy,
27–28, 39

Honolulu summit, 120–121

justification for presence in Vietnam,
146, 202–203

launch of Vietnam War, 1–4

on McNamara, 29

meeting with Eisenhower, 57

negotiation goals and attempts, 73–74,
114, 173, 202–203, 241–242, 276

pacification, 242–243

peace talks, 7, 9, 321, 325, 336–342,
346–347, 506, 533, 535

presidency, 25

press conference on Vietnam, 73–74

rationale for war, 67

reasons for escalation, 531–533

reelection campaign, 66, 179, 194–195,
203, 284, 535

reelection campaign suspended, 313,
317, 535

rules of engagement, 240

sand-table model of Khe Sanh, 253

search and destroy strategy, 5, 61–64

secret war in Laos, 151

State of the Union addresses, 117–118,
122, 145, 152

support for Thieu, 235

support for Westmoreland, 179

tax proposals, 51–52, 205

Tonkin Gulf Incident, 40–41

vice presidency, 25

"Vietnam-only Army," 187

War on Poverty, 2

war strategy, 145

"X file" on Chennault Affair, 347

Johnson administration, 31–32, 33, 38, 54,
129, 179

Joint Chiefs of Staff, 34, 35, 70, 74, 146, 151,
154, 158, 232, 272

Flaming Dart I operation, 55

Johnson's fear of, 27

Johnson's meetings with, 48, 61

Laotian Incursion support, 448

maximum-force options, 68, 116

McNamara's fear of, 18

search and destroy strategy, 78

Sigma I war game, 30

strategic reserve replenishment, 173–174

strategy planning, 28–29, 33, 43, 54, 173

Taylor as chairman of, 18, 22(photo),
27, 33

troop deployment recommendations, 57

Westmoreland's address to, 174

Wheeler as chairman of, 42, 46,
276, 284–285

Joint United States Public Affairs Office
(JUSPAO), 149, 156

jungle rot, 176–177

Just, Ward, 130–134, 149, 237

Kahn, Herman, 323–324

Kann, Peter, 376, 411

Kaplan, Phillip, 486

Katzenbach, Nicholas, 292

Kennan, George, 49, 120–121

Kennedy, Edward, 361–362, 473, 514

Kennedy, John F.

aid to South Vietnam, 15–16, 18–19, 21

assassination of, 1, 9, 25, 532

Berlin crisis, 68

communism fears, 1, 3

Kennedy, John F. *(continued)*
  coup against, 538
  coup authorization, 22–25
  election campaigns, 20, 339
  flexible response strategy, 29
  lack of winning strategy, 4, 5
  moon landing pledge, 2
  presidency, 145
  reasons for escalation, 531–532
  secret war in Laos, 151, 409
  tax cuts, 19, 52
Kennedy, Robert F, 21, 22(photo), 312,
    317, 335, 340
Kennedy administration, 16–17, 22–23, 31
Kent State University shootings, 421,
    439–441
Kerry, John, 439
Ketwig, John, 223, 261
Kham Duc, Battle of, 354–355
Khang, Le Nguyen, 281, 452
Khanh, Nguyen, 26, 27, 39, 53, 54, 55, 57, 65
Khe Sanh, Battle of
  border battle, 232
  casualties, 312, 314, 315
  end of, 315–316, 319
  financial costs of, 300
  hill fights, 215–217, 305
  Marine firepower, 307–308, 311
  Marine garrisons, 251–253, 305–306
  NVA siege, 304–307, 446
  Operation Niagara, 309–312
  supply runs during, 308
Khe Sanh plateau, 111–112
Khmer Rouge, 11, 113, 234, 351–352, 391,
    407, 417–418, 507–508, 520–523, 536
Khrushchev, Nikita, 46, 48

Kien Hoa province, 377–388
The Killing Fields (film), 521
Kim, Le Van, 25
Kim Il Sung, 286
King, Martin Luther, Jr., 195, 335, 432
Kissinger, Henry, 8, 114, 350(photo), 361,
    392, 397, 420, 450, 469, 475–476
  denounced by Reagan, 539
  military Vietnamization policy, 349–350
  Moscow trip, 488
  Nobel Peace Prize acceptance
    speech, 507
  opposition to troop withdrawals, 430
  Paris Peace Accords, 504–507
  peace talks, 366–367, 405, 411–412,
    498–499
  plot to derail LBJ peace talks, 337–341,
    345–347, 403, 536
Komer, Robert, 155–157, 197, 264, 369, 402
Kontum City, 486, 492, 493, 496, 517
Korean War, 2, 66, 77, 83, 90, 204, 392
Koster, Samuel, 219–220, 437–438
Kosygin, Alexei, 53, 58
Kovic, Ron, 400
Kraft, Joseph, 439
Kroesen, Fritz, 480–482
Krogh, Egil, 431
Krulak, Victor, 124, 209
Kubrick, Stanley, 43
Kulikov, Viktor, 511
Kung, Louis, 341
Ky, Nguyen Cao
  background of, 64–65
  barnstorming campaign, 196–197
  Cholon helicopter incident, 325
  Honolulu summit, 120–121

INDEX

Khang on, 281

Khanh's coup, 26

Lam's opposition to, 487

Nixon's Vietnam visit, 350(photo)

presidential election, 234–235

as prime minister, 125–127

return to VNAF, 473

as Vice President, 278

as VNAF Air Marshal, 55, 57, 119

Lai Khe Base Camp, 399–400

Laird, Melvin, 361, 392, 393, 397, 409, 415, 424, 430, 443, 448, 473, 477, 491, 500

Lam, Hoang Xuan, 278, 447, 452–455, 458–462, 467–470, 481–482, 485, 487, 489

landmines, 212, 302, 402

Lang Vei Special Forces camp attack, 306

Lansdale, Edward, 22, 86

Laos

air strikes against, 409

bombing halted in, 508

Hmong, 151, 523

Ho Chi Minh Trail, 3, 6, 37, 48, 76, 112, 147, 233, 446, 471–472

invasion of, 445–465, 456(fig.), 467–470, 471, 536

NVA in, 113–114, 151, 405–406, 447–451, 459

Pathet Lao, 11, 151, 233, 285, 405, 471, 523

People's Democratic Republic, 523

Route 9, 445–449

secret war in, 151, 409

secret war in Laos, 8

supply surge into, 318–319, 446–448

technical neutrality of, 3, 93

Westmoreland's plan to strike into, 112, 146–148, 151–153, 193–194, 245, 253, 283, 284, 446

Lawrence, T. E., 461

LeMay, Curtis, 27–28, 43–46, 48, 55, 335

"Lemon Tree" (Peter, Paul, and Mary), 429

Lewis, George, 381–383

Lich, Tran Quoc, 452

Life (periodical), 3, 84, 109, 141–142, 231, 362, 398, 425, 436, 495

Limbaugh, Rush, 428

Lincoln, Abraham, 179

Lindsay, John V., 440–441

Lippmann, Walter, 120

listening posts (LPs), 136

Loan, Nguyen Ngoc, 267–268, 324

Loc, Nguyen Van, 278

Loc, Vinh, 528

Loc Ninh, Battle of, 215

Lodge, Henry Cabot, Jr., 22–23, 25, 33, 70(photo), 119, 126, 149, 193, 296, 404

Logan Act (1799), 339–340

Long Binh Post, 81, 85, 268, 524

looting, 488, 490, 491

Lownds, David, 306–307

Lozada, Carlos, 224

Luat, Nguyen Trong, 453

Lucas, Andre, 422

Luce, Henry, 3

Luong, Duong Xuan, 452

MacArthur, Douglas, 90

machine guns, 82–83

MACV. *See* Military Assistance Command Vietnam

Maddox (destroyer), 40, 41

Mailer, Norman, 340

Manh, Nguyen Van, 264

Mansfield, Mike, 52, 54–55, 231, 409, 419

Mao Zedong, 2, 3, 8, 11, 189–190, 235, 321, 391, 478, 503

March Against Death, 397–398

marijuana, 431

Mark 81 bomb, 226

Marshall, George C., 147

Martin, Graham, 511, 520, 526–528

Maryknoll Seminary, 15

Matheson, Salve, 213–214

McCain, John, III, 240, 318, 497–498, 500–501

McCain, John, Jr., 393, 406–407

McCarthy, Eugene, 312, 317, 341

McCarthy, Joe, 1, 3, 12

McClellan, George, 179

McCone, John, 16, 49

McConnell, John P., 56

McGinniss, Joe, 351

McGovern, George, 42, 296, 347, 409, 419, 473, 497, 498

McGuire, Barry, 65

McNamara, Robert, 6, 16, 22(photo), 34, 43, 55, 66, 145, 178, 242, 533

  on air strikes, 59

  black ops, 39–40

  brilliance of, 29

  cost projections of, 122, 185, 300

  covert operations, 41–42

  defeatism, 112–113, 117, 139, 174–175, 282

  enlistment tactics, 425–427

  fear of Joint Chiefs, 18

  financial costs hidden by, 70–71

  graduated pressure strategy, 3–4, 18–20, 28–29, 33, 239–240

  Honolulu summit, 63, 121

  maximum-force options, 68

  on Operation Rolling Thunder, 58

  opposition to Diem coup, 22

  Pentagon Papers, 472

  resignation, 245

  search and destroy strategy, 80

  support for escalation, 52, 74–75, 535

  Systems Analysis Office, 20

  troop surge opposition, 194

  Vietnam tours, 18, 26–27, 139

McNamara Line, 217–218, 233, 311, 331

McNaughton, John, 32, 66, 74, 139, 173, 294

McPherson, Harry, 292

Meadlo, Paul, 303

Meany, George, 439

medevacs, 77, 83

Medina, Ernest, 301–303, 438

Mekong Delta, 37, 110, 175–178, 176(fig.), 375, 378

Michel, Werner, 370

Michelin Plantation, 141

Michener, James, 439–440

"Middle America," 439–440

Midway Conference, 388–389

Military Assistance Command Vietnam (MACV), 57, 97

  164th Aviation Group, 265

  525th Military Intelligence Group, 373

  ARVN analysis, 238

  Civic Action program, 156, 219

  Civil Affairs program, 156

  claims of success in Laos, 468–469

deactivation of, 506–507

establishment of, 17–19

mission statement, 388–389

MONEVALs, 59–60, 140–141

Objectives Plan, 356

press briefings, 149–150, 150(photo)

rules of engagement, 413

VC forces counts, 243–244

Westmoreland as commander of, 29,
    33–35, 37–38, 121–122

military bases, 77, 83–85

military efficiency, 534

military intelligence, 88–89, 244, 450

Miller, William H., 486

Mills, Wilbur, 70, 152, 205

Ming, Duong Van, 529

Minh, Duong Van, 23–24, 25, 26–27,
    196–197, 526

Minh, Ho Chi, 12, 26, 28, 49, 63, 141, 146,
    153, 197–200, 211, 241–242, 399,
    478, 538

Minh, Tran Van, 526

missing in action (MIA), 133, 189, 354, 506

Mitchell, John, 397

Montagnards, 100, 306, 354–355

moon landing, 2

Moore, Hal, 98–107

Moorer, Thomas, 481

morale problems, 428–436, 473

Moratorium to End the War in Vietnam,
    396–398

Morse, Wayne, 42

Murphy, Robert, 296

Murray, John, 513

Muscle Shoals, 311

Muskie, Edmund, 409, 477

My Khe massacre, 438

My Lai massacre, 302–304, 398, 436–438

napalm, 103, 104, 165, 226, 311

"Napalm Girl," 495

National Commitments Resolution, 394

National Council of Reconciliation and
    Concord, 505

National Guard, 420–421, 424, 439–440

National Intelligence Estimate, 31

National Leadership Council, 65, 127

National Liberation Front (NLF), 240, 330

National Police (Saigon), 156, 267–268,
    324, 370

National Press Club, 244

National Security Council (NSC), 32–33,
    53, 54, 69, 70(photo)

NATO, 75, 174, 205–206, 336, 419, 534

NBC, 293

Negroponte, John, 506, 537

neutralization of VCI, 369–375, 402

New Life Development, 288–289

New Republic (periodical), 86

New Standards Men, 426–427

Newsweek (periodical), 161, 237, 268,
    423, 439–440

New Yorker (periodical), 160, 219

New York Times (periodical), 53, 227, 231,
    235, 313, 361, 366, 394, 472, 488, 521

New York Times Magazine (periodical),
    235–236

New Zealand troops in Vietnam, 141

Nguyen Van Thieu, 7

Nhu, Ngo Diem, 21, 22–24

Nhung, Nguyen Van, 24, 26

Nitze, Paul, 294–298

Nixon, Richard
  air strike authorization, 352, 491–492,
    495, 499–501, 537
  approval ratings, 440, 469, 504
  on Calley's trial, 437–438
  Cambodian Incursion, 407–422,
    414(fig.), 445, 471, 536–537
  China trip, 478
  draft end pledge, 424
  draft lottery system, 9, 427–428
  election campaigns, 66, 195, 313, 335,
    338–339, 347, 439, 477, 535–536
  fears of losing a war, 1, 2
  Laotian Incursion, 448, 464–465, 536
  madman theory, 349, 392, 532
  Moscow trip, 478, 479, 492
  Nixon Doctrine, 394, 411
  peace plan, 359, 366–367, 388–389, 405,
    475–476, 478, 498–499, 503, 507
  Pentagon Papers, 472–473
  plot to derail LBJ peace talks, 339–341,
    345–347, 403, 536
  public plan to end war, 395
  reasons for escalation, 532
  resignation, 511, 512
  response to antiwar movement, 396–397
  Saigon aid request, 508–511
  secret bombing campaign, 392–394, 407
  "secret plan" to end war, 7–8, 349–351,
    360–361, 363–364, 366, 397–398, 412
  "silent majority" speech, 397, 450
  troop withdrawals, 363–364, 365, 389,
    401–402, 404, 408, 412–413, 430, 434,
    465, 476–477
  Vietnamization plan, 8–9
  Vietnam visit, 350(photo)

  warnings of NVA offensives, 477–478
  Watergate scandal, 347, 394, 473, 494,
    507, 511
Nol, Lon, 113, 351–352, 391, 407, 408–411,
  416–418, 470–471, 495–496,
  507–508, 520
Non, Lon, 522
North Korea, 11, 285
North Vietnam, 14(fig.)
  air strikes against, 28–29, 40–41, 43–46,
    54–55, 58–59, 116–117, 198, 294–295,
    491–492, 495, 499–501
  Cambodian strategy, 416
  Chinese aid to, 214
  demilitarized zone, 37, 110–112,
    217–218, 221, 476
  draft eligible population of, 74
  famine in, 198
  foreign aid promises to, 62–63
  French retreat from, 11
  graduated pressure strategy against, 3–4
  junta generals, 25–26
  lack of US troops to fight effectively in, 6
  leadership in, 197–200
  likelihood of American invasion of, 251
  negotiation goals and attempts, 73–74,
    76, 114, 117, 154, 202–203, 250, 337,
    477, 504
  resistance to Le Duan, 215
  search and destroy strategy against, 4–5,
    152–153
  Soviet aid to, 214
  sustained reprisal policy against, 58
North Vietnamese Army (NVA)
  1st Division, 134, 221, 223
  4th Regiment, 273

6th Regiment, 273

7th Division, 257, 486

9th Division, 164, 167, 257

29th Regiment, 356, 358

100th Division, 134

174th Regiment, 224

226th Regiment, 132

304th Division, 306, 311, 448

308th Division, 448

320th Division, 448

324th Division, 480

air strikes against, 537

atrocities by, 182

bombing halt supply surge, 318–319

in Cambodia, 113, 407, 410

casualties, 181, 217, 488, 493, 494, 529

DMZ operations, 111–112, 476, 481

draft law, 479

fighting tactics, 105–106

final offensives, 516(fig.)

high-speed trails, 135–136

"hugging tactics," 105–106, 133, 455

invisibility of, 111–116

in Laos, 151, 447–451, 453–458, 459

march into South Vietnam, 48, 76,
    247, 256

May Offensive, 394

military intelligence, 450

physical health of, 170–171

recruitment numbers, 229, 287

reorganization of, 511

resolve of, 329–330

Saigon occupation, 527–530

shadow supply system, 344, 355

in South Vietnam, 91–92, 141, 194,
    233, 318, 510

Soviet military assistance, 53

tactics, 135–138, 140, 169–170, 178–179,
    181, 187–188, 190, 200–202, 207–208,
    211, 230

toughness of, 102, 171(photo), 171–172

troop numbers, 203, 332–333

vagueness of strength of, 35, 76

VC support, 118

NVA. *See* North Vietnamese Army

Oberdorfer, Don, 263, 272

O'Brien, Tim, 302, 331–332

O'Connell, Michael Davis, 417

O'Connor, George, 176–177

oil embargo, 509

One China policy, 8

Operation Apache Snow, 355–356, 357–364

Operation Arc Light, 84

Operation Attleboro, 141–142, 158, 161,
    164, 166, 169

Operation Benton, 237

Operation Billings, 206–207

Operation Breakfast, 393

Operation Cedar Falls, 158–161,
    159(fig.), 168

Operation Chicago Peak, 421–422, 451

Operation Complete Victory, 322, 343–344

Operation Coronado I, 177–178

Operation Delaware, 319–321, 353–354

Operation Dessert, 393

Operation Dewey Canyon, 356

Operation Dewey Canyon III, 439

Operation Dinner, 393

Operation Duck Hook, 392, 395, 397

Operation Eagle Pull, 520

Operation El Paso, 283–284

Operation Enhance Plus, 499, 509

Operation Enterprise, 177

Operation Final Victory, 412

Operation Flaming Dart I, 54, 55

Operation Flaming Dart II, 55–56

Operation Francis Marion, 181, 186, 221

Operation Frequent Wind, 527

Operation Friendship, 98

Operation Greeley, 181–184, 221

Operation Happy Valley, 95–98

Operation Hawthorne, 130–134, 221

Operation Holly, 431

Operation Junction City, 159(fig.), 161–168,
    162(photo), 198–199, 255, 343

Operation Keystone, 430

Operation Lam Son 719, 449–465,
    456(fig.), 467–470

Operation Linebacker I, 491–492, 497

Operation Linebacker II, 499–501, 503–504

Operation Lunch, 393

Operation MacArthur, 223

Operation Masher, 118

Operation Menu, 351–352, 391–393

Operation Niagara, 254, 309–312

Operation Pacific Grove, 283–284

Operation Paul Revere, 134, 135–139,
    169, 170, 221

Operation Pegasus, 315–316

Operation Pershing, 179–180

Operation Recovery, 289

Operation Rolling Thunder, 28–29, 58–59,
    60, 62, 91, 116–117, 139, 191, 198, 238,
    241, 294–296, 346, 504, 539

Operation Russell Beach, 373

Operation Sam Houston, 169–172, 221

Operation San Angelo, 255

Operation Scotland, 253–254, 315

Operation Shenandoah II, 207–208

Operation Silver Bayonet, 95, 98–99, 106

Operations Massachusetts Striker, 356

Operation Snack, 393

Operation Speedy Express, 376, 377–388,
    399–400, 536

Operation Supper, 393

Operation Texas Star, 421–422

Operation Toan Thang, 470

Operation White Wing, 118–119, 345

OPLAN 34-A, 40

pacification, 79, 87, 90, 124, 154–157,
    242–243, 255, 288–289, 328, 334, 369,
    375, 389, 403

Palmer, Bruce, 167, 418

Pao, Vang, 523

paratroopers, 39, 226, 228, 358

Paris Peace Accords, 504–507, 512, 525

Pathet Lao, 11, 151, 233, 285, 405, 471, 523

patrol torpedo (PT) boats, 40–42

Patton (film), 412

Paul VI, Pope, 249

peace deal, 7, 9

peace talks, 321, 324, 336–342, 345–346,
    366, 388–389, 391, 394–395, 403–405,
    412, 449, 469, 475–476, 481, 497,
    503–504, 535–536

Pearson, Willard, 130

Peers, William, 181, 186–189, 224, 228, 229,
    437–438

Pence, Arthur, 452

Pentagon Papers, 472–473

People's Revolutionary Party (PRP), 88, 369

Perfume River, 273–274

petroleum, oils, and lubricants (POL)
    terminals, 84–85
Phantom III program, 379–388
Philippine troops in Vietnam, 141
Phoenix Program, 326, 327, 369–374,
    402, 529
Phouma, Souvanna, 471
Phu, Pham Van, 517
Phu Cuong City, 269–270
Phuoc Binh City, fall of, 513–514
Phuoc Long Offensive, 512, 513
Pike, Douglas, 504
Pilger, John, 430
"Pinkville," 301–304
Pleiku Campaign, 92, 94–96, 106, 109, 134
Policy Planning Council, 30
political prisoners, 529
Pol Pot, 113, 234, 351, 391, 407, 507, 521–523
popular opinion, 9, 205, 268
Popular Self-Defense Force (PSDF), 385
Powell, Enoch, 415
press
    criticism by, 9, 231–232, 237, 282,
        290–291, 293, 307, 361
    embedded reporters, 130, 159–160, 219,
        227, 276, 305–306
    international, 166–167, 330
    JUSPAO briefings, 149
    MACV briefings, 149–150, 150(photo)
    presence in South Vietnam, 21, 180, 184,
        218, 223–224, 272, 282
    televised execution, 268
    Tet Offensive reporting, 266, 282
prisoners of war (POWs), 171(photo), 189,
    240, 419, 475, 491–492, 497, 504–505
Project 100,000, 426

protests
    anti-American, 56, 500
    anti-Diem, 21–22
    anti-war, 8, 62, 65–66, 153, 222,
        222(photo), 284, 350, 361, 395–398,
        420–421, 439–440, 501
    Buddhist-led, 56, 125–126
    on college campuses, 222
    Democratic National Convention,
        340–341
    hard hats demonstrations, 440–441
Provincial Intelligence and
    Operation Coordinating Centers
    (PIOCCs), 372
Provincial Reconnaissance Units
    (PRUs), 327
PROVN study, 122–125
Proxmire, William, 296
psyops, 156, 170, 384, 387
Pueblo, USS, 205, 285, 304

Quang, Tran Van, 496
Quang Tri City, 488, 494, 517
Quayle, Dan, 428

Raborn, William, 63–64
race relations, 432–434, 437
race riots, 195, 335
Rach Nui River, 178
radio telephone operators (RTOs),
    207–208, 208(photo)
Rakkasans, 358, 359
Ranch Hand pilots, 140
Reagan, Ronald, 2, 66, 539
recondo platoons, 130–134, 131(photo)
Record, Jeffrey, 384–388

INDEX

Red Scare, 3

reeducation camps, 529

refugees, refugee camps, 159, 161, 214, 236, 236(photo), 288, 323, 384, 416, 488, 490, 517–519, 533

Regional Forces/Popular Forces (RF/PF), 156, 177, 211, 242, 328, 334, 342, 343, 365, 367–368, 368(photo), 377, 442, 538

Republicans, on communism, 2

restraint, opposition to, 384–385

Revolutionary Development, 156, 211, 242, 288–289

Rhodes, James, 440

Ridenhour, Ron, 304

Ridgway, Matthew, 12, 167, 296

Ripcord FSB, 422

Rockefeller, Nelson, 335, 338

Rocket Ridge, 485–486

Rockpile, 111–112

Rogers, William, 392, 397, 409, 418, 430, 505

Roman Catholicism. *See* Catholics, Catholicism

Rosson, Bill, 209, 212

Rostow, Walt, 148, 173, 242–243, 300, 336, 347, 533, 537

ruff-puffs, 156, 177, 211, 242, 328, 334, 342, 343, 365, 367–368, 368(photo), 377, 442, 538

rules of engagement, 177, 240, 413, 438–439, 533

Rusk, Dean, 3–4, 16, 22, 26, 31, 35, 39, 41, 52, 59, 66, 205, 272, 304, 338

Russell, Richard, 419

Russia. *See* Soviet Union

Saar, John, 84, 436, 495

Saigon, fall of, 526–530, 538, 539

Salisbury, Harrison, 117

sampans, 380

San Antonio Formula, 295

"Santa Fe Trail," 215

saturation patrols, 98

Schanberg, Sydney, 489–490, 521–523

Schell, Jonathan, 159–160, 219, 237

Schlesinger, Arthur, Jr., 24–25

Schlesinger, James, 510, 519

Schroeder, Patricia, 511

Scott, George C., 412

Seaman, Jonathan, 167

SEATO, 336

segregation, 432

Selective Service Act (1948), 75

The Selling of the President 1968 (McGinniss), 351

Senate Armed Services Committee, 129, 146, 203, 419

Senate Foreign Relations Committee, 41, 119, 231, 282, 408, 418, 439, 474, 495, 513

"Set Lt. Calley Free" (song), 437

17th parallel, 39, 55, 111

Sharbutt, Jay, 360

Shawcross, William, 508

Sheehan, Neil, 17, 26, 220, 329

Sigma I, 30

Sigma II, 43–46, 114

Sihanouk, Norodom, 113, 233–234, 351–352, 391, 407, 411, 421, 522–523

Sihanouk Trail, 405–406

Siri Matak, Sisowath, 351, 407, 522

Six-Day War, 199

Smith, Hedrick, 361

Smith, Jack, 104, 106–107

snipers, 379–380, 382

Snuffy FSB, 430

South Korea

  Korean War, 11

  military readiness of, 205

  North Korean attack on palace, 285

  troops in Vietnam, 75, 118–119, 141, 250

South Vietnam, 14(fig.)

  American aid to, 214

  American military bases in, 77, 83–85

  American military personnel in, 53, 54,
    236–237, 251, 428, 512

  America's commitment to, 11–13

  Catholics in, 12, 22

  Central Highlands region, 92, 93(fig.),
    100, 184–185, 221

  civil war, 125

  corps areas, 35, 36(fig.), 37, 81, 94,
    125–126

  counterinsurgency measures, 37–38, 57,
    61, 326–327

  coups, 22–27, 56, 59, 64, 538

  demilitarized zone, 37, 111–112, 217–218,
    221, 476

  destruction of, 4, 213–214, 235, 533

  drop in military power in, 480

  elections, 196–197, 234–235, 242,
    473–474, 476, 505

  elections cancelled, 13

  evacuations from, 526–530

  foreign aid promises to, 62–63

  French retreat from, 11

  graduated pressure strategy, 3–4

  Hamlet Evaluation System, 368–369

Ia Drang Valley, 91, 94–96

  lack of leadership in, 6

  militia forces, 59–60

  Ministry of Social Welfare, 289, 329

  National Police, 156, 267–268, 324, 370

  "no-breathing week," 64–65

  NVA forces in, 91–92, 141, 233, 318,
    399, 510

  pacification plans, 154–157

  Quang Ngai province, 236, 236(photo)

  rainy weather in, 80

  removal of NVA troops from, 505

  Saigon Circle, 256, 268–269

  search and destroy strategy, 5

  terrorism in, 287–288

  troop needs, 74

  troops in Vietnam, 286

  troop surge, 62–64, 66, 69, 73, 91, 141,
    175, 233

  VC forces in, 27, 53, 56, 109–110,
    110(fig.), 115, 127, 154, 318

Soviet Union

  aid to North Vietnam, 139, 189–190, 214

  invasion of Czechoslovakia, 285

  military assistance to NVA and VC, 53,
    238, 479, 511

  Nixon's trip to, 478, 479

  peace deal motives, 338–339

  pressure to end war by, 497

  risks of intervention by, 58, 61

  Sino-Soviet rift, 189–190, 199

Spellman, Francis, 143

State Department, Policy Planning
  Council, 30

Stennis, John, 129, 419–420

Stevenson, Adlai, 57, 66

Stewart, Brian, 190

St. Francis Xavier Church, 23

Stillwell, Dick, 35, 38, 355, 357

St. Louis Post-Dispatch (periodical), 398

Stockdale, James, 40

Stone, Dana, 223

Stone, Edward Durrell, 235

strategic reserve, 173–174, 284

Strong Point Obstacle System, 217–218, 233

Struggle Movement, 21–22, 125–127

Students for a Democratic Society (SDS),
    395–396, 498

Stud LZ, 315–316

success metrics, 212–213, 403, 536–537

Sun Tzu, 29

Suoi Tre, 164–166

"super gaggles," 308–309

surface-to-air missiles (SAMs), 48

Sutherland, Jock, 457, 460, 470

Systems Analysis Office, 415

Taber, Richard, 225–226

tactical air support (tac air), 83–84, 99

Tamarkin, Bob, 528

Tang, Truong Nhu, 505

Tan Son Nhut Air Base, 85, 256, 265,
    268–269, 501, 526

Task Force Oregon, 209–213, 219

Taylor, Maxwell, 120, 242, 252, 296, 538
  as ambassador to South Vietnam, 33–35,
    43–44, 47–48, 54, 56–57
  "The Cause in Vietnam is Being Won,"
    235–236
  as chairman of Joint Chiefs of Staff, 18,
    22, 22(photo), 27, 28, 33
  as White House military adviser, 16–18

Taylor, Telford, 438

Taylor, Zachary, 441

Terry, Michael, 303–304

Tet Nguyen Dan, 249

Tet Offensive, 262(fig.)
  aftereffects of, 286–289, 299, 301
  atrocities against civilians, 275–276
  attack plan, 255, 257–259, 269
  authorization of, 244
  casualties, 263, 266, 270–271, 274–275,
    278–279, 286–287, 289
  COSVN proposal, 214
  counterattacks, 270–271
  evidence of imminence of, 254–255, 264
  financial costs of, 300
  Hue battle, 271–279, 277(photo), 358, 535
  Mini-Tet, 321–325, 328, 354
  opening attacks, 261, 263
  planning of, 199–200, 216, 232, 247–251
  Saigon battle, 265–271
  US embassy attack, 265–266, 535
  VC infiltration of Saigon, 257–258

Thai, Hoang Van, 215, 250

Thanh, Nguyen Chi, 35, 141, 152, 197–198,
    206–208, 214–215

Thao, Pham Ngoc, 23, 64

Thi, Nguyen Chanh, 125–126

Thieu, Nguyen Van
  authoritarianism of, 510
  background of, 64–65
  Cambodian Incursion, 470
  Catholicism of, 23, 64, 493
  Chau arrest order, 327
  coups, 23, 26, 56–57, 196–197
  election campaigns, 451, 473–474
  Honolulu summit, 120–121

inauguration, 221

Khang on, 281

Laotian Incursion, 446–447, 452–455, 457–461, 464, 471

"most hated man in Vietnam," 524

Nixon's visit, 350(photo)

peace talks, 337–339, 345, 366, 388–389, 475, 498–499, 503

power network, 389, 442, 487

presidency, 238–240

presidential election, 234–235

replacement of Ky's men, 324

resignation, 525, 527

rise of, 538

Taiwan exile, 523–524, 525

Tet Offensive, 264–265, 279

troop increases, 193

The Things They Carried (O'Brien), 302

Tho, Le Duc, 197, 321, 338, 395, 405, 497, 523

Tho, Nguyen Ngoc, 25

Thompson, Hugh, 303

Thu, Ngo Viet, 234

Thurmond, Strom, 419

Thuy, Xuan, 324

Ticonderoga, USS, 40

Tiger Force recondo platoon, 130–131

Time (periodical), 3, 76, 109, 237, 316

Tonkin Gulf Incident, 40–41, 54

Tonkin Gulf Resolution, 41–42, 48, 120, 231, 418

Tower, John, 419

Tra, Tran Van, 486, 513, 529

troop carriers, 77

Truehart, Bill, 32

Truman, Harry, 2, 17, 66, 532

Trump, Donald, 428

Truong, Ngo Quang, 273, 279, 489, 494, 517

Tung, Van Tien, 480

Turner Joy (destroyer), 40, 41

Turse, Nick, 381

Tuy Hoa, 517

The Uncertain Trumpet (Taylor), 17

The Uncounted Enemy (TV show), 243

United States

  anti-American protests, 56, 500

  anti-war protests, 8, 62, 65–66, 153, 350, 361, 395–398, 420–421, 501

  domestic issues, 335

  federal deficit, 70, 205

  inflation, 7, 70, 173, 205, 300

  motivations of, 1

  opposition to war in, 125, 290–291, 335, 439

  perceived weakness of, 3

  spending by, 76–77, 85–87, 115–117

  support for war in, 47, 143, 145, 173, 234, 356, 439, 509, 531–532

  understanding of Vietnam policy in, 59

  wealth of, 2

  willingness to go to war, 9–10

United States Information Service (USIS), 56, 421

University of Michigan, 62

USAID, 156, 329

US Air Force, 12, 29, 43, 84, 226, 228, 239, 448, 483, 485, 501, 508

US Army

  1st Aviation Brigade, 268

  1st Cavalry Division, 78–79, 95–98, 118, 274–275, 278–279, 283, 319–321, 413

US Army *(continued)*

1st Cavalry Division, 3rd Brigade, 181, 274

1st Infantry Division, 159, 161, 200, 206–208, 269–270, 272, 334, 344, 428, 486

4th Cavalry Regiment, 269–270

4th Infantry Division, 136, 161, 169–170, 181, 186, 223–224, 229, 344–345, 389, 415

7th Cavalry Regiment, 1st Battalion, 99

7th Cavalry Regiment, 2nd Battalion, 101, 106

9th Infantry Division, 175, 177–178, 263, 269, 322, 322(photo), 377–382, 389, 399–400, 430

9th Infantry Division, 2nd Brigade, 177–178

9th Infantry Division, 3rd Brigade, 177

11th Armored Cavalry Regiment, 159, 413, 486

11th Light Infantry Brigade, 429(photo)

12th Infantry Division, 1st Battalion, 189

23rd American Infantry Division, 218–220, 436, 488

23rd American Infantry Division, 11th Brigade, 301–304

25th Infantry Division, 158, 161, 164–165, 255, 270, 322, 413, 428

25th Infantry Division, 3rd Brigade, 167

28th Infantry Regiment, 208

82nd Airborne Division, 174

101st Airborne Division, 130–134, 184–185, 255, 266, 269, 274–275, 283, 319–321, 334, 354, 357, 363, 415, 421–422, 436–437, 453, 476

101st Airborne Division, 1st Brigade, 213, 255, 279

101st Airborne Division, 2nd Brigade, 356

173rd Airborne Brigade, 159, 181–183, 223–224, 229–230, 232

187th Airborne Regiment, 358

196th Light Infantry Brigade, 158, 162(photo)

503rd Infantry Regiment, 224, 226

506th Infantry Regiment, 2nd Battalion, 422

antagonism with Marines, 216–217

casualties, 279, 377

combined action platoons (CAPs), 127–128

counter-guerrilla operations, 61–62

DEROS policy, 187–188, 188(photo), 200

desertions, 433

desire to attack VC, 29

evacuations from Saigon, 526–530

Green Berets, 306, 354

grunts, 96, 137(photo), 201(photo), 332, 429–430, 436

"no land wars in Asia" precept, 12

noncombat volunteers, 8, 424

reserves, 69, 173–174

Support Command, 84–85

Task Force Oregon, 209–213, 219

US Marines

1st Division, 212, 219

2nd Division, 174

3rd Division, 218, 253, 258, 342, 363, 514

5th Regiment, 1st Battalion, 277(photo), 277–278

9th Regiment, 1st Battalion, 218

26th Regiment, 251, 306

antagonism with Army, 216–217

casualties, 209, 216, 217–218, 279, 356

combined action platoons (CAPs), 124–125, 127–128, 334

deployment of, 46, 60, 77

DMZ operations, 110–112

"Marineland," 209, 210(photo)

reserves, 173–174

Task Force Oregon, 209–213, 219

troop numbers, 209

US Navy, 12, 29, 39–40, 483, 501

U.S. News & World Report (periodical), 237

Ut, Nick, 495

Utermahlen, Brian, 436

Valenti, Jack, 153

Vance, Cy, 296

Vann, John Paul, 17–20, 263, 288, 326, 376, 383, 485, 492

Variety (periodical), 347

Vatthana, Savang, 523

VC. *See* Viet Cong

vertical envelopment strategy, 78–80

Vien, Cao Van, 464, 526

Viet Cong (VC)

5th Division, 256, 257, 323

9th Division, 141, 323

271st Regiment, 270

272nd Regiment, 164–165, 270

273rd Regiment, 269–270

274th Regiment, 269

275th Regiment, 269

advance into South Vietnam, 27, 56

Alliance of Democratic, National, and Peace Forces, 301

atrocities by, 68, 155, 177, 182

attacks against Americans, 38–39, 47–48, 53, 55

casualties, 165–166, 377, 529

COSVN proposal, 214–215

employed inside US embassy, 266

growth of, 20–21

guerrilla support for, 88–89

Happy Valley operation response, 96–98

infrastructure (VCI), 369–375, 402

intelligence organizations, 371

invisibility of, 111–116

Iron Triangle, 158–161, 168

military intelligence, 450

naming of, 15

National Liberation Front, 240, 330

negotiation goals and attempts, 240–241

NVA support, 118

prisoners of war (POWs), 88(photo)

propaganda, 124, 214

protracted war strategy, 404–405

Provisional Revolutionary Government, 498, 505, 529

recruitments, 4, 5, 229, 287

reorganization of, 35

resolve of, 329–330

shadow governments of, 26

in South Vietnam, 318

South Vietnam control, 109–110, 110(fig.), 115, 127, 154

Soviet military assistance, 53

strategic terrorism of, 287–288, 328

support for, 175–176

tactics, 140, 142, 163–164, 166, 177–178, 201–202, 207–208, 211

troop numbers, 203

Viet Minh, 12, 13, 15–16, 271, 307, 538, 539. *See also* Viet Cong

Vietnam Christmas Tour, 48, 143, 143(photo), 347, 399–400, 431, 501, 537

Vietnamese Air Force (VNAF), 55, 64, 367, 453, 455, 510, 513–514

Vietnamization, 8–9, 89, 264, 342–343, 350, 367–369, 391, 394, 397–398, 401, 409, 415, 443, 448, 450, 460–461, 470, 509, 519, 532

Vietnam Veterans Against the War, 439

Vietnam War

    Americanization of, 60, 231, 460–461

    American opposition to, 125, 290–291, 335, 439

    American support for, 47, 143, 145, 173, 284, 356, 439, 509, 531–532

    American troop numbers, 6, 8–9, 141, 202, 203, 250, 350, 428

    anti-war protests, 8, 62, 65–66, 284

    casualties, 53, 54, 56, 83, 105–107, 115, 117, 119, 123, 145, 167, 170, 172, 194, 202, 204, 209, 229–231, 312, 322–323, 332, 343, 345, 361–362, 395, 404, 425, 473, 500, 507, 529

    congressional funding for, 55, 68–70, 497, 504, 508, 512

    congressional hearings on, 118–120

    "Denunciation of Communists Campaign," 15–16

    financial costs of, 6–7, 9, 70–71, 115–117, 122, 129, 145–146, 151–152, 185, 203, 204–205, 294, 300, 312, 313, 334, 342–343, 346, 390, 396, 420, 443, 448, 469, 507

    graduated pressure strategy, 3–4, 18–20, 28, 33, 56, 116–117

    Johnson's rationale for, 67

    lack of strategy in, 4, 94–95

    lesson of, 539

    as militarily "unlosable," 86, 153, 272, 295

    as a political war, 531–533

    popular opinion on, 9, 205, 268

    search and destroy strategy, 4–5, 61–64, 78–80, 90, 99, 101, 186, 333–334

    success metrics, 212–213, 403

    as unwinnable, 31

    as a war of choice, 1

VNAF. *See* Vietnamese Air Force

Vogle, Paul, 518

Walker, Glenn, 116

Walker, Harold, 440

Wallace, George, 317, 335

Wall Street Journal (periodical), 32, 291

Walsh, Lawrence, 404

Walt, Lewis, 111–112, 124, 128, 209, 251

Warnke, Paul, 294–299

War on Poverty, 2, 426, 532

Washington Post (periodical), 440

Watergate scandal, 347, 394, 473, 494, 507, 511

Weather Underground, 395–396

"We Gotta Get Out of This Place" (Animals), 433

Westmoreland, William "Westy"

    ARVN PR campaign, 238

    Attleboro operation, 141–142

    attrition strategy, 194, 233

    border sealing operations, 252, 255–256

on Cambodian invasion, 413, 415

Cedar Falls operation, 158–161

"Concept of Military Operations in South Vietnam," 127–128

Delaware operation, 319–321

disastrous tenure of, 331–334

disbelief in NVA spring offensive, 480–481

escalations by, 56–57, 59–60, 76–77, 139–140

Flaming Dart I operation, 53–54

Guam meeting, 152

Happy Valley operation, 95–98

Hawthorne operation, 130

Honolulu summit, 121

inflation of body counts by, 232, 316

Junction City operation, 161–168

Khe Sanh abandonment, 331

Khe Sanh battle, 251–253

lawsuit against CBS, 243

Lewis's letter to, 380–383

Life interview, 141–142

as MACV commander, 29, 33–35, 37–38, 121–122

Masher operation, 118

Niagara operation, 309–312

optimism of, 172, 179, 195–196, 223, 231, 232–233, 237, 244–245

pacification operations, 79, 87, 154–157, 334, 403

Paul Revere operations, 130, 134, 135–139

phony revision of enemy numbers, 237, 243–244

Pleiku Campaign, 92, 94–96, 106–107, 109, 134

PROVN study findings against, 122–125

reputation management, 333, 398

rules of engagement, 438–439

sacking of, 313

Sam Houston operation, 169–172

scissors theory, 95, 253, 272

search and destroy strategy, 4–6, 78–80, 87–90, 91–92, 96, 128, 152–154, 157, 161, 200, 333–334

Silver Bayonet operation, 95

strategy of the periphery, 211, 216–218

success metrics, 212–213

Tet Offensive, 269

Time "Man of the Year," 76, 109

troop requests, 35, 63, 146–148, 172–173, 174, 178–179, 194, 232, 282–285, 291–293, 298–300, 312

troop withdrawals, 431

two-fisted strategy, 148, 150–153

victory strategy, 63–64, 67, 114, 139, 142, 193–194, 534–535

Vietnamization plan, 89

White Wing operation, 118–119

Weyand, Fred, 149, 158, 255, 256–257, 265, 271, 328, 460, 462–463, 494, 506, 520

Wheeler, Earle "Bus," 42, 43–46, 51, 64, 66, 148, 277, 284–285, 291–293, 297(photo), 298–299, 314, 342, 362–363, 393

White, Edwin, 223

white phosphorous (WP), 102, 103

Wiedmaier, Marcel, 372–374

Wilson, Harold, 75

Winter Soldier Investigation, 439

"Wise Men" group, 296–298

Workers' Party Central Committee,
153, 167

World War II, 2, 9, 55, 83, 106, 147, 185,
204, 218–219, 291, 323, 332, 358, 425

Wright, Corey, 186–189

X-Ray LZ, 99–103

Xuan Loc, Battle of, 523–525, 527

Zais, Melvin, 334–335, 357, 361–363

Zorthian, Barry, 149, 238

Matias Wawro

Geoffrey Wawro is University Distinguished Research Professor and director of the Military History Center at the University of North Texas and the author of seven books, including *Quicksand: America's Pursuit of Power in the Middle East* and *Sons of Freedom: The Forgotten American Soldiers Who Defeated Germany in World War I.* Wawro lives in Dallas, Texas.